STATUTORY NUISANCE:
LAW AND PRACTICE

STATUTORY NUISANCE: LAW AND PRACTICE

ROSALIND MALCOLM

LLB (Hons), Barrister
University Director in Law, University of Surrey and
Field Court Chambers, Gray's Inn, London WC1R 5EP

JOHN POINTING

BA (Hons), MPhil, Dip Law, Barrister
Field Court Chambers, Gray's Inn, London WC1R 5EP

OXFORD
UNIVERSITY PRESS

Great Clarendon Street, Oxford OX2 6DP

Oxford University Press is a department of the University of Oxford.
It furthers the University's objective of excellence in research, scholarship,
and education by publishing worldwide in

Oxford New York

Auckland Bangkok Buenos Aires Cape Town Chennai
Dar es Salaam Delhi Hong Kong Istanbul Karachi Kolkata
Kuala Lumpur Madrid Melbourne Mexico City Mumbai Nairobi
São Paulo Shanghai Singapore Taipei Tokyo Toronto

with an associated company in Berlin

Oxford is a registered trade mark of Oxford University Press
in the UK and in certain other countries

Published in the United States
by Oxford University Press Inc., New York

© Rosalind Malcolm and John Pointing 2002

The moral rights of the author have been asserted
Database right Oxford University Press (maker)

First published 2002

Crown Copyright material is reproduced with the permission of the
Controller of Her Majesty's Stationery Office

All rights reserved. No part of this publication may be reproduced,
stored in a retrieval system, or transmitted, in any form or by any means,
without the prior permission in writing of Oxford University Press,
or as expressly permitted by law, or under terms agreed with the appropriate
reprographics rights organization. Enquiries concerning reproduction
outside the scope of the above should be sent to the Rights Department,
Oxford University Press, at the address above

You must not circulate this book in any other binding or cover
and you must impose this same condition on any acquirer

British Library Cataloguing in Publication Data
Data available

Library of Congress Cataloging in Publication Data
Data available

ISBN 0–19–924246–1

1 3 5 7 9 10 8 6 4 2

Typeset in Times by
Cambrian Typesetters, Frimley, Surrey

Printed in Great Britain
on acid-free paper by
Biddles Ltd., Guildford and King's Lynn

PREFACE

In writing this book we have aimed to provide a comprehensive and definitive account of the various types of statutory nuisance—noise, premises, smoke, etc that are included in section 79 of the Environmental Protection Act 1990. Common law nuisance is well covered in legal textbooks but this is the first book to analyse each of the statutory nuisances in depth. We have also organized the chapters with the needs of busy practitioners in mind and responded to the suggestion that each of the statutory nuisances has its own problems as well as those in common. This has meant that there is some repetition of material in chapters dealing with substantive nuisances and those dealing with procedural and conceptual matters. The concept and historical features of statutory nuisance continue to challenge the courts and we make no excuses for analysing them and providing our own interpretations.

Statutory nuisance is an interesting amalgam of social policy, common law nuisance and venerable statute law—originally enacted, in haste, in response to the cholera epidemics of the 1840s and the 1850s. Since then, there has been a barrage of not always consistent cases going back many decades. This is an area of law which is ripe for root and branch reform—a worthy candidate for the Law Commission. Attempts made by the appeal courts since *Network Housing v Westminster City Council* (1994) 93 LGR 280 to determine what Parliament intended in nineteenth-century sanitary statutes— much of which survives today in Part III of the Environmental Protection Act 1990 and virtually in the same form as in the 1850s—cannot amount to reform. Things have moved on and legislative reform is badly needed. Statutory nuisance is also the paradigm case of state intervention in private affairs. Its promulgators saw the legislation as part of a civilising process: to cleanse the environment in which the working and labouring classes lived and worked, and to make the owners of property more socially responsible by having to pay for the costs of clearing up filth and pollution and of preventing the spread of contagious diseases.

Besides the judiciary, others struggle to interpret statutory nuisance law. Pity the poor lay justices having to summon up their resources of wisdom and common sense to decide whether a nuisance has been established in a bitter dispute between neighbours. Local authorities are under a statutory duty to enforce the legislation and have to grapple—or their environmental health officers do—with the thousands of complaints made by the public every year. In 2000, there were over 120,000 domestic noise complaints made to councils in England and Wales, according to figures collated by the Chartered Institute of Environmental Health. Besides local authorities, private individuals can initiate statutory nuisance proceedings against their neighbours, or landlords—including local authority landlords.

The scope and depth of these practical problems have encouraged us to write this book. We have also benefited enormously from the questions, comments and views of the numerous lawyers and environmental health officers we have helped to train over the last 12 years. Their contributions have helped us appreciate how difficult the tasks of local authority officers are. To exercise discretion fairly and decide objectively over whether a complaint amounts to a nuisance or health risk, are quasi-judicial skills that require a great deal of professionalism.

Many individuals have helped in the book's preparation. We would like to acknowledge, in particular, the contributions of Howard Price, of the Chartered Institute of Environmental Health, Martin Wright, the criminal justice reformer, John Corkey, of Belfast City Council, Peggy Law, of the London Borough of Hillingdon, and the journalist, Rodney Malcolm, for providing us with material and advice on the enforcement of the legislation by local authorities. Thanks are due also to Leslie Blake, Barrister and Lecturer at the University of Surrey for his advice generally and for preparing the index, and to Tom May for his encouragement. Our colleagues at Field Court Chambers have always been supportive and encouraging in numerous ways. The staff at Lincoln's Inn library—still, probably, the best law library in the world—have been as helpful, knowledgeable and efficient as ever. We have been very lucky with our publishers. Chris Rycroft and his team at OUP have been both supportive throughout and handled the publication process admirably. For any errors or misinterpretations, the fault lies with us.

The law is as stated on 5 February 2002.

Rosalind Malcolm & John Pointing
University of Surrey, and, Field Court Chambers, Grays Inn
February 2002

CONTENTS

Table of Cases	xv
Tables of Legislation	xxxi

1 Synopsis
Introduction	1.01
Part I: Structure and Framework	1.05
Part II: The Specific Nuisances	1.08
Part III: Procedure and Evidence	1.09
Appendices	1.18

PART I: STRUCTURE AND FRAMEWORK

2 The Regulatory Framework
Enforcement authorities	2.01
Devolution	2.04
General powers of local authorities	2.07
Power of local authorities to prosecute	2.09
Local authority decisions	2.11
Appearance in legal proceedings	2.15
Limits to local authority powers	2.18
Local Government Ombudsman	2.20
Environmental health regulation by local authorities	2.27
Environment Agency	2.31
European dimension	2.34

3 The Historical Context of Statutory Nuisance and Public Health Legislation
Origins	3.01
Conceptual uncertainty	3.03
Legislative history	3.05
Early alternatives to statutory nuisance	3.06
Nuisance in the Industrial Revolution	3.07
Growth of a 'sanitary paradigm'	3.11
Present-day historicism	3.17
Legislative intention	3.21

4 The Concept of Statutory Nuisance
Introduction	4.01
The list of statutory nuisances	4.04
'Prejudicial to health or a nuisance'	4.08

Origins of the two limbs of statutory nuisance 4.09
The modern judicial approach 4.11
The nuisance limb 4.16
Public nuisance 4.25
Private nuisance 4.28
Public, private and statutory nuisances: differences and overlaps 4.34
The nuisance limb and the health limb 4.37
Is the nuisance limb limited to those matters which might also be 'prejudicial to health'? 4.41
Distinguishing the health and nuisance limbs 4.48
Reasonableness as a central concept of common law nuisance and its relevance to statutory nuisance 4.55
The health limb 4.82

PART II: THE SPECIFIC NUISANCES

5 Premises
Premises as a statutory nuisance 5.01
Meaning of 'premises in such a state . . .' 5.04
'State' of the premises 5.05
The meaning of 'premises' 5.30
Vessels 5.37
Premises suffering from dampness, condensation and mould 5.39
Can empty premises be prejudicial to health? 5.50
Identifying the premises 5.54
Liability for escape of the land itself 5.56
Public sewers 5.73
Defining 'premises' in other contexts 5.74
Defences 5.80
Alternative provisions relating to premises 5.83
Leasehold premises 5.106

6 Noise and Noise Nuisance
Introduction 6.01
Noise and statutory nuisance 6.09
Public nuisance 6.15
Legislative background of statutory noise nuisance 6.18
Section 79(1)(g) of the EPA 1990: 'noise emitted from premises so as to be prejudicial to health or a nuisance' 6.22
Legal requirements and the role of enforcement officers 6.32
Scope of noise nuisance 6.36
Neighbourhood and domestic noise 6.40
Noise Act 1996 6.51
Audible intruder alarms 6.63
Entertainment noise 6.65

CONTENTS ix

Entertainment noise and statutory nuisance		6.70
Drafting noise abatement notices under the EPA 1990		6.75
Noise emitted from industrial, commercial and business premises		6.79
The defence of best practicable means in noise cases		6.82
Noise in the street and other public places		6.91
Noise from construction sites		6.102
Statutory nuisance and other forms of noise control		6.119
Conclusion		6.138

7 Atmospheric Emissions
Origins 7.02
Smoke emitted from premises: application of subsection (1)(b) 7.05
Fumes or gases emitted from premises: application of
  subsection (1)(c) 7.14
Dust, steam, smell etc: application of subsection (1)(d) 7.17
Defences 7.28
Smoke, fumes or gases from vehicles, etc on a street: application
  of subsection (1)(gb) 7.29

8 Animals
Origins 8.02
Definition of 'animals' 8.03
Animals as a statutory nuisance 8.05
Bye-laws 8.18

9 Accumulations and Deposits
Origins 9.02
The waste management regime 9.04
Definitions 9.05
The obligation to remove accumulations 9.09
The nuisance or health limb requirement 9.11
The defence of 'best practicable means' 9.14

10 Miscellaneous Nuisances in Other Legislation
Statutory nuisances and watercourses 10.02
Meaning of watercourses 10.08
Persons who may be liable 10.19
Land Drainage Act 1991 10.22
Tents, vans, sheds and similar structures 10.26
Domestic water supply 10.30
Fencing of abandoned and disused mines and quarries 10.33

PART III: PROCEDURE AND EVIDENCE

11 Implications of the Human Rights Act 1998
Background to the Act 11.01
Applicable to all acts or decisions taken by public authorities 11.02

Application to acts of private individuals	11.07
Relationship between Convention rights and UK legislation	11.09
Persons entitled to bring judicial review proceedings under the Human Rights Act 1998	11.14
Impact of the Human Rights Act 1998 on local authority decision-making	11.17
The right to property	11.30
Article 8: Right to respect for private and family life	11.33
Article 7: No punishment without law	11.42
Article 6: Right to a fair trial	11.46
Regulation of Investigatory Powers Act 2000	11.69
Application of the Regulation of Investigatory Powers Act 2000 to statutory nuisance	11.72
Application of the Regulation of Investigatory Powers Act 2000 to statutory nuisance enforcement: Conclusions	11.87

12 Enforcement: Use of Abatement Notices

Introduction	12.01
Duty to inspect	12.02
Duty to respond to complaints	12.06
Is there a duty to consult?	12.12
Abatement notices: technical requirements	12.17
Time limit for undertaking work	12.58
Service of notices	12.60
Suspension of abatement notices	12.75
Withdrawing notices	12.78
Amending notices	12.81

13 Appeals against Abatement Notices

Introduction	13.01
Suspension of the notice	13.06
Grounds of appeal	13.12
Abatement notice is not justified by section 80 of the EPA 1990	13.13
Some informality, defect or error in, or in connection with, the abatement notice	13.17
The authority have refused unreasonably to accept compliance with alternative requirements, or the requirements of the abatement notice are otherwise unreasonable in character or extent, or are unnecessary	13.27
The time (or times) within which the requirements of the abatement notice are to be complied with is not reasonably sufficient for the purpose	13.37
Best practicable means were used to prevent, or to counteract the effects of, the nuisance (regulation 2(2)(e))	13.41

In the case of noise nuisance from premises or in the street, the requirements imposed by the notice are more onerous than those provided in other statutory notices or consents	13.47
Service on persons instead of the appellant or in addition to the appellant	13.49
Court's powers on appeal	13.57
Court's powers in respect of third parties	13.60
Amending the grounds of appeal	13.63
Pre-trial procedures	13.65
Procedures at trial	13.68
Costs	13.71
Appeals to the Crown Court	13.85
Appeals to the High Court	13.93

14 Offences and Prosecution for Breach of an Abatement Notice

Introduction	14.01
Offence of breach of abatement notice	14.04
Obstruction offences	14.13
Scope of 'obstruction'	14.17
Powers to seize and remove noise-making equipment	14.23
The decision to prosecute	14.26
Attorney-General's guidelines for bringing a prosecution	14.30
Public interest factors	14.34
Prosecutor's use of discretion	14.35
The *Enforcement Concordat*	14.37
Formal cautions	14.40
Who to prosecute	14.51
Corporate defendants	14.63
Crown immunity	14.66
Costs	14.68
Where the prosecution succeeds	14.71
Defence costs	14.82
Costs where the prosecution is brought improperly	14.87
Wasted costs	14.88
Compensation orders	14.91
Appeals to the Crown Court	14.94
Appeals to the Divisional Court	14.102

15 Defences

Defence of best practicable means	15.02
Without reasonable excuse	15.29

16 Section 82 Proceedings

Introduction	16.01
Section 82 and housing defects	16.04
Person aggrieved	16.08
Person responsible	16.11
Nature of the proceedings	16.15
The procedure	16.16
Abatement order	16.35
Compensation orders	16.41
Costs	16.52
Defences	16.57
Appeals	16.59
Default proceedings	16.61
Checklist for lay prosecutor starting proceedings under section 82	16.63

17 Other Remedies

Introduction	17.01
Alternative dispute resolution and mediation	17.02
Injunctions	17.11
Public nuisance	17.22
Judicial review	17.26
The *Wednesbury* principle and human rights	17.39
Applying for judicial review	17.52
Overlaps with other statutory regimes	17.57
Contaminated land	17.58
Authorization of nuisance by planning permission	17.61
Harassment	17.68

18 Overview of Evidential Issues and Preparation for Court

Introduction	18.01
The investigation	18.02
Using photographs	18.03
Using noise measurements	18.09
Using tape recordings	18.16
Using other technical and scientific data	18.17
Using documentary evidence	18.22
Using expert witnesses and opinion evidence	18.35
Officers' notebooks	18.43
Witness statements	18.46
Advance disclosure	18.55
Admissibility of evidence and the court hearing	18.78

Appendices 329

A. Environmental Protection Act 1990—Extracts 331
B. Statutory Nuisance (Appeals) Regulations 1955, SI 1995/2644 347
C. Other Legislation 351

Index 373

TABLE OF CASES

A Lambert Flat Management Ltd v Lomas [1981] 2 All ER 280;
  [1981] 1 WLR 898 .... 13.22, 15.38–15.40, 15.43
Aitken v South Hams DC [1995] 1 AC 262; [1994] 3 All ER 400;
  3 WLR 333; [1995] 159 JPR 25 .... 12.80
Allen v Gulf Oil Refinery Ltd [1979] 3 All ER 1008; revs'd [1981]
  AC 1001, HL 17.61–17.62, 17.64
AMEC Building Ltd v London Borough of Camden [1997] Env
  LR 330 .... 12.72, 14.07
Anderson v Dundee CC [2000] SLT (Sh Ct) 134; [1999] SCLR 518; [1999]
  Hous LR 82; [2000] EHLR Dig 96; [1999] GWD 1–52 .... 5.42
Anderson v Merseyside Improved Houses (QBD, CO/1792/95, 12 February
  1995, unreported) 5.42, 18.39
Andreae v Selfridge & Co Ltd [1938] Ch 1; [1937] 3 All ER
  255 .... 4.74, 4.79
Associated Provincial Picture Houses Ltd v Wednesbury
  Corporation [1947] 2 All ER 680; [1948] 1 KB 223 .... 12.13, 12.51, 13.11,
                                        14.103, 17.33, 17.39–17.40, 17.42
Attorney-General v Cole [1901] 1 Ch 205; 70 LJ Ch 148; 83 LT 725;
  65 JP 88 .... 4.55
Attorney-General v Great Eastern Rly (1880) 5 App Cas 473 .... 2.18
Attorney-General v PYA Quarries Ltd [1957] 2 QB 169 ...... 4.19, 4.26, 4.35,
                                                  6.15–6.16, 6.29, 17.23
Attorney-General v Tod Heatley [1897] 1 Ch 560 .... 4.35, 17.23
Attorney-General of the Gambia v N'Jie [1961] AC 617 .... 6.08
Attorney-General of Hong Kong v Ng Yuen Shiu [1983] 2 All ER 346;
  [1983] 2 AC 629 .... 12.14, 12.16
Attorney-General's Reference No 3 of 1979 [1979] 69 Cr App
  R 411 .... 18.44, 18.54
Autronic AG v Switzerland (1990) 12 EHRR 485 .... 11.16
Aviation & Shipping Co v Murray [1961] 1 WLR 974 .... 15.12

Bamford v Turnley (1862) 3 B&S 66; (1862) 31 LJQB 286 .... 4.55,
                                                              4.73, 6.45
Banbury Sanitary Authority v Page (1881) 8 QBD 97; 36 Digest 156;
  51 LMJC 21; 45 LT 759 .... 4.44
Bank of New Zealand v Greenwood [1984] 1 NZLR 525 .... 4.32
Barker v Herbert [1911] 2 KB 633 .... 5.60
Baroness Wenlock v River Dee Co (1885) 10 App Cas 354 .... 2.18

TABLE OF CASES

Barr & Stroud v West of Scotland Water Authority [1998]
    Env LR 3 D3 .... 7.22
Benjamin v Storr (1874) LR 9 CP 400 .... 4.75
Betts v Penge UDC [1942] 2KB 154; [1942] 2 All ER 61 .... 4.47
Birchall v Wirral UDC (1953) 117 JP 384 .... 16.06
Birmingham CC v Oakley [2001] 1 All ER 385; [2000] 3 WLR 1836;
    [2001] LGR 110; [2001] Env LR 37 .... 3.20–3.21, 3.24, 4.12–4.14,
                4.39, 4.49, 4.52, 4.86, 4.90, 5.05, 5.11, 5.13–5.14,
                          5.22, 5.26, 5.29, 5.84
Birmingham DC v Kelly (1985) 17 HLR 572 .... 5.12
Birmingham DC v McMahon (1987) 86 LGR 63; 151 JP 709;
    19 HLR 452 .... 5.55, 16.09
Bishop Auckland Local Board v Bishop Auckland Iron and Steel Co
    (1882) 10 QBD 138 .... 4.44, 9.06
Blackburn v ARC Ltd [1998] Env LR 469 .... 6.69
Blackpool BC v Johnstone; R v Blackpool Magistrates' Court,
    ex p Blackpool BC [1992] COD 463 .... 16.26
Bland v Yates (1914) 58 SJ 612 .... 9.06
Bliss v Hall (1838) 7 LJCP 122 .... 3.10
Bloodworth v Cormack [1949] NZLR 1058 .... 6.11
Bob Keats Ltd v Farrant [1951] 1 All ER 899 .... 2.15
Botross v London Borough of Hammersmith and Fulham [1995]
    Env LR 217; [1994] 16 Cr App Rep(s) 622; 27 HLR 179 .... 16.15, 16.41
Bowyer, Philpott & Payne Ltd v Mather [1919] 1 KB 419 .... 2.15
Bracey v Read [1963] Ch 88; [1962] 3 All ER 472; [1962] 3 WLR 1194;
    183 EG 773; [1962] EGD 292 .... 5.76
Bradford v Pickles [1895] AC 587 .... 4.71
Bradford City MC v Brown (1986) 84 LGR 731 .... 17.11
Bradford MBC v Booth (2000) 164 JP 485 .... 13.73–13.74
Brighton and Hove Council v Ocean Coachworks (Brighton) Ltd
    [2001] Env LR 4 .... 12.35, 12.43, 12.59
Briscoe v Drought (1860) 11 IRCom Law Rep 250 .... 10.09
Bristol City Football Supporters Club v The Commission [1975]
    VATRR 93 .... 5.78
British Celanese Ltd v Hunt [1969] 1 WLR 959 .... 4.76
Broadbent v Ramsbothom (1856) 11 Ex 602 .... 10.09
Brown v Bussell III (1867–8) LR 3 QB 251 .... 9.10
Budd v Colchester BC [1999] Env LR 739; [1999] JPL 717 ...... 4.61, 6.76,
                              12.51–12.52, 15.05
Butler v Standard Telephones and Cables Ltd [1940] 1 KB 399 ...... 15.64
Butuyuyu v London Borough of Hammersmith and Fulham (1996)
    29 HLR 584; [1997] Env LR D13 .... 13.02, 13.22, 15.41–15.43
Bybrook Barn Garden Centre Ltd v Kent CC [2001] Env LR 30 .... 10.21

Cambridge CC *v* Douglas [2001] Env LR 41 . . . . .6.75, 12.33, 12.40,12.75,
12.77, 13.08
Cambridge Water Company *v* Eastern Leather Counties plc [1994]
  2 AC 264; 1 All ER 53; 2 WLR 53 [1994] Env LR 105 . . . . .4.11, 4.34,
4.55, 4.76, 5.70, 6.45
Camden LBC *v* Gunby [2000] 1 WLR 465; [1999] 4 All
  ER 602 . . . . .10.32, 12.27
Carr *v* London Borough of Hackney (1995) 93 LGR 606; 28 HLR 749;
  160 JP 402 . . . . .16.13, 16.35
Central London Rly *v* Hammersmith BC (1904) 68 JP 217 . . . . .16.38
Chapman *v* Gosberton Farm Produce Company Ltd [1993]
  Env LR 191 . . . . .15.25–15.26
Christie *v* Davey [1893] 1 Ch 316 . . . . .4.71
City of London Corp *v* Bovis Construction Ltd [1992] 3 All ER 697;
  86 LGR 660 . . . . .6.109, 6.14, 17.15
Clayton *v* Sale UDC [1926] 1 KB 415 . . . . .14.57
Colam *v* Pagett (1883) 12 QBD 66 . . . . .8.03
Concentrate Manufacturing Company of Ireland (Trading as 7-Up International)
  v Coca-Cola Bottlers (Ulster) Ltd (6 October 1992, unreported) 5.74
Cook *v* Southend BC [1990] 2 QB 1 . . . . .17.55
Cooke *v* Adatia (1989) 153 JP 129 . . . . .18.42
Council of Civil Service Unions *v* Minister for the Civil Service [1985]
  AC 374; [1984] 3 All ER 935 . . . . .12.14, 17.37
Coventry CC *v* Cartwright [1975] 1 WLR 845; 2 All ER 99 . . . . . . .4.33, 4.93,
5.01, 5.40, 8.14, 9.08, 9.13
Coventry CC *v* Doyle [1981] 2 All ER 184; [1981] 1 WLR 1325;
  79 LGR 418; 125 Sol Jo 639 . . . . .5.52, 16.34
Cowl and Others *v* Plymouth CC, *The Times*, 8 January 2002 . . . . .17.03
Crowe *v* London Borough of Tower Hamlets, noted in LAG,
  May 1997 . . . . .16.35
Crown River Cruises *v* Kimbolton Fireworks [1996] 2 Lloyd's Rep
  533 . . . . .4.69, 4.74
Cunningham *v* Birmingham CC [1998] Env LR 1; (1997) 30 HLR 158;
  (1997) 96 LGR 231 . . . . 4.67, 4.84, 5.45
Curtis *v* Thompson (1956) 106 L Jo 61 . . . . .8.15

Davenport *v* Walsall MBC [1997] Env LR 24; (1995) 28 HLR 754; [1996]
  COD 107 . . . . .14.92, 16.15, 16.41, 16.43, 16.45, 16.56
Daventry DC *v* Olins (1990) 154 JP 478 . . . . .18.64
Davey *v* Harrow Corporation [1958] 1 QB 60 . . . . .5.64
De Freitas *v* Ministry of Agriculture [1999] 1 AC 69 . . . . .17.40
De Keyser's Royal Hotel Ltd *v* Spicer Bros Ltd (1914) 30 TLR 257 . . . . . .4.77
Debtor, Re A (No 490 of 1935) [1936] Ch 237 . . . . .15.13

Delaware Mansions Ltd and Flecksun Ltd v Westminster CC [2001]
    4 All ER 737; [2001] 3 WLR 1007; (2001) 44 EG 150 . . . . .4.31, 5.58,
                                                                5.64, 5.71, 12.29
Delcourt v Belgium (1979–80) 1 EHRR 355 . . . . .11.50
Dover DC v Farrar (1980) 2 HLR 32 . . . . .4.99, 5.47, 16.13
DPP v Denning and Pearce [1991] 2 QB 532 . . . . .14.82
Draper v Sperring (1861) 10 CB (NS) 113 . . . . .9.06
Dymond v Pearce [1972] 1 QB 496; [1972] 2 WLR 633; 116 SJ 62;
    [1972] 1 All ER 1142; [1972] RTR 169 . . . . .4.34, 4.55
Dudden v Clutton Union (1857) 26 LJ Ex 146 .10.09

East Devon DC v Farr (QBD Administrative Court, 30/1/2002,
    unreported) 11.57, 13.88
East Northamptonshire DC v Fossett [1994] Env LR 388 . . . . .4.74, 6.49,
                                                                12.32, 12.40
East Riding of Yorkshire Council v Yorkshire Water Services Ltd
    [2001] Env LR 113 . . . . .5.35, 5.73
East Staffordshire BC v Fairless [1999] Env LR 525 . . . . . .12.65, 16.28–16.29
Edgington v Swindon BC [1939] 1 KB 86 . . . . .6.125
Enfield LBC v B (a minor) and Another [2000] 1 All ER 255 . . . . .17.74

Farley v Skinner HL [2001] 4 All ER 801; [2001] 3 WLR 899 . . . . .6.120
Fernandez v Broad (QBD, CO/660/96) 10 July 1996,
    unreported 16.32–16.33
Field v Leeds CC [2000] EG 165; [2000] 1 EGLR 54 . . . . .5.43, 18.37
Fitzpatrick (AP) v Sterling Housing Association Ltd (1999) 32 HLR
    178 . . . . .5.10
Freda Gillings v Kirklees MBC [1999] 1 Env LR D2 . . . . .6.125

Galer v Morrissey [1955] 1 All ER 380; 1 WLR 110 . . . . .6.131, 8.05,
                                                                8.08, 8.14, 8.18
Gardiner v Sevenoaks RDC [1950] WN 260; 2 All ER 84 . . . . .5.75
Gaunt v Fynney (1872) 8 Ch App 8 . . . . .6.10
Gillingham BC v Medway Dock Co Ltd [1993] QB 343;
    [1992] 3 All ER 923; 3 WLR 449 . . . . .4.80, 6.69, 15.24, 17.63–17.65
GLC v London Borough of Tower Hamlets (1983)
    15 HLR 54 . . . . .4.100, 5.12, 5.39, 5.47, 16.13
GN Rly v Lurgan Town Commissioners [1897] 2 IR 340 . . . . .9.06
Godfrey v Conwy CBC [2001] Env LR 674 . . . . .4.16, 4.42, 4.47–4.48,
                                                                4.78, 6.07, 12.56
Goldman v Hargrave [1967] 1 AC 645; [1966] 2 All ER 989;
    [1966] 3 WLR 513 . . . . .5.62
Goodes v East Sussex CC [2000] 1 WLR 1356 . . . . .4.13

TABLE OF CASES

Grandi *v* Milburn [1966] 2 QB 263; [1966] 2 All ER 816; [1966] 3 WLR 90;
   64 LGR 375; 198 EG 1195; [1966] EGD 453 ....5.77
Gravesham BC *v* British Railways Board [1978] Ch 379 ....17.22
Great Western Rly Co *v* Bishop (1872) LR QB 550; 37 JP 5 ....4.41,
                                                            4.43, 4.93
Griffiths *v* Pembrokeshire CC [2000] Env LR 622 .....7.08, 7.10, 7.16, 14.75
Gwinnell *v* Eamer [1875] LR 10 CP 658 ....12.24

Halawa *v* Federation Against Copyright Theft (1995) 159 JP 816 ....18.78
Hall *v* Kingston upon Hull CC; Ireland *v* Birmingham CC; Baker *v* Birmingham
   CC [1999] 2 All ER 609; (1999) 96 LGR 184; [1999] Env LR D19;
   (1999) 31 HLR 1078 ....12.60, 12.64–12.65, 16.18, 16.23
Hall *v* Manchester Corporation (1915) 84 LJ Ch 732; 79 JP 385 ....16.06
Hammersmith LBC *v* Magnum Automated Forecourts Ltd [1978]
   1 WLR 50; 1 All ER 401 ....17.14
Hardman *v* North Eastern Rly (1878) 3 CPD 168 ....9.07
Haringey LBC *v* Hibbert [2001] Env LR 29 ....12.17, 12.61
Haringey LBC *v* Jowett (1999) LGR 667; 32 HLR 308 ....5.20
Harris *v* Hickman [1904] 1 KB 13 ....12.13
Harrison *v* Southwark and Vauxhall Water Co [1891] 2 Ch 409 ....4.69
Hatton and Others *v* United Kingdom (ECHR, No 36022/97,
   2 October 2001) 34 EHRR 1 ....6.122, 11.38
Hazell *v* Hammersmith & Fulham LBC [1992] 2 AC 1 ....2.08
Heap *v* Burnley Union Sanitary Authority (1884) 12 QBD 617 ....8.18
Heap *v* Ind Coope and Allsopp Ltd [1940] 2 KB 476 ....12.24
Heath *v* Brighton Corporation (1908) 98 LT 718 ....4.65
Herbert *v* Lambeth LBC (1991) 13 Cr App R (S) 489; 156 JP 389;
   24 HLR 299; 90 LGR 310 ....16.15, 16.41
Hester Dutch *v* Coventry CC [1996] Env LR D27 ....12.17
Hinchliffe *v* Sheldon [1995] 3 All ER 406 ....14.19
Hipperson *v* Electoral Registration Officer for the District of Newbury
   [1985] 3 WLR 61; 2 All ER 456; QB 1060 ....12.11
Holbeck Hall Hotel Ltd *v* Scarborough Council [2000] 2 All ER 705;
   [2000] 2 WLR 1396 ....5.66
Hollywood Silver Fox Farms *v* Emmett [1936] 2 KB 468 ....4.71
Howard *v* Walker [1947] KB 860; [1947] 2 All ER 197 ....4.18
Howarth *v* United Kingdom [2001] Crim LR 229 ....11.55
Hunter *v* Canary Wharf and London Docklands Development Corporation
   [1996] 1 All ER 482; aff'd [1997] 2 All ER 426; 2 WLR 684
   [1997] AC 655 ....4.11, 4.17, 4.23, 4.28–4.29, 4.31–4.32, 4.34, 4.79,
                        4.81, 6.45, 11.37, 12.11, 16.08, 16.43, 17.68, 17.70
Hussain and Another *v* Lancaster CC (1998) LGR 663; [2000] 1 QB 1
   (CA) 17.69

Ireland v United Kingdom (1979–80) 2 EHRR 25 ....11.06
Issa v London Borough of Hackney [1997] Env LR 157; 1 All ER 999;
    1 WLR 956 ....16.43

Jespers v Belgium (1981) 27 DR 61 ....11.60–11.61
Job Edwards Ltd v Birmingham Navigations Co Proprietors [1924]
    1 KB 341 ....5.63
Johnson v RSPCA (2000) 164 JPR 345 ....13.92
Johnsons News of London Ltd v London Borough of Ealing (1989)
    154 JP 33 ....13.04, 15.15
Jordan v Norfolk CC [1994] 4 All ER 218 ....12.07

Kenny v Preen [1963] 1 QB 499 ....6.27
Khan (Sultan) v United Kingdom [2000] Crim LR 684 ....11.49
Khorasandjian v Bush [1993] QB 727 ....17.68
Kirklees MBC v Field and Others [1998] Env LR 337; (1998) 30
    HLR 869 .... 5.02, 5.57, 12.39, 12.55–12.56
Kirklees MBC v Wickes Building Supplies [1993] AC 227 ....17.20
Kokkinakis v Greece (1994) 17 EHRR 397 ....11.43
Kruse v Johnson [1898] 2 QB 91 ....4.50

LB & SC Rly v Haywards Heath UDC (1899) 86 LT 266 ....9.06
Lambeth LBC v Mullings, *The Times*, 16 January 1990 ....12.61
Lambeth LBC v Stubbs (1980) 255 EG 789; 78 LGR 650 ....5.50
Lambie and Minter v Thanet DC [2001] Env LR 21 ......12.42, 12.47, 16.39
Leakey v The National Trust for Places of Historic Interest or Natural
    Beauty [1980] QB 485; [1980] 1 All ER 17; [1980] 2 WLR 65 ....5.57,
                                                                5.62–5.63
Leanse v Egerton [1943] KB 323 ....12.29
Leeds v London Borough of Islington [1998] Env LR 655; 31 HLR
    545 ....12.60, 16.18, 16.24
Lemmon v Webb [1894] 3 Ch 1; aff'd [1895] AC 1 ....5.64
Lewisham LBC v Fenner (1995) 248 ENDS Report 44 ....16.15
Lister v Pickford (1865) 34 Beav 576 ....6.61
Lithgow v United Kingdom (1986) 8 EHRR 329 ....11.16
Lloyds Bank plc v Guardian Assurance plc and Trollope & Colls Ltd (1986)
    35 BLR 34 ....6.102
London & Leeds Estates Ltd v Paribas Ltd (No 2) [1995] 1 EGLR
    102 ....18.37
London Borough of Camden v London Underground Ltd [2000] Env
    LR 369 ....4.16, 6.127, 12.49, 12.52, 12.81, 15.15

London Borough of Ealing Trading Standards v Woolworths plc
  [1995] Crim LR 58 ....18.79
London Borough of Southwark v Simpson [1999] Env LR 553;
  31 HLR 725 ....4.102, 5.42, 18.39–18.40
Lopez-Ostra v Spain (1994) 20 EHRR 277 ....11.23, 11.40
Lowe & Watson v South Somerset DC [1998] Env LR 143 ....4.37, 11.32,
                                                              12.37, 16.37

M & JS Properties Ltd v White [1959] 2 QB 25; [1959] 2 All ER 81;
  [1959] 2 WLR 525; 173 EG 675; [1959] EGD 90 ....5.79
McCann v UK (1995) 21 EHRR 97 ....11.15
McCombe v Read [1955] 2 QB 429 ....5.64
McGillivray v Stephenson [1950] 1 All ER 942 ....16.37
McKay v Secretary of State for the Environment and Others [1994]
  JPL 806 ....12.32
M'Nab v Robertson [1897] AC 129 ....10.09
McQuaker v Goddard [1940] 1KB 687 ....8.03
Malton Board of Health v Malton Manure Co (1879) 4 Ex
  D 302 ....4.43, 7.25
Manchester Corporation v Farnworth [1930] AC 171 ....15.23
Manley v New Forest DC [2000] EHLR 113; [1999] 4 PLR 36 .....6.86, 8.09,
                                                              15.05, 15.24, 15.27
Mannai Investment v Eagle Star [1997] AC 749 ....12.49
Marcic v Thames Water Utilities Ltd [2002] EWCA Civ 65 ....4.55, 5.63,
                                                              10.21, 11.25
Margate Pier and Harbour (Proprietors Co) v Margate Town Council (1869)
  20 LT 564; (1869) 33 JP 437 ....4.16, 5.71, 9.06, 9.10, 9.13
Masters v Brent LBC [1978] 1 QB 841 ....5.64
Maunsell v Olins [1975] AC 373 ....5.33
Medicaments and Related Classes of Goods (No 4), Re, *The Times*,
  7 August 2001 ....11.16, 14.90, 17.56
Millard v Wastall [1898] 1 QB 342 ....16.38
Miller-Mead v Minister of Housing and Local Government [1963]
  2 QB 196 ....12.32
Minelli v Switzerland (1983) 5 EHHR 554 ....14.86
Mint v Good [1951] 1 KB 517 ....12.24
Morgan v Khyatt [1964] 1 WLR 475 ....5.64
Morgan v Liverpool Corporation [1927] 2 KB 131 ....16.06
Munroe v DPP [1988] Crim LR 823 ....14.99
Murdoch v Glacier Metal Company Ltd [1998] Env LR 732 ....4.16,
                                                              6.27, 18.11
Murray v United Kingdom (1996) 22 EHRR 29 ....11.53
Myatt v Teignbridge DC [1994] Env LR 242 ....12.35, 12.51

TABLE OF CASES

National Coal Board v Neath BC (sometimes cited as National Coal Board v Thorne) [1976] 2 All ER 478; [1976] 1 WLR 543; 239 EG 121 ......4.33, 4.47, 4.97, 5.01, 6.26
National Justice Naviera SA v Prudential Assurance Co Ltd ('The Ikarian Reefer') [1993] 2 EGLR 183; [1993] 2 Lloyds Rep 68 ....18.37
National Rivers Authority v Shell UK [1990] 1 Water Law 40 ....15.21, 18.84
Neath RDC v Williams [1950] 2 All ER 625; [1951] 1 KB 115 ....10.20, 14.59
Network Housing Association v Westminster CC (1994) 93 LGR 280; 27 HLR 189; [1995] Env LR 176 ....12.44, 12.52
Neville v Gardner Merchant Ltd (1984) 83 LGR 577; (1983) 5 Cr App RCS 349 ....14.75
Nimmo v Alexander Cowan & Sons Ltd [1968] AC 106 ....15.33
Noble v Harrison [1926] 2 KB 332........................5.59, 5.69
North Cornwall DC v Welton and Welton [1997] 161 JP; (1997) LGR 114 ....12.19
Northern Ireland Trailers Ltd v Preston Corporation [1972] 1 All ER 260 ....16.31
Nottingham Corporation v Newton [1974] 2 All ER 760 ....16.37

O'Toole v Knowsley MBC [1999] Env LR D29; *The Times*, 21 May 1999 ....4.103, 5.42, 18.39
Overseas Tankship (UK) Ltd v Miller Steamship Co Pty, The Wagon Mound (No 2) [1967] 1 AC 617 ....17.22

Patel v Blakey (1987) 151 JP 532 ....14.82
Patel v Mehtab (1980) 5 HLR 78 ....4.96, 4.101, 5.01, 5.42, 18.36
Pearshouse v Birmingham CC [1999] Env LR 536; 96 (1999) LGR 169; (1999) JPL 725 ....5.46, 16.02, 16.18, 16.25, 16.27–16.28
Phillips v Crawford (1984) 82 LGR 199 ....8.20
Phonographic Performance Ltd v Pontin's Ltd [1968] Ch 290; [1967] 3 All ER 736 ....5.78
Pike v Sefton MBC [2000] Env LR D31 ....4.99, 5.47, 16.13
Pollway Nominees v London Borough of Havering (1989) 88 LGR 192; 21 HLR 462...........................5.40–5.41, 5.55, 12.23, 16.10
Polsue and Alfieri v Rushmer [1907] AC 121 ....4.79
Polychronakis v Richards & Jerrom Ltd [1998] Env LR 347 .....14.09, 15.06, 15.33–15.34, 15.43
Pontardawe RDC v Moore-Gwyn [1929] 1 Ch 656 ....5.02, 5.57
Powell and Rayner v United Kingdom (1990) 12 EHRR 355 ....11.25, 11.38
Practice Direction (Crime: Costs) [1991] 1 WLR 498; amended by [1999] 1WLR 1832; [2000] 1 Cr App Rep 60 ....14.83, 14.85–14.86

TABLE OF CASES

Quigley *v* Liverpool Housing Trust (1999) EGCS 94 ....5.47, 5.49, 16.12

R *v* Abadom [1983] 1 All ER 364 ....18.41
R *v* Ashford Justices, ex p Hilden [1993] QB 555 ....18.28
R *v* Associated Octel Co Ltd [1997] 1 Cr App Rep (S) 435 ......12.52, 14.73, 14.81, 14.84
R *v* Barnet and Camden Rent Tribunal, ex p Frey Investments Ltd [1972]
  2 QB 342 ....17.35
R *v* Beddoe (1893) 1 Ch 547 ....16.55
R *v* Birmingham CC, ex p Ferrero Ltd [1993] 1 All ER 530 ....12.12
R *v* Board of Trustees of the Science Museum [1993] 3 All ER 853;
  (1993) 158 JP 39 ....6.129, 17.57
R *v* Bolton Justices, ex p Wildish (1983) 147 JP 309 ....14.82
R *v* Breeze [1973] 1 WLR 994 ....15.13
R *v* Brentford Justices, ex p Wong [1981] QB 445 ....14.26
R *v* Briscoe (1993) 15 Cr App R (S) 699 ....16.44
R *v* Bristol CC, ex p Everett [1998] 1 WLR 92; 3 All ER 603; affd [1999]
  2 All ER 193; 1 WLR 1170; Env LR 587 ....3.21–3.24, 4.12, 4.49,
    4.52, 4.86, 4.88–4.89, 5.24–5.26, 5.29, 5.83, 5.85,
    12.17, 12.78, 13.81, 17.31
R *v* British Steel [1995] IRLR 310; 1 WLR 1356 ....6.128
R *v* Broadcasting Standards Commission, ex p British Broadcasting Corporation
  [2000] EWCA Civ 116 ....11.16
R *v* Bros (1901) LT 581 ....16.32
R *v* Cannock Justices, ex p Astbury (1972) 70 LGR 609; 224 Estates Gazette
  1037 ....12.78
R *v* Cardiff CC, ex p Cross (1982) 6 HLR 1 ....5.46, 16.04
R *v* Carr-Briant [1943] KB 607 ....15.06
R *v* Carrick DC, ex p Shelley [1996] Env LR 273; (1996) JPR
  912 (1996) 95 LGR 620; [1996] JPL 857 ....2.24, 4.16, 4.25, 4.36,
    4.47, 4.98, 9.04, 9.06, 12.13, 12.17, 13.74, 15.11, 17.07, 17.29, 17.44
R *v* Chappell (1984) CLR 574 ....16.45
R *v* Clarke [1969] 1 WLR 1109 ....15.32
R *v* Colohan, *The Times*, 14 June 2001 ....17.72
R *v* Cooper [1982] Crim LR 308 ....14.92
R *v* Cross (1826) 2 C&P 483; 172 ER 219 ....3.09
R *v* Crown Court at Canterbury, ex p Howson-Ball [2001] Env LR 36 ....6.77,
    11.57, 12.41, 13.88, 14.95, 15.28
R *v* Da Silva [1990] 1 WLR 31 ....18.54
R *v* Denton, *The Times*, 22 November 2000 ....11.63, 18.26
R *v* Devon CC, ex p Baker [1995] 1 All ER 73 ....12.14, 17.50
R *v* Donovan (1982) 3 Cr App R (S) 192; [1982] RTR 126 ....16.44
R *v* Dovermoss Ltd [1995] Env LR 258 ....10.09

R v Dudley Magistrates' Court, ex p Hollis and Another [1998] Env
  LR 354; 1 All ER 759; [1999] 1 WLR 642 ....16.52, 16.54–16.56
R v Dunmow Justices, ex p Nash (1993) 157 JP 1153 ....18.60
R v Edwards [1975] 1 QB 27 ....15.32
R v Epping (Waltham Abbey) Justices, ex p Burlinson [1948] 1 KB 79;
  [1947] 2 All ER 537; 63 TLR 628; 112 JP 3; 46 LGR 6;
  [1947] WN 274 ....9.06, 16.01
R v F Howe & Sons (Enginers) Ltd [1999] 2 All ER 249 ....15.21, 18.84
R v Fairfax [1995] Crim LR 949 ....18.29
R v Falmouth and Truro Port Health Authority, ex p South West Water Ltd
  [1989] Env LR 833; affd [2000] 3 All ER 306; 3 WLR 1464 ....3.05, 3.21,
        4.12, 4.52, 6.39, 6.78, 8.10, 10.05, 10.11, 10.13, 10.17, 11.27, 11.45,
            12.12, 12.15–12.16, 12.39, 12.48, 12.50–12.52, 12.55–12.56, 12.58,
                                    13.17, 13.25, 16.35, 17.44, 17.51
R v Fenny Stratford Justices, ex p Watney Mann (Midlands) Ltd [1976]
  2 All ER 888; [1976] 1 WLR 1101; 140 JP 474; 238 EG 417;
  75 LGR 72..12.40, 16.39
R v Friskies Pet Care (UK) Ltd [2000] 2 Cr App R (S) 401 ....18.84
R v Gough [1993] AC 646 ....17.47
R v Harrow Crown Court, ex p Dave [1994] 1 WLR 98; 1 All
  ER 315 ....13.88, 14.95
R v Hereford Corporation, ex p Harrower [1970] 1 WLR 1424 ....2.12
R v Highbury Corner Magistrates' Court, ex p Edwards [1994] Env
  LR 215 ....16.07
R v Home Secretary, ex p Ruddock [1987] 1 WLR 1482 ....17.49
R v Horseferry Road Justices, ex p Underwoods (Cash Chemists) Ltd [1985]
  81 Cr App R 334 ....14.86
R v Horseferry Road Magistrates' Court, ex p Prophet (DC, CO/1339/93,
  24 February 1994) (Transcript: Smith Bernal) 16.49
R v Horsham Justices, ex p Richards [1985] 1 WLR 986;
  2 All ER 1114 ....16.45
R v Hunt [1987] AC 352 ....15.32
R v Inland Revenue Commissioners, ex p Mead [1993] 1 All ER 772 ...14.35,
                                                                14.39
R v Inland Revenue Commissioners, ex p National Federation of Self Employed
  & Small Businesses Ltd [1982] AC 617 ....17.55
R v Inner London Crown Court, ex p Bentham [1989] 1 WLR 408 ......16.02
R v Ireland [1998] AC 147 ....4.13, 5.10
R v Jenkins (1923) 87 JP 115 ....15.06
R v Jones [1988] 10 Cr App R (S) 95 ....14.81
R v Keane [1994] 1 WLR 746; 2 All ER 478 ....18.56
R v Kennet DC, ex p Somerfield [1999] JPL 361 ....6.69
R v King (1895) 59 JP 571 ....8.06

R v Knightsbridge Crown Court, ex p Abdillahi [1999] 1 Env LR
 (D1) 16.46
R v Knightsbridge Crown Court, ex p Cataldi [1999] Env LR
 62 ....12.51–12.52
R v Kneeshaw [1975] QB 57; [1974] 1 All ER 896 ....16.42
R v Knowsley MBC, ex p Williams [2001] Env LR 28 ...14.100, 16.34–16.35
R v Lister and Biggs (1857) 26 LJMC 196; 21 JP 422 ....17.23
R v Liverpool Corp, ex p Liverpool Taxi Fleet Operators' Association
 [1972] 2 QB 299 ....12.14, 17.50
R v Liverpool Crown Court, ex p Cooke [1997] 1 WLR 700;
 [1996] 4 All ER 589 ....16.16, 16.25, 16.46–16.47, 16.52
R v Lloyd (1802) 4 Esp 200; 170 ER 691 ....6.29
R v London Borough of Tower Hamlets, ex p Tower Hamlets Combined
 Traders Association [1994] COD 325 ....11.16
R v Madden [1975] 3 All ER 155; [1975] 1 WLR 1379; 61 Cr App Rep 254;
 139 JP 685...4.26, 6.29
R v Manchester Stipendiary Magistrate, ex p Hill [1983] 1 AC 328 .....16.31
R v Mattey and Queeley [1995] 2 Cr App 409; [1995] Crim LR 308 .....18.34
R v Meath Justices (1899) 34 ILT 47 ....16.38
R v Mildenhall Magistrates' Court, ex p Forest Heath DC, *The Times*,
 16 May 1997 ....14.104
R v Milford Haven Port Authority [2000] Env LR 632 ....15.21, 18.84
R v Ministry of Defence, ex p Smith and Others [1996] QB 517 ....17.39
R v Newham Justices, ex p Hunt [1976] 1 WLR 420;
 1 All ER 839 ....16.15, 16.26
R v Newham Magistrates, ex p Newham (QBD, CO/2771/92, 29 June 1993,
 unreported)..5.14
R v Newton (1983) 77 Cr App R 13; [1983] Crim LR 198 ..1.18, 14.100, 18.86
R v Northallerton Magistrates' Court, ex p Dove [2000] 1 Cr App Rep (S)
 136; 163 JP 657 ....14.81
R v Nottingham Justices, ex p Brown [1960] 1 WLR 1315;
 3 All ER 625 ....16.31
R v O'Brian and Enkel [2000] Env LR 653 ....15.21, 18.84
R v Old Street Magistrates' Court, ex p London Borough of Hackney
 (QBD, 9 February 1994), (Transcript: Smith Bernal) 12.67
R v Pappineau (1726) 2 Stra 686; 93 ER 784 ....17.25
R v Parlby (1889) 22 QBD 520; 53 JP 327 ....5.36, 5.73
R v Ruffell [1992] 13 Cr App R(S) 204............................6.15
R v Sandhu [1997] Crim LR 288 ....14.02
R v Secretary of State for the Environment, ex p Hillingdon LBC
 [1986] 1 WLR 807; 2 All ER 273 ....2.14
R v Secretary of State for the Environment, ex p Ostler [1976]
 3 All ER 90; 3 WLR 288; affd [1977] 1 WLR 258, HL 13.02

R v Secretary of State for the Environment, ex p Watney Mann (Midlands) Ltd
 [1976] JPL 368 .... 16.37
R v Secretary of State for Foreign & Commonwealth Affairs, ex p World Devel-
 opment Movement Ltd [1995] 1 WLR 386; 1 All ER 611 .... 17.56
R v Secretary of State for the Home Department, ex p Daly [2001]
 UKHL 26 .... 17.40
R v Secretary of State for the Home Department, ex p Hargreaves
 [1997] 1 All ER 397; 1 WLR 906 .... 17.49
R v Secretary of State for the Home Department, ex p Swati [1986]
 1 WLR 477 .... 17.52
R v Senior [1899] 1 QB 283 .... 14.19
R v Shorrock [1994] QB 279; [1993] 3 WLR 698; 3 All ER 917;
 [1993] Env LR 500 .... 4.35, 4.69, 4.74, 6.15, 6.99, 17.23
R v Somerset CC, ex p Fewings [1995] 1 All ER 513 .... 2.08
R v South Ribble Magistrates, ex p Cochrane [1996] Cr App R 544 ..... 18.54
R v South Somerset DC, ex p DJB (Group) Ltd (1989) LGR 624 .... 2.11
R v Southend Stipendiary Magistrate, ex p Rochford DC [1995] Env
 LR 1 .... 13.72
R v Stewart 12 A&E 773 .... 9.10
R v Swansea Crown Court, ex p Stacey [1990] RTR 183; (1990)
 154 JP 185 .... 14.96
R v Swaysland [1987] BTLC 299 .... 15.06
R v Taylor [1991] 13 Cr App R(S) 466 .... 6.15
R v Thames Magistrates' Court, ex p Clapton Cash & Carry Ltd
 (1989) COD 518 .... 17.31
R v Thames Magistrates' Court, ex p Greenbaum (1957) 55
 LGR 129 .... 17.55
R v Tindall (1837) 6 Ad & El 143; 1 JP 139 .... 10.04
R v Tottenham Justices, ex p Joshi [1982] 1 WLR 631; [1982]
 2 All ER 507 .... 14.70, 14.81
R v Wakefield Magistrates' Court, ex p Wakefield MBC [2000] Env LR
 D18 .... 7.22
R v Walden-Jones, ex p Coton [1963] Crim LR 839 .... 8.15
R v Ward [1993] 2 All ER 577 .... 18.56
R v Waters [1997] Crim LR 823; 141 SJ LB 58; 161 JP 249 .... 18.27
R v West London Metropolitan Stipendiary Magistrate, ex p Klahn
 [1979] 1 WLR 933 .... 16.32
R v Wheatley, ex p Cowburn (1885) 16 QBD 34; 50 JP 424 .... 5.12, 12.39
R v Whitchurch (1881) 7 QB 534 .... 16.15
R v Wicks [1997] 2 All ER 801 .... 13.19
R v York City Justices, ex p Farmery (1988) 153 JP 257 .... 14.90
R (on the application of Aircraft Research Association Ltd) v Bedford BC
 [2001] Env LR 700 .... 6.07

R (on the application of Anne and Another) v Test Valley BC [2001]
  48 EG 127 (CS) 4.66, 4.84, 5.45, 12.08, 17.42
R (on the application of Knowsley MBC) v Williams (QBD (Divisional Court),
  CO/5010/1999, CO/1432/2000, 19 October 2000) (Transcript: Smith
  Bernal) 9.03
R (on the application of Mahmood) v Secretary of State for the Home
  Department [2001] 1 WLR 840 ....17.41
Railtrack plc v Wandsworth LBC, see Wandsworth LBC v
  Railtrack plc 17.23
Rapier v London Tramways [1893] 2 Ch 588 ....6.126
Rawstron v Taylor (1855) 11 Ex 369 ....10.09
Rayner v United Kingdom (1978) 14 DR 234 ....11.31
Reed, Bowen & Co, ex p Official Receiver, Re (1887) 19 QBD 178 .....16.08
Rhondda Waste Disposal Company Ltd, Re [2001] Ch 57 ....12.72, 14.64
Richards Hewlings v McLean Homes East Anglia Ltd [2001] Env LR 323;
  [2001] 2 All ER 281 ....12.60, 12.65, 16.18
Ridehalgh v Horsefield [1994] 3 All ER 848; Ch 205; 3 WLR 462 ......14.89
Rioters' Case (1683) 1 Vern 174 ....17.26
Robertson v Watson (1949) JC 73 ....15.06
Robinson v Kilvert (1889) 41 Ch D 88 ....4.64
Rolls v Miller (1894) 27 Ch D 71 ....15.13
Runnymede BC v Ball [1986] 1 All ER 629; 1 WLR 353 ....17.14
Rushmer v Polsue and Alfieri Ltd [1906] 1 Ch 234 ....6.79
Rylands v Fletcher (1868) LR 3 HL 330; [1861–73] All ER
  Rep 1 ....4.76, 5.62, 5.70

Saddleworth UDC v Aggregate and Sand Ltd [1970] 69 LGR 103 ......15.33
St Helen's Smelting Co v Tipping (1865); [1865]
  12 LT 776; 11 ER 1483 ....3.08, 4.78
St Leonard Vestry v Holmes (1886) 50 JP 132: 2.15, n 26 ....2.15
Salford CC v McNally [1976] AC 379; [1975] 2 All ER 860;
  [1975] 3 WLR 87; 139 JP 694; 73 LGR 408; 236 Estates Gazette 555;
  119 Sol Jo 475 ....4.38, 4.45, 4.47, 4.49, 4.93, 4.96,
                                     4.101, 4.104, 6.28, 12.09, 16.37
Sampson v Hodson-Pressinger [1981] 3 All ER 710 12 HLR 40 ....12.29
Sandwell MBC v Bujok [1990] 3 All ER 385; [1990] 1 WLR
  1350 ....16.08, 16.26, 16.52
Saunders v United Kingdom (1997) 23 EHRR 313 ....11.67
Saunders, Ex p (1883) 11 QBD 191 ....4.96, 5.12
Scarborough Corporation v Scarborough Rural Sanitary Authority (1876) 1 Ex
  D 344; 34 LT 768; 40 JP 726; 36 Digest 235, 745 ....9.06
Schofield, Ex p (1891) 2 QB 428 ....16.15
Schofield v Schunck (1855) 19 JP 84 ....13.34, 15.23

SCM (United Kingdom) Ltd v WJ Whittal & Sons Ltd [1970] 1 WLR
   1017 .... .4.76
Sedleigh-Denfield v O'Callaghan [1940] AC 880; [1940] 3 All ER
   349 .... 5.62–5.63, 10.21, 12.29, 14.59
Sevenoaks DC v Brands Hatch Leisure Group Ltd [2001] Env LR 86 .... .6.75,
                                              12.40, 12.51, 12.56, 16.39
SFI Group plc (formerly Surrey Free Inns plc) v Gosport BC [1999] Env LR
   750; (1999) LGR 610 .... 5.50, 5.52, 6.76, 12.51–12.52, 13.04,
                                              13.14, 13.43, 15.15
Sheringham UDC v Halsey (or Holsey) (1904) 68 JP 395 ....17.22
Shoreham-by-Sea UDC v Dolphin Canadian Proteins (1972) 71 LGR
   261 .... .4.35, 17.23
Sidebotham, Re (1880) 14 Ch D 458 ....16.08
Silles v Fulham BC [1903] 1 KB 829 ....12.13
Skinner v Jack Breach [1927] 2 KB 220 ....15.12
Slater v Worthington's Cash Stores (1930) Ltd [1941] 1 KB 488;
   3 All ER 28 .... .9.09
Smith v Marrable (1843) 11 M&W 5 ....5.106
Smith v United Kingdom [1998] EHRLR 499 ....17.39–17.40
Smith v Waghorn (1863) 27 JP 744 ....9.06
Snape v Mulvenna, The Times, 28 December 1994 ....14.19
Société Stenuit v France (1992) 14 EHHR 509 ....11.16
Soering v UK (1989) 11 EHRR 439 ....11.25
Solihull MBC v Maxfern Ltd [1977] 2 All ER 177; [1977] 1 WLR 127 ...2.10
Solloway v Hampshire CC (1981) 79 LGR 449 ....5.62
Somersetshire Drainage Commissioners v Bridgwater (1899) 81 LT
   729 ....10.08
South Eastern and Chatham Rly Company's Managing Committee
   (1902) 24 MCC 343 ....9.06
Southwark LBC v Ince (1989) 153 JP 597; (1989) 21 HLR 504 ....5.14,
                                              5.16–5.18, 5.21–5.22, 5.28
Southwark London Borough Council v Tanner and others; Baxter v Camden
   London Borough Council (No 2), House of Lords, [2001] 1 AC 1;
   [1999] 4 All ER 449; [1999] 45 EG 179; [1999] 3 WLR 939;
   [1999] 3 EGLR 35; [2000] LGR 138; 32 HLR 148 .... .4.11, 4.34,
                                              5.106, 6.45, 6.47
Sovereign Rubber Ltd v Stockport MBC [2000] Env LR 194 ....12.15, 12.32,
                                 12.34, 12.76, 13.06, 13.11, 13.20, 13.59, 15.15
Spicer v Smee [1946] 1 All ER 489 ....4.76
Spruzen v Dossett (1896) 12 TLR 246 ....6.11
Stanley v London Borough of Ealing [2000] Env LR D18; (1999)
   32 HLR 753 .... 5.41, 9.03, 9.06, 12.32, 12.35, 12.45–12.46, 12.68
Steel v UK (1999) 28 EHRR 603 ....12.56

TABLE OF CASES

Sterling Homes (Midlands) Ltd v Birmingham CC [1996] Env LR 121 ... .6.75, 12.39,12.52, 13.28
Stevenage BC v Wilson [1993] Env LR 214 .... .5.32
Stoke-on-Trent CC v B & Q (Retail) Ltd [1984] AC 754; 2 WLR 929;
   2 All ER 332 .... .17.13
Stollmeyer v Trinidad Lake Petroleum Co [1918] AC 485 .... .10.09
Stone v Bolton [1950] 1 KB 201; [1949] 2 All ER 851;
   affd [1951] AC 850; 1 All ER 1078 .... .4.58, 4.60, 4.63
Sturges v Bridgman (1879) 11 Ch D 852 .... .4.79
Sunday Times v United Kingdom (1979–80) 2 EHRR 245 .... .11.28
SW v UK (1995) EHRR 363 .... .12.56

Tadema Holdings Ltd v Alan Ferguson (1999) EGCS 138 .... .12.69
Tarry v Ashton [1876] LR 1 QBD 314 .... .4.22
Tate & Lyle Food and Distribution Ltd v GLC [1983] 2 AC 509;
   2 WLR 649; [1983] 1 All ER 1159 .... .4.22
Taylor v St Helens Corporation (1877) 6 Ch D 264 .... .10.08
Taylor v Walsall & District Property & Investment Co Ltd
   [1998] Env LR 600 .... .16.53–16.54
Thompson-Schwab v Costaki [1956] 1 WLR 335 .... .4.32
Todd v Flight (1860) 9 CB (NS) 377; 3 LT 325 .... .12.24
Tough v Hopkins [1904] 1 KB 805 .... .16.38
Tower Hamlets LBC v Creitzman (1984) 148 JP 360; 83 LGR 72 ...... .6.94
Town Investments Ltd v DOE [1976] 3 All ER 479; [1976]
   1 WLR 1126 .... .15.14
Tulkington and Others v Times Newspapers (Northern Ireland) [2000]
   3 WLR 1670 .... .5.10

Universal Salvage Ltd and Robinson v Boothby [1984] RTR 289;
   (1984) 148 JP 347 .... .14.103

Vale of White Horse DC v Allen & Partners [1997] Env LR
   212 .... .17.12–17.13
Van der Mussele v Belgium (1984) 6 EHRR 163 .... .11.06
Vel v Chief Constable of North Wales [1987] Crim LR 498; (1987)
   151 JP 510 .... .18.78

Walter v Selfe (1851) 20 LJ Ch 433; (1851) 4 DeG & Sm 315;
   64 ER 849 .... .4.64
Wandsworth LBC v Railtrack plc [2001] 1 WLR 368; [2001] Env LR 23;
   affrmd in Railtrack plc v Wandsworth LBC (2001) LGR 544,
   CA 5.71, 8.07, 9.03, 9.09, 17.23
Wanstead Local Board of Health v Wooster (1874) 38 JP 21 .... .8.18

TABLE OF CASES

Warner v London Borough of Lambeth (1984) 15 HLR 42 ....12.26
Wealden BC v Hollings (1992) 4 Land Management and Env LR 126 ....7.22
Wellingborough BC v Gordon [1993] Env LR 218; (1990) 155 JP 494 ...6.44,
    12.79, 15.16, 15.36–15.37, 15.43
Welton v North Cornwall DC [1997] 1 WLR 570 ....6.85, 13.34
Westminster CC v Select Management Ltd [1985] 1 WLR 576 ....5.103
Whatling v Rees (1940) 79 JP 209 ....16.39
Wheeler v Saunders [1996] Ch 19; [1995] 2 All ER 697;
   [1995] 3 WLR 466 ....4.81, 6.69, 7.22, 15.24, 17.65–17.66
Whitehouse v Jordan [1981] 1 WLR 246; 1 All ER 267 ....18.38
Wiggins v United Kingdom (1978) 13 DR 40 ....11.37
Wilkinson, Re [1922] 1 KB 584 ....15.13–15.14
Wilson's Music and General Printing Co v Finsbury BC [1908]
   1 KB 563; 72 JP 37 ....12.13
Wiltshier Construction Ltd v Westminster CC [1997] Env LR 321 ......12.34
Wincanton RDC v Parsons [1905] 2 KB 34; 69 JP 242 ....14.58
Wivenhoe Port v Colchester BC [1985] JPL 176 ......4.47, 7.20, 15.21–15.22
Wycombe DC v Jeffways and Pilot Coaches (1983) 81 LGR 662 ...4.55, 15.21

Young and Harston's Contract, Re (1885) 31 Ch D 168 ....14.57

TABLES OF LEGISLATION

UK STATUTES

Access to Neighbouring Land Act 1992
   s 1 . . . . .12.26
Airports Act 1986
   s 63 . . . . .6.122
Animals Act 1971 . . . . .8.17
   s 2 . . . . .8.05
      (2) 8.05
      3 . . . . .8.05
      4 . . . . .8.05
      11 . . . . .8.03
Audit Commission Act 1998
   s 17 . . . . .12.19
   18 . . . . .12.19
Building Act 1984 . . . . .3.01, 3.05, 5.10, 5.57, 5.84, 5.87,
                                                    5.97, 17.57
   s 76 . . . . .5.84, 5.85, 5.87, 5.94, 5.95
      (1) 5.87
        (b) 5.85
   77 . . . . .5.95
   78 . . . . .5.96
   94 . . . . .5.88
   95 . . . . .5.97
   96 . . . . .5.97
Celluloid and Cinematograph Film Act 1922 . . . . .5.75
Chancery Amendment Act 1858 . . . . .3.06
Civil Aviation Act 1982 . . . . .6.121, 6.123
   s 76(1) 6.120
Clean Air Act 1956
   s 16(1) 3.05
Clean Air Act 1968 . . . . .3.05
Clean Air Act 1993 . . . . .3.05, 7.02, 7.07
   s 1 . . . . .App C
   2 . . . . .App C
   3 . . . . .7.05, App C
      (2) 7.02
   64(1) 7.05
Common Law Procedure Act 1854 . . . . .3.06

xxxii TABLES OF LEGISLATION

Companies Act 1985
   s 431 (5) 11.67
Consumer Protection Act 1987 ....12.12
Contempt of Court Act 1981
   s 14 ....17.21
Control of Pollution Act 1974 ....3.18, 4.50, 6.19–6.21, 6.26, 15.38
   s 58 ....6.20, 6.26
     (1) 3.05
   59 ....16.02
     (2) 16.02
     (4) 16.02
   60 ....6.20–6.21, 6.69, 6.102, 6.111, 6.119, 17.15
     (1) 6.103
     (2) 6.104
     (3) 6.107
     (4) 6.110
     (5) 6.105
     (6) 6.108
     (7) 6.111
   61 ....6.116, 6.118–6.119
   62 ....6.100
     (1) 6.133
     (2) 6.100
      (d) 6.100
   71 ....6.110, 6.133, 15.04
   72 ....15.04
   74 ....6.104
   105(3) 6.106
Courts and Legal Services Act 1990
   s 1 ....17.24
Crime and Public Disorder Act 1998 ....1.16, 18.84
Criminal Justice Act 1967 ....14.65
   s 9 ....18.06, 18.08, 18.21, 18.46, 18.54
Criminal Justice Act 1988 ....11.62
   23 ....11.62, 18.24–18.25, 18.27–18.28, 18.34, 18.46
     (2) 18.22, 18.32
     (3) 18.23, 18.32
   24 ....11.62, 14.65, 18.31, 18.34, 18.46
   25 ....18.25, 18.33
   26 ....18.25, 18.27, 18.33
   30 ....18.21
Criminal Justice and Public Order Act 1994 ....6.96, 6.97–6.99
   s 34 ....11.68, 18.51, App C

63	6.96, 6.98
(1)	6.137
ss 64–7	6.98
s 64	6.96
65	6.96
ss 66–7	6.96

Criminal Law Act 1977
s 16	4.36, 17.25
Sch 2	4.36

Criminal Procedure and Investigations Act 1996 . . . .11.61, 18.57–18.61, 18.66
s 3	11.59–11.60, 18.75
(1)	18.55, 18.59, 18.70
5	18.71
6	18.70–18.71
7	11.59, 18.71
9	18.65

Dangerous Wild Animals Act 1976	8.17
Defective Premises Act 1972	5.104
s 1	5.104
(5)	5.104
Deregulation and Contracting Out Act 1994	14.38

Dogs (Fouling of Land) Act 1996
s 1	8.15
3	8.15

Dogs (Protection of Livestock) Act 1953	8.17
Environment Act 1995	6.19, 6.106
Pt I	2.31
ss 1–56	2.31
s 4(1)	2.33
107	6.19
120(3)	6.19
Sch 17	6.19

Environmental Protection Act 1990 . . . . .1.03, 1.14, 2.29, 3.01, 3.20,
4.50, 4.104, 6.26, 6.32, 6.37, 6.39, 6.53, 6.56–6.57, 6.70, 6.88, 6.92,
6.127, 8.03, 8.20, 9.02, 9.05, 10.07, 10.11, 11.20, 11.60, 12.01, 12.03,
12.06, 12.23, 12.80, 13.11, 13.52, 13.60, 13.63, 13.83, 13.85, 14.24, 14.42,
14.51, 14.66, 15.08, 15.14, 15.38, 16.34, 17.10, 17.32
Pt I	7.02, 7.12, 7.24
s 33	9.04
34	9.04
44	14.02
70(4)	3.05
78A	17.58

Environmental Protection Act 1990 (*cont.*):
- (2) 17.59
- 78H(1) 12.12
- Pt IIA 12.27, 17.58–17.60
- Pt III ....1.01, 1.24, 2.02–2.03, 3.18, 4.01, 4.07, 4.15–4.16, 5.03, 5.56, 5.86–5.87, 6.19, 6.36, 6.53, 6.80, 6.85, 6.119, 8.03, 9.04, 11.09, 11.31, 11.46, 12.19, 12.21, 12.31, 12.39, 12.47, 12.65, 14.14, 14.17, 14.20, 15.04–15.05, 15.11, 15.24, 16.06, 16.43, 16.52, 18.10, 18.79, App A
- s 79 ....4.01–4.03, 4.15, 4.28, 4.83, 5.18, 5.25, 5.84, 6.20, 6.28, 6.120, 6.127, 7.01, 10.17, 11.32, 13.82, 17.05, 17.18, 17.67, App A
  - (1) 1.08, 4.04, 4.29, 5.02, 7.17, 7.23, 9.06, 11.32, 12.03, 12.08, 12.21, 12.32, 12.35, 13.13, 13.41, 16.03, 16.30, 16.63, 17.23
    - (a) 3.05, 3.21, 3.23–3.24, 4.39, 4.49, 4.52, 4.82, 4.90, 4.96, 5.01, 5.04–5.05, 5.07, 5.10, 5.14–5.15, 5.17, 5.20, 5.26, 5.30, 5.35, 5.38–5.39, 5.54, 5.67, 5.72–5.73, 5.80–5.81, 12.53, 13.41
    - (b) 3.05, 7.01–7.02, 7.06, 7.08, 7.10–7.11, 7.14, 7.19, 7.23, 8.15, 13.41
    - (c) 3.05, 7.01–7.02, 7.15, 7.17
    - (d) 3.05, 7.01, 7.03, 7.15, 7.17–17.18, 7.22–7.23, 7.27–7.28, 13.41
    - (e) 3.05, 8.07, 9.01, 9.04, 9.13–9.14, 13.41
    - (f) 3.05, 8.01, 8.04, 8.07–8.09, 8.13, 8.15, 8.16, 13.41
    - (g) 2.03, 3.05, 4.52, 6.19, 6.22, 6.25, 6.30, 13.07, 13.41, 13.47–13.48, 16.17
    - (ga) 2.03, 4.04, 4.54, 5.20, 6.19, 6.24, 6.92, 6.124, 13.07, 13.41, 13.47–13.48, 14.55, 16.17
    - (gb) 7.01, 7.04
    - (h) 3.05, 4.06, 10.01
  - (1A) 17.58, 17.60
  - (2)
    - (a) 7.11
    - (b) 7.11
  - (3) 3.06, 7.06
    - (i) 13.42
  - (4) 7.15
  - (5) 7.21
  - (6) 6.121
  - (6A) 6.24, 6.93, 6.124
  - (6B) 7.29
  - (7) 2.01, 4.09, 4.85, 5.30, 5.37, 5.61, 6.03, 6.22, 6.94, 7.05–7.06, 7.10, 7.13–7.15, 7.19, 7.29, 10.19, 12.22, 12.28, 14.56, 15.11
  - (8) 2.03, 10.07

(9) 15.04
(10) 7.12
(11) 5.38
(12) 5.37
80 .... 1.16, 2.01, 2.13, 5.44, 5.85, 5.87, 5.92, 6.17, 6.33, 6.35, 6.56,
           6.121, 10.32, 11.03–11.04, 11.26, 12.65, 13.03, 13.15, 13.47, 14.04,
           16.03, 16.11, 16.35, 16.57, 17.01, 17.18, 17.29, 17.46, 17.67,
           17.71, App A
  (1) 6.20, 6.75, 11.29, 12.39, 12.58, 13.16, 13.37, 14.05, 14.07, 17.44
    (a) 6.75, 6.77, 11.45
    (b) 12.47–12.48, 12.77, 13.08
  (2) 14.51, 14.54
    (a) 5.87
    (b) 5.87, 12.23, 16.10
    (c) 5.61, 5.87, 12.25
  (3) 5.50, 13.01–13.02, 14.01, 15.07, 15.09, 15.20, 17.46, 18.01
  (4) 4.57, 5.51, 6.58, 14.03–14.04, 14.08, 14.52, 14.59–14.60,
              15.09, 15.20, 15.29, 15.34–15.35, 16.10, 16.41, 17.11, 17.21,
              18.01, 18.83
  (5) 6.38, 14.11
  (6) 14.12
  (7) 6.82, 6.88, 15.09, 15.39
  (8) 15.09, 15.39, 16.61
  (c) 10.01
  (9) 6.69
80A .... 16.11, App A
  (1)
    (a) 12.28
    (b) 12.28
  (2) 14.55
    (a) 12.28
    (b) 12.28
  (3) 12.28
  (4) 12.28
  (7) 14.54
81 .... 1.16, 13.85, 12.19, 14.14, App A
  (1) 12.30
  (3) 6.56, 6.71, 12.26, 14.21
  (4) 14.22
  (5) 6.17, 6.72, 17.11, 17.45
81A .... App A
  (9) 5.37
81B .... App A

Environmental Protection Act 1990 (cont.):
  82 ....1.15–1.16, 2.01, 4.30, 5.06, 5.44, 5.46, 5.52–5.53, 5.81,
           6.118, 9.04, 11.04, 11.08, 12.06, 12.08–12.09, 12.31, 12.65–12.66,
           13.03, 14.04, 14.71, 14.91, 15.28, 16.01–16.02, 16.04, 16.06–16.07,
           16.09–16.10, 16.12, 16.15, 16.18, 16.20, 16.24–16.25, 16.27–16.28,
           16.35, 16.41, 16.46–16.47, 16.51–16.52, 17.01–17.02, App A
    (1) 16.02, 16.08, 16.15, 18.01
    (2) 5.44, 5.52, 14.04, 15.09, 15.20, 16.02, 16.05, 16.15, 16.35,
                                            16.51–16.52, 16.58, 18.83
    (3) 16.02, 16.05, 16.36
    (4) 16.11, 16.52
    (5) 16.14
    (6) 16.16, 16.23–16.27, 16.29
    (7)(b) 16.17
    (8) 15.09, 15.20, 16.02, 16.15, 16.40, 16.51, 18.83
    (11) 16.61
    (12) 16.52, 16.55
    (13) 16.62
  157 ....14.63, App A
    (2) 14.64
  159 ....App A
    (1) 14.66
    (2) 12.31, 14.66
    (3) 12.31
    (4) 14.67
  160 ....12.60, 12.64, 12.67, 16.21, 16.23–16.24, App A
    (2) 16.21
    (3) 16.22, 16.24
    (4) 16.22
    (5) 12.64, 16.23–16.24
  162 ....6.19
    (1) 5.87
    (2) 17.57
  164(4) 2.02
  Sch 3 ....App A
    para 1(3) 13.85
    para 2 ....14.20
      (1) 14.14
       (b) 12.47
      (2) 14.15
      (3) 14.16
      (4) 14.17–14.18
    para 3 ....14.02

(1) 14.13
  para 4 ....12.05, 12.08
  para 5 ....12.19
  Sch 15, para 24 ....5.87
  Sch 16 ....6.19
Factories Act 1844 ....13.34
Finance Act 1972 ....5.78
Food Safety Act 1990 ....12.12, 14.41, 18.79
  s 1(3) 15.13
  8(1) 14.52
  40 ....14.41
Government of Wales Act 1998
  s 22 ....2.06
  125 ....2.20
  Sch 2 ....2.06
  Sch 12 ....2.20
Health and Safety at Work Act 1974 ....5.103, 6.31, 6.81, 6.128, 12.12,
                                                      13.80, 17.57
  ss 2–7 ....11.44
  s 2 ....6.129, 17.57
  3 ....17.57
    (1) 17.57
  5 ....17.57
  15 ....6.128
  18
    (1) 6.128
    (7)(a) 6.128
  20
    (2)(j) 11.67
    (7) 11.67
Housing Act 1985 ....3.05, 16.06, 17.57
  s 189 ....5.100
  190 ....5.100
  264 ....5.100
  265 ....5.100
  338 ....13.21
  352(1) 5.102
  369 ....5.102
  604 ....5.101
  Pt IV 5.94
Housing Act 1988
  s 8 ....12.69
Housing Act 1996 ....1.16, 6.50, 12.69, 17.73

Housing Act 1996 *(cont.)*;
　s 152 ....17.74
　　(1) 17.73
　　(6) 17.73
Housing of the Working Classes Act 1885
　s 9(1) 3.05
Human Rights Act 1998 ....1.10, 2.10, 5.13, 11.01–11.05, 11.07, 11.14,
　　　　　　11.27, 11.29, 11.36, 11.56, 11.69, 12.47, 14.83, 17.39, 17.47,
　　　　　　　　　　　17.56, 18.26, 18.48, 18.57, 18.60
　s 3(1) 11.01, 11.09
　　4 ....11.10
　　6 ....11.24, 11.69, 11.71, 11.79
　　　(1) 11.01, 11.21
　　　(2) 11.20–11.22
　　　(3) 11.07
　　　　(b) 11.06
　　　(4) 11.05
　　7(7) 11.15
　　10 ....11.11
　　18 ....11.01
　　19 ....11.01, 11.09
　　20 ....11.01
　　21(5) 11.01
　　22 ....11.01
　　56 ....11.05
　Sch 1 ....11.02
Insolvency Act 1986
　s 10 ....12.72
　　(1)(c) 12.72
　　11 ....12.72
　　(3)(d) 12.72
Interpretation Act 1978
　s 5 ....5.31
　　7 ....12.61
　Sch 1 ....5.31
Land Compensation Act 1973 ....4.80
Land Drainage Act 1991 ....10.22
　s 1 ....10.22
　　23 ....10.22
　　24 ....10.22
　　25 ....10.22–10.23
　　　(3) 10.23
　　28 ....10.25

(1)	10.24
(5)	10.24
Landlord and Tenant Act 1954	5.76
Pt II	5.76
Landlord and Tenant Act 1985	5.41
s 11	5.41, 5.108, 12.23, 16.07, 16.43
Landlord and Tenant Act 1987	16.24
Licensing Act 1964	6.135

Limitation Act 1980

s 2	5.104
4	5.104
32	5.104
Local Government Act 1858	8.18

Local Government Act 1933

s 249	8.13
Local Government Act 1972	2.01, 2.13, 12.67
s 2	2.08
101	2.11, 17.45
111	2.18
222	4.22, 6.14, 8.07, 17.11, 17.22
(1)	2.09
223	2.15, 2.17
233	6.104
235	6.130, 8.19

Local Government Act 1974

Pt III	2.20
Local Government Act 1985	2.01

Local Government Act 1988

s 29	2.21
Sch 3, para 5	2.21

Local Government Act 1992

s 17	2.02

Local Government and Housing Act 1989

s 20(1)	2.12
ss 22–8	2.20

Local Government etc (Scotland) Act 1994

s 2	2.02

Local Government (Miscellaneous Provisions) Act 1976

s 16	5.41, 12.25, 12.68
Local Government (Miscellaneous Provisions) Act 1982	6.136

Local Government (Wales) Act 1974

s 2	2.08
Local Government (Wales) Act 1994	2.02

London Building Acts 1930–1939 .... 5.95
London Government Act 1963 .... 6.136
London Local Authorities Act 1996
   s 24 .... 4.04, 7.04, 7.29
London Local Authorities Act 2000 .... 5.95
Magistrates' Courts Act 1980 .... 13.71
   s 1(3) 16.32
     17(1) 4.36, 17.25
     40 .... 16.41–16.42
       (1) 14.93
     64 .... 13.71, 13.80
     75 .... 14.80
     101 .... 15.06
     108 .... 14.94
       (1) 14.97
     111 .... 14.102, 14.108
       (4) 14.105
     123 .... 16.32
     127(1) 16.34
   Sch 1, para 1 .... 4.36, 17.25
Mental Health Act 1983 .... 12.69
Mines and Quarries Act 1954 .... 10.01
   s 151
     (1) 10.33
     (2)
       (a) 10.33
       (b) 10.33
       (c) 10.34
   181
     (1) 10.35
     (2) 10.35
     (4) 10.35
Noise Abatement Act 1960 .... 3.05, 3.18, 4.50, 4.52, 6.13–6.14, 6.18,
                                                    6.102, 8.14
   s 1 .... 6.18
Noise Act 1996 .... 6.04, 6.49, 6.51, 6.56–6.58, 6.60–6.61, 6.73,
                                              11.87, 17.57, 18.10
   s 1 .... App C
   ss 2–9 .... 6.60
   s 2 .... App C
     3 .... 6.59, App C
     4 .... 6.58, 6.60, App C
     5 .... 6.55, App C

UK STATUTES

8	App C
10	6.53, 6.55, 6.58–6.59, 6.71, 17.71
(1)(b)	6.62
(2)	6.53, 14.23
(4)	6.62
(7)	6.56, 6.71, 14.23–14.24
(8)	6.62, 14.23, 14.25
11(2)(b)	6.61
Sch	App C
para 1(a)	6.58
para 2(1)(a)	6.58
Noise and Statutory Nuisance Act 1993	4.50, 4.54, 5.20, 6.24
s 2	3.05, 6.24, 6.92
(2)(b)	4.04
(4)(c)	6.94
8	6.101
9	6.63
Sch 2, para 1	6.101
Sch 3	
para 5(1)	6.63
para 6	6.64
para 7	6.64
Northern Ireland Act 1998	2.04
s 5	2.04
Nuisances Removal and Diseases Prevention Act 1848	3.14, 4.09, 5.09, 7.25
Nuisances Removal and Diseases Prevention Act 1849	3.14, 4.09
Nuisances Removal and Diseases Prevention Act 1855	3.02–3.03, 3.14, 3.17, 3.22, 4.16, 4.41, 5.09, 8.02, 8.14, 10.12, 10.14
s 8	3.02–3.03, 3.05, 5.35, 9.02
Occupiers' Liability Act 1957	5.105
Police and Criminal Evidence Act 1984	1.17, 11.54, 11.66, 14.60, 18.48–18.49, 18.52, 18.79
s 67	App C
69	18.08, 18.24, 18.31, App C
76	18.79, App C
78	1.17, 11.49, 11.65, 14.18, 18.25, 18.33, 18.79, App C
Code B	18.79, App C
Code C	18.79, App C
para 10.1	18.49
10.4	18.50
11	18.52
Code E	18.52

TABLES OF LEGISLATION

Pollution Prevention and Control Act 1999 .... 7.02, 7.15
   s 2 .... 7.12
Powers of Criminal Courts Act 1973 .... 16.51
   s 35 .... 14.91, 16.41, 16.46, 16.56
      (1) 16.15, 16.42
         (A) 16.42
      (4A) 14.93
Prevention of Damage by Pests Act 1949 .... 9.03
   Pt I 8.05
   s 2 .... 9.03
Private Places of Entertainment (Licensing) Act 1967 .... 6.137
Prosecution of Offences Act 1985 .... 14.71
   s 10 .... 14.28
     16
      (1) 14.82
      (6) 14.83
      (7) 14.85
      (9)(b) 14.84
     17
      (2) 14.71
      (6)(c) 14.71
     18(1) 14.72
     19A(1)(c) 14.88
   Pt II 14.68
Protection from Harassment Act 1997 .... 1.16, 6.50, 17.57, 17.70
   s 1
      (1) 17.70
      (2) 17.72
      3 .... 17.72
Protection of Animals Act 1911 .... 8.16, 13.92
   s 15 .... 8.03
Public Health Act 1875 .... 3.04, 3.17
   s 35 .... 3.05
   ss 91–6 .... 16.15
   s 91 .... 3.05
      (4) 9.06
    96 .... 9.06
Public Health Act 1925 .... 10.15
   s 54
      (1) 3.05
      (2) 3.05
Public Health Act 1936 .... 1.08, 3.01, 3.05, 3.18, 4.38, 4.46, 4.52, 5.28,
                            6.18, 6.26, 6.102, 10.01, 15.09, 16.26

s 81(b) 8.18
    83 ....5.98
    92 ....3.18, 5.04
        (1)
            (a) 3.05, 5.55
            (b) 3.05, 8.13, 8.15
            (c) 3.05, 4.93, 9.02, 9.06
            (d) 3.05, 7.03, 7.20
    93 ....5.87, 16.10
    94(2) 5.52, 16.35
    95 ....15.33
    99 ....5.52, 12.09, 16.02, 16.15, 16.52
    101 ....3.05
    140 ....10.31
    141 ....3.05, 4.06, 10.30–10.32
    259 ....3.21, 4.06, 10.05, 10.16–10.17, 10.22
        (1) 4.06, 10.05
            (a) 3.05, 10.02, 10.05–10.06, 10.12, 10.19
            (b) 3.05, 10.03, 10.05, 10.12, 10.15, 10.19–10.20, 10.25
    260
        (1)
            (a) 10.02
            (b) 10.02
    268 ....3.05, 4.06, 10.26
        (2) 10.26–10.27
        (3) 10.27
        (4) 10.28
        (5) 10.29
    289 ....12.26
    343 ....4.93
        (1) 12.27
    Pt III 5.18
Public Health Act 1961
    s 74 ....8.07, 9.03
Public Health Acts Amendment Act 1907 ....3.05
Public Health (Ireland) Act 1878 ....2.02, 3.04
Public Health (Scotland) Act 1897 ....6.18–6.19
Public Order Act 1986 ....6.95
    s 16 ....6.95
Radioactive Substances Act 1993
    s 40 ....10.27, 10.32
Railways Act 1993
    s 122(3) 6.120, 6.127

Regulation of Investigatory Powers Act 2000 . . . . .1.10, 11.08, 11.69–11.70,
11.73, 11.79, 11.82–11.83, 11.87–11.89, 18.16
  Pt II . . . . .11.72, 11.85, App C
  s 26 . . . . .11.73, App C
    (2) 11.74
    (3) 11.78
    (4) 11.81
    (8) 11.85
    (9) 11.74
    (10) 11.74
  ss 27–37 . . . . .11.73
  s 27 . . . . .11.71, App C
    28 . . . . .App C
    29 . . . . .11.86, App C
    48 . . . . .11.84
    (2) 11.74, 11.82
    71(3)(a) 11.72
    Sch 1 . . . . .11.72
Rent Act 1957 . . . . .5.79
Road Traffic Act 1988
  Pt II 6.120
Road Traffic (Consequential Provisions) Act 1988
  s 7 . . . . .6.120
Sanitary Act 1866
  s 3 . . . . .6.86
  19 . . . . .3.03, 3.05
Scotland Act 1998 . . . . .2.05
  s 28 . . . . .2.05
    53 . . . . .2.05
    63 . . . . .2.05
    117 . . . . .2.05
Supreme Court Act 1981
  s 28A 14.106
    29(3) 17.26
    31(3) 17.55
    48
      (2) 13.92
      (4) 14.96
Territorial Sea Act 1987
  s 1 . . . . .5.38
Tunbridge Wells Improvement Act 1846
  s 138 . . . . .9.06
Vehicles (Excise) Act 1971 . . . . .12.28

Visiting Forces Act 1952 ....7.11
Water Resources Act 1991
    Pt III 10.02, 10.17
    s 85 ....10.09, 10.18

UK STATUTORY INSTRUMENTS

Air Navigation (General) Regulations 1993, SI 1993/1622 ....6.120
Building Regulations 2000, SI 2000/2531 ....5.10
Civil Procedure Rules 1998 SI 1998/3132 ....5.43, 17.53, 18.37
    Pt 54 ....11.15, 17.52
    r 54.0.9 ....17.53
    54.2 ....17.54
    54.3 ....17.54
    54.5 ....17.52
Contaminated Land (England) Regulations 2000, SI 2000/227 ....12.12, 17.58
Control of Noise (Appeals) Regulations 1975, SI 1975/2116
    reg 5(2) 6.111
Crown Court Rules 1982, SI 1982/1109 ....13.85, 13.92
    r 5 ....14.94
    7 ....13.85, 14.94
    12(2) 13.90
    13 ....13.91–13.92
Housing (Management of Houses in Multiple Occupation) Regulations
    1990, SI 1990/830 ....5.102
Human Rights Act 1998 (Commencement No 1) Order 1998, SI 1998/
    2882 ....11.01
Human Rights Act 1998 (Commencement No 2) Order 2000, SI 2000/
    1851 ....11.01
Magistrates' Courts Rules 1981, SI 1981/552
    r 14
        (1) 13.68
        (2) 13.68
        (3) 13.68
        (5) 13.69
    34 ....13.01
    76 ....14.108
    100 ....16.32
Magistrates' Courts (Advance Information) Rules 1985, SI 1985/601 ....18.62
Magistrates' Courts (Advance Notice of Expert Evidence) Rules 1997,
    SI 1997/705 ....18.73–18.76, App C
Magistrates' Courts (Forms) Rules 1981, SI 1981/553
    Sch 2

Magistrates' Courts (Forms) Rules 1981 (*cont.*):
    Forms 29, 30 ....14.50
    Form 1 ....16.32
Magistrates' Courts (Hearsay Evidence in Civil Proceedings) Rules 1999,
    SI 1999/691 ....13.68, App C
National Assembly for Wales (Transfer of Functions) Order 1999, SI 1999/672
    Sch 1 ....2.06
Regulation of Investigatory Powers Act 2000 (Commencement No 1 and Transitional Provisions) Order 2000, SI 2000/2543 ....11.72
Regulation of Investigatory Powers (Prescription of Offices, Ranks and Positions) Order 2000, SI 2000/2417 ....11.76
Rules of the Supreme Court 1965
    Ord 53 ....17.52
Statutory Nuisance (Appeals) Regulations 1995, SI 1995/2644 ...13.01, 13.11,
                        13.61, 13.63, 13.83, 15.08, App B
    reg 2 ....15.09, 15.38
        (2) 13.12, 13.47
           (a) 13.13–13.16, 13.29
           (b) 13.17–3.26, 13.37, 13.40
           (c) 13.27–13.36
           (d) 12.58, 13.37–13.40
           (e) 6.39, 13.41–13.46, 15.07, 15.39
              (ii) 13.42
           (f) 13.47–13.48, 15.39
           (g) 13.47–13.48
           (h) 13.21, 13.49–13.51, 13.56
           (i) 13.49, 13.52–13.53, 13.56, 13.60
           (j) 13.49, 13.54–13.56, 13.60
        (3) 13.18
        (5) 12.42, 13.01, 13.21, 13.32, 13.58, 13.87
        (6) 13.61
        (7) 13.62
    3 ....12.75, 13.38
        (1) 13.06–13.07
        (2) 13.08, 13.10
           (a)(i) 13.39
           (b) 12.77
        (3) 13.10
    4 ....13.60
Town and Country Planning (Applications) Regulations 1988, SI 1988/1812
    reg 4 ....15.25
Town and Country Planning (Use Classes) Order 1987, SI 1987/764 ....15.13

EU LEGISLATION

Directive 92/97/EEC (traffic-related noise) 2.35
Directive 94/62/EC (packaging and packaging waste) 2.36
Directive 96/62/EC (air quality framework) 2.35
Directive 2000/53/EC (end of life of vehicles) 2.36
Treaty of Amsterdam
   art 2 . . . . .2.35
      6 . . . . .2.35
     28 . . . . .2.35
     30 . . . . .2.35
    174(2) 2.35
Treaty of European Union 2.34

INTERNATIONAL CONVENTIONS

European Convention for the Protection of Human Rights and Fundamental
   Freedoms 1950 . . . . .11.01, 11.05, 11.07, 11.09,
                                       11.21–11.23, 11.25, 11.28, 12.47
   First Protocol, art 1 . . . . .11.30–11.31, 13.60
     art 6 . . . . .11.27, 11.49–11.50, 11.52, 11.57, 11.65, 11.67–11.68,
                       12.31, 13.24, 13.60, 14.18, 14.86, 16.29, 18.26
     (1) 11.46–11.48, 11.50, 11.55, 11.58
     (2) 11.47
     (3)
       (b) 11.59, 11.61
       (c) 11.53–11.54
       (d) 11.62–11.63
    7 . . . . .11.27, 11.44–11.45, 12.56, 13.24, 16.29
     (1) 11.42–11.43
    8 . . . . .6.122, 11.08, 11.32–11.34, 11.69–11.70
     (2) 11.35, 11.38–11.39, 11.71
    13 . . . . .17.39
    34 . . . . .11.15
International Covenant on Civil and Political Rights (United Nations, 1966)
   art 14(3)(g) 11.67

SYNOPSIS

Introduction 1.01
Part I: Structure and Framework 1.05
    Chapter 2: The Regulatory Framework 1.05
    Chapter 3: The Historical Context of Statutory Nuisance and Public
    Health Legislation 1.06
    Chapter 4: The Concept of Statutory Nuisance 1.07
Part II: The Specific Nuisances 1.08
Part III: Procedure and Evidence 1.09
    Chapter 11: Implications of the Human Rights Act 1998 . . . . .1.10
    Chapter 12: Enforcement: Use of Abatement Notices 1.11
    Chapter 13: Appeals against Abatement Notices 1.12
    Chapter 14: Offences and Prosecution for Breach of an Abatement
    Notice 1.13
    Chapter 15: Defences 1.14
    Chapter 16: Section 82 Proceedings 1.15
    Chapter 17: Other Remedies 1.16
    Chapter 18: Overview of Evidential Issues and Preparation for Court 1.17
Appendices 1.18

Introduction

This book is concerned with the law and practice of statutory nuisances falling under Part III of the Environmental Protection Act 1990 ('EPA 1990'). Statutory nuisance lies at the heart of the controls available to local councils with which to deal with environmental complaints. Situated at the front line of public health are to be found local authority environmental health professionals. Seldom does their work catch the public eye in the same way as that of the national enforcement agencies, but the moment a local resident finds himself embroiled in a public health issue, then it is the local council which is the first port of call. Whether a complaint is about noise, smells, accumulations of rubbish, or other such nuisances, it will be dealt with locally by publicly accountable authorities whose decisions and actions will have an immediate impact on the quality of life of ordinary residents and people working in the area. **1.01**

Statutory nuisance represents a mixture of civil, administrative and criminal procedures. At the heart of the procedure is the abatement notice: a form of protection which can be used, very effectively, by a local authority in seeking to achieve a **1.02** speedy remedy to an alleged nuisance. Failure to comply with a notice will have serious consequences: it may lead to a criminal prosecution against the perpetrator. If the notice is carelessly or improperly prepared and served, it may be appealed against.

1.03 Provision is also made in the EPA 1990 for ordinary individuals to bring their own proceedings in the magistrates' courts where a local authority fails to act, or where, perhaps, the local authority is itself the perpetrator of an alleged nuisance (most typically in disputes about the state of local authority housing).

1.04 This book is divided into three parts. Part I is concerned with the structure and framework of the law of statutory nuisance; Part II explores the specific nuisances in depth; and Part III covers matters of procedure and evidence. Relevant statutory material can be found in the Appendices to this book.

Part I: Structure and Framework

Chapter 2: The Regulatory Framework

1.05 Chapter 2 outlines the structural framework in which statutory nuisances are dealt with and prosecuted. It covers:

- the organization and powers of local authority environmental health departments;
- the Local Government Ombudsman;
- the impact of the Environment Agency; and
- the European background.

Chapter 3: The Historical Context of Statutory Nuisance and Public Health Legislation

1.06 This chapter covers the development of modern public health law and statutory nuisance. As recent case law has demonstrated, the interpretation of statutory nuisances in the twenty-first century owes much to their nineteenth-century origins. An understanding of the historical background is, therefore, essential for a complete grasp of the individual types of statutory nuisance today.

Chapter 4: The Concept of Statutory Nuisance

1.07 This chapter deals with the definition of a statutory nuisance and contrasts its use and availability with private and public nuisances. It covers:

- comparison with private and public nuisance;
- the meaning of 'prejudice to health or a nuisance'; and
- problems with the concept of statutory nuisance.

Part II: The Specific Nuisances

1.08 Chapters 5 to 9 each deal with a separate substantive nuisance. Chapter 10 covers miscellaneous nuisances in other legislation. All the nuisances under section

79(1) of the EPA 1990 and under the relevant parts of the Public Health Act 1936 are covered. The framework of each chapter includes the elements of the nuisance and technical issues arising in relation to the specific nuisance covered. The chapters are arranged as follows:

Chapter 5:   Premises;
Chapter 6:   Noise and Noise Nuisance;
Chapter 7:   Atmospheric Emissions (including smells);
Chapter 8:   Animals;
Chapter 9:   Accumulations and Deposits; and
Chapter 10: Miscellaneous Nuisances in other Legislation.

Part III: Procedure and Evidence

The final part of the book covers procedural and evidential matters of particular relevance to practitioners of statutory nuisance law. It identifies the various pitfalls, focusing on the problematic areas which can cause most difficulty for legal practitioners and environmental health professionals.

1.09

Chapter 11: Implications of the Human Rights Act 1998
Chapter 11 considers the implications of the Human Rights Act 1998 on substantive statutory nuisance law, procedural law and evidential issues. Much development remains in the future as the implications of this Act unfold. The chapter focuses on possible issues and pitfalls and seeks to highlight areas where the law of statutory nuisance might be obliged to change as a result of the implementation of the Act. The implications of the Regulation of Investigatory Powers Act 2000 are also considered.

1.10

Chapter 12: Enforcement: Use of Abatement Notices
This chapter examines the framework within which statutory nuisances are regulated by local authorities. It covers the extent of the duty of local authorities to inspect, to investigate complaints and to consult the prospective recipients of abatement notices. It also considers the technical requirements for the drafting of abatement notices and nuisance orders. In the light of recent judicial thinking about abatement notices, it concentrates on drafting issues and the various problems frequently encountered in drafting, amending and withdrawing notices. Finally, it considers issues surrounding service of notices, specifically on whom to serve notices and problems with service.

1.11

Chapter 13: Appeals against Abatement Notices
This chapter deals with each of the grounds of appeal that can be made to the magistrates' courts by those who are served with abatement notices. The chapter also examines the procedural aspects of appeals against notices, and further

1.12

appeals to the Crown Court and the High Court, together with a consideration of the costs issues involved.

Chapter 14: Offences and Prosecution for Breach of an Abatement Notice

1.13 This chapter deals with the procedural requirements for bringing a prosecution for statutory nuisance. It considers:

- enforcement policy;
- formal cautions;
- offences, including obstruction;
- whom to prosecute;
- penalties;
- costs; and
- compensation orders.

Chapter 15: Defences

1.14 This chapter considers the defences available under the EPA 1990. It is primarily concerned with the defences of 'best practicable means' and 'reasonable excuse'.

Chapter 16: Section 82 Proceedings

1.15 This chapter deals with the summary proceedings under section 82 of the EPA 1990 by 'persons aggrieved', including procedure, uses and actions against landlords, including local authorities. In particular, it covers:

- the definition of a person aggrieved;
- letter before action by a person aggrieved;
- uses and actions against landlords, including local authorities;
- proceedings in magistrates' courts, including the drafting of a nuisance order;
- appeals against orders;
- enforcement;
- costs and compensation orders; and
- a checklist for the lay prosecutor.

Chapter 17: Other Remedies

1.16 This chapter considers alternatives to prosecution, and other remedies, to the procedures under sections 80 and 82 of the EPA 1990. It covers:

- alternative dispute resolution and mediation;
- High Court injunctions under section 81 of the EPA 1990;
- public nuisance injunctions;
- judicial review;
- the Crime and Public Disorder Act 1998, the Housing Act 1996 and the Protection from Harassment Act 1997;
- contaminated land; and
- planning law.

Chapter 18: Overview of Evidential Issues and Preparation for Court
The final chapter deals with some of the evidential matters involved in preparing **1.17**
a statutory nuisance case for prosecution or appeal. It does not attempt to replace the standard works on procedure, but focuses on specific issues of importance to statutory nuisance practitioners. In particular, it covers:

- the discretion of a court to exclude evidence under section 78 of the Police and Criminal Evidence Act 1984;
- rebuttal evidence and uses to be made in court;
- statutory powers of investigation and collection of evidence;
- interviewing witnesses and suspects under the Police and Criminal Evidence Act 1984;
- advance disclosure;
- using expert witnesses and opinion evidence;
- using documentary and photographic evidence;
- using scientific and technical data;
- using tape recorders and noise measurements;
- preparation for court hearings, in particular the use of witness statements, exhibits and notebooks; and
- *Newton*[1] hearings.

Appendices

The statutory material most frequently referred to is reproduced in the **1.18**
Appendices to this book.

[1] *R v Newton* (1983) 77 Cr App R 13.

PART I

STRUCTURE AND FRAMEWORK

2

THE REGULATORY FRAMEWORK

Enforcement authorities 2.01
Devolution 2.04
General powers of local authorities 2.07
Power of local authorities to prosecute 2.09
Local authority decisions 2.11
    Standing orders 2.12
    Delegation 2.13
Appearance in legal proceedings 2.15
Limits to local authority powers 2.18
Local Government Ombudsman 2.20
Environmental health regulation by local authorities 2.27
    Organizational structure 2.27
    Environmental health qualification 2.29
Environment Agency 2.31
European dimension 2.34

Enforcement authorities

The enforcement of statutory nuisance legislation is done primarily by local authorities[1] using powers defined in section 80 of the Environmental Protection Act ('EPA 1990').[2] English local authorities enforcing the Act comprise district councils outside of Greater London and London borough councils in Greater London.[3] Unitary authorities in non-metropolitan counties are responsible for enforcement.[4] **2.01**

In Wales, enforcement is by the 22 unitary councils set up under the Local Government (Wales) Act 1994. In Scotland, since April 1996, 32 unitary councils **2.02**

---

[1] The Local Government Act 1972 created districts in shire and metropolitan counties. Metropolitan county councils, including the Greater London Council, were abolished by the Local Government Act 1985. The 1985 Act transferred their powers to metropolitan district councils and to London borough councils.
[2] Prosecution by private individuals, or 'persons aggrieved', is by the EPA 1990, s 82.
[3] EPA 1990, s 79(7). That subsection also includes as London local authorities: the Common Council of the City of London, and, as respects the Temples, the Sub-Treasurer of the Inner Temple and the Under-Treasurer of the Middle Temple. The Council of the Isles of Scilly is also a local authority.
[4] Established by orders of the Secretary of State made under the Local Government Act 1992, s 17.

have been responsible for enforcement and for providing environmental services.[5] District councils enforce statutory nuisance provisions in Northern Ireland, although there is a single local housing authority: the Northern Ireland Housing Executive.[6] However, Part III of the EPA 1990 does not apply in Northern Ireland where the Public Health (Ireland) Act 1878 is still in force.[7]

2.03 Additionally, for enforcing Part III of the EPA 1990, port health authorities have the functions of local authorities for their districts.[8] These authorities are empowered to enforce all statutory nuisance provisions except for noise.[9]

Devolution

2.04 New assemblies have been set up in Scotland and in Wales which hold powers previously exercised by the Westminster Parliament. Section 5 of the Northern Ireland Act 1998 gave the Northern Ireland Assembly the power to make laws, though this does not affect the power of the Westminster Parliament to legislate for that province.[10]

2.05 In Scotland, with effect from 1 July 1999, all matters relating to the environment have been devolved to the Scottish Parliament except for some reserved matters such as coal, nuclear energy and oil.[11] The Scotland Act 1998 transferred most functions to the Scottish Parliament from Westminster.[12] Thus, references to the 'Secretary of State' or 'Minister' in legislation are to be construed as including references to Scottish Ministers. Administrative functions and Orders exercisable by Ministers of the Crown were also transferred under the Act.[13]

---

[5] Local Government etc (Scotland) Act 1994, s 2. Responsibility for water and sewage was transferred to three water and sewerage authorities on 1 April 1996.

[6] In Northern Ireland, public health notices issued under the Public Health (Ireland) Act 1878 are used as a way of triggering mandatory repairs grants from the Northern Ireland Housing Executive. This applies both to the private rented sector and to owner-occupiers. Abatement notices are therefore welcomed and sometimes demanded by owners wishing to improve their properties. Clearly, this situation is inconsistent with the enforcement responsibilities of local authorities. It has arisen, at least in part, because of legislative underdevelopment in Northern Ireland, such that housing legislation as a separate field from statutory nuisance has not evolved as much as on the mainland, and the agencies resort to pragmatism to make the system work. [7] EPA 1990, s 164(4).

[8] ibid, s 79(8).

[9] ibid, s 79(1)(g) and (ga) do not apply to port health authorities, so noise in general and noise emitted from or caused by a vehicle, machinery or equipment in the street is excluded.

[10] Devolution has been periodically suspended in Northern Ireland since the Northern Ireland Act 1998 came into force on 1 January 2000. The Westminster Parliament has suspended and restored its operations by the use of statutory instruments.

[11] Scotland Act 1998, s 28; the reserved list is in Schedule 5 to the Act. [12] ibid, s 53.

[13] ibid, s 63. Section 117 of the Act makes clear that any pre-commencement enactment or prerogative instrument and any other instrument or document which refers to Ministers of the Crown should be read as to include a reference to Scottish Ministers.

In Wales, the Westminster Parliament retains exclusive competence to make primary legislation on environmental matters. However, the power to make secondary legislation by Orders in Council has been transferred to the Welsh National Assembly.[14]

2.06

General powers of local authorities

A local authority is an artificial entity existing as a corporation for an indefinite period, but which can be abolished by Act of Parliament. It functions by perpetual succession, as successive individuals act on its behalf and then cease to do so. Corporate status means that the acts of individual officers can become the acts of the local authority.

2.07

This corporate status provides local authorities with the capacity to act as an individual.[15] It allows them to own and dispose of property, enter into contracts and makes them capable of suing and being sued. It also means that local authorities can prosecute in their own name. Corporate status does not give local authorities the same general capacity to act as an ordinary individual.[16] As creatures of statute, local authorities can only do things which are expressly or impliedly authorized by Parliament. For example, they cannot act in the same way as a private landowner, but must hold and manage land in accordance with the statutory power whereby the land is held.[17]

2.08

Power of local authorities to prosecute

For the purpose of enforcing certain statutes, including statutory nuisance, local authorities are public prosecuting authorities. The Local Government Act 1972 empowers them to prosecute and to start (or defend) civil proceedings in their own name. Section 222(1) of this Act provides:

2.09

Where a local authority consider it expedient for the promotion or protection of the interests of the inhabitants of their area—
  (a) they may prosecute or defend or appear in any legal proceedings and, in the case of civil proceedings, may institute them in their own name . . .

---

[14] Government of Wales Act 1998, s 22 and Sch 2. In a few cases the power to make secondary legislation remains with Ministers of the Crown. The transfer of functions from the Secretary of State to the National Assembly for Wales applies to a large body of legislation; see the National Assembly for Wales (Transfer of Functions) Order 1999, SI 1999/672, Sch 1.
[15] For England, as provided in the Local Government Act 1972, s 2; for Wales, the Local Government (Wales) Act 1974, s 2.
[16] eg, where an unauthorized person makes a purported contract binding the local authority, this act will be *ultra vires* and the contract void (*Hazell v Hammersmith & Fulham LBC* [1992] 2 AC 1).
[17] *R v Somerset CC, ex p Fewings* [1995] 1 All ER 513.

2.10 This section allows a local authority to bring public nuisance proceedings in its own name and to seek civil remedies such as injunctions.[18] The decision to prosecute is discretionary and local authorities are subject to the ordinary principles of administrative law when making such decisions.[19] Further, for decisions made from 2 October 2000, local authorities are subject to the provisions of the Human Rights Act 1998.[20]

Local authority decisions

2.11 The acts of local authorities may be carried out by a committee or subcommittee, or by an officer employed by the council. The power to institute proceedings may be delegated to a subcommittee or officer with sufficient seniority.[21] Additionally, a local authority may make arrangements to discharge its functions by another local authority or to act jointly with it.[22] Delegation may be effected by Council resolution or standing orders.

Standing orders

2.12 Standing orders provide a general means whereby local authorities regulate their conduct and proceedings.[23] They may be used to define the remit and extent of delegation to each committee, subcommittee and officer. Standing orders can be changed, but if a local authority does not act in accordance with those in force such acts will be judicially reviewable.[24]

Delegation

2.13 The Local Government Act 1972 has the effect that authority for taking decisions on behalf of a council can be delegated to a properly authorized officer. This will apply to any action unless any statutory provision states otherwise. An officer with sufficient authority is able to make decisions on behalf of the council on such matters as service of an abatement notice under section 80 of the EPA 1990, whether to prosecute for breach of a notice, or to seek a High Court injunction.

2.14 Delegation to an officer does not include delegation to an individual council member, since the professional expertise, competence and accountability of the

---

[18] *Solihull MBC v Maxfern Ltd* [1977] 2 All ER 177. Before the 1972 Act was in force a local authority could only sue on the relation of the Attorney-General and not in its own name.
[19] Prosecution policies drawn from central government guidelines also act as a framework for the exercise of discretion. See further paras 14.37–14.39.   [20] See Chapter 11.
[21] *R v South Somerset DC, ex p DJB (Group) Ltd* (1989) LGR 624.
[22] Local Government Act 1972, s 101.
[23] The terms of standing orders are for the local authority to decide, though they may not be contrary to law and do not have the force of law. Central government has the power to require local authorities to include certain provisions or to make or to refrain from making certain modifications to their standing orders (Local Government and Housing Act 1989, s 20(1)).
[24] *R v Hereford Corporation, ex p Harrower* [1970] 1 WLR 1424.

employee is the rationale for the delegation.[25] Standing orders commonly provide for a power to be delegated to an officer acting in consultation with a specified member, but this would not extend to enabling the member to exercise the power alone or to play the dominant role. It is common practice for the decisions of local authorities about whether to prosecute or to issue a formal caution against an offender to be delegated to a senior officer acting in consultation with a member.

Appearance in legal proceedings

Section 223 of the Local Government Act 1972 allows any member or officer of an authority to prosecute or defend summary legal proceedings, provided that they were authorized to do so before commencement of those proceedings.[26] Proof of authorization—and also of authority to initiate proceedings by laying an information—is by production of the relevant council resolution: reliance on the officers's appointment or position is not sufficient.[27] Officers appearing in court should bring with them proof of authorization, such as a warrant card or a copy of the minutes of the relevant council resolution. **2.15**

This provision enables employees such as trading standards and environmental health officers without formal legal qualifications to appear in magistrates' courts. Such officers conducting cases are also competent to give evidence in the same proceedings. **2.16**

Section 223 applies to an officer responding to an appeal against an abatement notice as well as to a prosecution for breach of a notice. **2.17**

Limits to local authority powers

As a corporation a local authority's powers are limited to those expressly given by statute and to those which may be implied by statute.[28] Implied powers are fairly tightly construed, but may include anything 'reasonably incidental' to what the local authority has express or implied authority to do.[29] Section 111 of the Local Government Act 1972 empowers local authorities to do anything calculated to facilitate, or which is conducive or incidental to the discharge of, any of its functions. This statutory limitation applies to all acts carried out by or on behalf of the local authority, including the exercise of its powers and responsibilities and the prosecution of offenders. **2.18**

---

[25] *R v Secretary of State for the Environment, ex p Hillingdon LBC* [1986] 1 WLR 807.
[26] *Bowyer, Philpott & Payne Ltd v Mather* [1919] 1 KB 419. Proper authorization also applies to the service of notices. Where not properly authorized at the time of service, notices may not be cured by subsequent authorization. Evidently, such a defective notice cannot form the basis for any subsequent prosecution; see *St Leonard Vestry v Holmes* (1886) 50 JP 132.
[27] *Bob Keats Ltd v Farrant* [1951] 1 All ER 899.
[28] *Baroness Wenlock v River Dee Co* (1885) 10 App Cas 354.
[29] *A-G v Great Eastern Rly* (1880) 5 App Cas 473.

2.19 Where a local authority has acted beyond its powers such acts or decisions are *ultra vires* and subject to judicial review.[30]

Local Government Ombudsman

2.20 An important check on a local authority's use of its powers is the ability to make a complaint to the Local Government Ombudsman. A separate Commissioner exists for England and for Wales, England being divided into three areas, each with a local Commissioner.[31]

2.21 The purpose of the Ombudsman is to investigate complaints made by, or on behalf of, a member of the public who claims to have suffered injustice as a result of maladministration.[32] The scope of maladministration is wide and may include 'bias, neglect, inattention, delay, incompetence, ineptitude, perversity, turpitude, arbitrariness'.[33] The scope is wider than for a court case. A complaint can include not merely injury or loss redressible in court, but also the sense of outrage aroused by the unfair or incompetent administration.[34]

2.22 The subject of a complaint can be the actions of a committee, subcommittee, member or officer. It can include a person or body acting on behalf of a local authority.

2.23 Examples of suitable types of complaint against the local authority are given in *Complaint about the Council? How to Complain to the Local Government Ombudsman*, a leaflet published by the Commission for Local Administration in England which is available from the Local Government Ombudsman's website.[35] They include a local authority:

- taking too long to take action without good reason;
- not following its own rules or the law;
- breaking its promises; and
- giving wrong information.

2.24 Delay, which may be coupled with some other fault such as not complying with a legal requirement, seems to be the most common form of complaint. For example, a delay of five months between an initial visit to interview a complainant

---

[30] See further paras 17.26–17.56.
[31] The system was introduced by Part III of the Local Government Act 1974, as amended by the Local Government and Housing Act 1989, ss 22–8, and, for Wales, by the Government of Wales Act 1998, s 125, Sch 12.
[32] Since 1988, complaints can be made direct to the Commissioner; previously, they could only be made through a member of the local authority concerned (Local Government Act 1988, s 29, Sch 3, para 5).
[33] Rt Hon Richard Crossman, *Hansard*, HC Debates, 1966, Vol 754, col 51.
[34] S de Smith, Lord Woolf and J Jowell, *Judicial Review of Administrative Action* (5th edn, Sweet & Maxwell, 1995), para 1–102.   [35] www.lgo.org.uk/complain.htm.

and carrying out a technical evaluation was held to be excessive;[36] failure or excessive delay in responding to requests to monitor a clay pigeon shoot because it occurred on a Sunday was held to be a breach of duty.[37] And before *Ex p Shelley*,[38] the Commissioner had held that a delay of 20 months between deciding whether the activity constituted a nuisance and serving an abatement notice was excessive.[39]

The system is particularly appropriate to third parties affected by decisions who can show injustice suffered as a result of the maladministration. Actual loss need not be shown. With regard to statutory nuisance, the Commissioner has no power to quash or amend any notice. Recipients of abatement notices have other means of redress through a process of appeal against the service of notices.[40] 2.25

Where the Commissioner provides a report which upholds, at least in part, a complaint, the local authority is under a duty to consider the report and to notify him within three months of the basis of any action taken or to be taken. The report will be principally concerned with putting right the injustice and may include recommending a payment being made to the complainant. However, reports are not legally enforceable and the local authority cannot be obliged to accept the Commissioner's views. 2.26

Environmental health regulation by local authorities

Organizational structure

The regulation of environmental health by local authorities originated in the mid-nineteenth century.[41] Local councils had powers to appoint one or more sanitary inspectors, supervised by a medical officer of health. Until recently, environmental health departments were organized hierarchically. Councils would employ a chief environmental health officer heading up a department to whom various powers would be delegated. At the departmental level, chief officers formed the apex of a hierarchical pyramid, being assisted by managers with functional responsibilities who in turn managed teams of environmental health officers and other staff. 2.27

The above organizational model, which involved extended hierarchies between managers and field officers, has been out of favour for some years due to its high 2.28

---

[36] Complaint 88/A/1864 against London Borough of Barnet, 3 May 1990, Commission for Local Administration in England.
[37] Complaints 88/C/1571 and 88/C/182 against Rotherham MBC, 26 November 1990, Commission for Local Administration in England.
[38] *R v Carrick DC, ex p Shelley* [1996] Env LR 273.
[39] Complaint 88/C/1373 against Sheffield CC, 19 September 1989, Commission for Local Administration in England.   [40] See Chapter 13.
[41] See Chapter 3.

costs and perceived inefficiencies.[42] Nowadays, most local authorities have dispensed with several hierarchical layers, in favour of 'flat' organizational structures. Teams of environmental health officers and ancillary staff are managed by team leaders with managerial authority. More senior managers managing groups of activities may be responsible for trading standards and other services as well as for environmental health. These senior managers may or may not be qualified as environmental health officers.

Environmental health qualification

2.29 Environmental health officers are professionally qualified, being required to pass examinations accredited by the Chartered Institute of Environmental Health. Environmental health departments also employ technical and scientific officers at various levels who will often be qualified to degree (or postgraduate degree) level, but who have not obtained the approved professional qualification. Besides enforcing the statutory nuisance provisions in the EPA 1990, environment health departments are responsible for other areas of regulation including housing, pollution control, food safety and health and safety at work.

2.30 The qualification, coupled with sufficient experience, provides the basis to justify an officer serving an abatement notice and appearing in court, both as a witness of fact and of opinion. An experienced environmental health technician, or other employee lacking membership of the Chartered Institute of Environmental Health, could be challenged in court about the appropriateness of his serving a notice or about his credentials for giving expert evidence.[43]

Environment Agency

2.31 Local government is not the sole agency responsible for enforcing environmental legislation. Since April 1996, the Environment Agency (for England and Wales) and the Scottish Environmental Protection Agency have acquired powers in specified areas touching on statutory nuisance.[44] As central government agencies these bodies have responsibilities which exclude the remit of local authorities, although in some substantive areas both central and local government agencies have responsibilities, such as with contaminated land.[45] The central government agencies also possess scientific and other expertise which local authorities may draw upon for advice and information.

2.32 In April 1996 the Environment Agency acquired powers formerly exercised by two national bodies, HM Inspectorate of Pollution and the National Rivers

---

[42] J Stewart and G Stoker, *Local Government in the 1990s* (Macmillan, 1995).
[43] See paras 18.35–18.42.
[44] Environment Act 1995, Part I (ss 1–56). These central government agencies have no jurisdiction over statutory nuisances, however. [45] See further paras 17.58–17.60.

Authority. The Agency also took over the waste regulation functions of district councils and acquired the powers of the London Waste Regulation Authority. Some of the environmental protection functions of the Department of the Environment were also transferred.

The statute which established the Environment Agency sets out its role explicitly as being 'to protect or enhance the environment . . . to contribute towards attaining the objective of achieving sustainable development . . .'[46] By contrast, the Scottish Environmental Protection Agency lacks these statutory principles. In part, this is because its remit is limited to pollution control. In Scotland flood control remains with the local authorities and the Scottish Environmental Protection Agency has no responsibilities concerning water extraction from rivers or catchment areas.

2.33

European dimension

Statutory nuisance is an area of law developed in the United Kingdom from common law and statute, drawing extensively from both public and private law traditions. It remains notably free from any application of European law. The Treaty of European Union, while recognizing the centrality of public health and environmental law, has no direct application to the law relating to statutory nuisance.

2.34

The impact of European law on United Kingdom environmental law has been to introduce broad concepts such as sustainable development,[47] and the precautionary, preventive, proximity, and 'polluter pays' principles.[48] There has also been European legislation in areas having a potential overlap with statutory nuisance, for example directives on noise (such as Directive 92/97/EEC (traffic-related noise)) and atmospheric emissions (such as Directive 96/62/EC (air quality framework)). Such measures are for the protection of public health and, therefore, can override the fundamental freedom of the movement of goods.[49] It is possible that these principles and legal developments may influence enforcement policy at the local authority level and have some impact on the law and practice of statutory nuisance.

2.35

Proposals for a scheme of strict liability in civil law for waste and its impact on the environment have been made at the European level.[50] Likewise, European

2.36

---

[46] Environment Act 1995, s 4(1).
[47] Treaty of Amsterdam (2 October 1997, Cm 3780), arts 2 and 6. [48] ibid, art 174(2).
[49] ibid, arts 28 and 30.
[50] See further the European Commission's *White Paper on Environmental Liability*, Commission of the European Communities (9 February 2000, COM (2000) 66, available from the Commission's website at www.europa.eu.int/comm/off/white/index_en.htm). See also the earlier Commission proposal for a Directive on Civil Liability for Damage Caused by Waste (OJ C251/3, 4 October 1989), as amended by the 1991 proposal (OJ C192/6, 23 July 1991).

law has introduced a number of initiatives to enhance the responsibility of producers with regard to the environmental impacts of their products.[51] Whilst having no direct bearing on the law of statutory nuisance, such proposals may create a different attitude within industry as to potential liability for activities which impact on the environment.

[51] These initiatives include the area of legislation known as 'take-back' legislation, such as Directive 94/62/EC (packaging and packaging waste) and Directive 2000/53/EC (end of life of vehicles). See also the European Commission's *Green Paper on Integrated Product Policy* (February 2001, COM (2001) 68, available from the Commission's website at www.europa.eu.int/comm/off/green/index_en.htm).

3

THE HISTORICAL CONTEXT OF STATUTORY NUISANCE AND PUBLIC HEALTH LEGISLATION

Origins 3.01
Conceptual uncertainty 3.03
Legislative history 3.05
Early alternatives to statutory nuisance 3.06
Nuisance in the Industrial Revolution 3.07
    Judicial inconsistency 3.09
Growth of a 'sanitary paradigm' 3.11
Present-day historicism 3.17
Legislative intention 3.21

Origins

Statutory nuisance is a concept that originated in the huge changes and adverse environmental conditions brought about during the Industrial Revolution in Great Britain. It was fundamental to the social legislation that was first enacted in the 1840s and 1850s, and which continued into the twentieth century in the Public Health Act of 1936. Some of this early sanitary legislation continues in the Environmental Protection Act 1990 ('EPA 1990'), either virtually unaltered from its original formulation or in an amended form; some early formulations are to be found in other legislation, such as the Building Act 1984. **3.01**

The key statute in this period is the Nuisances Removal Act 1855, which listed statutory nuisances as *including*: **3.02**

Any Premises in such a State as to be a Nuisance or injurious to Health:
Any Pool, Ditch, Gutter, Watercourse, Privy, Urinal, Cesspool, Drain, or Ashpit so foul as to be a Nuisance or injurious to Health:
Any Animal so kept as to be a Nuisance or injurious to Health:
Any Accumulation or Deposit which is a Nuisance or injurious to Health . . .[1]

---

[1] Nuisances Removal and Diseases Prevention Acts 1855, s 8.

Conceptual uncertainty

3.03 The concept of statutory nuisance[2] had a wider meaning during this early period than today and great hopes were placed on it as the mechanism for resolving social problems. This was reforming legislation: forward looking, intended to lead society and to change social and economic conditions. The 1855 Act, when listing the nuisances in section 8, used the word 'including', suggesting that the list was not intended to be exhaustive. For example, the 1855 Act was amended in 1866 to include: 'Any House or Part of a House so overcrowded as to be dangerous or prejudicial to the Health of the Inmates'.[3]

3.04 Environmental provisions pertaining to the supply of clean water, the working conditions of factory hands, smoke control, building standards, and overcrowding both in dwellings and in factories all had their origins in Victorian public health legislation. They tended to be lumped together in general legislation such as the Public Health Act 1875, which set down virtually all the duties local authorities were required to carry out in the closing decades of the nineteenth century. In England and Wales—but not in Northern Ireland—provisions such as these have long since been repealed and replaced by other legislative schemes.[4]

Legislative history

3.05 The historical origins of present-day statutory nuisances are set out in Table 3.1 below. Matters which were previously statutory nuisances but which are now covered in other legislative regimes, such as the Housing Act 1985 and Building Act 1984, are not included.

Early alternatives to statutory nuisance

3.06 Before Parliament enacted sanitary statutes, the only way individuals could enforce their rights was by taking out proceedings for nuisance at common law. A private nuisance action could be launched by a plaintiff seeking damages from a neighbour who had caused some injury to his land. In practice, the scope for redress was limited, not least because of the need to have substantial financial resources in order to conduct litigation. To obtain an injunction to prevent a nuisance from occurring or continuing, the applicant had to seek relief from the Court of Chancery. He thus had to litigate in separate courts—to obtain judgment for damages and subsequently to seek an injunction—until the fusion of law and

---

[2] See Chapter 4 for a detailed consideration of the concept of statutory nuisance.
[3] Sanitary Act 1866, s 19.
[4] In Northern Ireland, public health legislation is still in force which is similar to the Public Health Act 1875, namely the Public Health (Ireland) Act 1878.

Table 3.1 *Legislative history of modern statutory nuisances in England and Wales*

Premises	1855: 'Any Premises in such a State as to be a Nuisance or injurious to Health'[a]	1936: 'Any premises in such a state as to be prejudicial to health or a juisance'[b]	1990: *ditto*[c]
Smoke	1866: 'Nuisances' . . . shall include . . . Any Fireplace or Furnace . . . Any Chimney (not being the Chimney of a private Dwelling House) sending forth Black Smoke in such Quantity as to be a Nuisance'[d]	1875: 'Any fireplace or furnace . . . Any chimney (not being a chimney in a private dwelling house) emitting smoke in such quantity as to be a nuisance . . . shall be a [statutory] nuisance'[e]	1936: '. . . (a) any installation for the combustion of fuel which is used in any manufacturing or trade process, or for working engines by steam, and which does not so far as practicable prevent the emission of smoke to the atmosphere; and (b) any chimney (not being a chimney in a private house) emitting smoke in such quantity as to be a nuisance . . . shall be a [statutory] nuisance'[f]	1956: 'Smoke other than—(a) smoke emitted from a chimney of a private dwelling; or (b) dark smoke from . . . [industry, for which stricter provisions apply] shall, if a nuisance to inhabitants of the neighbourhood, be deemed [to be] a statutory nuisance'[g] 1990: 'smoke emitted from premises so as to be prejudicial to health or a nuisance'[h]
Fumes or gases			1990: 'fumes or gases emitted from premises so as to be prejudicial to health or a nuisance'[i]
Dust, steam, smell or other effluvia		1936: 'any dust or effluvia caused by any trade, business, manufacture or process and being prejudicial to the health of, or a nuisance to, the inhabitants of the neighbourhood'[j]	1990: 'any dust, steam, smell or other effluvia arising on industrial, trade or business premises and being prejudicial to health or a nuisance'[k]
Accumulation or deposits	1855: 'Any Accumulation or Deposit which is a Nuisance or injurious to Health'[l]	1936: 'any accumulation or deposit which is prejudicial to health or a nuisance'[m]	1990: *ditto*[n]
Animals	1855: 'Any Animal so kept as to be a Nuisance or injurious to Health'[o]	1936: 'any animal kept in such a place or manner as to be prejudicial to health or a nuisance'[p]	1990: *ditto*[q]

Table 3.1 continued

Noise	1960: 'noise or vibration which is a nuisance shall be a statutory nuisance'[r]	1974: 'noise (including vibration) amounting to a nuisance'[s]	1990: 'noise emitted from premises so as to be prejudicial to health or a nuisance'[t]	1993: including 'noise emitted from or caused by a vehicle, machinery or equipment in a street'[u]

Any other matter declared by any other enactment to be a statutory nuisance:[v]

Insanitary Cisterns etc	1907: '(1) Any cistern used for supply of domestic water . . . (2) Any gutter, drain, shoot, stack-pipe or down spout . . . causing damp (3) Any deposit of material in or on any building or land . . . causing damp in such building or in an adjoining building so as to be dangerous or injurious to health shall be deemed to be a nuisance'[w]	1936: 'Any well, tank, cistern, or water-butt used for the supply of water for domestic purposes which is so placed, constructed or kept as to render the water therein liable to contamination or otherwise prejudicial to health, shall be a statutory nuisance'[x]	
Watercourses, ditches, ponds etc.	1855: 'Any Pool, Ditch, Gutter, Watercourse, Privy, Urinal, Cesspool, Drain, or Ashpit so foul as to be a Nuisance or injurious to Health'[y] 1925: 'Any part of a watercourse which . . . is so choked or silted up as to obstruct or impede the proper flow of water . . . and thereby to cause, or render probable, an overflow of the watercourse on to land and property adjacent to the watercourse, or to hinder the usual effective drainage of water through the same, shall be deemed to be a nuisance . . . notwithstanding that the same may not be injurious to health . . .'[bb]	1875: 'Any pool ditch gutter watercourse privy urinal cesspool drain or ashpit so foul or in such a state as to be a nuisance or injurious to health'[z] 1936: 'any part of a watercourse, not being a part ordinarily navigated by vessels employed in the carriage of goods by water, which is so choked or silted up as to obstruct or impede the proper flow of water and thereby cause a nuisance, or give rise to conditions prejudicial to health'[cc]	1936: 'any pond, pool, ditch gutter or watercourse which is so foul or in such a state as to be prejudicial to health or a nuisance . . .'[aa]

Tents, vans, sheds etc

1885: 'A tent, van, shed, or similar structure used for human habitation, which is in such a state as to be a nuisance or injurious to health, or which is so overcrowded as to be injurious to the health of the inmates whether or not members of the same family, shall be deemed to be a nuisance . . .'dd

1936: '[Any] tent, van, shed and similar structure used for human habitation [which] (a) is in such a state or so overcrowded, as to be prejudicial to the health of the inmates; or (b) the use of which, by reason of the absence of proper sanitary accommodation or otherwise, gives rise . . . on the site or on other land, to a nuisance or to conditions prejudicial to health [shall be deemed to be a nuisance]'ee

---

[a] Nuisances Removal Act 1855, s 8.   [b] Public Health Act 1936, s 92(a).   [c] EPA 1990, s 79(1)(a).   [d] Sanitary Act 1866, s 19.
[e] Public Health Act 1875, s 91.   [f] Public Health Act 1936, s 101.   [g] Clean Air Act 1956, s 16(1), as amended by the Clean Air Acts 1968 and 1993.
[h] EPA 1990, s 79(1)(b). Section 79(3) disapplies: (i) smoke emitted from a chimney of a private dwelling within a smoke control area (of Clean Air Act 1993, Part III), (ii) dark smoke emitted from industrial or trade premises, (iii) smoke from a railway locomotive steam engine for which provisions other than statutory nuisance apply (Clean Air Act 1993, ss 1 and 27).
[i] ibid, s 79(1)(c). Section 70(4) stipulates that the provision applies only to private dwellings.   [j] Public Health Act 1936, s 92(d).   [n] EPA 1990, s 79(1)(e).
[k] EPA 1990, s 79(1)(d).   [l] Nuisances Removal Act 1855, s 8.   [m] Public Health Act 1936, s 92(c).   [q] EPA 1990, s 79(1)(f).
[o] Nuisances Removal Act 1855, s 8.   [p] Public Health Act 1936, s 92(b).
[r] The Noise Abatement Act 1960 amended the Public Health Act 1936 to include noise nuisance.   [s] Control of Pollution Act 1974, s 58(1).
[t] EPA 1990, s 79(1)(g).
[u] The Noise and Statutory Nuisance Act 1993, s 2, amended the EPA 1990, s 79(1)(g) to include certain types of noise from the street (excluding traffic noise).
[v] EPA 1990, s 79(1)(h).   [w] The Public Health Acts Amendment Act 1907 inserted these provisions into the Public Health Act 1875, s 35.
[x] Public Health Act 1936, s 141.   [y] Nuisances Removal Act 1855, s 8.   [z] Public Health Act 1875, s 91.   [aa] Public Health Act 1936, s 259(1)(a)
[bb] Public Health Act 1925, s 54(1). This was the original form of the Public Health Act 1936, s 259(1)(b), which was judicially considered by Hale LJ in *R v Falmouth and Truro Port Health Authority; ex p South West Water Ltd* [2000] 3 All ER 306.
[cc] Public Health Act 1936, s 259(1)(b). This exclusion of ordinarily navigable watercourses originated in the Public Health Act 1925, s 54(2).
[dd] Housing of the Working Classes Act 1885, s 9(1).   [ee] Public Health Act 1936, s 268.

equity was finally brought about by the Supreme Court of Judicature Acts 1873 and 1875.[5] Besides civil proceedings, public nuisances could be prosecuted on indictment in criminal courts. Neither type of action was convenient, or, to use present-day jargon, 'user-friendly'.

Nuisance in the Industrial Revolution

3.07 Nuisance cases were rare even during the period of the Industrial Revolution when environmental changes were at their greatest—from the 1820s to the 1850s.[6] It has been estimated that 'on average in a ninety-year period (up to 1870) there were (in England) one or two actions for air pollution every ten years. Even allowing for actions which were not reported, appeal to the common law was minimal in the case of air pollution.'[7]

3.08 Cases involving industrial noise and water pollution were also rare. The cost of bringing proceedings acted as a powerful disincentive and the law of nuisance was ineffective in dealing with pollution problems. Arguably the most celebrated nuisance case of the mid-nineteenth century—*St Helen's Smelting Co v Tipping*[8]—had no practical consequences beyond the decision itself, even though it resulted in the plant emitting sulphuric acid fumes being forced to close down and relocate three miles away.[9]

Judicial inconsistency

3.09 Professor McLaren has argued that legal decisions in pollution cases during the Industrial Revolution were inconsistent.[10] Some judges were sympathetic to established use (or 'prior appropriation') arguments whilst others preferred not to impede manufacturing or industrial development. Even so, established user could support industrial polluters where the plant had existed for some time. For example, during the 1820s, in *R v Cross*[11] Abbott CJ considered the problem of an established slaughterhouse around which houses were subsequently built. It was held that as the plaintiff had come to the nuisance a defence could be made out; inconvenience caused by the slaughterhouse was not actionable, since the building of the houses was responsible for the nuisance not the operating of the plant.

3.10 The doctrine of 'prior appropriation' was one of several incompatible ideologies influencing judicial decision-making. Generally, it served to protect established landed interests from the new incursions of manufacturing industry. Clearly, a

---

[5] Some limited steps towards fusion were taken in the mid-nineteenth century with the Common Law Procedure Act 1854 and the Chancery Amendment Act 1858.
[6] A Briggs, *Victorian Cities* (Penguin, 1968).
[7] J P S McLaren, 'Nuisance Law and the Industrial Revolution' (1983) 3 OJLS 160.
[8] (1865) 11 HL Cas 642.
[9] A W Brian Simpson, *Leading Cases in the Common Law* (Clarendon Press, 1995), p 190.
[10] McLaren (n 7 above), p 183.   [11] (1826) 2 C&P 483.

conservative doctrine such as this, had it been applied widely and been left unchallenged, would have impeded industrial development. However, actions were rarely brought—not least because the owners of landed property stood to make huge financial gains by selling or leasing land for industrial and housing development.[12] If a neighbourhood was changing its character there were enormous incentives to cash in rather than to resist development through the courts. The position was complicated since older ideologies signifying entrenched rights co-existed with ones more favourable to industrial development. Thus, Tindal CJ could say in *Bliss v Hall*:

When a person becomes occupier of a house, he is entitled by common law, to all reasonable rights, easements, and appurtenances, amongst which good wholesome air is of course included.[13]

However, few individuals were in a position to enforce their common law rights, particularly to clean air. This was why sanitary reformers looked to the state and to the criminal law for a solution.

Growth of a 'sanitary paradigm'

During the first half of the nineteenth century, common law nuisance proceedings were ineffective in controlling pollution or for resolving public health problems. In the new urban and industrial environments the speed and scale of development were unprecedented. The problems that ensued were of a corresponding scale and difficulty. **3.11**

The law of nuisance constituted the paradigm for the statutory nuisance regime that was set up in the 1840s and 1850s to deal with public health matters, both in respect of housing and industry. From 1848,[14] a nationwide system of intervention by local authorities to control certain types of nuisance emerged in response to the very serious threats to public health posed by the Industrial Revolution and by urbanization. The underlying philosophy was driven by concerns for the environment and public health, the essential point being that the owners of property—both industrial and residential—were being expected to contribute to the costs of the adverse consequences of social and economic changes.[15] The owner—the person causing the nuisance or allowing it to occur on his land—was expected to put right something which threatened the health of his neighbours, his tenants, or **3.12**

---

[12] A Offer, *Property and Politics, 1870–1914: Landownership, Law, Ideology and Urban Development in England* (Cambridge University Press, 1981); D A Reeder, 'The Politics of Urban Leaseholds in Late Victorian England' (1961) 6 *International Review of Social History* 413–30.
[13] (1838) 7 LJCP 122, at 123.
[14] Nuisances Removal and Diseases Prevention Act 1848; Public Health Act 1848.
[15] Belief in the efficacy of 'responsible ownership' was an article of faith to those opposed to further state intervention. By the late-1880s it became associated with a 'conservative consensus' on housing policy. See J E Pointing and M A Bulos, 'Some Implications of Failed Issues of Reform' (1984) 8 *International Journal of Urban and Regional Research* 467–80.

the public generally. If he failed to do so, the local authority had powers to serve a notice, the breach of which rendered him liable to prosecution and fines.

3.13 Social reformers in the 1830s and 1840s who pursued the cause of sanitary reform, such as Edwin Chadwick,[16] sought to control social problems using the legal and political resources available at the time. This process included trying to persuade property owners to be socially responsible, setting up a local government machinery of inspection and enforcement, and utilizing a system based on aspects of public and private nuisance.

3.14 The social conditions prevailing in towns and cities in the 1840s and 1850s, when the first sanitary acts were passed by Parliament,[17] constituted a particular set of circumstances that do not apply today. In particular, the concept of what could amount to a statutory nuisance was bound up by disease-based public health considerations because these were so pressing in this period: infectious and contagious diseases, particularly cholera and typhoid, were very prevalent and their causes were little understood. Medical science could do little to combat disease at this time: the emphasis was on prevention. The difficulties were enormous. First, there was the prevalence and number of dangerous, life-threatening diseases; second, there was no effective system of personal medical care; and third, there was no adequate theory of disease. As late as the 1870s, the 'miasma' theory of disease prevailed, namely the idea that disease was caused by the transmission of minute faecal particles suspended in droplets of breath. The objectives of tackling overcrowding in housing and of separating human from animal habitations flowed from this theory. It is almost impossible today to comprehend the degree to which the Victorians feared disease and death. Sanitary reformers calculated that the average life expectancy for working-class Mancunians in the 1840s was only 17 years.[18]

3.15 As regards housing, sanitary legislation was enacted to deal with specific issues: overcrowding, serious disrepair, lack of a clean water supply, lack of adequate drainage, poor facilities for the removal of human and animal dung and rubbish.[19] Public concern at times reached panic levels, not least because there was an ever-present risk that the 'poison' infesting the slums might find its way to where the professional and middle classes lived, or even reach the town houses of the aristocracy.

3.16 This focus on property—particularly on insanitary housing posing a risk of disease to its neighbours—is consistent with the concepts of public and private

---

[16] See further S E Finer, *The Life and Times of Sir Edwin Chadwick* (Methuen, 1952).
[17] The full titles of these included disease prevention as well as nuisance; they were the Nuisances Removal and Diseases Prevention Acts 1848 and 1849, consolidated and amended by the Nuisances Removal and Diseases Prevention Act 1855.   [18] Briggs (n 6 above), p 101.
[19] A S Wohl, *The Eternal Slum: Housing and Social Policy in Victorian London* (Edward Arnold, 1977).

nuisance. But the scope of statutory nuisance was pushed further. For sanitary reformers, the risks were from diseases caused by smells, dampness and accumulations of filth. These were soon followed by smoke, dust and effluvia. Reformers pushed the boundaries of nuisance to include the conditions in which factory hands worked as well as the homes where they lived. The concerns were not solely, or even mainly, with the effects of these conditions on neighbouring properties, but included those who suffered directly from poor environmental conditions. The aim was to encourage the improvement of conditions where they had deteriorated to such an extent as to cause nuisance or injury to health. Whether the fit between the concept of a statutory nuisance and common law nuisance was neat and elegant was not a primary concern—sanitary reformers were practical people who wanted to get things done. What constituted a statutory nuisance was, therefore, firmly rooted in the 'here and now' in the minds of sanitary reformers and legislators.

Present-day historicism

Present-day law governing statutory nuisance owes much to these historical roots—arguably too much. The lineage of many of today's statutory nuisances are directly traceable to these early years, with certain sections using similar words to those found in the 1855 and 1875 Acts.[20] This has formed the basis, illustrated by a number of recent and important decisions, for the adoption by the courts of a narrow view of the scope of statutory nuisance.

3.17

Recourse by the higher courts to a narrow historicism has placed statutory nuisances enacted comparatively recently—such as noise which first became a statutory nuisance in 1960—in an anomalous position.[21] Part III of the EPA 1990 was enacted as a consolidating measure. This was deemed necessary partly in order to tidy up nuisances drawn from the Public Health Act 1936 and to consolidate these with noise. Prior to the EPA 1990, noise was a nuisance under the Control of Pollution Act 1974 and, from 1960 to when the 1974 Act came into force, noise nuisance was enforced under the 1936 Act. Does the now prevailing historicist interpretation of the scope of statutory nuisance mean that noise nuisance should be understood in terms of the intentions of Parliament when most of today's statutory nuisances were first enacted, as public health nuisances, in 1855? Or in 1960 when noise first became a statutory nuisance enforced under the 1936 Act? Or in 1990 when it was consolidated with the early public health nuisances under the EPA 1990?[22]

3.18

---

[20] ie the Nuisances Removal Act 1855 and the Public Health Act 1875. See Table 3.1 at para 3.05.
[21] The Noise Abatement Act 1960 amended the Public Health Act 1936, s 92, to include noise nuisance.
[22] In fact, none of the recent cases in which the courts have utilized an historical analysis has considered noise nuisance.

3.19 Recourse to historical analysis by the courts has gone hand in hand with judicial conservatism. This suggests a resistance amongst the higher judiciary to the doctrine of considering environmental legislation to be 'always speaking', that is orientated to present conditions as opposed to being fixed to the time of their original enactment.[23] Judicial conservatism is justified by a natural reluctance to encroach on the territory of Parliament to change the law.

3.20 This has not been a universal feature of judicial opinion, perhaps the most notable dissenting voice coming from Lord Steyn, who stated in his minority judgment in *Birmingham CC v Oakley*:

> The appeal to Victorian social history, and legislative history going back more than a 150 years, is in my view not appropriate to the context. The 1990 Act [the EPA 1990] must be given a sensible interpretation in the modern world.[24]

Legislative intention

3.21 Recent leading judgments, such as those in *R v Bristol CC, ex p Everett* [25] and *Birmingham CC v Oakley*,[26] have gone back to the legislative origins of some forms of statutory nuisance, notably those arising from the state of premises.[27] In *R v Falmouth and Truro Port Health Authority, ex p South West Water Ltd* [28] watercourses have been subjected to exhaustive judicial enquiry.[29]

3.22 In *Ex p Everett*[30] the Court of Appeal was concerned with whether the likelihood of an accident causing physical injury which arose because of the poor arrangement of an internal staircase in a house, was capable of amounting to a statutory nuisance. It decided that the correct approach to adopt for provisions originating in the 1855 Act and continuing in the present legislation, is that they should bear the same meaning as when originally enacted. A public health issue in the 1850s is held to be the same as a public health issue today, implying that a statutory nuisance is a fixed entity rather than open to revision because of changing social conditions.

3.23 The Court of Appeal adopted a very narrow approach to legislative intention in deciding that section 79(1)(a) of the EPA 1990—the state of the premises—must be read as a sanitary or public health provision, simply because the same words are used as originally appeared in the Victorian sanitary acts.[31] To Buxton LJ it

---

[23] F Bennion, *Statutory Interpretation* (3rd edn, Butterworths, 1997).
[24] [2001] 1 All ER 385, at 393.   [25] [1999] 2 All ER 193.   [26] n 24 above.
[27] EPA 1990, s 79(1)(a), defines this nuisance as 'any premises in such a state as to be prejudicial to health or a nuisance'.   [28] [2000] 3 All ER 306.
[29] Watercourses can constitute statutory nuisances under the Public Health Act 1936, s 259.
[30] n 25 above.
[31] No judicial comments were made in *Ex p Everett* regarding statutory nuisances originating in other legislation, such as noise nuisance. Applying the rules of statutory construction in the way the

'cried out from the page' that 'the successor provisions of 1990 are about disease or ill-health, not about physical danger' and that 'the target of the legislators was disease and not physical injury'.[32] As disease constitutes the same type of risk as existed during the original enactment, for his Lordship there was no basis for updating the construction of the statute to include the risk of personal injury. If Parliament intended to legislate for such risks—which are of a type that could be envisaged in 1855 as easily as today—they would have been included in the original legislation. Consequently, the provisions could not be construed as requiring continuous updating to allow for changes since their original enactment; and so they bear the same meaning today as in 1855.[33]

In *Birmingham CC v Oakley* the factual issue was whether the absence of a washbasin in the lavatory of premises that were old and of a poor standard meant that those premises could be prejudicial to health. A majority decided that such premises did not come within the scope of section 79(1)(a). Lord Hoffmann decided that '*Ex parte Everett* is authority for the proposition that the language of section 79(1)(a) must be construed in the light of its legislative history',[34] and this excluded lack of amenities as well as the layout of premises from coming within the scope of the section. **3.24**

Clearly, as the law presently stands, legal advisers need to be careful about adopting a more expansive, environmentally informed approach towards statutory nuisance. The alternative view advocated among environmental lawyers that 'it is no longer appropriate, if it ever was, to construe the references to statutory nuisances as necessarily being coloured by public health issues'[35] appears to be unsustainable. **3.25**

Court of Appeal has done produces the anomalous position that Part III of the 1990 Act, which was intended to provide a reformed and unitary system for dealing with statutory nuisances, is bifurcated depending on whether particular nuisances originated as public health provisions or in more recent legislation.

[32] n 25 above, at 204.
[33] Bennion (n 23 above), p 686.
[34] n 24 above, at 394.
[35] R Burnett-Hall, *Environment Law* (Sweet & Maxwell, 1995), p 1032.

4

THE CONCEPT OF STATUTORY NUISANCE

Introduction 4.01
The list of statutory nuisances 4.04
   Section 79 of the Environmental Protection Act 1990 . . . . .4.04
   Definitions in statutes 4.07
'Prejudicial to health or a nuisance' 4.08
Origins of the two limbs of statutory nuisance 4.09
The modern judicial approach 4.11
The nuisance limb 4.16
   Common law nuisance 4.17
   Distinguishing public from private nuisance 4.21
Public nuisance 4.25
Private nuisance 4.28
   Requirement that the claimant in private nuisance must have an
   interest in real property 4.28
   Classification of private nuisances 4.31
   The transmission of the offending activity 4.32
   Private nuisance and the nuisance limb 4.33
Public, private and statutory nuisances: differences and overlaps 4.34
The nuisance limb and the health limb 4.37
**Is the nuisance limb limited to those matters which might also be
'prejudicial to health'?** 4.41
Distinguishing the health and nuisance limbs 4.48
   Consequences 4.48
   Premises and the health limb 4.49
   Noise and the nuisance and health limbs 4.50
   Street noise and the nuisance and health limbs 4.54
**Reasonableness as a central concept of common law nuisance and
its relevance to statutory nuisance** 4.55
   'Give and take' 4.55
   Reasonableness and enforcement action 4.60
   Particular sensitivity 4.64
   Social utility of the defendant's conduct 4.68
   Motive of the defendant 4.70
   Duration and intensity 4.72
   Time of day 4.77
   Nature of locality 4.78

The health limb	.4.82
What is covered by 'prejudice to health'?	.4.85
The decision in *Everett*	.4.87
The decision in *Oakley*	.4.90
Earlier case law	.4.93
Reasonableness and 'prejudice to health'	.4.94
Cases where 'prejudice to health' is in issue	.4.96
Who caused the prejudice to health?	.4.99
Expert evidence	.4.101
The health limb post-*Everett*	.4.104

Introduction

4.01 Statutory nuisances are, as their name implies, creatures of statute, which are all now consolidated and re-enacted in Part III of the Environmental Protection Act 1990 ('EPA 1990'), or incorporated by reference into this Act. They are listed in section 79 of the 1990 Act.

4.02 The list contains a range of potentially offending activities with separate statutory origins.[1] Each statutory nuisance was passed to deal with different problems relating to public health and the quality of life. As a result, to discuss statutory nuisances in generic terms is not always possible since differences in application result from their distinct histories.[2] Chapters 5 to 10, therefore, deal separately with each category of statutory nuisance.

4.03 Nevertheless, there are some unifying characteristics of statutory nuisances which can be treated in generic terms. The primary commonality is that, in order for an offending activity to fall under the umbrella of the law of statutory nuisance it must first be identified as one of the listed matters in section 79 and secondly, must be either a 'nuisance' or 'prejudicial to health'.

The list of statutory nuisances

Section 79 of the Environmental Protection Act 1990
4.04 The list of statutory nuisances appears in section 79(1) of the Act as follows:

---

[1] For the genesis of each nuisance, see Chapter 3, and, in particular Table 3.1.
[2] A modern example of this approach is the proposal to incorporate the nuisance which can be created by tall hedges as a statutory nuisance under section 79 of the EPA 1990. This proposal was promoted in the Statutory Nuisances (Hedgerows in Residential Areas) Bill 1999, which would have inserted the following new paragraph, section 79(1)(aa), into the EPA 1990: 'any hedgerow planted in such a place, or maintained in such a manner, as to be prejudicial to health or a nuisance'. Such a nuisance is far removed from the problems of nineteenth-century industrial Britain and the public health issues of the day. See P H Kenny, 'Good Fences Make Good Neighbours' [2000] Conv March/April 73–4.

(a) state of the premises;
(b) smoke emitted from premises;
(c) fumes or gases emitted from premises;
(d) any dust, steam, smell or other effluvia arising on industrial, trade or business premises;
(e) any accumulation or deposit;
(f) any animal kept in such a place or manner;
(g) noise emitted from premises;
(ga) noise emitted from or caused by a vehicle, machinery or equipment in a street;[3]
(gb) smoke, fumes, or gases emitted from any vehicle, machinery or equipment on a street other than from any vehicle, machinery or equipment being used for fire brigade purposes;[4]
(h) any other matter declared by any enactment to be a statutory nuisance.

This list is limited and defined. There are nine categories which group different types of offending activities together. Some, such as effluvia and the keeping of animals, are drawn directly from the original Victorian legislation where they were first established. Others, such as noise, have a more modern origin.[5] **4.05**

One category, in section 79(1)(h), incorporates all the statutory nuisances which appear in other legislation. These are to be found in sections 141, 259 and 268 of the Public Health Act 1936.[6] They include such matters as: **4.06**

- ponds, ditches, gutters or watercourses;[7]
- wells, tanks, cisterns, or water-butts used for the supply of water for domestic purposes;[8]
- tents, vans, sheds and similar structures used for human habitation, accommodation or otherwise.[9]

Definitions in statutes
Some definitions of these listed statutory nuisances are to be found in Part III of the EPA 1990 and case law has further refined their meaning and extent. Until Parliament legislates further, the list is finite. **4.07**

'Prejudicial to health or a nuisance'

For an offending activity to fall under the statutory nuisance regime it must be 'prejudicial to health or a nuisance'. These two limbs are alternative requirements. This phrase is common to each of the listed statutory nuisances. **4.08**

---

[3] Paragraph (ga) was inserted by the Noise and Statutory Nuisance Act 1993, s 2(2)(b).
[4] This provision only applies to London boroughs and was inserted by the London Local Authorities Act 1996, s 24. It does not include smoke, fumes and gases emitted from vehicle exhausts.   [5] See Table 3.1 at para 3.05.   [6] See Chapter 10.
[7] Public Health Act 1936, s 259(1).   [8] ibid, s 141.   [9] ibid, s 268.

Origins of the two limbs of statutory nuisance

4.09 The origins of the two limbs can be traced from different sources. The concept 'prejudicial to health' is entirely a creature of statute developed in the nineteenth century as part of public health law. It has no historical links with the common law or with nuisance. It has a legislative origin in the virtually identical terms used in the Victorian statutes, the Nuisances Removal and Diseases Prevention Acts 1848 and 1849. In these statutes the phrase was 'a nuisance or *injurious* to health' (our emphasis). The modern phrase defined in section 79(7) of the EPA 1990, includes injury to health. Thus, no difference exists between the words used in the original legislation and the current expression.

4.10 Nuisance, on the other hand, owes its origins to the common law and must therefore, as a preliminary, satisfy the basic elements of public or private nuisance. In addition, it must have a link with a health matter to the extent that it must interfere with personal comfort. The determination of the extent of the nuisance limb rests, as a result, on the common law, which pre-dates and co-exists with the law of statutory nuisance. But the health limb can be defined exclusively in relation to case law under the sanitary statutes.

The modern judicial approach

4.11 The genesis of the phrase 'prejudicial to health or a nuisance' is not of mere academic interest. In decisions of the appeal courts both in statutory nuisance and common law nuisance, the judges have harked back to the original meaning of statutory words and the original purpose of the law.[10]

4.12 In statutory nuisance, the decision of the House of Lords in *Birmingham CC v Oakley*[11] and two judgments of the Court of Appeal, *R v Bristol CC, ex p Everett*[12] and *R v Falmouth and Truro Port Health Authority, ex p South West Water Ltd*,[13] evidence this approach.

4.13 In *Oakley* (a case about the lack of washing facilities[14]) it was held that, while a statute must be interpreted in the light of changing knowledge, technology or

---

[10] At common law, two decisions on private nuisance are noteworthy in this regard. The House of Lords, in both *Cambridge Water Co v Eastern Leather Counties plc* [1994] 2 AC 264 and *Hunter v Canary Wharf and London Docklands Development Corporation* [1997] AC 655, firmly cemented the law in its Victorian origins. Both cases emphasized the importance of the original purpose of the tort of private nuisance, namely the protection of property rights. These decisions have a policy background to them in that they reflect awareness by the judiciary that environmental matters are subject to much concerted action at national and European level. See, eg, *Southwark LBC v Tanner and Others*; *Baxter v Camden LBC (No 2)*, House of Lords [2001] 1 AC 1; and the comments of Lord Goff in *Cambridge Water Co v Eastern Counties Leather plc*, at 305.   [11] [2001] 1 All ER 385.
[12] [1999] 2 All ER 193.   [13] [2000] 3 All ER 306.
[14] See I Loveland, 'And Now Wash Your Hands: Statutory Nuisance Under the Environmental Protection Act 1990, section 79(1)(a)' [2001] JPL 1144. For a discussion of the public law principle that a statute is 'always speaking', see also paras 5.05–5.29.

social standards, the meaning of the statutory language remains unaltered. 'The content may change but the concept remains the same'.[15] Thus, evidence of what Parliament must have intended when the statute was enacted is relevant to its modern interpretation.[16]

The decision in *Oakley* highlights the intractable nature of the judicial approach to the interpretation of the meaning and extent of a statutory nuisance. Further, to extend the meaning of statutory nuisance would, in some cases,[17] impose heavy financial burdens on local housing authorities. Their Lordships have explicitly stated their reluctance to extend the meaning of the statutory words in a manner which they considered would go beyond what Parliament originally intended, the current words being an exact re-enactment of the language used in the nineteenth century.[18] **4.14**

Thus, in defining the terms used in Part III of the 1990 Act, close regard must be had to the history of that legislation and to the presumed legislative intent of Parliament at the time of the promulgation of the particular part of section 79 of the EPA 1990. Chapter 3 describes the precise legislative origin of each part of that section. It is important, therefore, to ascertain the legislative genesis of each of the statutory nuisances listed in section 79. The application of the law to any current problem will be determined in this manner. **4.15**

The nuisance limb

No further definition of 'nuisance' is to be found in Part III of the EPA 1990. The common law meaning of nuisance is to be imported into the statute, but it encompasses two different concepts: private and public nuisance. 'In principle, "nuisance" has its common law meaning, either a public or a private nuisance.'[19] In an earlier case on a predecessor statute (the Nuisances Removal Act 1855) it was said: 'I think that the section is not confined to the case of a public nuisance, it is enough if it is a private nuisance, or one affecting a considerable number of persons'.[20] **4.16**

Common law nuisance
Nuisance law is the branch of tort law which is most commonly associated with protection of the environment.[21] This association is, however, neither exclusive **4.17**

---

[15] n 11 above, per Lord Hoffmann at 396.
[16] *Goodes v East Sussex CC* [2000] 1 WLR 1356; *R v Ireland* [1998] AC 147, 158–9.
[17] Such as the circumstances in *Oakley* (n 11 above).
[18] *Oakley* (n 11 above) was a majority decision, their Lordships splitting 3–2 in favour of this interpretation.
[19] *R v Carrick DC, ex p Shelley* [1996] Env LR 273, per Carnwath J at 278. See also *Godfrey v Conwy CBC* [2001] Env LR 674, *London Borough of Camden v London Underground Ltd* [2000] Env LR 369 and *Murdoch v Glacier Metal Co Ltd* [1998] Env LR 732.
[20] *Proprietors of Margate Pier v Town Council of Margate* (1869) 33 JP 437, per Hayes J at 439.
[21] *Winfield & Jolowicz on Tort* (15th edn, Sweet & Maxwell, 1998), p 490.

nor intentional. Environmental protection may often be served as an incident of liability which is aimed primarily at the protection of property rights.[22]

4.18 The definitions of each type of common law nuisance are well established. Private nuisance has been defined in *Howard v Walker* by Lord Goddard CJ as:

> the unlawful interference with a person's use or enjoyment of land, or of some right over, or in connection with it.[23]

4.19 In *A-G v PYA Quarries Ltd* Denning LJ defined public nuisance as

> a nuisance which is so widespread in its range or so indiscriminate in its effect that it would not be reasonable to expect one person to take proceedings on his own responsibility to put a stop to it, but that it should be taken on the responsibility of the community at large.[24]

4.20 *Clerk and Lindsell on Torts* provides another definition which encompasses both private and public nuisance:

> The essence of nuisance is a condition or activity which unduly interferes with the use or enjoyment of land. In common parlance, stenches and smoke and a variety of different things may amount to a nuisance in fact but whether they are actionable as the tort of nuisance will depend upon a variety of considerations and a balance of conflicting interests. . . . Nuisance is an act or omission which is an interference with, disturbance of or annoyance to, a person in the exercise or enjoyment of (a) a right belonging to him as a member of the public, when it is a public nuisance, or (b) his ownership or occupation of land or of some easement, profit, or other right used or enjoyed in connection with land, when it is a private nuisance.[25]

Distinguishing public from private nuisance

4.21 In many respects, the incorporation of both public and private nuisance into the concept of statutory nuisance is odd. Public and private nuisance are not in reality generically linked at all.[26]

4.22 Public nuisance is a criminal offence. It may also be the subject matter of proceedings for an injunction brought by the Attorney-General on behalf of a person or by the local authority.[27] It is only actionable by a private individual in a civil claim where that person has suffered special damage over and above that suffered by the public at large. In such a case, the claimant need not show an interest in land.[28]

---

[22] *Hunter v Canary Wharf and London Docklands Development Corporation* (n 10 above).
[23] [1947] 2 All ER 197 at 199, quoting in approval Winfield, *Textbook on the Law of Tort* (3rd edn), p 426. [24] [1957] 2 QB 169, at 190–1.
[25] 18th edn, Sweet & Maxwell, 2000, para 19-01.
[26] See the discussion of public nuisance in *Salmond & Heuston on the Law of Torts* (21st edn, Sweet & Maxwell, 1996), ch 5, and in J R Spencer, 'Public Nuisance: A Critical Examination' [1989] CLJ 55. [27] Local Government Act 1972, s 222.
[28] *Tarry v Ashton* (1876) 1 QBD 314. Equally, having an interest in land is no bar to such an action; *Tate & Lyle Food and Distribution Ltd v GLC* [1983] 2 AC 509; [1983] 1 All ER 1159.

Private nuisance, on the other hand, is a civil wrong designed specifically to protect property rights from unreasonable interference. It protects the property owner[29] from offending activities which interfere with the enjoyment of his land and which emanate from neighbouring land. **4.23**

However, although there are distinctions to be drawn, there are also considerable areas of overlap between public and private nuisance.[30] Indeed, this overlap occurs between all three types of nuisance: public, private, and statutory. **4.24**

Public nuisance

Public nuisances often form the subject matter of a statutory nuisance.[31] In many respects, public nuisance bears a greater affinity with statutory nuisance than does private nuisance. A public nuisance is a criminal offence regulated by an administrative agency;[32] it relates to matters which materially affect the comfort or convenience of a class of people; it is a case where it is so indiscriminate in its effect that it is deemed to be a proper matter to be dealt with by the community at large; and, it is not related to private property rights. **4.25**

The persons affected by a public nuisance must be a cross-section of the community[33] or a considerable number of persons as distinct from individual persons.[34] The nuisance must be so widespread and indiscriminate in its effect that it would be unreasonable to expect an individual, as opposed to the state, to take action to deal with it.[35] **4.26**

It may sometimes be the case that the public nuisance route is more apposite for a local authority than the statutory nuisance regime. This is certainly the case where the offending activity falls outside the list in section 79 of the EPA 1990.[36] **4.27**

Private nuisance

Requirement that the claimant in private nuisance must have an interest in real property
An action in private nuisance is dependent on the claimant owning an interest in land which includes: freehold and leasehold interests,[37] legal and equitable interests, and, **4.28**

---

[29] *Hunter v Canary Wharf and London Docklands Development Corporation* (n 10 above).
[30] For a concise discussion on the differences between private and public nuisance, see G Price, 'Nuisance Values', *Estates Gazette*, 16 September 2000, pp 152–3. For a general discussion of public nuisance, including its relationship to private nuisance, see R A Buckley, *The Law of Nuisance* (2nd edn, Butterworths, 1996), ch 4.
[31] See, eg, *R v Carrick DC, ex p Shelley* (n 19 above) (accumulations and deposits on a public beach). [32] The Attorney-General or a local authority.
[33] *A-G v PYA Quarries Ltd* (n 24 above) (blasting operations and noise, dust, vibration).
[34] *R v Madden* [1975] 3 All ER 155 (bomb hoax actually affecting only individual persons).
[35] *A-G v PYA Quarries Ltd* (n 24 above). [36] See further paras 17.22–17.25.
[37] Including weekly, monthly or other periodic tenancies.

exceptionally, de facto licences with exclusive possession.[38] The purpose and object of the tort of private nuisance is to protect, and provide a remedy for interference with, real property rights.

4.29 This requirement for a property interest on the part of the claimant has no parallel in the statutory nuisance regime. The person affected by a statutory nuisance may include the broad category of persons excluded from the tort of private nuisance by the test established by the House of Lords in *Hunter v Canary Wharf and London Docklands Development Corporation*,[39] that is, spouses, children, lodgers and guests. Any persons living within the area may register a complaint with a local authority about the existence of a statutory nuisance.[40]

4.30 Under section 82 of the EPA 1990 which provides that an individual may bring summary proceedings before a magistrates' court in respect of a statutory nuisance in his own name, the prerequisite for bringing an action is simply that the applicant must be a 'person aggrieved'.[41]

Classification of private nuisances

4.31 Private nuisances may be classified as being one of three kinds:

- nuisance by encroachment on a neighbour's land;[42]
- nuisance by direct physical injury to a neighbour's land; and
- nuisance by interference with a neighbour's enjoyment of his land (sometimes known as amenity nuisances).[43]

The transmission of the offending activity

4.32 Each of the threefold classifications of private nuisance encompasses the transmission in some manner of the offending activity from one piece of land to another.[44] Encroachment suggests an intrusion of a physical kind, such as the foundations of a building, which it would be difficult to envisage forming the

---

[38] *Hunter v Canary Wharf and London Docklands Development Corporation* (n 10 above). For a discussion of the extent of the property interest required for an action in private nuisance, see R Malcolm, 'Suing in Private Nuisance: The Rights of the Property Owner' in Jackson and Wilde (eds), *Contemporary Property Law* (Ashgate Publishing, 1999), pp 254–82. [39] n 10 above.
[40] EPA 1990, s 79(1). This does appear to exclude a person *working* in the area; a result perhaps unintended by the draftsman of the Act. [41] See further paras 16.08–16.10.
[42] Not necessarily amounting to trespass. See *Delaware Mansions Ltd and Flecksun Ltd v Westminster City Council* [2001] 4 All ER 737.
[43] *Hunter v Canary Wharf and London Docklands Development Corporation* (n 10 above), per Lord Lloyd at 695. This category might also include obstruction of rights of way, or other easements.
[44] While an emanation from the defendant's land is almost always necessary in private nuisance, there are some exceptions. Two exceptions worthy of note are *Thompson-Schwab v Costaki* [1956] 1 WLR 335, where the sight of prostitutes and their clients entering and leaving premises was actionable; and (a New Zealand decision) *Bank of New Zealand v Greenwood* [1984] 1 NZLR 525, where a dazzling glare was reflected from the defendant's veranda into the plaintiff's buildings. See Lord Goff's analysis of these cases in *Hunter v Canary Wharf and London Docklands Development Corporation* (n 10 above), at 685–6.

basis for an action in statutory nuisance. But physical matter such as oil or other effluvia could encroach on neighbouring land. The land could be physically damaged by such an encroachment, and smell, dust and noise could interfere with the enjoyment of land.

Private nuisance and the nuisance limb
It is plain that the factual basis of a private nuisance will often form the subject matter of a complaint in statutory nuisance. In general, however, where there is no transmission of the offending activity from one plot of land to another, then the private nuisance limb in statutory nuisance will not be satisfied. So, if dampness and condensation occur in a property which arise as a result of a lack of adequate ventilation or heating from within the property itself, the nuisance limb will not be satisfied. In such a case, reliance must be placed on the health limb. In *National Coal Board v Neath BC*[45] it was said that the case could not fall under the nuisance limb if what had taken place affected only the person or persons occupying the premises where that nuisance was said to have taken place. A similar outcome occurred in *Coventry CC v Cartwright*[46] where the activity complained of—an accumulation of rubble on a waste site—did not fall under the nuisance limb as no transmission of the offending activity occurred.   **4.33**

Public, private and statutory nuisances: differences and overlaps

The same areas of activity can be covered by all three types of nuisance—smell, noise and atmospheric pollution are examples of this. The perpetrator of a nuisance can be subject to all three types of action. Reasonableness is a relevant factor[47] and the 'give-and-take' principle expounded in *Cambridge Water Company v Eastern Counties Leather plc*[48] and in *Hunter v Canary Wharf and London Docklands Development Corporation*[49] applies equally across the board.   **4.34**

Many cases which have been the subject of public nuisance proceedings could equally have been brought under the banner of a statutory nuisance.[50] Such cases include: quarry blasting;[51] bad smells from a chicken-processing factory;[52] an acid-house party;[53] and the deposit of filth and refuse.[54]   **4.35**

To include all types of common law nuisance into the statutory nuisance legislative regime would be excessive and contrary to the intention of Parliament. With   **4.36**

---

[45] *National Coal Board v Neath BC* (sometimes cited as *National Coal Board v Thorne*) [1976] 2 All ER 478.   [46] [1975] 1 WLR 845.   [47] *Dymond v Pearce* [1972] 1 All ER 1142.
[48] Per Lord Goff of Chievely (n 82 below), at 299. See also Lord Millett in *Southwark London Borough Council v Tanner and Others*; *Baxter v Camden LBC (No 2)*, House of Lords [2001] 1 AC 1, at 20.   [49] n 10 above, at 711.   [50] See paras 17.22–17.25.
[51] *A-G v PYA Quarries Ltd* (n 24 above).
[52] *Shoreham-by-Sea UDC v Dolphin Canadian Proteins* (1972) 71 LGR 261.
[53] *R v Shorrock* [1994] QB 279; [1993] 3 All ER 917.
[54] *A-G v Tod Heatley* [1897] 1 Ch 560.

some few exceptions,[55] the judges have made this plain over the centuries. But where is the borderline to be drawn?[56]

The nuisance limb and the health limb

4.37 The two limbs, the 'health' limb and the 'nuisance' limb, stand separately and must be distinguished.[57] The evidential requirements for proving the existence of a statutory nuisance under one limb or the other are different.[58]

4.38 In 1975, in *Salford CC v McNally*,[59] the House of Lords emphasized the different requirements for each of the limbs of statutory nuisance:

> ... confusion occurs in some of the cases through the use of the words 'personal comfort'. These words are appropriate enough in the context of what is a 'nuisance' for the purpose of the Public Health Act 1936 (see as to this the clear judgment of Stephen J in *Bishop Auckland Local Board v Bishop Auckland Iron Co*), but they are quite inappropriate in relation to the other limb 'prejudicial to health'. Health is not the same as comfort and interference with the latter does not bring a case within the 'health' limb of the 1936 Act.[60]

4.39 Further, in *Birmingham CC v Oakley*,[61] Lord Clyde opined that the definition of 'prejudice to health', 'covers what may be actually injurious as well as what may be likely to be injurious and in either case something over and above what may be seen as a "nuisance", since section 79(1)(a) includes not only what is "prejudicial to health" but also, in the alternative, what may be a nuisance'.[62]

4.40 So, it becomes necessary to analyse the differing requirements for the nuisance limb and the health limb.

Is the nuisance limb limited to those matters which might also be 'prejudicial to health'?

4.41 In *Great Western Rly Co v Bishop*,[63] the court held that the purpose of the statute was to deal with public health and private health issues and it was aimed at the

---

[55] See, eg, the *dicta* of Carnwath J in *R v Carrick DC, ex p Shelley* (n 19 above), at 279.

[56] The distinction in the availability of remedies should be borne in mind. A prosecution in the Crown Court for public nuisance can result in an unlimited fine and/or two years' imprisonment. Extremely serious statutory nuisances could, therefore, be prosecuted as a public nuisance; Criminal Law Act 1977, s 16, Sch 2; Magistrates' Courts Act 1980, s 17(1), Sch 1, para 1. See further para 17.25.

[57] For the sake of clarity and ease of reference the two limbs are described throughout this book as the 'nuisance limb' and the 'health limb'.

[58] Although the health limb and the nuisance limb are separate concepts, there is no requirement for an abatement notice to set out under which limb it is alleged the statutory nuisance takes effect; *Lowe & Watson v South Somerset DC* [1998] Env LR 143. See further paras 12.37–12.38.

[59] [1976] AC 379.   [60] ibid, per Lord Wilberforce at 389.   [61] n 11 above.

[62] ibid, at 399. (Lord Clyde gave a dissenting opinion in *Oakley* but not in relation to this point which was not in dispute.)

[63] (1872) LR QB 550. The case concerned water dripping from an overhead bridge and it was held that this was not the sort of mischief that the law of statutory nuisance was aimed at. The law was

health of urban and suburban dwellers in particular. It was not to be used to provide a method of abatement of private and public nuisances in general.

4.42 But, if the case is being brought under the nuisance limb then it cannot simply be said that it must also be prejudicial to health. After all, these are alternates.[64] The link with health where the case is being argued under the alternative nuisance limb, is more tenuous, amounting to an interference with personal comfort.

4.43 The issue arose again in *Malton Board of Health v Malton Manure Co*[65] where it was said that a statutory nuisance could arise even if it was not injurious to health. Effluvia was emanating from a factory where bones were being crushed and dissolved to make manure.[66] Stephen J, considering whether it was necessary to prove that, not only was a nuisance caused by the effluvium, but also that it was injurious to health, stated that 'such effluvium was a nuisance whether causing injury to health or not'.[67] The statute was not to be read as though it was a 'nuisance injurious to health'. Nuisance—and in this he was following *Great Western Rly Co v Bishop*—could not be given its fullest meaning.[68] It must be some matter 'affecting' public health, and he was prepared to extend this to include the 'diminution of comfort'. Clearly, nausea and the other effects of the effluvium, fell within this concept of public health.

4.44 This seems a sensible result because it is indisputable that to extend the meaning of the nuisance limb (as opposed to the health limb) any further would be absurd,

concerned with nuisances that affected public health and this was the point where a line had to be drawn. Cockburn CJ stated (at 552–3) that 'it was admitted that this Act [the Nuisances Removal Act 1855] cannot be considered as comprehending within its provisions all things which would amount to nuisances in point of law. Obstructions to a highway and a variety of other offences of that kind against public convenience, which are in point of law nuisances, never can have been intended to be within the scope of this legislation. It comes therefore necessary to draw a line somewhere. We can only discover that line by reference to the evident scope and purpose of the enactment. It is plain that the object was to protect the public health and private health of individuals living in towns, or in the neighbourhood of towns. I think that affords us a guiding principle by which to construe this Act, and that "nuisance", the general term used in the Act, must be taken to mean a nuisance affecting public health.' It is probably the case that this statement of the law goes too far in that it fails to distinguish fully between the two limbs.

[64] See, eg, *Godfrey v Conwy BC* [2001] Env LR 38 where Rose LJ at 23 accepted counsel's submission that 'it cannot have been Parliament's intention to have equated nuisance with prejudice to health. If it had been, the word nuisance would have been otiose'.

[65] (1879) 4 Ex D 302.

[66] A medical officer of health had certified that it was injurious to the health of the inhabitants of the area. This expert evidence was disputed and other medical witnesses alleged that though the effluvia might 'make sick people worse, and cause nausea', it would not cause permanent injury to health.

[67] n 65 above, at 306. The first judge (Kelly CB) commented was that he was sorry to put a construction on the statute so as to prevent traders from carrying on their business in a reasonable way. Nevertheless, he held that the effluvium did constitute a nuisance.

[68] Stephen J suggested that had the nuisance in *Great Western Rly Co v Bishop* (n 63 above) interfered with the permanent comfort of the neighbourhood then the result might have been different. A modern example of the sort of nuisance which Stephen J might have had in mind might be the problem of pigeon droppings falling from railway bridges and accumulating on pavements and the highway.

bringing the range of matters which properly should only be the subject of private or public nuisance proceedings at common law, within a statutory public health framework. There is a need to draw the line at some point so as to exclude matters which are no more than mere common law nuisances but certainly to include those nuisances which were aimed at by the legislature. It can also be adapted to modern conditions—what might only affect personal comfort today can be included in the scope of the legislation.[69]

4.45 The nineteenth-century cases have consistently indicated that the nuisance aimed at by the legislature must be something more than a mere common law nuisance but that it is not necessary to show injury to health—personal discomfort will do. This interpretation was confirmed by the House of Lords in 1975 in *Salford CC v McNally*,[70] where an occupier alleged that his house was in such a condition as to be prejudicial to health under the Public Health Act 1936.[71]

4.46 During the course of his judgment, Lord Wilberforce confirmed that the interpretation of the word 'nuisance' in the Public Health Act 1936 was capable of including personal discomfort. He clearly distinguished between the two limbs: personal comfort is relevant in defining 'nuisance' but not 'prejudice to health':

> These words (personal comfort) are appropriate enough in the context of what is a 'nuisance' for the purpose of the Public Health Act 1936 ... but they are quite inappropriate in relation to the other limb 'prejudicial to health'. Health is not the same as comfort and interference with the latter does not bring a case within the 'health' limb of the 1936 Act.[72]

4.47 *Salford CC v McNally* is authority for the proposition that personal comfort is an essential ingredient in defining the nuisance limb but would not be sufficient for the health limb.[73]

---

[69] Further nineteenth-century cases consolidated this approach; see, eg, *Bishop Auckland Local Board v Bishop Auckland Iron and Steel Co* (1882) 10 QBD 138; *Banbury Sanitary Authority v Page* (1881) 8 QBD 97.

[70] n 59 above. This case concerned the condition of premises which were part of a clearance area. The context of the case, markedly different from the earlier nineteenth-century cases, shows the changing social circumstances in which the statutory nuisance regime was, by then, operating.

[71] The House of Lords also held that statutory nuisance under the Public Health Act 1936 and 'fitness for human habitation' under the Housing Act 1957 were two different statutory codes and should be treated quite separately. Unfitness for human habitation was not an essential element of a statutory nuisance although a house which was unfit for humans to live in might well be prejudicial to health also.   [72] n 59 above, at 389.

[73] In reaching this decision Lord Wiberforce held *Betts v Penge UDC* [1942] 2KB 154 (where the action of a landlord who removed doors and sash windows was held to be a statutory nuisance) to have been wrongly decided. He considered that *Betts* was a harassment case, although it is arguable that the case is a borderline one. Carnwath J ventured briefly into the debate in *R v Carrick DC, ex p Shelley* (n 19 above) although the point is not resolved. See also *National Coal Board v Neath BC* (n 45 above); *Godfrey v Conwy CBC* (n 19 above); and *Wivenhoe Port v Colchester BC* [1985] JPL 175, at 178, where the judge concluded that 'to be within the spirit of the Act a nuisance to be a statutory nuisance had to be one interfering materially with the personal comfort of the residents, in the sense that it materially affected their well-being, although it might not be prejudicial to health'.

Distinguishing the health and nuisance limbs

Consequences

If the nuisance limb is being relied upon and the alleged nuisance does not have **4.48**
the characteristic of a public nuisance, then, as stated above, there must be a transmission of the offending activity to the affected premises from neighbouring property. This could be from one flat to another as in classic residential noise cases; or, fumes or smoke blowing from a factory over neighbouring houses. If that is the case, then the transmission of the offending activity plus interference with personal comfort will suffice to bring the case under the nuisance limb. This will frequently be appropriate in noise and smell cases where it may be difficult to establish direct health effects in the short term. Personal discomfort which may be followed by injury to health in the longer term, will suffice if the common law elements of nuisance are satisfied.[74]

Premises and the health limb

However, there is one common type of case where the nuisance limb can never **4.49**
be satisfied. These are the cases where the problem arises from within the premises themselves, as in the example of flats which suffer from, for example, chronic dampness, mould growth or condensation. These cases will fall under section 79(1)(a) of the EPA 1990 ('premises in such a state . . .').[75] The alleged nuisance is not transmitted from one property onto neighbouring property but arises from within the premises and affects only the health of the occupier. Therefore, the argument must always be brought under the health limb so as to show health effects—arguably a more complex standard than that required by the nuisance limb.[76]

Noise and the nuisance and health limbs

Noise nuisance cases raise a different point. Noise nuisance has a legislative **4.50**
origin distinct from other statutory nuisances. The first controls dealing with noise were bye-laws.[77] These gave local authorities power to suppress noise which interfered with personal comfort. The first comprehensive legislation which established noise as a statutory nuisance was the Noise Abatement Act 1960. This was repealed by the Control of Pollution Act 1974, which, in turn, was substantially amended by the EPA 1990 and the Noise and Statutory Nuisance Act 1993. Thus, noise nuisance does not have its origin in the sanitary statutes of the

---

[74] *Godfrey v Conwy CBC* (n 19 above).   [75] See Chapter 5.
[76] *Salford CC v McNally* (n 59 above), *R v Bristol CC, ex p Everett* (n 12 above) and *Birmingham CC v Oakley* (n 11 above) are all examples of internal nuisance cases which relied on the health limb.
[77] The famous case of *Kruse v Johnson* [1898] 2 QB 91 is an illustration of such a bye-law. The bye-law in question purported to prohibit the playing of musical instruments or singing in any public place within 50 yards of any dwelling house, after being ordered by a police constable, or by any inmate of the house, to desist.

nineteenth century. It has simply borrowed the clothing and modus operandi of the statutory nuisance procedure.[78]

4.51 Noise sits uneasily in the statutory nuisance framework to the extent that while it may cause a nuisance which interferes with personal comfort, it often would not fall within the definition pertinent to the health limb. Noise does not cause disease as it was understood in the nineteenth century. The health effects of noise are difficult to establish. Certainly, noise can interfere with the quality of life and the personal comfort of affected individuals and can be a nuisance in the common law tortious sense—it can interfere with the enjoyment of land.

4.52 None of the cases which have interpreted the meaning of a statutory nuisance as consistent with the intention of Parliament when passing the original nineteenth-century legislation have been concerned with noise nuisance. They have predominantly been concerned with 'premises' falling under section 79(1)(a) of the EPA 1990.[79] It is arguable, therefore, that, in interpreting the ambit of section 79(1)(g) of the EPA 1990, the intention of Parliament when passing the Noise Abatement Act 1960 is relevant, albeit that a subsequent Parliament saw fit to position noise nuisance within the statutory nuisance framework of an earlier era.

4.53 This would be relevant in determining what health effects were intended to be covered by the provision relating to noise nuisance. It could not be argued that disease in the nineteenth-century context was relevant.

Street noise and the nuisance and health limbs

4.54 A similar argument could be made in respect of section 79(1)(ga) which was inserted by the Noise and Statutory Nuisance Act 1993. It would be difficult to maintain that this paragraph which deals with street noise such as vehicles (other than traffic noise) and machinery, as well as intruder alarms, has any connection with the social circumstances of the nineteenth century. Again, it is simply the procedural approach for dealing with such nuisances which has been adopted. They do not fit within the public health model of the sanitary statutes.

Reasonableness as a central concept of common law nuisance and its relevance to statutory nuisance

'Give and take'

4.55 Reasonableness is a central concept in common law nuisance and is grounded in the recognition that nuisances arise from conflicting uses of land.[80] The law of

---

[78] For a critical discussion of noise law see, F McManus, 'Noise Law in the United Kingdom: A Very British Solution?' (2000) 20 Legal Studies 264; and see further Chapter 6.

[79] eg, *Birmingham CC v Oakley* (n 11 above) and *R v Bristol CC, ex p Everett* (n 12 above). *R v Falmouth and Truro Port Health Authority, ex p South West Water Ltd* (n 13 above) was a case on watercourses under the Public Health Act 1936, the provisions of which also date from earlier legislation.

[80] See R A Buckley, *The Law of Nuisance* (2nd edn, Butterworths, 1996). The centrality of the test of reasonableness has not gone unchallenged. In *A-G v Cole* [1901] 1 Ch 205 a public

nuisance attempts to balance these conflicting interests and achieve a compromise which recognizes the demands of living in a society. It is 'a rule of give and take, of live and let live'.[81] As Lord Goff stated in *Cambridge Water Co v Eastern Counties Leather plc*, 'if the user is reasonable, the defendant will not be liable for consequent harm to his neighbour's enjoyment of his land; but if the user is not reasonable, the defendant will be liable, even though he may have used reasonable care and skill to avoid it'.[82] In the statutory nuisance case of *Wycombe DC v Jeffways and Pilot Coaches*[83] the Court of Appeal was concerned with the balance of interests between a factory whose hours of operation were causing a noise nuisance, and the interests of local residents. The question was whether the restriction on the hours of operation of the factory, which the local authority had required, was reasonable or not. The court stated that it was necessary to undertake 'some sort of balancing operation of conflicting interests of two inhabitants of the area—or one inhabitant on one side and a lot of inhabitants on the other.'[84] Accepting the magistrates' decision that the curfew which the local authority had required was a little too restrictive to be reasonable, they acknowledged that the result in balancing the interests concerned was 'not to cure the nuisance but to restrict its occurrence or recurrence'.[85]

4.56 There is, further, the defence of 'best practicable means' available to trade, business and industrial users in some circumstances.[86] Again, this in effect permits an activity which might otherwise be unreasonable to continue since the creators of the nuisance have used the best (which might be interpreted as the 'most reasonable') means to avoid the nuisance.

4.57 In statutory nuisance cases an important additional factor is the defence that a person who failed to comply with an abatement notice might have a 'reasonable excuse'.[87] This emphasizes the test of reasonableness in statutory nuisance.

4.58 It is clear that defining what is reasonable in common law nuisance and under the nuisance limb of statutory nuisance is not a straightforward matter. It will depend on the nature of the case and the purpose of the activities engaged in. But, there are a number of matters which may be considered in reaching a view on the matter. These include: motive, duration, intensity and time of the

---

nuisance was caused by the owner of a fat smelter, who carried out his business reasonably but caused a nuisance to residents of nearby houses built after the business was established. It was stated by Kekewich J (at 207) that if a man 'commits a nuisance, then he cannot say that he is acting reasonably'. But in *Dymond v Pearce* (n 47 above), a lorry which was parked so as to cause an obstruction of the highway was deemed not to be a nuisance because it was parked in a highly visible way. This pragmatic approach is typical of the attitude to statutory nuisances. There is no absolute standard of what is reasonable—each case must be viewed in context and on its own particular merits.

[81] *Bamford v Turnley* (1862) 3 B&S 66, per Bramwell B at 83. See also *Marcic v Thames Water Utilities Ltd* [2002] EWCA Civ 65. [82] [1994] 2 AC 264, at 299.
[83] (1983) 81 LGR 662. [84] ibid, per Stephenson LJ at 674. [85] ibid.
[86] See further Chapter 15. [87] EPA 1990, s 80(4).

offending activity, sensitivity of the complainant and the nature of the locality. In *Stone v Bolton* Oliver J stated:

> Whether such an act does constitute a nuisance must be determined not merely by an abstract consideration of the act itself, but by reference to all the circumstances of the particular case, including, for example, the time of the commission of the act complained of; the place of its commission; the manner of committing it, that is, whether it is done wantonly or in the reasonable exercise of rights; and, the effect of its commission, that is, whether those effects are transitory or permanent, occasional or continuous; so that the question of nuisance or no nuisance is one of fact.[88]

4.59 There is no reason why the judiciary might not extend this list of factors which underline the concept of reasonableness and, indeed, this may well occur in situations where the public health effects or environmental impact of certain activities become better known or where it is becoming more acceptable that a precautionary approach should be taken.

Reasonableness and enforcement action

4.60 The concept of reasonableness in connection with the existence of a statutory nuisance under the nuisance limb is not unrelated to the reasonableness of the enforcement action specified in the abatement notice. The factors set out in the judgment of Oliver J in *Stone v Bolton* assist in determining whether, *a priori*, a statutory nuisance exists. But they will also play a role in determining the reasonableness of the prescribed works of abatement.

4.61 For example, there may be many ways of remedying a noise nuisance. These might range from closing down a factory, installing new equipment, changing the operating hours of a piece of machinery, double-glazing windows, and so on. Further, the remedy required might vary according to the nature of the perpetrator of the nuisance. Such persons might be private individuals, the sole proprietors of local workshops, publicans, large corporations, or public utilities. The means to remedy the problem in each case will vary according to the means and ability of the individual. Whereas one course of action, such as a requirement to install noise-measuring equipment, might be reasonable in one case, in another, a much simpler approach might be necessary. For instance, in *Budd v Colchester BC*[89] (a case over barking dogs), Swinton-Thomas LJ suggested several ways in which the dogs could be quietened:

> The most extreme would be to get rid of all six greyhounds, but that might well be an unreasonable requirement. A reduction in the number of dogs might abate the nuisance. Insulation of part of the house might be sufficient. It might be possible to send the dogs to an animal training centre to cure the problem. However, it might well not be reasonable for the local authority to require this appellant, for example, to take that course, because he might not be able to afford to do so.

[88] [1950] 1 KB 201, at 238–9.   [89] [1999] Env LR 739, at 747.

4.62 The extent to which the concept of reasonableness plays a role and the importance of balancing the requirements imposed against the particular recipient in question are plain. Reasonableness is a critical test both in relation to the primary question of whether a nuisance exists and to the enforceability of the works required by an abatement notice.

4.63 The factors underlying the concept of reasonableness as set out in the judgment from *Stone v Bolton*[90] are considered in further detail below.

Particular sensitivity

4.64 The classic formulation of this concept appears in *Robinson v Kilvert*: 'A man who carries on an exceptionally delicate trade cannot complain because it is injured by his neighbour doing something which would not injure anything but an exceptionally delicate trade'.[91] The test is objective:

> ought this inconvenience to be considered as more than fanciful, more than one of mere delicacy or fastidiousness, as an inconvenience materially interfering with the ordinary comfort physically of human existence, not merely according to elegant or dainty modes of living, but according to plain and sober and simple notions among the English people?[92]

4.65 In a noise nuisance case, *Heath v Brighton Corporation*,[93] the plaintiff failed in his action in respect of noise from a generator as it was established that he had hypersensitive hearing. It was held that the test for determining whether a statutory nuisance existed is an objective one and should be judged according to the standards of the average man. The courts should not have regard to the abnormal sensitiveness of particular occupiers.

4.66 In neighbourhood noise disputes this may present a problem since the courts may not recognize sufficiently the cumulative effect of multiple instances of annoyance. Often, a complainant becomes sensitized over a long period to noise disturbance. This may not be evidence of a hyper-sensitivity peculiar to that occupier but rather a pattern of sensitivity which would affect the ordinary person. To deal with a case like this in the courtroom, techniques such as the collation of a diary to show the continuous or repetitive nature of the disturbance, and the use of noise readings over a lengthy period, are useful.[94]

4.67 Further, there may be health effects which are present in a substantial minority of the population. Take asthmatic problems amongst children, for example.[95] This

---

[90] n 88 above.
[91] (1889) 41 Ch D 88, per Lopes J at 97.
[92] *Walter v Selfe* (1851) 4 DeG & Sm 315 at 322.
[93] (1908) 98 LT 718.
[94] See further Chapter 6. It has, however, been suggested that the objective test remains the same where a claimant had an unusually high sensitivity, whatever the reasons for the development of that sensitivity. See *R (on the application of Anne and another) v Test Valley Borough Council* [2001] 48 EG 127 (CS) where the claimants alleged that honeydew, produced by aphids on a nearby lime tree and deposited on the claimants' roof, encouraged the growth of mould that caused increased allergic sensitivity. In such a case, the medical evidence may prove decisive.
[95] See the commentary to *Cunningham v Birmingham CC* [1998] Env LR 1, at 8.

affects a significant and rising number of children, as well as adults. There will clearly come a point where the health effect brings that group into an objective category.

Social utility of the defendant's conduct

4.68 Public benefit is a relevant issue in balancing the competing uses of land and in determining reasonableness. There is, however, no defined list of socially useful activities—the courts have eschewed such an approach preferring to deal with matters on a case-by-case basis.

4.69 In *Harrison v Southwark and Vauxhall Water Co* the court took into account the essential nature of the defendant's purpose:

> It frequently happens that the owners or occupiers of land cause, in the execution of lawful works in the ordinary user of land, a considerable amount of temporary annoyance to their neighbours; but they are not necessarily on that account held to be guilty of causing an unlawful nuisance. The business of life could not be carried on if it were so. For instance, a man who pulls down his house for the purpose of building a new one no doubt causes considerable inconvenience to his next door neighbours during the process of demolition; but he is not responsible for a nuisance if he uses all reasonable skill and care to avoid annoyance to his neighbour by the works of demolition.[96]

This kind of judicial thinking recognizes that it might be reasonable to tolerate a temporary annoyance where it is a useful and necessary act. This should be contrasted with the situation where a temporary annoyance has no public benefit or social usefulness.[97]

Motive of the defendant

4.70 In statutory nuisance, the presence of malice may result in the use of land being held unreasonable and, thereby, may bring the case under the nuisance limb. The presence of malice may deprive a use of any social usefulness or reasonableness. It may also be relevant in making an award for compensation to the victim of the nuisance.

4.71 Typical cases include those where noise is used as a weapon in a dispute between neighbours. In *Christie v Davey*[98] (deliberate noise to annoy the plaintiff) and *Hollywood Silver Fox Farms v Emmett*[99] (deliberate noise to disrupt fox-farming) both cases might be regarded as neighbour disputes. The noise nuisance would not have been actionable in either case unless it had interfered with the enjoyment of the neighbouring land. Equally, these cases, assuming the necessary element of

---

[96] [1891] 2 Ch 409, per Vaughan Williams J at 413–14.
[97] eg, *R v Shorrock* (n 53 above) (noise from acid-house party); and *Crown River Cruises v Kimbolton Fireworks* [1996] 2 Lloyd's Rep 533 (short period of burning debris from firework party). [98] [1893] 1 Ch 216.
[99] [1936] 2 KB 468.

disruption of personal comfort,[100] might have been actionable as statutory nuisance cases (had they been heard after 1960 when noise nuisance first became actionable as a statutory nuisance).

Duration and intensity

Duration will be a factor for the court in deciding whether an interference is sufficient to cause nuisance. Interference with the enjoyment of land must be of 'some degree of permanence. That which is temporary and evanescent cannot be a nuisance.'[101] **4.72**

The longer an offending activity lasts the more likely it is to be a nuisance: **4.73**

A clock striking the hour or a bell ringing for some domestic purpose may be a nuisance, if unreasonably loud and discordant of which the jury alone must judge; but although not unreasonably loud if the owner for some whim or caprice, made the clock strike the hour every ten minutes or the bell ring continually, I think a jury would be satisfied in considering it to be a very great nuisance.[102]

Even if an offending activity only lasts for a short period, it can amount to a nuisance, particularly where there is no social utility or public benefit to the activity. In *Andreae v Selfridge & Co Ltd*[103] it was said that the loss of a single night's sleep from noise could amount to a nuisance: 'I certainly protest against the idea that, if persons, for their own profit and convenience, choose to destroy even one night's rest of their neighbours, they are doing something which is excusable.'[104] In *R v Shorrock*[105] a public nuisance arose from noise from a one-night acid-house party and in *Crown River Cruises v Kimbolton Fireworks*[106] burning debris from a fireworks display which lasted less than 20 minutes was held to be a nuisance. Further, in *East Northamptonshire DC v Fossett*[107] a single event (an all-night 'rave' party) was held to be a statutory nuisance. **4.74**

While the duration of the nuisance in these cases was fleeting, the nature of the nuisance was such that it was not trivial. The fact that a nuisance must be 'of a substantial character; not fleeting or evanescent'[108] is of evidential importance in indicating whether it is sufficiently serious to be actionable. **4.75**

---

[100] The element of personal discomfort may not have been present in *Hollywood Silver Fox Farms v Emmett* where the firing of guns affected the breeding success of the silver foxes on the fur farm. On the other hand, it does seem to have been present in *Christie v Davey* where the banging of trays on the wall interfered with the daily life and activities of the inhabitants of the house. See also *Bradford v Pickles* [1895] AC 587 where the defendant drained his land for the sole purpose of ensuring that no water percolated on his neighbour's land. This was not actionable in private nuisance since there is no proprietary right in percolating water until it has been appropriated. Therefore, no right had been infringed.
[101] F H Newark, *The Boundaries of Nuisance* [1949] LQR 480, at 489.
[102] *Bamford v Turnley* (1862) 31 LJQB 286, per Pollock CB at 346.
[103] [1937] 3 All ER 255.   [104] ibid, per Sir Wilfrid Greene MR at 261.
[105] n 53 above.   [106] n 97 above.   [107] [1994] Env LR 388.
[108] *Benjamin v Storr* (1874) LR 9 CP 400, per Brett J at 407.

4.76 An isolated escape will be actionable as a nuisance either if it falls within the principles established in *Rylands v Fletcher*[109] or if it arose from the condition of the defendant's land or premises or property or the activities engaged in thereon.[110] Thus, a single escape of polluting fumes from a factory could amount to a nuisance, both at common law and as a statutory nuisance.[111]

Time of day

4.77 The time when the alleged nuisance is carried out will be relevant since it may affect the reasonableness of the action. In *De Keyser's Royal Hotel Ltd v Spicer Bros Ltd*[112] pile-driving through the night for building purposes was deemed unreasonable and an injunction was granted. However, where there is a substantial justification for night-time working in the particular circumstances of the case, such activity may be found reasonable.

Nature of locality

4.78 At common law, locality is relevant in determining whether a nuisance exists when the matter complained of affects personal comfort. Thus, locality will be disregarded when the complaint is in respect of matters producing 'sensible injury to the value of property' or 'material injury' but not when the matter causes personal discomfort.[113] Personal comfort is always relevant when relying on the nuisance limb of statutory nuisance. It follows, therefore, that locality will always be relevant.[114]

4.79 In cases of personal comfort, the classic expression of this principle is to be found in *Sturges v Bridgman*: 'What would be a nuisance in Belgrave Square would not necessarily be so in Bermondsey'.[115] This does not mean that people living in an area adjoining an industrial area will receive no protection under the nuisance limb. The degree of nuisance to be tolerated will be measured against what is

---

[109] (1868) LR 3 HL 330. That is, if there is an escape of something likely to do harm which has been brought onto the land and which is not part of the natural use of the land. These principles are part of the tort of private nuisance; *Cambridge Water Co Ltd v Eastern Counties Leather plc* (n 10 above).

[110] *SCM (United Kingdom) Ltd v WJ Whittal & Sons Ltd* [1970] 1 WLR 1017, per Thesiger J at 1031. *British Celanese Ltd v Hunt* [1969] 1 WLR 959. See also *Spicer v Smee* [1946] 1 All ER 489 where defective electrical wiring which caused a fire was evidence of a dangerous state of affairs existing on the defendant's premises.

[111] *Cambridge Water Co v Eastern Counties Leather plc* (n 10 above).

[112] (1914) 30 TLR 257.

[113] *St Helen's Smelting Co v Tipping* (1865) 11 ER 1483, per Lord Westbury LC at 1487.

[114] *Godfrey v Conwy CBC* (n 19 above).

[115] (1879) 11 Ch D 852, per Thesiger LJ at 865. (There is some difficulty in this analysis since matters which might be perceived as causing personal discomfort such as smell and noise, may also have an effect on property values. Indeed, it was considered in *Hunter v Canary Wharf and London Docklands Development Corporation* (n 10 above) that in a personal discomfort case damages are to be awarded on the basis of the damage to the amenity value of the land.) See also *Polsue and Alfieri v Rushmer* [1907] AC 121; *Andreae v Selfridge & Co Ltd* (n 103 above); and *Milner v Spencer* (1976) 239 EG 573.

reasonable—the 'give and take' approach to balancing the interests of competing uses will apply.

The nature of a locality may change. This will occur when, for example, industrial development changes an area which was previously primarily residential. It can also occur more immediately where the effect of a planning permission is so extensive that it alters the character of a neighbourhood. In *Gillingham BC v Medway Dock Co Ltd*[116] a public nuisance action failed on these grounds. Operators of a commercial dock had been granted planning permission for their activities. This involved the passage of heavy lorries around the clock which caused serious disturbance to the residents of an adjoining district. Buckley J held that the planning permission had altered the character of the neighbourhood and, while the activity might have been a nuisance if judged against the previous nature of the locality, this was no longer the case.[117] **4.80**

This does not mean that a single and limited planning permission can give immunity from action. In *Wheeler v Saunders*[118] planning permission was given for the expansion of a pig farm. When a complaint was made about the smell from the expanded farm, it was held that the effect of the planning permission was not to grant immunity against a nuisance action.[119] **4.81**

The health limb

While the nuisance limb is closely linked with common law nuisance, the second of the two limbs, the health limb, stands alone. The health limb is particularly relevant when considering cases which fall under section 79(1)(a) of the EPA 1990 ('premises in such a state as to be . . .'), the so-called 'internal premises' cases.[120] **4.82**

However, it is not limited to such cases. If injury to health in the sense of disease can be shown to arise from any offending activity that falls under section 79 of the EPA 1990 then the case could be argued under the health limb. **4.83**

The test to be applied in determining whether premises were in such a state as to be prejudicial to health is an objective one.[121] **4.84**

What is covered by 'prejudice to health'?
The definition of the health limb appears in section 79(7) of the EPA 1990, as 'injurious, or likely to cause injury, to health'. Otherwise, there is no further definition **4.85**

---

[116] [1993] QB 343.
[117] In some cases of 'public works', property owners might be entitled to compensation for a limited list of nuisance—known as 'the seven deadly sins'—under the Land Compensation Act 1973.
[118] [1996] Ch 19. See also *Hunter v Canary Wharf and London Docklands Development Corporation* (n 10 above) on this point.   [119] See further paras 17.61–17.67.
[120] See further para 4.49 and, generally, Chapter 5.
[121] *Cunningham v Birmingham CC* (n 95 above) and *R (on the application of Anne and another) v Test Valley Borough Council* (n 94 above).

of 'injury' or 'health' in the 1990 Act. None of the elements of common law nuisance are relevant in determining whether an offending activity is prejudicial to health. The health limb derives exclusively from the public health legislation of the nineteenth century and the body of case law which has interpreted it.

4.86 A dictionary meaning of 'injury to health' is broad enough to include a single dramatic accident. The *Shorter Oxford Dictionary* defines health as 'a state of complete physical, mental and social well-being and not merely the absence of disease or infirmity'. It could be said, however, that on the basis of such a definition the whole population lives in a state of unhealthiness. Judicial interpretation of the phrase is unsurprisingly much narrower. The two cases of particular note in this context are the decision of the House of Lords in *Birmingham CC v Oakley*[122] and that of the Court of Appeal in *R v Bristol CC, ex p Everett*.[123]

The decision in Everett

4.87 It was held that the threat of injury from falling down a narrow and steep staircase was not to be considered as a statutory nuisance. The interpretation of the health limb was drawn directly from the Victorian cases and the Victorian context of the law. The health effect was limited to the risk of disease. Injury, such as a broken ankle, was not the type of health effect intended to be covered by the Act.

4.88 This decision hinged solely on statutory interpretation and the application of the purposive approach, which involved an historical analysis of the statutes commencing with the Nuisances Removal Act 1855 leading to the present legislation.[124] The Court of Appeal in the *Everett* case concluded that the purpose of these earlier statutes was to control disease rather than the prevention of accidental physical injury arising from the dangerous condition of premises.

4.89 In the Divisional Court, Richards J, whose judgment on this point was approved by the Court of Appeal, expressed the following view:

> When one looks, however, at the legislative history summarised above, it seems reasonably clear that the expressions were not intended to be so wide in their scope. When powers to take action against premises that were 'prejudicial to health' or 'injurious to health' were conferred by the mid-nineteenth century statutes, the object of concern was plainly the direct effect on people's health of filthy or unwholesome premises and the like: in particular, the risk of disease or illness. There is nothing to suggest that the powers were intended to protect against the danger of accidental physical injury. Looking at the legislation as a whole it seems to me that that kind of problem fell outside the legislative purpose. I do not discern in the subsequent legislative history any material change in the legislative intention, such as to justify the attribution of an enlarged scope to the current powers, based as they are on essentially the same language as used in the original legislation.[125]

---

[122] n 11 above. [123] n 12 above. [124] See Chapter 3.
[125] [1999] Env LR 256 at 369.

4: THE CONCEPT OF STATUTORY NUISANCE

The decision in Oakley

The second case of note is the House of Lords' decision in *Birmingham CC v Oakley*.[126] This confirms the interpretation of the health limb in the *Everett* case.[127]

4.90

A purposive approach to statutory interpretation in the context of the full legislative history was applied. Lord Slynn emphasized that he was influenced by the earlier statutes dealing with premises in a 'filthy and unwholesome condition' or

4.91

> ... the collection of noxious matter or a foul or offensive drain or privy. All of these were in themselves prejudicial to health because of the germs or smells or the risk of disease ... They are directed to the presence in the house of some feature which is in itself prejudicial to health in that it is a source of possible infection or disease or illness such as dampness, mould, dirt or evil smelling accumulations or the presence of rats.[128]

In reaching this view their Lordships concluded that the premises themselves must evince some such state of filthiness. Prejudice to health could not arise from the layout of premises, albeit that that layout could give rise to cross-infection.[129]

4.92

Earlier case law

The case of *Coventry CC v Cartwright*[130] had adopted the same approach. This case was concerned with a derelict site where fly-tipping had occurred and it was alleged that the site was prejudicial to health in that people might trip over the rubble and injure themselves, and that the site had an unattractive visual impact. The Divisional Court considered that, while the words of the section were broad enough to include such injury, nonetheless the

4.93

> underlying conception of the section is that that which is struck at is an accumulation of something which produces a threat to health in the sense of a threat of disease, vermin or the like.[131]

The fact that trespassers on the site, who included children using it as a short cut to school, might injure themselves on the rubble, was not enough to bring the case within the type of health problems anticipated by the legislation.

---

[126] n 11 above.
[127] It also considers the scope of section 79(1)(a) ('premises in such a state ...') which is considered in greater detail in Chapter 5.   [128] n 11 above, at 392.
[129] The decision of the House of Lords was finely balanced (3–2) with powerful dissenting judgments; see further paras 5.05–5.29. See also Loveland (n 14 above), who argues that the House of Lords, in a future case, might reach a different view.
[130] n 46 above, per Lord Widgery CJ at 851. The case was an action brought under the Public Health Act 1936, ss 92(1)(c) and 343. See also *Great Western Rly Co v Bishop* (n 63 above).
[131] It does seem to be the case that Lord Widgery, in the extract from his judgment quoted here from *Coventry CC v Cartwright* (n 46 above), at 849C, appears to be suggesting that the requirement for a threat to health underlies both limbs of the definition of statutory nuisance. This does appear to be contrary to the House of Lords' view expressed in *Salford CC v McNally* (n 59 above), which preserves the distinction between nuisance and prejudice to health.

Reasonableness and 'prejudice to health'

4.94 The reasonableness of the offending activity is an element in examining the existence of a statutory nuisance falling under the nuisance limb. It will not be relevant when a statutory nuisance has been committed which falls under the health limb. Where there is a threat of disease, no question can arise as to the reasonableness of the action giving rise to the statutory nuisance. Indeed, the reverse might be argued in that an activity which produces a risk of disease could not, *per se*, be reasonable.

4.95 In this, therefore, the health limb again bears a distinction from the nuisance limb. The reasonableness of the offending activity is not in question where prejudice to health is established. This would include reference to all the factors which go towards determining whether an action is reasonable. So, for example, a sudden and brief escape of fumes which causes ill health would not be rendered reasonable because of its duration.

Cases where 'prejudice to health' is in issue

4.96 There are a number of cases which illustrate the extent and meaning of the health limb. Most of these are cases falling under section 79(1)(a) of the EPA 1990 or preceding legislation. In *Ex p Saunders*[132] the prejudice to health arose from the smells and risks to health which came from defective drains, lack of ventilation and defective flushing facilities. In *Salford CC v NcNally*[133] the defects alleged to exist by the complainant included: an accumulation of refuse, dampness, defective sanitary fittings, unsealed drains allowing egress of rats, defective windows and/or doors, leaking roof, defective drainage, defective plasterwork and defective floors. The house was in a slum condition and had been designated for clearance. The magistrate found that there was rising damp and perished plaster, that the rear door was rotten and unhinged; that there was severe dampness on the first floor, and that the water-closet pipe was cracked and insanitary. These matters were deemed to cause the state of the house to be prejudicial to health, and their extensiveness and seriousness warranted this decision. Similarly in *Patel v Mehtab*[134] it was held that defects which included dampness, leaks, inadequate ventilation, the presence of fungus, coldness and draughts, and a defective water heater were injurious to health.

4.97 On the other hand, in *National Coal Board v Neath BC*[135] it was held that there was no injury to health. Here, guttering and skirting boards were defective but were not in such a condition as to present a threat to health. The case could not succeed under the health limb because the problems in the premises were not a health risk. The claim also failed under the nuisance limb as the elements of common law nuisance were not made out as only the occupiers of the defective building were inconvenienced.

---

[132] (1883) 11 QBD 191.
[134] (1980) 5 HLR 78.
[133] n 59 above.
[135] n 45 above.

4: THE CONCEPT OF STATUTORY NUISANCE

In *R v Carrick DC, ex p Shelley*[136] accumulations and deposits on a public beach of sewage-related material (on average one kilogram per day) comprising sanitary towels (79 per cent), condoms (11 per cent) and weed (10 per cent) was considered to be prejudicial to health. It was held that the presence of this material was capable of amounting to a statutory nuisance because of the risk to health that was presented, even though there was no evidence of actual injury. **4.98**

Who caused the prejudice to health?
It is necessary to ascertain the cause of the health problem to ensure that it arises because of the action of the recipient of a notice. In *Pike v Sefton MBC*[137] a health problem arose from the presence of condensation-related mould growth because of the unwillingness of a tenant to use the heating which had been provided. Had the heating been used the condensation would have been avoided. There was, therefore, no actionable statutory nuisance against the landlord. This followed the decision in *Dover DC v Farrar*[138] where it was held that a landlord was not responsible for what might otherwise have been a statutory nuisance where the tenant's health problem was induced by his failure to use heating facilities provided by the landlord. **4.99**

Conversely, in *GLC v Tower Hamlets LBC*[139] the cause of dampness was the failure of the landlord to take necessary precautions in a building which was exceptionally vulnerable to condensation. **4.100**

Expert evidence[140]
Where an allegation of prejudice to health is made, there must be some expert evidence to substantiate that claim. The magistrates may not reach a view based on their own expertise on such a matter and should not substitute their views for that of experts.[141] Evidence such as illness, stiffness, cramps and backache and headaches may be acceptable as evidence of health injury resulting from the state of the premises.[142] In premises cases the test is not whether the premises are uninhabitable but whether they are a health hazard.[143] **4.101**

An expert witness does not have to be medically qualified in order to be able to give evidence about whether a nuisance was prejudicial to health although he must have some experience in the field. In *London Borough of Southwark v Simpson*[144] a chartered surveyor would have been able to give evidence about injury to health if he had had some relevant experience in the field.[145] **4.102**

---

[136] n 19 above. [137] [2000] Env LR D31. [138] (1980) 2 HLR 32.
[139] (1983) 15 HLR 54. [140] See also paras 18.35–18.42.
[141] *Patel v Mehtab* (n 134 above). [142] ibid.
[143] *Salford CC v McNally* (n 59 above). [144] [1999] Env LR 553.
[145] As the chartered surveyor said he had no such experience his evidence was of no greater weight than a layman and the magistrates should have disregarded his evidence. It was said that an environmental health officer would have had the relevant expertise.

4.103 In *O'Toole v Knowsley MBC*[146] it was held that it was not necessary for environmental health officers to have medical qualifications in order to express an opinion as to whether premises were prejudicial to health.

The health limb post-Everett

4.104 Accidental physical injury is not covered. It can be seen that the interpretation of the health limb is to be narrowly defined. The EPA 1990 is to be viewed as the latest link in an unbroken chain of sanitary statutes. There is no statutory code under the 1990 Act. However, reference may be made to codes established by other bodies. For example, the Building Research Establishment Medical Advice Panel publishes a list of hazards affecting 'health' as opposed to 'safety'.[147] However, these must be treated with caution since they are aimed at the Housing Health and Safety Rating System,[148] a system that is concerned with the habitability of houses not the existence of statutory nuisance.[149] While some of the identified hazards such as damp, inadequate sanitation and ventilation might clearly lead to the likelihood of injury to health, others, such as inadequate means of securing the dwelling against entry by intruders, do not. For this reason, it is not recommended that these lists should be used as anything other than guidance on what constitutes a hazard to health in the context of the housing laws.

4.105 Problems such as defective electrical wiring or gas installations, exposed hot pipes, dangerously thin glass, slippery surfaces, inadequate stair handrails and banisters and unhygienic kitchen layouts will not fall within the remit of the statutory nuisance regime. The underlying test for whether a matter is prejudicial to health must be whether it results in ill health in the form of disease not accidental physical injury. The health limb, therefore, demands more than mere discomfort or annoyance, and requires proof of harmful effects or the risk of such effects.

---

[146] [1999] Env LR D29. [147] *Building Regulations and Health* (CRC, 1995).
[148] See *The Guidance (Version 1)* (The Stationery Office, 2000).
[149] This was specifically warned against in *Salford CC v McNally* (n 59 above): the two systems of housing standards and of statutory nuisance must not be confused; a house that is unfit for human habitation might also be a statutory nuisance but the two regimes must be considered separately.

PART II

THE SPECIFIC NUISANCES

5

PREMISES

Premises as a statutory nuisance 5.01
Meaning of 'premises in such a state . . .' 5.04
'State' of the premises 5.05
    The decision in *Birmingham CC v Oakley* 5.05
    The dissenting judgments 5.11
    The problem of 'fine distinctions' 5.13
    State of premises and external factors 5.14
    Nature of defects 5.24
The meaning of 'premises' 5.30
    Statutory definitions 5.30
    Judicial definitions 5.33
Vessels 5.37
Premises suffering from dampness, condensation and mould 5.39
    The nature of the problem 5.39
    Satisfying the health limb 5.42
    Bringing an 'internal premises' case under section 82 .... 5.46
    Identifying the person responsible for the nuisance 5.47
Can empty premises be prejudicial to health? 5.50
Identifying the premises 5.54
Liability for escape of the land itself 5.56
    Relevance to statutory nuisance 5.68
Public sewers 5.73
Defining 'premises' in other contexts 5.74
    Caves 5.75
    Gallops 5.76
    Petrol tanker 5.77
    Holiday camp 5.78
    Incorporeal rights 5.79
Defences 5.80
Alternative provisions relating to premises 5.83
    Building Act 1984 .... 5.84
    Public Health Act 1936 .... 5.98
    Housing Act 1985 .... 5.100
    Health and Safety at Work Act 1974 .... 5.103
    Defective Premises Act 1972 .... 5.104
    Occupiers' Liability Act 1957 .... 5.105

Leasehold premises 5.106
    Common law 5.106
    Contractual obligations 5.107
    Landlord and Tenant Act 1985 .... 5.108

Premises as a statutory nuisance

5.01 Premises may be in such a state that they constitute a statutory nuisance to the occupier of those premises (an 'internal nuisance') or to an adjoining occupier. When premises fall into the internal nuisance category, this will, normally, fall under the health limb of section 79(1)(a) of the Environmental Protection Act 1990 ('EPA 1990') since there is no element of a private or public nuisance present.[1] Some actual or threatened injury to health must then be shown.[2]

5.02 When the state of the premises causes a statutory nuisance to a neighbour or group of neighbours then it may fall under either the nuisance or the health limb. This type of statutory nuisance may arise from an escape of part of the land itself, such as a rock fall. Emissions resulting from a process taking place on the land are more likely to fall under other categories of statutory nuisance, such as, for example, fumes or smoke. If, however, there is a threat of a landslip, for instance, then the nuisance is posed by the premises themselves and the category in the first paragraph of section 79(1) of the EPA 1990 would be the relevant one.[3]

5.03 'Premises', which includes land under Part III of the EPA 1990, is an apparently wide term. But not all premises fall within the category so some analysis of its meaning and extent is necessary.

Meaning of 'premises in such a state ...'

5.04 The formulation in section 79(1)(a) of the EPA 1990 is 'premises in such a state as to be prejudicial to health or a nuisance'.[4] There are two elements to consider in relation to the meaning and extent of this provision:

(1) the extent and meaning of 'state' of the premises; and,
(2) the identification of 'premises'.

---

[1] *National Coal Board v Neath BC* (sometimes cited as *National Coal Board v Thorne*) [1976] 2 All ER 478; *Coventry CC v Cartwright* [1975] 1 WLR 845. See also para 4.49.
[2] See, eg, *Patel v Mehtab* (1980) 5 HLR 78.
[3] See, eg, *Kirklees MBC v Field and Others* [1998] Env LR 337, where houses were built into the rock face and were in danger of collapsing; and *Pontardawe RDC v Moore-Gwyn* [1929] 1 Ch 656 where an outcrop of rock broke away onto neighbouring land.
[4] This is an exact re-enactment of the equivalent paragraph of the Public Health Act 1936, s 92.

'State' of the premises

The decision in Birmingham CC v Oakley[5]

In the important House of Lords' decision in *Birmingham CC v Oakley*, the meaning of 'state' of the premises was considered. The key part of the House of Lords' decision was that section 79(1)(a) of the EPA 1990 needs to be considered as a whole. Premises are a statutory nuisance when they are 'in such a state' as to fall under the health or the nuisance limb. If the premises are, as they stand, clean and hygienic and pose no threat from their current state then there is no statutory nuisance.

5.05

The case concerned the layout of premises which were owned by Birmingham City Council and occupied by tenants, the Oakley family. A lavatory without a washbasin led off from the kitchen. In order to wash their hands, the family would either have to pass through the kitchen into the bathroom, which led off from the other side of the kitchen, or wash their hands in the kitchen sink. It was undisputed that this was unhygienic as it could lead to germs being transmitted into an area where food was prepared. The action was brought by Mr Oakley as a 'person aggrieved' under section 82 of the EPA 1990 against the landlords, Birmingham City Council.[6]

5.06

The House of Lords[7] held that it was the practice which was unhygienic, not the state of the premises, and, therefore, the premises could not constitute a statutory nuisance. They accepted that the words of section 79(1)(a) were capable of having a broad meaning attached to them as well as a narrow meaning, and that the paragraph is ambiguous. A broad meaning of the words would include consideration of the layout and the use of the premises in the context of the layout.

5.07

In reaching their conclusion that a narrow meaning should be adopted which excluded consideration of the layout, they held that the paragraph must be interpreted according to the original purpose of the statute. Further, where there was ambiguity, they should adopt a narrow construction.

5.08

The original Act[8] used phrases such as:

5.09

---

[5] [2001] 1 All ER 385.

[6] This problem in the layout of premises affects much of the older housing stock in the hands of local authorities.

[7] [2001] Env LR 37. The Divisional Court had upheld the decision of the magistrates to the effect that a statutory nuisance existed at the house because of the absence of a hand basin in the lavatory. Simon Brown LJ (at 38) concluded that 'in cases like this the way the premises are used is the direct result of their layout, and if, as it was found here, that use is predictably so unhygienic as to create a health risk, then it is the state of the premises which is injurious to health'. The Divisional Court certified that a point of general public importance arose from their decision. The question was whether the arrangements in the house fell within the words 'the state of the premises'.

[8] The Nuisances Removal and Diseases Prevention Act 1848.

the filthy and unwholesome condition of any dwelling house or other building, or of the accumulation of any offensive or noxious matter, refuse, dung, or offal, or of the existence of any foul or offensive drain, privy, or cesspool

and

any dwelling house ... in such a filthy and unwholesome condition

to describe a statutory nuisance affecting the state of the premises. By 1855, the words of the Nuisances Removal Act 1855, which consolidated the 1848 Act, as amended, had been changed to their modern form: 'premises in such a state as to be prejudicial to health or a nuisance', thereby changing the word 'condition' to 'state'.

5.10 Their Lordships concluded that there was an unbroken history of parliamentary intention which indicated that there must be a factor relating to the premises which in itself is prejudicial to health.[9] The arrangement of rooms which are otherwise not in themselves insanitary, is not something which falls within the health limb of section 79(1)(a).

In my view the Public Health Acts are concerned with the *state* of the premises, not with their *layout* or with the facilities which ought to be installed in them. In the present case the risk to health can be variously ascribed to the layout of the premises (because the lavatory was poorly sited) or to the absence of a desirable facility (a washbasin in reasonable proximity to the lavatory). But it does not derive from the *state* of the premises.[10]

They also considered that other legislation[11] was available to regulate the layout of the premises and that the use of statutory nuisance to achieve an improvement in the condition of the property was inappropriate.

The dissenting judgments

5.11 The decision in *Oakley* was a majority decision (three to two). The main dissenting judgment was given by Lord Clyde, with whom Lord Steyn agreed. Their Lordships preferred the broad approach to the interpretation of the phrase 'state of the premises' in that the whole purpose of the legislation had been the prevention of illness and risks to health. This would, in their view, include consideration of a layout, or absence of a facility, which was injurious to health.

---

[9] Lord Hoffmann, n 5 above, at 396, referred to the 'always speaking' principle which requires a statute to be interpreted as it is currently understood. He concluded, however, that to interpret the concept of 'premises in such a state as to be ...' to include the absence of facilities, would be an illegitimate extension of the statutory meaning. On this principle of public law, see *R v Ireland* [1998] AC 147; *Fitzpatrick (AP) v Sterling Housing Association Ltd* (1999) 32 HLR 178; *Tulkington and ors v Times Newspapers (Northern Ireland)* [2000] 3 WLR 1670; R Cross (ed), *Statutory Interpretation* (3rd edn, Butterworths, 1995); F Bennion, *Statutory Interpretation* (3rd edn, Butterworths, 1997); and I Loveland, 'And Now Wash Your Hands: Statutory Nuisance Under the Environmental Protection Act 1990, section 79(1)(a)' [2001] JPL 1144.   [10] Lord Millett, n 5 above, at 401.
[11] Such as the Building Act 1984 and the Building Regulations 2000, SI 2000/2531.

Lord Clyde referred to *The Queen v Wheatley*[12] and *Ex p Saunders*[13] in support 5.12
of the broad approach. *Wheatley* concerned an untrapped drain which was held to
be a statutory nuisance, as was a water closet situated in the centre of a house in
Saunders. Both cases involved the layout of the premises, Lord Clyde argued.
Further, he relied on *GLC v London Borough of Tower Hamlets*[14] and
Birmingham DC v Kelly.[15] Both of these cases concerned the provision of facilities. In the first, it was the provision of proper ventilation, insulation and heating.
In the second, it was the provision of fixtures, fittings and facilities. Lord Clyde
considered that his adoption of the broad approach to the interpretation of the
subsection, that the state of premises included such layout as gave rise to a health
risk, was supported not only by statutory history, but also, by case law.

The problem of 'fine distinctions'
Lord Clyde urged that the public health provisions should not give rise to fine 5.13
distinctions. Unfortunately, by the adoption of a narrow approach by the majority of their Lordships in *Oakley*, this is precisely what has happened.[16] The question then arises: when will premises be in such a state as to be prejudicial to
health?

State of premises and external factors
The clear effect of the decision in *Oakley* has been to exclude from the consider- 5.14
ation of section 79(1)(a) of the EPA 1990 factors which occur which are external
to the current condition of premises, whether or not the premises in question are
equipped to counter the effect of those external factors. This has the effect of
throwing doubt on the decision in *Southwark LBC v Ince*.[17]

In *Ince* it was held that premises not properly equipped to deal with the problems 5.15
created by external factors were in a state which constituted a statutory nuisance
under what is now section 79(1)(a) of the EPA 1990. The case concerned traffic
noise and vibration from road and rail traffic running near the building. The
tenants obtained an order from the magistrates that the landlords, the London
Borough of Southwark, should abate the statutory nuisance by properly sound-
insulating the building. It was held on appeal that the magistrates were justified in
finding that the premises were in such a state by reason of the noise that they were
prejudicial to health. It was found as a fact that, at the time of the conversion of

[12] (1885) 16 QBD 34. [13] (1883) 11 QBD 191. [14] (1983) 15 HLR 54.
[15] (1985) 17 HLR 572.
[16] It may be that a future House of Lords might consider *Oakley* to have been wrongly decided. A
differently constituted panel of their Lordships might take a different view on the 'always speaking'
application of the principle of statutory interpretation (see n 9 above). Further *Oakley* was decided
prior to the implementation of the Human Rights Act 1998 which might make sufficient advances in
the future to affect the outcome of cases such as this which concern basic living conditions.
[17] (1989) 153 JP 597. See also *R v Newham Magistrates, ex p Newham* (CO/2771/92; 29 June
1993) (unreported).

the block into flats, no adequate sound-insulation measures had been taken by the landlords given the proximity of the road and rail to the premises. Therefore, the Divisional Court considered that the magistrates were entitled to conclude that the premises were in such a state as to be prejudicial to health because of the 'act, default, or sufferance' of the local authority, the owners and the persons responsible for the conversion, even though the noise originated from outside the premises. It was a crucial finding to the outcome of the case that the fault had occurred because the block had not been properly converted with due attention to noise insulation.

5.16　It was accepted in *Ince* that if premises are properly and reasonably equipped against external factors, then if those external factors change through no fault of the owner, he cannot be made liable for them since in those circumstances they would not have arisen as a result of his 'act, default or sufferance'.

5.17　Similarly, if the external factors were always in existence, then the owner, provided the premises are in a reasonable condition, cannot be made liable under section 79(1)(a) of the EPA 1990 if the external factors constitute a nuisance. Thus, if the block of flats in *Ince* had been properly converted at the outset, then the court would have been unlikely to have come to the same decision.

5.18　The difficulty inherent in the judgment of finding that external factors can affect the state of the premises where the premises are not equipped to counter them, so as to make the owner liable in statutory nuisance, was expressly recognized in *Ince*. As to the matter of policy, Lord Justice Woolf stated:

> I recognise that the decision could be regarded as having wide implications, and I also recognise that it is possible to have come to a different conclusion as to the proper interpretation of the relevant provisions contained in Part III of the Public Health Act 1936 [the predecessor section to section 79 of the EPA 1990].[18]

5.19　Lord Justice Woolf went on to urge that magistrates should exercise 'discretion and common sense' in deciding what the contents of the abatement notice should be and should not place unreasonable obligations on local authorities.

5.20　It is clear from the decision in *Haringey LBC v Jowett*[19] that the decision in *Ince* has, in any event, been affected by the insertion of section 79(1)(ga) of the EPA 1990 by the Noise and Statutory Nuisance Act 1993 which specifically excludes traffic noise from the ambit of paragraph (ga). It was held in *Jowett* that, since 1994, the ambit of section 79(1)(a) of the EPA 1990 must be regarded as restricted so as to exclude traffic noise from vehicles, machinery and equipment in the street.

5.21　However, the fundamental issue of whether premises could be rendered into a state which constituted a statutory nuisance as a result of external factors (other than noise from the street) remained part of the *ratio* of *Ince*. As Saville J had

[18] n 17 above.　　[19] (1999) LGR 667.

stated, premises may be in such a state as to be prejudicial to health 'for a whole variety of external factors, be they weather, noise, the incursion of sewage, or indeed anything else'.[20]

5.22 In *Oakley*, the issue was whether the absence of a facility, or the layout of premises could render a house prejudicial to health. In deciding that these factors could not have that effect, their Lordships have cast doubt on the correctness of the decision in *Ince*.[21]

5.23 It is, therefore, the case that a strict and narrow approach to the interpretation of 'state of the premises' is to be applied. The premises must be in an unhealthy state. The absence of facilities (unless that absence could render the premises as they stand unhealthy) will not be sufficient. External factors will equally not be sufficient even where the premises are not equipped properly to counter their effect.

Nature of defects

5.24 The nature of the defects which are likely to place premises in such a state as to be prejudicial to health or a nuisance has also been significantly limited by the Court of Appeal's decision in *R v Bristol CC, ex p Everett*.[22] Not any defect will do. It must be a defect which is likely to place the premises in such a state that they are likely to be prejudicial to health in a manner which fits the public health model of the nineteenth-century sanitary statutes. The Court of Appeal concluded that the purpose of these statutes was to control disease rather than the prevention of accidental physical injury arising from the dangerous condition of premises. In that respect, the physical state of the premises is not relevant.

5.25 *Everett* concerned a steep staircase in a house. The Court of Appeal held that a risk of physical injury arising from the state of the premises did not render them in such a state as to be 'prejudicial to health' under section 79 of the EPA 1990 and they could not, therefore, constitute a statutory nuisance.

5.26 *Everett* is specifically concerned with the interpretation of the phrase 'prejudice to health', but leaves untouched the question of the meaning of the term 'nuisance' in the context of statutory nuisance. It can only be assumed that this was what the court intended in that reference is made to the intention behind the whole section.[23]

---

[20] n 17.

[21] It is interesting to note the change in judicial approach from the decision in *Ince* to that in *Oakley*. In the former, while the enormity of the obligation which was being imposed on local authorities was recognized, it was felt sufficient to temper it with an instruction to magistrates to act reasonably and with common sense. In *Oakley*, it seems that the policy implications of requiring structural changes to local authority housing were not to be contemplated. [22] [1999] 2 All ER 193.

[23] In *Birmingham CC v Oakley* (n 5 above), at 394, Lord Hoffmann refers to *Everett* as a case where 'the words which fell to be interpreted were "prejudicial to health"'. It is arguable that *Everett* can be confined to its particular facts; that is, that it relates to a statutory nuisance brought under the health limb of the EPA 1990, s 79(1)(a), in relation to the state of premises. In *Everett* the allegation fell under the prejudice to health limb not the nuisance limb since there was no migration of the offending circumstances from one piece of land to another.

5.27 The premises must be in such a state as to cause actual or likely prejudice to health in the sense of disease, not mere accidental injury. The sort of defects which might cause premises to be in such a state that they are prejudicial to health will, therefore, include such matters as dampness, mould growth, pests, inadequate sanitation, drainage and contaminated domestic water.[24]

5.28 It is arguable whether such matters as the emission of carbon monoxide from heaters or the presence of asbestos will now be considered to render premises in such a state as to be prejudicial to health given the emphasis of the judiciary on a purposive approach to statutory interpretation in a nineteenth-century context. In *Ince*, Saville J said:

> It may well be the case that in 1936 when the Public Health Act was enacted it was not appreciated that noise could be prejudicial to health. No more, of course, was it appreciated, or at least to the same extent as today, that asbestos could be prejudicial to health but it could hardly be suggested that because of this the Public Health Act does not apply to premises prejudicial to health through the presence of asbestos.[25]

5.29 It may be questioned whether this view has survived the decisions in *Oakley* and *Everett*. However, to the extent that the concept of statutory nuisance recognizes, at least under other heads, the threats to public health posed by the emission of fumes, gases and effluvia, it is suggested that the presence of such dangers will still be considered to render premises in such a state as to be prejudicial to health.

The meaning of 'premises'

Statutory definitions

5.30 'Premises', within the context of section 79(1)(a) of the EPA 1990, includes land and any vessel (unless powered by steam-reciprocating machinery).[26] There is no further definition within the Act.

5.31 Section 5 of the Interpretation Act 1978 provides:

> In any Act, unless the contrary intention appears, words or expressions listed in Schedule 1 to this Act are to be construed according to that Schedule.

Although there is no definition of 'premises' in the Interpretation Act 1978 there is a definition of 'land'. In relation to this, the Schedule states:

> 'Land' includes any buildings and other structures, land covered with water and any estate, interest, easement, servitude or right in or over land.

5.32 There are also a number of cases which have considered the meaning of 'premises' in a variety of contexts, both statutory and at common law.[27]

---

[24] See paras 4.82–4.105 for an analysis of the health limb.   [25] n 17 above.
[26] EPA 1990, s 79(7).
[27] In *Stevenage BC v Wilson* [1993] Env LR 214, the meaning of 'dwelling' was considered by the judge as 'apt to include the premises, ie the garden as well as the house'.

Judicial definitions

In *Maunsell v Olins* a case concerning the meaning of 'premises' in a leasehold conveyance, Viscount Dilhorne said: **5.33**

'Premises' is an ordinary word of the English language which takes colour and content from the context in which it is used. A reference to *Stroud's Judicial Dictionary* . . . shows this to be the case. It has, in my opinion, no recognised and established primary meaning . . . I do not think that it is right, when Parliament uses that word in a statute to conclude that it is intended to have the meaning that conveyancers attach to it unless a contrary intention appears.[28]

In the same case, Lord Wilberforce said: **5.34**

I think that I would not be alone in finding that the key word 'premises' invites reflection. It is true that it is a general word or, rather, a word of some generality but I know of no rule of construction which requires general words to be interpreted literally regardless of their context. If appeal is made to the principle that the plain meaning of a word should be taken, unless at least some other indication appears, it must be said that a word does not necessarily have a plain meaning just because it appears to be general—certainly not such a word as 'premises'.[29]

In defining the meaning of 'premises' in the context of section 79(1)(a) of the EPA 1990, the judicial history of the section must be called in aid. Section 79(1)(a) derives directly from the provisions in section 8 of the Nuisances Removal Act 1855. It therefore follows that judicial interpretation will follow previous authorities defining the meaning and extent of this subsection.[30] These authorities are concerned with the public health context of the sanitary statutes of the nineteenth century. **5.35**

In *R v Parlby*,[31] a decision on whether public sewers were premises, it was said that the expression did not simply apply to any premises on which a nuisance exists. Otherwise, there would be no need to specify other heads of statutory nuisance. Furthermore, it was stated that the provision was to be confined to cases in which **5.36**

the premises themselves are decayed, dilapidated, dirty, or out of order, as, for instance, where houses have been inhabited by tenants whose habits and ways of life have rendered them filthy or impregnated with disease, or where foul matter has been allowed to soak into walls or floors, or where they are so dilapidated as to be a source of danger to life and limb.[32]

Vessels

Vessels are specifically included in the definition of 'premises'.[33] So houseboats, yachts, and other ships will be included. **5.37**

---

[28] [1975] AC 373, at 383. [29] ibid, at 385–6.
[30] *East Riding of Yorkshire Council v Yorkshire Water Services Ltd* [2001] Env LR 113.
[31] 22 QBD 520. [32] ibid, per Wills J at 525.
[33] EPA 1990, s 79(7). Vessels driven by steam-reciprocating machinery are, however, excluded (EPA 1990, s 79(12)). (Note that vessels are excluded from the provisions of EPA 1990, s 81A(9), so recoverable expenses may not be charged against a vessel.)

5.38 The area of a local authority includes the territorial sea lying seawards from that part of the shore.[34] The UK territorial sea is 12 nautical miles in width.[35] Thus, a vessel within this area of sea will be covered as 'premises' within section 79(1)(a) of the EPA 1990. The master of such a vessel is deemed to be the occupier.[36]

Premises suffering from dampness, condensation and mould

The nature of the problem

5.39 Many of the cases which are brought under section 79(1)(a) of the EPA 1990 relate to the internal state of residential premises.[37] These are typically cases where condensation problems arising from the condition of the dwelling cause dampness, black mould and other fungal growth within the property.[38] This problem can arise from a lack of proper heating or ventilation, or it could be caused by structural problems such as lack of a damp-course or cavity walls, or defective plumbing, or from several causes. Complaints about dampness are common and need to be investigated carefully to see whether they are likely candidates for proceedings for statutory nuisance. These cases usually arise in relation to tenanted properties and may give rise to a clash of viewpoints between landlord and tenant. The former may tend to blame the lifestyle of the latter, while the latter may consider the situation to be a case of neglect or indifference on the part of the landlord.

5.40 In these cases there is normally no transmission of the nuisance from neighbouring property to the affected property.[39] The problem arises internally to the premises. Consequently, as these cases do not satisfy the requirements of common law nuisance, private or public, they must be brought under the health limb of statutory nuisance.[40]

5.41 It might be the case that, if the dampness is caused by a structural problem, the remedy lies in the hands of another person responsible for the structure and exterior of the building.[41] In a chain of leases for example, the superior landlord

---

[34] EPA 1990, s 79(11).
[35] Territorial Sea Act 1987, s 1.
[36] EPA 1990, s 79(11).
[37] See, eg, *GLC v London Borough of Tower Hamlets* (n 14 above).
[38] For the problems caused by condensation, see P Adams and L W Blake, 'The Curse of the Black Spot: Condensation and the Law' (1995) *Estates Gazette*, 1 April, pp 128–9, and, 15 April, pp 103–5. See also J Brown and M Pawlowski, 'Liability of Landlords for Condensation Dampness' [2001] 65 Conv 184–91.
[39] Unless the problem arises on other premises. See, eg, *Pollway Nominees v London Borough of Havering* (1989) 88 LGR 192.
[40] *Coventry CC v Cartwright* (n 1 above).
[41] But see *Pollway Nominees v London Borough of Havering* (n 39 above).

might be responsible.[42] The correct person must be identified as being responsible for the nuisance so that the appropriate notice may be served properly.[43]

Satisfying the health limb
To satisfy the health limb premises must be in such a state that they are injurious, or likely to cause injury, to health. It may be necessary to give informed expert evidence relating to the health risk to assist magistrates. This evidence need not necessarily be given by medical practitioners.[44] The evidence of environmental health officers, housing officers or surveyors, for example, will be accepted as expert evidence, provided that these professionals have relevant experience.[45] So, if a case concerns a building in imminent danger of collapsing onto the people living in it, the best person to give such expert evidence would be a structural engineer.[46]

5.42

The fact that these officers may be employed by the local authority does not prevent them from acting as experts although the court would need to be satisfied that they were objective in regard to their evidence. Indeed, it is desirable that employed experts are given training as to the requirements for giving expert evidence before a court.[47] These include the requirements that it must be demonstrated, firstly, that such persons have sufficient and relevant expertise in regard to the relevant issues in the case and, secondly, that they are aware of their primary duty to the court if they give expert evidence. It is, therefore, essential when selecting an expert to give evidence relating to the health risk, that that person's experience, credentials and his understanding of an expert witness's role should be carefully examined.

5.43

If the case is brought under section 82 of the EPA 1990 by a tenant, as a 'person aggrieved', then there is a limitation on proof of the health limb: only actual injury or its likely recurrence is acceptable.[48] This limitation does not apply if the

5.44

---

[42] Note the effect of the Landlord and Tenant Act 1985. Where a tenancy is for less than seven years, the Landlord and Tenant Act 1985, s 11, implies certain lessor's duties into the lease. The obligation is to keep in repair the structure and exterior of all residential premises; to put and keep in repair and proper working order the installations for the supply of gas, water, electricity, and for sanitation and space- and water-heating.
[43] *Stanley v London Borough of Ealing* [2000] Env LR D18. The local authority has power to make requisitions on the land; Local Government (Miscellaneous Provisions) Act 1976, s 16.
[44] *O'Toole v Knowsley MBC* [1999] Env LR D29.
[45] For the principles on giving expert evidence as to the health risk, see, eg, *Patel v Mehtab* (n 2 above); *Anderson v Dundee CC* [2000] SLT (Sh Ct) 134; *London Borough of Southwark v Simpson* [1999] Env LR 553. See further paras 18.35–18.42.
[46] *Anderson v Merseyside Improved Houses* (CO/1792/95; 12 February 1995, QBD) (unreported), per Saville LJ.
[47] *Field v Leeds CC* [2000] EG 165. Although *Field* was a case concerning a claim in private nuisance brought in the county court under the Civil Procedure Rules 1998, SI 1998/3132, it would be equally applicable on an appeal against an abatement notice. The principles regarding the necessity for expert witnesses to be objective apply equally to civil and criminal cases; see further paras 18.35–18.42.
[48] EPA 1990, s 82(2). See further Chapter 16.

case is brought by a local authority under section 80 of the EPA 1990 where a threat of injury is actionable.

5.45 To determine whether the health limb has been made out, an objective test will be applied. The individual health circumstances of the occupier will not be taken into account, however significant they might be.[49]

Bringing an 'internal premises' case under section 82[50]

5.46 As these cases often relate to social housing owned and managed by local authorities, they frequently fall under the procedure contained in section 82, in that they are brought by way of a complaint by a 'person aggrieved'.[51] Where such a person brings a case under section 82, he must specify the premises affected and give the owner enough information so that he has an opportunity to remedy the problem. Technical language is not required.[52]

Identifying the person responsible for the nuisance

5.47 An issue to be considered under this heading is whether the internal condensation problem is caused by the failure of the landlord to provide proper heating or ventilation facilities, or the failure of the tenant to use them (*Pike v Sefton MBC*[53]). As noted above, where a tenant fails to heat the premises efficiently, or to allow a landlord/owner access to undertake the work, then the tenant (and not the landlord) is the person responsible.[54] Where a landlord makes a reasonable offer of alternative accommodation to rehouse a tenant for a short period while necessary work is done, and that offer is refused by the tenant, the landlord is not then responsible for causing the nuisance.[55] The legal issue is whether the tenant or the landlord is responsible for causing the state of the premises to amount to a statutory nuisance. It is important, therefore, to identify the person who has *control* over them, not merely who is the *owner.*

5.48 It is also vital to identify the actual cause or causes of the problem.[56] Is it lack of sufficient heating facilities or is it because an occupier fails to switch the heater on? If it arises because the occupier dries clothes indoors, are there facilities to enable him to do otherwise? Or, would it be reasonable to expect the occupier to take laundry to a launderette?

---

[49] *Cunningham v Birmingham CC* [1998] Env LR 1 and, *R (on the application of Anne and Another) v Test Valley BC* [2001] 48 EG 127 (CS). [50] See also paras 16.04–16.07.
[51] It would seem that an environmental health officer may not serve an abatement notice on the housing department (as landlord) of the same local authority using the procedure under the EPA 1990, s 80, as a local authority may not serve proceedings on itself (*R v Cardiff CC, ex p Cross* (1982) 6 HLR 1).
[52] *Pearshouse v Birmingham CC* [1999] Env LR 536. The procedure under section 82 is separate from the summary procedure in section 80 where a local authority, in the first instance, serves an abatement notice. See further Chapter 16.
[53] [2000] Env LR D31. See also *GLC v London Borough of Tower Hamlets* (n 14 above) and *Dover DC v Farrar* [1980] 2 HLR 32. [54] See further paras 5.39–5.41.
[55] *Quigley v Liverpool Housing Trust* (1999) EGCS 94.
[56] If there is more than one cause of a nuisance it may be necessary to identify different persons responsible and serve abatement notices setting out different remedial work on each.

At the outset of 'internal premises' cases, an expert evaluation of the problem 5.49
should be undertaken. The occupier should clearly inform the landlord of the
nature of the problem taking care to identify the premises with clarity, thus
enabling him to remedy the situation within a reasonable time. An occupier might
reasonably be expected to accept a temporary offer of suitable alternative accommodation
while the work is done.[57]

Can empty premises be prejudicial to health?

The premises in which it is alleged a statutory nuisance arises may be empty or 5.50
may become unoccupied at some stage in the course of an investigation or court
hearing. Whether this affects its status as a statutory nuisance depends on the
nature of the proceedings. If the proceedings constitute an appeal against an
abatement notice brought under section 80(3) of the EPA 1990, then the appropriate
time to consider this specific point is at the time of service of the notice. In
SFI Group plc (formerly Surrey Free Inns plc) v Gosport BC[58] the Court of
Appeal held that the proper time to consider the validity of an abatement notice
is the time when it is served, not the date of the magistrates' court hearing (or
decision). The fact that occupants have been removed does not constitute an
abatement of a nuisance although the position might be different if the premises
were rendered uninhabitable so that there was no possibility that new occupiers
might be moved in.[59]

If the proceedings are brought under section 80(4) of the EPA 1990 – prosecution 5.51
for failure to comply with an abatement notice—then the issue is whether
compliance has been effected with the terms of the notice. (Thus, if, for example,
the notice required abatement of the nuisance within a set period of time, the state
of occupancy of the premises would be relevant at the expiry of this period.)

If the procedure under section 82 is followed, and a notice or letter of intent has 5.52
been served by a person aggrieved, the relevant time is the date of the hearing (or
decision) in the magistrates' court. *Coventry CC v Doyle*[60] concerned housing
which was zoned for demolition or radical refurbishment.[61] The decision in
Doyle was based on the relevant legislation which stated 'If on the hearing of the
complaint it is proved that the alleged nuisance exists, or that although abated it
is likely to recur . . .'[62] The decision has not been affected by the ruling in *SFI
Group plc (formerly Surrey Free Inns plc) v Gosport BC*.[63] The requirements of

---

[57] *Quigley v Liverpool Housing Trust* (n 55 above).   [58] [1999] Env LR 750.
[59] *Lambeth LBC v Stubbs* (1980) 255 EG 789.
[60] *Coventry CC v Doyle* [1982] 2 All ER 184 was actually one of three cases where council tenants laid informations against the council.
[61] The case was brought under the procedure available to tenants and private persons under the Public Health Act 1936, s 99. This procedure has its replacement in the EPA 1990, s 82, where a person aggrieved by a nuisance may apply to the court for an abatement order.
[62] Public Health Act 1936, 94(2).   [63] n 58 above.

section 82(2) of the EPA 1990 are that a nuisance must be in existence at the date of the hearing or, if abated, likely to recur.

5.53 The point will, however, only really be relevant in a situation where premises have been rendered uninhabitable so that prejudice to health cannot occur or recur because the presence of humans in the premises is an impossibility. Demolition would clearly satisfy this point. Even where a house is in a gross state of dereliction and has been abandoned, it might still be capable of being squatted. There is no reason why a squatter might not bring proceedings under section 82 as a 'person aggrieved'.

Identifying the premises

5.54 A careful analysis must be made of the extent of the premises which are intended to be covered by the proceedings under section 79(1)(a) of the EPA 1990 and from which the statutory nuisance is alleged to emanate. 'Premises' may include a single dwelling within a block or the entire block. However, where a complaint is made, or an abatement notice served, in respect of a statutory nuisance, then that must relate to the exact premises where the nuisance is said to have occurred.

5.55 In *Birmingham DC v McMahon*[64] a finding was made under section 92(1)(a) of the Public Health Act 1936 that a block of flats was in such a state that it was prejudicial to health in relation to an information filed by some of the tenants. It was held on appeal that a person could only be a 'person aggrieved' in relation to his own flat, not the whole block.[65]

Liability for escape of the land itself

5.56 Does an escape of the land itself, whether by erosion or encroachment, fall under the statutory nuisance regime? If a house, for example, is in a dangerous state and at risk of collapse, or a landslip is likely to occur, could an action be brought under Part III of the EPA 1990?

5.57 Such examples are most likely to be actionable under the private law of nuisance where there is injury to neighbouring land. Where a building in a dangerous structural state is involved then other statutory regimes may be more appropriate for public control of the problem.[66] However, there have been cases of this sort where the statutory nuisance regime has been relied on.[67]

---

[64] (1987) 86 LGR 63.
[65] See also *Pollway Nominees v London Borough of Havering* (n 39 above) where premises were rendered prejudicial to health by problems emanating from the structural exterior of the building, premises which were under the control of another person.
[66] See, eg, the Building Act 1984.
[67] See, eg, *Kirklees MBC v Field and Others* (n 3 above) where houses were built into a rock face and were in danger of collapsing, and *Pontardawe RDC v Moore-Gwyn* (n 3 above) where an outcrop of rock broke away onto neighbouring land (although the reasoning in the latter case was not considered to be good law in *Leakey v The National Trust for Places of Historic Interest or Natural Beauty* [1980] QB 485).

5.58 The principles relevant to determination of liability in common law nuisance have been developed over a long period. Owners and/or occupiers of land will be liable in nuisance where they are aware of the defect which gives rise to the nuisance. The defect must be patent, not latent. There is no relevance in the distinction between things which occur naturally on the land and those which are brought onto the land once knowledge is present.[68]

5.59 In *Noble v Harrison*,[69] a private nuisance case, a branch overhanging a public highway which broke and damaged a passing coach was held not to be a nuisance. Nor had it become a nuisance when, at some unknown time in the past, the latent defect began and gradually developed by natural causes and without any human agency or any indication to human eyes.

5.60 The result was the same in *Barker v Herbert* where the nuisance was caused by the act of a trespasser:

> In a case where the nuisance is created by the act of a trespasser, it is done without the permission of the owner and against his will, and he cannot in any sense be said to have caused the nuisance; but the law recognises that there may be a continuance by him of the nuisance. In that case, the gravamen is the continuance of the nuisance, and not the original causing of it . . .[70]

5.61 Thus, if premises are rendered in such a state as to be a statutory nuisance by the action of a trespasser, the owner of the land on which the nuisance arises will not be liable in the first instance. The trespasser will have primary liability but in practice that may be of no avail if the trespasser cannot be found. The landowner will incur liability in one of two ways. Firstly, if he continues the nuisance begun by the trespasser. In this case, his liability has become primary.[71] Secondly, he will incur liability if the trespasser cannot be found by virtue of the provision in section 80(2)(c) of the EPA 1990 which renders the owner or occupier of the premises liable where the perpetrator of a nuisance cannot be found.

5.62 However, the position changes where the owner/occupier is either aware of the dangerous state of his land albeit that its condition results from things naturally on his land,[72] or has brought something onto his land which is not naturally there and which escapes causing damage.[73]

---

[68] *Delaware Mansions Ltd and Flecksun Ltd v Westminster CC* [2001] 4 All ER 737. For a critical discussion of the proposed distinction between liability for things which are naturally, as opposed to artificially, on land, see A L Goodhart 'Liability for Things Naturally on the Land' (1930) 3 CLJ 13.

[69] [1926] 2 KB 332. [70] [1911] 2 KB 633, per Fletcher-Moulton LJ at 642.

[71] Under the EPA 1990, s 79(7), the 'person responsible' for the nuisance is the person to 'whose act, default or sufferance the nuisance is attributable'.

[72] *Leakey v The National Trust for Places of Historic Interest or Natural Beauty* (n 67 above). See also *Goldman v Hargrave* [1967] 1 AC 645; *Sedleigh-Denfield v O'Callaghan* [1940] AC 880; and *Solloway v Hampshire CC* (1981) 79 LGR 449.

[73] *Rylands v Fletcher* (1868) LR 3 HL 330.

5.63 In *Leakey v The National Trust for Places of Historic Interest or Natural Beauty*[74] a landowner was held liable in nuisance where a large quantity of soil and rubble fell onto neighbouring land causing damage. The landowner had been aware of the instability of its land and that it was a threat to the plaintiffs' properties. It was held that a landowner owed a general duty of care to a neighbouring occupier in relation to a hazard occurring on his land whether it was natural or man-made. The duty was to take such steps as were reasonable in all the circumstances to prevent or minimize the risk of which the occupier knew or ought to have known:

... a duty existed under which the occupier of land might be liable to his neighbour for damage to his neighbour's land as a result of a nuisance spreading from his land to his neighbour's land, even though the existence and the operative effect of the nuisance were not caused by any non-natural use by the defendant of his own land.[75]

5.64 Problems may arise from encroaching tree branches[76] or tree roots.[77] Rights of abatement at common law are available to landowners to cut tree roots or branches where they encroach on neighbouring land. Liability is not strict. A reasonably foreseeable risk of damage by encroachment has to be established. The principles of reasonable neighbourly conduct were emphasized in *Delaware Mansions Ltd and Flecksun Ltd v Westminster CC*: 'If reasonableness between neighbours is the key to the solution of problems in this field, it cannot be right to visit the authority or owner responsible for a tree with a large bill for underpinning without giving them notice of the damage and the opportunity of avoiding further damage by removal of the tree.'[78]

5.65 The circumstances which will be relevant to the issue of liability include knowledge of the hazard, extent of the risk, practicability of preventing or minimizing foreseeable injury or damage, the time available to remedy the damage, the probable cost and the relative financial resources of the parties, that is, the basic principles of tortious liability.

5.66 A different scenario was posed in *Holbeck Hall Hotel Ltd v Scarborough Council*[79] where the claimant's hotel slipped into the sea when the seashore disappeared as a result of erosion. Here the damage resulted from the passive removal of support. The Court of Appeal held that the measured duty of care only

---

[74] n 67 above.
[75] ibid, per Megaw LJ at 77, who confirmed the approval by the House of Lords in *Sedleigh-Denfield v O'Callaghan* (n 72 above) of Scrutton LJ's judgment in *Job Edwards Ltd v Birmingham Navigations Co Proprietors* [1924] 1 KB 341. See also *Marcic v Thames Water Utilities Ltd* [2002] EWCA Civ 65 which confirmed this line of authority.
[76] *Lemmon v Webb* [1894] 3 Ch 1, affirmed [1895] AC 1.
[77] *Delaware Mansions Ltd and Flecksun Ltd v Westminster CC* (n 68 above); *Butler v Standard Telephones and Cables Ltd* [1940] 1 KB 399; *McCombe v Read* [1955] 2 QB 429; *Davey v Harrow Corporation* [1958] 1 QB 60; *Morgan v Khyatt* [1964] 1 WLR 475; and *Masters v Brent LBC* [1978] 1 QB 841.
[78] n 68 above, per Lord Clyde at 34.
[79] [2000] 2 All ER 705. See also J Wightman, 'Liability for Landslips: Should Landowners be Responsible for the Consequences of Erosion?' (2000) 2 Env L Rev 285–90.

arose where there was actual or presumed knowledge. Presumed knowledge would only arise where a reasonable landowner[80] would have discovered the defect without undertaking further investigation. Further, the extent of the damage which actually occurred must be foreseeable.[81]

5.67 To what extent will these factors be relevant in a statutory nuisance action under section 79(1)(a) of the EPA 1990 resulting from the state of the land?

Relevance to statutory nuisance

5.68 Many of these factors are entirely consistent with the approach taken under the nuisance limb of statutory nuisance cases where the concept of reasonableness is central.[82] Reasonableness is relevant because nuisance takes account of the conflicting uses to which land is put and seeks to derive a balance between them. Factors such as the time and manner of the commission of the nuisance, the locality, etc, are all relevant.

5.69 Knowledge of the defect sufficient to impose liability on the landowner means actual, constructive or imputed knowledge. A landowner cannot, therefore, avoid liability by shutting his eyes to the defect.[83]

5.70 Where a landowner has brought something onto his land which is not naturally there and which is liable to cause damage if it escapes then liability falls under the principle in *Rylands v Fletcher*[84] which is part of the general law of nuisance.[85]

5.71 Liability may also arise in circumstances where no unnatural or unreasonable use of the land has been made. Such liability arises where an owner or occupier fails to remedy something which has occurred on his own land without his own act or default. To avoid liability he must remedy it within a reasonable time after he discovered it or ought to have discovered it.[86]

5.72 Most of these cases illustrate the application of these principles in common law nuisance. To enforce statutory nuisance under section 79(1)(a) of the EPA 1990 it would be necessary to show that the nuisance affected the personal comfort of the neighbouring landowner or the broader community, or that it was prejudicial to health.

---

[80] This means that the defect was sufficiently patent that it could be discovered without the necessity of geological investigations—a reasonable landowner does not mean a professional engineer.
[81] See Wightman (n 79 above).   [82] See paras 4.55–4.81.
[83] *Noble v Harrison* (n 69 above) and *Barker v Herbert* (n 70 above).   [84] n 73 above.
[85] *Cambridge Water Company v Eastern Leather Counties plc* [1994] 2 AC 264.
[86] As in the presence of pigeons under a railway bridge in *Wandsworth LBC v Railtrack plc* [2001] 1 WLR 368 or seaweed on a beach in *Margate Pier and Harbour (Proprietors Co) v Margate Town Council* (1869) 20 LT 564, or encroaching tree roots in *Delaware Mansions Ltd and Flecksun Ltd v Westminster CC* (n 68 above).

Public sewers

5.73 It was held in *East Riding of Yorkshire Council v Yorkshire Water Services Ltd*[87] that the word 'premises' under section 79(1)(a) does not include a public sewer. This case followed *R v Parlby*[88] where it was held that the statutory nuisance provisions did not apply to nuisances arising from sewage tanks and works.

Defining 'premises' in other contexts

5.74 While the meaning of 'premises' depends on the context in which it is used, nevertheless judicial definitions of the word in other statutory contexts can be helpful.[89]

Caves

5.75 An enclosed place such as a cave formed by excavating and quarrying sandstone, which is accessed by means of a cutting and to which the entrance is closed by a wooden door, can be premises.[90]

Gallops

5.76 Gallops, or downlands, on which racehorses were trained and exercised were capable of being premises.[91]

Petrol tanker

5.77 A petrol tanker parked for four hours on a forecourt, from which petrol was transferred direct into the petrol tanks of cars owned by members of the public, was not 'premises'. To so describe a petrol tanker was to go beyond the ordinary meaning of the word which connoted 'land or buildings upon land'.[92]

Holiday camp

5.78 A holiday camp as a whole can be regarded as 'premises'.[93]

---

[87] n 30 above.
[88] n 31 above.
[89] See *The Concentrate Manufacturing Company of Ireland (Trading as 7-Up International) v Coca-Cola Bottlers (Ulster) Ltd* (CA, unreported, 6 October 1992).
[90] *Gardiner v Sevenoaks RDC* [1950] WN 260, a case on the meaning of 'premises' within the Celluloid and Cinematograph Film Act 1922.
[91] *Bracey v Read* [1963] Ch 88, a case which concerned the application of the Landlord and Tenant Act 1954 to business tenancies and, in particular, whether the gallops were 'premises' under Part II of that Act.
[92] *Grandi v Milburn* [1966] 2 QB 263, per James J at 274. In argument it was contended that 'If a tanker was premises, where was the line to be drawn? Was a hearse, a pram, a bicycle ... premises? No.' (at 266).
[93] *Phonographic Performance Ltd v Pontin's Ltd* [1968] Ch 290. See also *Bristol City Football Supporters Club v The Commission* [1975] VATRR 93 on whether buffets constituted separate premises to the whole of the football ground for taxation purposes under the Finance Act 1972.

Incorporeal rights

'Premises' have been held to refer only to premises which were capable of physical occupation not to ancillary incorporeal rights such as a right to use a garden in common with another tenant.[94] **5.79**

Defences

The defence of 'best practicable means' is only available, in relation to premises in such a state as to be a statutory nuisance under section 79(1)(a), where the nuisance arises on industrial, trade or business premises.[95] Since statutory nuisances under this provision will often, in practice, arise internally to domestic premises causing health problems for the occupiers, this defence will rarely be available. **5.80**

Where proceedings are brought under section 82 of the EPA 1990 in respect of a nuisance falling within section 79(1)(a) of the Act, the defence of best practicable means is not available at all if the nuisance makes the premises unfit for human habitation. **5.81**

In common with all statutory nuisances, it is a defence to a prosecution for failure to comply with an abatement notice to show that there was a 'reasonable excuse'.[96] **5.82**

Alternative provisions relating to premises

Alternative provisions for dealing with housing defects may be more appropriate than the statutory nuisance regime; or, the regime may not be available because of the nature of the defect which is complained of.[97] An outline of these alternative regimes is set out below. However, a detailed examination of them is beyond the scope of this work and reference should be made to relevant specialist texts. **5.83**

Building Act 1984

Section 76 of the Building Act 1984 provides an alternative procedure for local authorities to deal with premises which are in such a state as to be prejudicial to health or a nuisance. This is referred to in the Building Act 1984 as a 'defective state', and it seems that the interpretation of the phrase follows that of 'state' in section 79 of the EPA 1990. That is, it means that the existing state of the premises must be such as to represent a threat to health or a nuisance.[98] **5.84**

---

[94] *M & JS Properties Ltd v White* [1959] 2 QB 25, a case brought under the Rent Act 1957.
[95] The availability of this defence is discussed in greater detail at paras 15.02–15.28.
[96] See further paras 15.29–15.43.
[97] As, eg, in the case of accidental physical injury (*R v Bristol CC, ex p Everett* (n 22 above)).
[98] *Birmingham CC v Oakley* (n 5 above).

5.85 The procedure is available where an unreasonable delay would ensue in remedying the defect if the procedure under section 80 of the EPA 1990 were to be followed[99] and permits the local authority to undertake the work itself.[100]

5.86 A local authority must first be satisfied that there is a statutory nuisance in existence. The definition of 'prejudicial to health' is the same as in Part III of the EPA 1990; that is, 'injurious, or, likely to cause injury to health'.[101] 'Premises' are defined as including 'land, buildings, easements, and hereditaments of any tenure'.[102]

5.87 The procedure under the 1984 Act is that the local authority serves on the person responsible for the nuisance a notice setting out the local authority's intention to remedy the defective state of the premises and details of the alleged defects. Identification of the recipient of the notice is to be determined according to the same rules that apply under Part III of the EPA 1990. This will, therefore, be the person 'by whose act, default of sufferance' the nuisance has been occasioned except where the defect affects the structure of the building. In that case the correct recipient is the owner of the building. If the person responsible cannot be found then the owner or occupier of the premises is the correct recipient of the notice.[103] In typical cases to which section 76 of the Building Act 1984 applies, the defective state will be a structural defect and the usual recipient will, therefore, be the owner of the premises.

5.88 Service of the notice may be effected by personal delivery or, by leaving it at, or posting it to, the usual or last known place of residence. Where the recipient of the notice is a local authority, service should be made on the officer at the local authority office. Where the recipient is a company, the secretary or clerk at the registered or principal office should be served. Service on an agent (such as someone entitled to receive the rack rent) should be at the place of business. Provision is made, where the identity of owner and occupier cannot be ascertained after reasonable inquiry, for service of the notice on the 'owner' or 'occupier' of named premises and for leaving it with some person on the premises, or by affixing it or a copy on a conspicuous part of the premises.[104]

---

[99] Building Act 1984, s 76(1)(b).
[100] The question arises as to whether this alternative procedure is only available, when the case falls under the health limb, in respect of defects which are threatening to health in the sense of disease; *R v Bristol CC, ex p Everett* (n 22 above). It is arguable that the alternative procedure in section 76 of the Building Act 1984 is to be interpreted in this way, since it is linked so closely with statutory nuisance. However, this limitation is unlikely to apply to other parts of the Building Act 1984 which deals with a wide range of defects in buildings, including dangerous structures.
[101] ibid, s 126. [102] ibid.
[103] Building Act 1984, s 76, and EPA 1990, s 80(2)(a), (b) or (c). Updating amendments have been made to section 76 by the EPA 1990, s 162(1), Sch 15, para 24. Oddly, the amendments have not altered the reference to section 93 in the Building Act 1984, s 76(1), which is a reference to the Public Health Act 1936. It seems reasonable to assume an error and to take this as a reference to the EPA 1990, s 80. [104] Building Act 1984, s 94.

5: PREMISES

5.89 Nine days after service the local authority may execute such works as may be necessary to remedy the defective state. It may then recover such costs as have reasonably been incurred from the recipient of the notice.

5.90 Although there is no appeal procedure, the recipient of the notice may serve a counter-notice stating that he intends to carry out the work himself. He has seven days from service of the notice to do so.

5.91 The local authority is not then permitted to take action unless the recipient fails to begin the work within a reasonable time, or fails to make reasonable progress towards completion. The determination of what is a reasonable time or reasonable progress falls to the local authority.

5.92 The matter comes before the court for the first time when proceedings to recover expenses start. The court must then satisfy itself that the premises were in a defective state or that unreasonable delay would have followed had the procedure under section 80 of the EPA 1990 been used. If the recipient served a counter-notice but the local authority was still obliged to carry out the work, then the court must satisfy itself that the defendant did not begin work within a reasonable time, or did not make reasonable progress towards completion. The penalty for a finding against the local authority is that it will then not recover its costs whether in whole or in part.

5.93 During a hearing for recovery of the local authority's expenses, the court may apportion the costs between the defendant and some other person or determine that they ought to be borne wholly by some other person. However, this route is not open to the court if the other person has not had due notice of the proceedings and an opportunity to be heard.

5.94 The procedure under section 76 of the Building Act 1984 is open to the local authority even though it could have proceeded by way of service of a repairs notice under Part IV of the Housing Act 1985.[105]

5.95 In addition to the alternative procedure under section 76, there are various provisions to deal with the safety of buildings, structures and sites.[106] Section 77 of the Building Act 1984 provides a procedure whereby a local authority can apply to the magistrates' court for an order requiring the owner to remedy the problem, either by remedial works or by demolition. The court has power to order interim measures to prevent a building from being used or restricting its use until the work is done.

5.96 These provisions may be used in a case where a building or structure is in imminent danger of collapse but there is no express limitation to this type of defect. In

---

[105] See para 5.100.
[106] Note that Inner London is covered by the London Building Acts 1930–1939 and the London Local Authorities Act 2000.

line with that typical case is the provision in section 78 of the 1984 Act which permits a local authority to take such action as may be necessary. The local authority's costs are recoverable from the owner.

5.97 Local authorities have power to enter premises, where they have a duty to enforce the Building Act 1984, to ascertain whether there has been a contravention and to ascertain whether circumstances exist which involve the local authority in taking action, and to carry out work. Twenty-four hours' notice of the intention to enter (except where the premises are a factory or workplace) is required.[107]

Public Health Act 1936

5.98 Section 83 of the Public Health Act 1936 provides that, where a local authority is satisfied that premises are in such a filthy or unwholesome condition as to be prejudicial to health or are verminous, it may give a notice to the owner or occupier requiring him to take steps to remedy the problem.

5.99 The local authority may prosecute for failure to comply with the notice. It may also (or as an alternative) carry out the necessary works itself and recover the costs.

Housing Act 1985

5.100 These provisions centre on the concept of fitness for human habitation in residential housing.[108] Where a local authority determines that a house is unfit it may either serve a Repair Notice[109] requiring works to make it fit, or make a Closing or Demolition order.[110]

5.101 The standard for fitness includes a range of matters.[111] These may include factors which might result in physical injury. There is no comparable public health requirement as in the statutory nuisance regime.

5.102 Houses in multiple occupation ('HMOs') are also covered under the Housing Act 1985 which provides for fitness[112] for multiple occupation and management.[113]

Health and Safety at Work Act 1974

5.103 The primary purpose of this Act is to secure the health and safety of employees in the workplace. However, the Act is sufficiently extensive to include a duty to visitors to non-domestic premises to ensure that they are safe. In *Westminster CC*

---

[107] Building Act 1984, ss 95 and 96.
[108] This does not include council housing.
[109] Housing Act 1985, ss 189 and 190.
[110] ibid, ss 264 and 265.
[111] ibid, s 604; and, see the Department of the Environment's Circular 17/96 for guidance on the interpretation of the fitness standard.
[112] Housing Act 1985, s 352(1).
[113] See also ibid, s 369, and the Housing (Management of Houses in Multiple Occupation) Regulations 1990, SI 1990/830.

v Select Management Ltd[114] this was held to apply to lifts and installations in common parts of blocks of flats and houses in multiple occupation.

Defective Premises Act 1972

This Act imposes a duty on anyone involved in the construction of a property to ensure that it is fit for habitation when completed.[115] The action accrues at the date of completion so the Act is limited to dwellings up to six years old.[116] Problems of dampness and condensation are not so likely to be found in modern dwellings but where they are, then there may be a design fault and liability might fall on the architect. To bring a claim under the Act, a claimant must have a legal or equitable interest in the property. Thus a freeholder or leaseholder would be covered but not a guest or mere lodger.

5.104

Occupiers' Liability Act 1957

Under this Act, there is a duty to take reasonable care to ensure that all occupiers and visitors are reasonably safe from personal injury. Under the Act, 'injury' includes disease and impairment of physical or mental condition.

5.105

Leasehold premises

Common law

At common law the landlord and tenant relationship confers certain obligations on a landlord by implying covenants into a lease. Covenants such as the covenant for quiet enjoyment,[117] fitness for human habitation[118] and non-derogation from grant entitle the tenant to a peaceful occupation of the home.[119] These are private rights enforceable by the tenant against the landlord.

5.106

Contractual obligations

Similarly, the lease itself may provide for an arrangement of duties relating to such matters as the obligation to repair. Matters which might constitute a statutory nuisance might also be remediable through a private action brought by a tenant against his landlord.

5.107

Landlord and Tenant Act 1985

Where a tenancy is for less than seven years, section 11 of the Landlord and Tenant Act 1985 implies certain leasehold duties into the lease. The obligation is

5.108

---

[114] [1985] 1 WLR 576.
[115] Defective Premises Act 1972, s 1.
[116] ibid, s 1(5) and the Limitation Act 1980, ss 2, 4 and 32.
[117] *Baxter v Camden LBC (No 2)* [2001] 1 AC 1.
[118] This covenant is to be satisfied at the beginning of the lease; see *Smith v Marrable* (1843) 11 M&W 5.
[119] For a case on the extent of this covenant in a noise context, see *Southwark London Borough Council v Tanner and Others*; *Baxter v Camden LBC (No 2)* (n 117 above).

to keep in repair the structure and exterior of all residential premises, and to put and keep in repair and proper working order the installations for the supply of gas, water, electricity and for sanitation, and for space- and water-heating. Where a landlord fails to satisfy these repairing obligations after the tenant has complained, the tenant has a right of action in the civil courts for damages and specific performance.

6

NOISE AND NOISE NUISANCE

Introduction 6.01
   Noise as a form of pollution 6.01
   Increases in complaints 6.04
   Noise levels and measurement 6.05
   Problems of control 6.08
Noise and statutory nuisance 6.09
   Objective test 6.09
   Origins 6.13
Public nuisance 6.15
Legislative background of statutory noise nuisance 6.18
   Noise abatement zones 6.21
**Section 79(1)(g) of the EPA 1990: 'noise emitted from premises so as
to be prejudicial to health or a nuisance'** 6.22
   Noise in the street 6.24
   Nuisance or prejudicial to health 6.25
   Links to private nuisance 6.27
   Links to public nuisance 6.29
   Noise and prejudice to health 6.30
Legal requirements and the role of enforcement officers 6.32
Scope of noise nuisance 6.36
   The defence of best practicable means 6.38
Neighbourhood and domestic noise 6.40
   Establishing liability in statutory noise nuisance 6.42
   The 'give and take' principle 6.45
   The way property is used: 'normal use' 6.46
   One-off events 6.49
   Harassment 6.50
Noise Act 1996 . . . . .6.51
   Seizure of equipment 6.53
   The Noise Act 1996 and the EPA 1990 . . . . .6.56
   Procedure for seizing equipment under the Noise Act 1996 . . . . .6.59
   Other requirements for using the Noise Act 1996 .6.61
Audible intruder alarms 6.63
Entertainment noise 6.65
   Links between statutory nuisance, planning and licensing systems 6.66

Entertainment noise and statutory nuisance 6.70
    Serious noise problems 6.73
Drafting noise abatement notices under the EPA 1990 ....6.75
Noise emitted from industrial, commercial and business premises 6.79
The defence of best practicable means in noise cases 6.82
    Standard of abatement 6.85
    Specific works notices and industrial noise 6.87
Noise in the street and other public places 6.91
    Noise and Statutory Nuisance Act 1993 ....6.92
    Criminal Justice and Public Order Act 1994 ....6.96
    Public nuisance 6.99
    Control of loudspeakers in the street 6.100
Noise from construction sites 6.102
    Scope of works 6.103
    Notices 6.104
    Scope of the notice 6.107
    Injunctions 6.109
    Use of powers 6.110
    Appeals 6.111
    Consultation 6.113
    Prior consent 6.116
Statutory nuisance and other forms of noise control 6.119
    Aircraft, road traffic and railway noise 6.120
    Statutory authority 6.125
    Noise at the workplace 6.128
    Model bye-laws 6.130
    Regulatory codes of practice 6.133
    Licensing 6.134
Conclusion 6.138

Introduction

Noise as a form of pollution

6.01 There is no adequate legal definition of noise and its measurement and control are often complicated. Noise is also perceived differently by different individuals and in some respects is a social construct. Changes in lifestyle affect the ways in which problems are perceived and defined.

6.02 Significant increases in noise affecting a high proportion of the population have been caused by an ever-increasing volume of road traffic. Increases in the number of aircraft movements coming from more and larger airports have also caused substantial problems which are similarly difficult to resolve. Noise from public entertainment, from longer opening hours in pubs, clubs and restaurants has also increased substantially over the last few decades. Sometimes new sources of noise contribute to problems of alleged nuisances, for example from power boats and off-road motor tracks. Even the summer operas held on the lawns of Garsington Manor in Oxfordshire suburbia split a small community over whether the events constitute a nuisance or a pleasure.

Noise pollution emerged as a social problem in the 1960s and 1970s, partly in response to the growth in public awareness about environmental issues. As noise has become increasingly problematic, individuals' expectations have been raised about what constitutes a noise nuisance and when controls are needed. Noise was (and still is) perceived differently from most other forms of pollution because it has no lasting effects on the physical environment.[1] Noise will interfere with the victim's use of property and may even diminish its value but it does not result in physical damage, except in the most extreme circumstances such as explosions. Vibration which accompanies noise may cause physical damage, however, and this is included in the statutory definition of noise.[2] 6.03

Increases in complaints
Complaints to local authorities are on the increase. Over 120,000 complaints about domestic noise were recorded by local authorities in England and Wales during the period from 1999 to 2000.[3] Of these, about one-sixth amounted to a statutory nuisance in the opinion of the authorities concerned. Substantial increases in complaints about noise from commercial sources were also recorded, notably from construction and demolition sites, aircraft and railways. Much of the increase in noise complaints falls below the standard required for nuisance and other types of control are needed to improve matters. To this end, following a review of the Noise Act 1996, the Environment Minister, Michael Meacher, announced on 20 December 2001 that an amendment to the Act will be put before Parliament to enable councils to use powers more freely in respect of night-time noise and to deal more effectively with noisy neighbours. 6.04

Noise levels and measurement
At any particular place, noise varies over time and can be conceptualized as a sequence of more or less variable events. It occurs within an acoustic environment made up of other sources of noise which are themselves more or less variable. A particular noise may seem louder during the night, or it may be unobtrusive during windy weather or when masked by another noise source. At other times, it may appear unbearable, particularly if the person responsible has not cooperated to reduce it or has appeared churlish and insensitive to the victim of noise. 6.05

---

[1] Royal Commission on Environmental Pollution, *Tackling Pollution: Experience and Prospect* (10th report, Cmnd 9149, 1984), paras 2.5 and 6.16.   [2] EPA 1990, s 79(7).
[3] *Annual Report* (Chartered Institute of Environmental Health, 2000).

6.06 The technical measurement of noise is problematic. The introduction of British Standards has helped to ensure that consistent and comparable methods of measurement are employed. However, interpreting the results is a matter requiring expert evidence, and, when results are presented in court, few informed commentators would have much confidence in the ability of lay magistrates to draw proper legal inferences.[4]

6.07 An objective noise level comprises a scientifically based, averaged level measured over a defined period. It is expressed, in decibels, as an Leq: as an equivalent continuous level of fluctuating noise. This expression targets the period and level of noise causing the alleged nuisance and allows for scientific comparisons to be made. Used in conjunction with an industry standard, such as the British Standards Institution's 'Method for Rating Industrial Noise Affecting Mixed Residential and Industrial Areas',[5] it provides an objective basis for measuring noise which is appropriate to particular circumstances. This standard provides weightings for noise sources which possess aggravating characteristics, for example when noise is intermittent. Noise which is obtrusive, annoying and out of character with a neighbourhood is capable of being a nuisance even when its level is not measurably greater than the background level.[6]

Problems of control

6.08 Practical means of control may be expensive, perhaps disproportionately so in relation to the benefits. Sometimes there is no effective step available to control the alleged nuisance or annoyance, short of stopping the activity causing the problem or moving the source of the noise to a new location. It may be feasible to restrict the times allowing the activity causing the noise to take place. The social and economic value of the activity causing the problem is clearly very important. A court will often consider the impact made by the commercially useful noise producer rather differently from that of the neighbour playing loud music solely for his own enjoyment. Some forms of noise nuisance are easy to justify, others are not.

Noise and statutory nuisance

Objective test

6.09 Whereas to the lay person anything that annoys him is a nuisance, the legal test for noise nuisance is objective: the noise must be both excessive and unreasonable.

---

[4] In spite of these difficulties, the present Government remains resistant to demands for a specialist environment court, as recommended by a report commissioned by the Department of the Environment, Transport and the Regions ('the Grant Report') in 2000. In the House of Lords debate (9 October 2000) following its publication, Lord Bach, speaking for the Government, maintained that there was no consensus among the higher judiciary for change and said that there were 'problems with a knee-jerk reaction to proposals for change'. See *ENDS Report 309* (October 2000), pp 33–4.

[5] BS 4142, 1997. See also *R (on the application of Aircraft Research Association Ltd) v Bedford BC* [2001] Env LR 700.   [6] *Godfrey v Conwy CBC* [2001] Env LR 38.

Probably more than for any other form of statutory nuisance, with noise there are wide variations between the perceptions of individuals and their ability to tolerate it. Much depends on the personality of the person affected, their lifestyle and cultural background, and on other aspects of their life. There is a huge subjective element which nuisance law disregards.[7]

6.10 Courts may be slightly more sympathetic to the noise victim than in the past, but the sensitivities of particular individuals receive scant regard. As was said long ago by Lord Selborne LC in *Gaunt v Fynney*, 'a nervous, or anxious, or prepossessed listener hears sounds which would otherwise have passed unnoticed, and magnifies and exaggerates into some new significance, originating within himself, sounds which at other times would have been passively heard and not regarded'.[8] This case was concerned with noise and vibration produced from the working of a steam engine. The court found for the defendant, holding that the level of noise had not become worse over time but that the plaintiff's sensitivity to noise had increased.

6.11 These objective requirements mean that an invalid suffering from noise has no right to expect a higher standard of protection than a person in good health. However, illness would provide a good reason to ensure that he enjoyed his right to be protected from noise nuisance to the full.[9]

6.12 The consequences of this traditional conception of noise nuisance can lead to injustice. Variety of lifestyle is not merely a simple matter of choice. Necessity may force the manual worker to work night shifts and to sleep during the day. Whether his complaints about his neighbour's ordinary, daytime noise-making activities, which prevent him from sleeping, amount to a statutory nuisance will be problematic.

Origins

6.13 Noise as a form of statutory nuisance originated with the Noise Abatement Act 1960. Before then a private nuisance action could be pursued in the civil courts and public nuisances could be prosecuted either summarily or on indictment. Injunctions and damages have been available remedies for many years, both for private and public nuisances.[10]

6.14 Local authorities usually relied on bye-laws to deal with noise complaints before the 1960 Act was in force. These powers were used sporadically if at all. At no time have common law actions been widely used to deal with noise nuisance. Partly this has been because of the complexity of noise as a form of nuisance. The

---

[7] Notwithstanding the legal theory, in practice magistrates are often greatly influenced by subjective factors.   [8] (1872) 8 Ch App 8, at 13.
[9] *Spruzen v Dossett* (1896) 12 TLR 246. Cf *Bloodworth v Cormack* [1949] NZLR 1058, per Callan J at 1064: 'This branch of the law pays no regard to the special needs of invalids'.
[10] See further paras 6.99 and 17.11–17.25.

financial cost of bringing a civil action also acts as a powerful filter. The requirements for prosecuting public nuisance are onerous and few actions have been brought by the Attorney-General or by local authorities who have been entitled to bring proceedings in their own name since 1972.[11]

Public nuisance

6.15 Public nuisance is confined to serious instances of noise pollution, where the public at large are victims rather than a limited number of individuals.[12] The availability of prison sentences and fines (unlimited in the Crown Court) make it a more serious offence than statutory nuisance. In recent years 'raves' and 'acid-house parties' have sometimes been prosecuted as public nuisances.[13]

6.16 Public nuisance proceedings should be considered where the nuisance is particularly serious or where there is a substantial public health risk, such as when noise levels are dangerously high, or low-frequency noise is very obtrusive and poses a danger to health.[14] Such proceedings may also be used in respect of one-off nuisances.[15]

6.17 Local authorities generally restrict themselves to using their enforcement powers under section 80 of the Environmental Protection Act 1990 ('EPA 1990'), which apply to public as well as to private forms of nuisance. It should also be noted that the remedies for statutory nuisance include obtaining an injunction in the High Court[16] and this course is available where use of ordinary criminal proceedings is likely to be ineffective. It may be that the increasing frequency and seriousness of noise complaints, especially those involving residential noise, will result in more public nuisance actions being brought, but at present there is no evidence for this. A lack of familiarity amongst local authorities with the public nuisance procedure may be a factor.

Legislative background of statutory noise nuisance

6.18 Section 1 of the Noise Abatement Act 1960 introduced noise nuisance, for England and Wales, into the framework provided by the Public Health Act 1936. The Noise Abatement Act 1960 also applied in Scotland where it was enforced

---

[11] Under the Local Government Act 1972, s 222, which provides: 'Where a local authority consider it expedient for the promotion or protection of the interests of the inhabitants of their area— (a) they may prosecute or defend or appear in any legal proceedings and, in the case of civil proceedings, may institute them in their own name ...' The reference to 'civil proceedings' includes an injunction even though public nuisance is a crime; *City of London Corp v Bovis Construction Ltd* [1992] 3 All ER 697; 86 LGR 660. [12] *A-G v PYA Quarries Ltd* [1957] 2 QB 169.

[13] *R v Shorrock* [1993] 3 All ER 917; *R v Ruffell* [1992] 13 Cr App R (S) 204; *R v Taylor* [1991] 13 Cr App R (S) 466.

[14] P L Pelmear, 'Noise and Health', in W Tempest (ed), *The Noise Handbook* (Academic Press, 1985). [15] *A-G v PYA Quarries Ltd* (n 12 above).

[16] EPA 1990, s 81(5).

under the Public Health (Scotland) Act 1897. The history of the Noise Abatement Act 1960, which was introduced as a Private Members' Bill, backed by a small but well-organized pressure group, indicates noise pollution's lowly status at the time as a 'Cinderella pollutant'.[17]

6.19 This regime was replaced by the Control of Pollution Act 1974, which was itself repealed in England and Wales by section 162 of, and Schedule 16 to, the EPA 1990. Section 79(1)(g) of the EPA 1990 is the relevant current statutory provision regulating noise nuisance, though noise on construction sites is still governed by section 60 of the Control of Pollution Act 1974.[18] Section 79(1)(g) was amended in 1993 to include noise emanating from the street.[19] The Environment Act 1995 extended the noise nuisance provisions in Part III of the EPA 1990 to Scotland.[20]

6.20 The Control of Pollution Act 1974 was the first Act enabling enforcement action to take place regarding prospective nuisances, that is noise nuisances that are 'likely to occur or recur'.[21] This power to take action with regard to future nuisances now applies to all forms of nuisance covered by section 79 of the EPA 1990.[22]

Noise abatement zones

6.21 The Control of Pollution Act 1974 also introduced the concept of the noise abatement zone

to prevent gradual increases of 'creeping', background noise especially from industrial and commercial premises.[23] Although about 60 zones have been established in England and Wales (none in Scotland), they have been expensive, ineffective, and local authorities have not been encouraged by central government to set them up.[24]

Section 79(1)(g) of the EPA 1990: 'noise emitted from premises so as to be prejudicial to health or a nuisance'

6.22 The provisions regarding noise nuisance are contained in section 79(1)(g) of the EPA 1990, which states that a statutory nuisance occurs as a result of 'noise

---

[17] F McManus, 'Noise law in the United Kingdom: A Very British Solution' (2000) 20 Legal Studies 264. [18] See further paras 6.102–6.115.
[19] EPA 1990, s 79(1)(ga).
[20] The Environment Act 1995, s 107 and Sch 17, extended Part III of the EPA 1990 to Scotland. The Environment Act 1995, s 120(3), repealed the Public Health (Scotland) Act 1897 which gave the police powers to deal with nuisance complaints. [21] Control of Pollution Act 1974, s 58.
[22] EPA 1990, s 80(1). Note that a local authority may not institute proceedings for a statutory nuisance falling under s 79(1)(g) without the consent of the Secretary of State where proceedings might also be instituted under Part I, EPA 1990, or under regulations made under section 2 of the Pollution Prevention and Control Act 1999, (s 79(10)).
[23] Besides industrial and commercial premises, central government anticipated schemes being set up in 'places of entertainment or assembly, agricultural premises, transport and public utility installations' (Department of Environment Circular 2/76, App 2, paras 2.3 and 2.4).
[24] *ENDS Report 225* (October 1995), p 12. This report noted that 40 are no longer operational and of those surviving there was only minimal enforcement action by the local authorities.

emitted from premises so as to be prejudicial to health or a nuisance'. Vibration is included in the definition of noise.[25]

6.23 It is a requirement for the noise to be emitted from 'premises', which includes land and vessels.[26] It may be arguable whether noise made by a person or group at large in a public place comes within the Act where there is no evidence of control being exercised by a particular person over the property, such as would occur in an organized event.

Noise in the street

6.24 The noise provisions in the EPA 1990 were widened by section 2 of the Noise and Statutory Nuisance Act 1993 to include some forms of noise emanating from the street. Section 79(1)(ga) provides that 'noise that is prejudicial to health or a nuisance and is emitted from or caused by a vehicle, machinery or equipment in a street' is a statutory nuisance. Section 79(6A) of the EPA 1990, as amended by the 1993 Act, excludes traffic noise from this provision.

Nuisance or prejudicial to health

6.25 Although statutory noise nuisance is of comparatively recent origin, section 79(1)(g) is drafted in a similar fashion to long-established types of statutory nuisance which originated in the 1850s.[27] As with these earlier forms of statutory nuisance, section 79(1)(g) has two limbs—injurious (or prejudicial) to health or common law nuisance—only one of which needs to be established for a prosecution to succeed.

6.26 The 'prejudicial to health' limb does not appear in the Control of Pollution Act 1974, the preceding legislation to the EPA 1990 with respect to noise nuisance. Section 58 of the Control of Pollution Act 1974 applied only to noise amounting to a common law nuisance, whether private or public. ('A nuisance coming within the meaning of the Public Health Act 1936 must be either a private or public nuisance as understood by common law.'[28]) During the final reading of the Environmental Protection Bill, the Government saw the inclusion of an 'injury to health' limb as an important extension to the law of noise nuisance.[29] In practice it is hard to prove that a noise nuisance is prejudicial to health and this limb of the EPA 1990 is rarely applicable.

Links to private nuisance

6.27 Most instances of statutory noise nuisance will fall under the common law nuisance limb as a form of private nuisance.[30] The definition of private nuisance

---

[25] EPA 1990, s 79(7).   [26] ibid.   [27] See Chapter 3.
[28] *National Coal Board v Neath BC* (sometimes cited as *National Coal Board v Thorne*) [1976] 2 All ER 478, per Watkins J at 482.
[29] *Hansard*, 6th Series, Vol 178, 31 October 1990, col 1023. Unfortunately, Parliament did not see fit to provide a statutory definition of what might comprise injury to health.
[30] *Murdoch v Glacier Metal Company Ltd* [1998] Env LR 732.

means that the noise has to be emitted from the property of another and substantially interfere with the victim's enjoyment of his property. Besides residential occupiers, this includes business or other non-residential occupiers. In the tort of private nuisance, 'enjoy' refers to the exercise and use of the right to occupy land and having the full benefit of that right rather than deriving pleasure from it.[31]

Private nuisance is thus a tort against property and its scope is very wide. The wrong is different in statutory nuisance and amounts to the right of a wider category of individuals not to suffer significant personal discomfort arising from any of the nuisances set down in section 79 of the EPA 1990.[32] Accordingly, the noise victim need not be the owner or somebody having exclusive possession of the property and could be any person sufficiently affected by the noise. **6.28**

Links to public nuisance
A statutory nuisance may also be a public nuisance. In this situation it is necessary to prove that the noise materially affected the comfort and quality of life of a 'class' of the public.[33] 'Class' is not precisely defined, but it implies that a substantial number or a section of the public are being affected by the nuisance, even if they do not all suffer to the same degree.[34] When the inhabitants of three chambers in Clifford's Inn in *R v Lloyd*[35] complained of noise caused by a tradesman, it was held that an indictment will not lie for a nuisance suffered by only a few inhabitants; if there was a nuisance it could only be a private nuisance. **6.29**

Noise and prejudice to health
Most statutory noise nuisances consist of a form of private nuisance, although particularly serious ones may be public nuisances. Does this mean that the 'prejudicial to health' limb in section 79(1)(g) is redundant? The legal standard required to prove prejudice to health is objective: the court will not be concerned about the different ways in which individuals experience noise. International organizations see the issues more broadly and the World Health Organization has considered risks to health in individualist and subjective terms.[36] **6.30**

There is no guidance in the EPA 1990 or from court decisions about how serious injury to health needs to be in order to fall within the statutory definition. However, there is an accumulating body of scientific literature concerned with the effects of persistent noise on health. Particularly when combined with other sources of stress, such as work pressures or high population densities, there is **6.31**

---

[31] *Kenny v Preen* [1963] 1 QB 499, at 511.
[32] *Salford CC v McNally* [1976] AC 379, per Lord Wilberforce at 389.
[33] *A-G v PYA Quarries Ltd* (n 12 above). [34] *R v Madden* [1975] 3 All ER 155.
[35] (1802) 4 Esp 200.
[36] Thus the World Health Organization uses the *Shorter Oxford English Dictionary*'s definition of health as 'a state of complete physical, mental and social well-being and not merely the absence of disease or infirmity'.

scientific evidence that noise can damage an individual's health by, for example, interfering with sleep and causing cardiovascular disorders.[37] As with most factors which amount to a health risk, the causal chain is not simple: whether it is the noise which causes the injury will be a matter for expert evidence and will ultimately be an issue for the court to decide.[38]

Legal requirements and the role of enforcement officers

6.32 The provisions in the EPA 1990 concerning noise nuisance are not intended to provide a comprehensive regime to control noise pollution, and they would be wholly inadequate to perform such a task. Neither do they play an active part in improving the general noise climate in which people live and work. The extent of interference in personal comfort or the quality of life for the victims of noise are questions of fact for the court to decide. The standard is a high one; the approach needed is therefore robust[39] and enforcement action by the local authorities will often be challengeable.

6.33 The local authority has to form an opinion—that is, make a discretionary decision—about whether a matter or complaint amounts to a nuisance or is prejudicial to health before serving a notice under section 80 of the EPA. In practice, councils will rely on the professional opinions of environmental health officers in coming to such decisions. The scope for challenging the opinions of environmental health officers as to noise nuisance is considerable. Practitioners will need to consider the sufficiency and quality of evidence particularly carefully, both that supporting the officer's opinion in a particular case and that of any lay witnesses to the nuisance. Consideration will also need to be given to the question of whether to obtain expert evidence on noise levels and on abatement measures that may be required.[40]

6.34 Making a decision that a complaint amounts to a statutory nuisance will often mean that a number of factors need to be weighed up. Frequently, issues are not clear cut, so care and professionalism are needed if decisions are to be made properly and fairly. The relevant factors include:

- the level and type of noise,
- its duration;
- the time of day or night when the noise occurs;
- whether any aggravating characteristics are present;
- what measures could reduce or modify the noise;

---

[37] Pelmear (n 14 above), pp 32–7.
[38] Workplace noise is covered by enforcement of the Health and Safety at Work Act 1974 and regulations made thereunder.
[39] R A Buckley, *The Law of Nuisance* (2nd edn, Butterworths, 1996), p 23.
[40] See further paras 18.09–18.15.

- the characteristics of the neighbourhood where the noise occurs;
- the number of persons affected; and
- whether best practicable means have been used to control noise emanating from commercial, industrial or business premises.[41]

The local authority must take an objective view of the situation and not be over-influenced by the persuasiveness either of noise producers or their victims.

6.35 The approach adopted by a local authority to control noise problems should include advice and persuasion rather than proceeding overzealously along a road leading to prosecution. Balancing this, however, is a statutory duty to serve an abatement notice under section 80 of the EPA 1990 once the point has been reached that the local authority is satisfied that a nuisance exists. There is no legal duty to consult with noise producers, though there may be good practical reasons to do so. All this requires a great deal of professionalism, knowledge and time. Under-enforcement fails to protect the public and produces the risk that noise victims will complain to the local authority ombudsman; over-enforcement may result in damage to the local economy or the risk of losing appeals in the magistrates' courts.

Scope of noise nuisance

6.36 The scope of noise nuisance within Part III of the EPA 1990 is broad. The principal areas of complaints to local authorities comprise:

- neighbourhood and domestic noise;
- entertainment noise;
- noise emitted from industrial, commercial and business premises;
- noise in the street; and
- transportation noise.

These heads will be considered separately since different issues arise according to the context of the noise.

6.37 There is no universally accepted system of classification for noise. The Noise Advisory Council attempted to provide one in 1972, though its classification is flawed since it did not distinguish between domestic and entertainment noise.[42] There is nothing in the EPA 1990 which distinguishes the above areas in the sense that different types of noise nuisance are required to be treated differently by enforcement authorities. Indeed, such an approach would be contrary to the

---

[41] The availability of a defence of best practicable means may not mean that a statutory nuisance does not exist; see para 15.05.
[42] 'Neighbourhood noise' was defined in the Noise Advisory Council's report as all noise except that arising from road traffic, aircraft and industrial noise affecting the workforce; see *Neighbourhood Noise* (Noise Advisory Council, 1972), paras 54 and 55.

The defence of best practicable means

6.38 When deciding whether a noise problem amounts to a statutory nuisance, the local authority will need to consider as a part of that decision whether reasonable steps have been taken to mitigate it. For certain types of noise, the local authority needs to consider whether best practicable means have been used. This is a statutory defence, which is limited in section 80(5) of the EPA 1990 to noise emitted from industrial, commercial and business premises.[43] It includes noise from pubs and clubs since this would be emitted from commercial premises. Clearly, it would not be relevant to domestic noise, and probably not to 'pay parties'.

6.39 Whether best practicable means have been used needs to be considered at the stage when a local authority is contemplating serving an abatement notice, because this is relevant to the reasonableness of that decision. One of the grounds for appealing a notice is that best practicable means have been used.[44] This is a delicate area since an element of consultation may be required before the local authority can satisfy itself whether best practicable means have been used to mitigate the nuisance, or whether any further steps are required to reduce it. There is no requirement in the EPA 1990 or in any regulations to consult in statutory nuisance cases. Indeed, the Court of Appeal has warned that if local authorities choose to consult with potential notice-recipients they risk creating a legitimate expectation that such consultation will be comprehensive.[45] Councils who wish to avoid raising such an expectation should limit their requirements for information about best practicable means and make it clear that they are not engaging in a consultation exercise.

Neighbourhood and domestic noise

6.40 As mentioned above, neighbourhood noise comprises a large and growing body of complaints to local authorities.[46] These include complaints triggered by the playing of amplified music and musical instruments, noisy parties, DIY and car repairs, and barking dogs. The volume, quality of sound, the times, frequency and duration of the noise in dispute are all highly relevant to the question of establishing nuisance.

6.41 Neighbourhood noise may involve a large number of residents—whether as offenders or victims. Particular problems arise in residential areas with high population densities, particularly where the standard of noise insulation between

---

[43] See further paras 6.82–6.84 and 15.02–15.28.
[44] Statutory Nuisance (Appeals) Regulations 1995, SI 1995/2644, reg 2(2)(e).
[45] *R v Falmouth and Truro PHA, ex p South-West Water Ltd* [2000] 3 All ER 306.
[46] C Penn, *Noise Control: The Law and its Enforcement* (2nd edn, Shaw & Sons, 1995), p 73.

properties is inadequate. Inadequate sound insulation may make noise problems intolerable or mean that everyday sounds of ordinary living cause considerable annoyance and nuisance. This will often be the case with older flats and house conversions in both the private and social housing sectors. Close proximity of residents with very different social, class, cultural or ethnic backgrounds may exacerbate the problem and the perceptions which people have of it. Sometimes great conflict and hostility between neighbours is generated. Sociological factors play a very important part in determining how the problem is interpreted and defined. Supposedly, individuals expect to live in a quieter and more privatized environment nowadays and are less tolerant about other people's noise than was the case 20 or 30 years ago.[47]

Establishing liability in statutory noise nuisance
The legal requirements for establishing liability in statutory nuisance are objective. The threshold is a high one: either substantial personal discomfort or a health effect must be proved. The standard cannot be defined precisely and much will depend on the view taken by the bench of the seriousness of the harm. **6.42**

Statutory nuisance cases differ from those brought in private nuisance because it is the opinion of the local authority as set down in the abatement notice which defines the boundary of the nuisance. Crucial in establishing the reasonableness of that opinion is the quality of the evidence justifying service of the abatement notice. Evidence that will assist the court includes victims' noise diaries and noise monitoring, which should be supervised by competent persons employed by the local authority.[48] A contemporaneous note made by officers of the extent and type of noise will also be relevant.[49] **6.43**

A prosecution is founded upon a breach of the notice requirements rather than for directly causing a statutory nuisance. This sometimes produces strange results. In *Wellingborough BC v Gordon*[50] a noise abatement notice had been in force for several years and no complaints had been received by the local authority during this time. The person subject to the notice was then prosecuted for a breach after holding a noisy party. No neighbours had complained about the party, the noise was not prejudicial to health and the only evidence for a breach was that of two passing policemen who had witnessed the noise. On appeal to the Divisional Court, the conviction was upheld, albeit with judicial criticism, on the ground that the notice had been breached even though no nuisance was being caused. **6.44**

---

[47] See *Report of the Noise Review Working Party* (Department of the Environment Building Research Establishment, 1990); Penn (n 46 above); and McManus (n 17 above).
[48] Noise monitoring must not be undertaken where it infringes the family and privacy rights of those living in the property in question. See further paras 11.33–11.41.
[49] See paras 18.43–18.45.
[50] [1993] Env LR 218.

The 'give and take' principle

6.45 Noise cases are often about a neighbour's use of land causing personal discomfort to the victim and interfering with his enjoyment of property. Such cases—as with all forms of nuisance—are subject to the concept of 'reasonable user' or the principle of give and take.[51] This principle requires the person causing the alleged nuisance to consider not whether his own use of the land is reasonable but the effect this use has on his neighbour. The point was well made with regard to private nuisance by Lord Millett in *Southwark LBC v Tanner and others; Baxter v Camden LBC (No 2)*:

> It is not enough for a landowner to act reasonably in his own interest. He must also be considerate of the interest of his neighbour. The governing principle is good neighbourliness, and this involves reciprocity. A landowner must show the same consideration for his neighbour as he would expect his neighbour to show for him.[52]

The way property is used: 'normal use'

6.46 Does this mean that a statutory nuisance is established if the everyday noise of a resident interferes with his neighbour's use and enjoyment of property? Poor sound insulation between adjoining properties often triggers complaints. Whether or not this is a factor, neighbours often do cause annoyance to each other. Moreover, toleration of noise is variable and often there is an inequality between the maker and victim of the noise; for example, a disc jockey working in a night club is unlikely to perceive noise in the same way as his elderly, housebound neighbour.

6.47 Normal, everyday noise will not constitute a common law nuisance; therefore (absent injury to health) there will be no statutory nuisance. In other words it is not reasonable to expect neighbours to behave especially quietly because the sound insulation between their properties is poor. Lord Hoffmann in *Baxter v Camden LBC (No 2)*[53] argued that:

> I do not think that the normal use of a residential flat can possibly be a nuisance to the neighbours. If it were, we would have the absurd position that each, behaving normally and reasonably, was a nuisance to the other.

6.48 The key variable is 'normal use', so nuisance would require some additional, unreasonable aspect, such as placing domestic appliances against an adjoining wall unnecessarily and using such equipment during sleeping hours, or playing musical instruments loudly for long periods. The concept of 'normal use' does not address the issue that what is normal and everyday for one person may not be for another because of the differing lifestyles of neighbours.

---

[51] *Bamford v Turnley* (1860) 3 B&S 66; *Cambridge Water Company Ltd v Eastern Counties Leather plc* [1994] 2 AC 264; *Hunter and Others v Canary Wharf Ltd and London Docklands Development Corporation* [1997] AC 655.   [52] [2001] 1 AC 1, at 20.
[53] ibid, at 15.

One-off events
Complaints are frequently made about one-off events, such as noisy parties,[54] **6.49**
especially when these occur late at night. Many local authorities in urban areas
employ 'party patrols' in order to deal more effectively with such complaints.[55]
The use of statutory nuisance powers (and those available under the Noise Act
1996) to deal with one-off nuisances marks a difference compared with civil
private nuisance claims, which are usually concerned with ongoing problems.

Harassment
Neighbourhood and domestic noise may be frequent and repetitive, victimize a **6.50**
large number of people, and noise episodes may last for long periods. Sometimes
the noise is deliberate and used in order to intimidate or harass people. The police
should be involved where there is evidence of harassment, since it may be more
appropriate for them to investigate using powers available to them under the
Protection from Harassment Act 1997.[56] Additionally, local authorities have
powers under the Housing Act 1996 to deal with persistent and serious noise
producers residing in social housing.[57]

Noise Act 1996

A local authority in England and Wales (but not in Scotland) has adoptive powers **6.51**
under the Noise Act 1996 to regulate night-time domestic noise, that is noise
occurring between 11pm and 7am. The intention is for these powers to comple-
ment those available in the EPA to deal with certain kinds of neighbourhood noise
problems. The relevant powers under the 1996 Act can only come into effect
three months after the council in whose area the noise occurs has passed a resolution.

The Act utilizes a fixed standard of noise rather than being based on the concept **6.52**
of nuisance. These powers are rarely used because very few local authorities have
adopted them or believe them to be necessary. Further, enforcement officers may
have become overly attached to the nuisance paradigm.[58] This attachment is not
necessarily a bad thing since the traditional nuisance approach requires an objective assessment of whether a complaint constitutes a nuisance. For most
enforcers, reliance on a fixed and rigid standard is difficult to justify except when
the noise nuisance is very obvious.

---

[54] In *East Northamptonshire DC v Fossett* [1994] Env LR 388 the local authority brought a successful prosecution for holding a one-off 'rave party'.
[55] In 1999, 140 local authorities reported they operated an out-of-hours noise complaints service; *Annual Report* (Chartered Institute of Environmental Health, 2000).
[56] See further paras 17.70–17.72.   [57] See further paras 17.73–17.74.
[58] McManus (n 17 above), pp 282–5.

Seizure of equipment

6.53 Section 10 of the Noise Act 1996 applies to all local authorities in England and Wales;[59] it comes into effect generally and does not require a council resolution. It provides additional powers to those available in Part III of the EPA 1990 for enforcement officers to enter dwellings and to seize equipment causing noise. Section 10(2) provides that an officer, or authorized person:

> may enter the dwelling from which the noise . . . is being, or has been, emitted and may seize and remove any equipment which it appears to him is being, or has been, used in the emission of the noise.

6.54 Having the power to seize equipment after the noise has stopped is important, since officers can deal effectively when faced with situations of transient compliance followed by further usage of the offending equipment.

6.55 The power to seize equipment under section 10 of the Noise Act 1996 is confined to dwellings and does not require a local authority to form an opinion that the matter complained of is a statutory nuisance, only that the level of noise exceeds the 'permitted level'.[60] However, use of this power in the absence of nuisance would probably constitute an abuse of power by the local authority. Use of this power is triggered by the local authority issuing a warning notice following a complaint from a neighbour. The purpose of the provision is to provide a simple, quick and effective remedy to deal with neighbours making an excessive amount of noise, such as the playing of amplified music.

The Noise Act 1996 and the EPA 1990

6.56 The Noise Act 1996 makes clear that its seizure provisions also apply to abating noise nuisance under the EPA 1990. Section 10(7) of the Noise Act 1996 states that the local authority has the power under section 81(3) of the EPA 1990 to seize noise-making equipment from premises. 'Premises' is obviously a wider term than 'dwelling', so this provision also applies to seizing equipment from a commercial venue. It requires that an abatement notice has been served under section 80 of the EPA 1990 and that it has not been complied with. Use of section 81(3) of the EPA 1990 is not conditional on any prosecution for breach of the notice requirements.

6.57 From an enforcer's point of view, the main advantage of using the Noise Act 1996 rather than the EPA 1990 to seize equipment is that there is no requirement for an abatement notice to be in place. Additionally, there is no provision for appeals in the Noise Act 1996, so the only challenge to the local authority's decision is by

---

[59] The Act applies in modified form to Northern Ireland but not to Scotland.

[60] Section 5 of the Act gives the Secretary of State the power to determine the maximum level of permitted noise in the form of written directions. These are determined by Circular 8/97 and 41/97 for Wales. Currently, the level set is 35 dB above the background level.

way of judicial review. Arguably, however, this makes this use of the Noise Act 1996 inconsistent with the Human Rights Act 1998.[61]

The Noise Act 1996 gives a power to retain any equipment for 28 days beginning with the date of the seizure,[62] or until the conclusion of proceedings for a 'noise offence'.[63] A noise offence includes a breach of section 80(4) of the EPA as well as of section 4 of the Noise Act 1996. **6.58**

Procedure for seizing equipment under the Noise Act 1996
The local authority's powers under section 10 are exercisable after a warning notice has been served. The requirements for serving a warning notice are: **6.59**

(1) that the noise is emitted from the offending dwelling at night-time;
(2) that it exceeds, or may exceed, the permitted level as measured from the complainant's dwelling;
(3) that a warning has been given to the person responsible for the noise that he may be guilty of an offence.[64]

What constitutes an offence in this last requirement is not clear when the purpose of issuing the warning notice is to seize equipment where the local authority has not adopted sections 2 to 9 of the Noise Act 1996. An offence can only be committed where the council has passed a resolution to adopt the Noise Act 1996, since breach of the warning notice is only an offence under section 4, one of the adoptive sections. It follows that when a warning notice is served under the Noise Act 1996 to seize equipment in a situation where no EPA 1990 abatement notice is in force, and, secondly, where the council has not made a resolution to adopt the Noise Act 1996, there can be no offence for breaching the warning notice. **6.60**

Other requirements for using the Noise Act 1996
The Noise Act 1996 is limited to noise emitted from the 'offending dwelling' which has exceeded the 'permitted level'. 'Dwelling' includes any garden, yard, outhouse or other appurtenance.[65] 'Appurtenance' includes a garden or yard, but does not extend outside the curtilage.[66] **6.61**

The location for taking noise measurements must be from within the complainant's dwelling.[67] Refusal to allow seizure of the equipment leaves the noise offender open to a charge of obstruction.[68] Where refusal is anticipated or has already occurred, the local authority may apply for a warrant to a magistrate to enter the premises, if necessary by force.[69] **6.62**

---

[61] See further Chapter 11.
[62] Noise Act 1996, s 10, Sch, para 2(1)(a).
[63] ibid, Sch, para 1(a).
[64] ibid, s 3.
[65] ibid, s 11(2)(b).
[66] *Lister v Pickford* (1865) 34 Beav 576.
[67] Noise Act 1996, s 10(1)(b).
[68] ibid, s 10(8).
[69] ibid, s 10(4).

Audible intruder alarms

6.63 Section 9 of the Noise and Statutory Nuisance Act 1993 gives local authorities adoptive powers to regulate the installation and operation of audible intruder alarms in premises. The operation of such alarms requires compliance with prescribed standards, notification to the police of the names, addresses and telephone numbers of the current keyholders, and informing the local authority of the address of the police station to which such notification has been given.[70]

6.64 Where an alarm has been sounding for more than an hour and is causing annoyance to persons working or living in the vicinity, an authorized officer of the council can enter the premises and turn off the alarm.[71] Where, additionally, the authorized officer has taken steps to obtain the assistance of keyholders and needs to use force to enter the premises, he may obtain a warrant from a magistrate to enter the premises and turn off the alarm. When entering with a warrant he must be accompanied by a police constable.[72]

Entertainment noise

6.65 Entertainment noise covers a wide range of situations. Noise problems, which may be ongoing and regularly occurring, often arise from social activities in permanent premises such as pubs and clubs. Live events, such as music or sporting activities, also trigger noise complaints. Such events may be one-off, or take place in permanent premises at more or less regular intervals. Although permanent premises where entertainment is provided may have been designed to contain sound efficiently this will not always be the case, particularly where older buildings have been converted to new uses. One-off events, particularly those taking place in the open air, often produce serious noise problems where residential property is located nearby. Entertainment noise from one-off events or events which occur regularly may be dealt with under the statutory nuisance provisions.

Links between statutory nuisance, planning and licensing systems

6.66 Separate enforcement regimes underpin planning consent, licensing and statutory nuisance controls. However, not all noise events are covered by planning conditions and licensing regulations. Entertainment noise is regulated by various forms of licensing by local authorities; there may also be planning conditions to restrict noise-producing activities.

6.67 Licensing is targeted to specific types of activity or premises and licensing and planning controls are primarily directed towards the permission to undertake the activity causing the noise rather than with regulating the noise itself. There is,

---

[70] Noise and Statutory Nuisance Act 1993, s 9, Sch 3, para 5(1). [71] ibid, para 6.
[72] ibid, para 7.

therefore, less of an overlap with statutory nuisance than might at first appear. Further, the licensing and planning systems do not cover all eventualities and statutory nuisance is relevant to gaps in provision.

Government advice to planning authorities contained in *Planning Policy Guidance Note 24: Planning and Noise* (PPG 24)[73] is principally intended to ensure that new, noise-sensitive development is not incompatible with existing activities. The guidance notes also provide indicators on levels of noise that might be permitted with new development and with measures which might be taken at source to restrict noise and to protect properties from external noise sources. Planning authorities are also advised to consider the impact of future levels of noise from new development.[74]

6.68

Where noise limits have been specified in a planning consent this does not provide immunity in respect of a statutory nuisance prosecution. A planning authority is entitled to specify noise limits and PPG 24 provides guidance on levels.[75] Neither a planning consent[76] nor a waste management licence[77] can be defences against a statutory nuisance prosecution.[78] But planning permission may change the character of a neighbourhood so that what would have been a nuisance before the grant of permission is no longer so afterwards. In *Gillingham BC v Medway Dock Co Ltd*[79] road traffic levels increased substantially as a result of planning permission being given for a change of use from a naval base to a commercial port. The court found that the increases in noise levels due to the major change of use did not constitute a public nuisance. However, a major change of use is required before a court should decide against a nuisance and the general rule remains that planning consent does not provide a defence to nuisance.[80]

6.69

Entertainment noise and statutory nuisance

Noise from pubs and clubs and one-off events will often be dealt with under the noise nuisance provisions in the EPA 1990. These are applicable to events where the noise is excessively loud and/or of long duration, or where there is some aggravating or irritating quality to the noise. Such cases often include some kind of failure of control by the person responsible for the noise. This may be the result of incompetence, ignorance, a lack of genuine concern regarding the effects of the noise on neighbours, or because maximizing profits excludes other considerations.

6.70

---

[73] Issued by the Department of the Environment in September 1994.   [74] ibid, para 12.
[75] In *R v Kennet DC, ex p Somerfield* [1999] JPL 361 the court accepted that the planning authority was entitled to specify noise limits of 41dB as a condition for planning consent.
[76] *Wheeler v Saunders* [1996] Ch 19.   [77] *Blackburn v ARC Ltd* [1998] Env LR 469.
[78] In contrast to noise on construction sites, where, under the EPA 1990, s 80(9), if a local authority serves a notice under the Control of Pollution Act 1974, s 60, or gives prior consent under section 61, this provides a defence to proceedings under the EPA 1990, s 80.
[79] [1993] QB 343.   [80] See further paras 17.61–17.67.

6.71 A local authority is empowered to seize equipment causing the noise from commercial premises, whether or not prosecution proceedings are contemplated or have commenced.[81] The basis for doing so is lack of compliance with an abatement notice, since section 81(3) of the EPA 1990 empowers the authority to do whatever may be necessary in the execution of an abatement notice. Powers of seizure under section 81(3) only come into effect once an abatement notice has been served on the person responsible for the nuisance and are restricted to noise emitted from premises.[82]

6.72 In appropriate cases, including where the abatement notice procedure is likely to be ineffective, a local authority may apply to the High Court for an injunction.[83]

Serious noise problems

6.73 As mentioned above, it seems that the incidence of serious noise disturbances is on the increase. The enforcement regime characterized by serving abatement notices and prosecuting breaches is slow and not always effective. It is for this reason that measures which rely on simple noise levels for enforcement—such as the Noise Act 1996—rather than on the law of nuisance have proved popular with legislators. However, these measures have been limited in scope and effectiveness.[84]

6.74 An issue for local authorities with serious noise problems in their areas is the risk of personal injury to enforcement officers. Noise offenders may be extremely drunk, may also be under the influence of drugs, and may possess various antisocial characteristics and behavioural disorders which render them dangerous to others and especially to enforcement officers. A large number of noisy, intoxicated individuals acting as a group can be particularly dangerous and may prevent enforcement officers from carrying out their responsibilities, even when accompanied by police officers. Throughout the UK, public order offences, as well as nuisances, accompany behaviour in and around pubs and clubs. Disturbances may spill over outside these premises, rendering parts of many towns and city centres noisy and dangerous places in the evenings. According to recent Home Office research, the police play a diminishing role in controlling such disorder, choosing to adopt a more 'low-profile' approach.[85]

---

[81] Noise Act 1996, s 10(7).

[82] A local authority also has powers of seizure under Noise Act 1996, s 10, in respect of noise emitted from a dwelling; see further para 6.53. [83] EPA 1990, s 81(5); see paras 17.11–17.21.

[84] See para 6.51.

[85] This has left the field open to the largely unregulated private security industry to maintain public order, both inside and outside premises and on the public highway. Business practices of the private security industry are sometimes dubious and include employing untrained and unaccountable 'bouncers', some of whom have serious criminal records; see Dick Hobbs and Steve Hall, *Bouncers: The Art and Economics of Intimidation* (ESRC Research Programme on Violence, University of Durham, 2000).

Drafting noise abatement notices under the EPA 1990

The local authority has a discretion about which type of notice to serve: a specific **6.75** works notice or a simple abatement notice.[86] If it chooses to specify works, they must be sufficiently specified so as to make it clear precisely what the recipient must do to conform to the requirements.[87] Alternatively, a local authority can serve a simple notice without specifying works, leaving it up to the recipient to decide how to fulfil the requirements, and can decide not to suspend such a notice pending an appeal.[88] Stipulating noise limits in an abatement notice and specifying how monitoring should be undertaken do not constitute 'steps' under section 80(1) of the EPA 1990.[89] Therefore, a simple notice served in the section 80(1)(a) form which specifies noise limits in the body of the notice, will be sufficient.

The width of a local authority's discretion[90] means that there is little scope to **6.76** appeal on the grounds that the authority should have served a specific works form of notice.[91] This applies particularly in entertainment noise cases where it will always be possible to stop causing the nuisance by turning down the noise source or by not holding the event. In the notice served by the local authority in *SFI Group plc (formerly Surrey Free Inns plc) v Gosport BC* it was stated that the recipient was required 'to cease the playing of amplified music at levels which cause a nuisance at neighbouring premises'.[92] The choice of how to comply with the notice was left up to the noise producer: it could cease playing the music, keep the volume down, or undertake works to prevent the noise from leaving the premises. The validity of the notice was upheld by the Court of Appeal.

Subsequent cases have confirmed that service of simple notices in the section **6.77** 80(1)(a) EPA 1990 form—specifying noise limits but leaving the choice of how to keep within those limits to the recipient of the notice—is sufficient. In *R v Crown Court at Canterbury, ex p Howson-Ball*[93] a notice required that no noise nuisance be caused from amplified, live or recorded musical entertainment, or other amplifying equipment, to any adjoining or neighbouring residential occupier. The second part of the notice specified a limitation of noise levels at a two-metre distance from any loudspeaker of 75dB LAeq (1 minute). This form of the abatement notice was approved by the court.

---

[86] EPA 1990, s 80(1), stipulates that the abatement notice should include 'all or any of the following requirements—(a) requiring the abatement of the nuisance or prohibiting or restricting its occurrence or recurrence; (b) requiring the execution of such works, and the taking of such other steps, as may be necessary for any of those purposes . . .'
[87] *Sterling Homes (Midlands) Ltd v Birmingham CC* [1996] Env LR 121. For abatement notices generally, see Chapter 12. [88] *Cambridge CC v Douglas* [2001] Env LR 41.
[89] *Sevenoaks DC v Brands Hatch Leisure Group Ltd* [2001] Env LR 86.
[90] See further paras 12.39–12.56. [91] *Budd v Colchester BC* [1999] Env LR 739.
[92] [1999] Env LR 750, per Stuart-Smith LJ at 753. [93] [2001] Env LR 36.

6.78 It is up to the person running the event or in control of the premises to pay for any preventative measures needed to avoid committing a statutory nuisance. The choice of measures will be entirely up to him, unless the local authority chooses to specify any works required. The local authority is not under a duty to consult with the notice-recipient about how the nuisance might be avoided.[94] If, in relation to a specific works notice, alternative, or less expensive, ways to deal with the problem are proposed, the local authority will be under a duty to consider them. Where these would be sufficient to avoid a statutory nuisance from occurring or recurring then it would be unreasonable—and therefore a ground for appeal—for the local authority to insist on more expensive measures being taken.[95]

Noise emitted from industrial, commercial and business premises

6.79 The fact that a locality is a noisy one or of an industrial character does not in itself constitute a defence to nuisance. In *Rushmer v Polsue and Alfieri Ltd* Cozens-Hardy LJ said:

> It does not follow that because I live, say in the manufacturing part of Sheffield I cannot complain if a steam-hammer is introduced next door, and so worked as to render sleep at night almost impossible, although previously to its introduction my house was a reasonably comfortable abode, having regard to the local standard; and it would be no answer to say that the steam-hammer is of the most approved pattern and is reasonably worked.[96]

6.80 Noise produced by industrial and manufacturing processes or by using equipment associated with such activities is a complicated area of control. Particularly problematic are cases involving low-frequency noise, where the technical solutions may be elusive and the cost of abatement considerable. One might expect such noise problems to be dealt with at source, but this does not always solve the problem. Consequently, enforcement using Part III of the EPA 1990 is important and becomes relevant when the noise affects residents or other neighbours.

6.81 Where the noise affects a large number of people then it may be a public nuisance.[97] Exposure of a workforce—and other individuals having sufficient proximity to the site—to noise ('occupational noise') is regulated by the Health and Safety at Work Act 1974 and regulations made under that Act.

The defence of best practicable means in noise cases[98]

6.82 Statutory noise nuisances are subject to the defence of best practicable means, which is available in relation to noise emitted from industrial, commercial and

---

[94] *R v Falmouth and Truro PHA, ex p South-West Water Ltd* (n 45 above).
[95] For appeals against notices, see Chapter 13.   [96] [1906] 1 Ch 234, at 250.
[97] See further paras 17.22–17.25.
[98] Generally, for best practicable means defences, see Chapter 15.

business premises.[99] It can be raised at two stages: when appealing against an abatement notice or as a defence in a prosecution. In either case, it will be up to the noise producer to prove, to a civil standard, that best practicable means have been used to prevent or to counteract the effects of the nuisance.

Local authorities will wish to consider whether best practicable means have been used before serving an abatement notice. This may require expert advice, in which case the authority will need to consider whether to accept expert advice obtained from the noise producer or to instruct its own, independent expert. Such advice may be needed to decide whether a nuisance has been caused, and, if so, to determine the form, if any, of notice the authority should serve on the noise producer. **6.83**

A particular difficulty arises when the noise producer has taken all reasonable steps to reduce the level of noise, but the problem remains and still constitutes a nuisance in the eyes of the local authority. The extent of the nuisance may have been diminished by steps taken by the noise producer and the noise may only marginally constitute a nuisance. This situation, though not uncommon, seems to be rarely litigated, probably because companies and local authorities usually cooperate to find a solution which avoids expensive and time-consuming litigation. The opinion of the local authority as to whether there is, or continues to be, a nuisance is likely to be to some extent elastic and this may have implications for the human rights of persons affected by the noise.[100] **6.84**

Standard of abatement
Local authorities need to avoid interpreting their duty under Part III of the EPA 1990 as a way of obliging businesses to adopt too high a standard of abatement. They have no powers to require the most expensive, best available, or 'state of the art' technology to reduce noise problems to a minimum.[101] The requirement is that enough is done to reduce the problem to below the nuisance threshold: a somewhat elastic concept. **6.85**

The defence of best practicable means is available to protect commercial interests; sometimes this results in allowing a nuisance to continue. The origins of the defence were to prevent such interference in the activities of the manufacturing and business classes as would have harmful economic consequences.[102] Some of this philosophy still attaches. *Manley v New Forest DC*[103] illustrates this point. This case concerned the commercial keeper of a pack of Siberian huskies, who **6.86**

---

[99] EPA 1990, s 80(7).
[100] See further Chapter 11.
[101] *Welton v North Cornwall DC* [1997] 1 WLR 570.
[102] eg, in respect of smoke nuisances, the Sanitary Act 1866, s 3, stated that 'the Justices may hold that no Nuisance is created . . . if they are satisfied that such Fireplace or Furnace is constructed in such Manner as to consume as far as practicable, having regard to the Nature of the Manufacture or Trade, all Smoke arising therefrom, and that such Fireplace or Furnace has been carefully attended to by the Person having the Charge thereof.'
[103] [2000] EHLR 113.

had a licence going back many years allowing the dogs to be kennelled in a mixed residential and commercial area. The problem arose from the howling of the pack. The Divisional Court accepted the findings of the Crown Court (on appeal from the magistrates' decision) that measures to abate the noise, such as glazing the kennels, would not be a practicable solution. However, it rejected the judge's finding that best practicable means requirements would be satisfied if the kennels were relocated elsewhere—this being considered too onerous a requirement to impose upon a legitimate business. The Divisional Court accepted that the nuisance would continue but that it was not actionable as a statutory nuisance.[104] The decision in *Manley* confirms that great care is needed before serving a notice in noise cases where the defence of best practicable means is available.

Specific works notices and industrial noise

6.87 Low-frequency noise from generators, air-conditioning plant or from other industrial machinery sometimes produces intrusive, low-frequency noise which is very difficult to reduce to below a level causing nuisance. Very often, companies will already have taken ameliorative measures, but the nuisance remains. Should a local authority serve a notice in this situation and, if so, in what form?

6.88 It is doubtful whether an actionable statutory nuisance can be said to exist where the noise producer has taken all reasonable steps to reduce the noise. This is an area of difficulty because the EPA 1990 does not require a local authority to consider best practicable means before service of the notice or in deciding whether something is a statutory nuisance. Best practicable means is a statutory defence, and it is for the court to decide whether it has been made out. Practitioners should note that the best practicable means requirements under the Act include 'counteracting the effects' of the noise, so full abatement is not the test.[105]

6.89 Although currently there is no authority on the point, it would be inadvisable for a local authority to decide in a low-frequency noise case that a statutory nuisance existed and then to serve a simple abatement notice where it was unable to specify what further steps were required to abate the nuisance. Despite having a discretion to serve a notice in the simple form, it could form the basis of an appeal on the grounds that it was unreasonable.[106]

---

[104] This judgment also implies that the requirements needed to prove a statutory nuisance may be higher than for common law nuisance, whether private or public. In the words of Newman J: 'it is . . . important to remember the distinctive legal actions or processes available in connection with the law of nuisance. There are distinctive aspects of the law of nuisance: private nuisance, public nuisance and now, as one sees in this Act, statutory nuisance. Proof of private or public nuisance will generally lead to the cessation of the nuisance, but the provisions of the 1990 Act are penal and they give rise to criminal proceedings in the event that a notice is not complied with. They affect the way in which a permitted lawful business is being carried on. Parliament plainly thought it right to give the operator of a business the benefit of the principle of "best practicable means", otherwise, in my judgment, it would be obvious that great hardship could be caused to businesses . . .'   [105] EPA 1990, s80(7).
[106] See further paras 13.27–13.40.

Local authorities should consider very carefully whether to specify the works **6.90** required to be carried out. This may mean that councils have to pay for expert advice early on to enable them to specify precisely what is required to be undertaken by the noise producer. Service of a simple notice which is unspecific risks losing on appeal, either on the grounds that the notice is unreasonable or that the matter complained of is not a statutory nuisance. In these specific circumstances, it is suggested that it would be difficult for a local authority to convince a bench as to the validity or reasonableness of a notice, or that a prosecution was justified, unless it could specify what measures or additional steps are required of the noise producer to reduce a noise problem to below the nuisance threshold.

Noise in the street and other public places

There are various statutory provisions applicable to noise in streets and in other **6.91** public places which are considered below.

Noise and Statutory Nuisance Act 1993
The noise provisions in the EPA 1990 were amended by section 2 of the Noise **6.92** and Statutory Nuisance Act 1993 to include certain forms of street noise. The 1993 Act inserted section 79(1)(ga) into the EPA 1990, which provides that 'noise that is prejudicial to health or a nuisance and is emitted from or caused by a vehicle, machinery or equipment in a street' is a statutory nuisance.

Section 79(6A) of the EPA 1990, as amended by the 1993 Act, excludes the **6.93** following types of noise from this provision:

(1) traffic noise;
(2) noise made by any naval, military or air force of the Crown or by a visiting force; and
(3) noise made by a political demonstration or a demonstration supporting or opposing a cause or campaign.

'Street' is defined in section 2(4)(c) of the 1993 Act to mean a highway and any **6.94** other road, footway, square or court that is for the time being open to the public.[107] An open space where members of the public regularly go to attend a market may be regarded as a 'street'.[108]

Noise in other public places may be controlled under local bye-laws, which tend **6.95** to be narrow in scope, rarely enforced and ineffective. Control of demonstrations is exercised by the police under the Public Order Act 1986, which has a wider ambit than noise, the purpose being to control the route of a demonstration and to prevent public disorder. The 1986 Act applies to any 'public place', a term which

---

[107] Section 2(c) of the 1993 Act amended EPA 1990, s 79(7), to include this definition of 'street'.
[108] *Tower Hamlets LBC v Creitzman* (1984) 148 JP 630; 83 LGR 72.

includes the highway and also any place to which the public, or a section of the public, has access (on payment or otherwise) as of right or by virtue of express or implied permission.[109] It can, therefore, include private land.

Criminal Justice and Public Order Act 1994

6.96 Quite draconian controls in respect of 'raves' are available to the police under the Criminal Justice and Public Order Act 1994.[110] They include powers:

(1) to remove persons attending or preparing for a rave (section 63);
(2) of entry and seizure (section 64);
(3) to stop persons proceeding to a rave (section 65); and
(4) to retain, charge for and forfeit sound equipment (sections 66–7).

6.97 These provisions give the police powers to control unlicensed, open-air events where serious disturbance is anticipated, including the playing of loud music during the night at a volume likely to cause serious distress to the inhabitants of the locality. Offences under the above sections of the Act are summary only.

6.98 These sections in the 1994 Act were arguably enacted in response to a moral panic rather than a real social need and the police have been sparing in their use of such draconian powers. Between 1996 (when the relevant sections came into force) and 1998, there were five convictions under section 63 and none under sections 64 to 67.[111]

Public nuisance

6.99 Before the Criminal Justice and Public Order Act 1994 created summary offences in respect of 'raves', the police could only seek an injunction and/or prosecute offenders in public nuisance.[112] An injunction in public nuisance remains available in appropriate cases such as when law enforcement using statutory powers would be ineffective. Prosecution for public nuisance, being indictable, imprisonable and without limit to the level of fines in the Crown Court, would be appropriate for very serious offences.

Control of loudspeakers in the street

6.100 Section 62 of the Control of Pollution Act 1974 prohibits the operation of loudspeakers—with some exceptions[113]—in the street between 9pm and 8am the following morning. This prohibition is for 24 hours a day where the use of loudspeakers is for advertising any entertainment, trade or business. Loudspeaker

---

[109] Public Order Act 1986, s 16.
[110] Local authorities can also control such events through the licensing laws; see further paras 6.134–6.137.
[111] Criminal Justice Unit (CCJU). (The CCJU is based in the Research, Development and Statistics (RDS) Directorate of the Home Office.)   [112] *R v Shorrock* (n 13 above).
[113] Control of Pollution Act 1974, s 62(2), cites the following exceptions: police, fire brigade and ambulance services, water and sewerage undertakers, local authorities.

systems in vehicles are exempt from these provisions, provided that they are operated so as not to give reasonable cause for annoyance to persons in the vicinity.[114] These offences are summary only.

Licences to vary these time limits can by granted by local authorities using their adoptive powers under section 8 of the Noise and Statutory Nuisance Act 1993. Consent cannot include the operation of loudspeakers used for any election or for advertising any entertainment, business or trade.[115]

6.101

Noise from construction sites

Local authorities are empowered to serve notices under section 60 of the Control of Pollution Act 1974 on persons carrying out works on construction sites. These powers are used frequently to control noise levels. The intention of the Act is for the authority and the noise producer to settle questions about noise before the works commence.[116] This provision was made in response to the failure of powers based on statutory nuisance to deal with transient forms of noise.[117] Where a section 60 notice is in force, a person who is suffering the noise nuisance is not prevented from applying to the High Court (or county court) for an injunction to restrict the works further than is allowed by that notice.[118]

6.102

Scope of works
Works falling within the scope of section 60(1) of the Control of Pollution Act 1974 are wide and comprise:

6.103

(a) the erection, construction, alteration, repair or maintenance of buildings, structures or roads;
(b) breaking up, opening or boring under any road or adjacent land in connection with the construction, inspection, maintenance or removal of works;
(c) demolition or dredging work; and
(d) any work of engineering construction.

Notices
A local authority may serve a notice[119] imposing requirements as to how the works should be carried out and may publish such a notice.[120] If the activities covered by any notice extend beyond the premises stipulated, then a fresh notice

6.104

---

[114] Control of Pollution Act 1974, s 62(2)(d).
[115] Noise and Statutory Nuisance Act 1993, s 8, Sch 2, para 1.
[116] Department of Environment Circular 2/76, para 24.
[117] Prior to the Control of Pollution Act 1974, enforcement was by statutory nuisance under the Public Health Act 1936, as amended by the Noise Abatement Act 1960, to include noise nuisance.
[118] *Lloyds Bank plc v Guardian Assurance plc and Trollope & Colls Ltd* (1986) 35 BLR 34, per Sir John Arnold P, at 41.
[119] Rules under the Local Government Act 1972, s 233, apply to service.
[120] Control of Pollution Act 1974, s 60(2).

should be served in respect of that extension. The power to serve notices is discretionary and does not depend on whether a statutory nuisance has occurred or is believed to be likely to occur or recur. Breach of a notice without 'reasonable excuse' constitutes a summary only offence, on level 5 of the standard scale.[121] Financial penalties apply for each day the offence continues.

6.105 It is usual to serve a notice on the promoter of the works before they are commenced and on the main contractor once they have begun. Service should be on the person who appears to be carrying out, or going to carry out, the works. Service should include any others who appear responsible for or who have control over works, or anyone who retains supervisory responsibilities or an element of control.[122] Thus, besides developers and main contractors, notices should also be served on any subcontractors or their agents with responsibility for works. Site agents, surveyors or architects will frequently have responsibilities which bring them within the scope of the Act, in which case they should also be served. In cases of difficulty, the contractual arrangements between operators may assist in deciding who should be served.

6.106 Since April 1998 Crown exemption no longer applies to the Control of Pollution Act 1974, so notices may now be served, for example, on the contractors of trunk roads.[123]

Scope of the notice

6.107 A local authority has a wide discretion on the scope of the notice, which may specify:

(a) the plant or machinery which may or may not be used;
(b) the hours when works can be carried out; and
(c) the level of noise which may be emitted from the premises in question.[124]

The noise levels allowed may be specified at any point on the premises during the hours when works are permitted. These levels do not have to satisfy requirements in nuisance but do have to be reasonable. The authority has a duty to consider the effects of the noise on residents or people working in the vicinity. It will also take into consideration the urgency of the works and any other relevant factors.

6.108 The notice may provide for any change in circumstances and the period within which compliance is required may also be stipulated.[125]

Injunctions

6.109 A local authority may obtain an injunction to prevent infringements of a notice. The test is for the authority to show that the unlawful operations are likely to

---

[121] Currently, a maximum of £5,000; Control of Pollution Act 1974, s 74.
[122] ibid, s 60(5). [123] ibid, s 105(3), as amended by the Environment Act 1995.
[124] Control of Pollution Act 1974, s 60(3). [125] ibid, s 60(6).

continue unless the offender is restrained by injunction. Repeated infringements of a notice, provided they were material, would suffice. The standard is not so high as to require a deliberate and flagrant flouting of the law to be proved.[126]

Use of powers
Besides being under a general duty to act reasonably, a local authority must also have regard to any code of practice issued under section 71 of the Control of Pollution Act 1974 and ensure that best practicable means are employed to minimize noise. The authority should consider before drafting a notice whether there are alternative and cheaper methods, plant or machinery available to minimize noise. These should be 'substantially as effective' as the ones being contemplated by the authority and the intended recipient of the notice is entitled to be consulted about this.[127]

6.110

Appeals
A person served with a notice may appeal to a magistrates' court within 21 days of service.[128] Grounds of appeal include that:

6.111

- the notice is not justified by section 60 of the Control of Pollution Act 1974;
- it is defective or contains some material error or informality;
- the requirements are unreasonable or excessive;
- the notice fails to have regard to best practicable means;
- the authority has unreasonably refused to accept alternative requirements;
- the authority has allowed insufficient time for compliance with the notice; and
- service of the notice should have been on persons other than or in addition to the appellant.[129]

On hearing the appeal, the court may quash the notice, vary it in favour of the appellant, or dismiss the appeal.

6.112

Consultation
In principle, it is a good idea for a local authority to consult as early as possible with the intended recipient of a notice. The local authority will be more confident that the scope of the notice is not too wide and that there are no other justified grounds for appeal if the terms can be agreed at an early stage. Where a notice is served later and without sufficient consultation, a contractor risks having to pay additional costs if planned or operating working practices need to be changed. He may then calculate that appealing the notice is worthwhile.

6.113

Consultation may not work where, for example, a contractor fails to cooperate or where a local authority is trying to impose too high a standard of control. With

6.114

---
[126] *City of London Corp v Bovis Construction Ltd* [1992] 3 All ER 697.
[127] Control of Pollution Act 1974, s 60(4).   [128] ibid, s 60(7).
[129] Control of Noise (Appeals) Regulations 1975, SI 1975/2116, reg 5(2).

some very large companies there is an inequality of bargaining power and the local authority may accept a poor standard, perhaps exposing the public to an excessive volume or duration of noise.

6.115 In all cases there is a legal requirement to consult with potential notice-recipients and to consult adequately. The authority is obliged to consider best practicable means and whether there are alternative and cheaper equivalent works to the ones they envisage specifying in the body of the notice.

Prior consent

6.116 Section 61 of the Control of Pollution Act 1974 allows a person intending to carry out works to seek the local authority's prior approval. The local authority must give consent within 28 days of the application being received, if, having regard to the codes of practice and best practicable means, it would not serve a section 60 notice in those specific circumstances. The local authority may attach conditions to its consent, which are appealable to a magistrates' court, as is a refusal to give its consent.

6.117 This licensing provision is rarely invoked, ostensibly because of a strongly held belief in the construction industry that local authorities are restrictive in what they are prepared to allow.[130]

6.118 Works carried out in accordance with consent given under section 61 of the Control of Pollution Act 1974 cannot be the subject of a subsequent prosecution. However, as the consent only applies with respect to the local authority, it does not provide a defence in proceedings brought under section 82 of the EPA 1990 by a 'person aggrieved' by noise nuisance.[131]

Statutory nuisance and other forms of noise control

6.119 Using enforcement powers under Part III of the EPA 1990 for noise nuisance and those under sections 60 and 61 of the Control of Pollution Act 1974 to control noise from construction sites are not the only ways enforcement authorities are able to deal with noise problems. There are a number of other measures which to some extent overlap and the enforcement field has been described as something of a 'hotchpotch'.[132] The type and level of interference by noise and what is meant by 'interference' will not be the same in all provisions. Measures designed to prevent excessive noise at source, including the design of equipment and machinery, can build in fixed noise limits which set an industry standard, at least in some spheres.

---

[130] *Report of the Noise Review Working Party* (Department of the Environment Building Research Establishment, 1990).   [131] See Chapter 16.
[132] McManus (n 17 above), p 264.

Aircraft, road traffic and railway noise
There are certain kinds of noise, such as aircraft,[133] road traffic[134] and railway[135] **6.120**
noise for which specific legislative provisions apply which exclude any action or
prosecution in nuisance, including statutory nuisance. Even in these areas
covered by separate legislation, practitioners should not ignore statutory nuisance
because associated or auxiliary activities may come within the scope of section
79 of the EPA 1990.

Section 79(6) specifically disapplies the EPA 1990 from aircraft noise other than **6.121**
from model aircraft. But this does not mean that the EPA 1990 has no role to play
in ancillary activities. For example, ground activities in airports are not included
in regulations made under the Civil Aviation Act 1982 dealing with airport noise
and complaints may be made to a local authority about such matters as excessively loud information announcements or noise produced by the ground staff
servicing aeroplanes. The local authority will have to consider such complaints in
terms of its duties under section 80 of the EPA 1990.

Some auxiliary activities may be covered by other legislation. Section 63 of the **6.122**
Airports Act 1986 gives airport operators powers to make bye-laws regulating the use
and operation of the airport. Action by the operator may be a relatively simple as well
as a more effective way of dealing with a problem, for example by imposing fines on
aircraft companies who breach fixed noise limits on the take-off of aeroplanes.[136]

Noise from aerodromes not coming within the scope of the Civil Aviation Act **6.123**
1982 will be subject to planning controls. Guidance notes are provided in *Planning
Policy Guidance Note 24: Planning and Noise* (PPG 24) regarding the siting of
such aerodromes and on limiting their hours of operation and the number and type
of aircraft which may be used. However, this guidance only applies to proposed
aerodromes and planning controls cannot be imposed on existing ones.[137]

---

[133] The Air Navigation (General) Regulations 1993, SI 1993/1622, regulate the permitted noise and vibration from aircraft. The Civil Aviation Act 1982, s 76(1), states that no action shall lie in nuisance in respect of the flight of an aircraft where there has been compliance with any Air Navigation Order and provided that there has been no dangerous flying of the aircraft. Exemption is not given where the aircraft flies below a reasonable height above the ground, or to air displays. See also *Farley v Skinner* HL [2001] 4 All ER 801, [2001] 3 WLR 899, at 30, in which Lord Steyn held, notwithstanding the exemption of aircraft noise from statutory nuisance, that 'aircraft noise could arguably constitute a nuisance' and 'is capable of causing inconvenience and discomfort'.

[134] Part II of the Road Traffic Act 1988 gives the Secretary of State powers to make regulations regarding noise emissions from vehicles. Note that the Road Traffic (Consequential Provisions) Act 1988, s 7, provides that nothing in the Road Traffic Acts authorizes a person to use a vehicle so as to cause a nuisance. However, provisions prohibiting the causing of excessive noise by drivers are rarely enforced.

[135] Railways Act 1993, s 122(3), provides a defence of statutory authority to any proceedings in nuisance, whether civil or criminal.

[136] Actions against the British Airports Authority over aircraft noise may receive a fillip in the wake of *Hatton and Others v United Kingdom* (2002) 34 EHRR 1 where the court held that night flights in UK airports interfered with the rights of residents to a good night's sleep and that the Government's policy on night flights breached article 8 of the European Convention on Human Rights (Rome, 4 November 1950; TS 71 (1953); Cmd 8969).   [137] n 73 above, para 15.

6.124 As regards noise from motor vehicles, traffic noise and measures that need to be taken to combat these, the basic system of enforcement is through the road traffic legislation, which includes detailed regulations made by the Secretary of State. Noise emitted from vehicles on the street, such as loud music and car alarms, is subject to statutory nuisance control,[138] but traffic noise is expressly excluded by section 79(6A) of the EPA 1990. Off-road uses such as scrambling are subject to statutory nuisance provisions as are other uses off the highway or noisy activities taking place on private land, such as the use of vehicles in the yards of storage depots.

Statutory authority

6.125 Statutory authority can provide a defence to activities which would otherwise be a nuisance. Statutory authority will be sufficient justification particularly where the public benefit is great and the nuisance comparatively small.[139] The scope of the defence depends on the statute which provides the statutory authority.

6.126 Railway operations are generally exempt from common law nuisance actions, subject to operators exercising reasonable diligence in avoiding making unnecessary noise.[140] Statutory authority does not apply to all operations, however. Thus, a statute authorizing tramways did not authorize the setting up of stables for horses. Even though such stables were necessary to the operation of the tramway, they were not included in the statute and therefore they did not attract statutory authority.[141] Where a nuisance is incidentally committed whilst carrying out an authorized act and the nuisance was a necessary consequence of the act, then the courts have been prepared to find that statutory authority will apply.

6.127 To what extent can statutory authority provide a defence to statutory nuisance proceedings? Usually the position for statutory nuisance will be the same as for common law nuisance but the situation is not beyond doubt. *London Borough of Camden v London Underground Ltd*[142] involved service of an EPA 1990 notice on the company in respect of noise emanating from the lift-winding mechanism and generator at Russell Square underground station. The court gave a 'provisional view' that the defence to common law nuisance provided in section 122(3) of the Railways Act 1993 did not apply to all statutory nuisances. The court reasoned that the prejudice to health limb in section 79 of the EPA 1990 meant that a statutory nuisance differed from common law nuisance and that Parliament

---

[138] EPA 1990, 79(1)(ga), provides that 'noise that is prejudicial to health or a nuisance and is emitted from or caused by a vehicle, machinery or equipment in a street' is a nuisance.

[139] *Edgington v Swindon BC* [1939] 1 KB 86; *Freda Gillings v Kirklees MBC* [1999] 1 Env LR D2.

[140] Previous unreported cases indicate that railway companies have been successfully prosecuted for breach of section 80 notices for making excessive noise in associated activities, such as track repairs. In February 1993, the London borough of Kensington and Chelsea successfully prosecuted the British Railways Board for disturbing the sleep of local residents because of track realignment works (cited in Penn (n 46 above), p 78).

[141] *Rapier v London Tramways* [1893] 2 Ch 588.

[142] [2000] Env LR 369.

could not have intended to authorize a defence where prejudice to health was shown. However, this part of the decision was *obiter* since the court had decided that the notice served by the council was invalid on other grounds.

Noise at the workplace
Employees and others present on work premises are protected from the effects of noise by the Health and Safety at Work Act 1974 and regulations enforced under section 15 of that Act. The duty of care required of employers, and imposed on occupiers, is a high one which cannot be delegated.[143] Enforcement is primarily the responsibility of the Health and Safety Executive, though for many activities and sectors local government is responsible.[144]

6.128

Section 2 of the 1974 Act requires an employer to provide and maintain a working environment that is, so far as is reasonably practicable, safe, without health risks and adequate as regards facilities and arrangements for the workforce. The Act imposes duties of care widely on employers and others and these extend to protecting members of the public who are not actually present on the premises.[145]

6.129

Model bye-laws
For certain forms of noise, controls can be applied by local authorities using model bye-laws. These are issued by central government for the guidance of local authorities under section 235 of the Local Government Act 1972. They are comparatively simple to enforce and the financial penalties are limited.

6.130

Model bye-laws are not a substitute for a general statute. If a problem could be dealt with under an Act or under a model bye-law then it should be dealt with under the Act. The reason for this is that if the statute deals with precisely the same matter, the bye-law would be superfluous and *ultra vires*; and if the bye-law goes beyond the statute then it is bad.[146]

6.131

The scope of bye-laws tends to be restricted and aimed at dealing with transient noise problems. It is essential that the alleged breach fits the bye-law exactly. Examples include:

6.132

- singing or playing a noisy musical instrument in the street;
- operating amplified musical instruments in a street, public place or in a shop;
- noisy hawking;
- noisy conduct in the street at night-time; and
- keeping noisy animals.

---

[143] *R v British Steel* [1995] IRLR 310.
[144] Health and Safety at Work Act 1974, s 18(1), (7)(a).
[145] *R v Board of Trustees of the Science Museum* [1993] 3 All ER 853.
[146] *Galer v Morrissey* [1955] 1 All ER 380.

Regulatory codes of practice

6.133 A small number of codes of practice have been issued by central government under powers provided by section 71 of the Control of Pollution Act 1974. These deal with highly specific situations, such as regulating the use of model aircraft and the playing of chimes in ice-cream vans. As with bye-laws, the scope is narrow and breaches are relatively simple to prosecute. Contraventions are summary only; any fines imposed are usually low.[147]

Licensing

6.134 The playing of amplified music on commercial premises may be subject to statutory nuisance controls. This is not the only way problems of entertainment noise can be dealt with. Licensing deals with wider issues concerning use—with permission to cause noise and with the controls required to prevent unnecessary noise. Besides having this preventative value, the threat or actuality of being refused or of losing a licence can be a powerful deterrent to potential noise offenders.

6.135 Conditions can be imposed on public houses and licensed clubs by justices using their powers under the Licensing Act 1964 to restrict the playing of music, or the use of particular instruments, such as drums. Objections to the renewal of licences can be made by residents as well as by the police where there is evidence of rowdy behaviour. Local authorities can also make objections and will often do so if there is a record of noise complaints.

6.136 Control of music and dancing establishments in public places also operates through a licensing system. In Greater London, the London Government Act 1963 applies, and elsewhere, the Local Government (Miscellaneous Provisions) Act 1982.

6.137 Licensing in private places of entertainment is provided by the Private Places of Entertainment (Licensing) Act 1967. This provision allows the local authority to control events such as 'warehouse' and 'acid-house' parties, and, possibly, pay parties in domestic premises.[148]

Conclusion

6.138 Noise occupies a curious position as a pollutant. Government regards it (or claims to) as one of the most significant environmental problems of the time.[149] It might

---

[147] Control of Pollution Act 1974, s 62(1).

[148] This terminology was used in the *Report of the Noise Review Working Party* (n 130 above) and appears in recent case law to describe large-scale events, often in the open air, and one-off events. 'Raves' is the term used in the Criminal Justice and Public Order Act 1994, defined in section 63(1) as 'a gathering on land in the open air of 100 or more persons (whether or not trespassers) at which amplified music is played during the night (with or without intermissions) and is such as, by reason of its loudness and duration and the time at which it is played, is likely to cause serious distress to the inhabitants of the locality . . .' See also paras 6.96–6.98.

[149] *Annual Report, 1997* (Cmnd 3556), p 12, on *This Common Inheritance: Britain's Environmental Strategy* (Cm 1200, 1990).

be thought that the Government has the incentive to produce a well-thought out and coherent policy strategy. However, existing measures sometimes rely on the concept of nuisance, sometimes on fixed standards and there is no consistent strategy to tackle noise at source. The state of the law in this field has been described as a 'confused hotchpotch of measures', lacking focus or direction and set to drift.[150]

Many noise problems result from everyday human activities and are not confined to a limited sphere which can be comprehensively tackled with a battery of regulations, codes of practice and guidance from central government. It is therefore very difficult to regulate such behaviour using very directive approaches such as the criminal law, unless the behaviour is in some way extreme or deviant. In many parts of the UK today, social relations exist in a state of vague ideological drift and it is not possible for state agencies to impose uniform and consistent standards of behaviour. **6.139**

Equally difficult is deciding who should be punished for being a noise offender and how. The very term 'noise offender' sounds strange and artificial. Despite the social costs of noise pollution, only very rarely will noise-polluting activities attract the opprobrium normally accorded to the perpetrators of 'real crime'.[151] It is the same with nearly all environmental crime. **6.140**

[150] M Adams and F McManus, *Noise and Noise Law* (Wiley, 1994), p 151.
[151] G Slapper and S Tombs, *Corporate Crime* (Longman, 1999).

7

ATMOSPHERIC EMISSIONS

Origins 7.02
Smoke emitted from premises: application of subsection (1)(b) 7.05
    Definition 7.05
    Crown property 7.11
    Overlaps with other statutory regimes 7.12
    Defences 7.13
Fumes or gases emitted from premises: application of subsection (1)(c) ... 7.14
    Definition 7.14
Dust, steam, smell etc: application of subsection (1)(d) 7.17
    Dust, steam, smell or other effluvia arising on industrial, trade or business premises 7.17
        Dust 7.19
        Steam 7.21
        Smell 7.22
        Effluvia 7.25
Defences 7.28
Smoke, fumes or gases from vehicles, etc on a street: application of subsection (1)(gb) 7.29

This chapter examines the following heads of statutory nuisances under section 79 of the Environmental Protection Act 1990 ('EPA 1990') which cause emissions to the atmosphere as follows: **7.01**

- section 79(1)(b): smoke emitted from premises;
- section 79(1)(c): fumes or gases emitted from premises;
- section 79(1)(d): dust, steam, smell or other effluvia arising on industrial, trade or business premises; and
- section 79(1)(gb): smoke, fumes or gases emitted from any vehicle, machinery or equipment on a street so as to be prejudicial to health or a nuisance (other than from any vehicle, machinery or equipment being used for fire brigade purposes).

Origins

Section 79(1)(b) (smoke nuisance) is an early form of statutory nuisance, dating from 1866 in respect of dark smoke and 1875 in other cases. Section 79(1)(c) **7.02** (fumes and gases), which applies only to domestic premises, originated in the EPA 1990. Smoke nuisances have also been controlled through other legislation in the past, notably the Clean Air Acts, and continue to fall subject to this statute and other environmental controls. Thus, primary controls over smoke are to be found in the Clean Air Act 1993 and Part I of the EPA 1990.[1] The Clean Air Act 1993 regulates the emission of smoke from chimneys and some open sites. It prohibits the emission of dark smoke from chimneys.[2]

7.03 Section 79(1)(d) is partly new. Dust and effluvia appeared in predecessor sections,[3] while steam and smell appeared for the first time in the EPA 1990.

7.04 Section 79(1)(gb) was inserted by section 24 of the London Local Authorities Act 1996 and only applies to London boroughs.

Smoke emitted from premises: application of subsection (1)(b)

Definition

7.05 'Smoke' is defined in the EPA 1990 as follows:

'Smoke' includes soot, ash, grit or gritty particles emitted in smoke.[4]

The definition of 'dark smoke', found in section 3 of the Clean Air Act 1993, is smoke which:

if compared in the appropriate manner . . . would be as dark or darker than shade 2 on the Ringelmann Chart.

7.06 Section 79(1)(b) of the EPA 1990 does not apply to:

(i) smoke emitted from a chimney[5] of a private dwelling within a smoke control area,
(ii) dark smoke emitted from a chimney of a building or a chimney serving the furnace of a boiler or industrial plant attached to a building or for the time being fixed to or installed on any land,
(iii) smoke emitted from a railway locomotive steam engine, or
(iv) dark smoke emitted otherwise than as mentioned above from industrial or trade premises.[6]

---

[1] Note also the Pollution Prevention Control Act 1999.
[2] Dark smoke is usually determined according to a measure known as the Ringelmann Chart. This is a card with cross-hatching in black on a white background. When viewed from a distance the cross-hatching merges to give a uniform shade. The extent to which the white background is obscured, when matched against the smoke, determines its colour—ranging from black, to dark and so on. Dark smoke is shade 2 on the chart. It is not, in fact, essential to use the Ringelmann Chart for the purpose of court proceedings (Clean Air Act 1993, s 3(2)). [3] Public Health Act 1936, s 92(1)(d).
[4] EPA 1990, s 79(7). 'Smoke' is also defined as including 'soot, ash, grit and gritty particles emitted in smoke' by the Clean Air Act 1993, s 64(1).
[5] 'Chimney' includes structures and openings of any kind from or through which smoke may be emitted (EPA 1990, s 79(7)). [6] EPA 1990, s 79(3).

7.07 Thus, there are a number of limitations for use of the statutory nuisance procedure in respect of the control of smoke. Most of the exclusions[7] prevent overlaps with the atmospheric controls contained in the Clean Air Act 1993 and other legislation. Thus, most smoke nuisances (particularly involving dark smoke) arising on industrial premises will be dealt with under other legislation.

7.08 It might be considered that smoke emanating from a bonfire, which fell below the 'dark smoke' criteria might not amount to a statutory nuisance. The decision in *Griffiths v Pembrokeshire CC*,[8] however, makes it clear that even though no smoke can be seen with the naked eye, if it is possible to smell the smoke then that may constitute a smoke nuisance falling under section 79(1)(b). *Griffiths* concerned the burning of bones and other residues from animal carcasses together with bedding used by a pack of hounds. It was alleged in evidence that the smoke passed over neighbouring property at too high a level to cause a nuisance. It was held that, while the primary dictionary meaning of smoke was 'the visible volatile product given off by burning or smouldering substances', nevertheless, the smell of smoke was included in a smoke nuisance under section 79(1)(b) of the EPA 1990.

7.09 The definition of a smoke nuisance does apply to domestic smoke (from a fire or grate) emitted from a chimney outside a smoke control area.[9]

7.10 Section 79(1)(b) specifies that the nuisance is committed where smoke is emitted from 'premises'. 'Premises' include land and any vessel.[10] This would encompass everything within the curtilage of the property.[11]

Crown property

7.11 Proceedings in respect of a smoke nuisance under section 79(1)(b) are not available in respect of premises that are occupied on behalf of the Crown for naval, military or air force purposes or for defence purposes.[12] Neither are they available where the premises are occupied by a visiting military force.[13]

Overlaps with other statutory regimes

7.12 If the premises in question are controlled under Part I of the EPA 1990 or under regulations made under section 2 of the Pollution Prevention and Control Act 1999, then the consent of the Secretary of State must be sought and obtained by the local authority before summary proceedings for statutory nuisance can be instituted.[14] This ensures that the two systems of control—statutory nuisance

---

[7] With the notable exception of the exclusion in favour of steam engines which was included at the behest of steam-engine enthusiasts.   [8] [2000] Env LR 622.
[9] It follows that in this case, a best practicable means defence would be applicable.
[10] EPA 1990, s 79(7).
[11] *Griffiths v Pembrokeshire CC* (n 8 above). For a further discussion of the extent of the meaning of 'premises' see paras 5.30–5.36.   [12] EPA 1990, s 79(2)(a).
[13] A 'visiting force' is defined under the Visiting Forces Act 1952 (EPA 1990, s 79(2)(b)).
[14] EPA 1990, s 79(10) which also applies to nuisances falling under s 79(1)(d), (e) or (g) and (in relation to Scotland) paragraph (ga).

administered by the local authority and integrated pollution prevention control administered by the Environment Agency—do not inadvertently collide.

Defences

7.13 The defence under section 79(7) of the EPA 1990, that the 'best practicable means' were used, is available in all cases where the smoke was emitted from a chimney.[15] Bonfires, whether on commercial premises or otherwise, are excluded therefore.

Fumes or gases emitted from premises: application of subsection (1)(c)

Definition

7.14 'Fumes' are defined as 'any airborne matter smaller than dust'.[16] The definition of dust does not include 'dust emitted from a chimney as an ingredient of smoke'. This prevents an overlap with smoke nuisance under section 79(1)(b) of the EPA 1990. 'Gas' includes 'vapour and moisture precipitated from vapour'.[17] Thus the definition of 'fumes' is comprehensive but that of gas is not necessarily so.

7.15 Section 79(1)(c) of the EPA 1990 is limited[18] to private dwellings only which are defined as any building or part of a building, used or intended to be used as a dwelling.[19] Fumes or gases arising from commercial premises are likely to be controlled under other legislation.[20]

7.16 It may also be arguable, on the authority of *Griffiths v Pembrokeshire CC*[21] in relation to smoke nuisances,[22] that smells caused by fumes or gases would also be covered under this paragraph.

Dust, steam, smell etc: application of subsection (1)(d)

Dust, steam, smell or other effluvia arising on industrial, trade or business premises

7.17 Subsection (1)(d) is expressly limited to industrial, trade and business premises. It is not, therefore, available in respect of emanations of dust, steam, smell and other effluvia from domestic premises.[23] It is the only paragraph of section 79(1) of the EPA 1990 which is limited in this way. It may be contrasted with section 79(1)(c) (fumes and gases) which is expressly limited to private dwellings. The two paragraphs might, therefore, be seen as parallel provisions to be used in the appropriate setting—homes or businesses.

---

[15] For the definition of 'chimney' see n 5 above.   [16] EPA 1990, s 79(7).
[17] ibid, s 79(7).   [18] ibid, s 79(4).   [19] ibid, s 79(7).
[20] eg, the Pollution Prevention and Control Act 1999. Alternatively, they may fall under section 79(1)(d) ('dust, steam, smell or other effluvia arising on industrial, trade or business premises').
[21] n 8 above.   [22] See para 7.05.
[23] For a definition of 'industrial, trade and business premises', see paras 15.10–15.11. See also n 14 above.

7.18 Subsection (1)(d) also applies where the statutory nuisance *arises* on the premises. This suggests that, provided the statutory nuisance falls under the health limb, it may be actionable where it affects the occupiers of, and visitors to, the premises.[24]

Dust 'Dust' does not include dust emitted from a chimney as an ingredient of smoke which would fall under section 79(1)(b) as a smoke nuisance.[25] Otherwise, 'dust' is not defined in the EPA 1990. **7.19**

7.20 Dust was the subject matter of the statutory nuisance in *Wivenhoe Port v Colchester BC*.[26] Here, the nuisance arose from the discharge from moored vessels and the handling and loading of soya meal into lorries from within the port. These operations caused a great deal of dust in the environs of the docks.

Steam 'Steam' is not defined in the Act except that steam emitted from a railway locomotive engine is expressly excluded from the subsection.[27] **7.21**

Smell 'Smell' is one of the key elements of section 79(1)(d) of the EPA as odour nuisances have become increasingly unacceptable among an affluent urban population with high environmental expectations. The alleged nuisance typically arises either where an industrial site is close to a residential area or where there is less tolerance of countryside smells in a rural area.[28] In *Wealden BC v Hollings*,[29] for example, smell was produced by manure spread on farmland. The farmer appealed against the abatement notice which had prohibited the practice. He asked for the right to spread it for a limited period of time (40 days per year). The magistrates' court allowed his appeal to the extent that he was permitted to spread manure for 15 days per year, excluding weekends and bank holidays. Something of a balance was, thus, achieved between the commercial interests of the farmer and the rights of the residents to be free from the odour nuisance. The conflict, as is often the case, is between the economic interests of those creating the nuisance and the rights of the general population to be free of nuisances.[30] **7.22**

---

[24] It would not be actionable under the nuisance limb in these circumstances since the definition of nuisance requires that the offending activity leaves the land and affects neighbouring land or a section of the community. [25] EPA 1990, s 79(7).

[26] [1985] JPL 176. The case was brought under the Public Health Act 1936, s 92(d) ('any dust or effluvia'). The decision, frequently referred to judicially and by academic writers because of the quality and perceptiveness of the judge's analysis of the issues is, in fact, the hearing of an appeal by the Crown Court from a decision of the magistrates and, as such, is not binding.

[27] EPA 1990, s 79(5).

[28] Pig farms are a notorious instance of such odour nuisances; see, eg, *R v Wakefield Magistrates' Court, ex p Wakefield MBC* [2000] Env LR D18 and *Wheeler v Saunders* [1996] Ch 19.

[29] (1992) 4 Land Management and Env LR 126.

[30] See the Scottish case, *Barr & Stroud v West of Scotland Water Authority* [1998] Env LR 3 D3, for an example of a refusal to grant an interlocutory injunction in a nuisance action where the economic and environmental issues outweighed the balance of convenience in respect of the odour problem caused by a sewage plant to nearby residents.

7.23 Where a smell is one of the results of the offending activity, there may be a choice of paragraph of section 79(1) of the EPA 1990 under which to bring the nuisance proceedings. In *Griffiths v Pembrokeshire CC*[31] smoke from burning residue was not always visible to the naked eye although its smell could still be detected. The court held that, 'in common parlance', an allegation of a smoke nuisance could include its smell. The case had, therefore, been properly brought under section 79(1)(b) of the EPA 1990. The court did not suggest that it would have been improper to have brought the case under section 79(1)(d) as an odour nuisance.

7.24 While there are olfactory methods of assessing and quantifying odour,[32] as with other areas, there are not as yet, any uniform standards.[33] There remains a problem about the subjectivity of odours. Different residents might have different responses to smells. Essentially, this is a problem which will fall to the professional opinion of the environmental health officers as to whether, in the particular circumstances of the case, the smell amounts to a nuisance. It may be sensible to subject the officers to an olfactory test first to ensure that none are overly sensitive to smells.[34]

7.25 Effluvia The *Oxford English Dictionary Online* defines 'effluvium' as 'chiefly applied to the (real or supposed) outflow of material particles too subtle to be perceived by touch or sight', or 'an "exhalation" affecting the sense of smell, or producing effects by being received into the lungs. In modern popular use chiefly a noxious or disgusting exhalation or odour.' It was the subject matter of the statutory nuisance proceedings in *Malton Board of Health v Malton Manure Co*[35] although it was not specifically defined in that case. The *Malton* case concerned the process or manufacture of artificial manures. These included bone manures and the dissolving of bones and coprolites[36] with sulphuric acid, but not the burning or boiling of bones. During the manufacturing process, or while the hot product was being moved, or during storage, 'effluvia was thrown off in large quantities'.[37] This escaped from the premises and, depending on the wind direction, was carried into

---

[31] n 8 above.

[32] The Committé Européen Normalisation (CEN) working group, CEN/TC264/WG2 ('Odours'), was established in 1993 to standardize odour-concentration measurements using dynamic olfactometry. Their draft standard, PREN 13725:1999E (*Air Quality: Determination of Odour Concentration by Dynamic Olfactometry*) was published in October 1999 and is slowly progressing through the stages of CEN standardization; see further www.odournet.com/ON_news.htm.

[33] One advance is that, under the system of integrated pollution prevention and control (IPPC), which will eventually replace the system of integrated pollution control under Part I of the EPA 1990, smells are to be assessed prior to licensing by the Environment Agency. While this will not lead to the total elimination of smells, and will only apply to those installations subject to IPPC, it will nonetheless lead in many cases to a greater emphasis on the need to anticipate and prevent unacceptable odour nuisances.

[34] For an interesting discussion of a case in West Devon concerning odours emanating from a milk products factory, see D Jones, 'Statutory Nuisance Appeals with Special Reference to Smells' [1995] JPL 797.   [35] (1879) 4 Ex D 302.

[36] 'Coprolites' are various kinds of rounded stony nodules thought to be the fossilized faeces of Mesozoic reptiles.   [37] n 35 above, at 302.

a nearby town. The presence of effluvia on the inhabitants was thought to cause nausea and make sick people worse, but it was also thought that it would not cause permanent injury to health.[38]

In modern parlance, 'effluvia' might seem to be little more than a smell. But its historical derivation from Victorian legislation betrays its meaning. It originates in the concept of the 'miasma' theory. The idea behind this theory was that disease was caused by the transmission of minute faecal particles suspended in droplets of breath. This theory prevailed until the late 1870s.[39] **7.26**

Thus, the distinction between smell (which was added in the EPA 1990) and effluvia would seem to be that effluvia is the presence of minute particles in air (which might be accompanied by a smell) whereas smell is just that—the smell emanating from the particles. Section 79(1)(d) lists effluvia as a catch-all expression at the end of the list: 'dust, steam, smell *or other effluvia*'. This suggests that it is to be considered as an emanation from a process within the context of the preceding words and should be defined in like fashion.[40] **7.27**

Defences

The defence that best practicable means were used to prevent, or to counteract the effects of the nuisance is available in respect of paragraph (d). This follows from the fact that it is limited to industrial, trade and business premises. **7.28**

Smoke, fumes or gases from vehicles, etc on a street: application of subsection (1)(gb)

This provision only applies to London boroughs and was inserted by section 24 of the London Local Authorities Act 1996. It applies to vehicles, machinery and equipment in a street. It does not include smoke, fumes and gases emitted from vehicle exhausts[41] and there is a general exemption for the fire brigade. **7.29**

---

[38] Effluvia causing cholera was defined by the Marquess of Lansdowne in the House of Lords at the Second Reading of the Nuisances and Contagious Diseases Bill 1848 (which became the Nuisances and Diseases Prevention Act 1848) as follows: '(the cause of cholera) was atmospheric: that it was influenced by the exhalation of rivers, the currents of air, and certain meteoric changes and vicissitudes; that the disturbing causes which promoted the disorder resided principally, if not altogether, in the atmosphere' (*Hansard*, 3rd Series, Vol 101, col 614).
[39] See Chapter 3 for a further discussion of this theory.
[40] The rule of statutory interpretation, the *eiusdem generis* rule, favours this approach.
[41] EPA 1990, s 79(6B). A 'vehicle' means 'a mechanically propelled vehicle intended or adapted for use on roads, whether it is in a fit state for such use, and includes any trailer intended or adapted for use as an attachment to such vehicle, any chassis or body, with or without wheels, appearing to have formed part of such a vehicle or trailer and anything attached to such a vehicle or trailer' (EPA 1990, s 79(7), as amended).

8

ANIMALS

Origins 8.02
Definition of 'animals' 8.03
Animals as a statutory nuisance 8.05
    Feral pigeons 8.07
    Scope of section 79(1)(f) and other remedies 8.08
    Where section 79(1)(f) is appropriate 8.09
    Noisy animals 8.11
    Uses against pets 8.15
Bye-laws 8.18
    Model bye-laws 8.19

Section 79(1)(f) of the Environmental Protection Act 1990 ('EPA 1990') defines **8.01** this statutory nuisance as 'any animal kept in such a place or manner as to be prejudicial to health or a nuisance'.

Origins

Nuisances caused by animals were common before and during the Industrial **8.02** Revolution. They were one of the first kinds of statutory nuisance, the wording in its present form being changed only slightly from that used in the 1855 Nuisances Removal Act.[1] Nuisance from animals became particularly acute in towns and cities from the 1840s. An influx of unskilled labourers and service workers who brought pigs, fowl, donkeys and horses with them caused nuisances where humans and animals shared the same domestic space. This added to the overcrowding already prevalent in urban environments and was seen as a health risk as well as a nuisance.

Definition of 'animals'

The EPA 1990 does not provide a definition of 'animals'. The purpose of Part III **8.03** would suggest importing a wide definition. Nothing in the Act confines it to livestock or even to domestic animals, though these are quite widely defined in other legislation. Wild animals would need to be kept on premises, such as in cages, in

---

[1] See further para 3.02.

order to come within the subsection. Trained wild animals, as distinct from those which are merely caged, are domestic animals.[2] Section 15 of the Protection of Animals Act 1911 includes livestock within its definition of 'domestic animals'. A modern definition of 'livestock' mentions: cattle, horses, asses, mules, hinnies, sheep, pigs, goats, poultry, domesticated deer, and pheasants, partridges and grouse provided such game is kept in captivity.[3] Dogs and cats are domestic animals,[4] as are pet birds.[5] Implicit in these definitions are the animals' utility to man and some degree of tameness or domestication. Feral animals, such as pigeons, would therefore be excluded.

8.04 Invertebrates do not appear in general lists of animals in the above statutes, but do in specialized secondary legislation. It would seem nonsensical to argue that animals such as snakes and crocodiles do not come within the scope of section 79(1)(f) of the EPA 1990. Given the lack of a definition of 'animals' in the EPA, importing the ordinary meaning of the term is, it is suggested, justifiable and this would imply that no class of animals is excluded.

Animals as a statutory nuisance

8.05 This type of statutory nuisance focuses on the premises, on the place where an animal is kept or on the way it is kept. It does not extend to the activities of an animal off the premises, such as livestock trespassing and causing damage on another's land[6] or pest damage.[7] The suitability of the premises where animals are kept and the conditions of their keeping are what this provision is aimed at. A key question is: is there anything defective or insanitary about the premises which causes nuisance or prejudice to health to arise from the keeping of animals?[8]

8.06 The focus on premises in cases of nuisance from animals is illustrated by a Victorian case, *R v King*[9] (which was heard by a stipendiary magistrate and is obviously not binding authority). Mr King kept snakes which repeatedly escaped into his neighbour's house. His conviction for a statutory nuisance was on the basis that he had failed to ensure that the snakes could not escape from his premises. The problem did not arise from the risk of disease or a public health

---

[2] *McQuaker v Goddard* [1940] 1KB 687.   [3] Animals Act 1971, s 11.
[4] Protection of Animals Act 1911, s 15.   [5] *Colam v Pagett* (1883) 12 QBD 66.
[6] Animals Act 1971, s 4, imposes strict liability on the owners for damage caused by livestock trespass. This Act extends such liability to the keepers of dangerous animals causing damage (s 2) and to the keepers of dogs injuring or killing livestock (s 3). Animals which, though not dangerous, are known to be likely to cause damage, and which have characteristics making this likely, are also covered under section 2(2) of the Act.
[7] Local authorities are empowered under Part I of the Prevention of Damage by Pests Act 1949 to destroy rats and mice and to require owners to take treatment measures or to carry out repairs to property to prevent damage and nuisance from these pests.
[8] *Galer v Morrissey* [1955] 1 All ER 380.   [9] (1895) 59 JP 571.

nuisance from the snakes, which were described as harmless, agreeable grass snakes. The main problem for the neighbouring householder arose from his wife's fear that the snakes might enter her bed whilst she was asleep and so cause her to have a heart attack.

Feral pigeons
Feral or wild pigeons—or, more particularly, their faeces—can be a nuisance where such birds roost on the roofs and in the eaves of buildings and underneath bridges.[10] Such birds cannot be said to be 'kept' by the owners of buildings or other structures, so section 79(1)(f) of the EPA 1990 ought not to be used for this type of nuisance. Where pigeons or other feral birds cause a statutory nuisance, the local authority can better deal with the matter as accumulations or deposits under section 79(1)(e) of the Act.[11] Alternatively, civil proceedings in public nuisance are available to a local authority where it decides it needs to protect the interests of the community[12] and the nuisance is such as to interfere substantially with the comfort and convenience of a significant class or part of the public.[13]

8.07

Scope of section 79(1)(f) and other remedies
Section 79(1)(f) has been interpreted in a restricted way by the courts. For example, it has been held not to include noise nuisance from animals kept on premises.[14] An enforcement authority will sometimes need to consider other types of action to deal with nuisances caused by animals because this is not a comprehensive or widely drawn type of statutory nuisance. In some instances, public nuisance proceedings should be considered instead of statutory nuisance. For example, an action in public nuisance could arise for an obstruction of the highway by animals.[15] This would not be a statutory nuisance, since it would not be connected to the manner in which the animals were kept on premises. Where a problem is caused solely by a lack of control being exercised by the owner or keeper of the animals, the requirements for a statutory nuisance are not fulfilled.

8.08

Where section 79(1)(f) is appropriate
Section 79(1)(f) is particularly useful where a local authority decides to serve a specific works notice in order to control the conditions in which animals are kept. This might apply when the living conditions of domesticated animals are producing a number of problems, such as excessive smell, noise or flies. The

8.09

---

[10] Public Health Act 1961, s 74, empowers local authorities to cull house doves, pigeons, starlings or sparrows where sufficient numbers cause annoyance, damage or nuisance.
[11] See Chapter 9.
[12] Its authority to do so derives from its powers to commence civil proceedings under the Local Government Act 1972, s 222.
[13] *Wandsworth LBC v Railtrack plc* [2001] 1 WLR 368. The application in this case was for a declaration, injunction, and damages to recover the cost of sluicing the pavement.
[14] *Galer v Morrissey* (n 8 above).
[15] P M North, *The Modern Law of Animals* (Butterworths, 1972), p 172.

provision cannot be used, however, for animal welfare purposes, such as to control overcrowding. But where the overcrowding is the cause of an alleged nuisance, then the local authority could impose restrictions on the number of animals kept. A local authority's powers do not extend to forcing owners to relocate their businesses. In *Manley v New Forest DC*,[16] a case of noise nuisance arising from a dog-breeding business, it was held that taking 'best practicable means' to reduce a nuisance did not extend to relocating the business to other premises.

8.10 In deciding to specify precisely the works required to reduce the nuisance, although there is no requirement for the local authority to consult with the potential notice recipient, in practice it may prove difficult not to do so.[17] The advantage of serving a specific works notice is that it is easier to enforce, even though the local authority has to justify the particular measures required.[18]

Noisy animals

8.11 It might be thought that if animals were kept on premises and the ensuing noise amounted to a nuisance that section 79(1)(f) of the EPA 1990 should be used for enforcement. However, it is recommended that for noisy animals section 79(1)(g) is used instead, namely noise emitted from premises such as to cause a statutory nuisance.[19] The reason for focusing on the noise rather than on the animals is historical rather than logical and follows from the decision of the Divisional Court in *Galer v Morrissey*.[20]

8.12 Where the scope of the nuisance is wider than, but includes, noise then it might be feasible to use the animals paragraph. For example, a pack of dogs might be kept on premises from which they regularly escaped to foul outside the curtilage; additionally, they might bark a great deal and cause noise nuisance. These facts would seem to bring it within the scope of the section 79(1)(f) since the premises appear to be unsuitable for kennelling. The doubt arising from *Galer v Morrissey*[21] has resulted in some councils, faced with an animals nuisance involving noise and the manner in which the animals are kept, serving two notices.

8.13 *Galer v Morrissey* was a case of noisy greyhounds causing a nuisance to the villagers of Harrietsham, in Kent. It was brought under a bye-law because there was no statute in force at that time (1955) dealing with noise nuisance.[22] The point for consideration by the Divisional Court was whether the statutory

---

[16] [2000] EHLR 113.
[17] *R v Falmouth and Truro Port Health Authority, ex p South West Water Ltd* [2000] 3 All ER 306.
[18] See Chapter 12 for notice requirements generally.   [19] See Chapter 6.
[20] n 8 above.   [21] n 8 above.
[22] The bye-law was made under the Local Government Act 1933, s 249, and provided that 'No person shall keep within any house, building, or premises any noisy animal which shall be or cause a serious nuisance to residents in the neighbourhood'.

provision for nuisance from animals under section 92(1)(b) of the Public Health Act 1936[23] could include noise. If it could, then the bye-law would be superfluous and *ultra vires*. Lord Goddard CJ was clear that the statute dealt with public health matters which were different from noise, so the bye-law was good. In his Lordship's view, the statute was confined to nuisances caused by keeping animals in premises, such as nuisance from effluvia, smells and faeces.

When *Galer v Morrissey* was decided noise could not be a statutory nuisance; it first became one with the Noise Abatement Act 1960. Doubts have been expressed about this case. In *Coventry CC v Cartwright* Lord Widgery said 'I would have thought . . . that a noisy animal could as much be prejudicial to health as a smelly animal'.[24] However, it seems that the purpose of the comment was not to cast doubt on the correctness of *Galer v Morrissey* but to approve the construction given by Lord Goddard concerning the public health requirements for a statutory nuisance.[25] Both judges were concerned to justify restricting the scope of a statutory nuisance to its public health origins. 8.14

Uses against pets
The owner of a dog which repeatedly fouls a neighbour's land could be held liable in private nuisance because the fouling interferes with the neighbour's enjoyment of his land.[26] A person in charge of a dog which defecates on designated land and who fails to remove the faeces commits an offence under section 3 of the Dogs (Fouling of Land) Act 1996.[27] The Act is enabling legislation and local authorities have the power to designate land coming within its provisions. It could also be a statutory nuisance where a complaint arises from a failure to keep the animal on premises in such a way as to prevent it from causing a nuisance. In *R v Walden-Jones, ex p Coton*,[28] a case brought under section 92(1)(b) of the Public Health Act 1936 (the predecessor animals provision to EPA, s 79(1)(f)), the premises were defective so enabling cats to stray. The Divisional Court held that such a nuisance came within the scope of paragraph (b). The owner of the cats was ordered to bury all excreta, keep the cats 8.15

---

[23] EPA 1990, s 79(1)(f) is identical to the provision in the 1936 Act.
[24] [1975] 1 WLR 845, at 850.
[25] *Galer v Morrissey* (n 8 above) was concerned about animals and *Coventry CC v Cartwright* with accumulations, ie both forms of nuisance in the Nuisances Removal Act 1855 and both being public health types, unlike noise. Some commentators, however, have placed a different construction, believing that Lord Widgery was expressing judicial doubts concerning the correctness of *Galer v Morrissey*; see N Hawke, *Environmental Health Law* (Sweet & Maxwell, 1995), p 423.
[26] *Curtis v Thompson* (1956) 106 L Jo 61.
[27] 'Designated land' is defined by section 1 of the Act as any land which is open to the air and to which the public are allowed access, with or without payment. Exceptions include highways where the speed limit is more than 40 mph, land used for agriculture or woodlands, land which is predominantly marshland, moor or heath and common land. [28] [1963] Crim LR 839.

within the boundaries of her premises and to prevent the escape of all offensive smells.

8.16 The keepers of exotic pets could be prosecuted under section 79(1)(f) where the requirements for statutory nuisance are made out. However, prosecutions are usually brought under specific welfare legislation directed to more general failures to look after animals properly. Thus, offences involving cruelty to animals are prosecuted under the Protection of Animals Act 1911.

8.17 Other legislation is available for specific matters. The keeping of dangerous wild animals is regulated by the Dangerous Wild Animals Act 1976. The owner of a dog found worrying livestock on agricultural land is liable under the Dogs (Protection of Livestock) Act 1953. Civil liability for damage caused by animals is provided by Animals Act 1971. These are examples of legislation dealing with specific groups of animals and the circumstances in which they are kept and utilized.[29]

Bye-laws

8.18 Bye-laws preventing the keeping of animals so as to be prejudicial to health can be made under section 81(b) of the Public Health Act 1936. This provision re-enacts powers going back to the mid-nineteenth century. A bye-law made under Local Government Act 1858 which stipulated that 'no occupier . . . shall keep any pigs within . . . 100 feet from any dwelling' was held to be reasonable in an urban area in *Wanstead Local Board of Health v Wooster*,[30] but not in a rural area in *Heap v Burnley Union Sanitary Authority*.[31] Nowadays, use of such bye-laws is rare. They may also be challengeable both on grounds of reasonableness and for going beyond the scope of the statute and thus being *ultra vires*.[32]

Model bye-laws

8.19 Model bye-laws to control nuisances made under section 235 of the Local Government Act 1972 are sometimes used to deal with noisy animals. The model noise bye-law provides that 'no person shall keep within any . . . premises any noisy animal which shall be or cause a serious nuisance to residents of the neighbourhood'.

8.20 Generally, use of the noise nuisance provisions in the EPA 1990 is preferred by local authorities to enforcement by bye-laws because the abatement notice procedure is more effective. Prosecution for keeping noisy animals under the model bye-laws requires continuation of the nuisance for two weeks from date of service

---

[29] See 2 *Halsbury's Statutes* (4th edn, 1992 reissue) for a full list. [30] (1874) 38 JP 21.
[31] (1884) 12 QBD 617. Here the limitation was 50 feet, but it is clear from the decision that the bye-law was not reasonable in a country area. [32] *Galer v Morrissey* (n 8 above).

of a notice, which must be signed by not less than three householders residing in the neighbourhood and who suffer the nuisance. Intermittent noise nuisance, which will usually be the case with noisy animals, may require service of one or more fresh notices under the bye-laws.[33] Consequently, the model bye-laws are rarely an effective solution.

[33] *Phillips v Crawford* (1984) 82 LGR 199.

9

ACCUMULATIONS AND DEPOSITS

Origins 9.02
The waste management regime 9.04
Definitions 9.05
The obligation to remove accumulations 9.09
The nuisance or health limb requirement 9.11
The defence of 'best practicable means' 9.14

9.01 Section 79(1)(e) of the Environmental Protection Act 1990 ('EPA 1990') provides that the list of statutory nuisances includes:

any accumulation or deposit which is prejudicial to health or a nuisance.

This statutory nuisance may arise on private domestic, commercial or public property.

Origins

9.02 This statutory nuisance has its origins in the earliest public health legislation. It first appeared in section 8 of the Nuisances Removal Act 1855: 'Any Accumulation or Deposit which is a Nuisance or injurious to Health.' It was consolidated in section 92(c) of the Public Health Act 1936: 'any accumulation or deposit which is prejudicial to health or a nuisance' and, is now contained in the EPA 1990 with the same wording.

9.03 Its appearance in the 1855 legislation reflects the need of that age to deal with nuisances such as smell, dampness and accumulations of filth, and the frequent proximity of the living situations of animals and humans. Lack of proper means of disposal of human sewage was also a factor. Today, although it is not among the most common of the statutory nuisances, it may be used to deal with accumulations of rubble which attract vermin,[1] pigeon droppings[2] or collections of household waste.[3]

---

[1] Where vermin are attracted because of the presence of an accumulation on land, a local authority may use its powers under the Prevention of Damage by Pests Act 1949. Section 2 of the 1949 Act prescribes that a local authority has a duty to take such steps as are necessary to keep its district free from rats and mice. The Public Health Act 1961, s 74, gives local authorities power, at their own expense, to deal with nuisances from birds.
[2] *Wandsworth LBC v Railtrack plc* (2001) LGR 544 (a public nuisance action where pigeon infestation and the consequent fouling amounted to a substantial interference with the comfort and convenience of the public).
[3] See *Stanley v London Borough of Ealing* [2000] Env LR D18 and *R (on the application of Knowsley MBC) v Williams* (CO/5010/1999, CO/1432/2000; 19 October 2000, QBD) (transcript:

The waste management regime

9.04 The raft of legislation which regulates the management of waste and which prescribes a range of offences for their breach, means that accumulations of matter which also fall within the definition of waste, are more likely to be dealt with under those provisions than as a statutory nuisance under s 79(1)(e) of the EPA 1990.[4] However, Parts II[5] and III of the EPA 1990 are not mutually exclusive so a local authority, or a 'person aggrieved' by the presence of an accumulation, is not prevented from bringing an action in respect of a statutory nuisance simply because the matter may also fall under the waste legislation and thus be enforced by the Environment Agency.[6] The service of an abatement notice may, in fact, be the swifter mechanism for dealing with the problem. For an individual faced with the problem of accumulations of waste in the neighbourhood and the consequent risk of disease, the availability of the procedure under section 82 whereby an individual can bring proceedings for the abatement of a statutory nuisance in the magistrates' court, may be the most expeditious manner of dealing with the problem.

Definitions

9.05 There is no definition in the EPA 1990 of 'accumulation or deposit'. The *Oxford English Dictionary Online* defines 'accumulation' as 'an accumulated mass; a heap, pile, or quantity formed by successive additions'. 'Deposit' is defined as 'something deposited, laid or thrown down; a mass or layer of matter that has subsided or been precipitated from a fluid medium, or has collected in one place by any natural process'.

9.06 Past cases have held that 'accumulations and deposits' included such matters as:

- a deposit of sewage and sewage-related material on a beach;[7]
- an accumulation of seaweed in a harbour;[8]
- a pile of garden manure which gave off smells and attracted flies;[9]
- sheep droppings on a pavement;[10]

Smith Bernal), where the accumulation consisted of miscellaneous refuse including carpets, soil, old furniture and garden waste which was a potential harbourage for rodents and flies.

[4] See Part II of the EPA 1990 and, for the waste offences, sections 33 and 34 of that Act.
[5] Part II of the EPA 1990 establishes the waste management framework.
[6] The Environment Agency for England and Wales (in Scotland the relevant body is the Scottish Environment Protection Agency) is responsible for the enforcement of waste offences falling under Part II of the EPA 1990. Overlapping jurisdictions may cause enforcement difficulties in practice, especially where delays might occur in resolving the problem; see *R v Carrick DC, ex p Shelley* [1996] Env LR 273. If proceedings in respect of an accumulation or deposit might be brought under Part I, EPA 1990 or under regulations under section 2 of the Pollution Prevention and Control Act 1999 the local authority must obtain the consent of the Secretary of State before instituting proceedings under Part III. [7] *R v Carrick DC, ex p Shelley* (n 6 above).
[8] *Margate Pier and Harbour (Proprietors Co) v Margate Town Council* (1869) 33 JP 437.
[9] *Bland v Yates* (1914) 58 SJ 612 (a private nuisance case).
[10] *Draper v Sperring* (1861) 10 CB (NS) 113.

- an accumulation of dung;[11]
- an accumulation of cinders and ashes which were continually smouldering and were the source of strong fumes and effluvia; in addition, the accumulations stood in part on sewers and the fumes passed along the sewers through the water-closets into nearby dwellings;[12]
- the deposit by an urban sanitary authority of refuse, manure, and cinders into a heap from where it was collected by farmers who had bought it;[13]
- refuse deposited in a compound against the front boundary wall of a property;[14] and
- railway trucks standing at a station and loaded with manure.[15]

An accumulation may also give rise to a nuisance where it alters the level of the land so as to cause rainwater to drain onto neighbouring land.[16]

9.07

Many of these cases date from the nineteenth century and focus on problems relating to accumulations of dung or manure. In *Coventry CC v Cartwright*,[17] a more recent case, an accumulation was considered to be 'something which produces a threat to health in the sense of a threat of disease, vermin or the like'.[18]

9.08

The obligation to remove accumulations

The obligation to deal with an accumulation arises whether or not it has been caused by the action of the owner or occupier of the land. Liability is triggered by a failure to remove it given a reasonable time to do so from when knowledge that it constitutes a public nuisance first arose. This will follow whether or not the accumulation has arisen as a result of human intervention or by an act of nature.[19] On this basis, in *Wandsworth LBC v Railtrack plc*[20] the Court of Appeal held that the presence of pigeon droppings under a railway bridge which crossed Balham High Road, interfered with the right of the public to enjoy the

9.09

---

[11] *Smith v Waghorn* (1863) 27 JP 744 (a case brought under the Tunbridge Wells Improvement Act 1846, s 138, a local Act, which imposed a penalty on offensive matter being kept so as to be a nuisance).
[12] *Bishop Auckland Local Board v Bishop Auckland Iron and Steel Co* (1882) 10 QBD 138. This case was brought under the Public Health Act 1875, s 91(4) ('an accumulation or deposit of cinders, ashes and refuse which was a nuisance or injurious to health').
[13] *Scarborough Corporation v Scarborough Rural Sanitary Authority* (1876) 1 Ex D 344 (a case brought under the Public Health Act 1875, s 96). See also *R v Epping (Waltham Abbey) Justices, ex p Burlinson* [1948] 1 KB 79 (a case brought under the Public Health Act 1936, s 92(1)(c), a predecessor section to EPA 1990, s 79(1)). [14] *Stanley v London Borough of Ealing* (n 3 above).
[15] *LB & SC Rly v Haywards Heath UDC* (1899) 86 LT 266; *South Eastern and Chatham Rly Company's Managing Committee* (1902) 24 MCC 343; *GN Rly v Lurgan Town Commissioners* [1897] 2 IR 340. [16] *Hardman v North Eastern Rly* (1878) 3 CPD 168.
[17] [1975] 1 WLR 845. [18] ibid, per Lord Widgery CJ at 849.
[19] *Slater v Worthington's Cash Stores (1930) Ltd* [1941] 1 KB 488. [20] n 2 above.

highway in reasonable comfort and convenience and amounted to a public nuisance.[21]

9.10 In *Margate Pier and Harbour (Proprietors Co) v Margate Town Council*[22] a nuisance arose from the presence of seaweed in the harbour. The action of the tide caused an accumulation of seaweed which decomposed over the summer months causing an offensive smell. It affected the business interests of local hoteliers and, in the evidence of a surgeon, caused harm to health. Indeed, it was said by another witness to have caused 'relaxation of the bowels'. The harbour authority argued that because the accumulation arose as a result of the action of the sea, it was part of the law of nature and did not result from the act or default of the respondent.[23] Nevertheless, it was held that it was the duty of the harbour authority to abate the nuisance: 'whether it was brought from the sea or comes from any other quarter, if it is an accumulation which endangers health'.[24] No distinction was to be made between accumulations or deposits arising on land naturally, or by the owner's act or that of another, where that accumulation gave rise to a statutory nuisance.

The nuisance or health limb requirement

9.11 It is axiomatic that the accumulation or deposit must constitute a statutory nuisance, that is, it must fall under the nuisance or the health limb.

9.12 In *Coventry CC v Cartwright*[25] a demolition site had attracted a certain amount of opportunistic fly-tipping. This included the deposit of household refuse—which was regularly removed by the council—and, large quantities of building material such as brick ends, tarmacadam, old reinforcements, earth, scrap iron, and broken glass—which was not. The question was whether inert material could fall under the definition of a statutory nuisance. The answer hinged on whether the accumulation of inert rubble was prejudicial to health. The Divisional Court held that such matter which might only be hazardous because it might cause physical harm to people coming onto the site was not prejudicial to health.[26] Nor did the visual impact of the site constitute a statutory nuisance since that too fell outside the public health considerations of the legislation.

9.13 The accumulation in *Coventry CC v Cartwright* could not fall under the nuisance limb because there was no transmission of harm from the demolition site to

---

[21] Liability in public nuisance will arise where the defendant is aware of the nuisance, had had a reasonable opportunity to abate it; had the means to abate it; and, had chosen not to do so: *Wandsworth LBC v Railtrack plc* (n 2 above); *A-G v Tod Heatley* [1897] Ch 560.
[22] n 8 above.
[23] Citing in support *Brown v Bussell* III (1867–8) LR 3 QB 251, 439 Lush J pointed out that if a dead body is on premises the occupier was bound by the common law to carry it away and bury it; *R v Stewart* 12 A&E 773. This followed a question from Hayes J as to whether an obligation to remove a dead horse thrown into the harbour by the action of the tide would fall on the harbour authority.
[24] n 8 above, per Lush J at 439.   [25] n 17 above.
[26] See the discussion on the meaning of 'prejudicial to health' at paras 4.82–4.105.

surrounding land, neither did it affect a sufficient cross-section of the public so as to constitute a public nuisance. Its visual impact could not constitute a statutory nuisance and there was no evidence as to smell. So, the only harm which could be caused was to people going onto the site. Since the potential harm to such people was physical injury, it could not constitute a statutory nuisance. Thus, again, the importance of the historical origins of section 79(1)(e) can be seen. The type of harm aimed at by the legislation was disease and ill health such as that evidenced in the *Margate Pier* case.

The defence of 'best practicable means'

9.14 In relation to statutory nuisances falling under section 79(1)(e), the defence that best practicable means were used to prevent or counteract the nuisance is available but it is limited to such nuisances arising on industrial, trade or business premises.[27]

9.15 In common with all statutory nuisances, it is a defence to a prosecution for failure to comply with an abatement notice to show that there was a 'reasonable excuse'.[28]

[27] For further detail on the availability of this defence, see Chapter 15.
[28] See further Chapter 15.

10

MISCELLANEOUS NUISANCES IN OTHER LEGISLATION

Statutory nuisances and watercourses 10.02
    Statutory nuisance and port health authorities 10.07
Meaning of watercourses 10.08
    The decision in *South West Water* 10.11
Persons who may be liable 10.19
Land Drainage Act 1991 ....10.22
Tents, vans, sheds and similar structures 10.26
Domestic water supply 10.30
Fencing of abandoned and disused mines and quarries 10.33

Some miscellaneous statutory nuisances under section 79(1)(h) of the Environmental Protection Act 1990 ('EPA 1990') remain from the Public Health Act 1936 and from the Mines and Quarries Act 1954. In none of these is the defence of 'best practicable means' available.[1] The miscellaneous statutory nuisances comprise nuisances from: **10.01**

- watercourses;
- tents, vans, sheds and similar structures used for human habitation;
- domestic water supply; and
- unfenced abandoned mines and quarries.

Statutory nuisances and watercourses

Section 259(1)(a) of the Public Health Act 1936 defines as a statutory nuisance: **10.02**

any pond, pool, ditch, gutter or watercourse which is so foul or in such a state as to be prejudicial to health or a nuisance ...

This form of statutory nuisance dates, in a slightly modified form, from 1855.[2] Section 259(1)(a) of the 1936 Act makes it an offence to throw rubbish into ponds, streams and the like where this causes a nuisance or poses a risk to health.[3] Without prejudice to its taking enforcement action against a person causing a

---

[1] EPA 1990, s 80(8)(c).   [2] See further para 3.14.
[3] Part III of the Water Resources Act 1991 provides for offences of disposing of polluting matter in streams.

statutory nuisance, the local authority is also empowered to drain, cleanse, cover, or otherwise prevent such water sources from being prejudicial to health.[4] It can also execute any works, including maintenance and improvement works, in relation to such actions.[5]

10.03 Section 259(1)(b) of the Public Health Act 1936 adds a further statutory nuisance:

> any part of a watercourse, not being a part ordinarily navigated by vessels employed in the carriage of goods by water, which is so choked or silted up as to obstruct or impede the proper flow of water and thereby cause a nuisance, or give rise to conditions prejudicial to health.

10.04 Obstruction of a public navigable river can be a public nuisance.[6]

10.05 Section 259(1) of the Public Health Act 1936 provides for two different statutory nuisances, paragraphs (a) and (b), each having separate legislative histories until consolidated by the 1936 Act. Nevertheless, these provisions are closely linked, forming a single subsection of the Act and are contained within a single sentence. In view of such proximity, the Court of Appeal has held that the term 'watercourse' has the same meaning in both types of nuisance stipulated in section 259.[7]

10.06 Note that the watercourse must *be* in such a state as to be a nuisance under section 259(1)(a) of the Public Health Act 1936. This provision is concerned with the watercourse itself and not with what might be *caused* by the nuisance, such as any flooding resulting from an obstruction.

Statutory nuisance and port health authorities

10.07 Enforcement powers can be exercised by port health authorities, who are in the same position as local authorities for taking action in respect of statutory nuisances occurring within their areas. The EPA 1990 excludes noise nuisances from the jurisdiction of port health authorities.[8]

Meaning of watercourses

10.08 At common law the meaning of 'watercourse' is fairly wide and depends on the context in which it is used. In *Taylor v St Helens Corporation*[9] it was held to be capable of meaning either a right or easement to the running of water, or the channel through which the water runs, or the land over which the water flows. It can include the tidal stretches of a river.[10]

---

[4] Public Health Act 1936, s 260 (1)(a).
[5] ibid, s 260 (1)(b).
[6] *R v Tindall* (1837) 6 Ad & El 143.
[7] *R v Falmouth and Truro Port Health Authority, ex p South West Water Ltd* [2000] 3 All ER 306.
[8] EPA 1990, s 79(8).
[9] (1877) 6 Ch D 264.
[10] *Somersetshire Drainage Commissioners v Bridgwater* (1899) 81 LT 729.

Watercourses are normally limited to water flowing between more or less defined banks; containment within a definite channel is characteristic, but it is not essential for the channel to be permanent.[11] A watercourse does not cease from being so merely because it is dry at any particular time, or for quite a lot of the time.[12] An essential characteristic is the existence of flowing as distinct from stable waters.[13] Controlled waters, as provided for under section 85 of the Water Resources Act 1991, can apply to any watercourse.[14]

10.09

The common law definition is not without difficulties. It is not clear, for example, whether an artificial lake, from which a stream exits and carries on its natural course, is a watercourse.

10.10

The decision in South West Water
The meaning of a watercourse in a statutory nuisance context has recently been considered by the Court of Appeal in *R v Falmouth and Truro Port Health Authority, ex p South West Water Ltd*.[15] The case concerned the discharge of sewage into the Carrick Roads stretch of the Fal estuary by South West Water, and in particular whether the point of discharge was into a watercourse and thus capable of amounting to a statutory nuisance.[16] The EPA 1990 provides no statutory definition of 'watercourse'.

10.11

One of the issues before the Court of Appeal was whether the scope of 'watercourse' was limited by its original enactment in a public health statute—the Nuisances Removal Act 1855. This would import a very narrow scope, applying to a limited body of water as implied by section 259(1)(a) of the 1936 Act. Alternatively, could 'watercourse' be extended to cover a much larger body of water, such as an estuary, as the later provision in section 259(1)(b) might suggest?

10.12

Following the leading judgment on watercourses by Hale LJ, the Court of Appeal in *South West Water* decided on a fairly narrow interpretation. This was another decision grounded in a detailed historical analysis of statutory nuisance coupled with a narrow determination of legislative intention.[17]

10.13

The first part of the Court of Appeal's reasoning was based on the correct assumption that a tidal section of a river would not have been contemplated as

10.14

---

[11] *Briscoe v Drought* (1860) 11 IRCom Law Rep 250; *Rawstron v Taylor* (1855) 11 Ex 369; *Broadbent v Ramsbothom* (1856) 11 Ex 602; *Dudden v Clutton Union* (1857) 26 LJ Ex 146.
[12] *Stollmeyer v Trinidad Lake Petroleum Co* [1918] AC 485.
[13] *M'Nab v Robertson* [1897] AC 129.   [14] *R v Dovermoss Ltd* [1995] Env LR 258.
[15] n 7 above. See particularly the judgment of Hale LJ at 337–44.
[16] For a wider consideration of the implications of this case see J Pointing, '*Falmouth and Truro Port Health Authority v South West Water Ltd*: Have Specific Works Notices Finally Run their Course?' [2000] ELM 99; and R Malcolm, 'Statutory Nuisance: The Validity of Abatement Notices' [2000] JPL 894.
[17] See Chapter 4 for a detailed analysis of the concept of statutory nuisance.

coming within the scope of a watercourse in the Nuisances Removal Act 1855, when this form of statutory nuisance was first enacted.[18] Relying on tidal action at that time to dispose of human waste was conventional and acceptable. It would not have been considered a nuisance but a wholesome alternative to polluting a non-tidal stretch of a river or a stream. For Hale LJ (at 342) this meant that 'by no stretch of the imagination could it [a watercourse] have included an estuary such as Carrick Roads or indeed any tidal waters'.

10.15 The Court of Appeal could not have left matters there because the scope of statutory nuisance in watercourses was extended by the Public Health Act 1925 to include what is now section 259(1)(b) of the 1936 Act. This paragraph expressly brings the generally not navigated stretches of rivers within the scope of statutory nuisance. Thus, the scope of 'watercourse' when the 1936 Act was enacted was broad enough to include a stretch of water capable of navigation by ships, if not ordinarily used in such a way. There is no mention in this provision of a large body of water, such as a lake or the tidal stretch of a river.

10.16 In essence, the Court of Appeal decided that the legislature's intention in 1936 should prevail as to the meaning of 'watercourse'. Included in this was a decision that its meaning had to be the same for both parts of section 259 of the Public Health Act 1936. The location of both types of nuisance within the same subsection of the Act and even in the same sentence meant that 'watercourse' could bear only one meaning. Had Parliament intended differently, it would have been obvious to the draftsman and two meanings would have been provided in the statute.

10.17 However, the decision in *South West Water* is very cautious and it would appear that a tidal stretch of a river with banks on both sides does not come within the scope of a statutory nuisance. Despite the careful analytical approach taken by Hale LJ, it is not clear from her judgment why she did not adopt a broader approach, taking into account developments in the common law and societal changes since 1936. One reason given was that in recent decades the protection of estuaries and tidal waters from health hazards could be achieved in different ways; in this case the Environment Agency could have refused to have given its consent to the discharge under Part III of the Water Resources Act 1991. Her decision does not attach significance to the fact that section 259 of the Public Health Act 1936 only became consolidated with other forms of statutory nuisance in section 79 of the EPA 1990.[19]

---

[18] This is apparent from the wording of section 8 of the 1855 Act: 'Any Pool, Ditch, Gutter, Watercourse, Privy, Urinal, Cesspool, Drain, or Ashpit so foul as to be a Nuisance or injurious to Health'.

[19] PHA 1936, s 259, was separated from other statutory nuisances in that Act. In part, this was because legislators still thought about statutory nuisances in various ways, as they had in the 1850s, depending on the type of nuisance.

10.18 Although the decision of the Court of Appeal seems altogether cautious, it is still not clear where the line is to be drawn on watercourses. Coastal waters and estuaries are clearly excluded, but what of inland lakes or tidal parts of rivers upstream of their estuaries?[20] Enforcement authorities will need to consider very carefully whether action should be taken under other provisions than statutory nuisance, notably section 85 of the Water Resources Act 1991 which deals with river pollution.

Persons who may be liable

10.19 With regard to nuisances falling under section 259(1)(b) of the Public Health Act 1936, proceedings can only be taken against the person responsible by reason of his *act* or *default* for the nuisance arising or continuing. 'Default' includes a failure to discharge an obligation or duty; merely doing nothing will not suffice. This restricts serving notices on the landowner or riparian owner unless he is also responsible for causing the nuisance in the above ways. This contrasts with liability in other forms of statutory nuisance—including under section 259(1)(a) of the Public Health Act 1936—where proceedings can also be taken against a person by whose *sufferance* the nuisance is attributable.[21]

10.20 In *Neath RDC v Williams*[22] a riparian owner was not liable to maintain a watercourse and so he could not be guilty of default if he failed to clear an obstruction that had been naturally caused. Williams merely suffered the nuisance of a choked watercourse to continue and so could not be served with an abatement notice because of the proviso in section 259(1)(b) of the Public Health Act 1936. The decision in this case was influenced by the common law position restricting liability of riparian owners to artificial obstructions, whether or not they were responsible for creating them. A common law duty may also arise where the watercourse itself is artificial, such as a canal, rather than naturally occurring.

10.21 This contrasts with the situation where the obstruction is the result of non-natural causes, in which case liability could arise. In *Sedleigh-Denfield v O'Callaghan*[23] a pipe had been inserted into a ditch to carry away excess water and it was the pipe that had been allowed to get choked by the landowner. It was held that a local authority could be held liable in a civil action for damage resulting from a blocked culvert, however the blockage was caused, where it could be shown that it had allowed the nuisance to continue. It would need to be proved that the local authority knew or ought to have known of the obstruction. A local authority could also be held liable for flood damage from a culvert which though not a nuisance

---

[20] See R Macrory, 'Statutory Nuisances and Watercourses', *ENDS Report 303*, April 2000.
[21] EPA 1990, s 79(7).   [22] [1950] 2 All ER 625.   [23] [1940] AC 880.

when constructed became one when changes in the area caused the flow to increase beyond its capacity.[24]

Land Drainage Act 1991

10.22 Section 259 of the Public Health Act 1936 overlaps to a certain extent with the Land Drainage Act 1991, which contains various provisions for dealing with obstructions to watercourses. Section 23 of the Land Drainage Act 1991 requires that written consent is obtained from the drainage board[25] before any mill, dam, weir, or similar structure is erected that obstructs the flow of any watercourse. Consent is also required to erect a culvert where this is likely to affect the flow. Contravention of section 23 constitutes a nuisance, for which the person having the power to remove the obstruction is liable to be served with an abatement notice, breach of which is an offence under section 24.

10.23 The drainage board or local authority concerned may also serve a notice under section 25 of the Land Drainage Act 1991 requiring the relevant person to remedy a condition where the proper flow of water is impeded in a watercourse. A 'relevant person' is any person having control of the watercourse where the impediment occurs, an adjoining occupier or landowner, or a person whose act or default is responsible for the impediment.[26]

10.24 Where a ditch is in such a condition as to cause injury to any land or where it prevents improvement to drainage, the owner or occupier may apply for an order from the Agricultural Land Tribunal for named persons to carry out specified works.[27] These works are restricted to cleansing and protecting the ditch and are based on powers to protect adjoining land from injury. A 'ditch' may include a culverted and a piped ditch, but not a watercourse vested in or controlled by a drainage body.[28]

10.25 Where a landowner has been served with a notice in respect of section 28 of the 1991 Act, a failure to comply may constitute a default arising from a failure to discharge an obligation. This may make him liable to proceedings under section

---

[24] *Bybrook Barn Garden Centre Ltd v Kent CC* [2001] Env LR 30. In this case there was no obstruction of the culvert. The problem arose because the culvert, having been built in the 1930s, had become inadequate in removing surface water after exceptionally heavy rainfall from an area that had become built up in the meantime, including the construction of the M20 motorway. The Court of Appeal held that once the highway authority became aware of the deficiency it was under a duty to enlarge the culvert if it was reasonable to do so, which in this case it was. See also *Marcic v Thames Water Utilities Ltd* [2002] EWCA 65.

[25] Section 1 of the Act deals with the composition of local drainage boards. Jurisdiction may be with the Environment Agency, such as where rivers as distinct from minor streams are involved. Where local authorities are involved, as with section 25 notices, they should notify their internal drainage district or the Environment Agency, depending on which has jurisdiction over the watercourse in question. [26] Land Drainage Act 1991, s 25(3).

[27] ibid, s 28(1). [28] ibid, s 28(5).

10: MISCELLANEOUS NUISANCES IN OTHER LEGISLATION

259(1)(b) of the Public Health Act 1936 even though the default is one in which he has *suffered* the obstruction to have arisen.[29]

Tents, vans, sheds and similar structures

10.26 Section 268 of the Public Health Act 1936 controls the use of temporary and other unsuitable structures for housing. One of the prime objectives of mid-Victorian nuisance legislation—to prevent domestic overcrowding—is reflected in this section.[30] Section 268(2) provides that a statutory nuisance shall occur where:

... a tent, van, shed or similar structure used for human habitation—
(a) which is in such a state, or so overcrowded as to be prejudicial to the health of the inmates; or
(b) the use of which, by reason of the absence of proper sanitary accommodation or otherwise, gives rise, whether on the site or on other land, to a nuisance or to conditions prejudicial to health ...

10.27 Where a local authority is satisfied that a statutory nuisance has resulted under this section, an abatement notice should be served on the occupier.[31] This provision is intended to deal with contamination arising from filth and other insanitary conditions of habitation; contamination by radioactive materials is excluded.[32] The statutory definition of 'occupier' includes any person for the time being in charge of the habitation in question.[33] An occupier can raise the statutory defence that he did not authorize the structure to be stationed or erected on the land.[34]

10.28 The local authority has powers under section 268(4) of the Public Health Act 1936 to make bye-laws for promoting cleanliness in, and the habitable condition of, these structures when used for human habitation. This can include bye-laws to prevent the occurrence of nuisances.

10.29 Under section 268(5) of the Public Health Act 1936, the local authority has a power to prohibit the use of such structures for human habitation.

Domestic water supply

10.30 Section 141 of the Public Health Act 1936 defines as statutory nuisance:

Any well, tank, cistern, or water-butt used for the supply of water for domestic purposes which is so placed, constructed or kept as to render the water therein liable to contamination or otherwise prejudicial to health ...

10.31 Section 141 of the Public Health Act 1936 complements section 140, which empowers a local authority to obtain an order from a magistrates' court directing

---

[29] See para 10.19.
[31] Public Health Act 1936, s 268(3).
[33] Public Health Act 1936, s 268(2).
[30] See further Chapter 3.
[32] Radioactive Substances Act 1993, s 40.
[34] ibid, s 268(3).

that the domestic water supply be temporarily or permanently closed or cut off where the water is, or is likely to become, so polluted as to be prejudicial to health.

10.32 Section 141 is restricted to the plant or equipment used for supplying domestic water and is particularly useful where there is a problem with the water supply from communal tanks to flats. It can be used where water tanks are contaminated by dead animals, but not by radioactive materials.[35] The local authority can serve an abatement notice under section 80 of the EPA 1990 on the owner, or the managing agent in control of flats.[36]

Fencing of abandoned and disused mines and quarries

10.33 By section 151(1) and (2)(a) of the Mines and Quarries Act 1954 a statutory nuisance includes a shaft or outlet of an abandoned mine, or of a mine which has not been worked for a period of twelve months, the surface entrance to which is not provided with a 'properly maintained efficient enclosure, barrier, plug or other device' designed and constructed to prevent any person from accidentally falling down the shaft or from accidentally entering the outlet. The intention of this provision is to place a duty on the owners of abandoned mines to provide suitable fencing to prevent accidents.[37]

10.34 Section 151(2)(c) of the Mines and Quarries Act 1954 provides another statutory nuisance, namely a quarry (whether in course of being worked or not) which is not provided with an efficient and properly maintained barrier so designed and constructed as to prevent any person from accidentally falling into the quarry; and which, by reason of its accessibility from a highway or place of public resort, constitutes a danger to the public.

10.35 Service of abatement notices should be on the 'owner' of a mine or quarry. The 'owner' means the person who is for the time being entitled to work the mine or quarry.[38] However, a contractor wholly working a quarry on behalf of such a person is deemed the owner.[39] And by section 181(4) of the 1954 Act a liquidator, receiver or manager carrying out the business of the owner is an 'additional owner'.

---

[35] Radioactive Substances Act 1993, s 40.
[36] *Camden LBC v Gunby* [2000] 1 WLR 465.
[37] Where the mine is not a mine of coal, stratified limestone, shale or fireclay and has not been worked for the purpose of extracting minerals since 9 August 1872, this provision only applies where the shaft or outlet constitutes a danger to the public because of its accessibility from the public highway or place of public resort (Mines and Quarries Act 1954, s 151(1) and (2)(b)).
[38] ibid, s 181(1).   [39] ibid, s 181(2).

PART III

PROCEDURE AND EVIDENCE

11

IMPLICATIONS OF THE HUMAN RIGHTS ACT 1998

Background to the Act 11.01
Applicable to all acts or decisions taken by public authorities 11.02
    Proceedings taken by 'persons aggrieved' 11.04
    The scope of the Act 11.05
Application to acts of private individuals 11.07
Relationship between Convention rights and UK legislation 11.09
    Declaration of incompatibility 11.10
Persons entitled to bring judicial review proceedings under the
Human Rights Act 1998 ....11.14
Impact of the Human Rights Act 1998 on local authority
decision-making 11.17
    Priority of primary legislation 11.20
    Where a local authority acts through a private body 11.23
    Proportionality 11.25
    Implications of the Human Rights Act 1998 for drafting abatement
    notices 11.26
The right to property 11.30
Article 8: Right to respect for private and family life 11.33
    The article 8(2) qualification 11.38
    Companies or natural persons? 11.41
Article 7: No punishment without law 11.42
    Conflict with section 80 of the EPA 1990 ....11.45
Article 6: Right to a fair trial 11.46
    Fair trial 11.47
    Width of article 6 ....11.49
    Boundary between criminal and civil law 11.51
    Access to a lawyer 11.53
    Delay 11.55
    Right to reasons 11.56
    Duty of disclosure 11.58
    Disclosure of unused material 11.59
    Hearsay evidence 11.62
    Unlawfully obtained evidence 11.65
    Right to silence 11.67

Regulation of Investigatory Powers Act 2000 . . . . .11.69
**Application of the Regulation of Investigatory Powers Act 2000 to
statutory nuisance** 11.72
    Directed surveillance 11.74
    Authorization 11.76
    Intrusive surveillance 11.78
    Directed or intrusive surveillance? 11.80
    Does noise-monitoring equipment amount to a surveillance device? 11.82
    Tape recorders 11.84
    Covert human intelligence sources 11.85
**Application of the Regulation of Investigatory Powers Act 2000 to
statutory nuisance enforcement: Conclusions** 11.87

Background to the Act

11.01 The principal provisions of the Human Rights Act 1998 came into force on 2 October 2000.[1] Extending to England, Wales, Scotland and Northern Ireland, it incorporates into UK law the rights and freedoms set out in the European Convention on Human Rights.[2] In basic terms this means that:

- so far as possible, legislation, whenever passed, must be read and given effect to in a way compatible with the Convention;[3]
- public authorities—including the courts—must not act (or fail to act) if that conduct would be incompatible with Convention rights;[4] and
- when interpreting Convention rights domestic courts must take into account any judgment of the European Court of Human Rights.

Applicable to all acts or decisions taken by public authorities

11.02 The Human Rights Act 1998 applies to all public authorities. The effect of this is that the articles set out in Schedule 1 to the Act shape the way individuals should be treated by public authorities. The 1998 Act is, therefore, potentially relevant to every act or decision taken by a local authority.

11.03 With regard to statutory nuisance enforcement, this means that decisions whether to serve an abatement notice, or whether to commence (or discontinue with) a prosecution under section 80 of the Environmental Protection Act 1990 ('EPA 1990'), have to be made in the light of the Act. Other decisions relevant

---

[1] Human Rights Act 1998 (Commencement No 2) Order 2000, SI 2000/1851. (Sections 18, 20, 21(5) and 22 (which concerned the appointment of judges to the European Court of Human Rights and order-making powers under the Act) came into force on Royal Assent (9 November 1998); section 19 (statements of compatibility) was brought into force on 24 November 1998 by the Human Rights Act 1998 (Commencement No 1) Order 1998, SI 1998/2882.)
[2] Rome, 4 November 1950; TS 71 (1953); Cmd 8969.
[3] Human Rights Act 1998, s 3(1).
[4] ibid, s 6(1).

to statutory nuisance enforcement may come within the scope of the Human Rights Act 1998, including:

- enforcement policy;
- prosecution policy;
- policy on inspections and investigating complaints;
- service provision, such as party noise patrols;
- use of discretion in the type of abatement notice served;
- withdrawal of abatement notices; and
- disclosure of unused material.

Proceedings taken by 'persons aggrieved'
Proceedings taken under section 82 of the EPA 1990 by private persons who are 'aggrieved' by a statutory nuisance may also be affected by the Human Rights Act 1998.[5] This might apply, for example, where a local authority has withdrawn an abatement notice, thus rendering proceedings under section 82 more difficult or less likely to succeed in court. A local authority which encourages aggrieved persons to take their own proceedings in order to save themselves the trouble of enforcing section 80 of the EPA 1990 may also be caught by the 1998 Act.

11.04

The scope of the Act
The Human Rights Act 1998 is intended to apply quite widely and the definition of a public authority and of the state are given a wide meaning in the Act.[6] This includes local government, public regulators including the Environment Agency, courts and tribunals. Both Houses of Parliament are expressly excluded, except for the House of Lords when acting in its judicial capacity.[7] Otherwise, the Act applies to decisions made by central government. The devolved assemblies in Wales and Scotland—in contrast to the Westminster Parliament—have no powers to act or to legislate incompatibly with the Convention.

11.05

The Act applies to 'any person certain of whose functions are ... of a public nature'.[8] The acts of privatized utilities come within its scope where these are of a public nature, but not their private acts.[9] The state is strictly liable for the

11.06

---

[5] See Chapter 16.
[6] During debate, the Home Secretary justified not providing a tight or an exhaustive definition of a public authority, asserting that: 'The [Bill] had to have a definition of a public authority that went at least as wide and took account of the fact that, over the past 20 years, an increasingly large number of private bodies, such as companies or charities, have come to exercise public functions that were previously exercised by public authorities ... What was needed ... was a statement of principle ... [Human Rights Act 1998, s 56] therefore adopts a non-exhaustive definition of a public authority.' (*Hansard*, HC Debs, 16 February 1998, col 775).   [7] Human Rights Act 1998, s 6(4).
[8] ibid, s 6(3)(b).
[9] In debate, the distinction was made using Railtrack as an example of a hybrid body, with public functions relating to safety and private ones involving land sales. See Lord Williams, *Hansard*, HL Debs, 24 November 1997, col 758.

conduct of its subordinates[10] and it cannot absolve itself by delegating responsibilities to private bodies or individuals.[11]

Application to acts of private individuals

11.07 Arguably, the Human Rights Act 1998 applies to some acts of certain private individuals. This is an area in which it is difficult to generalize since it is a developing area of law, applicable on a case-by-case basis.[12] Applicability to private acts may occur in situations where there is a positive obligation on the state to secure compliance with a Convention right. Where there is a breach of such a right, then the court's duty not to act in a way that is incompatible with a Convention right applies.[13]

11.08 An example where this might apply would be where a person's rights to privacy—protected by article 8 of the Convention—were being violated by a neighbour who was covertly collecting evidence of noise nuisance. The noise victim may be collecting evidence on behalf of the local authority, in which case the provisions of the Regulation of Investigatory Powers Act 2000 arguably apply.[14] Alternatively, the noise victim may be collecting evidence about the activities of the noise producer, intending to use it in his own proceedings under section 82 of the EPA 1990.[15] The court's duty in both these examples is to ensure that the noise producer's rights to privacy are not violated, so any evidence collected which breaches such a right should be found inadmissible on Convention grounds. Probably, such a ruling would apply both in civil proceedings, in an appeal against service of an abatement notice, and in a prosecution for breach of a notice.

Relationship between Convention rights and UK legislation

11.09 It might be thought that the potential for conflict between Convention rights and primary legislation, such as Part III of the EPA 1990, is enormous. Legislation passed before the Human Rights Act 1998 came into force is, to a considerable extent, saved from such difficulties. This is because of the presumption that Parliament intended its Acts to be compatible with the Convention.[16] Compatibility is also implied between Convention rights and the mass of statutory provisions in existence before the Human Rights Act 1998 came into effect.[17]

[10] *Ireland v United Kingdom* (1979–80) 2 EHRR 25, at para 159.
[11] *Van der Mussele v Belgium* (1984) 6 EHRR 163.
[12] S Grosz, J Beatson and P Duffy, *Human Rights: The 1998 Act and the European Convention* (Butterworths, 2000). [13] Human Rights Act 1998, s 6(3).
[14] See further paras 11.69–11.89. [15] See Chapter 16.
[16] This includes pre- Human Rights Act 1998 legislation. Section 19 of the 1998 Act stipulates that new Bills should include a statement of compatibility/incompatibility with the Convention.
[17] This is the most significant effect of the Human Rights Act 1998, s 3(1). It is analogous to the position with European Union law: domestic courts are obliged to interpret UK law in accordance with EU provisions.

Declaration of incompatibility

It is only where it proves impossible to interpret UK legislation compatibly with a Convention right that the higher courts can make a declaration of incompatibility.[18] This may occur in proceedings for judicial review. A declaration of incompatibility cannot be made during a prosecution in the magistrates' courts nor in an appeal heard in the Crown Court.

11.10

A High Court declaration of incompatibility ought to encourage the Government to remedy the offending parts of the legislation. This might have retrospective effect for a person whose rights had been breached.[19]

11.11

The court's duty is to strive to interpret domestic legislation consistently with Convention rights. This duty applies equally to magistrates' courts and Crown Courts as to the higher courts. A breach of Convention rights can be raised in the lower courts, even though these courts cannot make a declaration of incompatibility.

11.12

Convention rights do not override incompatible domestic legislation; they lack the power of an Act of Parliament, which expressly or impliedly will repeal inconsistent earlier legislation. Because of this a local authority could be required to act under incompatible domestic legislation. Only Parliament is able to repeal such legislation and no court can oblige it to do so.[20]

11.13

Persons entitled to bring judicial review proceedings under the Human Rights Act 1998

The Human Rights Act 1998 operates at different levels. Besides shaping the way public authorities should treat individuals, an individual who believes that his Convention rights have been breached by a public authority may bring proceedings in the High Court directly to enforce his rights. Previously such actions had to be referred to the European Court of Human Rights in Strasbourg.

11.14

An applicant will only be able to bring judicial review proceedings against a public authority for acting incompatibly with a Convention right if he is a victim according to article 34 of the Convention.[21] This is the 'sufficient interest' test in which the victim needs to show that he is *directly* affected by the act or omission in question.[22] A victim includes someone directly placed at risk by the act or omission. Indirect victims are included only where they can show that they have

11.15

---

[18] Human Rights Act 1998, s 4. [19] ibid, s 10.
[20] This situation is in contrast to European Union law, where the incompatibility of UK legislation would mean that EU law prevailed over it. [21] Human Rights Act 1998, s 7(7).
[22] This may be more restrictive than the 'sufficient interest' test for seeking judicial review in cases brought other than on Convention grounds. Here the procedure for judicial review is governed by the Civil Procedure Rules 1998, SI 1998/3132, Pt 54.

suffered some injury and where the direct victim cannot himself bring an action.[23]

11.16 A victim may include a company,[24] a non-government organization or a group of individuals, including a representative body, or an unincorporated association.[25] A company (or other body) can be a victim,[26] inter alia, of a breach of rights to a fair criminal trial,[27] or of the right to property.[28] Such groupings need to show that they, as bodies, were directly affected by the decision or omission in question. If a representative body brings an action on behalf of its members, but is not itself directly affected by the decision, it has no right to bring a complaint.[29]

Impact of the Human Rights Act 1998 on local authority decision-making

11.17 The key provision in the Human Rights Act 1998 is section 6(1) which states that 'it is unlawful for a public authority to act in any way which is incompatible with a Convention right'. From this wording it is clear that there is no positive requirement on the public authority to promote Convention rights, but an authority must avoid acting incompatibly with them.

11.18 Local authorities need to consider carefully what impact Convention rights might have on the decisions they take and on the way they are taken. There are no restrictions on the types of act open to challenge. Decisions, such as whether to prosecute, policies, such as on enforcement, and actions, such as the way an investigation was carried out, are all potentially challengeable on Convention grounds. Bye-laws made by a local authority are similarly open to challenge.

11.19 Decision-making is often complicated by a need to weigh what might be conflicting factors or priorities. It will be rare for a decision involving human rights issues to be clear cut. For instance, in cases of neighbourhood noise nuisance, both perpetrators and victims have rights of non-interference in their private and family life and the right to enjoy the use of their respective properties. Where the line is drawn in deciding that a complaint is justified is a matter of judgment or opinion.

---

[23] eg, in *McCann v UK* (1995) 21 EHRR 97 where relatives of IRA suspects killed by the SAS in Gibraltar were able to bring claims under article 2 (the right to life).
[24] *Autronic AG v Switzerland* (1990) 12 EHRR 485.
[25] *R v London Borough of Tower Hamlets, ex p Tower Hamlets Combined Traders Association* [1994] COD 325.
[26] A company cannot be a victim of a breach of privacy rights under the Convention, although its rights under other legislative provisions can provide it with some protection; see *R v Broadcasting Standards Commission, ex p British Broadcasting Corporation* [2000] EWCA Civ 116.
[27] *Société Stenuit v France* (1992) 14 EHRR 509.
[28] *Lithgow v United Kingdom* (1986) 8 EHRR 329.
[29] *Re Medicaments and Related Classes of Goods (No 4)*, The Times, 7 August 2001.

Priority of primary legislation

11.20 Notwithstanding the Convention, local authorities are required to act in accordance with domestic law. If, by acting in accordance with the EPA 1990, the local authority believes it may be breaching a Convention right, what should it do? The answer is provided by section 6(2) of the Human Rights Act 1998 which makes it clear that primary legislation has priority, including provisions made under Acts of the Westminster Parliament, such as statutory instruments.

11.21 Section 6(2) of the 1998 Act states that section 6(1)—the requirement not to act incompatibly with the Convention—is disapplied if:

(a) as the result of one or more provisions of primary legislation, the authority could not have acted differently; or
(b) in the case of one or more provisions of, or made under, primary legislation which cannot be read or given effect in a way which is compatible with the Convention rights, the authority was acting so as to give effect to or enforce those provisions.

11.22 Section 6(2) implies that a local authority has to strive to ensure that it does not act incompatibly with the Convention. It would be advisable to operate according to the presumption that domestic legislation and the Convention are compatible and it is only when this proves impossible that section 6(2) applies.

Where a local authority acts through a private body

11.23 The prohibition on public bodies acting incompatibly with the Convention includes a situation where a local authority contributes indirectly to or facilitates a breach committed by another party, including a private body. This would apply, for example, where a local authority provided the land and a subsidy for an industrial plant which causes the pollution breaching the rights of residents to respect for their homes. In *Lopez-Ostra v Spain*[30] the state was held responsible for the pollution caused by a private waste-disposal plant because the local council had granted permission for the facility to be built and had subsidized its construction.

11.24 Section 6 of the Human Rights Act 1998 would also apply to a local authority which relied on a private body to carry out its duties where that private body breached a person's Convention rights. This might apply, for example, where a local authority relied on a householder to collect evidence intended to be used in a prosecution.[31] If the householder breached his neighbour's rights in these circumstances the local authority could be deemed to have acted unlawfully.

Proportionality

11.25 Local authority decisions often involve balancing the rights of individuals against the interests of the community at large. Such a balancing act will often apply in statutory nuisance cases, where an individual's use of land interferes with his

---

[30] (1994) 20 EHRR 277.   [31] See para 11.85.

neighbour's use and enjoyment of his land. Striking a fair balance requires the application of the principle of proportionality which is inherent to the Convention.[32] Even where it is clear that a local authority has a legitimate purpose for restricting a Convention right, it must also show that the actual restrictions it employs do not go beyond what is strictly necessary to achieve that purpose.[33]

Implications of the Human Rights Act 1998 for drafting abatement notices

11.26 There will often be circumstances to justify some variation in how restrictive abatement notices need to be to prevent nuisances. Recent UK case law has shown that local authorities have a wide discretion as to how specific the terms need to be when drafting abatement notices under section 80 of the EPA 1990.[34] The principle of proportionality reinforces what should be good practice in any event, that is drafting a notice that requires the minimum interference necessary to prevent or curtail a nuisance.

11.27 In practice, achieving such an ideal for nuisances such as noise is often difficult. Arguably, this principle of minimum interference is inconsistent with a local authority having a wide discretion to specify notice requirements. This is because the council may choose to require specific changes which go beyond the minimum, that is the simplest form of notice that could reduce the problem to below the level of causing a nuisance.[35] This issue impinges on other Convention rights, since breach of an abatement notice provides the foundations for a criminal prosecution.[36]

11.28 Besides the principle of minimum interference, it is arguable that in order not to fall foul of the Convention, certainty is required which should be reflected in the terms of abatement notices. This point is strengthened by the position that in domestic law breach of an abatement notice lays the foundation for a criminal prosecution. The recipient of a notice needs to know precisely how his conduct needs to change in order to avoid breaching the terms of the notice. European Court of Human Rights case law suggests that in order not to offend against the Convention principle of legality, the law or rule in question must be formulated with sufficient clarity to enable those affected by it both to understand it and regulate their conduct to avoid breaking it.[37]

11.29 Convention rights have had little impact on cases in which the terms of abatement notices have been considered by the UK higher courts. This is partly because of

---

[32] *Soering v UK* (1989) 11 EHRR 439, n 18 at para 89. See also the comments of Lord Phillips MR in *Marcic v Thames Water Utilities Ltd* [2002] EWCA Civ 65, at 105–111 and 116–119.
[33] *Powell and Rayner v United Kingdom* (1990) 12 EHRR 355.   [34] See Chapter 12.
[35] This is the position following the Court of Appeal's decision in *R v Falmouth and Truro Port Health Authority, ex p South West Water Ltd* [2000] 3 All ER 306, which, it is suggested, may be inconsistent with the Human Rights Act 1998.
[36] Article 6 (right to a fair trial) and article 7 (certainty in the definition of a crime). See further para 11.45.   [37] *Sunday Times v United Kingdom* (1979–80) 2 EHRR 245.

the short period of time in which the Human Rights Act 1998 has been in effect. Practitioners should be aware, however, of the potential for section 80(1) of the EPA 1990 to be in conflict with the Convention and for legislative change to result from this.

The right to property

Article 1 of the first Protocol of the European Convention concerns the right to property. It provides that every natural or legal person is entitled to the peaceful enjoyment of his possessions. Interference with this right can involve deprivation or control of property. **11.30**

Only interferences which touch on the financial value of property and possessions will engage article 1 of the first Protocol. This may have a restrictive effect with regard to statutory nuisances. For example, it means that noise nuisance will be considered only where a diminution in the value of the property can be shown.[38] This is often difficult to prove and something which local authorities enforcing Part III of the EPA 1990 are not normally concerned about. **11.31**

The impact of this article on the substantive law of statutory nuisance is likely to be limited and victims suffering personal discomfort from statutory nuisances, which do not also diminish the value of their property, will not be able to use it to bring a claim under the Convention. However, article 8 may be engaged where a person's enjoyment of his property is seriously disrupted or where prejudice to health can be shown. The decision of a local authority about which limb of statutory nuisance to use in drafting a notice under section 79(1) of the EPA 1990—common law nuisance or prejudice to health—could be important in relevant cases.[39] **11.32**

Article 8: Right to respect for private and family life

Article 8 is probably the most important provision in regard to the impact of the European Convention on the law of statutory nuisance. Article 8 is concerned with wider matters than property rights; its scope extends to the population as a whole and is not restricted to property owners or those with exclusive possession. **11.33**

Article 8 states: **11.34**

> (1) Everyone has the right to respect for his private and family life, his home and his correspondence.

---

[38] *Rayner v United Kingdom* (1978) 14 DR 234.
[39] In *Lowe & Watson v South Somerset DC* [1998] Env LR 143, the Divisional Court found that the local authority did not have to decide under which limb of section 79 a statutory nuisance fell in order to serve a valid notice. This, it is suggested, makes the decision potentially in conflict with the Convention.

(2) There shall be no interference by a public authority with the exercise of this right except such as is in accordance with the law and is necessary in a democratic society in the interests of national security, public safety or the economic well-being of the country, for the prevention of disorder or crime, for the protection of health and morals, or for the protection of the rights and freedoms of others.

11.35 This article has been construed as imposing a positive obligation on states to protect individuals against incursions by other parties, whether public or private. This means that the protection of the state can be required to protect victims of nuisance from the activities of perpetrators. Secondly, there is a negative obligation not to interfere with rights unless this can be justified in terms provided in article 8(2).

11.36 The first of these obligations is of particular importance for statutory nuisance. For example, where a local authority can be shown not to have used its enforcement powers properly or sufficiently to protect victims of nuisance caused directly by third parties, such victims will be able to engage the Human Rights Act 1998.

11.37 'Home' includes any premises used by an individual as his home in which he has a legal interest. An owner without a right to occupy the home will be included within this definition,[40] as well as, possibly, caravan dwellers squatting on land. 'Home' from a human rights perspective is a wider concept than in private nuisance law, which is concerned with rights of ownership.[41] It includes the rights of persons who are living with (or without) the legal owner in his property, including children, servants, au pairs and elderly relatives. Probably, it excludes a company, since the home is where a person lives: 'the scene of domestic life, with its emotional associations'.[42]

The article 8(2) qualification

11.38 The way article 8(2) operates can be shown by *Powell and Rayner v United Kingdom*.[43] The case concerned complaints about aircraft noise at Heathrow Airport, which were held by the European Court of Human Rights to be material. However, the abatement measures taken to deal with the noise and the economic importance of the airport meant that the noise was justified.[44]

11.39 A fair balance needs to be struck where a right is infringed. The infringement must be weighed against any public benefit justification for it. Causing a serious health risk cannot be justified by article 8(2), and pollution may be so severe or serious, or affect so many people that it cannot be justified.

---

[40] *Wiggins v United Kingdom* (1978) 13 DR 40.
[41] *Hunter and Others v Canary Wharf Ltd and LDDC* [1997] AC 655.
[42] *Chambers Twentieth Century Dictionary* (W & R Chambers, 1964).   [43] n 33 above.
[44] These justifications did not persuade the European Court of Human Rights in respect of noise from night flights in UK airports. In *Hatton and Others v United Kingdom* (2002) 34 EHRR 1, the court held that such flights interfered with the rights of residents to a good night's sleep and that the government's policy on night flights breached article 8.

A serious health risk is not the threshold for article 8. As was stated in *Lopez-* **11.40**
Ostra v Spain:

... severe environmental pollution may affect individuals' well-being and prevent them from enjoying their homes in such a way as to affect their private and family life adversely, without, however, seriously endangering their health.[45]

Companies or natural persons?
It is not clear whether companies can be the victims of breaches of article 8 and **11.41**
further litigation is likely before this issue is resolved. Some cases suggest that only natural persons can experience nuisance or disturbance and therefore companies are excluded. This does not apply to the English concept of private nuisance which requires an interference with rights of property, so the owner can be a victim whether as a natural person or not. On the other hand, interference falling under the nuisance limb of statutory nuisance—that is where it is not injurious to health—requires a material degree of *personal discomfort* rather than merely an interference in property rights. It is difficult to contemplate a company suffering from personal discomfort or injury to health.

Article 7: No punishment without law

Article 7(1) protects individuals from punishment for acts that were not criminal **11.42**
at the time they were committed. It states that:

No one shall be guilty of any criminal offence on account of any act or omission which did not constitute a criminal offence under national or international law at the time when it was committed.

This article is also concerned with certainty in the definition of crime and its **11.43**
scope is broader than at first appears from this wording. A broad interpretation was made in *Kokkinakis v Greece*[46] which held that:

... article 7(1) of the Convention is not confined to prohibiting the retrospective application of the criminal law to an accused's disadvantage. It also embodies, more generally, the principle that only the law can define a crime and prescribe a penalty ... and the principle that the criminal law must not be extensively construed to an accused's detriment; ... it follows from this that an offence must be clearly defined in law.

Article 7 requires an offence be clearly defined in law so that a person when **11.44**
charged knows precisely what acts or omissions render him liable. The requirement is for an individual to know from the wording of the relevant provision (if need be, with the assistance of the court's interpretation) what acts and omissions will make him liable.[47]

---

[45] n 30 above, at note 3.   [46] (1994) 17 EHRR 397, at para 52.
[47] The same point can be made for all criminal charges founded on a breach of a duty of care, such as the Health and Safety at Work Act 1974, ss 2–7.

Conflict with section 80 of the EPA 1990

11.45 Article 7 may conflict with domestic law on abatement notices served under section 80(1)(a) of the EPA 1990, notably the discretion of a local authority to serve notices which do not specify any works that may be needed for abatement.[48] A prosecution founded on a simple abatement notice, particularly where it is obvious that works are needed to achieve its intention could, possibly, be in breach of article 7. This is an area where there seems to be a conflict between domestic law and Convention rights. Recent case law, confirming that a local authority has a simple choice about which kind of notice to serve, has not considered the position in relation to article 7.[49]

Article 6: Right to a fair trial

11.46 An important aspect of human rights concerns court procedure, fairness and the evidence that can be admitted in prosecutions, including those brought under Part III of the EPA 1990. In fact, article 6(1) is wider than this and includes civil rights and obligations. The relevant part of the provision states:

> (1) In the determination of his civil rights and obligations or of any criminal charge against him, everyone is entitled to a fair and public hearing within a reasonable time by an independent and impartial tribunal established by law . . .
> (2) Everyone charged with a criminal offence shall be presumed innocent until proved guilty according to law.
> (3) Everyone charged with a criminal offence has the following minimum rights:
> (a) to be informed promptly, in a language which he understands and in detail, of the nature and cause of the accusation against him . . .

Fair trial

11.47 Rights to a fair trial are wide-ranging and likely to prove of great importance in all legal proceedings. Article 6(1) applies also to civil proceedings, including appeals against abatement notices[50] and High Court matters.[51] Statutes where a reversal of the burden of proof is provided for—such as where a defendant is required to prove that he has used 'best practicable means' to abate or reduce a statutory nuisance—are not in breach of article 6(2).[52]

11.48 The requirements under article 6(1) include:

- the right to an independent and impartial tribunal;
- the right to disclosure;
- the right to an adversarial hearing;

---

[48] See further paras 11.26–11.29.
[49] *R v Falmouth and Truro Port Health Authority, ex p South West Water Ltd* (n 35 above).
[50] See Chapter 13.
[51] See paras 17.11–17.21.
[52] See Chapter 15.

- the right to reasons being given for decisions; and
- the right to have decisions made within a reasonable period.

Width of article 6
Of course, all these rights are provided for by UK common law and statute, but in certain respects they have been enhanced by the Convention.[53] Article 6 does not contain an exhaustive list of rights and the European Court of Human Rights and Commission have read into it other rights and guarantees to protect the fairness of proceedings. **11.49**

Article 6 stipulates a minimum standard and it should not be interpreted narrowly. It was decided in *Delcourt v Belgium* that '. . . a restrictive interpretation of article 6(1) would not correspond to the aim and the purpose of that provision' bearing in mind the prominent place which the right to a fair trial holds 'in a democratic society within the meaning of the Convention'.[54] **11.50**

Boundary between criminal and civil law
Actions which are civil in domestic law may be construed as criminal by the European Court and Commission. An important factor in deciding this is the practice in other states. Severity of fines or imprisonment being imposed as a penalty are indicative of crimes. However, proceedings imposing a fine or imprisonment for breach of an injunction have been held to be civil. **11.51**

Service of an abatement notice is an administrative act and the notice itself is not a document whose primary purpose is the commencement of legal proceedings. Appeals against abatement notices, which are civil in domestic law, are arguably criminal under article 6, though there are no reported cases as yet on the point. It is unlikely, it is suggested, that the present division whereby criminal proceedings may start only after there has been a breach of an abatement notice will be found to be in breach of article 6. Provided the recipient of a notice is made aware when served with the notice that its breach may involve a criminal prosecution, there does not seem to be an infringement of his human rights. However, bearing in mind that an abatement notice has an indefinite life, a person prosecuted many years after service of the notice could argue that this factor alone amounted to unfairness. **11.52**

Access to a lawyer
Article 6(3)(c) guarantees everyone charged with a criminal offence the right to legal assistance. It applies to pre-trial stages, including interviews. Where adverse inferences may be drawn from silence 'it is of paramount importance for the **11.53**

---

[53] Breach of a Convention right, as distinct from breach of a domestic statute (such as the Police and Criminal Evidence Act 1984, s 78) or of a Code made under the 1984 Act, may be accorded a higher value. See the European Court of Human Rights case of *Khan (Sultan) v United Kingdom* [2000] Crim LR 684, commentary at 686.   [54] (1979–80) 1 EHRR 355, at para 25.

rights of the defence that an accused has access to a lawyer at the initial stages of police interrogation'.[55]

11.54 Article 6(3)(c) is relevant to the enforcement of regulatory offences, notably the conduct of interviews carried out by local authority officers in accordance with the Police and Criminal Evidence Act 1984. Where the prosecution asks the court to draw an adverse inference from silence, it is essential that at the time of interview the suspect was legally represented or, at least, warned about the consequences of not being represented.

Delay

11.55 The reasonableness of the length of proceedings depends on the circumstances of each case, in particular its complexity and the conduct of the defendant and prosecuting authorities. Where a delay is excessive and no convincing explanation is given to justify it, a defendant will be able to argue that article 6(1) has been violated.[56]

Right to reasons

11.56 Until the Human Rights Act 1998 came into force magistrates were not required to give reasons for decisions, except in family proceedings. With the Act in place, defendants are entitled on conviction to be given reasons. Besides fairness, this will be helpful in drafting grounds for any further appeal.

11.57 The requirement to give reasons also applies to reasons for admitting or excluding evidence in criminal trials as well as to decisions in appeals against notices. The standard expected of magistrates in providing reasons and the situations where they must be given will no doubt occupy the higher courts before long.[57]

Duty of disclosure

11.58 'Equality of arms' between prosecution and defence implies that the prosecuting authority is required to gather relevant evidence in favour of the accused as well as that against him. The requirement for fairness under article 6(1) means that the prosecutor should disclose to the defence all relevant evidence for or against the accused and a failure to do so can give rise to a defect in the trial proceedings. Both kinds of evidence should be disclosed sufficiently early to allow the accused enough time to prepare his defence. For a summary only trial, such as for breach of an abatement notice, this means that witness statements which the prosecution is intending to rely on are required to be disclosed in advance of the trial.[58]

[55] *Murray v United Kingdom* (1996) 22 EHRR 29, at para 66.
[56] *Howarth v United Kingdom* [2001] Crim LR 229.
[57] In *R v Crown Court at Canterbury, ex p Howson-Ball* [2001] Env LR 36 the Crown Court's decision was quashed as inadequate reasons were given; the Divisional Court's grounds included fairness at common law as well as a breach of article 6. However in *East Devon DC v Farr* (30/1/2002, QBD Administrative Court unreported), the Court dismissed an appeal even though the justices failed to give reasons for their decision to quash an abatement notice.
[58] 'Disclosure of Information in Criminal Proceedings', *Attorney-General's Guidelines* (2000), para 43, available from the Legal Secretariat to the Law Officers' website (www.lslo.gov.uk).

Disclosure of unused material

11.59 The disclosure of unused material, as required by sections 3 and 7 of the Criminal Procedure and Investigations Act 1996, continues to pose problems for local authorities who may comply with their duties late or incompletely.[59] Article 6(3)(b) provides that everyone charged with an offence is entitled to have adequate time and facilities to prepare his defence, so late and/or incomplete disclosure may raise Convention issues as well as those following non-compliance with domestic legislation.

11.60 The scope of disclosure includes the results of investigations carried out throughout the proceedings.[60] Where an investigation for breach of an EPA 1990 abatement notice has not indicated a nuisance or shows that the notice had not been breached on that particular occasion, disclosure of the results of the investigation should take place as this arguably undermines the prosecution case.[61]

11.61 Besides being disclosable under the Criminal Procedure and Investigations Act 1996, the results of such an investigation are relevant to mitigation at trial. The scope of disclosure is wider under article 6(3)(b) than in the 1996 Act as it includes material pertaining to mitigation.[62] It is for this reason that the disclosure guidelines produced by the Attorney-General should be followed as they are fully consistent with the Convention. These state that the prosecutor must consider disclosing any material which is relevant to sentence.[63]

Hearsay evidence

11.62 Under article 6(3)(d) a defendant is entitled to examine witnesses against him and to obtain the attendance and examination of witnesses on his own behalf under the same conditions as the prosecution enjoys. Evidence admitted with the leave of the court under the Criminal Justice Act 1988, to be read out during the trial, may infringe this principle. Such evidence includes oral hearsay (under section 23 of the 1988 Act) as well as business documents or documentary hearsay (under section 24).[64]

11.63 Where the defence is denied an opportunity to test the evidence in cross-examination, any conviction based solely or mainly on such hearsay evidence may violate article 6(3)(d). This will depend principally on the weight of the evidence, but also on whether a defendant had requested attendance of the witness at trial and whether there had been opportunities to challenge the evidence prior to trial.[65]

---

[59] See further paras 18.55–18.77.
[60] *Jespers v Belgium* (1981) 27 DR 61, note 106 at para 56.
[61] Criminal Procedure and Investigations Act 1996, s 3.
[62] *Jespers v Belgium* (n 60 above), note 106 at para 58.
[63] 'Disclosure of Information in Criminal Proceedings', *Attorney-General's Guidelines* (n 58 above), para 44.
[64] See further paras 18.22–18.34.
[65] *R v Denton*, *The Times*, 22 November 2000.

11.64 It is doubtful whether a case which depended on the admissibility of hearsay evidence to such an extent that without it there was little chance of a successful conviction would pass the evidential test required to bring or to continue with a prosecution.

Unlawfully obtained evidence

11.65 Reliance on unlawfully obtained evidence runs the risk of its exclusion at trial for breach of article 6.[66] Although the use of unlawfully obtained evidence is not necessarily ruled out by the Convention, if such evidence is the sole or principal evidence against the accused then a breach of his rights is likely.

11.66 The scope of unlawfully obtained evidence includes the way it was obtained. Thus, evidence obtained in breach of a code of practice, such as those provided by the Police and Criminal Evidence Act 1984, may be excluded where the breach is significant and/or where the evidence obtained from the breach is crucial, particularly if it is uncorroborated.

Right to silence

11.67 The Convention position is that 'in the determination of any criminal charge against him', everyone is entitled 'not to be compelled to testify against himself or to confess guilt'.[67] Where investigating officers have a statutory power to oblige a person to answer their questions his answers cannot be used against him in subsequent criminal proceedings. To use such powers to found a criminal charge based on his answers to questions would involve a clear breach of article 6.[68]

11.68 The drawing by the court of an adverse inference from silence, as is permitted by section 34 of the Criminal Justice and Public Order Act 1994, will not necessarily involve a breach of article 6. However, if an adverse inference is to be drawn, it is essential that the accused has sufficient opportunity to take legal advice at the relevant time. The implication of this for investigating officers is that suspects should be urged strongly to have a solicitor present during a formal interview, otherwise the court may decide not to draw any inference from silence.

---

[66] Of course it may also be excluded under the Police and Criminal Evidence Act 1984, s 78.

[67] Based on the International Covenant on Civil and Political Rights, art 14(3)(g).

[68] This protection of the right not to incriminate oneself applies even to situations where legislation provides that such answers can be used against their maker. In *Saunders v United Kingdom* (1997) 23 EHRR 313, the Companies Act 1985, s 431(5), which provided for the use of such incriminating evidence, was held to be in breach of article 6. Subsequently, the Attorney-General issued guidelines to prosecutors that they should not, except in very limited circumstances, rely on such evidence at trial; see (1998) 148 NLJ 208. By contrast, the Health and Safety at Work Act 1974, s 20(2)(j), gives inspectors the power to require answers to relevant questions, but section 20(7) specifically prohibits the use of such answers against their maker (or a spouse) in any subsequent proceedings.

Regulation of Investigatory Powers Act 2000

The Regulation of Investigatory Powers Act 2000 was enacted as a result of the 'revolution in communications technology' and to protect human rights in the wake of the Human Rights Act 1998 coming into force in October 2000.[69] As already noted, the key section in the 1998 Act is section 6, which makes it unlawful for a public authority to act in a way which is incompatible with a Convention right. Article 8 of the Convention, which stipulates the right to respect for private and family life, is the most likely to be invoked in statutory nuisance cases.

11.69

So, for example, there will be a potential breach of article 8 where a local authority is investigating a case of neighbourhood noise nuisance and is monitoring and obtaining recordings of noise levels. Whether there is an actual breach will depend, firstly, on whether the activity itself amounts to surveillance. Section 48 of the Regulation of Investigatory Powers Act 2000 defines surveillance as including 'monitoring, observing or listening to persons, their movements, their conversations or their other activities or communications'. It includes 'recording anything monitored, observed or listened to in the course of surveillance'.

11.70

Where an activity does amount to covert surveillance being carried out by a public authority it will need to be justified according to article 8(2)[70] and authorized by a designated person under section 27 of the 2000 Act. Article 8(2) includes the protection of the rights and freedoms of others as a justification for interference in the right to respect for private and family life, so the rights of noise victims will be included. Article 8(2) also requires that any interference must be in accordance with law, and it was partly for this reason that the Regulation of Investigatory Powers Act 2000 was enacted. Conduct which is not authorized by the Act is rendered unlawful under section 6 of the Human Rights Act 1998. Any evidence collected in an unauthorized manner is at risk of being inadmissible in court.

11.71

Application of the Regulation of Investigatory Powers Act 2000 to statutory nuisance

Part II of the 2000 Act[71] is the relevant part which might apply to routine statutory nuisance investigations. It is primarily directed to such bodies as the police, security services and HM Customs and Excise, but Part II also applies to local authorities.[72] Draft codes of practice issued under section 71(3)(a) of the Act have not considered local authority investigations.

11.72

---

[69] Home Secretary's foreword to *Interception of Communications in the United Kingdom* (Cm 4368, 1999).   [70] See paras 11.33–11.41.
[71] In effect since 25 September 2000; Regulation of Investigatory Powers Act 2000 (Commencement No 1 and Transitional Provisions) Order 2000, SI 2000/2543.
[72] Regulation of Investigatory Powers Act 2000, Sch 1.

11.73 Section 26 of the Regulation of Investigatory Powers Act 2000 applies to:

- directed surveillance;
- intrusive surveillance; and
- the conduct and use of covert human intelligence sources.

The Regulation of Investigatory Powers Act 2000 is intended to ensure that surveillance is carried out properly and proportionately; authorization is required to facilitate these objectives and to ensure that no breach of human rights occurs.[73]

Directed surveillance

11.74 'Directed surveillance' is defined by the Act as covert[74] but not intrusive, when undertaken as a specific investigation or operation and carried out in such a way as to make it likely that private information is obtained about a person.[75] 'Private information' includes any information relating to a person's private or family life.[76] 'Surveillance' includes monitoring, observing or listening to persons and any recordings made as a result of such activities.[77]

11.75 Noise nuisance involving residents or neighbours would appear to come within this definition when an investigation has been carried out covertly. However, it is not clear cut whether the evidence obtained from such an investigation comprises private information. For example, evidence which shows that music was played loudly or persistently enough to cause a nuisance could be interpreted simply as evidence of excessive noise. Does such evidence constitute information relating to family or private life? Arguably not. If it does, then it comes within the Act.

Authorization

11.76 Directed surveillance must be authorized in each case by a 'designated person'. A designated person must be an Assistant Chief Officer or an officer responsible for the management of an investigation.[78]

11.77 Authorization must be obtained for *each* investigation. If neighbourhood noise investigations do come within the scope of directed surveillance then the burden placed upon local authorities could be very great. The burden would be particularly great where, for example, a council provides a night-time party patrol service where many complaints may need to be investigated during a shift, each requiring separate authorization if directed surveillance is involved.

---

[73] Regulation of Investigatory Powers Act 2000, ss 27–37.
[74] ibid, s 26(9), states that surveillance shall be covert 'if, and only if, it is carried out in a manner that is calculated to ensure that persons who are subject to the surveillance are unaware that it is or may be taking place'.
[75] ibid, s 26(2).
[76] ibid, s 26(10).
[77] ibid, s 48(2).
[78] Regulation of Investigatory Powers (Prescription of Offices, Ranks and Positions) Order 2000, SI 2000/2417.

Intrusive surveillance

11.78 'Intrusive surveillance' is covert surveillance that is carried out on any residential premises or in any private vehicle, and which involves the presence of an individual on those premises or in that vehicle, or is carried out by means of a surveillance device.[79]

11.79 Local authorities are not authorized by the Regulation of Investigatory Powers Act 2000 to carry out intrusive surveillance. If a court were to decide that the type of surveillance employed to obtain information was intrusive, the evidence would have been obtained without authorization and in breach of section 6 of the Human Rights Act 1998 and should not be admissible.

Directed or intrusive surveillance?

11.80 It is important that the distinction between directed surveillance, which can and must be authorized, and intrusive surveillance, which a local authority is not authorized to conduct, is understood. Covert surveillance undertaken by a person off the premises of the person causing the nuisance, would be directed not intrusive surveillance, unless it involved the use of a surveillance device.

11.81 For the use of a surveillance device to be intrusive, it would either have to be placed covertly in the premises of a person causing the alleged nuisance, which would be improper as this would not be authorized by statute. Alternatively, to be intrusive, a device would have to be of a type that 'consistently provides information of the same quality and detail as might be expected to be obtained from a device actually present on the premises'.[80]

Does noise-monitoring equipment amount to a surveillance device?

11.82 It is conceivable that this second possibility might apply in a statutory nuisance case, provided that it can be established that a noise-monitoring device is a surveillance device for purposes of the 2000 Act. Whether the measurement and recording of noise levels is capable of amounting to surveillance is problematic and the question is not resolved by the definition provided in the Act.[81]

11.83 It is suggested that it would only be in limited circumstances that a monitoring instrument:

- was a surveillance device, that also
- consistently provided data of equivalent detail and quality to one used on the premises in question,

where the sections in the Regulation of Investigatory Powers Act 2000 on intrusive surveillance would have any relevance to a statutory nuisance investigation.

---

[79] Regulation of Investigatory Powers Act 2000, s 26(3).
[80] ibid, s 26(4).
[81] ibid, s 48(2).

Were the use of a monitoring device to be deemed intrusive, the result would be that the evidence obtained from it was not authorized by the 2000 Act and ought not to be admitted in court.

Tape recorders

11.84 In contrast to a noise-monitoring device, a tape recorder, which records the actual sounds made by the noise producer, including conversation, fits more closely with the intention of the Act and is included in section 48 of the Regulation of Investigatory Powers Act 2000. It is suggested that the covert use of a tape recorder which is installed in a neighbour's premises, could be 'intrusive surveillance'.

Covert human intelligence sources

11.85 The final category of surveillance covered by Part II of the Regulation of Investigatory Powers Act 2000 concerns the conduct and use of covert human intelligence sources. Where the neighbour of a person causing an alleged statutory nuisance is asked by an investigating officer to collect evidence covertly concerning the nuisance, arguably he could be acting as a covert human intelligence source for the purposes of the Act.[82] This would apply to the keeping of a 'noise diary', for example, where a victim cultivated a relationship with a noisy neighbour in order to obtain information about him. Similarly, in cases of neighbourhood noise nuisance where a paid witness is used by a local authority to collect evidence, the provisions of the 2000 Act arguably apply.

11.86 Authorization for the use of covert human intelligence sources is provided by section 29 of the Regulation of Investigatory Powers Act 2000 and the process is similar to that applying in respect of directed surveillance.[83]

Application of the Regulation of Investigatory Powers Act 2000 to statutory nuisance enforcement: Conclusions

11.87 Without guidance from the Secretary of State it is unclear whether the Regulation of Investigatory Powers Act 2000 applies to routine local authority investigations of statutory nuisances or to noise investigations carried out under the Noise Act 1996.[84] However, as argued above, it is suggested that the covert use of a tape recorder off the premises could constitute a form of intrusive surveillance.[85]

11.88 But there is no certainty whether routine investigations are covered by the provisions of the 2000 Act. The Act's primary purpose is to regulate services for whom surveillance operations are often central, such as the police and HM Customs and

---

[82] As provided in the Regulation of Investigatory Powers Act 2000, s 26(8), where the investigating officer establishes or maintains a personal or other relationship with a person for the covert purpose of obtaining or disclosing information about that person.
[83] See para 11.76.
[84] See paras 6.51–6.62.
[85] See para 11.84.

11: IMPLICATIONS OF THE HUMAN RIGHTS ACT 1998

Excise. Including local authorities may have been an afterthought and so the implications were not properly thought through. This raises some doubt whether Parliament intended to extend these regulatory provisions to cover routine local authority investigations. On the other hand, there is a plausible argument that any lack of such regulation would mean that the 2000 Act was not fully compatible with the Convention. This would require the legislation to be amended to ensure that routine local authority investigations which comprise a surveillance element are included.

In practical terms, the basic areas of uncertainty are over whether: **11.89**

- the evidence produced by a covert investigation comprises private or family information;
- noise-monitoring devices are capable of amounting to surveillance devices;
- the keeping of 'noise diaries' by victims makes them covert human intelligence sources; and
- the use of paid witnesses makes them covert human intelligence sources.

If local authority investigations do come within the scope of the Regulation of Investigatory Powers Act 2000, a system for authorization needs to be established. An officer of sufficient rank and experience will need to make authorization decisions; this should be a different individual from the one running the investigation for which authorization is sought. A procedure for recording the reasons for authorization decisions being made will also be needed to ensure that decisions are made consistently, transparently and proportionately in the spirit of human rights legislation.

12

ENFORCEMENT: USE OF ABATEMENT NOTICES

Introduction 12.01
Duty to inspect 12.02
Duty to respond to complaints 12.06
Is there a duty to consult? 12.12
    Discretion to consult 12.13
    Raising a legitimate expectation 12.14
    Conflict between consultation and the statutory duty to serve an
    abatement notice 12.16
Abatement notices: technical requirements 12.17
    Dependence on the opinion of the environmental health officer 12.17
    Form of abatement notice 12.21
    Who is the person responsible? 12.22
    Crown immunity 12.31
    Stating the opinion that a statutory nuisance has occurred/is
    likely to occur/recur 12.32
    Identifying the premises 12.34
    Specifying the nuisance 12.35
    Separate notices 12.36
    Separation of the limbs in the abatement notice 12.37
    Specifying works of abatement 12.39
    Specific works or simple notices: the discretion 12.50
    Checklist for validity of specific works notices 12.57
Time limit for undertaking work 12.58
Service of notices 12.60
    Methods of service 12.60
    Problems for local authorities when serving notices 12.68
Suspension of abatement notices 12.75
Withdrawing notices 12.78
Amending notices 12.81

Introduction

The key procedural impact of the Environmental Protection Act 1990 ('EPA **12.01** 1990'), was the introduction of the abatement notice as a method of controlling statutory nuisances through administrative action. The abatement notice, once served, requires the recipient to remedy the nuisance. At the centre of control is the local authority, which has a duty to inspect for statutory nuisances and to respond to complaints. Once the authority has formed the view that there is a statutory nuisance, it must serve a notice. The question of the extent to which the authority must consult arises at this stage. Further, since the abatement notice exposes the recipient to the risk of prosecution, the notice itself must be carefully drawn within the powers of the local authority. Finally, it must be properly served.

Duty to inspect

12.02　There are two triggers to the service of an abatement notice: the duty to inspect and the duty to respond to complaints. The first duty enables a local authority to act independently without the necessity for a complaint from the public.[1]

12.03　The EPA 1990 specifies that a local authority must inspect its area from time to time in order to detect any statutory nuisances, which ought to be dealt with.[2] The Act is no more specific than this, so it is for a local authority to determine the frequency of its inspections. The availability of local authority resources might well have a bearing but it would clearly not be sufficient for an authority to be inactive or to conduct merely a single inspection. Failure to inspect adequately, or at all, could result in an action for judicial review.[3]

12.04　A reasonable approach would be for a local authority to adopt a risk-based approach. Firstly, it should identify those areas which have a high, medium or low risk of nuisances occurring. Secondly, they should adopt an inspection procedure, which reflects this perceived level of risk. So, an industrial area, which lies cheek-by-jowl with a residential area, might be considered a high-risk area, and should, therefore, merit relatively frequent inspection. Where an authority has adopted a strategy of this sort, it would be more difficult for a challenge to be made as to the extent to which it is fulfilling its statutory duty. Another factor in the strategy might be the occurrence of complaints, thus linking the two triggers which precede the service of an abatement notice. So, where there is a history of complaints and, perhaps, enforcement action, it would be appropriate for an authority to adopt a more frequent level of inspection.

12.05　Paragraph 4 of Schedule 3 to the EPA 1990 provides that, where a local authority fails to carry out its duty to inspect, the Secretary of State may make an order declaring the authority to be in default. This order may include a direction to

---

[1] It should be appreciated that mid-nineteenth century nuisance legislation was passed in the teeth of opposition from the property-owning classes, especially the owners of urban housing. See further A S Wohl, *The Eternal Slum: Housing and Social Policy in Victorian London* (Edward Arnold, 1977) and J E Pointing and M A Bulos, 'Some Implications of Failed Issues of Reform' (1984) 8 *International Journal of Urban and Regional Research* 467–480.　　[2] EPA 1990, s 79(1).
[3] See Chapter 17.

undertake the inspection in a specified manner and at a specified time. If the authority still fails to comply, the Secretary of State may transfer the function of the authority to himself. The authority may be liable for any resulting expenditure incurred by the Secretary of State.

Duty to respond to complaints

In reality, most enforcement action is likely to result from a complaint, the second trigger, since nuisances are likely to arise in a neighbourhood context where people are affected. This duty on a local authority, introduced by the EPA 1990 is: **12.06**

where a complaint of a statutory nuisance made to it by a person living within its area, to take such steps as are reasonably practicable to investigate the complaint.[4]

The duty is to investigate. It is a preliminary to a decision to serve an abatement notice. So, a local authority might be entitled to decide that, having investigated the matter, there is no nuisance and, therefore, no obligation to serve a notice. It might also imply, should further complaints be made, that there is no further obligation to investigate. This would leave a complainant with the option of pursuing the complaint himself via section 82 of the EPA 1990. Then it would be for the magistrates to determine whether a nuisance existed.

A local authority must take such steps as are 'reasonably practicable' to investigate a complaint. This indicates that the duty to investigate is not absolute. It may be mitigated by considerations relating to physical feasibility and what is reasonably affordable in terms of cost-effectiveness and the proper use of a local authority's resources.[5] **12.07**

If a complainant felt that an authority had not taken reasonable steps to investigate a complaint, perhaps in circumstances where the alleged nuisance had increased because of the intensification of use of industrial premises, then other options would be: summary proceedings by the individual under section 82 of the EPA 1990,[6] an application for judicial review,[7] or a complaint to the Commissioner for Local Administration (the Ombudsman).[8] **12.08**

There is no guidance or code of practice to assist a local authority in deciding what it is reasonable to do in relation to its duty to investigate. It would be reasonable for a complainant to be notified of the state of an investigation and receive **12.09**

---

[4] EPA 1990, s 79(1).
[5] *Jordan v Norfolk CC* [1994] 4 All ER 218.
[6] See Chapter 16.
[7] See *R (on the application of Anne and another) v Test Valley BC* [2001] 48 EG 127 (CS), and for judicial review generally, see paras 17.26–17.56.
[8] There is no comparable power to that contained in paragraph 4 of Schedule 3 for the Secretary of State to declare the authority in default where they have failed to investigate a complaint; see para 12.02.

copies of any abatement notices that were served. It would be advisable for any local authority to have a procedure in place for dealing with complaints. There would need to be evidence of an approach to the investigation of complaints based on rational criteria. For instance, it would not be reasonable to decide, as a matter of policy, that no response would be made, unless there was more than one complaint, or, only if the matter were taken up by local councillors. Although an individual has a fallback position in that he may take proceedings in his own name under section 82 of the EPA 1990, this is not altogether satisfactory, and might be deemed to show that the authority is failing in its duty in relation to its public health obligations.[9]

12.10 The duty of a local authority to respond to complaints is confined to complaints emanating from 'a person living within its area'. This suggests that a person who works in the area is not entitled to have a complaint of a nuisance investigated. However, such a complaint might be sufficient to trigger a local authority's duty to inspect. It would be likely to be deemed an unreasonable action if a local authority declined to investigate or inspect following a complaint from a person who was not living in the area. 'Residence' is a question of fact and would include all persons living in the area provided their residence had some degree of permanence. An absence, provided it was temporary, would not mean that a person could not be classified as living in the area.

12.11 There is no requirement that the person living in the area should have a legal interest in the property they are occupying.[10] Thus a squatter would be classified as 'living in the area'.[11] However, it is unlikely that someone occupying a property as a holiday letting would fall within the category.

Is there a duty to consult?

12.12 Unlike other areas of public health legislation,[12] there is no obligation to consult the alleged perpetrator of an alleged nuisance (or, indeed, anyone else), prior to service of the notice. Consultation is neither required as part of the statutory code,

---

[9] It was stated, however, in *Salford CC v McNally* [1975] 2 All ER 860 by Lord Edmund-Davies, at 865, 'as a local authority may fall down in its duty to deal with statutory nuisances within its area [the Public Health Act 1936, s 99, the predecessor to EPA 1990, s 82] enables any person aggrieved by the nuisance to make complaint to a justice of the peace'. This would seem to give judicial approval to this practice.

[10] There is no restriction, equivalent to that in private nuisance, that such a person should have a proprietary right in the land; see *Hunter v Canary Wharf Ltd and London Docklands Development Corporation* [1997] AC 655.

[11] *Hipperson v Electoral Registration Officer for the District of Newbury* [1985] 3 WLR 61, 2 All ER 456.

[12] See, eg, the EPA 1990, s 78H(1), and the Contaminated Land (England) Regulations 2000, SI 2000/227. (Provisions made under the Food Safety Act 1990 requiring local authorities to serve 'minded-to' notices have been repealed.)

nor is it to be implied at common law in order to achieve fairness.[13] The duty to take reasonably practicable steps to investigate a complaint of an alleged nuisance does not include any obligation to consult. Any decision to consult remains part of a local authority's discretion. It might be the case that there is a need for urgent action because of a health risk, or because the alleged perpetrator is not amenable to a consultation, but there will be a variety of circumstances where it would not be appropriate for an authority to exercise its discretion to consult. Indeed, one of the reasons why it is not considered appropriate to impose such a duty on an authority is the difficulty in determining a precise set of circumstances when the duty would arise.[14] Even in situations where there is a health risk so that an appeal will not suspend the effect of an abatement notice, no duty to consult arises. In the *Falmouth* case Simon Brown LJ said:

Often, certainly, it will be appropriate to consult the alleged perpetrator, at least on some aspect of the matter, before serving an abatement notice, but the enforcing authority should be wary of being drawn too deeply and lengthily into scientific or technical debate, and warier still of finding itself fixed with all the obligations of a formal consultation process.[15]

Discretion to consult
If the local authority does exercise its discretion to consult then it must exercise that discretion in a rational manner.[16] It might also be argued that there are cases where the complexity of the circumstances leads to a situation where it would be unreasonable for the authority to do anything other than consult. Such circumstances might arise, for example, where an alleged nuisance requires remedial action of an extraordinarily expensive and time-consuming nature. Some older authorities cite the use of an 'intimation notice' which was used as part of a consultation process in such a context. However, this informal notice has no status in law, and it is arguable that service of it today would amount to an abuse of process. It is clear, after all, that once the authority has determined that a statutory nuisance exists, it is under an obligation to serve an abatement notice.[17] While there may well be some delay occasioned whilst an abatement notice is being drafted, the delay incurred by going down an informal route may be considered unreasonable and could expose the local authority to a judicial review by an aggrieved person. Further, use of an intimation notice to set out the requirements of an abatement notice would result in action which is entirely voluntary and

12.13

---

[13] *R v Falmouth and Truro Port Health Authority, ex p South West Water Ltd* [2000] 3 All ER 306.
[14] *R v Birmingham CC, ex p Ferrero Ltd* [1993] 1 All ER 530, where it was held that there was no duty to consult traders before serving a suspension notice under the Consumer Protection Act 1987.
[15] *R v Falmouth and Truro Port Health Authority, ex p South West Water Ltd* (n 13 above), at 318.
[16] *Associated Provincial Picture Houses Ltd v Wednesbury Corporation* [1948] 1 KB 223.
[17] *R v Carrick DC, ex p Shelley* [1996] Env LR 273.

which may have consequences in terms of the recovery of any expenditures wrongly applied.[18]

Raising a legitimate expectation

12.14 A difficulty might arise where a local authority creates in the mind of an alleged perpetrator, an expectation that a consultation process will precede the service of an abatement notice.[19] Such an expectation might arise as a result of an express promise or assurance[20] or arise impliedly because of an established practice to consult.[21] Where such an expectation arises then a public authority is bound to go through with the practice in the interests of fairness and good administration as long as the promise does not prevent the authority from fulfilling its statutory duty. Such promises must be clearly made before they will give rise to such an expectation.

12.15 It is likely that in many cases, particularly those of a complex nature, some correspondence will take place between a local authority and the perpetrator of an alleged nuisance prior to the service of an abatement notice. It would be reasonable, for example, 'to expect some sensible co-operation between the persons served and the local authority in producing an intelligent and workable abatement notice'.[22] Such an exchange will not, of itself, give rise to a legitimate expectation that formal consultation will follow.[23]

Conflict between consultation and the statutory duty to serve an abatement notice

12.16 It is clear from the judicial authorities that a legitimate expectation will only arise where it does not conflict with the statutory duty.[24] However, it may be that consultation may properly take place prior to the service of the abatement notice for various reasons.[25] It may be that the authority needs to consult in order to determine the initial question of whether a statutory nuisance exists; it might need to evaluate the availability of a defence of 'best practicable means'; it might need to consult to decide whether to specify works in the abatement notice (and, if so, what works) or to determine the length of time to be given for those works to be undertaken.

---

[18] See, eg, *Harris v Hickman* [1904] 1 KB 13; *Wilson's Music and General Printing Co v Finsbury BC* [1908] 1 KB 563; *Silles v Fulham BC* [1903] 1 KB 829.
[19] *R v Devon CC, ex p Baker* [1995] 1 All ER 73 at 89.
[20] *Re Liverpool Taxi Owners' Association* [1972] 2 QB 299 and *A-G of Hong Kong v Ng Yuen Shiu* [1983] 2 AC 629.
[21] *Council of Civil Service Unions v Minister for the Civil Service* [1985] AC 374.
[22] *Sovereign Rubber Ltd v Stockport MBC* [2000] Env LR 194, per Sedley LJ at 198.
[23] *R v Falmouth and Truro Port Health Authority, ex p South West Water Ltd* (n 13 above). A local authority might expressly state in any correspondence that it is merely seeking views not undertaking a formal consultation.
[24] See *A-G of Hong Kong v Ng Yuen Shiu* (n 20 above), per Lord Fraser of Tullybelton at 638.
[25] *R v Falmouth and Truro Port Health Authority, ex p South West Water Ltd* (n 13 above).

Abatement notices: technical requirements

Dependence on the opinion of the environmental health officer
Once an officer of a local authority has formed the view that a statutory nuisance exists, a duty arises to serve an abatement notice.[26] The opinion will rest, both on the legal question of whether the activity fits the category of a statutory nuisance[27] and whether, as a question of fact, a nuisance exists.[28] **12.17**

The opinion on which the decision to serve a notice is based must be justified on a professional basis. The officer forming the opinion must have sufficient qualifications and experience to support the decision. It would usually be inappropriate for councillors or technical officers, who do not have the requisite level of qualifications or experience, to form this opinion. Although at the point of service of a notice the procedure is administrative in that the approval of the court is not required, eventually, if an appeal or prosecution follows, the opinion may be subject to judicial scrutiny. It is important, therefore, that it is justifiable at a professional level at the time of service. **12.18**

If an officer is negligent in forming and acting upon his opinion, a civil claim for negligence could follow. Such an action is likely to be brought against the officer's employer.[29] However, for it to succeed, the officer would need to have fallen seriously below professional standards, since the courts are normally unwilling to impose liability on an officer carrying out statutory duties. Further, an officer acting in good faith has the protection of statute: **12.19**

Nothing done by . . . any officer of . . . a local authority shall, if done in good faith for the purpose of executing Part III, subject them . . . personally to any action, liability, claim or demand whatsoever (other than any liability under section 17 or 18 of the Audit Commission Act 1998 (powers of district auditor and court).[30]

In certain cases, the defence of best practicable means may be available to the perpetrator of a nuisance.[31] It may be that an officer considers that, although a nuisance exists, the defence will succeed in the particular case. Whether the defence is made out is a matter for the court, but it may be appropriate for an officer to take its availability into account when forming a view as to whether a nuisance exists. For instance, the taking of best practicable means may suggest **12.20**

---

[26] *R v Carrick DC, ex p Shelley* (n 17 above).
[27] eg, in *R v Bristol CC, ex p Everett* [1999] 2 All ER 193 an abatement notice was withdrawn on the basis of legal advice that the risk of falling down a steep staircase was not 'prejudicial to health' within the meaning of the EPA 1990. See further Chapter 4.
[28] eg, determining whether a noise level is such as to constitute a nuisance or whether the source of an alleged nuisance has been properly identified; see *Hester Dutch v Coventry CC* [1996] Env LR D27 and *Haringey LBC v Hibbert* [2001] Env LR 29.
[29] *North Cornwall DC v Welton and Welton* (1997) LGR 114.
[30] EPA 1990, s 81, Sch 3, para 5.
[31] See Chapter 15.

that the activity is reasonable and that, therefore, there is no statutory nuisance. However, the absence of authority on this point does leave the issue open. If an officer wrongly forms a view that the use of best practicable means suggests that a nuisance does not exist, then the authority is potentially exposed to an action for judicial review by a complainant, or, a complaint to the Local Commissioner for Administration. It would seem that the balance of opinion must be in favour of serving a notice where a nuisance is considered to exist, unless very clear evidence is available that best practicable means have been used.

Form of abatement notice

12.21 There is no statutory form for the notice but local authorities usually adopt variations of the style reproduced in Figure 12.1 below.[32]

Who is the person responsible?

12.22 An abatement notice is addressed to the person responsible for the nuisance. This is defined in section 79(7) of the EPA 1990 as: 'the person to whose act, default or sufferance the nuisance is attributable'. An 'act' implies a positive intervention; 'default' implies a permissive or passive act; and, 'sufferance' implies that the person responsible has tolerated the nuisance.

12.23 Where a nuisance arises from any defect of a structural character, the owner of the premises is the person responsible.[33] 'Owner' is not defined in the EPA 1990. It may be the freeholder in a purpose-built block of flats, or a long leaseholder, or the head leaseholder. The EPA 1990 does not require a local authority to ascertain who is responsible for the structure of the building, but it may be helpful to investigate this question by examining the liabilities in any lease where the building is occupied by tenants. There is no obligation for a freeholder to supply information on a lease, but a tenant may be willing, in such circumstances, to supply a copy.[34]

12.24 Where the nuisance does not arise from a structural defect, but the property where the nuisance arises is subject to a tenancy, then the person responsible is likely to be the occupier. If the nuisance arises from a repairing obligation then, again, the lease will be conclusive. Where a tenant has covenanted to do repairs, then he is

---

[32] A pro forma in common use is that published by Shaw & Sons.
[33] EPA 1990, s 80(2)(b); and see *Pollway Nominees v London Borough of Havering* (1989) 88 LGR 192.
[34] Where a tenancy is for less than seven years, the Landlord and Tenant Act 1985, s 11, implies certain leasehold duties into the lease. The obligation is to keep in repair the structure and exterior of all residential premises and to put and keep in repair and proper working order the installations for the supply of gas, water, electricity and for sanitation, and for space- and water-heating.

12: ENFORCEMENT: USE OF ABATEMENT NOTICES

ABATEMENT NOTICE IN RESPECT OF STATUTORY NUISANCE

ENVIRONMENTAL PROTECTION ACT 1990 PART III: ('THE ACT')

To: ....

Of: ....

TAKE NOTICE that the .... ('the Council') being satisfied of [the existence] [likely occurrence] [recurrence] of a statutory nuisance under section 79(1) of the Act at the premises known as:

....

In the borough of:

....

By reason of:

....

Hereby require you as:
[the person responsible for the nuisance] [(owner) (occupier) of the premises]
(A) [to abate the nuisance and thereafter neither to cause, permit nor otherwise allow its recurrence] and to that end require you to

(B) ....

Time for compliance:

(A) ....

(B) ....

from the date of the service of this notice

WARNING:

(1) If without reasonable excuse you contravene or fail to comply with any requirement of this notice you will be committing an offence under section 80(4) of the Act. On summary conviction fines on Level 5 may be imposed. Further fines up to one tenth of that level may be imposed for each day on which the offence continues after conviction. Fines up to £20,000 may be imposed in respect of industrial, trade or business premises.

(2) If you fail to comply with this notice the Council may abate the nuisance and do whatever is required to achieve compliance.

(3) The Council being of the opinion that the nuisance to which this notice relates (is injurious to health) (is likely to be of limited duration such that suspension of the notice would render it of no practical effect) (the expenditure which would be incurred by any person in the carrying out of works in compliance with this notice before any appeal has been decided would not be disproportionate to the public benefit to be expected in the period from such compliance) this notice shall not in the event that you appeal against it be suspended until the appeal has been decided by the court or abandoned.

STATUTORY NUISANCE (APPEALS) REGULATIONS

RIGHT OF APPEAL: An appeal may be made against this notice to a magistrates' court within 21 days beginning with the date of the service of this notice. The grounds of appeal prescribed in the Regulations are [reproduced overleaf] [attached].

Signed on behalf of the Council: ....

Dated: ....

FIG. 12.1. Typical form used by local authorities as an abatement notice in respect of a statutory nuisance

liable even where the nuisance arose prior to the letting.[35] In the absence of a contractual obligation to repair, a landlord may be liable if he has reserved the right to carry out necessary repairs.[36] It may also be implied that a landlord has reserved a right to enter premises to do repairs in the case of a weekly tenancy.[37]

12.25 There is a further default provision, which places responsibility on the owner or occupier of the premises where the person responsible cannot be found.[38] Reasonable enquiries must have been made by a local authority before this default provision becomes operative. This may include a requisition on the property for information under section 16 of the Law of Property (Miscellaneous Provisions) Act 1976.

12.26 Where the owner is the person responsible, an issue might arise where the owner has no right of entry or is otherwise prevented by an occupier from undertaking the work required. In that case, a complaint may be made to the magistrates' court for an order that the occupier must permit the work in question.[39] Where an occupier has refused to allow work to be done, then the owner may cease to be the person responsible for the nuisance.[40] If access is required to neighbouring land, then it may be possible to obtain an access order from the High Court or county court.[41] In practice, where the person responsible is unable to undertake the work because of difficulty in obtaining access, then it may be necessary for the local authority to use its default powers under section 81(3) of the EPA 1990.

12.27 Where an owner employs a managing agent to collect rent on his behalf, then the agent may be served instead of (or as well as) the owner.[42]

12.28 In the case of a statutory nuisance arising in respect of noise in the street, which has not yet occurred,[43] or in respect of noise from an unattended vehicle, machinery or equipment,[44] the person to be served is the person responsible for the vehicle, machinery or equipment.[45] If that person cannot be found, or when the local authority so determines, then the notice shall be served by fixing it to the vehicle, machinery or equipment.[46] This last provision is aimed at the situation where a

---

[35] *Gwinnell v Eamer* [1875] LR 10 CP 658. Conversely, in the absence of a contractual obligation to do repairs, a landlord will be liable if the nuisance existed at the time of the letting; *Todd v Flight* (1860) 9 CB (NS) 377.   [36] *Heap v Ind Coope and Allsopp Ltd* [1940] 2 KB 476.
[37] *Mint v Good* [1951] 1 KB 517.   [38] EPA 1990, s 80(2)(c).
[39] Public Health Act 1936, s 289.
[40] *Warner v London Borough of Lambeth* (1984) 15 HLR 42.
[41] Access to Neighbouring Land Act 1992, s 1.
[42] *Camden LBC v Gunby* [2000] 1 WLR 465. This decision rested on the definition of 'owner' in the Public Health Act 1936, s 343(1), and Part IIA of the EPA 1990, where it includes 'a person entitled to receive rack rent for the premises'.   [43] EPA 1990, s 80A(1)(a).
[44] ibid, s 80A(1)(b).
[45] ibid, s 80A(2)(a). In relation to a vehicle, the person responsible includes the person in whose name the vehicle is for the time being registered under the Vehicles (Excise) Act 1971 and any other person who is for the time being the driver of the vehicle (EPA 1990, s 79(7)).
[46] EPA 1990, s 80A(2)(b).

vehicle alarm on an unattended car is causing a statutory nuisance. If the person responsible is then found within an hour of the notice being affixed, then a copy is served on that person.[47] The time for compliance can then be extended in the copy of the notice that has been served on the responsible person.[48]

The object of the legislation is to serve the notice on the person who is responsible for the nuisance. This may be someone who causes the nuisance either by his act or failure to act. So, an owner who allows a nuisance to continue, having been alerted to its existence, may be responsible alongside the occupier who is, in fact, the person directly causing it. This would also apply where a trespasser had caused the nuisance.[49] There may be a question as to whether the owner knew of the nuisance (or ought to have known of it). If he does have knowledge then his delay in remedying it will be a relevant factor in determining his liability.[50]

12.29

More than one person can be responsible for a nuisance, so more than one person can be served with a notice.[51] In such a case, unless separate notices are served on each person responsible, then an appeal by one will have the effect of suspending the notice against all, until the appeal is resolved.

12.30

Crown immunity
The Crown is subject to the provisions of Part III of the EPA 1990, except that it cannot be made criminally liable.[52] So, an abatement notice may be served on the Crown but it would not be possible to bring a prosecution for non-compliance. In such circumstances, the appropriate procedure is for the local authority to seek a declaration in the High Court that the Crown has acted unlawfully.[53]

12.31

---

[47] ibid, s 80A(3). [48] ibid, s 80A(4).
[49] See *Leanse v Egerton* [1943] KB 323 where the owner of a property damaged in an air raid failed to repair the broken windows. He was held liable for continuing the nuisance and for injury to a passer-by who was hurt by falling glass.
[50] 'The occupier continues a nuisance if, with the knowledge or presumed knowledge of its existence, he fails to take reasonable means to bring it to an end, though with ample time to do so'; *Sedleigh-Denfield v O'Callaghan* [1940] AC 880, per Viscount Maugham at 894. See also *Sampson v Hodson-Pressinger* [1981] 3 All ER 710; 12 HLR 40 where it was held that a purchaser of a freehold, who buys with knowledge that a leaseholder is causing a nuisance to another, may also acquire liability in nuisance; and *Delaware Mansions Ltd and Flecksun Ltd v Westminster CC* [2001] 3 WLR 1007 where there was continuing liability for damage caused by encroaching tree roots once the local authority had been made aware of the problem.   [51] EPA 1990, s 81(1).
[52] ibid, s 159(2), (3).
[53] ibid, s 159(2). This provision is only concerned with giving to a public or local authority a limited power to require the Crown to conform with the requirements of the EPA 1990. It does not provide a means for a 'person aggrieved' in proceedings under section 82 of the 1990 Act to obtain a declaration in the High Court where an alleged nuisance is caused by the Crown. Some commentators have argued, since they assume that there should be equivalence between the powers of a public authority and a private individual, that this position may constitute a breach of article 6 (right to a fair trial) of the European Convention on Human Rights (Rome, 4 November 1950; TS 71 (1953); Cmd 8969) (*pace* McCracken et al, *Statutory Nuisance* (Butterworths, 2001), p 260).

Stating the opinion that a statutory nuisance has occurred/is likely to occur/recur

12.32 The name of the local authority serving the notice is set out and a statement is made that it is satisfied that a nuisance falling under section 79(1) of the EPA 1990 exists or is likely to occur or recur within its area. Where a standard form is used, the inapplicable parts should be deleted since this may affect the clarity of the notice even though, in the particular circumstances, such a defect might not be held to invalidate a notice.[54] A notice must expressly or impliedly state that a recurrence of the alleged nuisance is prohibited before such a recurrence could be actionable.[55]

12.33 The test for determining the validity of a notice which has been poorly drafted in the sense that the standard form has not been completed fully, rests on a common-sense approach. If it is ambiguous as a result of unprofessional drafting, or fails to specify matters which should have been set out, then it may be quashed by the magistrates. However, it will often be the case that such defects are not considered to affect the purport of the notice and can be cured, in any event, by amendment by the magistrates.[56] Nevertheless, poor drafting will affect the professional standing of a local authority, its ability to carry out its statutory duties and may be used as a reason for an appeal which will suspend the effect of a notice. Procedures should, therefore, be adopted to avoid these consequences.

Identifying the premises

12.34 The premises, which are the origin of the alleged nuisance, must be clearly described so that the recipient of a notice can identify them. A misdescription, which puts the recipient at a serious disadvantage, will cause a notice to be quashed except where the recipient was well aware of the misdescription and clearly understood which site was the subject of the notice.[57] It has been held that, where a misdescription can be varied in favour of an appellant, this can include a change in the area to which the abatement notice applies.[58]

Specifying the nuisance

12.35 The nature of the alleged nuisance must be specified. For example:

---

[54] See *East Northamptonshire DC v Fossett* [1994] Env LR 388; and *Sovereign Rubber Ltd v Stockport MBC* (n 22 above) where the draftsman failed to delete one of the words 'prohibit' and 'restrict' in the notice. Sedley J criticized the poor quality of the drafting of the notice by the local authority but considered that it gave rise to no possibility of ambiguity and could be cured by the deletion of the word 'prohibit'. See also *McKay v Secretary of State for the Environment and others* [1994] JPL 806 and *Miller-Mead v Minister of Housing and Local Government* [1963] 2 QB 196.
[55] *Stanley v London Borough of Ealing* [2000] Env LR D18.
[56] *Cambridge CC v Douglas* [2001] Env LR 41.
[57] *Wiltshier Construction Ltd v Westminster CC* [1997] Env LR 321.
[58] *Sovereign Rubber Ltd v Stockport MBC* (n 22 above).

noise from the use of tools and machinery for vehicle repairs and from associated general activities, including the use of a radio in the workshop[59]

or

Refuse deposited in a 'compound' against the front boundary wall of the property ...[60]

The description needs to be practical and clear so that the recipient of the notice understands the exact nature of the alleged nuisance that is the subject of the notice. The relevant paragraph of subsection 79(1) of the EPA 1990 may also be identified.[61] A technical approach to describing the nuisance is not required; it must simply be described sufficiently so that the recipient knows the nature of the problem.[62]

Separate notices
A single notice which includes different types of statutory nuisance emanating from the same premises will not be defective. However, it might make the notice unnecessarily complex if it includes nuisances of different types since the time limits and remedial works might vary. Further, since an appeal normally suspends the effect of a notice, an appeal against one aspect only would lead to suspension of the notice in relation to every nuisance listed. Best practice dictates, therefore, that a local authority should serve separate notices in these circumstances.

12.36

Separation of the limbs in the abatement notice
Although the health limb and the nuisance limb are separate concepts, there is no requirement for an abatement notice to set out under which limb it is alleged the statutory nuisance takes effect.[63]

12.37

In *Lowe & Watson v South Somerset DC*, it was considered that if such a requirement were imposed, local authorities would simply include both limbs in the alternative, a solution which would not be an advantage in terms of specification: '... it seems to me that a notice which specifies that noise is prejudicial to health will almost inevitably include an allegation of nuisance actionable at common law, since in the latter, interference with personal comfort will be sufficient.'[64]

However, it might be considered inappropriate for an abatement notice not to specify under which limb the alleged statutory nuisance falls since the limb might affect the nature and standard of the work required to remedy it. The standard

12.38

---

[59] *Brighton and Hove Council v Ocean Coachworks (Brighton) Ltd* [2001] Env LR 4.
[60] *Stanley v London Borough of Ealing* (n 55 above).
[61] The EPA 1990 does not, in fact, require the relevant paragraph of EPA 1990, 79(1), under which the nuisance falls, to be specified. Normally, however, a local authority will identify the particular provision and would be advised to do so on the grounds of clarity and specificity.
[62] *Myatt v Teignbridge DC* [1994] Env LR 242.
[63] *Lowe & Watson v South Somerset DC* [1998] Env LR 143.
[64] ibid, per Gage J at 148.

required to ensure that an activity is not 'prejudicial to health' may well be higher than, or different from, that required to prevent the nuisance interfering with the enjoyment of property and the personal comfort of persons affected by the nuisance. However, given that such notices are not generally drafted by lawyers and that determination of such a question is frequently legalistic in nature, the decision not to require such a specification might be a sensible result in the circumstances.

Specifying works of abatement

12.39 By Part III of the EPA 1990 a local authority must serve a notice:

imposing all or any of the following requirements—
(a) requiring the abatement of the nuisance or prohibiting or restricting its occurrence or recurrence;
(b) requiring the execution of such works, and the taking of such other steps, as may be necessary for any of those purposes.[65]

The words 'all or any' indicate that a local authority can choose the requirements of the notice. The local authority has a discretion whether to serve a specific works notice or a simple abatement notice.[66] If the former is served, then the local authority must specify the works clearly so that there is no ambiguity as to what is required.[67]

12.40 In the case of abatement notices in respect of noise nuisances, the practice of specifying noise limits in the notice while leaving the method of abating the notice unspecified has been held to be valid.[68] So, for example, the following requirements have been held to be valid:

Reduce the noise from tyre squeal as measured at any point along the boundary marked red on the attached plan:
(1) to a level not exceeding 50dB at 1,000Hz, provided that such level may be exceeded on not more than two occasions within any one hour period whilst communication is being made with any vehicle driver causing the said noise in order to prevent the recurrence of such noise:
(2) to a level not exceeding 45dB at 1,000Hz, before 9am or after 6pm on any day. All Sound Level Pressure measurements specified above are to be taken in the open air

---

[65] EPA 1990, s 80(1).
[66] *R v Falmouth and Truro Port Health Authority, ex p South West Water Ltd* (n 13 above) overruling *Kirklees MBC v Field and Others* [1998] Env LR 337.
[67] *Sterling Homes (Midlands) Ltd v Birmingham CC* [1996] Env LR 121; *R v Wheatley, ex p Cowburn* (1885) 16 QBD 34.
[68] *Sevenoaks DC v Brands Hatch Leisure Group Ltd* [2001] Env LR 86. See also paras 6.75–6.78. The earlier case of *R v Fenny Stratford Justices, ex p Watney Mann (Midlands) Ltd* [1976] 2 All ER 888, is also of interest on this point. Note, however, that the converse is also true: there is no obligation to provide an objective test as to when a nuisance has been committed by inserting a decibel reading into a noise-abatement notice; *East Northamptonshire DC v Fossett* (n 54 above) and *Cambridge CC v Douglas* (n 56 above).

with a Type 1 sound level meter set on fast response, and measured using one-third octave filters.[69]

Although the notice apparently required steps to be taken, the court held that this did not trigger the requirement in section 80(1)(b) of the Act so as to oblige the authority to specify the work to be undertaken to abate the nuisance. The recipient of the notice could decide on the way in which the noise was to be prevented from causing a nuisance and the notice simply prescribed a yardstick against which the occurrence of the nuisance could be tested.

12.41 Similarly, in *R v Crown Court at Canterbury, ex p Howson-Ball*[70] an abatement notice which specified that the sound-pressure level of noise from the playing of live or recorded amplified music when measured 'at a distance of 2 (Two) metres from any speaker shall not exceed 75dB Laeq (1 minute) slow response', was considered valid and enforceable.

12.42 It is important to note that, in the above examples, the position where the measurements were to be taken was clearly specified. If this position were not carefully defined then the notice would be vulnerable to challenge for lack of certainty. Similarly, a practice favoured by some local authorities is to require noise to be limited so that it does not cause a nuisance in 'neighbouring premises'. Such a reference might be acceptable in that, in practice, those premises can be defined. But, a less precise definition might not work, as, for example, a paragraph in an abatement notice, which required the recipient:

within 14 days (to) ensure that the noise from the public address system or amplified music from the premises does not exceed at any time the one-third octave Leq (15 minutes) as measured *in any residential premises*.[71] (our emphasis)

The court accepted that the reference to 'any residential premises' was unclear.[72] It would clearly be desirable, in such a case, to include in an abatement notice the precise address of the affected premises for the avoidance of doubt, although many local authorities are not anxious to do this to avoid exacerbating neighbourhood disputes.

12.43 The courts have taken a robust view of the requirements of specific works notices and emphasize the importance of practical common sense in interpreting requirements. So, for example, a notice required the recipient:

---

[69] *Sevenoaks DC v Brands Hatch Leisure Group Ltd* (n 68 above).
[70] [2001] Env LR 36.
[71] *Lambie and Minter v Thanet DC* [2001] Env LR 21. It was also held in this case that a requirement to permit an environmental health officer to enter premises to install a noise limiter was valid.
[72] However, in *Lambie and Minter v Thanet DC* (n 71 above), the court was willing to amend the notice under the Statutory Nuisance (Appeals) Regulations 1995, SI 1995/2644, para 2(5), and substituted the exact address of the premises neighbouring the nuisance which were most affected by the noise.

to keep the main workshop entrance door fully closed except when it necessarily has to be opened from time to time for the moving of vehicles into and from the workshop or for other genuine business reasons.[73]

The court was happy to interpret this 'not as an abstract document, but one which relates to the carrying out of activities on these premises and it would be well understood by those who worked there and who received it'.[74]

12.44 Nevertheless, a specific works notice must be clear and free from ambiguity, not least because of the criminal sanctions that might follow a breach. The inclusion of unnecessary and superfluous words might throw doubt on such a notice. So, notices which specify certain works to be undertaken, but which then include words which suggest that the recipient may choose other unspecified means to abate the nuisance, might lead a court to view them as ambiguous.[75] If alternative work is to be proposed to that specified in the notice, then the notice should either be withdrawn and a new one issued, or the authority should accede to a request to undertake alternative work in writing. Rather than draft an open-ended notice, the authority might consider serving a simple abatement notice. But if a notice makes reference to particular works, then they must be clearly and unambiguously specified.

12.45 The degree of particularity in specifying works will depend on the complexity of the case. The more complex the work required, the greater the particularity. It might be sufficient in a straightforward case to require something to be done 'in an appropriate manner'. For example, in *Stanley v London Borough of Ealing*[76] a notice required the recipient to 'ensure that refuse is stored *appropriately*' (our emphasis). In the particular circumstances of the case, which concerned a residential dwelling, the judge concluded that it was reasonable to leave it to the recipient to decide what was appropriate. However, such a conclusion is only likely to follow in the simplest of cases. The storage of domestic waste in a residential context does not permit many options. But, an industrial case concerning complex odour emissions, for example, might permit many choices as to the method of abatement. An authority which chose to specify works in such a notice but then failed to do so with particularity, leaving a non-specific choice to the recipient, might well be at risk of an appeal on the ground of unreasonableness and lack of clarity.

12.46 Some notices include a reference to a benchmark for the abatement of the nuisance. In particular, it is a practice for some local authorities to include a statement that the work must be done according to the requirements of the officer

---

[73] *Brighton and Hove Council v Ocean Coachworks (Brighton) Ltd* (n 59 above).
[74] ibid, per Astill J at para 17.
[75] *Network Housing Association v Westminster CC* [1995] Env LR 176.
[76] n 55 above.

without specifying in the notice what those requirements entail. Typical clauses used include the following:

provide suitable refuse storage for the property to comply with the requirements of the environmental health officer.[77]

In this case, the court held that this clause did not render the notice too vague, but in other circumstances such wording might be challengeable. The fact that some of the requirements are not spelt out in the notice does not, of itself, render the notice invalid. Provided it can be shown as a matter of fact that the requirements were made known to the recipient and that they were not unclear, unreasonable or impracticable then a notice will be valid. However, these matters may be difficult to establish and it would seem that a notice could be more easily challenged if all the requirements are not spelt out on its face.

12.47 A novel approach was taken in *Lambie and another v Thanet DC*[78] where a notice included the following requirement:

Within 14 days from the service of this Notice install and have set by officers from the Environmental Service Department a sound restricting device which shall be operational any time music is played in the function room.

An authorized officer has the power to enter premises at any reasonable time

for the purpose of taking any action, or executing any work, authorised or required by Part III.[79]

In *Lambie* it was held that this provision, coupled with the power to specify the taking of such steps as may be necessary,[80] was sufficiently wide to include a power of entry for an officer to set a sound restricting device. This is a convenient provision enabling officers to deal with the installation and setting of equipment designed to abate a nuisance.[81]

12.48 While this route to the abatement of a nuisance might be acceptable, the requirement favoured by some authorities, and sometimes included in abatement notices, that the recipient should engage a consultant to inquire into the manner in which a nuisance might be effectively abated, may not be. Although it is arguable that such a requirement falls within the scope of section 80(1)(b) of the EPA 1990 as a necessary step, it might well be regarded as unreasonable. Further, since the decision in the *Falmouth*[82] case confirms that there are no limits to a local authority's discretion to serve simple abatement notices, it would be advisable for an authority not to include such a requirement.

---

[77] *Stanley v London Borough of Ealing* (n 55 above).
[78] [2001] Env LR 21.
[79] EPA 1990, Sch 3, para 2(1)(b).
[80] ibid, s 80(1)(b).
[81] Subject to any potential challenge since the coming into force of the Human Rights Act 1998 for breach of article 8 (the right to respect for private and family life) of the European Convention on Human Rights (n 53 above).
[82] n 13 above.

12.49 Where some of the requirements are contained in a separate letter or schedule then that document will be considered to be part of the notice and will be subject to the same principles for validity as the principal part of the notice.[83] The letter or schedule will be called in aid when construing the notice. This is because there is no prescribed form for notices and it is considered sensible to look at any accompanying documents in order to determine objectively how the notice would be understood by its recipient.[84]

Specific works or simple notices: the discretion

12.50 The Court of Appeal were clear in their decision in *R v Falmouth and Truro Port Health Authority, ex p South West Water Ltd*[85] that a local authority has a discretion to choose whether to draft a simple abatement notice or one specifying works. It might, therefore, be asked why an authority would ever choose to specify works when the complexity of drafting such a notice might render it susceptible to a successful appeal? After all, by specifying works a local authority might make itself more vulnerable to objection on the ground of uncertainty than if it served a simple abatement notice.[86]

12.51 However, there may be circumstances where it might be deemed irrational on *Wednesbury* principles[87] for a local authority to serve a simple abatement notice. In the *Falmouth* case, such a possibility was contemplated, albeit as a very marginal one:

> even if I was prepared . . . to recognise a class of case where it was irrational for the local authority not to use its discretion to require specific works for the abatement of the nuisance, the present case would not fall into it.[88]

In most cases, the question of administrative irrationality will not arise. Where, for instance, the act can simply be stopped so as to abate the nuisance, a simple

---

[83] *London Borough of Camden v London Underground Ltd* [2000] Env LR 369.
[84] *Mannai Investment v Eagle Star* [1997] AC 749, per Lord Steyn at 767.
[85] n 13 above.
[86] See also R Malcolm, 'Statutory Nuisance: The Validity of Abatement Notices' [2000] JPL 894 and J Pointing, '*Falmouth and Truro Port Health Authority v South-West Water Ltd*: Have Specific Works Notices Finally Run their Course?' [2000] ELM 99 for a further analysis of the decision in *R v Falmouth and Truro Port Health Authority, ex p South West Water Ltd* (n 13 above) and the preceding case law.
[87] As to judicial review, see further paras 17.26–17.56.
[88] n 13 above, per Simon Brown LJ at 328–9. Although this aspect of the decision is of profound importance, it is *obiter*, since the case fell on the point that the waters subject to the nuisance, the Carrick Roads, were not a watercourse within the meaning of the Public Health Act 1936. Note also, in *Sevenoaks DC v Brands Hatch Leisure Group Ltd* (n 68 above), at 91, the comment of Laws LJ in which he refers to the decision in *R v Falmouth and Truro Port Health Authority, ex p South West Water Ltd*: 'With very great deference to Simon Brown LJ, I venture to think that there may well be some utility in recognising a class of case, as he puts it, where it may be irrational for the local authority not to specify works, but no such point arises in the present case in which no *Wednesbury* challenge to the notice was launched'.

notice, which leaves the recipient to decide whether to cease the offending activity or to undertake works of abatement, will often suffice.[89]

In other situations, the perpetrator of the alleged nuisance will be in a better position than the local authority to know how to remedy the nuisance.[90] These are the cases where, in the past, a local authority may have sought to require the recipient to engage a consultant as a step towards abating the nuisance.[91] The cost of undertaking the exercise of determining the abatement works necessary, can be prohibitive for a local authority.[92] In industrial cases, abatement will usually be effected by works, rather than cessation of the activity. Closing down a factory or a process will not usually be a reasonable option. It will normally be fairer and more practical to permit the recipient, in such cases, to choose the manner of abatement rather than for an authority to impose a solution on them.

12.52

In some cases, local authorities may continue to serve specific works notices because that has been their traditional practice. This is particularly apparent in housing repair cases taken under section 79(1)(a) of the EPA 1990 where local authorities are accustomed to specifying a schedule of works. As a matter of fairness and public policy, it may be appropriate for local authorities to continue this practice, not least because these are cases where the 'do nothing' option cannot apply.

12.53

A potential difficulty in choosing to serve a simple abatement notice, and thereby leaving the choice of abatement to the recipients, is the danger that the recipients' work may be ineffective to resolve the nuisance. This leaves the recipient at risk of prosecution for failure to comply with the notice. Where the *authority* specifies steps or works which fail to abate the nuisance, then there can be no prosecution for failure to comply with the notice if those prescribed steps are taken but prove ineffective. It would be for the authority to start again and serve a second notice specifying different works.

12.54

---

[89] *Budd v Colchester BC* [1999] Env LR 739; *SFI Group plc (formerly Surrey Free Inns plc) v Gosport BC* [1999] Env LR 750; *R v Knightsbridge Crown Court, ex p Cataldi* [1999] Env LR 62; *Myatt v Teignbridge DC* (n 62 above).

[90] *Sterling Homes Ltd v Birmingham CC* (n 67 above); *Network Housing Association v Westminster CC* (n 75 above); and *R v Falmouth and Truro Port Health Authority, ex p South West Water Ltd* (n 13 above).

[91] In *London Borough of Camden v London Underground Ltd* (n 83 above) an accompanying letter contained a list of acoustic consultants 'who may be of assistance in aiding you to resolve the above problem'. The danger for a local authority in including such a piece of advice is that it might be argued that the notice requires works to be undertaken without specifying them with sufficient particularity, a route not permitted following the decisions in *R v Falmouth and Truro Port Health Authority, ex p South West Water Ltd* (n 13 above), *Budd*, *SFI Group* and *Cataldi* (all n 89 above).

[92] Such costs would not be recoverable by the local authority in any subsequent criminal proceedings since they would not have been undertaken subsequent to a decision to prosecute; *R v Associated Octel Co Ltd* [1997] 1 Cr App Rep (S) 435.

12.55 However, there is one category of cases, where it might be arguable that a simple notice might be irrational. These are cases where the recipient has no special expertise, but, nonetheless, some work must be done to abate the nuisance. These are not cases where the activity could simply be abandoned, or where the solution is obvious.[93] Where, for example, some work of a complex or expensive nature is required, but the recipient is an ordinary domestic householder without any special expertise, then service of a simple notice might be irrational.[94]

12.56 The Court of Appeal in *R v Falmouth and Truro Port Health Authority, ex p South West Water Ltd* did not contemplate this possibility. Nor was the impact of article 7 of the European Human Rights Convention (which requires certainty in the definition of crimes) considered. The service of an abatement notice is an administrative act. But failure to comply with a notice exposes the recipient to the possibility of a criminal prosecution. Where a simple notice is served, then, the recipient is not informed of the precise manner in which he can avoid criminal prosecution.[95] This might be considered an argument for the greater use of specific works notices except in the most straightforward of cases. However, the decision of the Divisional Court in *Godfrey v Conwy CBC*[96] supports the contention that a challenge under article 7 on this point will fail. It is unclear, however, whether *Falmouth* will have much impact on local authority policies on which types of notice to serve.

Checklist for validity of specific works notices

12.57 Abatement notices are tested for their validity, in the first instance, by way of appeal to a magistrates' court. The emphasis is on the application of common sense to this interpretative process. It might, therefore, be appropriate to consider a checklist against which the elements of a specific works notice might be tested:

Practicality:
- Is the solution practical?
- Can the solution be achieved by *this* recipient?
- Can it be achieved in the time the local authority has allowed?

---

[93] As, eg, in a noise nuisance case, where the solution might be to reduce the volume of amplified music, or close doors and windows, etc.

[94] *Kirklees MBC v Field and Others* (n 66 above) illustrates the problem. Here ordinary householders were faced with a complex and expensive task of shoring up a dangerous rock face and wall into which their houses were built. The Court of Appeal in *R v Falmouth and Truro Port Health Authority, ex p South West Water Ltd* (n 13 above) overruled the decision in *Kirklees* which had decided that, where it was clear on the face of the notice that works were required, then those works must be specified.

[95] This point was argued in *Kirklees MBC v Field and Others* (n 66 above), but on common law grounds without reference to the European Convention on Human Rights (n 53 above). It was also raised in argument before the Divisional Court in *Sevenoaks DC v Brands Hatch Leisure Group Ltd* (n 68 above), although it was not referred to in the judgment.

[96] [2001] Env LR 38. On this point see also *Steel v UK* (1999) 28 EHRR 603, *SW v UK* (1995) EHRR 363, and Chapter 11.

- Has the local authority used a standard form of words without applying them to fit the circumstances of the particular case?
- Consider the likely attitude of magistrates to the notice—use a common-sense approach.

Enforceability:
- Is the notice enforceable?
- Can the local authority enforce the notice?
- How will the notice be enforced?
- Will it be clear—to the local authority, those residing in the neighbourhood, to the notice recipient—if there has been a breach of the notice?
- Is there any vagueness which would make it difficult to know if the notice has been breached?

Fairness:
- Overall, is the notice fair?
- Consider the underlying principle of fairness in court proceedings. Does the notice and the proposed way the nuisance is to be controlled by the notice have the 'feel' of fairness about it?
- Have the officers involved in the case acted fairly throughout? (This question applies to the collection of evidence, the use of statutory powers, the way decisions are made, etc.)

Time limit for undertaking work

12.58 The notice must include a time limit within which the work must be completed.[97] An unreasonable time limit is a potential ground of appeal,[98] so a local authority should exercise care in determining the time limit, and, it might be a proper matter for consultation with the recipient prior to service of the notice.[99]

12.59 A recipient may be required to abate the nuisance immediately. A requirement to the 'person responsible for the said nuisance *forthwith* to abate the said nuisance' (our emphasis) was held to be valid in the particular circumstances of the case.[100] However, care should be taken by a local authority to determine realistic and reasonable time limits. The time limit must define the period within which compliance is to be effected. Thus, it must permit sufficient time for any work to be completed. If a nuisance can be abated by simple cessation of the activity, then a requirement to abate with immediate effect will suffice. However, if any work needs to be carried out, then, even where a simple notice is served, some evaluation

---

[97] EPA 1990, 80(1): '... and the notice *shall* specify the time or times within which the requirements of the notice are to be complied with' (our emphasis).
[98] Statutory Nuisance (Appeals) Regulations 1995, SI 1995/2644, reg 2(2)(d).
[99] *R v Falmouth and Truro Port Health Authority, ex p South West Water Ltd* (n 13 above).
[100] *Brighton and Hove Council v Ocean Coachworks (Brighton) Ltd* (n 59 above).

of the time necessary to complete the work, or carry out the steps, must be done.[101]

Service of notices

Methods of service

12.60 The methods of service are set out in section 160 of the EPA 1990. These methods of service are permissive rather than mandatory.[102]

12.61 The notice may be given to the person responsible for the nuisance, left at his proper address,[103] or sent by post[104] to him at that address.

12.62 In respect of a company, the notice should be served on the secretary or clerk of the company. In the case of a partnership, it should be served on the partner having control or management of the partnership business.

12.63 The proper address is the last known address, except in the case of a company or the company secretary or clerk, where it is the registered or principal office; and, in the case of a partnership, or the person having control of the partnership business, it is the principal office of the partnership. Where the company is registered outside the UK (or the partnership is carrying on business outside the UK) the proper address is the principal office within the UK.

12.64 If the person to be served has specified an address (other than his proper address) as the one at which he (or someone on his behalf) will accept such notices, then that address and addressee will suffice for the purposes of section 160 of the EPA 1990. Where this person is a local authority it has been held that the person who may specify an alternative address or addressee is not confined to the secretary or clerk or equivalent person.[105] By analogy, where the person to be served is a company, then it, too, may rely on section 160(5) of the EPA 1990 to specify an alternative address and/or addressee for service. That specification may be

---

[101] Where work is required (or expected to be needed) to abate the nuisance then, normally, a minimum of 21 days would be appropriate.

[102] *Richards Hewlings v McLean Homes East Anglia Ltd* [2001] 2 All ER 281. See also *Hall v Kingston upon Hull CC; Ireland v Birmingham CC; Baker v Birmingham CC* [1999] 2 All ER 609 and *Leeds v London Borough of Islington* [1998] Env LR 655.

[103] Leaving the notice in the letterbox of the proper address is good service; *Haringey LBC v Hibbert* (n 28 above) and *Lambeth LBC v Mullings, The Times*, 16 January 1990.

[104] This may be recorded delivery or first class post. The Interpretation Act 1978, s 7, provides that where a statute provides that a document may be served by post then 'unless the contrary intention appears, the service is deemed to be effected by properly addressing, prepaying and posting a letter containing the document and, unless the contrary is proved, to have been effected at the time at which the letter would be delivered in the ordinary course of post.' However, it would be good practice for a local authority to establish proof of posting by obtaining a certificate of posting where ordinary post is used.

[105] See *Hall v Kingston upon Hull CC; Ireland v Birmingham CC; Baker v Birmingham CC* (n 102 above), per Mitchell J at 619–20.

made, not only by the secretary or clerk to the company, but by any authorized person.

Much of the case law on service under Part III of the EPA 1990 relates to notices served by tenants against local authorities, in the capacity as their landlord, under section 82 of the EPA 1990.[106] This case law indicates that a greater degree of latitude will be given to an ordinary individual serving a notice of intention under section 82, than a local authority serving an abatement notice under section 80 of the EPA 1990: **12.65**

... local authorities, who are entitled to serve abatement notices, have access to legal and technical advice. It is understandable that greater particularity should be required in such a notice served by a public body, with penal consequences, if it is not complied with or appealed against.[107]

This extract from the judgment relates to the content of a letter of intention under section 82 of the EPA 1990 rather than to the manner of service but it indicates the approach which the judiciary are inclined to take when distinguishing between a private citizen and a public body. **12.66**

In relation to the power of a local authority to serve an abatement notice, the authority may also rely on the provisions of section 233 of the Local Government Act 1972. This section is, for the most part, in identical terms to the provisions of section 160 of the EPA 1990. However, there is an additional provision that, where the name or address of the owner, lessee or occupier of the land (on whom the notice should be served) cannot be found after reasonable enquiry, the notice may be served by giving it to, or leaving it with, a person who appears to be resident or employed on the land.[108] Alternatively, it could be affixed in a conspicuous place on the land. **12.67**

Problems for local authorities when serving notices
It may be difficult to ascertain the identity of the person responsible for a nuisance. Various methods of detection might reveal the answer. For instance, recourse to an electoral, council tax or business rate register, a requisition on the land under section 16 of the Local Government (Miscellaneous Provisions) Act 1976,[109] or a search of the Land Registry may reveal evidence of occupation or ownership. In business premises, records relating to employment such as wage **12.68**

---

[106] See *Richards Hewlings v McLean Homes East Anglia Ltd* (n 102 above). See also *Hall v Kingston upon Hull CC; Ireland v Birmingham CC; Baker v Birmingham CC* and *Michelle Leeds v London Borough of Islington* (n 102 above). See also paras 16.19–16.24.
[107] *East Staffordshire BC v Fairless* [1999] Env LR 525, per Sullivan J at 534.
[108] Where the recipient is a company, then the person who receives the notice must be connected with the company, *R v Old Street Magistrates' Court, ex p London Borough of Hackney* (QBD, 9 February 1994) (transcript: Smith Bernal).
[109] Such requisitions can be served on the occupier, freeholder, mortgagee or lessee, or on any person who directly or indirectly receives the rent. They can also be served on the agent of anyone with an interest in the land or premises; *Stanley v London Borough of Ealing* (n 55 above).

slips or employers' liability insurance may be helpful. Care should be taken that these enquiries identify the person responsible—who may not be the same person as the landowner. It is only after reasonable enquiries have been made, but without success, as to the identity of the person responsible, that service may be made on the owner and/or occupier of the land in lieu.

12.69 Sometimes difficulties arise where the perpetrator of a nuisance is mentally unwell. Where resolution of the nuisance in these cases is sought by service of an abatement notice, there is no requirement to ensure that the recipient understood, or even read, the notice—the only obligation is to ensure that proper service was made.[110] If the person is committed under the mental health legislation or is subject to a guardianship order, then service should be made on the custodian.

12.70 A notice may be served on a minor but this may not be the most effective remedy. In the case of a noise nuisance caused by minors, the usual procedure would be to serve the notice on the parent or guardian, as the person responsible. In fact, this might be the appropriate route even where the children of the family are 18 and above but are living as members of the family with parents resident. It might be possible for a parent to appeal in such a case on the ground that the notice has been wrongly served, but this could be resisted by a local authority on the ground that as the owner of the house, the parent, has 'suffered' the nuisance to continue.

12.71 There is no obligation to translate a notice for a person who cannot read English. The obligation is to serve the notice properly, not to ensure that the recipient reads or understands it.

12.72 Where complex company structures may be involved, such as in the privatized public utility industries, then a careful identification of the company responsible for the nuisance needs to be undertaken. Service of a notice on a sister company, even where the correct company indicates an intention to deal with it, will not be good service.[111] Where a failing company is in the hands of administrators, service of an abatement notice comes within the scope of 'other proceedings' under sections 10 and 11 of the Insolvency Act 1986 with the effect that when an administration order is in force, service requires the consent of the company's administrator or the leave of the court.[112]

---

[110] In *Tadema Holdings Ltd v Alan Ferguson* (1999) EGCS 138 a tenant suffered from a mental disorder as defined under the Mental Health Act 1983. He had not even opened his letters, which included a notice under the Housing Act 1988, s 8 (as amended by the Housing Act 1996). The Court of Appeal held that 'service' had its ordinary meaning of delivery of a document to a particular person.
[111] *AMEC Building Ltd v London Borough of Camden* [1997] Env LR 330.
[112] In *Re Rhondda Waste Disposal Company Ltd* [2001] Ch 57 it was held that the scope of 'other proceedings' in sections 10 and 11 of the Insolvency Act 1986 was not limited to remedies available to the creditors of the company or to those relating to the company's assets. Accordingly, in a prosecution (in this case of a waste company by the Environment Agency), leave of the court was required to commence prosecution of a company in administration under section 10(1)(c) of the Act, and, under section 11(3)(d), permission of the company's administrator should be obtained to continue a prosecution, or leave of the court was required.

Where the industry in question has been fragmented through a franchising struc- **12.73**
ture, then the issue of responsibility may be resolved by identifying the point at
which control lies for the activity causing the nuisance. The answer may be that
more than one person should be identified as being responsible for the nuisance
and, therefore, separate notices should be served. Control and, therefore, responsibility might lie at different levels of the structure. However, although this approach
may succeed in identifying the correct recipient(s), it may mean that some recipients have been incorrectly identified and may appeal. In such a case, if it has subsequently become possible to identify the person(s) responsible, then a local authority
might choose to withdraw those notices wrongly served prior to an appeal.[113]

Hospitals are now organized into health trusts, which are autonomous and inde- **12.74**
pendent. Service should, therefore, be made on the person responsible, namely,
the Chief Executive.

Suspension of abatement notices

Normally, suspension of an abatement notice is automatic when an appeal is **12.75**
launched. However, it is provided that an abatement notice shall not be suspended
if the nuisance is injurious to health, or of a limited duration so that suspension
would render it of no practical effect, or the expenditure to be incurred on the carrying out of work is not disproportionate to the benefit to be achieved in the period
before the appeal is determined.[114] This applies whether the notice is a simple
abatement notice or one specifying works.[115]

A local authority, when drafting an abatement notice, should take care to indicate **12.76**
whether the suspension provisions are to be disapplied and, if so, on what
grounds, since the recipient of the notice is entitled to know why the case is so
important as to require compliance pending an appeal. However, the fact that the
reasons are specified gives the recipient no rights to challenge or disregard the
disapplication of these provisions. The only remedy for a recipient in these
circumstances is to seek the earliest possible hearing of the statutory appeal. The
local authority should delete any provisions which are not applicable even though
failure to do so may not render the notice invalid.[116]

The inclusion of a provision in the notice stating that it will not be suspended **12.77**
because the expenditure on works is not disproportionate to the benefit to be
achieved,[117] is not to be taken as suggesting that a local authority is proceeding

---

[113] Arguably, although effective in practical terms, this procedure might be considered not to be good practice.
[114] Statutory Nuisance (Appeals) Regulations 1995, SI 1995/2644, reg 3. For further discussion of this point, see Chapter 13. [115] *Cambridge CC v Douglas* (n 56 above).
[116] In *Sovereign Rubber Ltd v Stockport MBC* (n 22 above) at 202, Sedley LJ considered such a fail-ure to be 'slapdash drafting on any view'.
[117] Statutory Nuisance (Appeals) Regulations 1995, SI 1995/2644, reg 3(2)(b).

under section 80(1)(b) of the EPA 1990 and must, therefore, have specified the relevant works in the notice.[118]

Withdrawing notices

12.78 There is no express power in the EPA 1990 to withdraw a notice once served.[119] However, it was held in *R v Bristol CC, ex p Everett*[120] that there is an implied power to withdraw notices. So, where a local authority concludes that a notice was improperly served for whatever reason, it may withdraw it and avoid thereby the prospect of an appeal.

12.79 There is no requirement to withdraw a notice once a nuisance has been abated. A local authority is entitled to leave a notice in existence and may act upon it at any time in the future provided that the circumstances pertaining when it was originally served are still extant. For example, in *Wellingborough BC v Gordon*[121] an abatement notice, which had been served three years before, was successfully relied upon when a noisy party took place, even though there had been no breach in the preceding period of time.

12.80 Provided that there has been no change in circumstances, notices issued under previous legislation continue to be enforceable under the EPA 1990.[122]

Amending notices

12.81 While a notice may be amended on appeal by the magistrates[123] there is neither an express nor an implied power, recognized by the courts, which enables a local authority to amend a notice prior to appeal. Should the parties agree a variation to a notice, say, for example, to extend the time period allowed for the works of compliance, then there are two options. A local authority may withdraw the first notice and substitute a second. Alternatively, the authority may write a letter, which records the agreed amendment. The letter would then be read as part of the notice.[124] Further, in such a situation, the authority would be estopped from denying the existence of the agreed variation.

---

[118] *Cambridge CC v Douglas* (n 56 above).

[119] Prior to the 1990 Act, if a recipient consented, it was possible to withdraw the notice. However, no costs would be recoverable by a recipient if this option was taken, so recipients would often be inclined to proceed to an appeal (*R v Cannock Justices, ex p Astbury* (1972) 70 LGR 609).

[120] n 27 above.   [121] [1993] Env LR 218.

[122] *Aitken v South Hams DC* [1995] 159 JPR 25.   [123] See Chapter 13.

[124] *London Borough of Camden v London Underground Ltd* (n 83 above).

13

APPEALS AGAINST ABATEMENT NOTICES

Introduction 13.01
   Time limits 13.02
   Who may bring an appeal? 13.03
   Purpose of the appeal 13.04
Suspension of the notice 13.06
   Appeal against a decision to serve a non-suspended notice 13.11
Grounds of appeal 13.12
**Abatement notice is not justified by section 80 of the EPA 1990
(regulation 2(2)(a))** 13.13
**Some informality, defect or error in, or in connection with, the
abatement notice (regulation 2(2)(b))** 13.17
   Void and invalid notices 13.19
   Prosecution after failure to appeal the notice 13.22
   Scope of 'informality, defect or error' 13.25
**The authority have refused unreasonably to accept compliance with
alternative requirements, or the requirements of the abatement
notice are otherwise unreasonable in character or extent, or are
unnecessary (regulation 2(2)(c))** 13.27
   Alternative requirements 13.28
   What is unreasonable? 13.30
   Requirements stipulated in the notice 13.33
**The time (or times) within which the requirements of the
abatement notice are to be complied with is not reasonably
sufficient for the purpose (regulation 2(2)(d))** 13.37
**Best practicable means were used to prevent, or to counteract the
effects of, the nuisance (regulation 2(2)(e))** 13.41
   Relevant date 13.43
   Use of expert evidence 13.44
   Implications in a future prosecution 13.45
**In the case of noise nuisance from premises (section 79(1)(g) of the
EPA 1990) or in the street (section 79(1)(ga) of the EPA 1990),
the requirements imposed by the notice are more onerous than those
provided in other statutory notices or consents (regulations
2(2)(f) and 2(2)(g))** 13.47
**Service on persons instead of the appellant (regulations 2(2)(h)
and 2(2)(i)) or in addition to the appellant (regulation 2(2)(j))** 13.49
   Regulation 2(2)(h) 13.50

200   PROCEDURE AND EVIDENCE

    Regulation 2(2)(i) 13.52
    Regulation 2(2)(j) 13.54
    Effect of successfully appealing notices 13.56
Court's powers on appeal 13.57
Court's powers in respect of third parties 13.60
Amending the grounds of appeal 13.63
Pre-trial procedures 13.65
Procedures at trial 13.68
    Order of speeches and evidence 13.68
    Burden and standard of proof 13.70
Costs 13.71
    Costs should follow the event? 13.73
    Where the terms of a notice are varied 13.76
    Where the appellant wins 13.78
    Where the local authority wins 13.80
    Position when the local authority withdraws a notice before the
    appeal is heard 13.81
Appeals to the Crown Court 13.85
    Powers of the court 13.87
    Inconsistent evidence 13.89
    Costs 13.90
Appeals to the High Court 13.93

Introduction

13.01 The recipient of an abatement notice may appeal to a magistrates' court[1] to have it quashed or to have the requirements varied to make them less onerous.[2] The appeal is a civil matter which is commenced by way of making a complaint to the court.[3] The grounds for appealing the notice need to be specified and are set down in the Statutory Nuisance (Appeals) Regulations 1995.[4] All relevant grounds of appeal should be included. If in doubt whether a particular ground is relevant, it should be included. It can subsequently be withdrawn if the appellant decides not to pursue the point at the hearing, in which case it should be withdrawn as early as possible to avoid wasting legal costs or the court's time.

Time limits

13.02 The appeal should be lodged with the court within 21 days of the date of service of the abatement notice.[5] Time begins to run from the date the recipient was properly

---

[1] EPA 1990, s 80(3). In Scotland, appeal is by summary application to the sheriff.
[2] Statutory Nuisance (Appeals) Regulations 1995, SI 1995/2644, reg 2(5).
[3] Magistrates' Courts Rules 1981, SI 1981/552, r 34.
[4] SI 1995/2644, set out in full in the Appendix to this work.
[5] EPA 1990, s 80(3). Where the last day falls on a Sunday, Good Friday or Christmas Day, the appeal should be lodged by the day before.

served with the notice, not from the date the local authority issued it. The court does not have an express power to extend the time limit for appeal; neither should such a power be implied.[6] This time limit may lead to an injustice where a person served with a notice was unaware of its existence until after the 21-day period had elapsed.[7]

Who may bring an appeal?
Only recipients of a notice may appeal against notices. Third parties aggrieved about the terms of a notice cannot be made parties to an appeal. A 'person aggrieved' can take his own proceedings under section 82 of the Environmental Protection Act 1990 ('EPA 1990') against a person causing a statutory nuisance.[8] He will not be prevented from doing so because a local authority has served a notice under section 80 of the EPA 1990, irrespective of whether that notice is appealed against. Further, a person who claims that his proprietary interest in premises is harmed by a statutory nuisance is not prevented from taking civil proceedings in private nuisance to obtain an injunction and/or damages because the procedure under section 80 for serving a notice has been invoked.

13.03

Purpose of the appeal
The purpose of bringing an appeal is to test the local authority's justification for serving the abatement notice. The time when the court has to consider this is the date the notice was served not the date of the court hearing.[9] The local authority becomes the defendant in an action brought by the person served with the notice, who is the appellant. The court should not be considering whether a breach of the notice has occurred. The court is concerned about such matters as whether a notice is needed to control a statutory nuisance and, if so, whether it is drafted in the correct form and was properly served on the right person or persons.

13.04

Magistrates (and sometimes their clerks) may be inexperienced or confused about this appellate role and not used to the court functioning as a civil tribunal.[10] For example, courts in appeals against notices sometimes treat the local authority as

13.05

---

[6] *R v Secretary of State for the Environment, ex p Ostler* [1976] 3 All ER 90.
[7] *Hope Butuyuyu v London Borough of Hammersmith* [1997] Env LR D13. In a prosecution the defendant may be able to argue that he had a reasonable excuse for non-compliance with a notice.
[8] See Chapter 16.
[9] *SFI Group plc (formerly Surrey Free Inns plc) v Gosport BC* [1999] Env LR 750. The Court of Appeal concurred with the decision of the Divisional Court to reverse *Johnsons News of London Ltd v London Borough of Ealing* (1989) 154 JP 33 which had held that the date of hearing the appeal was the relevant date. Appellants can no longer succeed in an appeal because they have abated the nuisance or employed best practicable means between service of the notice and the date of the hearing.
[10] Licensing applications and family proceedings are 'bread and butter' areas of work in magistrates' courts, but specialist regulatory areas involving both civil and criminal law are comparatively rare, as are cases involving disputed expert evidence.

though it were the prosecutor rather than the defendant in a civil action. Advocates for either party may be called upon to assist the court on matters of procedure as well as law.[11]

Suspension of the notice

13.06 The effect of bringing an appeal will sometimes be that a notice is suspended until either the appeal has been abandoned or has been decided by the court. Regulation 3(1) of the 1995 Regulations is drafted in such a way that the local authority has no discretion whether to suspend a notice, provided that all the requirements are met.[12] In some situations, such as when a perpetrator is causing an alleged nuisance only for a limited period, appealing the notice may be a tactic to buy time to delay enforcement.

13.07 The grounds set out in regulation 3(1) for suspending a notice are either:

- because compliance would involve expenditure in carrying out works before the appeal is heard; or
- in the case of noise nuisances (under section 79(1)(g) or (ga) of the EPA 1990) such noise is necessarily caused in the performance of some duty imposed by law on the appellant.[13]

13.08 Suspension of a notice does *not* apply where the nuisance:

- is injurious to health; or
- is likely to be of limited duration such that suspension would render the notice of no practical effect; or
- the expenditure in carrying out works required by the notice before any appeal has been decided would not be disproportionate to the public benefit to be expected in that period from compliance.[14]

13.09 These requirements give a local authority quite a lot of scope to decide that a notice should not be suspended pending the appeal. Provided a criterion is met, this provision prevents the deleterious effects of a nuisance continuing during the period leading up to an appeal hearing.

---

[11] In one of the authors' experience, a stipendiary magistrate needed to be persuaded not to combine in a single hearing an appeal against an abatement notice with a prosecution for breach of the notice requirements.

[12] A local authority should be careful to delete those parts of a standard notice form which do not apply, even though a failure to do so may not render the notice invalid; see *Sovereign Rubber Ltd v Stockport MBC* [2000] Env LR 194.

[13] For statutory authority in cases of noise nuisance, see paras 6.125–6.127.

[14] Statutory Nuisance (Appeals) Regulations 1995, SI 1995/2644, reg 3(2). Where this reason is given the local authority is not restricted to serving a specific works form of notice under the EPA 1990, s 80(1)(b), the details of which have been contained in the notice; see *Cambridge CC v Douglas* [2001] Env LR 41.

13: APPEALS AGAINST ABATEMENT NOTICES

When a local authority serves an abatement notice and wishes to revoke suspension, it must include in the body of the non-suspended notice: **13.10**

- a statement that it is not suspended pending the appeal, and
- the relevant regulation that applies (regulation 3(2)), and
- the grounds in regulation 3(2) on which the local authority is relying.[15]

Appeal against a decision to serve a non-suspended notice
There is no provision in the EPA 1990 or in the 1995 Regulations giving a right of appeal against a local authority's decision to serve a non-suspended notice. Clearly there is a risk of injustice from this, which will be reduced where the magistrates' court is willing and able to hear the substantive appeal very quickly. This may not be feasible, for example if expert evidence is going to be called by either party. In the words of Sedley J in *Sovereign Rubber Ltd v Stockport MBC* the 'only remedy for the disapplication of the suspensory provision is to seek the earliest possible hearing of the statutory appeal'.[16] Otherwise, the only method of challenging this non-suspension would be by way of judicial review if *Wednesbury* grounds could be established.[17] **13.11**

Grounds of appeal

There are a number of grounds of appeal, discussed below, which are set out in regulation 2(2) of the 1995 Regulations. Any one or more of these grounds need to be stipulated in the notice of appeal lodged with the court, which then forms the complaint against the local authority. The appellant is not required to give detailed particulars of each ground of appeal, at this or any other stage of the proceedings before the day of the hearing. **13.12**

Abatement notice is not justified by section 80 of the EPA 1990 (regulation 2(2)(a))

This ground can cover such matters as: **13.13**

- whether the alleged nuisance comes within the categories of statutory nuisance in section 79(1) of the EPA 1990; and
- whether the interference complained of is sufficient to amount to a nuisance.

The central issue here is over whether the matter which the local authority seeks to control amounts to a statutory nuisance. This is a matter of fact for the magistrates **13.14**

---

[15] Statutory Nuisance (Appeals) Regulations 1995, SI 1995/2644, reg 3(3).
[16] n 12 above, at 202.
[17] *Associated Provincial Picture Houses Ltd v Wednesbury Corporation* [1948] 1KB 223. Where a breach of human rights is being claimed, a lower threshold than the *Wednesbury* standard may be arguable; see further para 17.36.

to decide; and they are not bound by the local authority's view when serving the notice. In *SFI Group plc (formerly Surrey Free Inns plc) v Gosport BC*, Stuart-Smith LJ held:

> The notice is not justified if no statutory nuisance existed or was likely to occur or recur at the date of its service; that is a question of fact to be determined by the magistrates' court if it is in dispute. The court is not bound to accept the subjective view of the [council] in the absence of bad faith or *Wednesbury* grounds.[18]

13.15 The concept of a statutory nuisance is considered fully in Chapter 4. Whether a notice is justified by section 80 of the EPA 1990 is a very general ground; any reason for doubting that a notice is properly grounded in nuisance or that prejudice to health is involved can trigger an appeal under this regulation.

13.16 This ground of appeal is not only conceptual. The choice of words used in drafting the notice may also give grounds for appeal.[19] Section 80(1) only allows a notice to be served where the local authority is satisfied that a statutory nuisance exists, or is likely to occur or recur. If, for example, the notice purported to deal with a nuisance that could not recur, then this would be a ground for appeal.

Some informality, defect or error in, or in connection with, the abatement notice (regulation 2(2)(b))

13.17 This is the most important ground associated with drafting notices, a topic which is fully considered in Chapter 12. Appeals based on the argument that a particularized form of notice should have been served rather than a simple one are unlikely to succeed.[20] This argument had often been deployed until the Court of Appeal in *R v Falmouth and Truro Port Health Authority, ex p South West Water Ltd*[21] decided that a local authority has a wide discretion, for all forms of statutory nuisance, whether to require the carrying out of specified works.

13.18 The informality, defect or error in the notice in question must be significant or material, otherwise the court should dismiss this ground of appeal.[22]

Void and invalid notices

13.19 Where a defect or error is fundamental, or where a notice is manifestly unreasonable, it could be argued that the notice is a nullity, or nothing but a 'mere piece of paper'. Here the proper course is to seek judicial review against the local authority for serving so manifestly defective a notice.[23]

---

[18] *SFI Group plc (formerly Surrey Free Inns plc) v Gosport BC* (n 9 above), at 763.
[19] For drafting of notices generally, see Chapter 12.
[20] See J Pointing, 'Have Specific Works Notices Finally Run their Course?' [2000] ELM 99; R Malcolm, 'Statutory Nuisance: The Validity of Abatement Notices' [2000] JPL 894.
[21] [2000] 3 All ER 306.
[22] Statutory Nuisance (Appeals) Regulations 1995, SI 1995/2644, reg 2(3).
[23] *R v Wicks* [1997] 2 All ER 801.

But judicial review must only be sought on proper grounds and should not be resorted to as an optional form of appeal. In *Sovereign Rubber Ltd v Stockport MBC*, Sedley LJ stated: **13.20**

> I do not doubt that an abatement notice may . . . be quashed as a nullity in an extreme case, for example where bad faith can be shown or serious non-compliance with requisite procedures or such deficiency that the document cannot be described as an abatement notice at all. But any quashing on such grounds must be by way of judicial review. A recipient of an abatement notice who appeals to the Justices . . . is appealing against a notice which, though arguably deficient, is valid. If it is so deficient that it cannot be cured by variation in favour of the appellant, the Justices have jurisdiction to quash it, but this is the quashing of an abatement notice, not of a nullity.[24]

Magistrates do not have the power to declare an abatement notice null and void; this would require a judicial review of the local authority's decision to issue it. Cases where an abatement notice is so defective as to be a nullity will be rare. More often, the informality, defect or error is such that the notice can be varied and, if not, then the court may quash it.[25] Generally with defective notices the proper course is to appeal to the magistrates rather than to seek judicial review.[26] For example, a notice naming the wrong premises or served on the wrong company could be dealt with, firstly, by the local authority being invited to withdraw it.[27] If the local authority refuses, then the magistrates can be asked to quash the notice on appeal.[28] **13.21**

Prosecution after failure to appeal the notice
The recipient of a defective notice is not under a duty to inform the local authority that it is defective. The risk he takes is that a failure to appeal may result in his breaching the notice and so becoming liable to prosecution. The recipient of the notice, as defendant, may not be able to run a 'reasonable excuse' defence, where the prosecution convinces the court that he could and should have raised an issue about the notice's validity in an appeal.[29] *A Lambert Flat Management Ltd v Lomas*[30] is authority for the proposition that a defendant cannot raise in a prosecution a defence which ought to have been raised in an appeal against the notice. This does not mean that a prosecution founded upon a fundamentally flawed notice can be justified. **13.22**

---

[24] n 12 above, at 203–4.
[25] Statutory Nuisance (Appeals) Regulations 1995, SI 1995/2644, reg 2(5).
[26] cf the situation where there are no statutory grounds for appealing a notice (eg a notice served in respect of an overcrowded dwelling under the Housing Act 1985, s 338). In these circumstances, challenging the notice by judicial review may be the only remedy.
[27] The scope for the local authority withdrawing notices is wider since the decision in *R v Bristol CC, ex p Everett* [1999] 2 All ER 193.
[28] Statutory Nuisance (Appeals) Regulations 1995, SI 1995/2644, reg 2(2)(h), provides a ground of appeal based on service on the wrong person.
[29] *A Lambert Flat Management Ltd v Lomas* [1981] 2 All ER 280; *Hope Butuyuyu v London Borough of Hammersmith* (n 7 above) and see also paras 15.35–15.43.   [30] [1981] 2 All ER 280.

13.23 Generally, where a local authority cannot be persuaded to withdraw a defective notice, the recipient will be best advised to appeal. There may be other grounds on which the recipient wishes to appeal. It will save time and money if he can persuade the court to give a preliminary ruling on the validity of the notice since, if successful, this may obviate the need to appeal on the other grounds. However, this may result in the local authority serving a fresh, technically correct notice. Where the result of seeking a preliminary ruling on a technical ground of appeal is that the process of serving a fresh notice and appealing against it is merely repeated, an appellant may decide to proceed with all his grounds of appeal in one hearing to pre-empt subsequent service of a fresh notice.

13.24 A fundamentally flawed notice could not be used as the basis for a prosecution. Magistrates who decided to allow such a prosecution to continue could have their decision judicially reviewed. The position is not so clear where breach of a less obviously defective notice forms the basis for a prosecution. However, human rights challenges could be raised pertaining to the fairness of the proceedings, including whether there had been alleged breaches of articles 6 (right to a fair trial) and 7 (certainty in the definition of a crime) of the Convention.[31] Human rights challenges in respect of prosecutions founded upon dubious notices are likely to occur over the next few years.

Scope of 'informality, defect or error'

13.25 The ground of appeal in regulation 2(2)(b) is not restricted to what is stated in the notice, since the regulation also refers to an informality, defect or error made *in connection with* the notice. It would apply, it is submitted, to a failure to consult with a recipient who has been given a legitimate expectation to be consulted about the terms of the notice.[32]

13.26 It is difficult to ascertain the scope of 'in connection with' in this regulation. There remains an absence of authority on whether an unlawful state of mind, such as bad faith, possessed by a local authority at the time of service amounts to a defect made in connection with a notice. There is also a lack of authority on whether an innocent mistake made by a council at the time of service amounts to a defect or error made in connection with the notice. It is suggested that both these examples would be arguable on this ground of appeal.

---

[31] See further paras 11.42–11.52.
[32] *R v Falmouth and Truro Port Health Authority, ex p South West Water Ltd* (n 21 above). The Court of Appeal decided that there is no express or implied right to be consulted about what terms a local authority is contemplating specifying in a notice. It is only where the local authority has clearly provided the potential notice recipient with the expectation of consultation that any right arises.

The authority have refused unreasonably to accept compliance with alternative requirements, or the requirements of the abatement notice are otherwise unreasonable in character or extent, or are unnecessary (regulation 2(2)(c))

This is another complicated ground of appeal. It is needlessly complicated further by the legislative draftsman appearing to combine two separate processes: **13.27**

- where the notice recipient has suggested alternative requirements to those stipulated in the notice; and
- those requirements stipulated by a local authority in the body of the notice.[33]

Alternative requirements

Appeal on this ground presupposes that the recipient of a notice accepts that a nuisance exists; but disagrees over what needs to be done about it. The recipient of a notice may be better placed than a local authority to know how to abate or restrict the nuisance.[34] Alternative methods of dealing with a problem may be cheaper or more convenient for the recipient to put into effect. Possibly, the local authority's solution is more expensive without there being a corresponding benefit. In these kinds of situation, the notice recipient may suggest alternatives which a local authority will be under a duty to consider. Discussion may take place before a local authority has served a notice, particularly when there has been some negotiation between the parties as to what form of notice the authority is contemplating serving. **13.28**

If, subsequently, a notice is served with more onerous or different conditions than those suggested by the recipient, he may wish to appeal, additionally, on some other ground denying the existence of a nuisance, such as regulation 2(2)(a).[35] When suggesting alternative requirements, it is advisable for the potential notice recipient to avoid admitting causing the alleged nuisance, and so to reserve his position in the event of a future appeal.[36] **13.29**

What is unreasonable?

A refusal by an authority even to consider an alternative proposal would in itself be unreasonable. Evidence that an alternative proposal had not been considered **13.30**

---

[33] It has been suggested by McCracken et al in *Statutory Nuisance: Law and Practice* (Butterworths, 2001), p 87, that this regulation ought to be construed as two limbs, each giving rise to independent grounds of appeal. We agree. However, it is plausible that three limbs were intended by the draftsman.

[34] *Sterling Homes v Birmingham CC* [1996] Env LR 121, at 133–4.

[35] See para 13.13.

[36] The wording used in formal pleadings may assist in correspondence with the local authority, such as: 'If, which is denied, a statutory nuisance does exist, then the following alternative provisions are being proposed . . .'

properly should also result in this ground succeeding in an appeal. However, this would depend on the court accepting that an alternative solution proposed by an appellant would be sufficient to deal with the nuisance.

13.31 If a local authority disagrees that a proposed alternative solution is adequate to combat the nuisance it will need to formulate its reasons for refusing it.

13.32 If, on hearing an appeal, magistrates decide to incorporate some or all of any conditions suggested by the appellant, they should vary the notice, which will then have effect as though it had been served by the local authority.[37]

Requirements stipulated in the notice

13.33 The second ground of appeal in regulation 2(2)(c) applies after a notice has been served and can be made when the notice requirements are thought to be unreasonable in character or extent, or are unnecessary.

13.34 An appeal on this ground may be made where a local authority specifies that 'state of the art' equipment be installed, whereas a lower specification would be good enough to reduce a problem to below the level at which it continues to cause a nuisance.[38] Regulatory law should not, generally, be used as a means to improve standards beyond those normally found in a particular field or industry.[39]

13.35 What magistrates would consider unreasonable or unnecessary depends on the particular facts of each case, particularly on the effects the interference has on the appellant's neighbours. It is submitted that the onus on the appellant to prove that requirements in a notice are unreasonable or unnecessary is quite a high one. The appellant is likely to succeed where he can show that the cost of installing expensive equipment is out of proportion to the benefit, and it may be advisable to employ an expert if this strategy is pursued.

13.36 In view of the similarity between this ground of appeal and one based on using 'best practicable means', appellants who are able to avail themselves of the best practicable means defence should consider carefully whether to appeal under both these grounds.[40]

---

[37] Statutory Nuisance (Appeals) Regulations 1995, SI 1995/2644, reg 2(5).
[38] This problem is often found in food safety enforcement. For an extreme example in which an environmental health officer required the installation of kitchen equipment far in excess of what could reasonably be required, see *Welton v North Cornwall DC* [1997] 1 WLR 570.
[39] There is venerable authority, decided with reference to the Factories Act 1844, that precautions ordinarily adopted in the trade do not amount to best practicable means: *Schofield v Schunck* (1855) 19 JP 84. However, this case was decided at a time when normal standards in industry were considered by most informed commentators to be inherently dangerous. [40] See para 13.41.

The time (or times) within which the requirements of the abatement notice are to be complied with is not reasonably sufficient for the purpose (regulation 2(2)(d))

13.37 Stipulating the time (or times, when several matters are included) needed for carrying out the terms of the notice is a basic requirement.[41] Failure by a local authority to do so will render a notice invalid under regulation 2(2)(b) of the 1995 Regulations.

13.38 This ground of appeal is available when a recipient accepts that a notice is justified except for the time allowed to carry out its requirements. Where an appeal is limited to this issue, particularly where a notice is not suspended,[42] the case should be heard quickly in fairness to all parties.

13.39 An appellant will need to provide evidence that the time requirements in the notice are unreasonable. For example, evidence that it will take longer than the notice stipulates to order and install a piece of equipment would probably be considered a reasonable ground for appeal, whereas an inability to find the purchase money would not. In most cases in which compliance involves expenditure, the notice will be suspended until the appeal has been decided by the court. However, this will not always be the case, for example, where the nuisance is injurious to health.[43]

13.40 Appealing on this ground may appear inconsistent with also challenging the validity of the notice under regulation 2(2)(b).[44] If an appellant does wish to do this, the notice of appeal should make it clear that in any event the times required to meet the requirements are considered unreasonable.[45]

Best practicable means were used to prevent, or to counteract the effects of, the nuisance (regulation 2(2)(e))

13.41 An appeal grounded in best practicable means is limited to certain situations. Firstly, it only applies to the following statutory nuisances under section 79(1) of the EPA 1990:

- premises (section 79(1)(a));
- smoke from a chimney (section 79(1)(b));
- dust, steam, smell or other effluvia (section 79(1)(d));

---

[41] EPA 1990, s 80(1).
[42] Statutory Nuisance (Appeals) Regulations 1995, SI 1995/2644, reg 3.
[43] ibid, reg 3(2)(a)(i).
[44] See para 13.17.
[45] Care is needed in selecting which grounds of appeal are to be pursued and it is better to abandon hopeless grounds sooner rather than later. Otherwise, an appellant risks irritating the bench, who may think that the appellant is wasting the court's time. The court may impose penalties in costs for those pursuing hopeless grounds of appeal.

- accumulation or deposit (section 79(1)(e));
- keeping of animals (section 79(1)(f));
- noise from premises (section 79(1)(g)); and
- noise in the street caused by a vehicle, machinery or equipment (section 79(1)(ga)).

13.42 Secondly, an appeal on best practicable means grounds is only available in the above cases, with one exception, for nuisances emitted from or caused on industrial, trade or business premises.[46] The exception is that a best practicable means appeal is available for a statutory nuisance caused by smoke emitted from a chimney in a private dwelling, where the dwelling is located outside a smoke control area.[47]

Relevant date

13.43 The relevant date for deciding whether best practicable means have been used is the date the notice was served.[48] Steps taken after that date would not be relevant in an appeal, and, where a notice is suspended pending an appeal,[49] implementing measures to reduce a nuisance at this stage would be likely to undermine an appellant's case, its basis being that best practicable means had been employed before service of the notice.

Use of expert evidence

13.44 The magistrates' decision on whether best practicable means were employed will depend on the facts of each particular case. Expert evidence on the suitability of measures taken may well assist the court in all but very simple cases. Bearing in mind that disputes about best practicable means are often based on technically complex issues, both parties will need to consider whether to employ experts.[50] Experts should be able to assist in narrowing the issues in dispute, thus enabling both the advocates and the court to focus on relevant matters.

Implications in a future prosecution

13.45 Best practicable means is also a defence in a prosecution brought for breach of an abatement notice.[51] In an appeal in which an appellant fails to convince the court that best practicable means have been used, what are the chances of succeeding on these grounds later on, when defending a prosecution for breach of the abatement notice? The burden and standard of proof on the person causing the nuisance would be the same in both proceedings, namely, the civil standard, on

---

[46] See Chapter 15 and Table 15.1 at para 15.09. Note that this defence is never available for miscellaneous nuisances falling under s 79(1)(h) regardless of where they arise.
[47] Statutory Nuisance (Appeals) Regulations 1995, SI 1995/2644, reg 2(2)(e)(ii), enables an appeal on best practicable means grounds to be made for smoke nuisance from domestic premises. EPA 1990, s 79(3)(i), disapplies the smoke nuisance provision where the dwelling is in a smoke control area. For further details on smoke nuisance, see Chapter 7.
[48] *SFI Group plc (formerly Surrey Free Inns plc) v Gosport BC* (n 9 above).
[49] See para 13.06.
[50] See further paras 18.35–18.42.
[51] See Chapter 14.

the balance of probabilities. On the other hand, not all the evidence in the appeal would necessarily be admissible in criminal proceedings.[52] It is worth bearing in mind that the reasons why magistrates arrive at decisions are sometimes perplexing or obscure, perhaps especially when they are asked to decide complex issues such as those often raised in appeals against notices.

13.46 Appealing the magistrates' decision in the Crown Court and not succeeding in either venue will not necessarily persuade a company that it has failed to manage the nuisance effectively. In practice, the court may adopt a more sympathetic attitude to a company being prosecuted than one bringing an appeal against the notice. It may be worthwhile, then, defending a prosecution on best practicable means grounds even though an earlier appeal on these grounds had failed.

In the case of noise nuisance from premises (section 79(1)(g) of the EPA 1990) or in the street (section 79(1)(ga) of the EPA 1990), the requirements imposed by the notice are more onerous than those provided in other statutory notices or consents (regulations 2(2)(f) and 2(2)(g))

13.47 This summarizes two separate paragraphs of regulation 2(2) of the 1995 Regulations concerning notices under section 80 of the EPA 1990: those served in relation to noise emitted from premises and those served where the noise has been caused by equipment, machinery or vehicles in the street. Where a local authority has given its consent to a level of noise by issuing a notice restricting noise levels or by granting a licence, it cannot then serve an abatement notice under section 80 which imposes more onerous conditions. If it does so, a recipient can appeal.

13.48 An appeal on these grounds is limited to only a few situations, such as noise on construction sites[53] and noise emitted from loudspeakers in the street.[54] It does not apply to planning consents specifying noise levels; noise nuisance and planning consent operate as separate statutory regimes.[55]

Service on persons instead of the appellant (regulations 2(2)(h) and 2(2)(i)) or in addition to the appellant (regulation 2(2)(j))

13.49 Regulations 2(2)(h), 2(2)(i) and 2(2)(j) provide grounds of appeal based on disputed service.

Regulation 2(2)(h)
13.50 Under regulation 2(2)(h), an appellant can appeal where he believes that a notice should have been served on some other person instead, that person being:

---

[52] See paras 18.22–18.34 and 18.78–18.82.
[54] See further paras 6.91–6.95.
[53] See further paras 6.102–6.115.
[55] See further paras 17.61–17.67.

(i) the person responsible for the nuisance; or
(ii) the person responsible for the vehicle, machinery or equipment; or
(iii) in the case of a structural defect, the owner of the premises; or
(iv) in the case where the person responsible for the nuisance cannot be found or the nuisance has not yet occurred, the owner or occupier of the premises.

13.51 This ground of appeal applies where the appellant believes someone else is wholly responsible for the nuisance.

Regulation 2(2)(i)
13.52 Regulation 2(2)(i) is available to an appellant who believes that instead of him someone else might have been lawfully served with the notice and that it would have been equitable for the local authority so to do. How the court should make a judgement about a local authority exercising its powers equitably is unclear and neither the EPA 1990 nor the 1995 Regulations provides any guidance.

13.53 This ground applies when an appellant believes that he ought not to have been served with the notice because some other person is truly responsible for the nuisance. The question for the bench is whether it would have been equitable, or fair, to have served the notice on that other person rather than on the appellant. It only applies in cases:

- where the appellant is the owner of the premises, in which case service might, instead, have been on the occupier; or
- vice versa.

Regulation 2(2)(j)
13.54 This regulation applies when an appellant believes that some other person in addition to the appellant might have been served with the notice and that it would have been equitable so to do. The purpose of the regulation is to provide a notice recipient with a way of ensuring that others also responsible share the responsibility for ensuring that the terms of the abatement notice are adhered to, including sharing the costs of compliance.

13.55 The categories of person who might also have been served are those who are also:

(i) responsible for the nuisance; or
(ii) the owner of the premises; or
(iii) the occupier of the premises; or
(iv) responsible for the vehicle, machinery or equipment.

Effect of successfully appealing notices
13.56 A successful appeal under regulation 2(2)(h) or 2(2)(i) would result in an abatement notice being quashed since the person named would be the wrong person. Success on regulation 2(2)(j) grounds would mean that a notice served on an

appellant was good (unless successfully appealed on other grounds), but a further notice would need to be served on any third party.

Court's powers on appeal

The notice of appeal upon which a formal complaint to the magistrates' court is based may include one or more grounds of appeal. In cases involving multiple grounds of appeal, if only one succeeds then the appellant wins his appeal. **13.57**

On hearing the appeal the court may: **13.58**

- quash the notice; or
- vary the notice in favour of the appellant in such manner as it thinks fit; or
- dismiss the appeal.

The effect of the court making an order varying a notice is that the notice 'shall have effect as though it had been made by the local authority'.[56]

The court has no power to vary a notice by making its terms more onerous for an appellant. Arguably, a notice which is varied to make its terms clearer, or more readily enforceable, is not a variation in favour of the appellant. If this is correct, the court does not have the power to vary it for these reasons. An alternative, more pragmatic view is that it is in the appellant's interest for the court to vary a notice to make its terms clearer, since he will then know more clearly whether the notice has been breached.[57] It is suggested that the latter view is to be preferred, but the issue is arguable. **13.59**

Court's powers in respect of third parties

Third parties must be named by an appellant appealing on regulation 2(2)(i) or 2(2)(j) grounds when lodging a notice of appeal with the court; they must also be served with a copy of a notice of appeal.[58] Although both the EPA 1990 and the 1995 Regulations are silent on this point, it is suggested that such third parties are entitled to be represented and heard in an appeal. If this is refused, then, clearly, any order made by a court which affects a third party may have consequences for his property rights and rights to a fair hearing. A refusal would then seem to amount to a breach of the third party's rights under article 6 (right to a fair trial) **13.60**

---

[56] Statutory Nuisance (Appeals) Regulations 1995, SI 1995/2644, reg 2(5).
[57] *Sovereign Rubber Ltd v Stockport MBC* (n 12 above).
[58] Statutory Nuisance (Appeals) Regulations 1995, SI 1995/2644, reg 4. In addition, this regulation states that the appellant *may* serve a copy of the notice of appeal on any other person having an estate or interest in the premises, vehicle, machinery or equipment in question.

and article 1 (protection of property) of the First Protocol of the European Convention on Human Rights.[59]

13.61 In respect of third parties, a court can make an order rendering them liable to pay, whether wholly or in part, the costs of any works that are required for abatement. The 1995 Regulations provide that:

> on the hearing of an appeal the court may make such order *as it thinks fit—*
> (a) with respect to the person by whom any work is to be executed and the contribution to be made by *any* person towards the cost of the work, or
> (b) as to the proportions in which any expenses which may become recoverable by the authority . . . are to be borne by the appellant *and by any other person.*[60]

13.62 Regulation 2(7) of the 1995 Regulations requires the court to have regard to contractual or statutory conditions as between owner and occupier and to the nature of the works required. It provides also that the court must be satisfied that a third party had received a copy of the appellant's notice of appeal. The paucity of regulatory provisions to protect third parties' basic rights on this matter is deplorable.

Amending the grounds of appeal

13.63 There is no provision in the EPA 1990 or in the 1995 Regulations for amending the grounds of appeal. As the grounds contained in the notice of appeal must be lodged within 21 days of service of the notice, arguably a court hearing an appeal has no power to allow any amendment. This would be inflexible since an appellant can subsequently withdraw any of his grounds; but can he substitute other, perhaps more relevant ones? It is difficult to see any justification for refusing an amendment, provided that no unfairness is caused to the defendant. Other areas of civil litigation allow amendments to be made at various stages of the proceedings, sometimes requiring the leave of the court.

13.64 The better view is that the court has a discretion to allow amendments to the grounds of appeal. Where this is done late, perhaps necessitating a wasted hearing date, the appellant can be penalized in costs.[61] However, there is no direct authority on this issue so it is clearly arguable.

Pre-trial procedures

13.65 There is a paucity of procedural rules to regulate the conduct of appeals against abatement notices. This affects both parties and in a complex case can mean that

---

[59] European Convention on Human Rights (Rome, 4 November 1950; TS 71 (1953); Cmd 8969). See further, respectively, paras 11.46 and 11.30.
[60] Statutory Nuisance (Appeals) Regulations 1995, SI 1995/2644, reg 2(6) (our emphasis).
[61] See further paras 13.71–13.84 on costs generally.

court proceedings risk becoming very stressful and even farcical. In particular, there are no rules about disclosure of evidence, whether assertions of fact in witness statements or of expert reports. Theoretically, either party can introduce an expert on the day of a hearing without prior service of his report. This ought to result in the opposing party being granted an adjournment, with the costs of the wasted hearing being borne by the side wishing to introduce the evidence. But the practice in different courts varies enormously, and regulations are required if appeals are to be conducted fairly to both parties. An especially robust court may decide to refuse to hear such evidence but the legal basis for such a refusal is not firm and an appellant whose expert had been prevented from giving evidence on this ground could claim that his rights to a fair trial had been violated.[62]

13.66 Magistrates' courts can only exercise powers drawn from statute and do not have any inherent authority to invent their own procedure. However, if the parties can agree directions between themselves, such as the dates for exchanging witness statements, the court can be invited to endorse the agreement. The court cannot enforce any agreement, however, and neither can it penalize either party for a failure to comply with it. Such endorsement could be sought at a directions hearing when the court is setting times for the final hearing.

13.67 Given the problems posed by the lack of rules for the conduct of cases, co-operation between the parties is obviously sensible and it helps the court to concentrate on the relevant issues during an appeal hearing. Where co-operation proves impossible, then disclosure should not be one-sided. A local authority faced with an appellant, or his legal representative, who refuses to particularize the grounds of appeal or fails to provide any witness statements or expert reports, should:

- not serve any of its own evidence;
- write to the appellant telling him why this decision has been made;
- inform the appellant that the correspondence between the parties will be put before court to justify any adjournment that might be needed; and
- add that the local authority will be seeking costs for the wasted hearing.

Procedures at trial

Order of speeches and evidence

13.68 The appellant opens his case and presents his evidence first.[63] The defendant may address the court whether or not he subsequently calls evidence.[64] After the defendant's evidence is heard, the appellant may call evidence in rebuttal.[65] As the appeal is a civil matter, there are no restrictions on the admissibility of relevant hearsay evidence provided that the 1999 Rules are adhered to.[66]

---

[62] See further para 11.46. [63] Magistrates' Courts Rules 1981, SI 1981/552, r 14(1).
[64] ibid, r 14(2). [65] ibid, r 14(3).
[66] Magistrates' Courts (Hearsay Evidence in Civil Proceedings) Rules 1999, SI 1999/691.

13.69 Closing speeches are then made, with the defendant addressing the bench first. Addressing the court for a second time requires leave which should not normally be refused. If one party is allowed to address the court in a closing speech, the other must be allowed to do so.[67] The appellant should always have the last word.

Burden and standard of proof

13.70 The appellant has the burden of proving his case to the ordinary civil standard of the balance of probabilities. Should the appellant be unable to establish a *prima facie* case at the close of his evidence, the court may dismiss an appeal at this stage, either on application by the local authority or of its own motion.

Costs

13.71 The Magistrates' Courts Act 1980 gives magistrates a wide discretion to decide at the conclusion of an appeal whether to make an order for costs. Neither party has a right to recover his costs. If the court does decide to award costs, the amount will be such as the court thinks is 'just and reasonable'.[68]

13.72 In view of this discretion, both the party seeking costs and the party resisting them will need to consider carefully their submissions. These will be made at the conclusion of the appeal, after the court has announced its decision. Once it is made, challenging a costs order will be very difficult.[69]

Costs should follow the event?

13.73 The general rule in civil proceedings is that the party who wins receives his reasonable costs from the losing party. However, there is recent authority concerning civil appeals, confirming that the magistrates' discretion is wider and that they need not consider it just and reasonable for costs to follow the event.[70]

13.74 The general rule of costs following the event is not directly applicable to appeals against notices because a local authority issuing an abatement notice is acting under a statutory duty to protect persons within its area from statutory nuisances and not as a claimant in a civil dispute. Penalizing a local authority which loses an appeal by making a costs order is likely to deter future enforcement action and to act against the public interest.[71] Further, a local authority has no discretion whether to serve a notice once it is satisfied that a statutory nuisance exists;[72] it

---

[67] Magistrates' Courts Rules 1981, SI 1981/552, r 14(5).
[68] Magistrates' Courts Act 1980, s 64.
[69] *R v Southend Stipendiary Magistrate, ex p Rochford DC* [1995] Env LR 1.
[70] *Bradford MBC v Booth* (2000) 164 JP 485. This was a licensing appeal from the magistrates' decision, which, it is submitted, is similar in principle to statutory nuisance enforcement.
[71] *Bradford MBC v Booth* (n 70 above).
[72] *R v Carrick DC, ex p Shelley* [1996] Env LR 273.

may have acted reasonably and properly in serving the notice; it may have lost the appeal on technical grounds; and the recipient may not have been co-operative.

The possible outcomes of an appeal against an abatement notice are more complicated than one side winning and the other losing. In deciding on costs, magistrates should base their decisions on the realities of each case. **13.75**

Where the terms of a notice are varied
The court may decide simply to vary the terms of a notice in favour of an appellant. Such a variation may be relatively minor or profound. How should a court use its discretion to award costs wisely? The argument that no costs should be awarded where the court decides to vary a notice, rather than to quash it or to dismiss the appeal, may often be appropriate. But as a general rule it could also lead to injustice, for example where a variation was profound or when a local authority had been inept in its drafting. In these cases, it would be hard to justify making no order for costs. **13.76**

When an appeal results in a court varying the terms of a notice the court can decide: **13.77**

- to award costs to the appellant; or
- to award costs to the local authority; or
- to make no order for costs.

The decision should be based on the realities of the case and all the above options should be considered.

Where the appellant wins
If the local authority had acted in a blameworthy way in serving an abatement notice, usually it would be just and reasonable for them to pay the appellant's reasonable costs in full. In other circumstances where the appellant wins and the court decides to quash a notice, there may be grounds for the local authority to argue for a reduction in the award of costs to the appellant, or even for no costs to be awarded. **13.78**

An appellant may win on some grounds, but lose on others. Or a successful appellant may have included a number of irrelevant grounds of appeal along with germane ones. In both these instances, a local authority could argue for a reduction in the award of costs, or even for no costs, depending on the circumstances. **13.79**

Where the local authority wins
A local authority cannot avoid responding to an appeal against a notice. The argument that costs should follow the event is, perhaps, stronger where a local authority succeeds in resisting the appeal. However, there is a counter-argument that **13.80**

this would penalize the notice recipient and deter individuals from pursuing their legal rights if they had to pay the full costs of losing.[73] It is suggested that the wording of section 64 of the Magistrates' Courts Act 1980 allows the court to make a costs order which can accommodate all the circumstances of a case, including reducing the size of the costs awarded to the successful local authority, or awarding no costs.

Position when the local authority withdraws a notice before the appeal is heard

13.81 Since the Court of Appeal's decision in *R v Bristol CC, ex p Everett*,[74] a local authority has an implied power to withdraw an abatement notice. Should it do so in the period after the recipient lodges an appeal but before the case is heard, the question whether the recipient can obtain costs arises. The costs implications for the recipient of withdrawing an abatement notice were not considered by the Court of Appeal in *Ex p Everett*.

13.82 There are different circumstances in which a local authority could decide to withdraw a notice. In *Ex p Everett*, the council did so after it had changed its mind and decided that the risk of physical injury caused by steep stairs could not be prejudicial to health in the sense required by section 79 of the EPA 1990. On the other hand, withdrawing a notice might be undertaken because a local authority subsequently believes it to be misconceived or deficient in some way and wishes to avoid losing on appeal.

13.83 The situation might arise, for example, where a non-suspended notice was served because a local authority believed that a statutory nuisance was injurious to health and the notice required works to be carried out. If a recipient carries out such works and appeals against a notice which is subsequently withdrawn, can he claim costs, including the costs of those works? The answer is probably not. If the council had acted in bad faith then some other redress, such as a complaint to the Ombudsman or judicial review, might be feasible. If the recipient can prove that a local authority was negligent in serving the notice then he might succeed in a civil action and claim damages. There is nothing in the EPA 1990 or in the 1995 Regulations that deals with this problem.

13.84 It would appear, at present, that the magistrates' court has no jurisdiction to hear an application for costs where there is no appeal before it. This could lead to injustice for recipients who are put to unnecessary expenditure which they cannot recover.

---

[73] There has been a practice in appeals against Health and Safety at Work Act 1974 improvement notices for costs not to be awarded to the local authority or to the Health and Safety Executive where they succeed in resisting appeals.

[74] n 27 above.

Appeals to the Crown Court

13.85 Either party may appeal, without leave, to the Crown Court against any decision of the magistrates' court.[75] The procedures set down in the Crown Court Rules on appeals apply to all types of appeal against the magistrates' decision, whether civil or criminal.[76] Notification of the appeal and of the grounds must be made within 21 days of the date of the decision in the magistrates' court.[77] The recipient of a notice cannot introduce fresh grounds of appeal, but may appeal to the Crown Court on selected grounds from his previous appeal to the magistrates.

13.86 The Crown Court appeal, which will be a rehearing, is heard by a judge sitting with two magistrates. Because it is a rehearing, the court will be free to assess the facts anew and the parties will not be confined to presenting their evidence in the same way as earlier in the magistrates' court. Different or additional evidence may be called by both parties.

Powers of the court

13.87 The Crown Court has similar powers to the magistrates who first heard the appeal against the abatement notice. The court may:

- quash the notice; or
- vary the notice in favour of an appellant in such manner as it thinks fit; or
- dismiss the appeal.

The effect of the court making an order varying the notice is that a notice has effect as though it had been made by the local authority.[78]

13.88 The court should give reasons for its decisions; a failure to do so will be grounds for judicial review.[79]

Inconsistent evidence

13.89 Where there are inconsistencies in a person's evidence between hearings these can be put to their maker. As the Crown Court appeal is also a civil matter, there are not the restrictions in doing so that would apply in a criminal prosecution. Unless witness statements were prepared for the earlier hearing, in practice it is difficult to put to a witness his inconsistencies of evidence. This would depend on

---

[75] EPA 1990, s 81, Sch 3, para 1(3).
[76] Crown Court Rules 1982, SI 1982/1109. These general rules apply unless they are inconsistent with Acts of Parliament, including, therefore, the EPA 1990.
[77] Crown Court Rules 1982, SI 1982/1109, r 7.
[78] Statutory Nuisance (Appeals) Regulations 1995, reg 2(5).
[79] *R v Harrow Crown Court, ex p Dave* [1994] 1 WLR 98; *R v Crown Court at Canterbury, ex p Howson-Ball* [2001] Env LR 36. But see *East Devon DC v Farr* (QBD Administrative Court; 30/1/2002; unreported).

220   PROCEDURE AND EVIDENCE

having available an accurate note of the oral evidence heard in the magistrates' court. The accuracy of any note is not likely to be accepted by the party against whom it is intended to be used. Generally, note-taking skills in the magistrates' courts are not as well developed as they might be; the clerk's note, if available, is not likely to be very full.

Costs

13.90 The Crown Court may make 'such order for costs as it thinks just' in a civil appeal from the decision in the magistrates' court.[80] The issues on apportioning costs outlined above in relation to the magistrates' court are relevant to a rehearing in the Crown Court.[81] However, the costs of conducting proceedings in the Crown Court will generally be higher than in the magistrates' court and there is probably a greater tendency for costs to follow the event.

13.91 The decision in the Crown Court may have implications for the costs previously ordered by the magistrates. Where the appeal in the Crown Court is successful, the court may vary the magistrates' costs order and can make any order which the magistrates' court was empowered to make in relation to those proceedings.[82]

13.92 The position is different where an appellant fails in his appeal to the Crown Court. Where an appeal fails, the Crown Court does not have a specific power to modify a magistrates' costs order in a civil matter, although it is empowered to vary 'any part of the decision appealed against'.[83] This wording has been held to include costs in an appeal against conviction. In *Johnson v RSPCA*,[84] an appeal against conviction under the Protection of Animals Act 1911, it was held that the Crown Court could increase a magistrates' costs order made against the defendant/failed appellant, though it should hesitate before doing so.

This decision is probably inapplicable to a civil appeal, where either party can seek to change the magistrates' decision, and it is suggested that the Crown Court does not have the power to modify a magistrates' costs order where the party appearing before it fails in a civil appeal.[85]

---

[80] Crown Court Rules 1982, SI 1982/1109, r 12(2).   [81] See para 13.71.
[82] Crown Court Rules 1982, SI 1982/1109, r 13.
[83] Supreme Court Act 1981, s 48(2). This Act applies generally to the Crown Court, both in its criminal and civil jurisdictions.   [84] (2000) 164 JPR 345.
[85] Had Parliament intended to give the Crown Court a power to modify magistrates' costs orders in unsuccessful civil appeals, it would have made provision for this in the Crown Court Rules 1982, r 13. Rule 13 is only concerned with modifying magistrates' costs orders in successful Crown Court appeals. (*Pace* those who wish to extend the ratio of *Johnson v RSPCA* (n 84 above) to include civil appeals; see, eg, McCracken et al (n 33 above), p 181.)

Appeals to the High Court

The procedure and requirements for stating a case on a point of law for the opinion of the High Court are the same in an appeal against an abatement notice as against a conviction. Purely civil matters may be heard by a single judge in the Divisional Court, whereas a case stated from a prosecution requires at least two judges to hear it. The procedure is considered in more detail in Chapter 14.[86]

13.93

[86] See further paras 14.102–14.110.

14

OFFENCES AND PROSECUTION FOR BREACH OF AN ABATEMENT NOTICE

Introduction 14.01
Offence of breach of abatement notice 14.04
    Type of abatement notice 14.05
    What the prosecution has to prove 14.08
    Where the offence takes place 14.10
    Penalties 14.11
Obstruction offences 14.13
    Powers of entry to premises 14.14
    Entry by warrant 14.16
Scope of 'obstruction' 14.17
    Wilfully obstructs 14.19
    Obstruction in carrying out works 14.20
Powers to seize and remove noise-making equipment 14.23
The decision to prosecute 14.26
Attorney-General's Guidelines for bringing a prosecution 14.30
Public interest factors 14.34
Prosecutor's use of discretion 14.35
The *Enforcement Concordat* 14.37
Formal cautions 14.40
    Cautioning for statutory nuisance breaches 14.42
    Requirements for deciding whether to caution 14.44
    Grounds for administering a caution 14.45
        Offenders' age and health 14.46
        Previous offence history and attitude to the offence 14.47
    Administering the caution 14.48
    Records of cautions 14.49
Who to prosecute 14.51
    Service of notice requirements 14.54
    Noise in the street 14.55
    Meaning of 'person responsible' 14.56
    Default or sufferance 14.57
    Where more than one defendant is prosecuted 14.61
Corporate defendants 14.63
Crown immunity 14.66
Costs 14.68

Where the prosecution succeeds 14.71
    Itemizing costs 14.73
    What can be claimed? 14.75
    Costs incurred in serving abatement notices 14.76
    Full costs? 14.77
    Ability to pay 14.80
Defence costs 14.82
Costs where the prosecution is brought improperly 14.87
Wasted costs 14.88
    Against legal representatives 14.88
    Costs against justices 14.90
Compensation orders 14.91
Appeals to the Crown Court 14.94
    Powers of the Crown Court 14.96
    Grounds of appeal 14.97
    Appeal against conviction 14.98
    Appeal against sentence 14.99
    Costs 14.101
Appeals to the Divisional Court 14.102
    Powers 14.106
    Judicial review 14.107
    Procedure in stating a case 14.108
    Content of the case 14.109

Introduction

14.01 Local authority prosecutions for breach of an abatement notice invoke the rules of evidence and procedure of the magistrates' courts acting in their criminal capacity. These rules are more restrictive than apply in appeals against abatement notices under section 80(3) of the Environmental Protection Act 1990 ('EPA 1990') where the rules and procedures are based on civil law.[1] Hearsay evidence that would be admissible in an appeal is subject to much more stringent conditions in criminal proceedings.

14.02 Although prosecuted in the same courts and governed by similar rules and procedures, there are important differences between a local authority prosecution for a regulatory offence and a typical prosecution by the Crown Prosecution Service for a 'true' crime. Except for such offences as obstruction or knowingly making a false statement,[2] proof that a defendant had a guilty mind (or *mens rea*) is rarely a requirement in a regulatory offence. Usually it is merely an act of commission

---

[1] For appeals against abatement notices, see Chapter 13.
[2] eg, the offences under the EPA 1990, Sch 3, para 3 (obstructing an officer carrying out an inspection) and s 44 (statements made in waste licensing applications) which require proof of a guilty mind.

or of omission which constitutes the offence, so evidence as to motive or culpability will not be relevant to guilt, and, where not relevant, such evidence ought not to be admitted.[3]

Offences which do not require proof of a guilty mind—sometimes called offences of strict liability—are subject to statutory defences. In a statutory nuisance prosecution, a defendant can raise the defence of having had a 'reasonable excuse' for failing to comply with a notice requirement.[4] Further, the defence of taking 'best practicable means' to avoid causing some types of statutory nuisance can be raised during a prosecution as well as in an appeal against an abatement notice.[5] **14.03**

Offence of breach of abatement notice

In local authority proceedings under section 80 of the EPA 1990 the offence is not one of causing, allowing or permitting a statutory nuisance to occur, but of failure to comply with the requirements stipulated in an abatement notice.[6] Section 80(4) of the EPA 1990 provides that: **14.04**

If a person on whom an abatement notice is served, without reasonable excuse, contravenes or fails to comply with any requirement or prohibition imposed by the notice, he shall be guilty of an offence.

Type of abatement notice

A local authority has a discretion about whether to serve a simple notice requiring the recipient to abate the nuisance, or to prohibit or restrict its occurrence or recurrence. With simple notices, what the prosecution will be required to prove depends on the particular wording of the notice, that is the parts of the statute which the local authority selected to use in drafting.[7] With more complicated notices stipulating works required to be carried out within a specific time, it is the failure to carry out those works within the time allowed that constitutes the offence. **14.05**

The manner in which a notice is drafted forms the basis for identifying breaches. It is important for a prosecutor to identify all the ways in which a notice has been breached. Where a notice requires a nuisance to be abated and also requires certain steps to be carried out to achieve that result, a failure to abate the nuisance and a failure to carry out specified steps will constitute separate breaches. **14.06**

---

[3] *R v Sandhu* [1997] Crim LR 288. Evidence concerning mental elements may be relevant to sentencing, whether aggravating or mitigating the offence.
[4] EPA 1990, s 80(4); on defences, see Chapter 15.   [5] See further paras 13.41–13.46.
[6] By contrast, causing a statutory nuisance does constitute an offence (under the EPA 1990, s 82(2)) in proceedings taken by a 'person aggrieved' under the EPA 1990, s 82; see Chapter 16.
[7] EPA 1990, s 80(1), (see n 9 below) and see Chapter 12 for drafting issues and use of abatement notices generally.

14.07 Where a notice requires specific works or steps to be carried out the prosecution has to prove that those works or steps have not been carried out within the time allowed in the notice. It is not necessary also to prove that the nuisance has not been abated.[8] Such flexibility follows from the way section 80(1) of the EPA 1990 was drafted.[9] The provision allows a local authority to serve a form of notice stipulating the works required to prevent a nuisance from occurring without the need for any nuisance to have occurred already.

What the prosecution has to prove

14.08 Breach of section 80(4) of the EPA 1990 constitutes a criminal offence. The prosecution is required to prove all the elements of the offence to the criminal standard of 'beyond reasonable doubt'. Section 80(4) requires proof that an abatement notice was served on the defendant.

14.09 The prosecution also has to prove that there was no 'reasonable excuse' for breaching the abatement notice. The burden is initially on the defendant to raise the nature of the excuse. It then falls on the prosecution to prove, beyond reasonable doubt, that the excuse is not reasonable.[10]

Where the offence takes place

14.10 The place where the offence occurs is relevant to defences and to penalties. The defence of best practicable means is generally available for certain types of nuisances occurring on industrial, business or trade premises.[11]

Penalties

14.11 Section 80(5) of the EPA 1990 distinguishes between a person who commits an offence on or off industrial, business or trade premises. Where an offence does not occur on such premises he:

> ... shall be liable on summary conviction to a fine not exceeding level 5 on the standard scale[12] together with a further fine of an amount equal to one-tenth of that level for each day on which the offence continues after the conviction.

14.12 With an offence committed on industrial, trade or business premises, the maximum level of fine is £20,000.[13] For this category of offence there is no provision

---

[8] *AMEC Building Ltd v London Borough of Camden* [1997] Env LR 330.

[9] EPA 1990, s 80(1), provides: 'Where a local authority is satisfied that a statutory nuisance exists, or is likely to occur or recur ... [it] shall serve a notice ... imposing all or any of the following requirements—(a) requiring the abatement of the nuisance or prohibiting or restricting its occurrence or recurrence; (b) requiring the execution of such works, and the taking of such other steps, as may be necessary for any of those purposes, and the notice shall specify the time or times within which the requirements of the notice are to be complied with.'

[10] *Polychronakis v Richards & Jerrom Ltd* [1998] Env LR 347. For defences, see Chapter 15.

[11] A best practicable means defence is also available for domestic smoke nuisance from a chimney where the alleged nuisance is caused outside a smoke control area.

[12] Currently a maximum of £5,000.

[13] EPA 1990, s 80(6).

for additional fines to be imposed for an offence which continues after conviction.

Obstruction offences

Paragraph 3(1) of Schedule 3 to the EPA 1990 provides that a person who wilfully obstructs any person acting in the exercise of any statutory powers authorized by Part III is liable to a fine not exceeding level 3[14] on the standard scale. **14.13**

Powers of entry to premises
Officers authorized by a local authority have powers to enter any premises: **14.14**

- in order to ascertain whether or not a statutory nuisance exists; or
- for the purpose of taking any action, or exercising any work, authorized or required by Part III of the EPA 1990.[15]

No notice is required for entry to non-residential premises, but the time must be reasonable, such as during normal working hours or times when the premises are open. Except for emergencies, 24 hours' notice should be given to an occupier for entry to premises used mainly or wholly for residential purposes.[16] **14.15**

Entry by warrant
There is no right to forced entry, even to unoccupied premises. Where a sworn information is placed before a magistrate a warrant to enter by force may be issued. The magistrate must be satisfied that: **14.16**

- admission to any premises has been refused, or
- refusal is apprehended, or
- the premises are unoccupied, or
- the occupier is temporarily absent, or
- the case is an emergency, or
- an application for admission would defeat the object of the entry.

Additionally, in all cases, the magistrate must be satisfied that there is a reasonable ground for entry into the premises for the purpose for which entry is required.[17]

Scope of 'obstruction'

The scope of 'obstruction' is wider than interfering with an officer's powers to enter premises to carry out an inspection. It extends to obstructing an authorized person in the carrying out of any duties authorized or required by the statutory **14.17**

---

[14] Currently £1,000.
[15] EPA 1990, s 81, Sch 3, para 2(1).
[16] ibid, para 2(2).
[17] ibid, para 2(3).

nuisance provisions in the EPA. In addition to entry itself, these comprise the power to:

- take with him such other persons and such equipment as may be necessary;
- carry out such inspections, measurements and tests as he considers necessary for the discharge of any of the local authority's functions under Part III; and
- take away such samples or articles as he considers necessary for that purpose.[18]

14.18 It should be noted that there is no express power to take any documents or records or to make copies of them. This is in contrast to other areas of enforcement such as the regulatory regimes concerned with food safety and health and safety at work. Furthermore, such a power should not be implied from the wording of paragraph 2(4). Where such materials are sought, then, they can only be obtained on a voluntary basis and potential notice recipients or potential defendants should be informed of their right to refuse to produce them.[19]

Wilfully obstructs

14.19 Obstruction does not require a physical act or violence but extends to anything making it more difficult for an authorized person to carry out his duty.[20] As a matter of proportionality and common sense, the interference should be material and not trivial. The prosecution has to prove that the obstruction was done not accidentally or inadvertently, but deliberately and intentionally.[21] It is immaterial whether a person obstructing appreciated that the act amounted to obstruction. Where a trading standards officer was entitled to ask for information from a checkout assistant, it was no defence to fail to give the information because the assistant was instructed not to do so by her supervisor.[22]

Obstruction in carrying out works

14.20 The scope of obstruction is wider than obstructing an officer carrying out an inspection of premises to find out whether a statutory nuisance has occurred, is continuing, or is likely to occur or recur in the future. Paragraph 2 of Schedule 3 to the EPA 1990 refers to taking *any* action or executing *any* work authorized or required by Part III of the 1990 Act.

14.21 Obstruction can apply to situations where a local authority has decided to execute the requirements of an abatement notice itself and that process is being hindered. This power is available to a local authority under section 81(3) of the EPA 1990, which states:

---

[18] EPA 1990, s 81, Sch 3, para 2(4).

[19] Where a prosecutor seeks to introduce such materials as evidence, the defence can also object to their admission on the grounds of fairness because they were obtained without statutory authority. Both the Police and Criminal Evidence Act 1984, s 78, and article 6 (right to a fair trial) of the European Convention on Human Rights (Rome, 4 November 1950; TS 71 (1953); Cmd 8969) are relevant; see further paras 11.65 and 11.66.   [20] *Hinchliffe v Sheldon* [1955] 3 All ER 406.

[21] *R v Senior* [1899] 1 QB 283.   [22] *Snape v Mulvenna, The Times*, 28 December 1994.

Where an abatement notice has not been complied with the local authority may, whether or not they take proceedings for an offence ... abate the nuisance and do whatever may be necessary in execution of the notice.[23]

14.22 Where a local authority has undertaken works to carry out the requirements of a notice it can recover its reasonable costs from the person causing the nuisance or from the owner of premises.[24]

Powers to seize and remove noise-making equipment

14.23 Section 10(8) of the Noise Act 1996 provides that:

A person who wilfully obstructs any person exercising any powers conferred under subsection (2) or by virtue of subsection (7) is liable, on summary conviction, to a fine not exceeding level 3 on the standard scale.

14.24 Section 10(7) of the Noise Act 1996 makes it clear that a local authority's powers regarding the seizure and removal of noise-making equipment apply both for breaches of the Noise Act 1996 and for abating noise nuisances under the EPA 1990.[25]

14.25 Obstruction of an officer wishing to enter a dwelling to enforce the Noise Act 1996 constitutes an offence. An offence will also be committed where a person obstructs an officer who is in the process of carrying out the seizure and removal of any equipment that has been or is emitting noise. Both are offences under section 10(8) of the Noise Act 1996.

The decision to prosecute

14.26 The decision whether or not to prosecute is an exercise in the use of discretion by a local authority. The way in which a decision is taken and the reasons for taking it are crucial. These require proper and sufficient consideration by the person or persons responsible for making the decision on behalf of the local authority.[26] It would be an abuse of process to commence proceedings before a decision to prosecute had been taken.[27] Magistrates have a discretion to refuse to hear a summons founded on an abuse of process.

14.27 Underlying a decision to prosecute is an absolute requirement that the evidential test for bringing the prosecution is satisfied before a prosecution is commenced. This should be followed by a proper consideration being given to the public interest factors. No matter how serious the breach or the harm which follows from it, if the evidence is not sufficient to provide a realistic prospect of conviction then it would be improper to commence or to continue with a prosecution.

---

[23] In Scotland this provision applies whether or not proceedings *have* been taken for an offence.
[24] EPA 1990, s 81(4).
[25] See further paras 6.51–6.62.
[26] See further paras 2.09–2.14.
[27] *R v Brentford Justices, ex p Wong* [1981] QB 445.

14.28 These principles, which are derived from the Attorney-General's Guidelines[28] and are binding upon Crown Prosecution Service prosecutors, are equally applicable to local authorities. Local authorities should have regard to them even though not formally bound by them. Similar principles apply to the *Enforcement Concordat*, which sets out the principles for enforcement policy and practice procedures which local authorities should employ.[29]

14.29 It is usual practice for local authorities to publish their enforcement policy, including the basis for taking the decision to prosecute. Such policies will be derived from the Attorney-General's Guidelines and should be consistent with the *Concordat*. Practitioners are advised to scrutinize these local policies very carefully because sometimes they include omissions or variations having unintended consequences for enforcement.[30]

Attorney-General's Guidelines for bringing a prosecution

14.30 The Guidelines for Crown prosecutors comprise a two-stage test:

(1) Is there enough evidence to provide a realistic prospect of conviction, taking into account the likely defence case and the reliability and admissibility of the prosecution evidence?
(2) Is prosecution in the public interest?

14.31 It is only once the first of these tests is satisfied that public interest considerations need be considered. In order to satisfy the evidential test, legal advice should normally be sought and must be where issues of admissibility and the consistency or quality of evidence are involved.

14.32 The evidential test implies that a prosecutor should take into account the likelihood of the offender being able to establish a best practicable means defence.[31]

14.33 After the decision to prosecute has been taken it is important that it is kept under review. Fresh information may come to light suggesting that a reassessment of the strength of the case is required, or that the decision to prosecute should be reconsidered.

Public interest factors

14.34 Public interest factors relevant for a prosecutor in deciding whether to bring a prosecution include:

---

[28] *The Code for Crown Prosecutors* (2000), issued pursuant to the Prosecution of Offences Act 1985, s 10.   [29] See para 14.37.
[30] eg, one London authority once committed itself to prosecute regulatory offences only when there was a 'deliberate and flagrant breach of the law', thereby apparently ruling out its discretion to prosecute unless a case included *mens rea*.   [31] See further paras 15.02–15.28.

- seriousness of the alleged offence;
- whether it was deliberately or accidentally committed;
- consequences of the offence;
- foreseeability of the circumstances leading to the offence;
- attitude of the offender, including:
  - any explanation offered for the offence;
  - willingness to prevent recurrence; and
  - how investigating officers were treated.
- whether the breach was put right quickly;
- whether there is a history of offences;
- health and age of offender;
- deterrent effect of prosecution, both on offender and society at large; and
- delay between offence and decision to prosecute.

Prosecutor's use of discretion

A prosecutor's duty is to exercise discretion properly and to act in a quasi-judicial manner. He should take into account only the public interest factors that are relevant to the matter under consideration. There may be others not mentioned above that are relevant and these should also be included. Irrelevant considerations should be excluded. Weighing the various relevant factors and assessing them as a whole ought to ensure that the decision to prosecute is based on proper grounds.[32] **14.35**

The scope for challenging a decision to prosecute by judicial review[33] is limited because the higher courts will always recognize that the exercise of discretion necessarily involves some width and the possibility of error. The size of any error needs to be significant and material for judicial review to have a realistic chance of success. In practical terms, where the above approach to decision-making is followed, the scope for judicially reviewing a decision will be small. **14.36**

The *Enforcement Concordat*

The scope of the *Enforcement Concordat*[34] is wider than the decision to prosecute. It covers the whole relationship between local authorities and those who are subject to their enforcement activities. The *Concordat* is a policy document setting out the broad principles of regulation by local authorities of the activities of businesses in the environmental health field. It includes consideration of the circumstances in which informal enforcement activity, the service of formal notices and the prosecution of breaches of the law will be undertaken. The document defines **14.37**

---

[32] *R v Inland Revenue Commissioners, ex p Mead* [1993] 1 All ER 772.
[33] See further paras paras 17.26–17.56.
[34] *Enforcement Concordat* (Cabinet Office, March 1998).

enforcement to include: 'advisory visits and assisting with compliance as well as licensing and formal enforcement action'.[35] Formal enforcement includes the service of abatement notices and envisages prosecution as coming at the end of the enforcement process.

14.38 The *Concordat* originates in the Conservative government's deregulation initiatives of the mid-1990s.[36] It reflects the adoption of a restrained approach to enforcement and a political climate sympathetic to economic liberalism. The *Concordat* is geared towards industry and business and, perhaps arguably, is intended to make the lives of people running such organizations easier. Similar principles apply to statutory nuisances caused by the general public, though the economic benefits of deregulation are not so obvious with nuisances such as neighbourhood noise.

14.39 The approach to enforcement is based on principles of proportionality, consistency and transparency in which local authorities are encouraged to:

- adopt and publish a policy on initiating prosecutions;
- apply the policy fairly and consistently, in good faith and taking into account all relevant circumstances;[37]
- not apply the policy rigidly, particularly in reaching a decision to prosecute.

In other words, a local authority should apply its policy exercising common sense and ensuring that it uses its discretion in a quasi-judicial manner.

Formal cautions

14.40 An alternative to prosecution is for a local authority[38] to issue the offender with a formal caution. The principal advantage of doing so from a public policy point of view is that this will save the time and expense required to bring a prosecution. Issuing a caution is an entirely separate procedure from giving a written warning that unless a person complies with a requirement then some form of enforcement action may follow.

14.41 A formal caution can only be administered when certain conditions are fulfilled; it should be seen as equivalent to the decision to prosecute. Like the decision to prosecute, issuing a caution is an exercise in the use of discretion by a local authority. Since the early 1990s cautioning has been employed extensively in dealing with Food Safety Act 1990 offences and breaches of regulations made under the Act. In part this has been because codes of practice issued under section 40 of the Food Safety Act 1990 promoted the use of cautions, as did the Local

---

[35] *Enforcement Concordat* (Cabinet Office, March 1998), para 3.01.
[36] As exemplified by the Deregulation and Contracting Out Act 1994.
[37] *R v Inland Revenue Commissioners, ex p Mead* (n 32 above).
[38] In England and Wales only.

Authority Co-ordinating Body on Food and Trading Standards (LACOTS) which issued local authorities with detailed guidance on the use of cautions and model letters. More recently, the Health and Safety Commission[39] has promoted the use of cautioning by inspectors, including those employed by local authorities.

Cautioning for statutory nuisance breaches
The use of cautions in enforcing the statutory nuisance provisions in the EPA 1990 is more restricted than for these other areas. This is because minor and technical breaches of regulatory statutes—which are a common reason for issuing a caution—are not a cause for prosecution in statutory nuisance. As we have seen, except for obstruction offences, it is only with a breach of an abatement notice that a statutory nuisance offence can be committed.[40] Where a breach of the notice is trivial, the protection afforded by the notice remains in place and most authorities would decide to take no additional formal enforcement action. **14.42**

There is no reason in principle, however, why formal cautions should not be issued in statutory nuisance cases and the general grounds for doing so are the same as for other criminal offences. **14.43**

Requirements for deciding whether to caution
All the following requirements must be fulfilled before a caution can be issued. **14.44**

(1) Is there sufficient admissible evidence to justify a prosecution? The standard required for administering a caution is the same as for deciding whether to prosecute, that is are there reasonable prospects for a conviction? The evidential test is similar to the Attorney-General's guidelines.[41] Administering a caution where the evidence is insufficient to justify prosecution would be improper.

(2) There must be an admission of guilt.

(3) The offender must give his informed consent to the caution. If the caution is refused then the likely result will be a decision to prosecute. However, this is not automatic and prosecution should not be used as a sanction in respect of a refusal to accept a caution. Prosecuting *automatically* for refusal to accept a caution is arguably improper, possibly oppressive and a breach of human rights.[42] If the refusal to accept a caution occurs because the person is mentally ill, but not so ill that he cannot give his informed consent, then prosecution would most probably not be in the public interest. It may be that an offence is so trivial that a prosecution is not merited. It would be better for the local authority to adopt a prosecution policy which allows the decision to prosecute to be reconsidered after

---

[39] *Health and Safety Commission's Policy Statement on Enforcement* (Health and Safety Executive, July 2000), para 2. Traditionally the Commission was reluctant to recommend cautioning, possibly because it did not fit into the tradition of enforcement by central government agencies.
[40] See paras 14.08 and 14.09.   [41] *Code for Crown Prosecutors* (n 28 above).
[42] See Chapter 11.

a person proposed to be dealt with by caution has had the opportunity of accepting or rejecting the caution.

Grounds for administering a caution

14.45 Once the evidential test is satisfied, the local authority will need to consider relevant public interest factors. These include:

- the nature and seriousness of the offence; and
- the likely penalty.

Trivial offences, where it is decided that formal action is required, such as a minor breach of an abatement notice, could be dealt with by caution. On the other hand, it may be hard to justify administering a caution for a serious or repeated breach of the notice since this would tend to bring into question why a notice was issued in the first place.

14.46 Offenders' age and health Youth or old age are positive factors in favour of cautions, as are frailty in physical health, mental illness or mental disability.

14.47 Previous offence history and attitude to the offence A person with previous cautions or offences for related offences to the instant offence would be unlikely to respond positively to a caution. Someone who trivializes their offence, or is abusive to investigating officers, or is contemptuous of complainants, is unlikely to change their offending behaviour. In such instances it would be difficult to justify administering a caution.

Administering the caution

14.48 This can be done orally or, more usually, by letter, which should be signed by an officer with sufficient authority. A company as well as a natural person may receive a caution. Cautions can also be administered at court, even on the day of the trial.

Records of cautions

14.49 Cautions will be relevant to any penalty made after a finding of guilt in future proceedings. The Office of Fair Trading maintains a register of cautions from information provided by local authorities who issue them. Cautions will also be relevant to any future decision whether to prosecute for a fresh offence.

14.50 If during a subsequent prosecution a defendant asserts previous good character, a record of cautions, as well as previous convictions, may also be introduced into the trial as rebuttal evidence.[43] A copy of both should be served on the defendant in advance of the trial.[44]

---

[43] See further paras 18.80–18.82.

[44] Notice to cite previous convictions should be served at least seven days before the hearing, using forms 29 and 30 of the Magistrates' Courts (Forms) Rules 1981, SI 1981/553, Sch 2.

Who to prosecute

The EPA 1990 provides certain requirements to identify who may be prosecuted for a statutory nuisance offence, which also apply in deciding who may receive a caution as an alternative to prosecution. The object of the Act is to make the person who is responsible for causing the nuisance, or for allowing it to happen, liable to prosecution. Where such a person cannot be found, then the owner or occupier—the person having control over the premises—is deemed responsible. Where the nuisance is structural or due to a defect in the premises then the owner can be made liable.[45]

14.51

Any person who is prosecuted for a statutory nuisance offence must have been properly served with an abatement notice[46] since the offence is one of contravening or not complying with the notice requirements.[47] This makes the decision about who to prosecute more complicated than would be the case with offences involving a direct breach of a statute or regulation.[48] In a statutory nuisance offence, the person who directly breaches the notice may not be the person who was served with the notice, in which case only the latter person may be prosecuted. Should this person have a reasonable excuse[49] for the notice not being complied with then neither person should be found guilty.

14.52

The prosecuting authority needs to take great care in matching who can be an offender to whoever was served with the notice. With continuing nuisances caused by different individuals on the same premises, this may mean that notices need to be served on different individuals over a period. It will be crucial to identify the person having control over the premises and usually this will be the person liable to be prosecuted for breaching the notice requirements.

14.53

Service of notice requirements
Service requirements are more fully dealt with elsewhere.[50] In summary:

14.54

- anyone prosecuted for a statutory nuisance offence must have been properly served with an abatement notice, unless the offence is one of obstruction or removal of a fixed notice;[51]
- service should be on the person responsible for the nuisance, except where the nuisance arises from any defect of a structural character on the premises, in which case service should be on the owner;[52]

---

[45] EPA 1990, s 80(2).
[46] See further paras 12.60–12.74.
[47] EPA 1990, s 80(4).
[48] eg, selling food not complying with the food safety requirements, contrary to the Food Safety Act 1990, s 8(1).
[49] EPA 1990, s 80(4).
[50] See paras 12.60–12.74.
[51] EPA 1990, s 80A(7).
[52] ibid, s 80(2).

- where the person responsible for the nuisance cannot be found or the nuisance has not yet occurred, service should be on the owner or occupier of the premises.[53]

Noise in the street

14.55 A person served with a notice who is responsible for a vehicle, machinery or equipment causing noise nuisance in the street—a statutory nuisance under section 79(1)(ga) of the EPA 1990—is the person liable to be prosecuted.[54]

Meaning of 'person responsible'

14.56 An abatement notice should be served under section 79(7) of the EPA 1990 on the person, or persons 'to whose act, default or sufferance the nuisance is attributable'. Where the use of machinery or equipment is involved, this 'includes any person who is for the time being the operator of the machinery or equipment'. The meaning of 'person responsible' is wider than the person who directly caused the nuisance and there are indirect ways of committing an offence.

Default or sufferance

14.57 Default encompasses both contractual and statutory obligations; it 'means nothing more, nothing less, than not doing what is reasonable under the circumstances'.[55] A failure to act to prevent a nuisance which a notice recipient could and should have prevented amounts to default. The nature of the default must be connected to the nuisance which is subject to enforcement.[56]

14.58 There is a complex body of case law which considers the relationship between landlord and tenant in deciding who is liable for a failure to repair that may cause a nuisance arising from the state of the premises.[57] However, contractual liabilities do not necessarily determine statutory responsibilities; the issue of who exercises, in a practical sense, control over the premises is crucial.[58] It is possible for more than one person to be in default, or for one of them to have been in default and the other to have suffered the nuisance. Sometimes, both landlord and tenant may be held responsible for continuing a nuisance.

14.59 Sufferance, or allowing a nuisance to arise or continue, occurs when a person fails to take steps to end a nuisance when he has ample time to do so.[59] Merely doing nothing might amount to sufferance.[60] This is because the abatement notice, in effect, has placed the recipient on notice that he is under a duty to prevent a

---

[53] EPA 1990, s 80(2).
[54] ibid, s 80A(2).
[55] *Re Young and Harston's Contract* (1885) 31 Ch D 168.
[56] *Clayton v Sale UDC* [1926] 1 KB 415.
[57] See Chapter 5.
[58] *Wincanton RDC v Parsons* [1905] 2 KB 34.
[59] *Sedleigh-Denfield v O'Callaghan* [1940] AC 880.
[60] *Neath RDC v Williams* [1950] 2 All ER 625.

particular nuisance from occurring or recurring. Where it would not be reasonable to expect him to act, he has available the defence of 'reasonable excuse'.[61]

14.60 For example, in a case of neighbourhood noise nuisance, a notice might have been served on a householder/parent. Should, for example, the notice be breached by the householder's son or daughter playing excessively loud music which disturbs the neighbours, the local authority may decide to prosecute the householder for default or sufferance in allowing the nuisance to continue. Conversely, where the householder has taken all reasonable steps to prevent breach of the notice but it is nevertheless breached by the child, he or she may have a 'reasonable excuse' and thus a defence to any charge under section 80(4) of the EPA 1990. In these situations, where the local authority has quite a difficult task to decide who is responsible for the nuisance, interviewing suspects under the Police and Criminal Evidence Act 1984 will be necessary.[62]

Where more than one defendant is prosecuted

14.61 More than one person may be responsible for breach of an abatement notice. Provided that they have all been served with the notice, then all, some, or only one of them, may be prosecuted. The grounds for liability may be different, for example, one person being responsible by default and another by sufferance.

14.62 The prosecutor has to prove in court precisely how a notice has been breached by each person charged. This exemplifies the importance of ensuring that a notice is properly drafted since its terms determine what the prosecution needs to prove.[63]

Corporate defendants

14.63 A company can be guilty of breaching a notice and hence can commit a criminal offence, as can an officer of the company. Section 157 of the EPA 1990 states:

(1) Where an offence . . . committed by a body corporate is proved to have been committed with the consent or connivance of, or to have been attributable to any neglect on the part of, any director, manager, secretary or other similar officer of the body corporate or a person who was purporting to act in any such capacity, he as well as the body corporate shall be guilty of that offence . . .

14.64 Section 157(2) of the EPA 1990 provides that where the affairs of the corporation are managed by its members, then a member fulfilling a managerial function shall be liable similarly. A company in the hands of administrators may be prosecuted but the requirements of section 11 of the Insolvency Act 1986 will apply, so the consent of the company's administrator must be given or leave obtained from the court.[64]

---

[61] EPA 1990, s 80(4).
[62] See further paras 18.47–18.52.
[63] See further paras 14.04–14.09.
[64] *Re Rhondda Waste Disposal Company Ltd* [2001] Ch 57. The leave of the High Court is required for the prosecution to be commenced or continued in the magistrates' court.

14.65 A prosecution can proceed against an officer of a company as well as against the company itself where it can be proved that the officer was a decision-maker in the company and was himself, at least partly, personally responsible for the breach. A formal admission made under section 10 of the Criminal Justice Act 1967, the entry on the company register or similar documentary evidence will be needed to prove in court his position in the company.[65]

Crown immunity

14.66 Section 159(1) of the EPA 1990 binds the Crown to the Act and to any regulations or orders made under it. Abatement notices may be served on the Crown but they cannot be enforced in the criminal courts. This is because the Crown cannot be prosecuted. However, an application can be made to the High Court by a local authority for a declaration that any act or omission by the Crown is in contravention of the EPA 1990.[66]

14.67 The Secretary of State has the power to certify that particular Crown premises are exempt, for reasons of national security, from the right of the local authority to exercise powers of entry.[67]

Costs

14.68 Unlike appeals against abatement notices, which are civil, costs in criminal proceedings are governed by statute. Part II of the Prosecution of Offences Act 1985 deals with awards of costs out of central funds, where payments are made by central government.

14.69 Applications for costs should be made at the conclusion of the case. In a successful prosecution, this will be immediately after the court has announced its decision on sentence, including any compensation order to a victim that it may make.[68] Depending on the outcome, either party can make a costs application at the conclusion of the trial. The court is extremely unlikely to grant an adjournment merely to allow a costs application to be made, and both parties will need to come to court fully prepared to apply for and justify their costs.

14.70 Appeals to the Divisional Court by way of case stated[69] are rare since an error of law is required to overturn a costs order.[70] A costs order made by magistrates cannot of itself be appealed against in the Crown Court. However, where an

---

[65] Business documents admitted under the Criminal Justice Act 1988, s 24, can only be admitted with the leave of the court. Printouts of entries of registered companies held at Companies House can be obtained at www.companies_house.gov.uk.
[66] EPA 1990, s 159(2).
[67] ibid, s 159(4).
[68] See further paras 14.91–14.93.
[69] See further paras 14.102–14.110.
[70] *R v Tottenham Justices, ex p Joshi* [1982] 1 WLR 631.

appeal against sentence and/or a finding of guilt is allowed in the Crown Court, the costs order made by the magistrates can be reconsidered.[71]

Where the prosecution succeeds

Where a defendant pleads guilty or is found guilty, then the prosecutor will be entitled to his costs. However, a public prosecutor—including a local authority[72]—is unable to obtain any of his costs from central funds.[73] Further, the Prosecution of Offences Act 1985 is confined to indictable offences, so this provision will not apply to statutory nuisance proceedings brought by a private prosecutor under section 82 of the EPA 1990.[74]   **14.71**

Magistrates have the power to award costs against the person convicted. Their discretion is wide, the sum awarded being what they consider 'just and reasonable'.[75] In the past, costs orders made against defendants were often disproportionately small. More recently, courts have shown a greater willingness to bring them more in line with reality. However, many magistrates still need to be persuaded to perceive costs issues in economically realistic terms.[76]   **14.72**

Itemizing costs
In order to recover a high proportion of the costs of bringing a successful prosecution, local authorities (and private prosecutors) should follow the guidelines provided by the Court of Appeal in *R v Associated Octel Co Ltd*[77] which are applicable generally to regulatory offences. Each item of costs should be broken down, showing the task, times and the hourly rate claimed for each task. The process is similar to the way costs schedules are prepared in civil proceedings.   **14.73**

The schedule should be served on the defence in advance of the trial to give them the opportunity to challenge the reasonableness of any item claimed. The defence need to use this opportunity to prepare any challenge to a claim since, as noted above, it is very difficult to appeal against a decision on costs.   **14.74**

What can be claimed?
Associated Octel also provides guidance as to what can be claimed: **14.75**

- prosecution costs can include salaried investigating officers' time before charging the defendant, where these were incurred in collecting evidence and investigating whether an offence had been committed;[78]

---

[71] See further para 14.101.
[72] Prosecution of Offences Act 1985, s 17(6)(c).
[73] ibid, s 17(2).
[74] See Chapter 16.
[75] Prosecution of Offences Act 1985, s 18(1).
[76] J Pointing, 'Problems in Company Prosecutions' (1999) 163 JP 704.
[77] [1997] 1 Cr App Rep (S) 435.
[78] *Neville v Gardner Merchant Ltd* (1984) 83 LGR 577. See also *Griffiths v Pembrokeshire CC* [2000] Env LR 623.

- costs of carrying out routine inspections may not be claimed; and
- costs expended in the investigation and prosecution should be paid in full, provided these are reasonable.

Costs incurred in serving abatement notices

14.76 It is suggested that costs in statutory nuisance prosecutions start to run from the stage of investigating whether an abatement notice was breached. As the costs of serving the abatement notice form part of routine statutory duties and are not part of an investigation leading to prosecution they are not recoverable.[79]

Full costs?

14.77 In addition to investigatory officers' costs and lawyers' fees, payment can be made for the costs of obtaining expert evidence, including reports and the attendance of expert witnesses, and witnesses' expenses. The costs of fulfilling duties associated with the litigation, such as drafting summonses and providing advance disclosure should also be included. As with any item, these have to be reasonable both in amount and in relation to the conduct and importance of the case.

14.78 Defence solicitors should bear in mind that if their tactics are deemed to be unreasonable or unnecessarily aggressive, resulting in extra time being required or an excessive amount of correspondence passing between solicitors, then this will need to be explained to the court to justify why the defendant ought to pay such extra costs. There is also a risk that the prosecutor may be able to persuade the court to make a wasted costs order against the defendant's solicitor personally.[80]

14.79 Where defendants are companies or natural persons who have benefited financially from committing the nuisance for which they have been convicted, a court may decide to award a relatively high proportion of costs claimed.

Ability to pay

14.80 The court should take account of an individual's ability to pay, in which case some proof of means and outgoings ought to be provided by the defendant and it is very much in his interests to do so. Courts will expect to see copies of audited accounts for registered companies and accounts for sole traders and partnerships. These should be up to date and preferably cover a period of three or four years. The court can order the payment of costs by instalments, where a lump sum would place a person in difficulties.[81]

14.81 Costs should never be seen in a punitive way and should not be 'grossly disproportionate' to the level of fine. The connection made in *R v Northallerton Magistrates' Court, ex p Dove*[82] between the level of fine and costs is not strictly

---

[79] These costs may be recovered in an unsuccessful appeal against service of an abatement notice, where such costs are triggered by the appeal and not by the performance of a routine statutory duty.
[80] See paras 14.88 and 14.89.   [81] Magistrates' Courts Act 1980, s 75.
[82] [2000] 1 Cr App Rep (S) 136.

logical, particularly in view of the statutory limits on fines in the magistrates' courts. However, earlier decisions also indicate a requirement for proportionality between the size of costs and fines.[83] Even with the *Associated Octel*[84] guidelines, magistrates' courts continue to behave inconsistently on costs, and are unlikely to change this practice without much more specific guidelines and, perhaps, some curtailment of their discretion being imposed.

Defence costs

14.82 A court may make a costs order in favour of the accused, to be paid out of central funds, where an information laid before the court is not proceeded with or is dismissed.[85] Failure to proceed includes a situation where an information was laid out of time,[86] where the prosecution was withdrawn,[87] or discontinued.[88]

14.83 The amount of costs to be paid if a case is not proceeded with or where the defendant is found not guilty should be 'reasonably sufficient to compensate him for any expenses properly incurred by him in the proceedings'.[89] Although the court should award all his costs unless there are positive reasons for not doing so,[90] the above wording permits interpretative scope.

14.84 In practice, the amount allowed in a regulatory offence where a defendant employs an experienced solicitor often falls some way below the sum actually charged. The detailed breakdown of charges, which is required of the prosecution following the *Associated Octel* decision,[91] should be prepared by defence solicitors hoping to persuade the bench to order a high proportion of the amount claimed. Where a defendant does not agree with the court's assessment of his costs he can ask to have them determined by taxation by the justices' clerk.[92] A detailed breakdown of costs by the defence solicitor will also prove helpful for taxation.

14.85 The court is empowered to reduce the amount of a defendant's award, where it is of the opinion that this would be just and reasonable.[93] This could apply where:

- the defendant's conduct brought suspicion on himself and the prosecution was misled into thinking that the case against him was stronger than it actually was;

---

[83] *R v Tottenham Justices, ex p Joshi* (n 70 above); *R v Jones* (1988) 10 Cr App R (S) 95.
[84] *R v Associated Octel Co Ltd* (n 77 above).
[85] Prosecution of Offences Act 1985, s 16(1).   [86] *Patel v Blakey* (1987) 151 JP 532.
[87] *R v Bolton Justices, ex p Wildish* (1983) 147 JP 309.
[88] *DPP v Denning and Pearce* [1991] 2 QB 532.
[89] Prosecution of Offences Act 1985, s 16(6).
[90] *Practice Direction (Crime: Costs)* [1991] 1 WLR 498, amended by [1999] 1WLR 1832 so as to be consistent with Human Rights Act 1998.
[91] *R v Associated Octel Co Ltd* (n 77 above); see para 14.73.
[92] Prosecution of Offences Act 1985, s 16(9)(b).   [93] ibid, s 16(7).

- there was ample evidence to support a conviction and the defendant was acquitted on a technicality having no merit; and
- the defendant was convicted on some charges and acquitted on others.[94]

Another example would be where a defendant employed an expert whose report showed a lack of objectivity such as to justify the court discounting his findings. The court ought not to allow costs in respect of such a document.

14.86 The court needs to be satisfied that it has before it sufficient evidence to justify making a reduction in an award or when refusing to make a costs order. Otherwise the decision is judicially reviewable and arguably a breach of the defendant's right to a fair trial under article 6 of the European Convention on Human Rights.[95] The court should have proper regard to the Practice Direction on costs,[96] otherwise the Divisional Court can remit the case back to the magistrates to reconsider the costs order in the light of these guidelines.[97]

Costs where the prosecution is brought improperly

14.87 Where a prosecution has been brought improperly, or continued with when it should not have been, the court can make a costs order against a local authority. A material breach of the Attorney-General's guidelines,[98] such as prosecuting when there was not a reasonable prospect of obtaining a conviction, or bringing a prosecution in contravention of the local authority's own prosecution policy might justify costs being awarded against the local authority.

Wasted costs

Against legal representatives

14.88 In criminal proceedings magistrates may make a wasted costs order against a legal or other representative.[99] The person concerned must have incurred the costs as a result of an act or omission that was improper, unreasonable or negligent. Either his own costs can be disallowed, in part or wholly, or he can be ordered to pay the costs unnecessarily incurred by the other side.

14.89 'Improper' amounts to a substantial breach of professional conduct or a code; the magistrates can also make a formal complaint to the relevant professional body. 'Unreasonable' conduct includes tactics designed to harass the other side. 'Negligence' denotes a failure to act competently, according to the standard the public could normally expect of members of the profession.[100]

---

[94] *Practice Direction (Crime: Costs)* (n 90 above).
[95] *Minelli v Switzerland* (1983) 5 EHHR 554.
[96] *Practice Direction (Crime: Costs)* (n 90 above).
[97] *R v Horseferry Road Justices, ex p Underwoods (Cash Chemists) Ltd* [1985] 81 Cr App R 334.
[98] *The Code for Crown Prosecutors* (n 28 above).
[99] Prosecution of Offences Act 1985, s 19A(1)(c).
[100] *Ridehalgh v Horsefield* [1994] 3 All ER 848.

Costs against justices
Where magistrates or court staff have acted negligently, incompetently or with extreme inefficiency, there is no procedure to obtain costs from the Lord Chancellor's Department in criminal proceedings. Neither is the Lord Chancellor liable to pay a party's costs of a wasted hearing which had to be abandoned by reason of the appearance of bias by a member of the court.[101] Magistrates can be liable for the costs of their acting perversely and in flagrant breach of elementary principles of justice, but cost orders can only be made against them in judicial review proceedings.[102]

14.90

Compensation orders

Magistrates (or the Crown Court in an appeal) may order a person convicted for breach of an abatement notice to pay compensation to a victim who has suffered personal injury, loss or damage as a result of the offence.[103] A prosecutor or the court of its own motion may raise the issue of compensation.[104] Compensation orders can also be made to benefit 'persons aggrieved' bringing proceedings under section 82 of the EPA 1990.[105] This includes tenants of social housing landlords, including local authorities.

14.91

The power to make a compensation order should only be used in straightforward cases where the issues can be dealt with quickly and an exhaustive investigation by the court is not appropriate.[106] Evidence of injury, loss and damage will need to be produced. In complicated or high-value claims victims may commence civil proceedings in the county courts.[107]

14.92

The maximum amount of compensation that can be ordered by the court is £5,000.[108] The levels actually awarded tend to be quite modest and smaller than would be the case in a civil action for damages. Besides assessing the level of compensation according to the injury, loss or damage sustained as a consequence of the nuisance, the court should also take into account the convicted person's ability to pay. Where a defendant is ordered to pay a fine as well as compensation, but is unable to pay both, the compensation order should be given preference by the court.[109] Payments can be made by instalments.

14.93

---

[101] *Re Medicaments and Related Classes of Goods (No 4)*, *The Times*, 7 August 2001 (this case was heard in the Restrictive Practices Court).
[102] *R v York City Justices, ex p Farmery* (1988) 153 JP 257.
[103] Powers of Criminal Courts Act 1973, s 35.   [104] ibid.
[105] See paras 16.41–16.51.   [106] *Davenport v Walsall MBC* [1997] Env LR 24.
[107] *R v Cooper* [1982] Crim LR 308.   [108] Magistrates' Courts Act 1980, s 40(1).
[109] Powers of Criminal Courts Act 1973, s 35(4A).

Appeals to the Crown Court

14.94 A person convicted may appeal against the magistrates' decision to the Crown Court,[110] which sits as a three-person tribunal with a judge and two magistrates. These magistrates must not have heard the case previously in the magistrates' court.[111] Leave to appeal is not required, but notification of the appeal and whether it is against conviction or sentence only must be made within 21 days of the date of sentencing in the magistrates' court.[112] The grounds of appeal should also be provided. The notice of appeal is sent to the clerk of the magistrates' court. An extension to the 21-day limit may be granted by the Crown Court. The Crown Court will notify the parties of a hearing date.

14.95 The Crown Court is presided over by a judge, whose views on the law will bind the magistrates sitting with him. The court should give reasons for its decisions; a failure to do so may amount to a breach of the defendant's human rights and constitute grounds for judicial review.[113] All three members of the tribunal have equal weight as regards decisions of fact.

Powers of the Crown Court

14.96 The Crown Court is empowered to confirm, reverse or vary any part of the decision appealed against. It can increase or reduce the sentence passed by the magistrates, or the level of compensation to be paid to a victim, but no sentence may exceed that which the magistrates could have given.[114] Its powers are not identical to the court below. For example, unlike the magistrates' court the Crown Court does not have the power to amend a defective information.[115]

Grounds of appeal

14.97 A person who pleaded guilty in the magistrates' court can only appeal against sentence.[116] This includes the level of fine and any compensation order that the magistrates might have made. A person found guilty after a trial can also appeal on these grounds. Additionally, he can appeal against conviction.

Appeal against conviction

14.98 An appeal against conviction in the Crown Court is a rehearing, so evidence heard during the trial below will be heard anew. This does not mean that the Crown Court trial is merely a repetition of the previous trial. Fresh evidence may have come to light or evidence which had not been adduced previously. The

---

[110] Magistrates' Courts Act 1980, s 108.
[111] Crown Court Rules 1982, SI 1982/1109, r 5. [112] ibid, r 7.
[113] *R v Harrow Crown Court, ex p Dave* [1994] 1 WLR 98; *R v Canterbury Crown Court, ex p Howson-Ball* [2001] Env LR 36. [114] Supreme Court Act 1981, s 48(4).
[115] *R v Swansea Crown Court, ex p Stacey* [1990] RTR 183.
[116] Magistrates' Courts Act 1980, s 108(1). Unless the convicted person pleaded guilty under duress or the plea was not genuine.

Crown Court is also likely to be stricter regarding the admissibility of evidence than the magistrates below had been.

Appeal against sentence
Where the Crown Court is hearing an appeal against conviction as well as against sentence, it should base its decision on sentence according to the facts elicited during the appeal. Where the appeal is against sentence alone, the court should base its decision on the magistrates' court's findings of fact.[117] If the Crown Court takes a significantly different view of the offence based on those facts, it should alter the sentence of the court below to reflect this.

14.99

In practice it may be difficult for the Crown Court to discover the factual basis for the magistrates' decision: there are cases where neither the parties, the clerk nor the magistrates manage to keep an accurate note.[118] The court has two options. Either it can remit the case back to the magistrates to determine the basis for their decision on sentence, or it can hear contested evidence in a *Newton* hearing and base its decision on this.[119]

14.100

Costs
A costs order made by the magistrates cannot on its own be appealed against in the Crown Court. However, depending on the outcome of the appeal, the Crown Court will consider costs for the appeal and can reconsider the costs order made previously by the magistrates.

14.101

Appeals to the Divisional Court

An appeal by either party on a point or points of law to the Divisional Court may be made by way of case stated.[120] This remedy is available where the magistrates have made an error of law or have exceeded their jurisdiction; it is not appropriate to re-litigate factual disputes. The court does not generally have jurisdiction to consider matters of fact and will take the facts as outlined by the magistrates in stating the case.

14.102

The way in which the magistrates exercised their discretion cannot be appealed, unless they exercised it *Wednesbury*[121] unreasonably, such that no reasonable bench could have made such a decision. Issues of sentence cannot be considered unless the sentence given below was so clearly beyond the normal range as to be an error of law.[122]

14.103

---

[117] *Munroe v DPP* [1988] Crim LR 823.
[118] For an example of the Divisional Court's patience in dealing with this problem, see *R v Knowsley MBC, ex p Williams* [2001] Env LR 28.
[119] *R v Newton* (1983) 77 Cr App R 13.   [120] Magistrates' Courts Act 1980, s 111.
[121] *Associated Provincial Picture Houses Ltd v Wednesbury Corporation* [1948] 1 KB 223.
[122] *Universal Salvage Ltd and Robinson v Boothby* [1984] RTR 289.

14.104 Magistrates may only refuse to state a case because it is frivolous: 'futile, misconceived, hopeless or academic'.[123] A refusal to state a case is itself judicially reviewable.

14.105 Where a person convicted appeals by way of case stated he cannot also pursue an appeal against conviction or sentence in the Crown Court.[124]

Powers

14.106 The Divisional Court must decide on the questions stated and may reverse, affirm or amend the justices' determination. The court can also remit the matter to the justices with its opinion. This can include a direction to convict. The court can also make an order for costs.[125]

Judicial review

14.107 Judicial review and appeal by case stated employ separate procedures addressing different issues. Where magistrates have made a procedural error or are thought to have acted unfairly, or exercised bias, denied natural justice, or made a decision that results in a person's human rights being infringed, then judicial review is the appropriate course of action.[126] Strictly speaking, judicial review is not an appeal against a decision of the court, but a mechanism whereby the High Court exercises its supervisory jurisdiction over public bodies, including courts, to ensure that they make decisions properly.

Procedure in stating a case

14.108 The magistrates can be asked by either party to state a case for consideration by the Divisional Court. This should be done in writing within 21 days after the date of the decision to be appealed against.[127] The points of law for consideration by the Divisional Court are usually initially drafted by the party wishing to appeal. The justices' clerk prepares the draft case, which will then have to be approved by the magistrates. It will also be sent to the parties for consultation, who have 21 days to make representations. The final form should then be sent to the parties. It is the applicant's responsibility to lodge the stated case with the High Court.

Content of the case

14.109 The content of the case stated should include:

- the facts as found by the court below;
- what the parties contended;
- the legal authorities referred to by the parties;

---

[123] *R v Mildenhall Magistrates' Court, ex p Forest Heath DC*, *The Times*, 16 May 1997.
[124] Magistrates' Courts Act 1980, s 111(4). [125] Supreme Court Act 1981, s 28A.
[126] See further paras 17.26–17.56.
[127] Magistrates' Courts Act 1980, s 111, and Magistrates' Courts Rules 1981, SI 1981/552, r 76.

- the decisions of the justices; and
- the questions upon which the opinion of the Divisional Court is sought.

Where one of the questions includes an allegation that there was no evidence upon which a particular conclusion could have been reached, a summary of the relevant evidence (if any) should also be submitted. Otherwise a record of evidence is not required in stating a case. **14.110**

15

DEFENCES

Defence of best practicable means 15.02
   Development of the defence 15.02
   Statutory definition 15.04
   Ambit of the defence 15.05
   Burden and standard of proof 15.06
   Use of the defence in appeals and prosecutions 15.08
   When is it available? 15.09
   'Industrial, trade and business purposes' 15.10
   Trade purposes 15.12
   Business purposes 15.13
   Time for establishing the defence: on an appeal against an
   abatement notice 15.15
   Time for establishing the defence: on a prosecution for failure to
   comply with an abatement notice 15.16
   The defence is a question of fact not law 15.17
   Financial implications 15.21
   Trade practices 15.23
   Intensification of business activity 15.24
   Where planning permission is required for the steps 15.25
   Moving the business 15.27
   Where the local authority prescribes steps 15.28
Without reasonable excuse 15.29
   Burden and standard of proof 15.30
   Rationale 15.34
   Definition of 'reasonable excuse' 15.35
   Wellingborough BC v Gordon 15.36
   A Lambert Flat Management Ltd v Lomas 15.38
   Butuyuyu v London Borough of Hammersmith and Fulham 15.41

This chapter,[1] is concerned with two defences available in statutory nuisance   **15.01**
proceedings:

---

[1] Procedures reelvant to statutory nuisance proceedings are covered in Chapters 12, 13 and 14.

(1) 'best practicable means'; and
(2) 'reasonable excuse'.

Defence of best practicable means

Development of the defence

15.02 The defence of best practicable means has been included in environmental health legislation since the nineteenth century when the approach was designed to achieve a balance between the needs of industry and the interests of the local population. An important feature of the defence has been its flexibility to take account of local and individual circumstances. Its use has also been marked by a degree of discretion to accommodate technical requirements. This approach has been the hallmark of public health controls in the past to the extent that they encouraged a conciliatory, rather than a confrontational, approach by regulators.

15.03 Its purpose is to provide businesses, which might otherwise be threatened with penal consequences for committing a statutory nuisance, with an opportunity to defend themselves on the basis that they have used the best practicable means to conduct their activities.

Statutory definition

Section 79(9) of the Environmental Protection Act 1990 ('EPA 1990') provides the following definition:

15.04 In this Part 'best practicable means' is to be interpreted by reference to the following provisions—
  (a) 'practicable' means reasonably practicable having regard among other things to local conditions and circumstances, to the current state of technical knowledge and to the financial implications;
  (b) the means to be employed include the design, installation, maintenance and manner and periods of operation of plant and machinery, and the design, construction and maintenance of buildings and structures;
  (c) the test is to apply only so far as compatible with any duty imposed by law;
  (d) the test is to apply only so far as compatible with safety and safe working conditions, and with the exigencies of any emergency or unforeseeable circumstances;
and, in circumstances where a code of practice under section 71 of the Control of Pollution Act 1974 (noise minimisation) is applicable, regard shall also be had to guidance given under it.

This definition applies wherever the expression 'best practicable means' is used throughout Part III of the EPA 1990. It is based on the definition of 'best practicable means' to be found in section 72 of the Control of Pollution Act 1974 which makes provisions for noise nuisances.

Ambit of the defence

15.05 It is not necessary to show that the means deployed brought the nuisance to an end. It is enough if they were adequate to 'prevent, or to counteract the effects of, the nuisance'. So, while it may be possible to show that use of the best practic-able means eliminated the nuisance, that is not essential. It would be enough to show that the effects of the nuisance were counteracted to a sufficient extent. Thus, in a case involving barking dogs, removal of the dogs would remove the nuisance. But it might be sufficient to reduce the number of dogs, thus reducing the level of the noise without eliminating it.[2] 'Short of eliminating the nuisance, the "best practicable means" concept involves consideration of the scope for counteracting the effects of the nuisance.'[3] Thus, the defence operates so that, although the nuisance may otherwise have been established, it is not actionable because the defendant has succeeded in showing that the best practicable means have been used to deal with it. No more can be required of the defendant, within the context of Part III of the EPA 1990, than this. A defence case, therefore, may accept that a nuisance has been committed, but focus exclusively on the means used to counteract its effects. This balancing of activities is designed to compromise the interests of the parties involved. It may well have the effect of enabling a business to carry on its activities, while leaving residents with a nuisance which they must tolerate. But, this balancing of interests will only work to some extent. Where the nuisance falls under the health limb, it is less likely that the defence of best practicable means could be made out, since the reasonableness of the offending activity will not be relevant.

Burden and standard of proof
This is a statutory defence and, as such, in a prosecution for breach of a notice, the burden of proving the best practicable means defence lies on the defendant.[4] The normal burden of proof is reversed. The standard is that a defendant must show, on the balance of probabilities, that the best practicable means have been used to abate or counteract the effects of the nuisance. This reversal of the burden of proof and the civil standard required in respect of statutory defences, is a general principle to be found across the range of regulatory offences.[5] The standard against which the defence must be measured remains the civil standard even in a criminal prosecution for failure to comply with the notice. The admissibility of evidence led in support of the defence will be tested on the basis of the criminal rules of evidence.

15.06

---

[2] See, eg, *Manley v New Forest DC* [2000] EHLR 113; *Budd v Colchester BC* [1999] Env LR 739.
[3] *Manley v New Forest DC* (n 2 above), per Newman J.
[4] Magistrates' Courts Act 1980, s 101, and see, eg, *Polychronakis v Richards & Jerrom Ltd* [1998] Env LR 347 at 349.
[5] See, eg, *R v Carr-Briant* [1943] KB 607; *Robertson v Watson* (1949) JC 73; *R v Jenkins* (1923) 87 JP 115; *R v Swaysland* [1987] BTLC 299.

15.07 An appellant, relying on the defence as a ground of appeal,[6] will obviously bear the burden of establishing the defence and the standard will also be the civil standard. An appeal against an abatement notice is to the magistrates' court and is a civil action. Thus, civil rules regarding the admissibility of evidence will apply to all aspects of the proceedings.

Use of the defence in appeals and prosecutions
15.08 The EPA 1990 and the Statutory Nuisance (Appeal) Regulations 1995 prescribe that the defence is available both in an appeal against an abatement notice and in answer to a prosecution. If the defence failed in such an appeal it can be raised again at a prosecution for failure to comply with the same abatement notice which had been unsuccessfully appealed. Both sets of proceedings would be brought in the magistrates' court. But the appeal is civil; the prosecution criminal. A defendant could not, therefore, automatically assume that the same evidence would be admissible in both proceedings. The likelihood is that the evidence admissible in the criminal prosecution would be more restricted than that admissible at the appeal.[7]

When is it available?
15.09 This defence is available:

- as a ground of appeal against an abatement notice;[8]
- in a prosecution under section 80(4) of the EPA 1990 for failure to comply with an abatement notice without reasonable excuse;[9]
- in a prosecution under section 82(8) of the EPA 1990 for failure to comply without reasonable excuse with an abatement order issued by the magistrates' court under section 82(2) of the EPA 1990.[10]

There are restricted circumstances for the availability of the defence, as shown in Table 15.1 below.

'Industrial, trade and business purposes'
15.10 It can be seen that the defence is mainly only available in respect of industrial, trade and business purposes. This provides the balance between the needs of the residents to live a peaceful live, free from deleterious health effects and nuisances, and the need of industry to function provided it has taken the best practicable steps to obviate any nuisances. The achievement of such a compromise may not be an easy matter.

---

[6] EPA 1990, s 80(3), and the Statutory Nuisance (Appeals) Regulations 1995, SI 1995/2644, reg 2(e).   [7] See Chapter 13.
[8] The Statutory Nuisance (Appeals) Regulations 1995, SI 1995/2644, reg 2. It is probably not strictly correct to describe this as a defence in these circumstances. But the principles remain the same.   [9] EPA 1990, s 80(7) and (8).
[10] The defence is also probably available in respect of an application for an abatement order under EPA 1990, s 82(2), by a 'person aggrieved'; see para 16.57.

Table 15.1 *The availability of the defence of best practicable means*

type of nuisance	appeal against abatement notice (section 80(3))	prosecution for failure to comply with abatement notice (section 80(4))	prosecution for failure to comply with abatement order (section 82(8))	notes
section 79(1)(a) ('premises')	ITB	ITB	ITB (but defence not available at all if the nuisance makes the premises unfit for human habitation)	
section 79(1)(b) ('smoke')	✓ (but only where smoke emitted from chimney—see note)	✓ (but only where smoke emitted from chimney—see note)	✓ (but only where smoke emitted from chimney—see note)	the following are not covered by this nuisance: (1) smoke from chimney of private dwelling within smoke control area; (2) dark smoke from chimney, etc; (3) smoke from steam engine; and (4) dark smoke from ITB premises
section 79(1)(c) ('fumes or gases')	+	+	+	this nuisance applies only to fumes arising from private premises
section 79(1)(d) ('dust, steam, smell, effluvia arising on industrial, trade, or business premises')	ITB	ITB	ITB	this nuisance applies only to dust, etc arising from ITB premises

Table 15.1 *continued*

type of nuisance	appeal against abatement notice (section 80(3))	prosecution for failure to comply with abatement notice (section 80(4))	prosecution for failure to comply with abatement order (section 82(8))	notes
section 79(1)(e) ('accumulations or deposits')	ITB	ITB	ITB	
section 79(1)(f) ('animals')	ITB	ITB	ITB	
section 79(1)(g) ('noise')	ITB	ITB	ITB	
section 79(1)(ga) ('noise from vehicles, etc, in street')	ITB	ITB	ITB	defence available where vehicle being used for ITB purposes
section 79(1)(h) (all other categories)	+	+	+	This includes those categories of statutory nuisance which fall under the Public Health Act 1936 (see Chap. 10)

ITB defence only available where nuisance arises on industrial, trade, or business premises
✓ defence available regardless of where the nuisance originates
+ defence not available in any circumstances

Section 79(1)(7) of the EPA 1990 defines 'industrial, trade and business **15.11**
purposes' as:

(i) premises used for any industrial, trade or business purposes, or,
(ii) premises not so used on which matter is burnt in connection with any industrial, trade or business process, or,
(iii) premises used for industrial purposes where they are used for the purposes of any treatment or process as well as where they are used for the purposes of manufacturing.

The definition is, therefore, wider than might be supposed. It includes premises where matter is burnt such as an open waste site. This may be a use of the site for which the appropriate permissions, such as waste management licences, are not in force. Thus, the local authority is able to take action under Part III of the EPA 1990 even though it may also be possible for other agencies to be involved.[11] Industrial purposes are not limited to the manufacturing sector.

Trade purposes
'Trade purposes' will cover commercial activities including buying and selling **15.12**
although it is not limited to such functions.[12] There appears to be no good reason why charitable activities in the nature of trade and business, such as charity shops, should be excluded from the definition.

Business purposes
'Business purposes' is wider than 'trade'[13] and has been said to mean 'anything **15.13**
which is an occupation, as distinguished from a pleasure'.[14] It will include offices used to provide professional[15] and financial services, and government departments.[16] A dwelling from where a business is carried out may also, arguably, be business premises, although the scale of use may be a relevant factor in determining this question. However, if it is the business activity (as opposed to the residential activity) which causes an alleged nuisance then it is likely that the argument that it is a business use will prevail. So, for example, if noise from a music lesson, as opposed to the radio playing, causes an alleged

---

[11] eg, if there is a breach of planning law the local authority planning department may take action; if there is a failure to have a waste management licence, or an integrated prevention pollution licence, the Environment Agency may take enforcement action. The fact that other agencies may get involved does not absolve a local authority's environmental health department from taking action if they conclude that there is a statutory nuisance (*R v Carrick DC, ex p Shelley* [1996] Env LR 273).
[12] *Skinner v Jack Breach* [1927] 2 KB 220; *Aviation & Shipping Co v Murray* [1961] 1 WLR 974.
[13] *Debtor, Re A (No 490 of 1935)* [1936] Ch 237.
[14] *Rolls v Miller* (1894) 27 Ch D 71 at 88.
[15] *Re Wilkinson* [1922] 1 KB 584; *R v Breeze* [1973] 1 WLR 994.
[16] It may be helpful in defining 'business purposes' to consider uses as classified in the Town and Country Planning (Use Classes) Order 1987, SI 1987/764, as amended. The Order also includes a definition of 'industrial process'.

nuisance then it may be arguable that the defence will be available in that this is a business use.[17]

15.14 Schools and hospitals may not be considered to be commercial activities.[18] Nevertheless, if a purposive approach is taken to the interpretation of the EPA 1990, it is arguable that they do fall into the category designed to benefit from the defence.

Time for establishing the defence: in an appeal against an abatement notice

15.15 The date for determining the validity of an abatement notice is the date at which it is served.[19] It follows, therefore, that in an appeal against an abatement notice, the date for determining whether the best practicable means have been used to abate or counteract the nuisance is also the date of service of the notice.[20] Subsequent attempts to operate the business using best practicable means will not be relevant to the determination of an appeal. This may be effective, if successful in limiting the nuisance, in that the local authority will not then proceed to a prosecution. However, if a company does appeal an abatement notice, subsequent attempts to operate using best practicable means will not be relevant to the determination of that appeal. In *Sovereign Rubber Ltd v Stockport MBC*[21] a company produced a protocol designed to limit the use of forklift trucks (which were causing the alleged noise nuisance) after an abatement notice had been served. (In fact, the court found that the company had not complied with its own protocol. The key question was whether the company could rely on the protocol as comprising best practicable means. It could not, as the protocol was not in operation at the time of the service of the notice. (Its use did backfire on the company, as the protocol demonstrated that it was possible to take steps to ameliorate the effects of the nuisance and it was then difficult for the company to argue that 'some such restriction was impracticable'.)[22]

Time for establishing the defence: in a prosecution for failure to comply with an abatement notice

15.16 The position is different when the defence is raised in a prosecution. A prosecution relates to a failure to comply with a notice and a defendant will potentially

---

[17] Other statutes may be helpful in defining a 'business', eg, the Food Safety Act 1990, s 1(3), provides the following definition: '"business" includes the undertaking of a canteen, club, school, hospital or institution, whether carried on for profit or not, and any undertaking or activity carried on by a public or local authority'. However, it is arguable that it would not be appropriate to use such a definition (where the object is to ensure food safety) in the context of statutory nuisance where the defence is mainly aimed at allowing some freedom of action for industrial and like activities.

[18] See, eg, *Re Wilkinson* (n 15 above); *Town Investments Ltd v DOE* [1976] 3 All ER 479.

[19] *SFI Group plc (formerly Surrey Free Inns plc) v Gosport BC* [1999] Env LR 750, overruling *Johnsons News of London Ltd v Ealing* (1989) 154 JP 33.

[20] *London Borough of Camden v London Underground Ltd* [2000] Env LR 369.

[21] [2000] Env LR 194.

[22] ibid, per Sedley LJ at 210.

be able to rely on the steps it had taken to operate the business using the best practicable means after the service of the notice—provided that the steps related to the period for which it was alleged it had failed to comply with the notice. A notice has no fixed time period before it elapses. A prosecution may be brought some time after the original service of the notice, provided the facts remain the same throughout the period between the original service and the subsequent prosecution.[23] So, if a notice required a business to abate a noise nuisance, and the company attempted to comply by introducing sound-reduction measures, if it were later prosecuted, the company could argue in its defence that it had adopted the best practicable means to counteract the effects of the nuisance—an argument which would not have succeeded in an appeal against the notice.

The defence is a question of fact not law
There is no prescribed legal standard of what constitutes best practicable means. The defence is to be judged primarily on common sense principles. Nor is any further statutory guidance to be found relating to the meaning and extent of the defence. The defence is a question of fact. As such, it is the primary responsibility of the magistrates' court to make findings of fact in relation to the defence when it is raised in any particular case. In an appeal to the High Court against the decision of the magistrates, the Court will only consider issues of fact where there has been insufficient evidence for the magistrates to have made a finding of fact.[24] On appeal to the Crown Court against the magistrates' decision, however, the Court will have to consider issues of fact afresh and will not be bound by how these had been decided by the magistrates.[25]

15.17

The determination of what constitutes best practicable means will also depend on whether the offending activity has an adverse health effect. If it does then the reasonableness of the activity will not be a consideration. If, on the other hand, the issue is one of nuisance and personal comfort, then whether it is reasonable to disallow the activity will be in issue.

15.18

Best practicable means are not a rigid standard. Trade and industry practices change and improve with new technology, and new national and European laws which require enhanced environmental standards become law. Thus, the operation of a factory might require periodic review, in the light of changing standards, to ensure that it continues to operate the best practicable means.

15.19

---

[23] A prosecution brought some time after the service of a notice may, although permissible, attract the criticism of the court; see *Wellingborough BC v Gordon* [1993] Env LR 218.
[24] See further paras 14.102–14.110.   [25] See further paras 13.85–13.92.

Reasonableness of the defence

15.20 Procedurally, where a party relies on the defence of best practicable means, then, as discussed above, the burden is on that party to establish it, whether the defence is being used to answer a prosecution under section 80(4) of the EPA 1990 for failure to comply with an abatement notice, or by an appellant in an appeal, brought under section 80(3) of the 1990 Act, against an abatement notice.[26] The standard of proof in both cases is the civil standard, that is the balance of probabilities.

Financial implications

15.21 The cost involved in preventing the nuisance is a factor which should be taken into account. The financial implications referred to are those involved in adopting the best practicable means—in other words, the cost of taking those means.[27] So, if nuisance can only be prevented by exorbitant expenditure the means cannot be practicable. However, it is important to bear in mind that the financial implications concerned are not those for the individual company.[28] The test is objective. If the expense of using the best practicable means risks forcing a particular company into liquidation then, if the reason is that the company was inefficient or uncompetitive, that is irrelevant to the defence. If, on the other hand, the company is forced out of business because the cost of taking measures is disproportionate, then that may be unreasonable and beyond what could be required of the company. If implementing the best practicable means forces the inefficient company out of business, then the magistrates may view that as unfortunate but necessary. These are difficult decisions for magistrates to make and in practice they may be very reluctant to make findings in which the likely economic consequences are very serious for a commercial undertaking, particularly where the business activity is perceived to be otherwise desirable or unexceptionable.[29]

15.22 A company which intends to rely on the defence on the basis of cost must be prepared to demonstrate why the cost is disproportionate. Such evidence may include the extent to which the purchase of new equipment, for example, will affect the profitability of the company. It needs to show that the increased expenditure goes beyond what is reasonable for a company in this industry or location

---

[26] The defence is available in a prosecution under the EPA 1990, s 82(8), for failure to comply with an abatement order. It is suggested that the defence could also be raised in an application for an abatement order under the EPA 1990, s 82(2), although the statute does not expressly grant this right; see para 16.58. [27] *Wycombe DC v Jeffways and Pilot Coaches* (1983) 81 LGR 662.
[28] *Wivenhoe Port v Colchester BC* [1985] JPL 175.
[29] The question of the appropriate level of fine for a business casts another light on this question. In cases such as *R v Milford Haven Port Authority* [2000] Env LR 632; *R v F Howe & Sons (Engineers) Ltd* [1999] 2 All ER 249; *National Rivers Authority v Shell UK* [1990] 1 Water Law 40; and *R v O'Brian and Enkel* [2000] Env LR 653 the fact that a fine might force a business to fail (and have consequential effects on the local workforce) is a relevant factor. (These cases concern heath and safety matters and water pollution offences.)

to incur. As an illustration, in *Wivenhoe Port v Colchester BC*[30] a nuisance was caused by the discharge of 'grab' from moored vessels and the handling and loading of soya meal into lorries. This created clouds of dust and effluvia. The company had installed machinery which, when in operation, alleviated the dust clouds. However, they were unwilling to use the machinery on every occasion because of the cost. The company alleged that were it to be used for all dusty cargoes then it would make the operation unprofitable and the company would have to cease trading. However, the court, while accepting that profitability was a relevant factor, did not consider that the company had succeeded in establishing that the cost of using the machinery on all occasions was prohibitive.

Trade practices
Evidence that a defendant was following industry standards or codes of practice is good evidence to establish a presumption that the best practicable means have been used. Where there are industry standards in existence, or codes of good practice, then these should be used to show that the practices adopted at the particular plant are consistent with the best that can be found in that particular industrial sector. While the existence of an industry standard is not necessarily probative of a good practice nevertheless it provides a benchmark against which magistrates can test the evidence of the company as to its general standards and practices. Evidence that the best industry practice has been implemented at a plant must then be countered by evidence by the prosecution that that practice is not good enough. Industry might, in general, have adopted a bad practice and a prosecutor may be able to establish that in cross-examination, or by leading their own expert evidence. Thus, a company defending a practice on these grounds must be able to show that it is a reasonable practice in the circumstances of the case.[31]

15.23

Intensification of business activity
Sometimes a nuisance might arise as a result of a business increasing its activities. This might, for example, be the result of increased hours of operation, expansion of premises with the benefit of planning permission,[32] or an increase in traffic movements. While the previous level of activity may have been able to benefit from the defence that the best practicable means were being used, it may not be assumed that it will still be available where the operation has intensified. It may be that the new level of activity is unreasonable in the locality. Hours of

15.24

---

[30] n 28 above.
[31] *Schofield v Schunck* (1855) 19 JP 84; *Manchester Corporation v Farnworth* [1930] AC 171.
[32] Note that planning permission does not grant immunity from action under the EPA 1990, Pt III (*Wheeler v Saunders* [1996] Ch 19), unless it can be argued that the effect of the planning consent was to allow a change in the character of the neighbourhood to occur (*Gillingham BC v Medway Dock Co* [1993] QB 343).

operation generating increased traffic movements may be unacceptable if a factory is located adjacent to a residential district. It may, therefore, in order to counteract the nuisance, be acceptable to impose a restriction on the activity which limits it to its pre-existing level of activity.[33]

Where planning permission is required for the steps

15.25 It may be the case that the person responsible for an alleged nuisance proposes to undertake works which will abate the nuisance but for which planning permission is required. Clearly, if the planning permission is obtained and the work undertaken, then the defence of best practicable means may be made out. But what if the planning permission is refused? Or, the person responsible is less than diligent in pursuing his application? In *Chapman v Gosberton Farm Produce Company Ltd*[34] an abatement notice was served in respect of noise arising from the dispatch of horticultural produce from the premises. Prior to the service of the abatement notice, the company had submitted a planning application for an intensification of activity on the premises. The application included acoustic bunding which it was agreed would have resolved the noise nuisance. However, the local planning authority called for more information on the application.[35] The information was never supplied by the company. The court held that the failure to supply this information was indicative of the failure of the company to take reasonably practicable means to remedy the nuisance.

15.26 What this case leaves unanswered is whether the defence would have been made out if the company had supplied the information but the application had been refused. Would a planning appeal to the Secretary of State have satisfied the onus of proof for the establishment of the defence? The difficulty with such speculation is that it was common ground that the proposed works constituted the best practicable means to solve the noise nuisance. It may be that in circumstances which fall outside the precise situation in the *Chapman* decision it would be arguable that alternative means could have been sought to abate the problem—such as a curfew on night-time deliveries. In this case it was not necessary to explore any other option. The failure to pursue the planning application was enough on its own to show that the defence was not made out.

Moving the business

15.27 Best practicable means can only be considered in relation to the premises currently being used for operating the business.[36] Where a business is able to argue, on the balance of probabilities, that it has taken the best practicable means to counteract the nuisance which still persists, then it is not open to the court to

---

[33] *Manley v New Forest DC* (n 2 above).   [34] [1993] Env LR 191.
[35] This formal procedure fell under the Town and Country (Applications) Regulations 1988, SI 1988/1812, reg 4.   [36] *Manley v New Forest DC* (n 2 above).

decide that it should relocate the business even though the nuisance persists. In *Manley v New Forest DC*[37] it was held that it was not open to a local authority to argue that best practicable means should include moving kennels, which held a 24-strong pack of Siberian Huskies, to a non-residential location. While there was a continuing nuisance, the facts showed that building the kennels at the rear of the property was the best practicable means of running the business on existing premises. No other steps were feasible since the kennels had to have ventilation and an outside run.[38]

Where the local authority prescribes steps
In many instances, the local authority may specify the steps required to abate the nuisance. Noise nuisance cases are a common example of this where officers typically specify sound levels in abatement notices and provide assistance in the selection and installation of equipment designed to achieve the sound levels specified.[39] If it is then alleged that a nuisance still persists, even where the equipment has been properly installed and is being correctly operated, can the defendant rely on the defence of best practicable means in a subsequent prosecution for failure to comply with an abatement notice? The argument might be that, since the local authority has provided assistance in the selection of the equipment (even where this is not specified in the notice), then, by implication, the best practicable means have been used. However, the fact that the local authority has specified the means to be used to abate the nuisance does not necessarily mean that those are the best practicable means. Evidence may be adduced to show that, in fact, the authority was wrong in suggesting the method adopted for the abatement of the nuisance. Nevertheless, an authority faced with such a result would be unable to pursue a prosecution since no breach of the notice had occurred. The local authority, where it believed that a nuisance was continuing, could serve a fresh notice specifying a higher standard, sufficient to abate or restrict the nuisance. In this situation the person responsible for the nuisance might be able to argue that the local authority had been negligent in providing its original advice. Furthermore, where the measures taken are deemed inadequate to control the nuisance, there is likely to be an aggrieved resident suffering from it. Such a person might choose (if the local authority fails to act) to bring summary proceedings under section 82 of the EPA 1990. The defence may be available in those proceedings and it may be open to the defendant to call the local authority to give evidence as to its rationale in offering suggestions and assisting in relation to the particular steps which were taken to abate the nuisance (albeit unsuccessfully).

15.28

---

[37] n 2 above.
[38] The judge, Newman J, expressed surprise that the local authority had not argued that a reduction in the number of dogs would have constituted the best practicable means to counteract the nuisance.
[39] See, eg, *R v Crown Court at Canterbury, ex p Howson-Ball* [2001] Env LR 36.

Without reasonable excuse

15.29 Section 80(4) of the EPA 1990, provides that:

> If a person on whom an abatement notice is served, without reasonable excuse, contravenes or fails to comply with any requirement or prohibition imposed by the notice, he shall be guilty of an offence.

The implications of this defence are considered below.

Burden and standard of proof

15.30 The burden may be considered to fall into two parts. Firstly, a defendant, who wishes to rely on this defence, must discharge an evidential burden by specifying the excuse. Secondly, the prosecutor must prove that the excuse is not a reasonable one.

15.31 The prosecutor must discharge this burden to the criminal standard, that is, beyond reasonable doubt.

15.32 It is important to note the distinction between this defence and that of best practicable means. The normal burden of proof in a criminal prosecution falls on the prosecutor to prove his case beyond reasonable doubt. With the defence of best practicable means, the burden is reversed. This is not the case with the defence of reasonable excuse. It follows the normal pattern in that, once it has been raised by the defence, the burden remains with the prosecution to negate it.[40]

15.33 This position was established in *Polychronakis v Richards & Jerrom Ltd*.[41] In this case, the defence argued that they had not complied with an abatement notice prohibiting the open burning of metal casting to remove oil and grease because the forklift truck which they used to pack it had been damaged.[42] The Divisional Court held that:

> once the defendant had laid the proper evidential basis for a contention that he has a reasonable excuse, it is for the prosecution to satisfy the court to the criminal standard of proof that the excuse is not a reasonable one.[43]

---

[40] See *R v Clarke* [1969] 1 WLR 1109 which concerned the interpretation of 'reasonable excuse' to supply a specimen under drink-driving legislation. See also *R v Edwards* [1975] 1 QB 27 and *R v Hunt* [1987] AC 352.

[41] n 4 above, following the decision in *Saddleworth UDC v Aggregate and Sand Ltd* [1970] 69 LGR 103 on the similar provision in the predecessor statute, the Public Health Act 1936, s 95, but not following the *obiter dictum* of Lord Pearson in *Nimmo v Alexander Cowan & Sons Ltd* [1968] AC 106, at 136–7.

[42] In fact, on appeal by way of case stated by the prosecutor, evidence which had been overlooked by the magistrates showed that the defendants were not able to rely on this excuse.

[43] n 4 above, per Brooke LJ at 351.

Rationale

The reason for the distinction between the defences of best practicable means and reasonable excuse is that the former constitutes a statutory defence where it is clear that the section imposes the burden of proof on the defendant. The latter, the defence of reasonable excuse, falls under section 80(4), which creates the offence, and there is nothing to disturb the normal principle that the burden of proving the offence falls on the prosecution. It was suggested in *Polychronakis* that, had there been an intention for the burden to shift to the defendant, then it would have been necessary for the draftsman to have created a separate and explicit defence.

15.34

Definition of 'reasonable excuse'

The statute provides no further definition and the question of whether an excuse is a reasonable excuse is one of fact. Case law provides some guidance. In particular, there are three cases which address the question of what amounts to a 'reasonable excuse' in section 80(4) of the EPA 1990.

15.35

(1) Wellingborough BC v Gordon[44]

In this case, a party was held to celebrate a birthday. Three years previously, an abatement notice had been served in respect of noise from a private dwelling. It was held that the fact that the nuisance occurred three years after the original notice had been served, without any intervening breach, was not a reasonable excuse. Nor was it a reasonable excuse that the event was the celebration of a birthday. The occasion was 'unforced and planned', 'there was no overwhelming or even difficult situation here which the respondent was not able to control and which led to the breach. It was a wholly free decision of his to play the music in a way which the notice clearly prohibited.'[45]

15.36

A number of factors had been put forward in support of the contention that the circumstances surrounding the commission of the noise amounted to a reasonable excuse. These circumstances included the fact that the noise occurred on one night only; that it was a special occasion; that the neighbours had been invited; those who did not attend did not complain (the only evidence of the breach was by two local policemen); and that steps were taken to minimize the effect on workers by holding the event on a Friday night. None of these factors were considered by the court to be relevant to the issue of whether there was a reasonable excuse for the failure to comply with the notice. (The court did, however, point out that these factors might have been relevant to primary question of whether the noise constituted an actionable nuisance.)

15.37

---

[44] [1993] Env LR 218.   [45] ibid, per Taylor LJ at 221

(2) A Lambert Flat Management Ltd v Lomas[46]

15.38 In this case, brought under the predecessor legislation to the EPA 1990 affecting noise nuisances (section 58, Control of Pollution Act 1974), it was held that a reasonable excuse did not include matters which could have been raised in an appeal against the notice, unless such matters arose after the appeal was heard or, if there was no appeal, after the time for lodging an appeal had expired. Thus, matters which constitute grounds of appeal,[47] and which do not appear as possible defences to a prosecution, cannot be argued as constituting a reasonable excuse for not complying with the notice.

15.39 There is some overlap between the grounds of appeal against a notice and the availability of defences to a prosecution. In particular, the defence of best practicable means appears as a defence to a prosecution under section 80(7) and (8) of the EPA 1990, and also as a ground of appeal under regulation 2(2)(e) and (f) of the Statutory Nuisance (Appeals) Regulations 1995. This point was not directly addressed in *A Lambert Flat Management Ltd v Lomas* but it is clear that even where there has been no appeal against a notice, section 80(7) provides that the defence of best practicable means can be raised. Since this defence is available as a separate statutory defence to that of reasonable excuse, then, technically, it is not being raised as a reasonable excuse but as an independent defence. The decision in *Lambert* applies in a prosecution where no appeal has been brought, but the defendant attempts to raise, as a reasonable excuse, the ground that the notice was not justified. The defendant cannot raise as a defence something he failed to appeal against in a notice.

15.40 In *Lambert*, it was suggested that there might be some 'special reason such as illness, non-receipt of the notice or other potential excuse for not entering an appeal'.[48] Failure to receive the notice because a recipient was ill or abroad, were cited as examples. These would amount to a special difficulty in relation to compliance with a notice which provided a reasonable excuse. It was not the purpose of the provision that the defendant should simply be able to choose whether to raise his reasons for non-compliance in an appeal or a prosecution. The first opportunity to raise these matters was the appeal and, if this opportunity was not taken, then there was not a second chance to do so in a prosecution.

(3) Butuyuyu v London Borough of Hammersmith and Fulham[49]

15.41 This case also concerned a noise nuisance caused by the playing of amplified music or musical instruments at a private dwelling. No appeal was made against the abatement notice. The defendant was subsequently prosecuted for failure to comply and raised her illness and that of her son as the reason for her failure to

---

[46] [1981] 2 All ER 280.
[47] See the Statutory Nuisance (Appeals) Regulations 1995, SI 1995/2644, reg 2, for the grounds of appeal.   [48] n 46 above, per Ackner J at 286.
[49] [1997] Env LR D13.

appeal and therefore an excuse for raising issues relating to the non-justification of the notice at the prosecution hearing.

15.42 It was held that a limitation of reasonable excuse to non-receipt of the notice was too restrictive. In the circumstances of this particular case, the illness of the recipient and the death of her son were exceptional factors to justify her failure to appeal. She could, therefore, raise non-justification of the notice (a ground of appeal) as a defence to her subsequent prosecution. It should be noted, however, that the court emphasized the extreme circumstances of the defendant's case which clearly excited the sympathy of the court. It must not be assumed that illness, *per se*, will suffice and *Butuyuyu* indicates that the scope for succeeding in raising this defence is very limited.

15.43 It can be seen from these cases that a 'reasonable excuse' can be argued in two ways:

- where a defendant in criminal proceedings seeks to rely, by way of reasonable excuse, on matters which would have provided him with a ground of appeal against the abatement notice;[50] and,
- where a defendant in criminal proceedings seeks to raise an excuse for his failure to comply with an abatement notice.[51]

As *Butuyuyu* shows, there is very limited scope for arguing a point that ought to have been the subject of an appeal. Failure to comply with a notice needs an exceptional excuse, such as an emergency or *force majeure*, to qualify as reasonable for the purposes of section 80(4) EPA 1990.

---

[50] *A Lambert Flat Management Ltd v Lomas* (n 46 above); *Butuyuyu v London Borough of Hammersmith and Fulham* (n 49 above).
[51] *Polychronakis v Richards & Jerrom Ltd* (n 4 above); *Wellingborough BC v Gordon* (n 23 above).

16

SECTION 82 PROCEEDINGS

Introduction	16.01
Section 82 and housing defects	16.04
Person aggrieved	16.08
Person responsible	16.11
Nature of the proceedings	16.15
The procedure	16.16
Notice in writing	16.18
Service	16.19
Content of the notice	16.25
Starting the proceedings in the magistrates' court	16.31
Laying an information and issuing the summons	16.32
Abatement order	16.35
Breach of the abatement order	16.40
Compensation orders	16.41
Availability of alternative remedies	16.43
Applying for a compensation order	16.44
Calculation of the award	16.46
Example	16.48
Matters to be included in the award	16.49
Procedure for making the claim	16.50
Powers to fine	16.51
Costs	16.52
What expenses can be recovered?	16.54
Defences	16.57
On breach of an abatement order	16.57
On the application for an abatement order	16.58
Appeals	16.59
Default proceedings	16.61
Checklist for lay prosecutor starting proceedings under section 82	16.63

Introduction

As a key mechanism for the local control of polluting activities which are harmful to people, the control of statutory nuisances lies principally with local authorities. However, there is also a route whereby a private individual may prosecute

16.01

such proceedings himself. This may be necessary where a local authority fails to act or where the action is against the local authority itself.[1]

16.02 Section 82 of the Environmental Protection Act 1990 ('EPA 1990') enables a 'person aggrieved' by a statutory nuisance to bring proceedings[2] in the magistrates' court against the person responsible.[3] The court may then issue an order requiring the abatement of the nuisance and/or prohibiting its recurrence.[4] The procedure is only available if a statutory nuisance is in existence at the date of the complaint.[5] The court has power to deal with a nuisance which is still in existence at the date of the hearing or, if abated, may recur.[6] There is no power to bring proceedings under section 82 in respect of a statutory nuisance which has not yet occurred.[7] The order may also include a provision prohibiting the use of the premises for human habitation until the nuisance has been abated.[8] Further, there are provisions which enable the court to fine the defendant.[9]

16.03 The procedure differs from that available to a local authority under section 80 in that an individual may not serve an abatement notice but must apply to a magistrates' court for an abatement order, having first warned the person responsible of his intention of so doing. However, the framework of statutory nuisance remains the same in that the nuisance complained of must fall within the list of categories of nuisance under section 79(1) of the EPA 1990 and must be prejudicial to health or a nuisance.

Section 82 and housing defects

16.04 Many proceedings under section 82 are brought by tenants, or occupiers, of local authority, or, housing association, housing stock. A tenant cannot approach the environmental health department to serve an abatement notice against the housing department since a local authority cannot bring proceedings against itself.[10] There appears to have been an increase in the number of section 82 proceedings, as they have been perceived as a viable method of achieving a speedy response to housing defects.[11]

---

[1] Local authorities may be defendants in section 82 proceedings in the same way as any other person; *R v Epping (Waltham Abbey) Justices, ex p Burlinson* [1948] 1 KB 79.
[2] For the position in relation to bringing proceedings against the Crown, see para 12.31.
[3] The Public Health Act 1936, s 99, provided a similar right although the EPA 1990, s 82, is, in fact, based on the Control of Pollution Act 1974, s 59, which was specific to noise nuisances. Proceedings under section 99 could lead to a fine and were therefore criminal and were commenced by laying an information and summons (*R v Inner London Crown Court, ex p Bentham* [1989] 1 WLR 408). Proceedings for an order made under the Control of Pollution Act 1974, s 59(2), were civil and were commenced by complaint. Section 59(4) provides for an offence for breach of an order made under s 59(2)
[4] EPA 1990, s 82(2).   [5] ibid, s 82(1).   [6] ibid, s 82(3).
[7] See *Pearshouse v Birmingham CC* [1999] Env LR 536, at 539.   [8] EPA 1990, s 82(3).
[9] ibid, s 82(2) and (8).   [10] *R v Cardiff CC, ex p Cross* (1982) 6 HLR 1.
[11] See, eg, *The Use of Section 82 of the Environmental Protection Act 1990 against Local Authorities and Housing Associations* (Department of the Environment, Transport and the Regions, Housing Research Paper No 59, 1996).

Where the existence of a nuisance is proved to the satisfaction of the magistrates, **16.05**
then if in their opinion the nuisance renders the premises unfit for human habitation they may make an order[12] prohibiting the use of the premises for human habitation.[13]

A tenant bringing proceedings under section 82 of the EPA 1990 may adduce **16.06**
evidence to establish what work is required to remedy the nuisance. A surveyor's (or other specialist's) expert report may be led in evidence. Such evidence, where the court has accepted it as having the status of expert evidence, may also include opinion evidence. This may go to establishing the existence of a statutory nuisance, but it may also consider the fitness for human habitation of the premises with a view to assisting the court in formulating an order stipulating works required. Within the statutory nuisance regime, there are no prerequisites for a test of fitness.[14] An expert report might, however, assist the court in forming an opinion as to fitness. If, by ordinary use, injury to the health of the occupier or his family might result, then a house is unfit.[15] Such a question, within Part III of the EPA 1990, is a question of fact[16] and will ultimately rest on a common sense approach.

Section 82 proceedings may be seen as an alternative, or an addition, to taking **16.07**
action through the normal landlord and tenant procedures to improve the quality of living accommodation. Section 11 of the Landlord and Tenant Act 1985 may be used as another route to seek a similar remedy. Actions under section 11 are civil actions and may be used by tenants to enforce a landlord's repairing obligations in respect of housing defects.[17] There is nothing to prevent a tenant bringing parallel actions under section 82 of the EPA 1990 and under section 11 of the Landlord and Tenant Act 1985.[18]

Person aggrieved

The requirement for action is that a person must be 'aggrieved' by the existence **16.08**
of a statutory nuisance.[19] There is no further definition of the expression a 'person aggrieved' in the Act. But it is to be drawn widely and is not limited as in, for example, the tort of private nuisance.[20] 'The words "person aggrieved" are of

---

[12] Under the EPA 1990, s 82(2).   [13] ibid, s 82(3).
[14] cf the regime and tests for fitness for human habitation under the Housing Act 1985. The test of fitness under the housing regime is not appropriate in these circumstances; *Birchall v Wirral UDC* (1953) 117 JP 384.   [15] *Morgan v Liverpool Corporation* [1927] 2 KB 131.
[16] *Hall v Manchester Corporation* (1915) 84 LJ Ch 732.   [17] See para 5.108.
[18] *R v Highbury Corner Magistrates' Court, ex p Edwards* [1994] Env LR 215.
[19] EPA 1990, s 82(1). In *Sandwell MBC v Bujok* [1990] 3 All ER 385 it was stated that 'an individual who is adversely affected by a statutory nuisance is a "person aggrieved"' (per Lord Griffiths at 391).
[20] *Hunter and Others v Canary Wharf and London Docklands Development Corporation* [1997] AC 655.

wide import and should not be subjected to a restrictive interpretation. They do not include, of course, a mere busybody who is interfering in things which do not concern him; but they do include a person who has a genuine grievance because an order has been made which prejudicially affects his interests.'[21]

16.09 In a block of flats, some or all of the tenants might have a similar grievance but they would each constitute separate persons with separate entitlements to bring an action under section 82, whether individually or as part of a combined action. It would not be appropriate for a single tenant to bring an action in respect of the state of all or some of the flats in the block where he is only affected by the condition of his own flat. He would have to confine his complaint to the state of his flat alone.[22] If, on the other hand, the cause of the grievance is the state of common parts in the block (where, for example, accumulations and deposits of filth in a stairwell present a risk to health) then, each individual tenant would be able to point to the accumulation as the source of the health risk and would be entitled to bring proceedings under section 82 as a person aggrieved.

16.10 It has been suggested that the section 82 route to the resolution of nuisances could be used in circumstances where an owner of a building deemed responsible for the state of the premises is, in fact, unable to get to the root of the nuisance—where, for example, ownership of that structural part of the property which is the original cause of the dampness is not his.[23] In *Pollway Nominees v London Borough of Havering*[24] it was suggested that such an owner could then bring proceedings as a 'person aggrieved' against the person responsible for the structural defect.[25] The difficulty with this suggestion is that the owner of the premises could plead that, as he could not remedy the defect himself, he had a reasonable excuse for failing to comply with the notice.[26]

Person responsible

16.11 The person responsible for the statutory nuisance must be identified. Section 82(4) defines the person responsible in the same terms as sections 80 and 80A of the EPA 1990.[27] Primary liability falls on the person 'to whose act, default or sufferance the nuisance is attributable'.[28] Where the nuisance is caused because

---

[21] *Re Reed, Bowen & Co, ex p Official Receiver* (1887) 19 QBD 178, per Lord Esher MR, at 177. In support of this preliminary objection, counsel referred to the judgment of James LJ in *Re Sidebotham* (1880) 14 Ch D 458 where he said at 465, 'A "person aggrieved" must be a man who has suffered a legal grievance, a man against whom a decision has been pronounced which has wrongfully deprived him of something, or wrongfully refused him something, or wrongfully affected his title to something.' See also *A-G of the Gambia v N'Jie* [1961] AC 617.
[22] *Birmingham DC v McMahon* (1987) 86 LGR 63.
[23] Under EPA 1990, s 80(2)(b), where the nuisance arises because of a structural defect, then the person responsible is the owner of the premises. (Formerly the Public Health Act 1936, s 93.)
[24] (1989) 88 LGR 192.   [25] ibid, per Saville J.
[26] EPA 1990, s 80(4). This point could also be made in respect of abatement orders (s 82(8)).
[27] See para 12.22.   [28] EPA 1990, s 79(7).

of a structural defect then liability falls on the owner of the premises. If the person responsible cannot be found, then liability falls on either the owner or occupier of the premises.

If the occupier of the premises which are alleged to constitute a statutory nuisance unreasonably prevents his landlord from undertaking necessary work to abate the nuisance, then liability may shift from the landlord to the tenant. It is likely that, where a landlord offers a tenant alternative accommodation for a short period in order to enable remedial work to be carried out to the property, but the tenant rejects all such offers, then proceedings under section 82 against such a landlord will fail.[29] In such a situation, the court is likely to consider how reasonable the offers of alternative accommodation were, and how necessary it was for the tenant to vacate the property while the work was undertaken. 16.12

In determining who is the person responsible for the nuisance, the root cause of the problem must be investigated. If, for example, condensation is caused because a tenant blocked the ventilation then the court may consider that a resulting statutory nuisance is not the fault of the landlord.[30] Likewise, if a tenant refused to use heating provided by the landlord because of the expense[31] or if he refused (again because of the expense) to allow the installation of a particular form of heating which would have prevented the nuisance,[32] then the landlord will not be liable for the resulting nuisance. Clearly, in cases of this sort, the reasonableness of the landlord's conduct will be a relevant issue.[33] 16.13

Section 82(5) of the EPA 1990 provides that if more than one person is responsible for the nuisance, even if on their own they would not be liable, then all may be served. In this case, the person aggrieved should serve separate letters before action on each person setting out his part in the activity which gives rise to the nuisance. Separate informations should then be laid in respect of each. 16.14

Nature of the proceedings

Proceedings brought under section 82 of the EPA 1990 in the magistrates' court are criminal. This is despite the fact that section 82(1) of the 1990 Act refers to the laying of a complaint.[34] The making of a complaint indicates a civil procedure whereas the laying of an information is the appropriate procedure for criminal wrongdoings. However, the references in the rest of the section are to 16.15

---

[29] *Quigley v Liverpool Housing Trust* (1999) EGCS 94.   [30] ibid.
[31] *Dover CC v Farrar & others* (1980) 2 HLR 32, at 39–40; *Pike v Sefton MBC* [2000] Env LR D31. See also *GLC v London Borough of Tower Hamlets* (1983) 15 HLR 54.
[32] *Carr v London Borough of Hackney* (1995) 93 LGR 606.   [33] See also para 5.47–5.49.
[34] *Botross v London Borough of Hammersmith and Fulham* [1995] Env LR 217. This anomaly arose because of a late amendment in the House of Lords at the third reading (*Hansard*, HL Debs, Vol 522, cols 1279–80), and see the note in the *Encyclopaedia of Environmental Health Law* (Sweet & Maxwell), para 2-2060.

criminal matters, such as, for example, the payment of a fine.[35] The implications of this are that rules of evidence pertinent to criminal proceedings will apply and that compensation orders will be available on the conviction of the person responsible.[36] The standard of proof will be the higher, criminal standard.[37]

The procedure

16.16 The procedure is started by a letter before action by the person aggrieved.[38] It is an obligatory part of the procedure. No proceedings can be instituted until after the expiry of the notice, and if the person responsible rectifies the nuisance before the hearing, the nuisance is abated and no offence is committed. If the court decides that a statutory nuisance is still in existence (or, if not, likely to recur) at the date of the hearing, an offence has been committed.[39]

16.17 The essential requirements of this notification are that:

- it must be in writing;
- it must be given to the person who is to be served with the proceedings;
- it must specify the matters complained of;
- in respect of a nuisance falling under section 79(1)(g)[40] (noise), or section 79(1)(ga)[41] (noise from a vehicle, etc, in a street), not less than three days' notice must be given;
- in respect of all other nuisances, not less than 21 days' notice must be given.[42]

Notice in writing

16.18 Subject to the requirement that it must be written, the notice need not be formal. There is no prescribed form. It can be a simple letter which warns of the intention to bring proceedings. This non-technical aspect of proceedings under section 82 has been emphasized by the courts.[43]

---

[35] EPA 1990, s 82(2) and (8). The point had been previously dealt with under former legislation: *R v Whitchurch* (1881) 7 QB 534; *Ex p Schofield* (1891) 2 QB 428 (proceedings under the Public Health Act 1875, ss 91–6 were criminal); *R v Newham Justices, ex p Hunt* [1976] 1 WLR 420; *Herbert v Lambeth LBC* (1991) 13 Cr App R (S) 489 (proceedings under the Public Health Act 1936, s 99, were criminal).
[36] Powers of Criminal Courts Act 1973, s 35(1), and *Davenport v Walsall MBC* [1997] Env LR 24.
[37] *Lewisham LBC v Fenner* (1995) 248 ENDS Report 44.   [38] EPA 1990, s 82(6).
[39] *R v Liverpool Crown Court, ex p Cooke* [1997] 1 WLR 700, per Leggatt LJ at 705.
[40] 'Noise emitted from premises so as to be prejudicial to health or a nuisance'.
[41] 'Noise that is prejudicial to health or a nuisance and is emitted from or caused by a vehicle, machinery or equipment in a street'.
[42] There is a provision that the Secretary of State may alter this period of notice by order (EPA 1990, s 82(7)(b)).
[43] *Richards Hewlings v McLean Homes East Anglia Ltd* [2001] Env LR 323; *Pearshouse v Birmingham CC* (n 7 above); *Hall v Kingston upon Hull CC; Ireland v Birmingham CC; Baker v Birmingham CC* [1999] 2 All ER 609; *Leeds v London Borough of Islington* [1998] Env LR 655.

Service

16.19 The letter must be served on the person against whom the proceedings are to be brought. As noted above, the period of notice (depending on the type of nuisance complained of) must be 21 or three clear days between the day on which the notice is served and the day on which proceedings are commenced.[44]

16.20 There is no right of appeal against a notice of intention or against the time periods contained in it—the latter are fixed by statute. The time periods are not to be equated with those given in an abatement notice—even if there is insufficient time to complete the work, the person aggrieved may still start proceedings under section 82 of the EPA 1990 when the time limit has expired.

16.21 The method of service for notices under this part of the EPA 1990, is prescribed by section 160 of the 1990 Act. Section 160(2) states that the method of service may be 'by delivering it to him, or by leaving it at his proper address, or by sending it by post to him at that address'.

16.22 Where the recipient is a company or partnership, then the rules are to be found in section 160(3):

Any such notice may—
  (a) in the case of a body corporate, be served on or given to the secretary or clerk of the body;
  (b) in the case of a partnership, be served on or given to a partner or person having the control or management of the partnership business.

The proper address is the last known address except in the case of companies, when it is the registered or principal office; and, in the case of partnerships, it is the principal office of the partnership.[45]

16.23 There is a provision that allows recipients of a notice to specify a further address for service.[46] In *Hall v Kingston upon Hull CC*[47] a tenant served a letter of intention under section 82(6) of the EPA 1990 on the local authority landlord. In this case, the terms and conditions of the tenancy specified that statutory nuisances must be reported to the local neighbourhood housing team and 21 days' notice must be given for the council to remove the nuisance. This was held to fall within section 160(5) in that the landlord had specified an alternative address for service. Because the provisions of section 160 are directory rather than mandatory[48] it was not necessary to show that someone in the position of 'secretary or clerk' to the council had formally given notice of an alternative address.

---

[44] Good practice suggests not counting Sundays, Good Friday or Christmas Day as the last days.
[45] EPA 1990, s 160(4).   [46] ibid, s 160(5).   [47] n 43 above.
[48] Use of the word 'may' rather than 'shall' throughout the section indicates this.

274   PROCEDURE AND EVIDENCE

16.24 Rules relating to service may trip up the professional adviser. Given that section 82 is designed to be a straightforward method for the lay person to achieve the abatement of a nuisance, and that it deals with problems of public health, to exact precise adherence to the requirements of section 160 may be unduly onerous. This has been the view of the courts.[49]

Content of the notice

16.25 While the notice of intention stands in the stead of an abatement notice,[50] it is not to be implied that the notice under section 82(6) of the EPA 1990 should conform with the requirements for an abatement notice. The primary difference between an abatement notice and a notice of intention is that only the former, if not complied with, can create a criminal offence. The second is procedural, an essential step which lays the basis for the institution of proceedings.[51]

16.26 The provision in section 82(6) was new to the 1990 Act so previous case law is unhelpful.[52] However, several robustly expressed decisions have made clear the requirements for the notice of intention.

16.27 The purpose of the notice under section 82(6) is to give the recipient an indication of what is the subject matter of the complaint so that he may have an opportunity to make any necessary inspection and deal with the problem as appropriate. Thus, as a bare minimum, it must contain enough information as is reasonable in the circumstances to explain the nature of the complaint. Brief reference to such matters as 'damp, or broken windows or slates or sashes, or a defective boiler, or

---

[49] Care must be taken, however, in the interpretation of these provisions. In *Leeds v London Borough of Islington* (n 43 above) a tenant sent a section 82(6) notice to an address of her local authority landlord which had been obtained from a rent card. This specified that legal notices under the Landlord and Tenant Act 1987 should be served at the address shown. This was deemed to be ineffective service since it could not be taken to have authorized the service of notices under any other statutory provisions. An important factor was that proceedings under section 82, as opposed to those under the Landlord and Tenant Act, were criminal. There was no proper authorization under section 160(5) and no proper service under section 160(3). The result may have been different if the rent card had been differently worded so as to lead to a reasonable conclusion that it authorized service to be made on the address there specified in respect of matters arising beyond those limited to the landlord and tenant relationship.

[50] See *R v Liverpool Crown Court, ex p Cooke* (n 39 above), at 705, where Leggatt LJ stated when considering the status of a section 82 notice: 'That is not an abatement notice in the sense that proof of a failure to comply with it is necessary as a precondition of the bringing of proceedings. But its effect is comparable, since no proceedings can be instituted until after the expiry of the notice, and if the person responsible rectifies the matter complained of before the hearing, the nuisance is abated and no offence is committed.'

[51] *Pearshouse v Birmingham CC* (n 7 above).

[52] Under the predecessor section in the Public Health Act 1936, the aggrieved person could commence proceedings before the magistrates without giving any warning of his intention to do so. Thus, the person responsible was given no opportunity to abate the nuisance in advance of the proceedings and before costs began to be incurred. This practice, however, was considered to be deplorable. See *R v Newham Justices, ex p Hunt* (n 35 above); *Sandwell MBC v Bujok* (n 19 above); *Blackpool BC v Johnstone; R v Blackpool Magistrates' Court, ex p Blackpool BC* [1992] COD 463.

draughts, or a lack of ventilation, or the presence of mould will be enough'.[53] It is not essential to attach a full itemized list of defects. Nor will it be fatal to the notice if it lists matters which might not technically constitute a statutory nuisance for the purpose of section 82 proceedings.[54]

In *East Staffordshire BC v Fairless*[55] Sullivan J emphasized the importance of ensuring that this procedure was not over-technical so as to deter tenants from making complaints about statutory nuisances. He contrasted the abatement notice with the section 82 notice and pointed out that local authorities, when drafting abatement notices, have access to legal and technical advice and thus should be expected to draft them to a higher standard.[56]

16.28

In the *Fairless* case, the tenant was represented by solicitors. They wrote a letter on the tenant's behalf, making a complaint of a statutory nuisance and attaching a report prepared by a housing consultant. The letter stated that the report was not an exhaustive schedule of matters which might constitute a statutory nuisance. Nevertheless, this was not considered to be defective. At this stage a complainant is not required to set out precisely the matters of which he is complaining. The fact was that the local authority knew full well what it had to do to abate the nuisance and the report was sufficiently specific.[57]

16.29

To summarize, a letter of intention should include:

16.30

- the name and address of the person served;
- address of premises affected;

---

[53] *Pearshouse v Birmingham CC* (n 7 above), per Lord Bingham at 552.
[54] In *Pearshouse v Birmingham CC* (n 7 above), the surveyor's report attached to the letter complained of matters which might become statutory nuisances at some future date. Such anticipatory nuisances are not actionable under section 82. However, this was held not to invalidate the notice.
[55] [1999] Env LR 525.
[56] The approach is characterized by a number of judicial pronouncements on the matter. For example: 'It would frustrate the clear intention of Parliament if the procedure provided by section 82 were to become bogged down in unnecessary technicality or undue literalism. It is important that the system should be operable by people who may be neither very sophisticated nor very articulate, and who may not in some cases, unlike this appellant, have the benefit of specialised and high quality advice' (*Pearshouse v Birmingham CC* (n 7 above), per Lord Bingham at 551). The approach is pragmatic. Since the purpose of the warning letter is to notify the recipient of matters constituting a nuisance, then, if there has been previous correspondence between the parties which means that the recipient knows what is wrong, a brief letter may suffice. If this is the first intimation of a problem, more detail may well be considered fair.
[57] However, in *East Staffordshire BC v Fairless* (n 55 above) the judge did state that, had further matters been raised in addition to those listed in the report, the magistrates could have refused to make an order in respect of them since the local authority had not been properly warned. A further question arises in that, if the proceedings are brought against a private landlord as opposed to a public body such as a local authority, will the courts be so ready to take such a robust attitude? A small landlord might be able to argue that a more specific warning notice is fairly required under the EPA 1990 particularly in view of the criminal proceedings which may eventually flow. Although the warning letter under section 82(6) is not in itself a criminal application nevertheless, as articles 6 and 7 of the European Convention on Human Rights imply, procedures which may lead to the possibility of a criminal conviction (as this does) must operate on fair principles; see further Chapter 11.

- address of premises on which the alleged nuisance originates (if different);
- the name and address of the person aggrieved;
- the nature of the nuisance (for example, 'premises in such a state as to be prejudicial to health or a nuisance'), preferably including under which paragraph of section 79(1) the nuisance arises;
- details of the matters complained of (for example, 'dampness and mould growth around the window frames in the kitchen');
- statement that the nuisance should be abated and/or prevented from recurring;
- the period of notice before proceedings may be commenced if:
  1) the nuisance is not abated and prevented from recurring, or
  2) if the person served does not provide a timetable setting out what steps are proposed to be taken and when.

It is not necessary to specify details of the work required to remedy the problem.

Starting the proceedings in the magistrates' court

16.31 Once the notice of intention has been served, the next step is to start the proceedings in the magistrates' court. These proceedings are criminal in character leading to the possibility of an abatement order, a fine, a compensation order and a costs award. The correct procedure is, therefore, to lay an information and for the magistrates' court to issue a summons.[58]

Laying an information and issuing the summons[59]

16.32 The information is laid before the magistrates' court in writing, orally or, under oath,[60] setting out the statutory basis for the proceedings and the existence of the statutory nuisance.[61] It should be accompanied by the notice of intention which will set out most of the necessary information about the offence which it is alleged has been committed. Once the information has been laid, the magistrates' court has a discretion to issue the summons. The laying of the information founds the magistrates' jurisdiction to try the alleged offence; the summons is the mechanism for bringing the defendant before the court.[62] The discretion will be exercised in favour of issuing the summons provided that the court is satisfied that the essential ingredients of the offence have been made out, that the proceedings are not out of time, that the court has jurisdiction, and that the prosecutor has the

---

[58] If, in error, a complaint is made, this may render any subsequent proceedings a nullity (*R v Nottingham Justices, ex p Brown* [1960] 1 WLR 1315; *R v Manchester Stipendiary Magistrate, ex p Hill* [1983] 1 AC 328; *Northern Ireland Trailers Ltd v Preston Corporation* [1972] 1 All ER 260).

[59] A detailed description of the procedure for starting criminal proceedings is beyond the scope of this work and reference should be made to the specialist practitioner texts such as Draycott, Carr and Starmer (eds), *Stones' Justices Manual* (Butterworths, published annually). See also C Andrews, *The Enforcement of Regulatory Offences* (Sweet & Maxwell, 1998).

[60] Magistrates' Courts Act 1980, s 1(3).

[61] For the correct form for the information see the Magistrates' Courts (Forms) Rules 1981, SI 1981/553, Sch 2, Form 1.

[62] *Fernandez v Broad* (CO/660/96, QBD) 10 July 1996, unreported.

necessary statutory authority.[63] The court may also consider whether the allegation has been made vexatiously.[64]

Since a prior notice has to be issued warning the defendant of the likelihood of proceedings and the nature of the alleged offence, then any defects in the information are likely to be treated as being capable of being cured by amendment provided that no real prejudice is caused.[65]

16.33

The information must be laid within six months of the offence being committed.[66] However, this point is unlikely to cause a problem since the nuisance must be proved to be in existence (or likely to recur) at the date of the hearing of the information.[67]

16.34

Abatement order[68]

If the court is satisfied that the nuisance exists (or, if abated, is likely to recur) it has a duty to make an order. The order may require the defendant to abate the nuisance (and/or prohibit its recurrence) within a specified time period, and carry out any necessary works.[69] The court must be satisfied as to the existence of the nuisance (or its likelihood of recurrence) at the date of the hearing.[70]

16.35

The magistrates may also order that the premises should not be used for human habitation until they are rendered fit for that purpose.[71] The court must be

16.36

---

[63] *R v West London Metropolitan Stipendiary Magistrate, ex p Klahn* [1979] 1 WLR 933. See the Magistrates' Courts Rules 1981, SI 1981/552, r 100, and the Magistrates' Courts Act 1980, s 123.

[64] *R v Bros* (1901) LT 581.

[65] *Fernandez v Broad* (n 62 above). See also *Blackpool BC v Johnstone; R v Blackpool Magistrates' Court, ex p Blackpool BC* (n 52 above) where the Divisional Court held that magistrates had properly exercised their discretion to amend the information. This case was heard under the previous legislative regime where there was no requirement to serve a notice of intention, a position which the court deplored.

[66] Magistrates' Courts Act 1980, s 127(1), applies as statutory nuisances are summary offences and there is no express provision in the EPA 1990 in relation to time limits.

[67] *R v Knowsley MBC, ex p Williams* [2001] Env LR 28; *Coventry CC v Doyle* [1981] 2 All ER 184.

[68] Public Health Act 1936, s 94(2), specifically referred to a 'nuisance order'. The EPA 1990 adopts no specific nomenclature in respect of this order which is, as a result, variously referred to as a 'nuisance order' and an 'abatement order'. [69] EPA 1990, s 82(2).

[70] *R v Knowsley MBC, ex p Williams* (n 67 above); *Coventry CC v Doyle* (n 67 above). As the prosecution under section 82 is concerned with the existence of the nuisance at the date of the hearing, this decision is unaffected by the decision in *R v Falmouth and Truro Port Health Authority, ex p South West Water Ltd* [2000] 3 All ER 306, where it was decided that the proper time for determining the validity of an abatement notice was at the date of service. There is, therefore, a difference in this respect between summary proceedings brought under section 82 and abatement notices served under section 80. The prosecution under section 80 is for non-compliance with the abatement notice; the prosecution under section 82 is for the existence of a statutory nuisance at the date of the hearing. Note also that, if the section 82 proceedings are commenced but adjourned, then the date for testing the existence of the nuisance is the date the trial started; *Carr v London Borough of Hackney* (n 32 above); *Crowe v London Borough of Tower Hamlets* (noted in LAG, May 1997).

[71] EPA 1990, s 82(3).

satisfied that they have been rendered fit so an application to this effect would need to be made to the court for this part of the order to be lifted.

16.37 The court has a wide discretion as to the terms of the order and should 'as common sense dictates, look at the whole of the circumstances of the case and ... try and make an order which is in its terms sensible and just having regard to the entire prevailing situation'.[72] The order should follow closely the wording of the Act in that it should specify whether the state of affairs is either a nuisance or prejudicial to health. So, they should state under which limb the nuisance falls.[73] Unlike the position in relation to the wording of abatement notices, an abatement order made by the magistrates under section 82 should be as specific as possible in preference to an order simply requiring abatement of the nuisance.[74]

16.38 If no specific works need to be undertaken to abate the nuisance, then a simple abatement order will suffice.[75]

16.39 The abatement order must be clear and free from ambiguity otherwise it is at risk of being quashed for uncertainty.[76] If a sound level is introduced into an abatement order then, it must be clear at what point the sound reading is to be taken and the level of background noise.[77]

Breach of the abatement order

16.40 Breach of an abatement order without reasonable excuse is an offence.[78] The person aggrieved would be entitled to lay an information for a subsequent breach of the order.

Compensation orders[79]

16.41 As proceedings brought under section 82 are criminal in nature, the power to make a compensation order under section 35 of the Powers of Criminal Courts

---

[72] *Nottingham Corporation v Newton* [1974] 2 All ER 760, per Lord Widgery CJ at 766.

[73] cf *Lowe & Watson v South Somerset DC* [1998] Env LR 143 where it was held that an abatement notice need not specify under which limb it is being served.

[74] *Salford CC v McNally* [1976] AC 379, per Lord Wilberforce at 389–90; *R v Secretary of State for the Environment, ex p Watney Mann (Midlands) Ltd* [1976] JPL 368; and *McGillivray v Stephenson* [1950] 1 All ER 942.

[75] *Millard v Wastall* [1898] 1 QB 342; *Tough v Hopkins* [1904] 1 KB 805; *Central London Rly v Hammersmith BC* (1904) 68 JP 217; *R v Meath Justices* (1899) 34 ILT 47.

[76] *Whatling v Rees* (1940) 79 JP 209; *R v Fenny Stratford Justices, ex p Watney Mann (Midlands) Ltd* [1976] 2 All ER 888.

[77] *R v Fenny Stratford Justices, ex p Watney Mann (Midlands) Ltd* (n 76 above). See also *Lambie and Minter v Thanet DC* [2001] Env LR 21 and *Sevenoaks DC v Brands Hatch Leisure Group Ltd* [2001] Env LR 86 for an equivalent provision in relation to abatement notices. See further Chapters 6 and 18.

[78] EPA 1990, s 82(8). For a discussion of what a 'reasonable excuse' might include, see Chapter 15.

[79] Compensation orders are also available in proceedings for breach of an abatement notice under EPA 1990, s 80(4). See paras 14.91–14.93.

Act 1973 applies.[80] There is no distinction to be made between the application of this Act to statutory nuisances and other criminal cases.[81]

The amount the magistrates may award is modest as there is a monetary limit.[82] Within this limit, the court has power to award such amount as is considered appropriate 'having regard to any evidence and to any representations made by the defendant or the prosecutor'.[83] The court is to give reasons on passing sentence if it does not make such an order where it has power to do so.[84]   **16.42**

Availability of alternative remedies
The person aggrieved by the statutory nuisance may also commence a civil action for an injunction and/or damages.[85] The criteria for bringing a civil action for private nuisance and for bringing summary proceedings for statutory nuisance are not identical. One important difference is that the claimant in a civil action must have an interest in property.[86] This will exclude a number of people who would otherwise satisfy the test for a 'person aggrieved'.[87] Remedies in landlord and tenant law under statute[88] and/or for breach of covenant are also available.   **16.43**

Applying for a compensation order
The principles for making an order are that the case must be clear, simple and straightforward and not for a large amount.[89]   **16.44**

The person aggrieved may make an application to the court for a compensation award, or the court may consider this question of its own motion. The court need   **16.45**

---

[80] 'Subject to the provisions of this part of the Act and of Section 40 of the Magistrates' Courts Act 1980, which imposes a monetary limit on the powers of the magistrates' court under this Section, a court by or before which a person is convicted of an offence, instead of or in addition to dealing with him in any other way, may, on application or otherwise, make an order (in this Act referred to as a Compensation Order) requiring him to pay compensation for any personal injury, loss or damage resulting from that offence or any other offence which is taken into consideration by the court in determining sentence.' See *Botross v London Borough of Hammersmith and Fulham* (n 34 above) and *Herbert v London Borough of Lambeth* (n 35 above).
[81] *Herbert v Lambeth LBC* (n 35 above); *Davenport v Walsall MBC* (n 36 above).
[82] Currently £5,000; the Magistrates' Courts Act 1980, s 40, as amended.
[83] Powers of the Criminal Courts Act 1973, s 35(1)(A). 'Even then the matter is discretionary, and the court should hesitate to embark on any complicated investigation of this kind'; *R v Kneeshaw* [1975] QB 57, per Lord Widgery CJ at 60.
[84] Powers of the Criminal Courts Act 1973, s 35(1).
[85] It would seem that there is no civil action available for breach of statutory duty in respect of the EPA 1990, Pt III: *Issa v London Borough of Hackney* [1997] Env LR 157.
[86] *Hunter and Others v Canary Wharf and London Docklands Development Corporation* (n 20 above).
[87] This means that persons aggrieved by the presence of mould and condensation in their flat may not have access to a suitable civil remedy, see *Davenport v Walsall MBC* (n 36 above).
[88] See, eg, the Landlord and Tenant Act 1985, s 11.
[89] 'A compensation order is designed for the simple, straightforward case where the amount of compensation can be readily and easily ascertained', *R v Donovan* (1982) 3 Cr App R (S) 192, per Eveleigh LJ. *Donovan* was endorsed by the Court of Appeal in *R v Briscoe* (1993) 15 Cr App R (S) 699.

not hear evidence before deciding whether to make an award since to do so might lead to a long and complicated investigation.[90] It may decide that the compensation is not easily quantifiable, and that it is not appropriate to make an order.[91] The decision is discretionary and applicants should be prepared to put in evidence, whether in the form of experts' reports or otherwise, regarding the losses occasioned by the statutory nuisance.

Calculation of the award

16.46 By section 35 of the Powers of Criminal Court Act 1973, the court may make a compensation award 'for any personal injury, loss or damage resulting from' the offence. The period for which compensation may be claimed is that between the expiry of the notice of intention and the date of the hearing. So, an applicant can never get compensation for the period before the date on which the notice expires, since that is the date from which the person responsible received warning of the possibility of criminal liability for the nuisance and payment of compensation.[92]

16.47 The general rule in criminal proceedings that the information must have been laid within six months of the offence having been committed applies to section 82 proceedings. So, if the person aggrieved delays more than six months in laying the information,[93] then, provided the nuisance is continuing the period of compensation will be calculated from a date six months before the laying of the information until the date of the hearing.[94]

Example

16.48 (1) Expiry of notice (1 January 2002)
Laying of information (1 February 2002)
Date of hearing (1 May 2002)
Period of compensation is from 1 January 2002 to 1 May 2002

(2) Expiry of notice (1 January 2002)
Laying of information (1 September 2002)
Date of hearing (1 December 2002)
Period of compensation is from 1 March 2002 to 1 December 2002.

---

[90] *R v Horsham Justices, ex p Richards* [1985] 1 WLR 986; *R v Chappell* (1984) CLR 574.
[91] *Davenport v Walsall MBC* (n 36 above).
[92] It might be considered that it would be fair to award compensation from the date when the person responsible became aware of the nuisance—which may well be a date earlier than the expiry of the notice of intention. However, this argument has been rejected on the basis that liability under section 82 is criminal. Had the liability been civil, then it would have been arguable that damages should flow from the period when the defendant became aware of the injury (*R v Knightsbridge Crown Court, ex p Abdillahi* [1999] 1 Env LR (D1) following *R v Liverpool Crown Court, ex p Cooke* (n 39 above)).
[93] Since the nuisance must be in existence or likely to recur at the date of the hearing, there is unlikely to be an argument that the information was laid out of time.
[94] *R v Liverpool Crown Court, ex p Cooke* (n 39 above).

Matters to be included in the award

16.49 The compensation claimed may be readily quantifiable if it consists of damage to clothes, furniture and other material items. The cost of such damage may be proved by the production of receipts. If the compensation so quantified exceeds the maximum awardable by the magistrates they should award the maximum and leave the balance to be sought in civil proceedings in the county court.[95] Other matters such as personal injury may also be covered by a compensation award. Appropriate medical reports should be produced as evidence in support of such a claim. The magistrates may exercise their discretion to award compensation even where the evidence before them is sparse. However, it is more likely that the court will exercise its discretion in favour of an applicant who is able to produce evidence in support of the claim.

Procedure for making the claim

16.50 The application would normally be made after the decision of the court on the statutory nuisance. The person aggrieved may make an application to the court, or the court may decide to make an award of its own motion. The decision will be in two parts:

(a) the determination of whether this is a proper case to make a compensation award; and
(b) the determination of the amount of the award.

Powers to fine

16.51 The magistrates' court has two separate powers to impose a fine under section 82 of the EPA 1990. Firstly, it has the power to fine under section 82(2).[96] This fine may be imposed at the application for an abatement order. Secondly, it has the power to impose a fine under section 82(8) of the EPA 1990. This provides that, where a person who has been made subject to an abatement order under section 82(2) of the 1990 Act, without reasonable excuse contravenes the order, he shall be liable on summary conviction to a fine.[97] There is power both to fine under section 82 of the EPA 1990 and to award a compensation order under the Powers of Criminal Courts Act 1973. The court is responsible for ensuring that any fine or compensation order is paid promptly and should specify a reasonable period for allowing the defendant to pay. Where there are difficulties over payment and orders were made for both, the court should give the compensation order priority over the fine.

---

[95] *R v Horseferry Road Magistrates' Court, ex p Prophet* (CO/1339/93; 24 February 1994, QBD) (transcript: Smith Bernal).
[96] Not exceeding level 5 on the standard scale (currently £5,000).
[97] This is to an amount not exceeding level 5 on the standard scale together with a further fine of an amount equal to one-tenth of that level for each day on which the offence continues after the conviction.

Costs

16.52 The statutory scheme in Part III of the EPA 1990 makes special provision for the payment of the costs of a person bringing summary proceedings under section 82. These provisions are to be found in section 82(12) of the 1990 Act. Under section 82(12), magistrates are bound to make a costs order in favour of the person aggrieved, once they have found that a statutory nuisance existed at the date of making of the complaint.[98] The date is crucial. If the nuisance was abated after the date of making of the complaint but prior to the hearing, then the power under section 82(12) to make a costs order is still available regardless of whether the nuisance is likely to recur. An aggrieved person may bring proceedings immediately after the notice period has expired simply for the purpose of recovering expenses.[99] It does not matter if the nuisance has been abated or work is underway.[100]

16.53 As in other areas of litigation, the complainant should give advance notice of any proposed claim for costs and the defendant should indicate whether the claim will be accepted or otherwise.[101] It has been suggested that *Calderbank* letters might be used to advantage.[102] The amount claimed should be provided to the court in an itemized list so that the various fees attributable to the different stages of the procedure can be identified. Thus, there should be listed the costs relevant to the preparation of the notice of intention; to the laying of the information; to the application in the court for the abatement order; and so on. While the court must make an order for costs, it must also take proper steps to investigate how a claim has been arrived at—particularly where it amounts to a substantial sum. Any unreasonable expenditure or expenditure resulting from unreasonable behaviour on the part of the complainant should be disallowed by the magistrates.[103]

What expenses can be recovered?

16.54 The costs recoverable are not limited to the costs of the hearing. They may include the costs of preparing the notice, providing a list of defects, obtaining experts' reports and so on. All the expenses incurred in establishing that the

---

[98] *R v Dudley Magistrates' Court, ex p Hollis* and another [1998] Env LR 354. Under the earlier provision of the Public Health Act 1936, s 99, the award of costs to a person aggrieved lay at the discretion of the magistrates; *Sandwell MBC v Bujok* (n 19 above).

[99] *R v Dudley Magistrates' Court, ex p Hollis and another* (n 98 above).

[100] 'There is no offence for which a person can be convicted in any proceedings for an order under section 82(2) if a nuisance has existed but has been abated before the hearing and is not likely to recur. All that the court may do in such a case if a nuisance existed at the making of the complaint is to order the defendants to pay the person bringing the proceedings compensation for any expenses properly incurred by him in the proceedings: see section 82(2), (4) and (12) of the Act of 1990'; *R v Liverpool Crown Court, ex p Cooke* (n 39 above), per Leggatt LJ at 703.

[101] *Taylor v Walsall & District Property & Investment Co Ltd* [1998] Env LR 600.

[102] ibid, per Simon Brown J at 606. A surprising suggestion given that this is a civil procedure.

[103] *Taylor v Walsall & District Property & Investment Co Ltd* (n 101 above).

nuisance existed at the time of the complaint, and up to and including the hearing, are recoverable.[104]

The limitation in the subsection is that it must compensate the person aggrieved only for 'expenses properly incurred'. This ensures that the amount to be paid by a defendant is not increased by any improper act by the person aggrieved or his representatives.[105] There will still, however, be a discretion for the magistrates to exercise in relation to whether an expense has been properly incurred. **16.55**

The magistrates' court should consider 'whether particular items of expenditure were unnecessary and as to whether the amounts claimed are more than those warranted by the particular proceedings before them, such as the engagement of unduly expensive solicitors or counsel or an excessive number of experts.'[106] The costs of an adjourned hearing in order to make a claim for compensation under section 35 of the Powers of Criminal Courts Act 1973, may be a proper expense to be recovered under section 82(12).[107] **16.56**

Defences

On breach of an abatement order
The availability of the defence of best practicable means is the same as under section 80 of the EPA 1990[108] except that it is not available where the premises would be rendered unfit for human habitation. **16.57**

On the application for an abatement order
Under section 82(2) a person aggrieved may apply to the magistrates' court for an abatement order. There is no express provision in the section which permits the person responsible for a statutory nuisance to plead a defence. However, arguably the same defences as are available for breach of an abatement order may be implied into section 82(2), in that proceedings under that subsection are criminal in nature. It would be unacceptable that the person responsible could be subject to criminal proceedings (carrying a potential fine and be unable to plead the defence) on the granting of an abatement order yet could successfully plead it in a prosecution for a subsequent breach of that same order. **16.58**

---

[104] *R v Dudley Magistrates' Court, ex p Hollis & another* (n 98 above); *Taylor v Walsall & District Property & Investment Co Ltd* (n 101 above).
[105] *Davenport v Walsall MBC* (n 36 above). See also *R v Beddoe* (1893) 1 Ch 547 (a case on the amount of costs which a trustee may properly recover).
[106] *R v Dudley Magistrates' Court, ex p Hollis and another* (n 98 above), per Moses J at 367.
[107] *Davenport v Walsall MBC* (n 36 above).
[108] See Chapter 15.

Appeals[109]

16.59 Provisions are available to appeal against:

(1) the abatement order;
(2) a conviction for failing to comply with the abatement order;
(3) a compensation order;
(4) a costs order; and
(5) the sentence.

16.60 Depending on the type of appeal, challenges to orders and decisions made by the magistrates' court may be brought by way of:

(1) an appeal to the Crown Court;
(2) an appeal to the Divisional Court by way of case stated by the magistrates;
(3) an application to the Divisional Court for judicial review of the magistrates' decision.

Default proceedings

16.61 There are two possibilities of default proceedings against a local authority. Firstly, under section 82(11) of the EPA 1990 where a person has been convicted[110] for breach of an abatement order, the magistrates have a discretion to direct the local authority responsible for the area in which the nuisance arose to carry out the abatement order. The local authority must have an opportunity to be heard in the proceedings. This may arise where it is plain that the convicted person responsible for the nuisance does not have the capacity, for whatever reason, to abate the nuisance. The liability of the authority reflects its ultimate responsibility for public health matters. Any argument the local authority could raise against such default liability would need to focus on the ability of the convicted person to abate the nuisance himself. The court may, for example, hear evidence regarding the financial means of the convicted person.

16.62 The second possibility of default proceedings against a local authority arises under section 82(13) of the EPA 1990. This occurs at an earlier part of the procedure. Where the person responsible cannot be found, the magistrates have a discretion to direct the relevant local authority to do anything which the court could have ordered the person to do.

---

[109] The procedure for appealing against an abatement order or against a conviction for failing to comply with an abatement order follows that applicable for appealing against an abatement notice and a conviction for failing to comply with an abatement notice. This is dealt with in detail in Chapters 13 and 14. The procedure for judicial review is dealt with in Chapter 17.

[110] Section 80(8).

Checklist for lay prosecutor starting proceedings under section 82 16.63

- Is my health or personal comfort (or that of my family) affected or is it a nuisance?
- Is the nuisance in existence or likely to recur?
- Does it fall under one of the listed categories in section 79(1)?
- Serve a notice of intention 21 days before court proceedings (3 days if a noise problem)
- Set out in notice of intention:
  - name and address of person to be served
  - address of premises affected
  - address of premises which are the source of the nuisance
  - description of the nuisance
  - paragraph of section 79(1) under which it falls
  - statement that nuisance should be abated or prevented from recurring
  - date after which proceedings will be brought:
    (a) if nuisance is not abated and prevented from recurring, or
    (b) if not provided with a timetable setting out what steps are proposed to be taken and when.
- Lay information in magistrates' court

17

OTHER REMEDIES

Introduction 17.01
Alternative dispute resolution and mediation 17.02
Injunctions 17.11
    Requirements for seeking an injunction under section 80(4) EPA 1990 ....17.12
    Requirements in construction noise notices 17.15
    Who can take the decision? 17.16
    Procedure 17.17
    Liability to give undertakings in damages 17.20
    Penalties 17.21
Public nuisance 17.22
Judicial review 17.26
    Grounds for judicial review 17.30
        Absence of a power to act 17.31
        Irrelevancy 17.33
        Irrationality 17.36
The *Wednesbury* principle and human rights 17.39
    Unlawful limitations of discretion 17.43
    Procedural breaches in court 17.47
    Legitimate expectation and fairness 17.49
Applying for judicial review 17.52
    Types of claim 17.53
    Standing 17.55
Overlaps with other statutory regimes 17.57
Contaminated land 17.58
    The lacuna 17.60
Authorization of nuisance by planning permission 17.61
    The current position 17.66
Harassment 17.68
    Protection from Harassment Act 1997 ....17.70
    Housing Act 1996 ....17.73

Introduction

This chapter considers alternatives to the use of the abatement notice procedure under section 80 of the Environmental Protection Act 1990 ('EPA 1990') and to 'persons aggrieved' taking their own proceedings under section 82 of the EPA **17.01**

1990. (However, a discussion of civil claims in nuisance, which constitutes a different legal regime from statutory nuisance, is beyond the scope of this work. Civil or private nuisances are property torts which do not apply to local authorities unless a council is taking action in its own right to protect its interests. Conceptual overlaps between private, public and statutory nuisance are analysed in Chapter 4.)

Alternative dispute resolution and mediation

17.02 A local authority has a discretion to prosecute for breach of an abatement notice.[1] A private person may wish to consider an alternative to invoking the procedure under section 82 of the EPA 1990.[2] The use of alternative dispute resolution, based on mediation, to try and find an acceptable compromise to all interested parties is a possible alternative to taking formal action through the courts.[3]

17.03 Mediation requires sufficient time to allow fresh solutions to emerge and a willingness from the relevant parties to accept a different kind of solution. At present, it is not built into the system of enforcement for regulatory offences so it has a limited impact.[4]

17.04 Mediation is intended to encourage the following:

- the exchange of views, information and knowledge about a problem;
- companies/neighbours and the local authority publicly to account for their positions to the victims of alleged nuisances;
- the parties to be prepared to change their positions, to seek out fresh solutions to problems, and to respond quickly to suggestions.

17.05 Various forms of nuisance dispute, especially noise-related ones—neighbourhood noise, entertainment noise, industrial noise, noise on construction sites, etc—are areas where mediation has been successfully tried. One voluntary organization is running a mediation scheme to resolve hedge nuisances—arising from the

---

[1] See further paras 14.26–14.39. [2] See Chapter 16.
[3] A mediation usually takes two to three weeks to arrange with a mediation agency. Mediations are not legally binding; the referring agency is only told the outcome not what was said during the sessions. The likelihood is that a successful mediation improves neighbourly relations, whereas a prosecution brought by a local authority or by a 'person aggrieved' may aggravate them.
[4] By contrast, mediation is an integral part of civil proceedings in family law and in commercial disputes. Increasingly in civil disputes, courts expect alternative dispute resolution to be attempted before the parties seek a resolution from the court. In *Cowl and Others v Plymouth CC*, *The Times*, 8 January 2002, an appeal against the dismissal by the High Court of an application for judicial review of a local authority's decision to close a care home, Lord Woolf CJ said, 'Without the need for the vast costs which must have been incurred, the parties should have been able to come to a sensible conclusion as to how to dispose of the issues which divided them. If they could not do that without help, then an independent mediator should have been recruited to assist. Today, sufficient should be known about alternative dispute resolution to make the failure to adopt it, particularly when public money was involved, indefensible.'

misplaced planting of leylandii trees—which are not within the scope of section 79 of the EPA 1990, although proposals to include them have been raised.[5]

Alternative dispute resolution is not inconsistent with prosecution guidelines, such as the *Enforcement Concordat*, but neither is it promoted by them. However, the *Concordat* does encourage local authorities to use informal methods to resolve disputes.[6] Such guidelines tend to see informal approaches as appropriate only in the early stages of a problem rather than later on, when positions have become entrenched to the collective detriment.

17.06

The use of mediation may conflict with legal requirements. If a local authority has already decided that something amounts to a statutory nuisance then it has no discretion to withhold serving a notice.[7] It could, however, draft the notice to allow sufficient time for mediation to be tried before the notice comes into effect. Mediation could not be offered as an alternative to serving an abatement notice, but it could be employed in addition, for example where a recipient of a notice wished to find out from neighbours their definition of the problem and what they believed would reduce it.

17.07

By contrast, generally, mediation could be considered as an alternative to prosecuting for breach of an abatement notice. It may not be appropriate at certain stages because breach of a notice may be so serious that prosecution becomes unavoidable. Some cases may require immediate action, such as seeking a High Court injunction.[8] Even in cases such as these, mediation may be helpful later on.

17.08

There are two situations where mediation is particularly relevant. Firstly, after there has been a breach of an abatement notice a local authority needs to make a decision about what should be done. The prosecutor has a discretion to prosecute or to do something else, for example, to refer to mediation, administer a formal caution or to take no further action. Whatever decision is made, the local authority should consider the grounds for making it properly and transparently. Where the person who has breached the notice has subsequently taken steps to ensure that this is unlikely to happen again, the local authority might consider it to be not in the public interest to prosecute.[9]

17.09

Secondly, mediation may be appropriate where a local authority or a 'person aggrieved' cannot invoke the statutory nuisance provisions in the EPA 1990. This may be because the problem is insufficient to constitute a nuisance or because it is incapable of being a statutory nuisance, for example, light pollution or

17.10

---

[5] Mediation UK. This organization also organizes mediations for neighbourhood noise complaints, which are mostly below the threshold of statutory nuisances.
[6] See further paras 14.37–14.39.   [7] *R v Carrick DC, ex p Shelley* [1996] Env LR 273.
[8] See further paras 17.11–17.21.
[9] A factor militating against prosecution in Crown Prosecution Service cases is where an offender has put right the loss or harm caused by the offence; see *Code for Crown Prosecutors* (2000), para 6.5(h).

nuisances arising from the rapid growth of leylandii hedges. In such circumstances, all the parties, especially the person responsible for causing the nuisance, need to know the basis upon which the mediation process is to be carried out and that formal enforcement action could not apply in such cases.

Injunctions

17.11 Injunctions are a civil remedy, granted at the discretion of the court, which a local authority is able to seek in its own name.[10] A local authority may apply to the High Court for an injunction[11] against the person responsible for a statutory nuisance[12] where it is of the opinion that criminal proceedings under section 80(4) of the EPA 1990 would afford an inadequate remedy.[13]

Requirements for seeking an injunction under section 80(4) EPA 1990

17.12 Care is needed to ensure that an injunction is being sought on proper grounds. The inconvenience of the abatement notice procedure would not in itself be sufficient grounds for making an application.[14] Where combined, however, with a reasonable belief that the perpetrator of the alleged nuisance was likely to ignore the requirements of a notice, then seeking an injunction would be justified. It would be unreasonable if an authority failed to consider, before applying for an injunction, whether the respondents might respond favourably to prosecution for breach of the abatement notice or to service of a new notice.[15]

17.13 A local authority must satisfy itself that without an injunction a statutory nuisance would continue, be repeated or would occur in the first place. The likely consequences of the nuisance, were it to occur, should also be serious. Examples of grounds appropriate for an injunction include:

- urgency, such as the holding of a 'rave' party in the very near future;
- where there has been a deliberate and flagrant flouting of the law, for example where previous proceedings have been tried but without effect;[16]
- evidence that the nuisance offender intends to carry on with the conduct complained of, come what may.[17]

17.14 However, there is no requirement that the abatement notice procedure should have been tried and failed before seeking an injunction, or that there must have

---

[10] Local Government Act 1972, s 222, provides this power in civil proceedings where 'a local authority consider it expedient for the promotion or protection of the interests of the inhabitants of their area . . .' [11] Statutory nuisance injunctions are only available in the High Court.
[12] *Bradford City MC v Brown* (1986) 84 LGR 731. As an alternative, a local authority can seek an injunction in public nuisance using its powers under the Local Government Act 1972, s 222.
[13] Under the EPA 1990, s 81(5).
[14] *Vale of White Horse DC v Allen & Partners* [1997] Env LR 212.   [15] ibid.
[16] *Stoke-on-Trent CC v B & Q (Retail) Ltd* [1984] AC 754.
[17] *Vale of White Horse DC v Allen & Partners* (n 14 above).

already occurred a deliberate and flagrant breach of the law.[18] In a suitable case, if an abatement notice has already been served a local authority can still seek an injunction.[19]

Requirements in construction noise notices
Where a local authority has imposed conditions in a notice to control noise from construction sites served under section 60 of the Control of Pollution Act 1974,[20] it can seek an injunction where local residents need protection which is not provided by the notice. A deliberate and flagrant breach of the law is not a requirement in these cases.[21] **17.15**

Who can take the decision?
A decision by a council to seek an injunction is no different in principle from any other council decision and it may be delegated to a subcommittee or officer with sufficient authority.[22] **17.16**

Procedure
The action is commenced by originating summons on a 'without notice' basis (previously termed an *ex parte* application). Access to the High Court is very speedy. In a case of sufficient urgency an injunction can be granted over the telephone. It is more usual for an application to be made before a High Court judge at the start of the day's business. **17.17**

An affidavit fully setting out the grounds for the application will be needed. This should include: **17.18**

- details of the nuisance, including whether it is occurring, recurring, or likely to occur or recur;
- the statutory basis of the nuisance in section 79 of the EPA 1990;
- the reasons why an injunction is being sought and why the criminal procedure under section 80 of the EPA 1990 provides an inadequate remedy; and
- the basis for the decision to seek the injunction, by whom it was made and under what authority.

Granting an injunction is a discretionary remedy in which the applicant must provide full and frank disclosure of the circumstances of the nuisance, including any factors suggesting that the remedy might not be appropriate. If granted, the injunction has immediate effect once it has been served on the person responsible for the nuisance. A return date will also be set by the court, since a without **17.19**

---

[18] *Runnymede BC v Ball* [1986] 1 All ER 629.
[19] *Hammersmith LBC v Magnum Automated Forecourts Ltd* [1978] 1 WLR 50.
[20] See further paras 6.102–6.115.
[21] *City of London Corp v Bovis Construction Ltd* (1992) 3 All ER 697.
[22] See further paras 2.11–2.14.

notice application will have a limited duration. This is to provide the respondent with the opportunity to say why the injunction should not continue or ought not to have been granted in the first place.

Liability to give undertakings in damages

17.20 A local authority is in the same position as central government and is not usually required to give undertakings in damages before an injunction is granted. The effect of this is that the authority will not have to pay the respondent for losses incurred as a result of the injunction being granted.[23]

Penalties

17.21 The penalty for contempt of court resulting from breach of an injunction order includes a prison sentence of up to two years and/or an unlimited fine.[24] These penalties are considerably greater than those available for a criminal prosecution under section 80(4) of the EPA 1990.[25] The power to order an unlimited fine normally acts as a disincentive to those commercial offenders who may be minded to make an economic calculation in deciding whether to cause or continue causing a nuisance.

Public nuisance[26]

17.22 A local authority[27] may bring a public nuisance action in its own name in two situations:

- when it has suffered special damage, that is particular, foreseeable and substantial damage over and above that sustained by the public at large;[28] or
- where the local authority considers it expedient for the promotion or protection of the interests of the inhabitants of its area.[29]

These can be combined in one action, where a local authority wishes to protect the inhabitants of its area and has suffered some special damage.[30]

17.23 The circumstances for initiating proceedings in public nuisance include where a local authority wishes to take action for a nuisance which does not fall within the categories of section 79(1) of the EPA 1990, or is thought not to do so, or for

---

[23] *Kirklees MBC v Wickes Building Supplies* [1993] AC 227.
[24] Contempt of Court Act 1981, s 14.
[25] See further paras 14.11, and 14.12 and 18.83 (Table 18.1).
[26] For noise nuisances which amount to public nuisance, see further paras 6.15–6.17, above. For a general analysis of public nuisance, including its relationship to private nuisance, see R A Buckley, *The Law of Nuisance* (2nd edn, Butterworths, 1996), ch 4.
[27] A private individual can bring an action where he has suffered special damage; see *Overseas Tankship (UK) Ltd v Miller Steamship Co Pty, The Wagon Mound (No 2)* [1967] 1 AC 617.
[28] *Sheringham UDC v Halsey (or Holsey)* (1904) 68 JP 395.
[29] Local Government Act 1972, s 222.
[30] *Gravesham BC v British Railways Board* [1978] Ch 379.

a nuisance which is particularly serious and affects a large proportion of the public.[31] In *Railtrack plc v Wandsworth LBC*[32] the local authority sought an injunction and a declaration that the company should be held responsible for the costs of cleaning the pavements from deposits of pigeons roosting in the girders underneath the railway bridge of a south London railway station. The council succeeded in obtaining a declaration and the court found that the company was liable in public nuisance for damage caused by the pigeons. Other cases where public nuisance proceedings have succeeded include:

- quarry-blasting;[33]
- emission of noxious smells from a chicken-processing factory;[34]
- storage of large amounts of inflammable material;[35]
- allowing refuse and filth to be deposited in a densely populated part of London;[36] and
- holding an all-night 'rave' in a field.[37]

17.24 Injunctive proceedings for public nuisance can be heard in the High Court or in the county court.[38] These courts have jurisdiction to make awards in damages, as well as to grant injunctions and make declarations.

17.25 Every public nuisance is an offence which may be prosecuted in the Crown Court if sufficiently serious, or summarily in the magistrates' court.[39] Besides having the power to fine and to imprison, the court may order abatement of the nuisance.[40]

Judicial review

17.26 Judicial review[41] is the process whereby the High Court supervises decisions made by public authorities including the courts,[42] central government and local authorities. Judicial review is not an appeal against the decision of the magistrates' court or of the Crown Court in the sense that a party disagrees with that

---

[31] *A-G v PYA Quarries Ltd* [1957] 2 QB 169.
[32] (2001) LGR 544.
[33] *A-G v PYA Quarries Ltd* (n 31 above).
[34] *Shoreham-by-Sea UDC v Dolphin Canadian Proteins* (1972) 71 LGR 261.
[35] *R v Lister and Biggs* (1857) 26 LJMC 196.   [36] *A-G v Tod Heatley* [1897] 1 Ch 560.
[37] *R v Shorrock* [1993] 3 All ER 917. A 'rave' is a form of noise nuisance; see para 6.137.
[38] Courts and Legal Services Act 1990, s 1.
[39] Criminal Law Act 1977, s 16 and Sch 2; Magistrates' Courts Act 1980, s 17(1) and Sch 1, para 1.
[40] *R v Pappineau* (1726) 2 Stra 686.
[41] There are a number of leading texts on judicial review, eg, H W R Wade and C F Forsyth, *Administrative Law* (8th edn, Oxford University Press, 2000); S de Smith, Lord Woolf and J Jowell, *Judicial Review of Administrative Action* (5th edn, Sweet & Maxwell, 1995).
[42] There can be no judicial review against a decision of a superior court: *The Rioters' Case* (1683) 1 Vern 174. The Supreme Court Act 1981, s 29(3), allows judicial review against a decision of the Crown Court except for a trial on indictment.

decision and wants it to be changed.[43] If a lower court or other public body makes a decision employing an improper procedure then it is the use of that procedure that may be scrutinized by judicial review, not the decision itself.

17.27 Judicial review cannot involve the High Court making a decision which is the responsibility of the body being supervised, or of substituting its own discretion for that of the public authority. Its role is supervisory, to ensure that a decision is made properly and legally. Where, for example, a court finds that the body being supervised has failed to take into account a relevant factor in coming to a decision, it may order it to reconsider its decision in the light of the court's findings and to take the decision properly. Judicial review of a determination by magistrates may mean that a case is remitted to the magistrates' court to be reheard by a different bench.

17.28 The High Court will recognize that the scope for disagreement or variation in making a discretionary decision will be considerable. The court will not intervene merely because it would itself have come to a different conclusion on the same facts.

17.29 Local authorities are empowered by statutes to act and to make discretionary decisions. Section 80 of the EPA 1990 sets out their duties in relation to statutory nuisances. Local authorities as public prosecutors have a discretion whether to prosecute for breach of an abatement notice, but have no discretion whether to serve a notice once they have decided that a statutory nuisance exists or is likely to occur or recur.[44] If they act beyond the scope of their powers or duties, or fail to perform a duty, or decide something without taking into account a relevant factor, or a decision has been taken on behalf of the council by an unauthorized person, then such failings are liable to judicial review.

Grounds for judicial review

17.30 There are many instances in which statutory nuisance enforcement may involve judicial review. Some examples are given below.

17.31 **Absence of a power to act** Usually this means that a local authority[45] has acted beyond its statutory powers rather than completely outside of any statutory framework. In *R v Bristol CC, ex p Everett*[46] the applicant sought judicial review of the council's decision to withdraw an abatement notice. This had been served on her landlord in respect of stairs in a dangerous state in the house in which Mrs

---

[43] See Chapter 13 for appeals against abatement notices and paras 14.94–14.110 for appeals against conviction. [44] *R v Carrick DC, ex p Shelley* (n 7 above).

[45] A court may have acted beyond its powers. In a food safety case, the magistrate had erred by ordering the destruction of food likely to become unfit for human consumption when there was only a power to do so if the food was unfit; *R v Thames Magistrates' Court, ex p Clapton Cash & Carry Ltd* (1989) COD 518. [46] [1999] 2 All ER 193.

Everett was the tenant. The council withdrew the notice after obtaining counsel's opinion that the matter complained of was not capable of amounting to a statutory nuisance. Mrs Everett argued that the council had no power to withdraw a notice and was acting beyond its powers in purporting to do so.

17.32 The case could only be brought by judicial review, quite properly as there is no express power in the EPA 1990 allowing a local authority to withdraw a notice. As it turned out Mrs Everett lost because the court decided that a local authority had an implied power to withdraw a notice.

17.33 Irrelevancy The local authority should consider relevant matters in making a decision and ignore irrelevant ones. The classic formulation is in the *Wednesbury* case:

> The court is entitled to investigate the action of the local authority with a view to seeing whether it has taken into account matters which it ought not to take into account, or conversely, has refused to take into account, matters which it ought to take into account.[47]

17.34 For example, a London authority once formulated a policy which stated that officers should pursue complaints of neighbourhood noise nuisance only if the nuisance was a public nuisance or if supported by the complainant's local councillor. A decision drawn from this policy could be judicially reviewed because it took into account irrelevant factors and failed to consider relevant ones; the policy could also be challenged on other grounds, such as irrationality.

17.35 There is a proportionality requirement to consider and the omission of a single relevant factor (or inclusion of a single irrelevant one) will often not be enough to justify judicial review.[48]

17.36 Irrationality A local authority may have taken into account all the relevant factors and discounted irrelevant ones but still make a perverse decision. For example, a local authority may have a prosecution policy which is consistent with the *Enforcement Concordat*[49] and is otherwise unexceptionable. It may have considered its policy in prosecuting a case and nevertheless acted against the policy in making its decision, such as deciding not to prosecute because the nuisance offender was the lead guitarist of an internationally renowned group of popular musicians. Such a decision would have been made irrationally, or '*Wednesbury* unreasonably'.

17.37 The threshold required is a high one. In the words of Lord Diplock in *Council of Civil Service Unions v Minister for the Civil Service*:

---

[47] *Associated Provincial Picture Houses Ltd v Wednesbury Corporation* [1948] 1KB 223, at 233–4.
[48] *R v Barnet and Camden Rent Tribunal, ex p Frey Investments Ltd* [1972] 2 QB 342.
[49] See further paras 14.37–14.39.

It applies to a decision which is so outrageous in its defiance of logic or of accepted moral standards that no sensible person who had applied his mind to the question to be decided could have arrived at it.[50]

17.38 Not all cases may require such a high threshold as this and perhaps the judge in this case had matters of national security in mind when choosing his words. Where the decision taken has implications that are adverse to human rights, the court would require more from the decision-maker to show that its decision was reasonable.

The *Wednesbury* principle and human rights

17.39 With the coming into force of the Human Rights Act 1998, some recent human rights cases involving decisions made by central government indicate a shift away from the traditional, *Wednesbury* approach. In *R v Ministry of Defence, ex p Smith and Others*[51] the reviewing court stated that where the decision-maker interfered with a fundamental right, the courts should adopt a 'heightened scrutiny' of the decision. Subsequently, in *Smith v United Kingdom*,[52] the European Court of Human Rights found that there had been a breach of article 13 (the right to an effective remedy) and held that the *Wednesbury* test for judicial review was too restrictive.

17.40 In the light of the decision in *Smith v United Kingdom*, in cases involving a breach of human rights the traditional *Wednesbury* approach is no longer sufficient. The extra ingredient is proportionality,[53] which has been held to be what the court *must* consider when it conducts a judicial review involving a breach of human rights.[54]

17.41 It was held in *Daly* that the intensity of review is greater under the proportionality approach. The reviewing court is required to consider how the decision-maker has reached a decision, not merely whether the decision is within the range of what could be rational or reasonable. The principles which the reviewing court should adopt in assessing claims which contain a human rights element have been stated by Lord Phillips MR in *R (on the application of Mahmood) v Secretary of State for the Home Department*[55] as follows.

---

[50] *Council of Civil Service Unions v Minister for the Civil Service* [1985] AC 374, at 410.
[51] [1996] QB 517. Here the Ministry of Defence was challenged about its treatment of homosexuals serving in the armed forces. [52] [1998] EHRLR 499.
[53] The elements of proportionality have been stated in the following terms in *De Freitas v Ministry of Agriculture* [1999] 1 AC 69, per Lord Clyde at 80: 'Whether (i) the legislative objective is sufficiently important to justify limiting a fundamental right; (ii) the measures designed to meet the legislative objective are rationally connected to it; and (iii) the means used to impair the right or freedom are no more than is necessary to accomplish the objective'.
[54] *R v Secretary of State for the Home Department, ex p Daly* [2001] UKHL 26.
[55] [2001] 1 WLR 840, at para 37.

(1) The court would only intervene where the decision fell outside the range of responses open to a reasonable decision-maker.
(2) In conducting a review of a decision affecting human rights, the court would subject the decision to the most anxious scrutiny.
(3) Where the decision interfered with human rights, the court would require substantial justification for the interference in order to be satisfied that the response fell within the range of responses open to a reasonable decision-maker. The more substantial the interference, the more that was required to justify it.

17.42 It is the last of these principles which local authorities should consider particularly carefully when considering any decisions they make which have human rights implications. It is a significant departure from the limitations of *Wednesbury* because it lowers the standard whereby the court can review an executive decision. The difference in standard should not be exaggerated however. Where a local authority carries out an investigation 'reasonably practicably' to decide whether a statutory nuisance exists, then a decision based on such an investigation is unlikely to be successfully judicially reviewed even though human rights elements may be present.[56]

Unlawful limitations of discretion
17.43 The relevant principles are:

- discretion must not be fettered;
- decision-making may not be delegated unless authorized; and
- the decision-maker must not adhere to a fixed policy without regard to the circumstances of the case.

17.44 An example of fettering discretion would be where a local authority decided never to serve a specific works notice under section 80(1) of the EPA 1990, its discretion being very wide whether to serve a notice in a detailed or in a simple form.[57] In *R v Carrick DC, ex p Shelley*[58] the local authority decided not to serve an abatement notice despite having concluded that a contaminated beach constituted a statutory nuisance. The council had fettered its discretion even though the decision not to serve a notice was taken in the knowledge that the problem was going to be dealt with by the water authority.

17.45 An officer taking the decision to apply to the High Court for an injunction under section 81(5) of the EPA 1990 must be authorized to do so under section 101 of the Local Government Act 1972. The decision, if unauthorized, would itself be judicially reviewable.

---

[56] *R (on the application of Anne and another) v Test Valley BC* [2001] 48 EG 127 (CS).
[57] *R v Falmouth and Truro Port Health Authority, ex p South West Water Ltd* [2000] 3 All ER 306.
[58] n 7 above.

17.46 A decision to prosecute made according to a fixed policy, which did not consider the particular circumstances of each case would be an unlawful limitation of discretion. The use of standard forms of abatement notice[59] without consideration of the particular circumstances of each case could be reviewable, although not if appealing the notice to the magistrates' court under section 80(3) of the EPA 1990 could achieve the desired result.[60]

Procedural breaches in court

17.47 The rules concerning natural justice are particularly relevant to court procedures. With the Human Rights Act 1998 now fully in force, issues concerning the fairness of proceedings continue to call for the attention of the High Court.[61] Even when a decision is made reasonably, if there is evidence of bias or other procedural unfairness then judicial review may be available. In all cases of apparent bias the test is: is there a 'real danger' of bias in favour or against?[62]

17.48 Examples of bias in proceedings include:

- where a disqualified person (such as by having a financial interest) participates in making a decision;
- where the case is pre-judged, such as by the magistrates knowing about the defendant's criminal record during the hearing; and
- where an interested party has private access to those hearing a case.

Legitimate expectation and fairness

17.49 Legitimate expectation is an emerging doctrine which for some commentators has become a substantive right.[63] The cases are not altogether consistent. In *R v Home Secretary, ex p Ruddock*[64] it was held that the doctrine imposed a general duty to act fairly; whereas in *R v Secretary of State for the Home Department, ex p Hargreaves*[65] it was limited to procedural fairness.

17.50 A legitimate expectation arises, for example, when consultation has been promised in a clear and unambiguous way.[66] If a local authority subsequently resiles from that promise then this can be judicially reviewed.[67] In *R v Devon CC, ex p Baker* Simon Brown LJ said:

---

[59] This particularly applies in respect of noise notices served under the EPA 1990, s 80.
[60] Seeking judicial review rather than appealing the notice because the time limit for an appeal had exceeded the 21 days allowed would not be allowed.   [61] See Chapter 11.
[62] *R v Gough* [1993] AC 646.
[63] R Gordon, *Judicial Review: Law and Procedure* (Sweet & Maxwell, 1996), para 2-026.
[64] [1987] 1 WLR 1482.   [65] [1997] 1 All ER 397.
[66] See further paras 12.12–12.16.
[67] *R v Liverpool Corp, ex p Liverpool Taxi Fleet Operators' Association* [1972] 2 QB 299.

[T]he claimant's right will only be found established when there is a clear and unambiguous representation upon which it was reasonable for him to rely. Then the ... public body will be held bound in fairness by the representation made unless only its promise or undertaking as to how its power would be exercised is inconsistent with the statutory duties imposed upon it.[68]

Resiling from a stated policy can be justified in appropriate circumstances, such as when an authority has an overriding statutory duty. Otherwise, the authority's discretion would be fettered. The crucial element is the clarity and unambiguity of the promise. It was this which saved the Falmouth and Truro Port Health Authority from giving the water company a legitimate expectation to be consulted in its action over the discharge of sewage into the Fal estuary.[69] **17.51**

Applying for judicial review

An application for judicial review requires permission[70] from the High Court, which will only be given if the case is arguable. The application must be made promptly and in any event within three months of the date when grounds for the claim first arose.[71] Permission will generally not be given where the applicant has failed to exhaust any alternative remedy which could decide the issue.[72] For example, if the magistrates' court hearing an appeal against an abatement notice operated in a somewhat haphazard and lackadaisical (but not hopelessly incompetent) way, the High Court might refuse to give permission for judicial review on the grounds that the applicant should appeal on the facts to the Crown Court. However, if the Crown Court operated in a similar way there would be no further route of appeal (unless by way of case stated on a point of law[73]) and permission to seek judicial review should be granted. **17.52**

Types of claim

A claim for judicial review is governed by the Civil Procedure Rules 1998. The claim is restricted to a review of the lawfulness of: **17.53**

---

[68] *R v Devon CC, ex p Baker* [1995] 1 All ER 73, at 88.
[69] *R v Falmouth and Truro Port Health Authority, ex p South West Water Ltd* (n 57 above). See further, R Malcolm, 'Statutory Nuisance: The Validity of Abatement Notices' [2000] JPL 894.
[70] Previously termed 'leave'. The Civil Procedure Rules 1998, SI 1998/3132, Pt 54, apply to applications filed from 2 October 2000, before then RSC Order 53 applied.
[71] Civil Procedure Rules 1998, SI 1998/3132, Pt 54.5.
[72] In *R v Secretary of State for the Home Department, ex p Swati* [1986] 1 WLR 477, Sir John Donaldson MR said, at 485: 'In giving or refusing leave to apply for judicial review, account must be taken of the alternative remedies available to the applicant ... the jurisdiction [will] not be exercised where there [is] an alternative remedy by way of appeal, save in exceptional circumstances. By definition, exceptional circumstances defy definition, but where Parliament provides an appeal procedure, judicial review will have no place, unless the Applicant can distinguish his case from the type of case for which the appeal procedure was provided.
[73] See further paras 14.102–14.110.

(i) an enactment; or
(ii) a decision, action or failure to act in relation to the exercise of a public function.[74]

17.54 A claimant can seek one or more of the following remedies:

- a mandatory order;
- a prohibiting order;
- a quashing order;
- an injunction; or
- a declaration.[75]

Standing

17.55 The claimant has to show at the permission stage and sometimes at the substantive hearing that he has sufficient interest in the matter to which the claim relates.[76] The issue of standing has been treated more liberally over the years. Besides persons served with an abatement notice, or a 'person aggrieved' by a statutory nuisance, it could include neighbours of the person causing a nuisance on whom a local authority had decided not to serve with a notice. In *R v Thames Magistrates' Court, ex p Greenbaum* standing applied to 'a member of the public who has been inconvenienced' as well as to a 'person who has a particular grievance of his own'.[77] A local authority who is the losing party in legal proceedings can have standing.[78]

17.56 Representative groups may have sufficient standing, but there is the additional hurdle of satisfying the 'victim test' for actions based on a breach of human rights.[79] Public-spirited bodies may have standing to bring a claim for judicial review, but not for breach of human rights unless the 'victim test' is satisfied.[80]

Overlaps with other statutory regimes

17.57 Statutory nuisance enforcement is the paradigm case of mid-nineteenth century state intervention.[81] Over the years a number of areas of regulation have become disassociated from statutory nuisance, for example health and safety at work, overcrowded dwellings and building control. These areas are now regulated by

---

[74] Civil Procedure Rules 1998, SI 1998/3132, r 54.0.9.   [75] ibid, rr 54.2 and 54.3.
[76] Supreme Court Act 1981, s 31(3). See *R v Inland Revenue Commissioners, ex p National Federation of Self Employed & Small Businesses Ltd* [1982] AC 617.
[77] (1957) 55 LGR 129, per Parker LJ at 135.   [78] *Cook v Southend BC* [1990] 2 QB 1.
[79] Representative groups or bodies will not have standing in the enforcement of substantive rights under the Human Rights Act 1998 unless the group or body itself is able to satisfy the 'victim test' and not only the individuals who are being represented; see *Re Medicaments and Related Classes of Goods (No 4), The Times*, 7 August 2001.
[80] *R v Secretary of State for Foreign & Commonwealth Affairs, ex p World Development Movement Ltd* [1995] 1 WLR 386; see further paras 11.15–11.16.   [81] See further paras 3.11–3.16.

entirely separate regimes, respectively the Health and Safety at Work Act 1974,[82] Housing Act 1985[83] and the Building Act 1984.[84] Additionally, some recent statutes impinge on nuisance, such as the Noise Act 1996[85] and the Protection from Harassment Act 1997. Brief consideration will also be given to overlaps between statutory nuisance and the new contaminated land regime, and secondly, with the planning system.

Contaminated land

Statutory nuisance and the contaminated land regime brought into effect under Part IIA of the EPA 1990 are mutually exclusive systems.[86] Both are concerned with a similar subject matter, namely land or accumulations which could be a pollution or a health risk. Section 79(1A) of the EPA 1990 provides that: **17.58**

No matter shall constitute a statutory nuisance to the extent that it consists of, or is caused by, any land being in a contaminated state.

The legislation is drafted with the intention of avoiding overlaps. For the purposes of Part IIA of the EPA 1990, 'contaminated land' comprises any land which appears to the local authority to be in such a condition that significant harm is being caused, or where there is the significant possibility of such harm, by reason of substances in, on, or under the land.[87] Included are situations where the pollution of controlled waters is being, or is likely to be, caused by the contamination. The Guidance provides examples of what is meant by significant harm and it is clear that the threshold is a very high one.[88] Part IIA of the EPA 1990 also requires there to be a 'significant pollution linkage': the pathway linking the contaminant to the human, property or other receptors suffering significant harm, or (to use the tortured language of the parliamentary draftsman) the significant possibility of suffering significant harm. **17.59**

---

[82] The Health and Safety at Work Act 1974, s 5 (repealed by EPA 1990, s 162(2), Sch 16, Pt 1), is an example showing the origins in statutory nuisance of sections now found in other regimes. Section 5 created a duty to use 'best practicable means' to prevent the emission from premises into the atmosphere of noxious or offensive substances. Persons to whom a duty of care is owed under the 1974 Act include not only employees (s 2) but also members of the public (s 3). Thus in *R v Board of Trustees of the Science Museum* [1993] 3 All ER 853, in which the trustees were prosecuted for breach of duty under section 3(1), it was the general public who were at risk of legionnaires' disease bacteria escaping from premises into the atmosphere.
[83] See further para 5.100–5.102. [84] See further paras 5.84–5.97.
[85] See further paras 6.51–6.62.
[86] The contaminated land regime came into force on 1 April 2000. EPA 1990, Pt IIA, is supplemented by the Contaminated Land (England) Regulations 2000, SI 2000/227, and the *Guidance Notes* issued under the EPA 1990, s 78A, as DETR Circular on Contaminated Land: 2/2000.
[87] EPA 1990, s 78A(2).
[88] DETR Circular on Contaminated Land: 2/2000, Annex 3, Pt 3, para 23.

The lacuna

17.60 The exclusion of contaminated land from being a statutory nuisance by section 79(1A) of the EPA 1990 is wider than the test for significant harm in Part IIA of the EPA 1990. The requirement in section 79(1A) is merely for land to be in a contaminated state. This produces a lacuna in which a large number of cases are expected to fall. For example, land may be contaminated but not to such an extent as to produce a real risk of significant harm to people or to property. As such, it fails to meet the criteria of the contaminated land regime and is also excluded from statutory nuisance enforcement action.

Authorization of nuisance by planning permission

17.61 Planning permission is crucial for the development and future use of land. Changes in land use may mean that established users experience annoyance and interference directly caused by such changes. There is the potential, therefore, for nuisances to result directly from development and changes of use. In *Allen v Gulf Oil Refinery Ltd*[89] the Court of Appeal affirmed two fundamental principles:

(1) a planning authority has no jurisdiction to authorize a nuisance; and
(2) the grant of planning permission can permit the change of character of a neighbourhood.

17.62 The *Gulf Oil* case establishes that where the scale and type of new development allowed by planning permission inevitably results in nuisance, which could not reasonably be avoided, then there can be no cause of action. This does not mean that the planning authority can authorize any nuisance, though, in effect, it can alter the neighbourhood standard against which one person's interference with his neighbour's use of land could be judged a nuisance.

17.63 The way tension between these two principles is reconciled is crucial for deciding what role statutory nuisance has when planning permission authorizes an activity which causes annoyance and interference. In *Gillingham BC v Medway Dock Co Ltd*[90] the redevelopment of Chatham Dock changed the whole character of the neighbourhood. Planning permission set a high threshold for disturbance; disturbance adverse to residents could not be avoided. The economic realities of change prevailed, and the scale of the change resulting from the grant of planning permission meant that claims in nuisance based on the previous standard could not be sustained.

17.64 The two principles cited in the *Gulf Oil* case were reconciled by Buckley J in *Gillingham* thus:

---

[89] [1979] 3 All ER 1008; subsequently affirmed by the House of Lords at [1981] AC 1001.
[90] [1993] QB 343.

In short, where planning consent is given for a development or change of use, the question of nuisance will thereafter fall to be decided by reference to a neighbourhood with that development or use and not as it was previously.[91]

After the *Gillingham* case, it appeared until *Wheeler v JJ Saunders Ltd*[92] that nuisance law was subordinated to, even subsumed by, planning legislation. The crucial difference between these cases was over the scale of change. *Wheeler* did not involve change in the whole character of a neighbourhood, even though the defendants had argued that there had been an intensification in the use of the land. The facts of this case were that of a typical and serious nuisance resulting from the housing of 800 pigs within a distance of 36 feet of the plaintiff's holiday cottages which caused a substantial interference in the enjoyment of that land. The extension of the pig farm did not amount to an intensification of use significant enough to indicate a change in the character of the neighbourhood. **17.65**

The current position
Since *Wheeler v JJ Saunders Ltd* the position has been that where the scale of development resulting from the grant of planning permission is such as to change the character of a neighbourhood, then, provided that reasonable steps are taken to minimize annoyance and inconvenience, the threshold for nuisance is raised to accommodate the change. This threshold may go down as well as up, as where a locality previously used for commercial purposes is re-zoned for residential use. Where a change is less substantial and there has not been a change in character, the standard for deciding whether a nuisance exists remains the same. **17.66**

This position only applies to the nuisance limb of statutory nuisance under section 79 of the EPA 1990. Where injury to health can be shown it cannot be justified by the grant of planning permission. It would be possible to serve an abatement notice under section 80 of the EPA 1990 where, following the grant of planning permission, injury to health resulted from changes in the character of a neighbourhood. **17.67**

Harassment

A person may be the victim of a course of action involving nuisance which amounts to harassment. The ability of the common law to provide a remedy for harassment from nuisance was dealt a blow by the House of Lords in *Hunter and Others v Canary Wharf and London Docklands Development Corporation*[93] which overruled the decision of the Court of Appeal in *Khorasandjian v Bush*.[94] Miss Khorasandjian had been subjected to a course of abusive telephone calls, but the *Hunter* case decided that, as she had no proprietary interest in the land, being **17.68**

---

[91] n 90 above, at 359.　　[92] [1996] Ch 19.
[93] [1997] AC 655.　　[94] [1993] QB 727.

merely the daughter of the householder, she ought not to have had a cause of action in nuisance.[95]

17.69 Subsequent cases have demonstrated the boundary between nuisance and harassment. In *Hussain and another v Lancaster CC* the Court of Appeal decided that a campaign of verbal and racial abuse and physical attacks directed against an Asian family of small shopkeepers by young white racists 'unquestionably interfered persistently and intolerably with the plaintiff's enjoyment of the plaintiff's land'.[96] However, because the harassment did not involve the perpetrators' use of their own land (as council tenants) there could be no tort of nuisance. *Hussain* also confirmed the limited nature of the local authority's liability in nuisance as landlord. Even if they had constituted acts of nuisance, the council as landlord could only be held liable for the acts of their tenants if they could be shown to have specifically authorised or adopted them; and that, it was insufficient for the council simply to have known of and failed to take sufficient steps to prevent the tenants committing the acts.[97]

Protection from Harassment Act 1997

17.70 The Protection from Harassment Act 1997 was enacted largely as a result of the decision in *Hunter and Others v Canary Wharf and London Docklands Development Corporation*.[95a] Section 1(1) creates a new summary offence of harassment, punishable by up to six months' imprisonment, a fine (on scale 5, currently a maximum of £5,000), or both. The offence is defined as a 'course of conduct which amounts to harassment of another and which he [the offender] knows or ought to know amounts to harassment of the other'.

17.71 Although investigated by the police, the offence is relevant to serious neighbourhood nuisances, such as where sound systems are used to harass, intimidate or punish neighbours. The offence is widely drawn and local authorities should consider referring to the police complaints of harassment as an alternative to taking a prosecution under section 80 of the EPA 1990 or under section 10 of the Noise Act 1996.

17.72 Section 3 of the Protection from Harassment Act 1997 enables a claimant to pursue a civil claim in the High Court or in the county court for damages and an injunction. What constitutes harassment is the same in criminal or civil cases and the test is objective.[98]

---

[95] As regards the common law, *Hunter and Others v Canary Wharf and London Docklands Development Corporation* (n 93 above) separates harassment (a tort against the person) from nuisance (a tort against land), a link which the Court of Appeal in *Khorasandjian v Bush* (n 94 above) had sought to make.   [95a] See n 93 above.   [96] [2000] 1 QB 1, per Hirst LJ at 23.
[97] ibid, at 2.
[98] The Protection from Harassment Act 1997, s 1(2), defines as harassment: '... if a reasonable person in possession of the same information would think the course of conduct amounted to harassment of another'. In *R v Colohan*, *The Times*, 14 June 2001, the Court of Appeal rejected an argument that the test of reasonableness was according to the standards of a mentally ill defendant.

Housing Act 1996

Additional powers were made available in the Housing Act 1996 to deal with unruly local authority tenants and members of their households. Section 152(1) of the 1996 Act enables a local authority to apply to the High Court or to the county court for an injunction, to which a power of arrest may be attached.[99] The authority may seek an injunction in respect of persons: **17.73**

engaging in and threatening to engage in conduct causing or likely to cause a nuisance or annoyance to a person residing in, visiting or otherwise engaged in a lawful activity in residential premises.

Besides being available to protect the neighbours of the behaviourally challenged or disordered, this protection also applies to persons, such as a postman or tradesman, working in the neighbourhood. However, in *Enfield LBC v B (a minor) and another*[100] the Court of Appeal held that an injunction under section 152 of the Housing Act 1996 was not available in respect of council employees whose office merely happened to be near local authority housing and who needed protection from a violent and deranged local authority tenant and her son. **17.74**

[99] Housing Act 1996, s 152(6).   [100] [2000] 1 All ER 255.

18

OVERVIEW OF EVIDENTIAL ISSUES AND PREPARATION FOR COURT

Introduction 18.01
The investigation 18.02
Using photographs 18.03
    Admissibility and continuity of evidence 18.04
    Digital cameras 18.07
Using noise measurements 18.09
    Checklist of items required in an expert report 18.14
Using tape recordings 18.16
Using other technical and scientific data 18.17
    Evidence of odour nuisance 18.17
    Analysing atmospheric emissions 18.21
Using documentary evidence 18.22
    Admissibility of evidence: section 23 of the Criminal Justice Act
    1988 .... 18.22
    Scope of 'fear' 18.27
    Admissibility of evidence: section 24 of the Criminal Justice Act
    1988 .... 18.31
Using expert witnesses and opinion evidence 18.35
    Environmental health officers as experts 18.37
    Duty of objectivity 18.38
    Scope of expert evidence 18.39
Officers' notebooks 18.43
Witness statements 18.46
    Interviewing suspects and witnesses 18.47
    When to caution 18.49
    The caution 18.50
    Implications of silence 18.51
    Interview records 18.52
    Editing a witness statement 18.53
    Use of witness statements in court 18.54
Advance disclosure 18.55
    Common law duties and the effects of the Criminal Procedure and
    Investigations Act 1996 .... 18.57
    The prosecutor's duty 18.59
    Civil proceedings 18.61

Advance information of prosecution case 18.62
Complainant's identity 18.64
Examples of material for disclosure 18.65
Procedure 18.67
Secondary disclosure 18.70
Sensitive material 18.72
Disclosure of expert evidence 18.73
Admissibility of evidence and the court hearing 18.78
Fairness 18.79
Rebuttal evidence 18.80
Sentencing, mitigation and *Newton* hearings 18.83

Introduction

18.01 The procedures for prosecuting for failure to comply with an abatement notice under section 80(4) of the Environmental Protection Act 1990 ('EPA 1990'), appealing against an abatement notice under section 80(3), or bringing summary proceedings under section 82(1), follow the usual procedural routes for such proceedings in magistrates' courts.[1] However, there are certain aspects in relation to statutory nuisance cases where particular problems and issues may arise. Notable amongst these are the evidential issues relating to the investigation of the nuisance and the use of expert technical and scientific evidence. The rules of advance disclosure can also frequently cause difficulties in practice. This chapter, therefore, focuses on the more problematic evidential and procedural issues which the practitioner may encounter when appealing an abatement notice, prosecuting or defending a statutory nuisance case, or appealing from a decision in the magistrates' court.[2]

The investigation

18.02 During the initial investigation, an environmental health officer collates evidence pertinent to proof of the nuisance which may lead to service of an abatement notice. This evidence would be relevant in an appeal since proof of the nuisance must be established at the time of the service of the notice. Later, where relevant, evidence may be collated for use at a prosecution for failure to comply with a notice. Equally, the recipient of an abatement notice may use such evidence at an appeal, or to defend a prosecution, perhaps by raising the defences of 'best practicable means' or 'reasonable excuse'. This evidence (depending on the nature of the nuisance) may include the following:

---

[1] These procedures are discussed further in Chapters 13, 14 and 16.
[2] A comprehensive examination of the general procedural and evidential matters that may arise is beyond the scope of this work. For general issues regarding the commencement of proceedings in a magistrates' court, specialist practitioner texts such as Draycott, Carr and Starmer (eds), *Stone's Justices' Manual* (Butterworths, published annually) should be consulted.

- photographic evidence;
- noise measurements;
- tape recordings;
- other scientific and technical data;
- exhibits;
- documentary evidence;
- expert evidence;
- officers' notebooks; and
- witness statements.

Using photographs

Photographs are an effective evidential tool for the prosecution trying to establish the factual and visual circumstances surrounding an alleged nuisance. They may also be useful to the defence to counter such an allegation or to support a defence plea of best practicable means. The same points apply to the use of video evidence, which may also be useful in conveying to the court a moving image, for example, of smoke drifting across a residential area. **18.03**

Admissibility and continuity of evidence

In criminal proceedings, the admissibility of photographs introduced by the prosecution may be challenged on the basis that they give the impression that the defendant has committed offences other than those with which he is charged. It is wise, therefore, for photographic evidence to be agreed between the legal representatives of both parties prior to the court hearing. Photographs which are confined to the particular item in issue in the trial (for example, a bonfire which it is alleged caused the nuisance) with no other infringements being depicted, are likely to be admissible. When these photographs are used in evidence, no labels or annotations should be used other than a number for identification purposes.[3] **18.04**

It is desirable to have one set of photographs available for each magistrate, as well as for the opposing side's lawyers and the witness. **18.05**

Continuity of evidence is always a key issue and unless there is an agreement between the parties, it will be necessary to produce a statement from the processor of the film that the photograph was printed from an untouched negative. This would not be applicable where a Polaroid camera is used as there will be one original set of photographs available for inspection by the court. Additional sets can be made from an inter-negative, or on a high quality photocopier.[4] **18.06**

---

[3] This avoids any question that such annotations might amount to hearsay evidence.
[4] Again, a statement from the individual, made under s 9 Criminal Justice 1967, who made the photocopies should be produced in court.

Digital cameras

18.07 Many local authorities now use digital cameras and there is some concern about the admissibility of photographs produced by these means.[5] In principle they will be admissible, but the difficulty relates to the ease with which the images can be manipulated. As with all such evidence, the issue is whether both the accuracy and the authenticity of the images can be established to the satisfaction of the court. So, evidence should be directed to the procedures involved in the creation of the digital images to establish that the picture produced in court is an accurate copy of the original.[6]

18.08 One difference in relation to digital cameras is that, as computers, they are subject to the requirements of section 69 of the Police and Criminal Evidence Act 1984. This prescribes that a statement in a document produced by a computer (which is broadly defined) shall not be admissible as evidence of any fact stated unless it is shown:

(1) that there are no reasonable grounds for believing that the statement is inaccurate because of improper use of the computer; and
(2) that at all material times, the computer was operating properly, or, if it was not, that any respect in which it was not operating properly, or was out of operation, was not such as to affect the production of the document or the accuracy of its contents.

This can be established by producing a statement[7] in the form of a certificate which can be produced in evidence by the officer using the camera.

Using noise measurements

18.09 Different noise measurements such as, for example, a decibel reading (a unit of sound-level intensity), a leq (a unit of sound energy) or a dB(A) (a basic indication of noise make-up) may be introduced in evidence.

18.10 However, there is no noise standard that defines a nuisance boundary in relation to Part III of the EPA 1990[8] so the usefulness of any noise measurement taken is limited by the fact that there is no objective standard against which it can be measured.[9]

---

[5] For an interesting article on the use of digital cameras and their benefits, see J Smith, 'Candid Camera?' *Environmental Health Journal*, 5 July 2000.

[6] See the House of Lords' Science and Technology Committee's reports, *Digital Images as Evidence* (5th report, 1997–8, HL Paper 64) and *Digital Images as Evidence: Government Response* (8th Report, 1997–8, HL Paper 121).

[7] Under the Criminal Justice Act 1967, s 9.

[8] cf the Noise Act 1996 where a 35-dB(A) difference between the background level and the noise source is defined as sufficient to justify taking legal action. See further paras 6.51–6.62.

[9] The British Standards Institution's 'Method for Rating Industrial Noise Affecting Mixed Residential and Industrial Areas' (BS 4142, 1997) is helpful in providing an indication of when

18: OVERVIEW OF EVIDENTIAL ISSUES

Guidelines have been introduced by the World Health Organization.[10] These suggest that disturbance of sleep becomes increasingly apparent when ambient noise levels exceed 35 dB(A). In *Murdoch v Glacier Metal Company Ltd*,[11] a private nuisance action, the noise night-time readings were at or marginally above the WHO guidelines. But the claim was dismissed, taking into account all the surrounding circumstances such as the proximity of a bypass and the paucity of complaints from others living nearby.

18.11

Given these uncertainties surrounding the use of noise measurements, they should not be used in isolation in court proceedings but should constitute one part of a body of evidence.

18.12

It is also imperative that such measurements are introduced in evidence in a manner which is appropriate for a lay court. An explanation of the measurements in a comprehensible form is essential. A visual display using charts and tables to illustrate numerical values may also be helpful. Some everyday comparator[12] may be helpful so that the impact of a certain noise level can be appreciated by the court.

18.13

Checklist of items required in an expert report
In relation to their admissibility and reliability as evidence, it is important for the witness (whether for the prosecution or defence) producing evidence of noise measurements to be able to establish the following points in a documented report:

18.14

- details of noise source being measured (for example, the location and type of machinery, speed of operation, task being carried out);
- details of measuring instruments: type and model number, calibration values;
- sketch plan showing noise source, position of recording microphones, location of complainants;
- relative measurements (that is, the measurement when noise is present and when it is not in relation to background noise);
- a record of weather conditions (cold, wet, foggy or windy weather can affect measurements);
- times when the measurements were taken and other relevant circumstances should also be noted (the absence of such matters in the environmental health officer's notebook, or in the record kept by a defence expert, may be used in cross-examination to test the reliability of the measurements);

---

complaints are likely, but, its usefulness is limited in that it only refers to mixed residential and industrial settings. It suggests a method of assessment which uses the rating level for the specific noise and subtracts from that the measured background noise level. It indicates that a difference of around 10 dB or higher means that complaints are likely.

[10] *Environmental Health Criteria No 12: Noise* (1980).
[11] [1998] Env LR 732.   [12] eg, comparison with the noise from a jet plane or a bus.

- position where the measurements were taken (they need to be taken one metre away from a facade);
- any possible interference with the noise (there are problems about taking noise measurements in a complainant's house because of interference from other noises; there is also a problem about isolating the noise source from other sources in the neighbourhood); and
- subjective assessment of character of noise. This is an acceptable part of the scientific methodology and may include such things as the annoyance value of the noise, or whether it has an irritating component.[13]

18.15 It can be seen that there are a number of potential problems about the introduction of noise measurements in evidence and, as a result, a number of local authorities now avoid using such measurements in order to establish a nuisance. While such an approach is understandable, the absence of such evidence may, in itself, raise questions by the defence as to whether the noise was not measurable because it did not constitute a nuisance.

Using tape recordings

18.16 An alternative (or addition) to a noise measurement is the use of a tape recording of the noise. It is difficult, however, to reproduce the exact acoustic conditions at the site of an alleged nuisance. An echoing court room can present such a difficulty. But, nevertheless, a tape recording can be effective in court. Where it is used it is essential to be able to prove its accuracy. So, there must be a documented procedure including calibration of the tape recorder and analysis procedures. 'Noise annoyance recorders', known as Digital Audio Tape recorders, are available which can be left on site and operated by a complainant or from a remote switch. This kind of equipment is good for recording intermittent noise such as domestic noise. In order to establish the reliability as evidence of recordings from such equipment, it must be shown that they have not been tampered with.[14]

Using other technical and scientific data

Evidence of odour nuisance

18.17 There are no generally agreed scientific standards against which smell can be evaluated and establishing the existence of a smell is perhaps even more complex than noise. Noise can, at least, be quantified according to established measurements. There are, however, scientific instruments available to trap and analyse

---

[13] 'Method for Rating Industrial Noise Affecting Mixed Residential and Industrial Areas' (BS 4142, 1997) (n 9 above).
[14] Note the impact of the Regulation of Investigatory Powers Act 2000 in relation to the surveillance of the nuisance. See paras 11.69–11.89.

smells known as odometers. The same points about the continuity of evidence and its reliability and admissibility as pertain to the taking of noise measurements, apply here.

18.18 As with all technical evidence, it is important for a prosecutor to use a range of techniques to establish a nuisance. In the case of an odour nuisance, evidence may be given for the prosecution by environmental health officers and by lay witnesses. Where the evidence is given by environmental health officers, their evidence may be rendered more reliable if they are first required to undertake an olfactory test to establish that they are not overly sensitive to smell.[15] Evidence of ordinary residents (both for the prosecution and the defence) is essential. The prosecution must show, firstly, that there is a smell and, secondly, that that smell is a nuisance. Clearly, if there is expert evidence to show that the smell is prejudicial to health, then that will be relied on by the prosecution. However, in many cases, such as those relating to rural smells like pig farms, the complainant will rely on the nuisance limb. In this case, a body of evidence from lay witnesses to demonstrate the effect that the smell had on their personal comfort will be pertinent. Such matters as interference with sleep and daily activities, inability to open windows, nauseous reactions, etc, will be relevant.

18.19 It is possible, in respect of any kind of nuisance, for the court to visit the site. Smell and noise may be cases where there is some merit in the practice. However, the professional opinion of the environmental health officers will be of significant importance in these cases.

18.20 The defence may argue that a smell does not constitute a nuisance in that it does not interfere with the personal comfort of local residents and that, on the basis of the give and take principle to be found in nuisance law, such smell as there is should be tolerated. Arguments such as these may be attractive to local magistrates' courts where a good deal of tolerance in relation to economic activities may be encountered. So, where an allegation that a pig farm, or the agricultural practice of spreading slurry, causes an odour nuisance, then, where this occurs within a rural district, a local bench may consider that the locality demands that such practices are to be tolerated by the local population.

Analysing atmospheric emissions
18.21 Other nuisances such as dust and smoke may also lead to the introduction of technical evidence. The analysis of grit particles in smoke, for example, may be a mechanism for establishing prejudice to health. As in all such cases, establishing continuity of evidence is crucial. So, evidence must be called from the chain of people who took the sample, who received it at the laboratory, who analysed it,

---

[15] For an interesting discussion of a case in West Devon concerning odours emanating from a milk products factory, see D Jones, 'Statutory Nuisance Appeals with Special Reference to Smells' [1995] JPL 797.

and so on. These witnesses must all be called to give evidence to establish the chain of evidence unless the defence is willing to agree to the submission of a written statement, where this evidence is uncontested.[16]

Using documentary evidence

Admissibility of evidence: section 23 of the Criminal Justice Act 1988

18.22 Evidence in criminal proceedings usually needs to be given orally so that the witness can be cross-examined and his demeanour assessed. A person's witness statement can be admitted as evidence without him appearing in the witness box, but the conditions for such admission are onerous. Under section 23(2) of the Criminal Justice Act 1988 these conditions are where the person is:

- dead or unfit to attend by reason of his bodily or mental condition; or
- outside the UK and it is not reasonably practicable for him to attend; or
- all reasonable steps have been taken to find him but he cannot be found.

18.23 Admissibility under this section applies to defence as well as to prosecution witnesses. Alternatively, a statement can be admitted under section 23(3) of the Criminal Justice Act 1988 provided:

- that it was made to a police officer or someone else (such as an environmental health officer) under a duty to investigate offences or charge offenders; and
- that the person who made it does not give oral evidence through fear or because he is kept out of the way.

18.24 Statements in the form of computer records[17] made under section 23 of the Criminal Justice Act 1988 are subject to the requirements of section 69 of the Police and Criminal Evidence Act 1984.

18.25 The admission of evidence under section 23 of the Criminal Justice Act 1988 is subject to the court giving leave under sections 25 or 26 of that Act. Section 25 deals with evidence otherwise admissible under the Act; section 26 with documents prepared for the purpose of pending or contemplated criminal proceedings. The court also has a general discretion to exclude otherwise admissible prosecution evidence under section 78 of the Police and Criminal Evidence Act 1984.[18]

18.26 Since the coming into force of the Human Rights Act 1998 the court should also consider whether to exclude the evidence in the light of article 6 (right to a fair trial) of the European Convention on Human Rights. Where the evidence is the sole or a major piece of evidence on which a defendant may be convicted then,

---

[16] Such statements are taken under the Criminal Justice Act 1967, s 9. Reports relating to expert evidence are taken under the Criminal Justice Act 1988, s 30. [17] See para 18.08.
[18] See para 18.79.

arguably, it should be excluded since it would be problematic whether the trial would be fair.[19]

Scope of 'fear'
'Fear' in statutory nuisance prosecutions may be present in serious neighbourhood disputes. The admission of statements under section 23 of the Criminal Justice Act 1988, because of fear preventing a witness from giving oral evidence, is likely to be rare. This is partly because the onus will be a high one (to the criminal standard[20]) on the prosecutor to convince the court to give leave under section 26 of the Criminal Justice Act 1988 to admit the statement. This will be especially so where the evidence is central to the prosecution case. Further, the witness will usually want anonymity and the court is unlikely to admit a written statement in evidence where the maker is anonymous (and is probably unable to).

18.27

Admitting a witness statement under section 23 of the Criminal Justice Act 1988 might arise either immediately before or during the trial, including the period when the witness is actually giving oral testimony. In the latter case, an application to admit will apply only to that part not given orally.[21]

18.28

'Fear' refers to a witness's state of mind, meaning fear of the consequences of giving evidence orally and need not be fear related to the offence.[22] It does not mean nervousness about giving evidence. 'Fear' could apply to an employee in fear of an employer/defendant, but probably not fear of losing one's job as this is not fear for one's safety. 'Fear' could also apply to fear for safety of family members and not merely the witness himself.

18.29

Although the provisions regarding the admissibility of a witness statement in lieu of the witness himself may be useful, the circumstances in which they should be relied on must be unusual. The weight of such evidence will be less than that of a witness who enters the witness-box and whose evidence is subject to cross-examination.

18.30

Admissibility of evidence: section 24 of the Criminal Justice Act 1988
Business documents created in the normal course of business are admissible, subject to the requirements of section 69 of the Police and Criminal Evidence Act 1984, when in the form of computer records. Section 24 requirements apply to both parties.

18.31

Any document prepared for the purposes of pending or contemplated criminal proceedings or for a criminal investigation has to fulfil the requirements of either section 23(2) or section 23(3) of the Criminal Justice Act 1988.

18.32

[19] *R v Denton, The Times*, 22 November 2000. See further Chapter 11.
[20] *R v Waters* [1997] Crim LR 823.
[21] *R v Ashford Justices, ex p Hilden* [1993] QB 555.
[22] *R v Fairfax* [1995] Crim LR 949.

18.33 The leave of the court is required under either section 25 or section 26 of the 1988 Act for admission of business or other documents. As mentioned above, the court has a general discretion to exclude otherwise admissible prosecution evidence under section 78 of the Police and Criminal Evidence Act 1984.

18.34 The standard of proof required for admitting a document under section 23 or section 24 of the Criminal Justice Act 1988 is the criminal standard for the prosecution and the civil standard for the defence.[23]

Using expert witnesses and opinion evidence

18.35 A witness either gives evidence as a witness of fact or as a witness of opinion. Environmental health officers may find themselves appearing in court to give evidence relating both to factual matters and to expert opinion. In the first place, evidence may be given as to what the officer saw and did (factual matters); secondly, technical evidence may be given and an opinion might be offered as to whether the matters were prejudicial to health or, otherwise constituted a statutory nuisance (a matter of opinion). It might be wise, considering the presentational problems in attempting to give evidence in both capacities, to separate out these functions. It is usual for the investigating officer to be called as the first witness.[24]

18.36 In deciding questions, magistrates are entitled to draw on their own personal experience, either of the locality or of life in general. But, in statutory nuisance cases, the essential question in contention will often depend on some form of technical or special knowledge.[25] This will frequently arise when the defence of best practicable means is in issue. In such a case, only an expert witness may give an opinion. It is for the court to decide whether any witness is to be treated as an expert and will consider the qualifications and experience of the witness before deciding the question. Where a court accepts a witness as a qualified expert and the evidence of this witness is undisputed, then the magistrates are not, in general, entitled to substitute their own view.[26]

Environmental health officers as experts

18.37 An environmental health officer may be qualified to give an expert opinion on a particular aspect of the case, such as whether the noise constituted a nuisance. The fact that a person is employed by one of the parties is not a bar to that person acting as an expert witness in the case.[27] However, it is important that such a

---

[23] *R v Mattey and Queeley* [1995] 2 Cr App 409.
[24] As the officer is also the client of the prosecutor, he will need to give instructions in the course of the trial to the trial lawyer and will need to remain in court after giving evidence.
[25] *Patel v Mehtab* (1980) 5 HLR 78.
[26] ibid.
[27] However, such an expert should be aware of the risks of his position, and should ensure that he is never acting as an advocate for his client (or employer) but rather as an expert whose task is to assist the court before whom he is appearing; see *London & Leeds Estates Ltd v Paribas Ltd (No 2)* [1995] 1 EGLR 102.

person can show he fully understands the role of an expert witness,[28] the necessity for objectivity, and that he owes his primary duty to the court not to his employer.[29]

Duty of objectivity

The expert owes a duty to the court of objectivity. Thus Lord Wilberforce in *Whitehouse v Jordan* said:

18.38

> Expert evidence presented to the court should be, and should be seen to be, the independent product of the expert, uninfluenced as to form or content by the exigencies of legislation. To the extent that it is not, the evidence is likely to be not only incorrect, but self-defeating. The expert's responsibility is to the court and not to the client in giving evidence or producing a report. This applies as much to defence as to prosecution experts and applies throughout the duration of the case.[30]

Scope of expert evidence

Care should also be taken in determining the width of experience of a particular witness to ensure that he does not seek to give an opinion outside his field of knowledge or expertise. Similarly, it is important to ensure that the right expert is selected for the particular case. It would be quite proper to call either a structural engineer or a chartered surveyor to give evidence of a structural defect at the premises which might create a condition which could cause an injury to health.[31] It is more questionable whether such a professional witness would be able to go further and offer an expert opinion of whether such a defect constituted prejudice to health. Environmental health officers will usually have acquired considerable experience investigating complaints of nuisances and would be expected to have expertise in judging whether particular circumstances pose a nuisance or are prejudicial to health. It would not be necessary to bring a medically qualified expert to court to establish this point.[32] Any other professional witnesses would need to offer evidence of relevant experience in judging such matters before the court is likely to consider they have the necessary expertise.

18.39

Where expert witnesses indicate that they do not have expertise in a particular area, then any answer given by that witness should be disregarded by the court on the basis that they have no more expertise than the layman.[33]

18.40

---

[28] See *National Justice Naviera SA v Prudential Assurance Co Ltd ('The Ikarian Reefer')* [1993] 2 EGLR 183, where Cresswell, J set out the duties of an expert witness.

[29] 'I would encourage the authority concerned to provide some training for such a person to which they can point to show that he has the necessary awareness of the difficult role of an expert'; *Field v Leeds CC* [2000] 17 EG 165, per Lord Woolf. This judgment was given in the context of a civil action for private nuisance and was particularly concerned with the Civil Procedure Rules 1998, SI 1998/3132. However, the comments regarding the role of the expert may equally be applied to criminal proceedings or appeals against notices.   [30] [1981] 1 WLR 246, at 256–7.

[31] *Anderson v Merseyside Improved Houses* CO/1792/95 DC.

[32] *London Borough of Southwark v Simpson* [1999] Env LR 553; *O'Toole v Knowsley MBC* [1999] Env LR D29.   [33] *London Borough of Southwark v Simpson* (n 32 above), at 559.

18.41 Where experts are permitted to give evidence of opinion, then such witnesses may ground their opinion in any accepted body of learning in which they have expertise, and refer to published works in their own evidence.[34]

18.42 Proof of the existence of a statutory nuisance can rest on the evidence of an expert alone.[35] However, it is desirable to call a complainant if his evidence is reliable, in addition to an expert, to show the effect of the nuisance on the neighbourhood.

Officers' notebooks

18.43 Environmental health officers and other staff, when carrying out any investigation should keep proper notes of visits. Besides providing a record of what took place, notebooks form an essential basis for any witness statement that might be required in any proceedings. Their reliability and accuracy are paramount. If the court has any reasonable doubt about their accuracy then an officer's evidence will lack credibility.

18.44 Notebooks can also be used, with the court's permission, as memory refreshing documents when giving oral evidence. In order to be acceptable to the court, the record needs to be made when fresh in the maker's memory.[36] If notes are not made as soon as practicable after the event, then the defendant may be able to claim that the account has been degraded by lapse of time. Officers giving evidence in court need to bring their notebooks with them.

18.45 If an audio tape is made which is later transcribed, the officer should check the accuracy of the transcription. It is better to make a written record of quantitative findings since this is likely to be more accurate. Where tapes are used it is a good idea to retain them in case of a future challenge about their accuracy in court. It is desirable that notes are written up in a form which does not require subsequent editing. Thus many local authorities use paginated notebooks which form the basis of any future case and which can be copied for advance disclosure and used as the basis of a witness statement. Where notebooks are edited, the originals should be kept and disclosed beforehand as a challenge in court may lead to an adjournment. If a notebook is edited, then this should be stated and the contents should be authenticated as a true statement.

Witness statements

18.46 A witness statement may be admitted in evidence and read out in court, subject to the court's permission, if the opposing party has been served with a copy under

---

[34] *R v Abadom* [1983] 1 All ER 364. This is an exception to the rule against hearsay.
[35] *Cooke v Adatia* (1989) 153 JP 129.
[36] *A-G's Reference No 3 of 1979* [1979] 69 Cr App R 411.

section 9 of the Criminal Justice Act 1967 and has not objected to its admission. To be admitted in this way, the statement must have been made within the United Kingdom. If an objection has been made, then the witness will have to be called to give oral evidence under oath, unless the statement is admissible under section 23 or section 24 of the Criminal Justice Act 1988.[37] A statement made outside the United Kingdom which is not contested may be admitted under section 23 of the Criminal Justice Act 1988.

Interviewing suspects and witnesses
A witness statement is usually taken for the prosecution by the investigating environmental health officer. Where the officer is interviewing a person suspected of the offence of a failure to comply with an abatement notice, then consideration needs to be given to the requirement to caution that person. If he is the recipient of a notice, then he may be at risk of being personally prosecuted. If a company has been served with the notice, then a director, officer or manager being interviewed may be sufficiently senior to be part of the 'brains' of the company and thus able to make admissions on its behalf. There will be no need to caution if the officer has decided not to use any answers given at the interview against the person in question, or the company he represents. **18.47**

Interviewing officers need to give particular regard to considering the rights of suspects and other interviewees and to adopt the principles underlying the Police and Criminal Evidence Act 1984 and the Human Rights Act 1998. Not least to reduce the risk of issues of fairness being raised in court, it is particularly important to ensure that suspects are strongly urged to have a legal representative present when being questioned. **18.48**

When to caution
Paragraph 10.1 of Code of Practice C (made under the Police and Criminal Evidence Act 1984) states that a caution must be given if there are grounds to suspect that the person being questioned has committed an offence. There is no obligation to caution a person being questioned merely as a witness. So, where an officer is inspecting premises to determine whether a statutory nuisance exists, or is generally seeking information whilst carrying out his statutory duties, there is no obligation to caution. If, during such an interview, the person makes an admission of guilt, the officer must then give a caution. If the person being interviewed then exercises the right of silence, any earlier answers given suggesting that he is responsible for the nuisance may not be used against him. **18.49**

The caution
Paragraph 10.4 of Code of Practice C states that the caution shall be in the following terms: **18.50**

---

[37] See paras 18.22–18.34.

You do not have to say anything. But it may harm your defence if you do not mention when questioned something which you later rely on in court. Anything you do say may be given in evidence.

Implications of silence

18.51 If the recipient of the notice is being interviewed and fails to mention the possibility of the defence of best practicable means at that stage, then the court may draw such inferences as appear to be proper from that failure if the defence is subsequently relied on.[38] However, it may be that at the time of the interview, it would not be reasonable to expect any defence of best practicable means to be offered, in which case, the court can draw no inferences from the silence. In order to obtain any benefit from this provision, interviewing officers will need to explain its implications fully to the person being interviewed. Again, the likelihood of misunderstanding will be reduced where an interviewee has a legal representative present.

Interview records

18.52 An accurate written record must be kept of interviews with persons suspected of committing an offence[39] or a tape recording may be made.[40]

Editing a witness statement

18.53 A witness statement may contain irrelevant, prejudicial or otherwise inadmissible evidence and so it may need to be edited. This will normally be done by the legal representative acting for the prosecution. The prosecutor is under a duty to put before the court only relevant, admissible evidence. He is under a positive duty, therefore, not to introduce irrelevant or prejudicial material and should consider whether to edit any statement he wishes to rely on in that light.

Use of witness statements in court

18.54 The general rule is that a witness statement may not be read out,[41] or referred to, by the witness while in the witness-box since it is unlikely to satisfy the rule that only documents produced contemporaneously can be used to refresh the memory.[42] The likelihood is that a witness statement will have been produced some time after the events which it recounts. There are limited exceptions to this in that a witness might be permitted by the court to look at his witness statement while giving evidence if he cannot recall the details because of lapse of time,[43] a

---

[38] Criminal Justice and Public Order Act 1994, s 34.
[39] Code of Practice C, para 11, made under the Police and Criminal Evidence Act 1984.
[40] Code of Practice E made under the Police and Criminal Evidence Act 1984.
[41] Unless this is agreed (such as under the Criminal Justice Act 1967, s 9).
[42] *A-G's Reference No 3 of 1979* (n 36 above).
[43] With the other side's permission, a witness can be led on facts which are not in dispute.

statement had been prepared reasonably close to the time of the events, he had not read the statement before entering the witness-box, and he wishes to look at the statement before continuing to give evidence.[44] However, a witness who relies on this exception may be subject to challenge during cross-examination that he is unable to recollect the events to which he is testifying at all. In the case of a professional witness such as an environmental health officer, this would be very unfavourable in respect of his credibility.

Advance disclosure

18.55 As soon as reasonably practicable after a plea of not guilty has been entered, the prosecution should disclose all relevant evidence to the accused. This includes evidence the prosecution intends to rely on at trial[45] as well as any evidence which undermines the prosecution case and which it does not wish to use, that is 'unused material'.[46]

18.56 Disclosure by prosecuting authorities of unused material had been problematic in the 1970s and early 1980s in cases involving misconduct by the police and incompetence by Home Office forensic experts. Evidence had been suppressed, which, had it come to light would have seriously undermined the prosecution case.[47] While cases of serious miscarriage of justice do not appear relevant to the circumstances of local authority prosecutions, nonetheless, the rules that have been devised to prevent abuses apply equally to them as they do to Crown Prosecution Service prosecutions.

Common law duties and the effects of the Criminal Procedure and Investigations Act 1996
18.57 The common law position in respect of unused material has been replaced entirely by provisions in the Criminal Procedure and Investigations Act 1996, which applies to investigations starting from 1 April 1997. However, common law principles intended to protect defendants against the abuse of power by the authorities continue to influence the general duty of disclosure. Moreover, the *Attorney-General's Guidelines*[48] provide additional safeguards to defendants, which go beyond the requirements of the 1996 Act, in order to ensure that public authorities conduct prosecutions fairly and act in accordance with the Human Rights Act 1998.

---

[44] *R v Da Silva* [1990] 1 WLR 31. But see also, *R v South Ribble Magistrates, ex p Cochrane* [1996] Cr App R 544.
[45] See *Attorney-General's Guidelines* (2000), para 43 ('Disclosure of Information in Criminal Proceedings'). [46] Criminal Procedure and Investigations Act 1996, s 3(1).
[47] See, eg, *R v Ward* [1993] 2 All ER 577 and *R v Keane* [1994] 1 WLR 746.
[48] n 45 above, para 4.

18.58 The essential difference between the common law position and that produced by the Criminal Procedure and Investigations Act 1996 is that before the Act, the scope of 'unused material' meant, in practical terms, that everything collected in an investigation was disclosable unless it was sensitive. This included all preparatory material needed for witnesses to make statements, working notes, and earlier versions of witness statements. The scale of such disclosure could reach absurd proportions, with defendants demanding to see every scrap of paper or every blurred photograph, and they were able to do so because it was up to the defendant to decide on materiality.

The prosecutor's duty

18.59 Under the Criminal Procedure and Investigations Act 1996 the prosecutor is charged with deciding what material should be disclosed. Under section 3(1) of this Act:

The prosecutor must—

(a) disclose to the accused any prosecution material which has not previously been disclosed to the accused and which in the prosecutor's opinion might undermine the case for the prosecution against the accused, or
(b) give to the accused a written statement that there is no material of (such) a description . . .

18.60 The prosecutor must exercise his discretion properly in selecting relevant material for disclosure that might undermine the prosecution case. If it can be shown that the discretion was improperly used, then the disclosure decisions would in appropriate circumstances be judicially reviewable.[49] Justices have no power to order disclosure of advance information.[50]

Civil proceedings

18.61 These rules of disclosure do not apply to civil proceedings.[51] Consequently, appeals against notices heard in the magistrates' court, or in the Crown Court following an appeal against the magistrates' decision, are not affected by the Criminal Procedure and Investigations Act 1996. It is to be deplored that there are no rules for disclosing evidence in appeals against abatement notices. It means that unless agreement can be reached by the parties then either party should be advised not to disclose any material prior to the hearing.[52]

---

[49] The difficulty of demonstrating an improper use of discretion and the placing of the duty of disclosure in the hands of the prosecutor renders the Criminal Procedure and Investigations Act 1996 inconsistent with the Human Rights Act 1998; see Chapter 11.
[50] *R v Dunmow Justices, ex p Nash* (1993) 157 JP 1153.
[51] The position is different in proceedings in the High Court and county courts where separate procedures apply, including disclosure provisions. [52] See paras 13.65–13.67.

Advance information of prosecution case

In magistrates' courts, for offences triable either way, the Magistrates' Courts (Advance Information) Rules 1985[53] apply. The prosecution must supply to the accused either a summary of the case or witness statements which it proposes to use in court. The usual practice is to supply witness statements. Any documents referred to in these statements should be exhibited. In summary only cases, such as statutory nuisance, although these 1985 Rules do not strictly apply, the usual practice is to adopt the same approach and serve statements on the accused. Indeed, the Attorney-General recommends disclosure of witness statements in all summary trials.[54]

18.62

Witness statements and copies of exhibits are often supplied earlier, around the time the informations are laid, as this may encourage the accused to take a considered view of the evidence and decide to plead guilty early on. In any event, evidence which the prosecution intends to rely on must be disclosed as soon as is reasonably practicable after a plea of not guilty is entered by the court.

18.63

Complainant's identity

The identity of a complainant should be revealed to the defendant well before advance disclosure, preferably soon after the time of the complaint. This is to prevent prejudice to the defendant that might arise from delay up to the time the case is heard.[55] Where there are good grounds to preserve confidentiality, this information can be delayed until the decision to prosecute is taken.

18.64

Examples of material for disclosure

It is essential for prosecutors to give serious consideration to their duty to disclose relevant material that might undermine the prosecution case. Under section 9 of the Criminal Procedure and Investigations Act 1996, this duty continues until acquittal or conviction. Examples of disclosure might include the following:

18.65

- expert reports; also the records of experiments and tests in respect of any issue in the case; such disclosure should be made whether or not the material supports the prosecution's case;
- knowledge in possession of the prosecutor of expert tests which supports the defendant's case;
- records of investigating officers of previous inspections to that forming the basis of present prosecution;
- officers' notebooks;
- internal reports of the facts concerning investigations, but not legal advice which attracts professional privilege;
- any written prosecution policy;

---

[53] SI 1985/601.   [54] *Attorney-General's Guidelines* (n 45 above), para 43.
[55] *Daventry DC v Olins* (1990) 154 JP 478.

- previous inconsistent statements of prosecution witnesses;
- statements of witnesses not relied upon; and
- any convictions or other facts impugning the credibility of a prosecution witness.

18.66 Other items may need to be disclosed and not everything in the above list may be relevant. Some items should be disclosed automatically, for example, any criminal convictions of prosecution witnesses. It would be extremely difficult to argue that such convictions did not undermine the prosecution's case since credibility issues would be unavoidable. Difficult issues remain under the Criminal Procedure and Investigations Act 1996. For example, should earlier versions of witness statements, or notes, of witnesses the prosecution is proposing to rely on be disclosed? Clearly, they should be disclosed if inconsistent with their final versions. But unless such earlier versions undermine the prosecution case, or could reasonably be interpreted to do so, then they need not be disclosed.

Procedure

18.67 The principles applying to the *Code of Practice for Crown Prosecutors* are relevant to local authority prosecutions. Police investigations include employing a disclosure officer to make decisions independently from investigating officers about what unused material should be disclosed to the accused. Separating these functions by setting up a 'Chinese wall' is especially important in local authority cases, as the prosecuting authority is the same body as the investigating authority.

18.68 The procedure to be adopted might include the following:

- on the basis of schedules prepared by the disclosure officer, the prosecutor has to decide what material should be disclosed to the defence;
- these schedules should include material which may be relevant to an investigation but which does not form part of the case against the accused; and
- the items in the schedule should be described clearly enough to enable the prosecutor to decide whether they should be disclosed.

18.69 Disclosure is effected by either giving a copy of the material to the accused or allowing him to inspect it. Where there is no material to disclose, the prosecutor should give the accused a written statement saying so.

Secondary disclosure

18.70 The prosecutor's judgment about primary disclosure, under section 3(1) of the Criminal Procedure and Investigations Act 1996 is subjective and not challengeable except by judicial review. Secondary disclosure must be considered by the prosecutor in a summary case after a defence statement has been provided under section 6.

The test for secondary disclosure under section 7 is any additional material 'which might be reasonably expected to assist the accused's defence as disclosed by the defence statement given under section 5 or 6'. This would be relevant where, for example, a defence of best practicable means has been raised. If there is no such material then a written statement should be served to this effect. The test for secondary disclosure is objective and subject to challenge under section 8 where the accused has reasonable grounds to believe that disclosure has not been satisfactory. **18.71**

Sensitive material
It is unlikely that a document which is relevant and material to a statutory nuisance prosecution would also be sensitive. Sensitive material would include material revealing the identity of undercover officers or paid informants, or material given in confidence. If sensitive material does arise then it should be itemized on a separate schedule from non-sensitive materials. If the prosecutor decides to resist disclosure, an application will need to be made to the court that disclosure is not in the public interest. **18.72**

Disclosure of expert evidence
For investigations commenced from 1 April 1997, both prosecution and defence are bound by the same rules for advance disclosure of expert evidence, namely the Magistrates' Courts (Advance Notice of Expert Evidence) Rules 1997, SI 1997/705. Note that the Rules are restricted to a criminal investigation and therefore do not apply to an appeal against an abatement notice. **18.73**

The position on advance disclosure of expert evidence is now the same in magistrates' courts as in the Crown Court. Disclosure applies to expert evidence of fact as well as opinion, and should take place as soon as reasonably practicable after a not guilty plea. Since the position of the parties is the same under the Rules, the prosecution as well as the defence are able to examine the results of any observations or tests forming the basis for the other parties' opinion. A party who fails to disclose expert evidence requires leave in order to adduce the expert evidence in court. **18.74**

Although the rules on disclosure of expert evidence are the same for both parties this does not apply to the whole duty of disclosure. Thus, if the defence decided not to rely on an expert's testimony—possibly because it supported the prosecution's case—then there is no duty to disclose it. This is because the duty under the 1997 Rules is for a party to disclose evidence which he proposes to adduce in court. However, the prosecution would be obliged to disclose an unfavourable expert report, which it chose not to rely on, because of its duty under section 3 of the Criminal Procedure and Investigations Act 1996 to disclose any material which undermines its case. **18.75**

18.76 However, if the defence did wish to rely on an expert whose conclusions were only partly favourable to his client, then the position is not clear cut. The Rules requires disclosure of 'any finding or opinion he proposes to adduce'. This seems to imply particular evidence rather than the opinion as a whole, including the unfavourable aspects.

18.77 The objection to the defence expert giving partial disclosure stems from the expert's duty to the court, which is to provide unbiased expert testimony not influenced by the exigencies of court proceedings. This duty overrides that to the expert's client. In principle, the expert's duty is the same whether the proceedings are criminal or civil. The defence expert who does not provide the full picture, including evidence unfavourable to his client, would appear to be misleading the court.

Admissibility of evidence and the court hearing

18.78 In various circumstances, issues about the admissibility of evidence during the court hearing may arise. This may relate, for example, to the admissibility of a business document or of photographs taken by the prosecution. The question of admissibility is a matter for the magistrates to decide. The difficulty inherent in this is that the magistrates are both judges of fact and of law. They will, therefore, become aware of the existence of potentially prejudicial material even though they may not know the exact content of it. The magistrates must either hold a short hearing at the outset, or, at the time the question arises to determine questions of admissibility, or, they may leave it to the end.[56] Where unfairness may result from leaving the decision to the end of the trial (given that the court will by then have heard the evidence) an earlier hearing (a *voir dire*) should be held to determine the question.

Fairness

18.79 There is an underlying principle of fairness in court proceedings and, in particular, section 78 of the Police and Criminal Evidence Act 1984 permits the court to refuse to allow any evidence obtained by the prosecution where, having regard to all the circumstances, its admission would have such an adverse effect on the fairness of the proceedings that it ought not to be allowed. This will also include circumstances pertaining to the manner in which the evidence has been obtained.[57] In other areas of environmental regulation, breach of section 78 may involve a failure to follow codes of practice passed under the relevant statute.[58] There are very few specific codes pertinent to the application of Part III of the EPA 1990. However, a failure by

---

[56] *Halawa v Federation Against Copyright Theft* (1995) 159 JP 816; *Vel v Chief Constable of North Wales* [1987] Crim LR 498.

[57] The Police and Criminal Evidence Act 1984, s 76, permits the exclusion of confessions which have been unfairly obtained, including by oppression, but this is rarely likely to apply to the investigation of statutory nuisances. [58] See, eg, the codes passed pursuant to the Food Safety Act 1990.

the prosecution to abide by the codes of practice authorized under the Police and Criminal Evidence Act 1984, may result in a defence application to have certain evidence declared inadmissible. This might include, for example, evidence obtained as a result of a search not carried out in accordance with Code B or a failure to caution under Code C.[59] The question for the court to determine would be whether the evidence was so obtained that it would have an adverse effect on the fairness of the proceedings.

Rebuttal evidence
In general, evidence of a defendant's previous convictions, warnings and bad character are not admissible. Previous abatement notices would also not be admissible unless they could be shown to relate to the same nuisance, in which case their relevance to the instant prosecution would have to be established. **18.80**

However, if a defendant asserts during the course of the trial that he is of good character, then if such evidence is believed to be untrue, the prosecution may use evidence in rebuttal. This may take the form of previous letters, warnings and notices. Such evidence, used in this way, will be very powerful for the prosecution since it will go to the credibility of the defendant. A defendant seeking to rely on a best practicable means defence must be advised of the risks of seeking to put misleading material before the court. **18.81**

As stated above, evidence of previous history or bad character may not be adduced by the prosecution as part of their evidence-in-chief. Such evidence may only be used in rebuttal. It is important, therefore, for the prosecution to ensure that office files are available in court should the need arise during cross-examination to produce evidence to counter any untrue allegations given in evidence by the defendant or the defendant's witnesses. Since the prosecution may not be aware of the full extent of any defence which is to be raised, prior to the hearing, it is unlikely that the use of this evidence can be anticipated precisely. **18.82**

Sentencing, mitigation and Newton *hearings*
The magistrates' court has sentencing powers as set out in Table 18.1 below. **18.83**

Factors which are relevant to the sentence include the culpability of the defendant, the seriousness of the nuisance and public health effects.[60] Culpability will **18.84**

---

[59] See, eg, *London Borough of Ealing Trading Standards v Woolworths plc* [1995] Crim LR 58.
[60] See, eg, *R v Milford Haven Port Authority* [2000] Env LR 632; *R v F Howe & Sons (Engineers) Ltd* [1999] 2 All ER 249; *National Rivers Authority v Shell* UK [1990] 1 Water Law 40; *R v Friskies Pet Care (UK) Ltd* [2000] 2 Cr App R (S) 401; and *R v O'Brian and Enkel* [2000] Env LR 653. (None of these cases deals with statutory nuisances. However, the principles are applicable in respect of all environmental regulatory cases.) See also the advice of the Sentencing Advisory Panel (set up under the Crime and Disorder Act 1998 to advise the Court of Appeal on sentencing) at http://www.sentencing-advisory-panel.gov.uk/advenv.htm; and M Davies, 'Sentencing for Environmental Offences' [2000] 2 Env LR 195.

Table 18.1 *Sentencing powers*

offence	maximum sentence
offence committed under EPA 1990, s 80(4) on industrial, trade or business premises	£20,000
offence committed under EPA 1990, s 80(4) other than on industrial, trade or business premises	£5,000 (level 5 on the standard scale); plus £500 for each day offence continues after conviction
abatement order issued under EPA 1990, s 82(2)	£5,000 (level 5 on the standard scale)
offence committed under EPA 1990, s 82(8)	£5,000 (level 5 on the standard scale); plus £500 for each day offence continues after conviction

include such factors as a deliberate and reckless breach of the law; a financial motive for the commission of the nuisance; failure to heed previous advice; knowledge of special risks; the attitude (such as obstruction of their duties) towards the local authority's environmental health officers.

18.85 Where a defendant has pleaded guilty or has been found guilty, a plea in mitigation may be made on his behalf. Mitigation can be put forward in respect of statutory nuisance offences on many bases and the court will take it into account in determining sentence. Such matters as the defendant's prompt reporting of an accident or escape and prompt clean-up, and his previous good record will be helpful to mitigation. A timely plea of guilty will also be a mitigating factor. However, where injury to health has been established, a plea in mitigation is less likely to achieve a reduction in the financial penalty. Where the offender is a public body, the court may view a severe financial penalty as not in the interests of the public if that would inhibit the proper performance of the public body's statutory duties.

18.86 The need to counter untrue statements made by the defence may also arise during mitigation. If during this plea, statements of fact are made, which the prosecution knows to be untrue, then the prosecution is entitled to dispute such assertions. Evidence will then be given on oath. The prosecution may call the environmental health officer or some other witness to give evidence. The defendant will also give evidence and both parties may be cross-examined. This type of hearing is known as a '*Newton* hearing',[61] and is appropriate where there is a serious discrepancy of facts relevant to sentencing.

---

[61] From *R v Newton* (1983) 77 Cr App R 13.

APPENDICES

CONTENTS

The legislation is reproduced as amended on 5 February 2002.

Appendix A: Environmental Protection Act 1990—Extracts	331
Part III—Statutory Nuisances and Clean Air	331
Section 79—Statutory nuisances and inspections therefor	331
Section 80—Summary proceedings for statutory nuisances	334
Section 80A—Abatement notice in respect of noise in the street	335
Section 81—Supplementary provisions	336
Section 81A—Expenses recoverable from owner to be a charge on premises	337
Section 81B—Payment of expenses by instalments	338
Section 82—Summary proceedings by persons aggrieved by statutory nuisances	339
Section 157—Offences by bodies corporate	341
Section 159—Application to Crown	341
Section 160—Service of notices	342
Schedule 3—Statutory Nuisances: Supplementary Provisions	343
Appendix B: Statutory Nuisance (Appeals) Regulations 1995, SI 1995/2644	347
Appendix C: Other Legislation	351
Police and Criminal Evidence Act 1984	351
Section 67—Codes of practice—supplementary	351
Section 69—Evidence from computer records	351
Section 76—Confessions	351
Section 78—Exclusion of unfair evidence	351
Code B—Seizure of Property	352
Code C—Treatment and Questioning of Persons	352
Clean Air Act 1993	355
Section 1—Dark Smoke—Prohibition of dark smoke from chimneys	355
Section 2—Prohibition of dark smoke from industrial or trade premises	356
Section 3—Meaning of "dark smoke"	357
Criminal Justice and Public Order Act 1994	357
Section 34—Effect of accused's failure to mention facts when questioned or charged	357
Noise Act 1996	358
Section 1—Adoption of these provisions by local authorities	358
Section 2—Investigation of complaints of noise from a dwelling at night	358

APPENDICES—CONTENTS

Section 3—Warning notices	359
Section 4—Offence where noise exceeds permitted level after service of notice	359
Section 5—Permitted level of noise	359
Section 8—Fixed penalty notices	360
Section 10—Powers of entry and seizure etc.	360
Schedule—Powers in Relation to Seized Equipment	362
Magistrates' Courts (Advance Notice of Expert Evidence) Rules 1997, SI 1997/705	364
Magistrates' Courts (Hearsay Evidence in Civil Proceedings) Rules 1999, SI 1999/681	365
Regulation of Investigatory Powers Act 2000—Part II	367
Section 26—Conduct to which Part II applies	367
Section 27—Lawful surveillance etc.	369
Section 28—Authorisation of directed surveillance	369
Section 29—Authorisation of covert human intelligence sources	370

APPENDIX A

Environmental Protection Act 1990—Extracts

Part III
Statutory Nuisances and Clean Air

Statutory Nuisances: England and Wales

Section 79—Statutory nuisances and inspections therefor

(1) [Subject to subsections (1A) to (6A) below,] the following matters constitute "statutory nuisances" for the purposes of this Part, that is to say—

- (a) any premises in such a state as to be prejudicial to health or a nuisance;
- (b) smoke emitted from premises so as to be prejudicial to health or a nuisance;
- (c) fumes or gases emitted from premises so as to be prejudicial to health or a nuisance;
- (d) any dust, steam, smell or other effluvia arising on industrial, trade or business premises and being prejudicial to health or a nuisance;
- (e) any accumulation or deposit which is prejudicial to health or a nuisance;
- (f) any animal kept in such a place or manner as to be prejudicial to health or a nuisance;
- (g) noise emitted from premises so as to be prejudicial to health or a nuisance;
- [(ga) noise that is prejudicial to health or a nuisance and is emitted from or caused by a vehicle, machinery or equipment in a street [or in Scotland, road];]
- (h) any other matter declared by any enactment to be a statutory nuisance;

and it shall be the duty of every local authority to cause its area to be inspected from time to time to detect any statutory nuisances which ought to be dealt with under section 80 [and section 80A] below and, where a complaint of a statutory nuisance is made to it by a person living within its area, to take such steps as are reasonably practicable to investigate the complaint.

[(1A) No matter shall constitute a statutory nuisance to the extent that it consists of, or is caused by, any land being in a contaminated state.

(1B) Land is in a "contaminated state" for the purposes of subsection (1A) above if, and only if, it is in such a condition, by reason of substances in, on or under the land, that—

- (a) harm is being caused by or there is a possibility of harm being caused; or
- (b) pollution of controlled waters is being, or is likely to be caused;

and in this subsection "harm", "pollution of controlled waters" and "substance" have the same meaning as in Part IIA of this Act.]

(2) Subsection (1)(b) and (g) above do not apply in relation to premises—

(a) occupied on behalf of the Crown for naval, military or air force purposes or for the purposes of the department of the Secretary of State having responsibility for defence, or

(b) occupied by or for the purposes of a visiting force;

and "visiting force" means any such body, contingent or detachment of the forces of any country as is a visiting force for the purposes of any of the provisions of the Visiting Forces Act 1952.

(3) Subsection (1)(b) above does not apply to—

(i) smoke emitted from a chimney of a private dwelling within a smoke control area,

(ii) dark smoke emitted from a chimney of a building or a chimney serving the furnace of a boiler or industrial plant attached to a building or for the time being fixed to or installed on any land,

(iii) smoke emitted from a railway locomotive steam engine, or

(iv) dark smoke emitted otherwise than as mentioned above from industrial or trade premises.

(4) Subsection (1)(c) above does not apply in relation to premises other than private dwellings.

(5) Subsection (1)(d) above does not apply in relation to steam emitted from a railway locomotive engine.

(6) Subsection (1)(g) above does not apply to noise caused by aircraft other than model aircraft.

[(6A) Subsection (1)(ga) above does not apply to noise made—

(a) by traffic,

(b) by any naval, military or air force of the Crown or by a visiting force (as defined in subsection (2) above), or

(c) by a political demonstration or a demonstration supporting or opposing a cause or campaign.]

(7) In this Part—

"chimney" includes structures and openings of any kind from or through which smoke may be emitted;

"dust" does not include dust emitted from a chimney as an ingredient of smoke;

["equipment" includes a musical instrument;]

"fumes" means any airborne solid matter smaller than dust;

"gas" includes vapour and moisture precipitated from vapour;

"industrial, trade or business premises" means premises used for any industrial, trade or business purposes or premises not so used on which matter is burnt in connection with any industrial, trade or business process, and premises are used for industrial purposes where they are used for the purposes of any treatment or process as well as where they are used for the purposes of manufacturing;

"local authority" means, subject to subsection (8) below,—

(a) in Greater London, a London borough council, the Common Council of the City of London and, as respects the Temples, the Sub-Treasurer of the Inner Temple and the Under-Treasurer of the Middle Temple respectively;

(b) [in England] outside Greater London, a district council;
[(bb) in Wales, a county council or county borough council;]
(c) the Council of the Isles of Scilly; [and
(d) in Scotland, a district or islands council constituted under section 2 of the Local Government etc (Scotland) Act 1994;]

"noise" includes vibration;
["person responsible"—
  (a) in relation to a statutory nuisance, means the person to whose act, default or sufferance the nuisance is attributable;
  (b) in relation to a vehicle, includes the person in whose name the vehicle is for the time being registered under [the Vehicle Excise and Registration Act 1994] and any other person who is for the time being the driver of the vehicle;
  (c) in relation to machinery or equipment, includes any person who is for the time being the operator of the machinery or equipment;]

"prejudicial to health" means injurious, or likely to cause injury, to health;
"premises" includes land and, subject to subsection (12) [and, in relation to England and Wales section 81A(9)] below, any vessel;
"private dwelling" means any building, or part of a building, used or intended to be used, as a dwelling;
["road" has the same meaning as in Part IV of the New Roads and Street Works Act 1991;]
"smoke" includes soot, ash, grit and gritty particles emitted in smoke;
["street" means a highway and any other road, footway, square or court that is for the time being open to the public;]
and any expressions used in this section and in the [Clean Air Act 1993] have the same meaning in this section as in that Act and [section 3 of the Clean Air Act 1993] shall apply for the interpretation of the expression "dark smoke" and the operation of this Part in relation to it.

(8) Where, by an order under section 2 of the Public Health (Control of Disease) Act 1984, a port health authority has been constituted for any port health district [or in Scotland where by an order under section 172 of the Public Health (Scotland) Act 1897 a port health authority or a joint port health authority has been constituted for the whole or part of a port], the port health authority ... shall have by virtue of this subsection, as respects its district, the functions conferred or imposed by this Part in relation to statutory nuisances other than a nuisance falling within paragraph (g) [or (ga)] of subsection (1) above and no such order shall be made assigning those functions; and "local authority" and "area" shall be construed accordingly.

(9) In this Part "best practicable means" is to be interpreted by reference to the following provisions—
  (a) "practicable" means reasonably practicable having regard among other things to local conditions and circumstances, to the current state of technical knowledge and to the financial implications;
  (b) the means to be employed include the design, installation, maintenance and manner and periods of operation of plant and machinery, and the design, construction and maintenance if buildings and structures;
  (c) the test is to apply only so far as compatible with any duty imposed by law;

(d) the test is to apply only so far as compatible with safety and safe working conditions, and with the exigencies of any emergency or unforeseeable circumstances;

and, in circumstances where a code of practice under section 71 of the Control of Pollution 1974 (noise minimisation) is applicable, regard shall also be had to guidance given in it.

(10) A local authority shall not without the consent of the Secretary of State institute summary proceedings under this Part in respect of a nuisance falling within paragraph (b), (d), (e) or (g) [and, in relation to Scotland, paragraph (ga),] of subsection (1) above if proceedings in respect thereof might be instituted under Part I [or under regulations under section 2 of the Pollution Prevention and Control Act 1999.]

(11) The area of a local authority which includes part of the seashore shall also include for the purposes of this Part the territorial sea lying seawards from that part of the shore; and subject to subsection (12) [and, in relation to England and Wales, section 81A] below, this Part shall have effect, in relation to any area included in the area of a local authority by virtue of this subsection—

(a) as if references to premises and the occupier of premises included respectively a vessel and the master of a vessel; and
(b) with such other modifications, if any, as are prescribed in regulations made by the Secretary of State.

(12) A vessel powered by steam reciprocating machinery is not a vessel to which this Part of this Act applies.

Section 80—Summary proceedings for statutory nuisances

(1) Where a local authority is satisfied that a statutory nuisance exists, or is likely to occur or recur, in the area of the authority, the local authority shall serve a notice ("an abatement notice") imposing all or any of the following requirements—

(a) requiring the abatement of the nuisance or prohibiting or restricting its occurrence or recurrence;
(b) requiring the execution of such works, and the taking of such other steps, as may be necessary for any of those purposes,

and the notice shall specify the time or times within which the requirements of the notice are to be complied with.

(2) [Subject to section 80A(1) below, the] abatement notice shall be served—

(a) except in a case falling within paragraph (b) or (c) below, on the person responsible for the nuisance;
(b) where the nuisance arises from any defect of a structural character, on the owner of the premises;
(c) where the person responsible for the nuisance cannot be found or the nuisance has not yet occurred, on the owner or occupier of the premises.

(3) [A person served with an abatement notice] may appeal against the notice to a magistrates' court [or in Scotland, the sheriff] within the period of twenty-one days beginning with the date on which he was served with the notice.

(4) If a person on whom an abatement notice is served, without reasonable excuse, contravenes or fails to comply with any requirement or prohibition imposed by the notice, he shall be guilty of an offence.

A: ENVIRONMENTAL PROTECTION ACT 1990—EXTRACTS

(5) Except in a case falling within subsection (6) below, a person who commits an offence under subsection (4) above shall be liable on summary conviction to a fine not exceeding level 5 on the standard scale together with a further fine of an amount equal to one-tenth of that level for each day on which the offence continues after the conviction.

(6) A person who commits an offence under subsection (4) above on industrial, trade or business premises shall be liable on summary conviction to a fine not exceeding £20,000.

(7) Subject to subsection (8) below, in any proceedings for an offence under subsection (4) above in respect of a statutory nuisance it shall be a defence to prove that the best practicable means were used to prevent, or to counteract the effects of, the nuisance.

(8) The defence under subsection (7) above is not available—

   (a)   in the case of a nuisance falling within paragraph (a), (d), (e), (f) or (g) of section 79(1) above except where the nuisance arises on industrial, trade or business premises;

   [(aa) in the case of a nuisance falling within paragraph (ga) of section 79(1) above except where the noise is emitted from or caused by a vehicle, machinery or equipment being used for industrial, trade or business purposes;]

   (b)   in the case of a nuisance falling within paragraph (b) of section 79(1) above except where the smoke is emitted from a chimney; and

   (c)   in the case of a nuisance falling within paragraph (c) or (h) of section 79(1) above.

(9) In proceedings for an offence under subsection (4) above in respect of a statutory nuisance falling within paragraph (g) [or (ga)] of section 79(1) above where the offence consists in contravening requirements imposed by virtue of subsection (1)(a) above it shall be a defence to prove—

   (a)   that the alleged offence was covered by a notice served under section 60 or a consent given under section 61 or 65 of the Control of Pollution Act 1974 (construction sites, etc.); or

   (b)   where the alleged offence was committed at a time when the premises were subject to a notice under section 66 of that Act (noise reduction notice), that the level of noise emitted from the premises at that time was not such as to a constitute a contravention of the notice under that section; or

   (c)   where the alleged offence was committed at a time when the premises were not subject to a notice under section 66 of that Act, and when a level fixed under section 67 of that Act (new buildings liable to abatement order) applied to the premises, that the level of noise emitted from the premises at that time did not exceed that level.

(10) Paragraphs (b) and (c) of subsection (9) above apply whether or not the relevant notice was subject to appeal at the time when the offence was alleged to have been committed.

Section 80A—Abatement notice in respect of noise in the street

[(1) In the case of a statutory nuisance within section 79(1)(ga) above that—

   (a)   has not yet occurred, or

   (b)   arises from noise emitted from or caused by an unattended vehicle or unattended machinery or equipment,

the abatement notice shall be served in accordance with subsection (2) below.

(2) The notice shall be served—

(a) where the person responsible for the vehicle, machinery or equipment can be found, on that person;

(b) where that person cannot be found or where the local authority determines that this paragraph should apply, by fixing the notice to the vehicle, machinery or equipment.

(3) Where—

(a) an abatement notice is served in accordance with subsection (2)(b) above by virtue of a determination of the local authority, and

(b) the person responsible for the vehicle, machinery or equipment can be found and served with a copy of the notice within an hour of the notice being fixed to the vehicle, machinery or equipment,

a copy of the notice shall be served on that person accordingly.

(4) Where an abatement notice is served in accordance with subsection (2)(b) above by virtue of a determination of the local authority, the notice shall state that, if a copy of the notice is subsequently served under subsection (3) above, the time specified in the notice as the time within which its requirements are to be complied with is extended by such further period as is specified in the notice.

(5) Where an abatement notice is served in accordance with subsection (2)(b) above, the person responsible for the vehicle, machinery or equipment may appeal against the notice under section 80(3) above as if he had been served with the notice on the date on which it was fixed to the vehicle, machinery or equipment.

(6) Section 80(4) above shall apply in relation to a person on whom a copy of an abatement notice is served under subsection (3) above as if the copy were the notice itself.

(7) A person who removes or interferes with a notice fixed to a vehicle, machinery or equipment in accordance with subsection (2)(b) above shall be guilty of an offence, unless he is the person responsible for the vehicle, machinery or equipment or he does so with the authority of that person.

(8) A person who commits an offence under subsection (7) above shall be liable on summary conviction to a fine not exceeding level 3 on the standard scale.]

Section 81—Supplementary provisions

(1) [Subject to subsection (1A) below, where] more than one person is responsible for a statutory nuisance section 80 above shall apply to each of those persons whether or not what any one of them is responsible for would by itself amount to a nuisance.

[(1A) In relation to a statutory nuisance within section 79(1)(ga) above for which more than one person is responsible (whether or not what any one of those persons is responsible for would by itself amount to such a nuisance), section 80(2)(a) above shall apply with the substitution of "any one of the persons" for "the person".

(1B) In relation to a statutory nuisance within section 79(1)(ga) above caused by noise emitted from or caused by an unattended vehicle or unattended machinery or equipment for which more than one person is responsible, section 80A above shall apply with the substitution—

(a) in subsection (2)(a), of "any of the persons" for "the person" and of "one such person" for "that person",
(b) in subsection (2)(b), of "such a person" for "that person",
(c) in subsection (3), of "any of the persons" for "the person" and of "one such person" for "that person",
(d) in subsection (5), of "any person" for "the person", and
(e) in subsection (7), of "a person" for "the person" and of "such a person" for "that person".]

(2) Where a statutory nuisance which exists or has occurred within the area of a local authority, or which has affected any part of that area, appears to the local authority to be wholly or partly caused by some act or default committed or taking place outside the area, the local authority may act under section 80 above as if the act or default were wholly within that area, except that any appeal shall be heard by a magistrates' court [or in Scotland, the sheriff] having jurisdiction where the act or default is alleged to have taken place.

(3) Where an abatement notice has not been complied with the local authority may, whether or not they take proceedings for an offence [or, in Scotland, whether or not proceedings have been taken for an offence,] under section 80(4) above, abate the nuisance and do whatever may be necessary in execution of the notice.

(4) Any expenses reasonably incurred by a local authority in abating, or preventing the recurrence of, a statutory nuisance under subsection (3) above may be recovered by them from the person by whose act or default the nuisance was caused and, if that person is the owner of the premises, from any person who is for the time being the owner thereof; and the court [or sheriff] may apportion the expenses between persons by whose acts or defaults the nuisance is caused in such manner as the court consider [or sheriff considers] fair and reasonable.

(5) If a local authority is of opinion that proceedings for an offence under section 80(4) above would afford an inadequate remedy in the case of any statutory nuisance, they may, subject to subsection (6) below, take proceedings in the High Court [or, in Scotland, in any court of competent jurisdiction] for the purpose of securing the abatement, prohibition or restriction of the nuisance, and the proceedings shall be maintainable notwithstanding the local authority have suffered no damage from the nuisance.

(6) In any proceedings under subsection (5) above in respect of a nuisance falling within paragraph (g) [or (ga)] of section 79(1) above, it shall be a defence to prove that the noise was authorised by a notice under section 60 or a consent under section 61 (construction sites) of the Control of Pollution Act 1974.

(7) The further supplementary provisions in Schedule 3 to this Act shall have effect.

Section 81A—Expenses recoverable from owner to be a charge on premises

[(1) Where any expenses are recoverable under section 81(4) above from a person who is the owner of the premises there mentioned and the local authority serves a notice on him under this section—

(a) the expenses shall carry interest, at such reasonable rate as the local authority may determine, from the date of service of the notice until the whole amount is paid, and

(b) subject to the following provisions of this section, the expenses and accrued interest shall be a charge on the premises.

(2) A notice served under this section shall—
   (a) specify the amount of the expenses that the local authority claims is recoverable,
   (b) state the effect of subsection (1) above and the rate of interest determined by the local authority under that subsection, and
   (c) state the effect of subsections (4) to (6) below.

(3) On the date on which a local authority serves a notice on a person under this section the authority shall also serve a copy of the notice on every other person who, to the knowledge of the authority, has an interest in the premises capable of being affected by the charge.

(4) Subject to any order under subsection (7)(b) or (c) below, the amount of any expenses specified in a notice under this section and the accrued interest shall be a charge on the premises—
   (a) as from the end of the period of twenty-one days beginning with the date of service of the notice, or
   (b) where an appeal is brought under subsection (6) below, as from the final determination of the appeal,

until the expenses and interest are recovered.

(5) For the purposes of subsection (4) above, the withdrawal of an appeal has the same effect as a final determination of the appeal.

(6) A person served with a notice or copy of a notice under this section may appeal against the notice to the county court within the period of twenty-one days beginning with the date of service.

(7) On such an appeal the court may—
   (a) confirm the notice without modification,
   (b) order that the notice is to have effect with the substitution of a different amount for the amount originally specified in it, or
   (c) order that the notice is to be of no effect.

(8) A local authority shall, for the purpose of enforcing a charge under this section, have all the same powers and remedies under the Law of Property Act 1925, and otherwise, as if it were a mortgagee by deed having powers of sale and lease, of accepting surrenders of leases and of appointing a receiver.

(9) In this section—

"owner", in relation to any premises, means a person (other than a mortgagee not in possession) who, whether in his own right or as trustee for any other person, is entitled to receive the rack rent of the premises or, where the premises are not let at a rack rent, would be so entitled if they were so let, and

"premises" does not include a vessel.

(10) This section does not apply to Scotland.]

Section 81B—Payment of expenses by instalments

[(1) Where any expenses are a charge on premises under section 81A above, the local authority may by order declare the expenses to be payable with interest by instalments within the specified period, until the whole amount is paid.

(2) In subsection (1) above—

"interest" means interest at the rate determined by the authority under section 81A(1) above, and

"the specified period" means such period of thirty years or less from the date of service of the notice under section 81A above as is specified in the order.

(3) Subject to subsection (5) below, the instalments and interest, or any part of them, may be recovered from the owner or occupier for the time being of the premises.

(4) Any sums recovered from an occupier may be deducted by him from the rent of the premises.

(5) An occupier shall not be required to pay at any one time any sum greater than the aggregate of—

    (a) the amount that was due from him on account of rent at the date on which he was served with a demand from the local authority together with a notice requiring him not to pay rent to his landlord without deducting the sum demanded, and

    (b) the amount that has become due from him on account of rent since that date.

(6) This section does not apply to Scotland.]

Section 82—Summary proceedings by persons aggrieved by statutory nuisances

(1) A magistrates' court may act under this section on a complaint [or, in Scotland, the sheriff may act under this section on a summary application,] made by any person on the ground that he is aggrieved by the existence of a statutory nuisance.

(2) If the magistrates' court [or, in Scotland, the sheriff] is satisfied that the alleged nuisance exists, or that although abated it is likely to recur on the same premises [or, in the case of a nuisance within section 79(1)(ga) above, in the street] [or, in Scotland, road], the court [or the sheriff] shall make an order for either or both of the following purposes—

    (a) requiring the defendant [or, in Scotland, defender] to abate the nuisance, within a time specified in the order, and to execute any works necessary for that purpose;

    (b) prohibiting a recurrence of the nuisance, and requiring the defendant [or defender], within a time specified in the order, to execute any works necessary to prevent the recurrence;

and [, in England and Wales] may also impose on the defendant a fine not exceeding level 5 on the standard scale.

(3) If the magistrates' court [or the sheriff] is satisfied that the alleged nuisance exists and is such as, in the opinion of the court [or of the sheriff], to render premises unfit for human habitation, an order under subsection (2) above may prohibit the use of the premises for human habitation until the premises are, to the satisfaction of the court [or of the sheriff], rendered fit for that purpose.

(4) Proceedings for an order under subsection (2) above shall be brought—

    (a) except in a case falling within paragraph (b), (c) [or (d)] below, against the person responsible for the nuisance;

    (b) where the nuisance arises from any defect of a structural character, against the owner of the premises;

(c) where the person responsible for the nuisance cannot be found, against the owner or occupier of the premises;

[(d) in the case of a statutory nuisance within section 79(1)(ga) above caused by noise emitted from or caused by an unattended vehicle or unattended machinery or equipment, against the person responsible for the vehicle, machinery or equipment.]

(5) [Subject to subsection (5A) below, where] more than one person is responsible for a statutory nuisance, subsections (1) to (4) above shall apply to each of those persons whether or not what any one of them is responsible for would by itself amount to a nuisance.

[(5A) In relation to a statutory nuisance within section 79(1)(ga) above for which more than one person is responsible (whether or not what any one of those persons is responsible for would by itself amount to such a nuisance), subsection (4)(a) above shall apply with the substitution of "each person responsible for the nuisance who can be found" for "the person responsible for the nuisance".

(5B) In relation to a statutory nuisance within section 79(1)(ga) above caused by noise emitted from or caused by an unattended vehicle or unattended machinery or equipment for which more than one person is responsible, subsection (4)(d) above shall apply with the substitution of "any person" for "the person".]

(6) Before instituting proceedings for an order under subsection (2) above against any person, the person aggrieved by the nuisance shall give to that person such notice in writing of his intention to bring the proceedings as is applicable to proceedings in respect of a nuisance of that description and the notice shall specify the matter complained of.

(7) The notice of the bringing of proceedings in respect of a statutory nuisance required by subsection (6) above which is applicable is—

(a) in the case of a nuisance falling within paragraph (g) [or (ga)] of section 79(1) above, not less than three days' notice; and

(b) in the case of a nuisance of any other description, not less than twenty-one days' notice;

but the Secretary of State may, by order, provide that this subsection shall have effect as if such period as is specified in the order were the minimum period of notice applicable to any description of statutory nuisance specified in the order.

(8) A person who, without reasonable excuse, contravenes any requirement or prohibition imposed by an order under subsection (2) above shall be guilty of an offence and liable on summary conviction to a fine not exceeding level 5 on the standard scale together with a further fine of an amount equal to one-tenth of that level for each day on which the offence continues after the conviction.

(9) Subject to subsection (10) below, in any proceedings for an offence under subsection (8) above in respect of a statutory nuisance it shall be a defence to prove that the best practicable means were used to prevent, or to counteract the effects of, the nuisance.

(10) The defence under subsection (9) above is not available—

(a) in the case of a nuisance falling within paragraph (a), (d), (e), (f) or (g) of section 79(1) above except where the nuisance arises on industrial, trade or business premises;

A: ENVIRONMENTAL PROTECTION ACT 1990—EXTRACTS

- [(aa) in the case of a nuisance falling within paragraph (ga) of section 79(1) above except where the noise is emitted from or caused by a vehicle, machinery or equipment being used for industrial, trade or business purposes;]
- (b) in the case of a nuisance falling within paragraph (b) of section 79(1) above except where the smoke is emitted from a chimney;
- (c) in the case of a nuisance falling within paragraph (c) or (h) of section 79(1) above; and
- (d) in the case of a nuisance which is such as to render the premises unfit for human habitation.

(11) If a person is convicted of an offence under subsection (8) above, a magistrates' court [or the sheriff] may, after giving the local authority in whose area the nuisance has occurred an opportunity of being heard, direct the authority to do anything which the person convicted was required to do by the order to which the conviction relates.

(12) Where on the hearing of proceedings for an order under subsection (2) above it is proved that the alleged nuisance existed at the date of the making of the complaint [or summary application], then, whether or not at the date of the hearing it still exists or is likely to recur, the court [or the sheriff] shall order the [defendant or defender (or defendants or defenders) in such proportions as appears fair and reasonable] to pay to the person bringing the proceedings such amount as the court [or the sheriff] considers reasonably sufficient to compensate him for any expenses properly incurred by him in the proceedings.

(13) If it appears to the magistrates' court [or to the sheriff] that neither the person responsible for the nuisance nor the owner or occupier of the premises [or (as the case may be) the person responsible for the vehicle, machinery or equipment] can be found the court [or the sheriff] may, after giving the local authority in whose area the nuisance has occurred an opportunity of being heard, direct the authority to do anything which the court [or the sheriff] would have ordered that person to do.

Section 157—Offences by bodies corporate

(1) Where an offence under any provision of this Act committed by a body corporate is proved to have been committed with the consent or connivance of, or to have been attributable to any neglect on the part of, any director, manager, secretary or other similar officer of the body corporate or a person who was purporting to act in any such capacity, he as well as the body corporate shall be guilty of that offence and shall be liable to be proceeded against and punished accordingly.

(2) Where the affairs of a body corporate are managed by its members, subsection (1) above shall apply in relation to the acts or defaults of a member in connection with his functions of management as if he were a director of the body corporate.

Section 159—Application to Crown

(1) Subject to the provisions of this section, the provisions of this Act and of regulations and orders made under it shall bind the Crown.

(2) No contravention by the Crown of any provision of this Act or of any regulations or order made under it shall make the Crown criminally liable; but the High Court or, in

Scotland, the Court of Session may, on the application of any public or local authority charged with enforcing that provision, declare unlawful any act or omission of the Crown which constitutes such a contravention.

(3) Notwithstanding anything in subsection (2) above, the provisions of this Act and of regulations and orders made under it shall apply to persons in the public service of the Crown as they apply to other persons.

(4) If the Secretary of State certifies that it appears to him, as respects any Crown premises and any powers of entry exercisable in relation to them specified in the certificate that it is requisite or expedient that, in the interests of national security, the powers should not be exercisable in relation to the premises, those powers shall not be exercisable in relation to those premises; and in this subsection "Crown premises" means premises held or used by or on behalf of the Crown.

(5) Nothing in this section shall be taken as in any way affecting Her Majesty in her private capacity; and this subsection shall be construed as if section 38(3) of the Crown Proceedings Act 1947 (interpretation of references in that Act to Her Majesty in her private capacity) were contained in this Act.

(6) References in this section to regulations or orders are references to regulations or orders made by statutory instrument.

Section 160—Service of notices

(1) Any notice required or authorised by or under this Act to be served on or given to an inspector may be served or given by delivering it to him or by leaving it at, or sending it by post to, his office.

(2) Any such notice required or authorised to be served on or given to a person other than an inspector may be served or given by delivering it to him, or by leaving it at his proper address, or by sending it by post to him at that address.

(3) Any such notice may—
- (a) in the case of a body corporate, be served on or given to the secretary or clerk of that body;
- (b) in the case of a partnership, be served on or given to a partner or a person having the control or management of the partnership business.

(4) For the purposes of this section and of section 7 of the Interpretation Act 1978 (service of documents by post) in its application to this section, the proper address of any person on or to whom any such notice is to be served or given shall be his last known address, except that—
- (a) in the case of a body corporate or their secretary or clerk, it shall be the address of the registered or principal office of that body;
- (b) in the case of a partnership or person having the control or the management of the partnership business, it shall be the principal office of the partnership;

and for the purposes of this subsection the principal office of a company registered outside the United Kingdom or of a partnership carrying on business outside the United Kingdom shall be their principal office within the United Kingdom.

(5) If the person to be served with or given any such notice has specified an address in the United Kingdom other than his proper address within the meaning of subsection (4) above as the one at which he or someone on his behalf will accept notices of the same description as that notice, that address shall also be treated for the purposes of this section and section 7 of the Interpretation Act 1978 as his proper address.

(6) The preceding provisions of this section shall apply to the sending or giving of a document as they apply to the giving of a notice.

SCHEDULE 3

Section 81

Statutory Nuisances: Supplementary Provisions

Appeals to magistrates' court

1.—(1) This paragraph applies in relation to appeals under section 80(3) against an abatement notice to a magistrates' court.

(2) An appeal to which this paragraph applies shall be by way of complaint for an order and the Magistrates' Courts Act 1980 shall apply to the proceedings.

(3) An appeal against any decision of a magistrates' court in pursuance of an appeal to which this paragraph applies shall lie to the Crown Court at the instance of any party to the proceedings in which the decision was given.

(4) The Secretary of State may make regulations as to appeals to which this paragraph applies and the regulations may in particular—

   (a) include provisions comparable to those in section 290 of the Public Health Act 1936 (appeals against notices requiring the execution of works);
   (b) prescribe the cases in which an abatement notice is, or is not, to be suspended until the appeal is decided, or until some other stage in the proceedings;
   (c) prescribe the cases in which the decision on appeal may in some respects be less favourable to the appellant than the decision from which he is appealing;
   (d) prescribe the cases in which the appellant may claim that an abatement notice should have been served on some other person and prescribe the procedure to be followed in those cases.

Powers of entry etc

2.—(1) Subject to sub-paragraph (2) below, any person authorised by a local authority may, on production (if so required) of his authority, enter any premises at any reasonable time—

   (a) for the purpose of ascertaining whether or not a statutory nuisance exists; or
   (b) for the purpose of taking any action, or executing any work, authorised or required by Part III.

(2) Admission by virtue of sub-paragraph (1) above to any premises used wholly or mainly for residential purposes shall not except in an emergency be demanded as of right unless twenty-four hours notice of the intended entry has been given to the occupier.

(3) If it is shown to the satisfaction of a justice of the peace on sworn information in writing—

(a) that admission to any premises has been refused, or that refusal is apprehended, or that the premises are unoccupied or the occupier is temporarily absent, or that the case is one of emergency, or that an application for admission would defeat the object of the entry; and

(b) that there is reasonable ground for entry into the premises for the purpose for which entry is required,

the justice may by warrant under his hand authorise the local authority by any authorised person to enter the premises, if need be by force.

(4) An authorised person entering any premises by virtue of sub-paragraph (1) or a warrant under sub-paragraph (3) above may—

(a) take with him such other persons and such equipment as may be necessary;

(b) carry out such inspections, measurements and tests as he considers necessary for the discharge of any of the local authority's functions under Part III; and

(c) take away such samples or articles as he considers necessary for that purpose.

(5) On leaving any unoccupied premises which he has entered by virtue of sub-paragraph (1) above or a warrant under sub-paragraph (3) above the authorised person shall leave them as effectually secured against trespassers as he found them.

(6) A warrant issued in pursuance of sub-paragraph (3) above shall continue in force until the purpose for which the entry is required has been satisfied.

(7) Any reference in this paragraph to an emergency is a reference to a case where the person requiring entry has reasonable cause to believe that circumstances exist which are likely to endanger life or health and that immediate entry is necessary to verify the existence of those circumstances or to ascertain their cause and to effect a remedy.

[(8) In the application of this paragraph to Scotland, a reference to a justice of the peace or to a justice includes a reference to the sheriff.]

[**2A.**—(1) Any person authorised by a local authority may on production (if so required) of his authority—

(a) enter or open a vehicle, machinery or equipment, if necessary by force, or

(b) remove a vehicle, machinery or equipment from a street [or, in Scotland, road] to a secure place,

for the purpose of taking any action, or executing any work, authorised by or required under Part III in relation to a statutory nuisance within section 79(1)(ga) above caused by noise emitted from or caused by the vehicle, machinery or equipment.

(2) On leaving any unattended vehicle, machinery or equipment that he has entered or opened under sub-paragraph (1) above, the authorised person shall (subject to sub-paragraph (3) below) leave it secured against interference or theft in such manner and as effectually as he found it.

(3) If the authorised person is unable to comply with sub-paragraph (2) above, he shall for the purpose of securing the unattended vehicle, machinery or equipment either—

(a) immobilise it by such means as he considers expedient, or

(b) remove it from the street to a secure place.

(4) In carrying out any function under sub-paragraph (1), (2) or (3) above, the authorised person shall not cause more damage than is necessary.

(5) Before a vehicle, machinery or equipment is entered, opened or removed under sub-paragraph (1) above, the local authority shall notify the police of the intention to take action under that sub-paragraph.

(6) After a vehicle, machinery or equipment has been removed under sub-paragraph (1) or (3) above, the local authority shall notify the police of its removal and current location.

(7) Notification under sub-paragraph (5) or (6) above may be given to the police at any police station in the local authority's area or, in the case of the Temples, at any police station of the City of London Police.

(8) For the purposes of section 81(4) above, any expenses reasonably incurred by a local authority under sub-paragraph (2) or (3) above shall be treated as incurred by the authority under section 81(3) above in abating or preventing the recurrence of the statutory nuisance in question.]

Offences relating to entry

3.—(1) A person who wilfully obstructs any person acting in the exercise of any powers conferred by paragraph 2 [or 2A] above shall be liable, on summary conviction, to a fine not exceeding level 3 on the standard scale.

(2) If a person discloses any information relating to any trade secret obtained in the exercise of any powers conferred by paragraph 2 above he shall, unless the disclosure was made in the performance of his duty or with the consent of the person having the right to disclose the information, be liable, on summary conviction, to a fine not exceeding level 5 on the standard scale.

Default powers

4.—(1) This paragraph applies to the following function of a local authority, that is to say its duty under section 79 to cause its area to be inspected to detect any statutory nuisance which ought to be dealt with under section 80 [and section 80A] and its powers under paragraph 2 [or 2A] above.

(2) If the Secretary of State is satisfied that any local authority has failed, in any respect, to discharge the function to which this paragraph applies which it ought to have discharged, he may make an order declaring the authority to be in default.

(3) An order made under sub-paragraph (2) above which declares an authority to be in default may, for the purpose of remedying the default, direct the authority ("the defaulting authority") to perform the function specified in the order and may specify the manner in which and the time or times within which the function is to be performed by the authority.

(4) If the defaulting authority fails to comply with any direction contained in such an order the Secretary of State may, instead of enforcing the order by mandamus, make an order transferring to himself the function of the authority specified in the order.

(5) Where the function of a defaulting authority is transferred under sub-paragraph (4) above, the amount of any expenses which the Secretary of State certifies were incurred by him in performing the function shall on demand be paid to him by the defaulting authority.

(6) Any expenses required to be paid by a defaulting authority under sub-paragraph (5) above shall be defrayed by the authority in like manner, and shall be debited to the like account, as if the function had not been transferred and the expenses had been incurred by the authority in performing them.

(7) The Secretary of State may by order vary or revoke any order previously made by him under this paragraph.

(8) Any order under this paragraph may include such incidental, supplemental and transitional provisions as the Secretary of State considers appropriate.

[(9) This paragraph does not apply to Scotland.]

Protection from personal liability

5. Nothing done by, or by a member of, a local authority or by any officer of or other person authorised by a local authority shall, if done in good faith for the purpose of executing Part III, subject them or any of them personally to any action, liability, claim or demand whatsoever (other than any liability under section 17 or 18 of the Audit Commission Act [1998] (powers of district auditor and court)).

Statement of right of appeal in notices

6. Where an appeal against a notice served by a local authority lies to a magistrates' court [or, in Scotland, the sheriff] by virtue of section 80, it shall be the duty of the authority to include in such a notice a statement indicating that such an appeal lies as aforesaid and specifying the time within which it must be brought.

APPENDIX B

Statutory Nuisance (Appeals) Regulations 1995, SI 1995/2644

1. Citation, commencement and interpretation

(1) These Regulations may be cited as the Statutory Nuisance (Appeals) Regulations 1995 and shall come into force on 8th November 1995.

(2) In these Regulations—

"the 1974 Act" means the Control of Pollution Act 1974;
"the 1990 Act" means the Environmental Protection Act 1990; and
"the 1993 Act" means the Noise and Statutory Nuisance Act 1993.

2. Appeals under section 80(3) of the 1990 Act

(1) The provisions of this regulation apply in relation to an appeal brought by any person under section 80(3) of the 1990 Act (appeals to magistrates) against an abatement notice served upon him by a local authority.

(2) The grounds on which a person served with such a notice may appeal under section 80(3) are any one or more of the following grounds that are appropriate in the circumstances of the particular case—

(a) that the abatement notice is not justified by section 80 of the 1990 Act (summary proceedings for statutory nuisances);
(b) that there has been some informality, defect or error in, or in connection with, the abatement notice, or in, or in connection with, any copy of the abatement notice served under section 80A(3) (certain notices in respect of vehicles, machinery or equipment);
(c) that the authority have refused unreasonably to accept compliance with alternative requirements, or that the requirements of the abatement notice are otherwise unreasonable in character or extent, or are unnecessary;
(d) that the time, or where more than one time is specified, any of the times, within which the requirements of the abatement notice are to be complied with is not reasonably sufficient for the purpose;
(e) where the nuisance to which the notice relates—
   (i) is a nuisance falling within section 79(1)(a), (d), (e), (f) or (g) of the 1990 Act and arises on industrial, trade, or business premises, or
   (ii) is a nuisance falling within section 79(1)(b) of the 1990 Act and the smoke is emitted from a chimney, or
   (iii) is a nuisance falling within section 79(1)(ga) of the 1990 Act and is noise emitted from or caused by a vehicle, machinery or equipment being used for industrial, trade or business purposes,

that the best practicable means were used to prevent, or to counteract the effects of, the nuisance;

(f) that, in the case of a nuisance under section 79(1)(g) or (ga) of the 1990 Act (noise emitted from premises), the requirements imposed by the abatement notice by virtue of section 80(1)(a) of the Act are more onerous than the requirements for the time being in force, in relation to the noise to which the notice relates, of—
  (i) any notice served under section 60 or 66 of the 1974 Act (control of noise on construction sites and from certain premises), or
  (ii) any consent given under section 61 or 65 of the 1974 Act (consent for work on construction sites and consent for noise to exceed registered level in a noise abatement zone), or
  (iii) any determination made under section 67 of the 1974 Act (noise control of new buildings);

(g) that, in the case of a nuisance under section 79(1)(ga) of the 1990 Act (noise emitted from or caused by vehicles, machinery or equipment), the requirements imposed by the abatement notice by virtue of section 80(1)(a) of the Act are more onerous than the requirements for the time being in force, in relation to the noise to which the notice relates, of any condition of a consent given under paragraph 1 of Schedule 2 to the 1993 Act (loudspeakers in streets or roads);

(h) that the abatement notice should have been served on some person instead of the appellant, being—
  (i) the person responsible for the nuisance, or
  (ii) the person responsible for the vehicle, machinery or equipment, or
  (iii) in the case of a nuisance arising from any defect of a structural character, the owner of the premises, or
  (iv) in the case where the person responsible for the nuisance cannot be found or the nuisance has not yet occurred, the owner or occupier of the premises;

(i) that the abatement notice might lawfully have been served on some person instead of the appellant being—
  (i) in the case where the appellant is the owner of the premises, the occupier of the premises, or
  (ii) in the case where the appellant is the occupier of the premises, the owner of the premises,

and that it would have been equitable for it to have been so served;

(j) that the abatement notice might lawfully have been served on some person in addition to the appellant, being—
  (i) a person also responsible for the nuisance, or
  (ii) a person who is also owner of the premises, or
  (iii) a person who is also an occupier of the premises, or
  (iv) a person who is also the person responsible for the vehicle, machinery or equipment,

and that it would have been equitable for it to have been so served.

(3) If and so far as an appeal is based on the ground of some informality, defect or error in, or in connection with, the abatement notice, or in, or in connection with, any copy of the notice served under section 80A(3), the court shall dismiss the appeal if it is satisfied that the informality, defect or error was not a material one.

(4) Where the grounds upon which an appeal is brought include a ground specified in paragraph (2)(i) or (j) above, the appellant shall serve a copy of his notice of appeal on any other person referred to, and in the case of any appeal to which these regulations apply he may serve a copy of his notice of appeal on any other person having an estate or interest in the premises, vehicle, machinery or equipment in question.

(5) On the hearing of the appeal the court may—
   (a) quash the abatement notice to which the appeal relates, or
   (b) vary the abatement notice in favour of the appellant in such manner as it thinks fit, or
   (c) dismiss the appeal;

and an abatement notice that is varied under sub-paragraph (b) above shall be final and shall otherwise have effect, as so varied, as if it had been so made by the local authority.

(6) Subject to paragraph (7) below, on the hearing of an appeal the court may make such order as it thinks fit—
   (a) with respect to the person by whom any work is to be executed and the contribution to be made by any person towards the cost of the work, or
   (b) as to the proportions in which any expenses which may become recoverable by the authority under Part III of the 1990 Act are to be borne by the appellant and by any other person.

(7) In exercising its powers under paragraph (6) above the court—
   (a) shall have regard, as between an owner and an occupier, to the terms and conditions, whether contractual or statutory, of any relevant tenancy and to the nature of the works required, and
   (b) shall be satisfied before it imposes any requirement thereunder on any person other than the appellant, that that person has received a copy of the notice of appeal in pursuance of paragraph (4) above.

3. Suspension of notice

(1) Where—
   (a) an appeal is brought against an abatement notice served under section 80 or section 80A of the 1990 Act, and—
   (b) either—
      (i) compliance with the abatement notice would involve any person in expenditure on the carrying out of works before the hearing of the appeal, or
      (ii) in the case of a nuisance under section 79(1)(g) or (ga) of the 1990 Act, the noise to which the abatement notice relates is noise necessarily caused in the course of the performance of some duty imposed by law on the appellant, and
   (c) either paragraph (2) does not apply, or it does apply but the requirements of paragraph (3) have not been met,

the abatement notice shall be suspended until the appeal has been abandoned or decided by the court.

(2) This paragraph applies where—

(a) the nuisance to which the abatement notice relates—
   (i) is injurious to health, or
   (ii) is likely to be of a limited duration such that suspension of the notice would render it of no practical effect, or
(b) the expenditure which would be incurred by any person in the carrying out of works in compliance with the abatement notice before any appeal has been decided would not be disproportionate to the public benefit to be expected in that period from such compliance.

(3) Where paragraph (2) applies the abatement notice—
   (a) shall include a statement that paragraph (2) applies, and that as a consequence it shall have effect notwithstanding any appeal to a magistrates' court which has not been decided by the court, and
   (b) shall include a statement as to which of the grounds set out in paragraph (2) apply.

APPENDIX C

Other Legislation
Police and Criminal Evidence Act 1984

Section 67—Codes of practice—supplementary

(11) In all criminal and civil proceedings any such code shall be admissible in evidence; and if any provision of such a code appears to the court or tribunal conducting the proceedings to be relevant to any question arising in the proceedings it shall be taken into account in determining that question.

Section 69—Evidence from computer records

(1) In any proceedings, a statement in a document produced by a computer shall not be admissible as evidence of any fact stated therein unless it is shown —
  (a) that there are no reasonable grounds for believing that the statement is inaccurate because of improper use of the computer;
  (b) that at all material times the computer was operating properly, or if not, that any respect in which it was not operating properly or was out of operation was not such as to affect the production of the document or the accuracy of its contents; . . .

Section 76—Confessions

(2) If, in any proceedings where the prosecution proposes to give in evidence a confession made by an accused person, it is represented to the court that the confession was or may have been obtained—
  (a) by oppression of the person who made it; or
  (b) in consequence of anything said or done which was likely, in the circumstances existing at the time, to render unreliable any confession which might be made by him in consequence thereof,
the court shall not allow the confession to be given in evidence against him except insofar as the prosecution proves to the court beyond reasonable doubt that the confession (notwithstanding that it may be true) was not obtained as aforesaid.

Section 78—Exclusion of unfair evidence

(1) In any proceedings the court may refuse to allow evidence on which the prosecution proposes to rely to be given if it appears to the court that, having regard to all the circumstances, including the circumstances in which the evidence was obtained, the admission of

the evidence would have such an adverse effect on the fairness of the proceedings that the court ought not to admit it.

Codes of Practice made under the Police and Criminal Evidence Act 1984—Extracts

Code B—Seizure of Property

1.3B This code does not apply to the exercise of a statutory power to enter premises or to inspect goods, equipment or procedures if the exercise of that power is not dependent on the existence of grounds for suspecting that an offence may have been committed and the person exercising the power has no reasonable grounds for such suspicion.

Code C—Treatment and Questioning of Persons

10 Cautions

(a) When a caution must be given

10.1 A person whom there are grounds to suspect of an offence must be cautioned before any questions about it (or further questions if it is his answers to previous questions which provide the grounds for suspicion) are put to him regarding his involvement or suspected involvement in that offence if his answers or his silence (i.e. failure or refusal to answer a question or to answer satisfactorily) may be given in evidence to a court in a prosecution. He therefore need not be cautioned if questions are put for other purposes, for example, solely to establish his identity or his ownership of any vehicle or to obtain information in accordance with any relevant statutory requirement (see paragraph 10.5C) or in furtherance of the proper and effective conduct of a search, (for example to determine the need to search in the exercise of powers of stop and search or to seek co-operation while carrying out a search) or to seek verification of a written record in accordance with paragraph 11.13.

10.2 Whenever a person who is not under arrest is initially cautioned or is reminded that he is under caution (see paragraph 10.5) he must at the same time be told that he is not under arrest and is not obliged to remain with the officer . . .

(b) Action: general

10.4 The caution shall be in the following terms:

You do not have to say anything. But it may harm your defence if you do not mention when questioned something which you later rely on in court. Anything you do say may be given in evidence.

Minor deviations do not constitute a breach of this requirement provided that the sense of the caution is preserved . . .

10.5 When there is a break in questioning under caution the interviewing officer must ensure that the person being questioned is aware that he remains under caution. If there is

C: POLICE AND CRIMINAL EVIDENCE ACT 1984

any doubt the caution shall be given again in full when the interview resumes. [See Note 10A]

(c) Juveniles, the mentally disordered and the mentally handicapped
10.6 If a juvenile or a person who is mentally disordered or mentally handicapped is cautioned in the absence of the appropriate adult, the caution must be repeated in the adult's presence.

(d) Documentation
10.7 A record shall be made when a caution is given under this section, either in the officer's pocket book or in the interview record as appropriate.

Notes for Guidance
10A In considering whether or not to caution again after a break, the officer should bear in mind that he may have to satisfy a court that the person understood that he was still under caution when the interview resumed.

10C If it appears that a person does not understand what the caution means, the officer who has given it should go on to explain it in his own words.

11 Interviews: general

(a) Action
11.1A An interview is the questioning of a person regarding his involvement or suspected involvement in a criminal offence or offences which, by virtue of paragraph 10.1 of code C is required to be carried out under caution.

11.3 No police officer may try to obtain answers to questions or to elicit a statement by the use of oppression. Except as provided for in paragraph 10.5C, no police officer shall indicate, except in answer to a direct question, what action will be taken on the part of the police if the person being interviewed answers questions, makes a statement or refuses to do either. If the person asks the officer directly what action will be taken in the event of his answering questions, makes a statement or refuses to do either, then the officer may inform the person what action the police propose to take in that event provided that action is itself proper and warranted.

11.4 As soon as a police officer who is making enquiries of any person about an offence believes that a prosecution should be brought against him and that there is sufficient evidence for it to succeed, he shall ask the person if he has anything further to say. If the person indicates that he has nothing more to say the officer shall without delay cease to question him about that offence.

(b) Interview records
11.5 (a) An accurate record must be made of each interview with a person suspected of an offence, whether or not the interview takes place at a police station.
    (b) The record must state the place of the interview, the time it begins and ends, the time the record is made (if different), any breaks in the interview and the names

of all those present; and must be made on the forms provided for this purpose or in the officer's pocket book.

(c) The record must be made during the course of the interview, unless in the investigating officer's view this would not be practicable or would interfere with conduct of the interview. and must constitute either a verbatim record of what has been said or, failing this, an account of the interview which adequately and accurately summarises it.

11.7 If an interview record is not made during the course of the interview it must be made as soon as practicable after its completion.

11.8 Written interview records must be timed and signed by the maker.

11.9 If an interview record is not completed in the course of the interview the reason must be recorded in the officer's pocket book.

11.10 Unless it is impracticable the person interviewed shall be given the opportunity to read the interview record and to sign it as correct or to indicate the respects m which he considers it inaccurate. If the interview is tape recorded the arrangements set out in Code E apply. If the person concerned cannot read or refuses to read the record or to sign it, the senior police officer present shall read it to him and ask him whether he would like to sign it as correct (or make his mark) or to indicate the respects in which he considers it inaccurate. The police officer shall then certify on the interview record itself what has occurred.

11.11 If the appropriate adult or the person's solicitor is present during the interview, he shall also be given an opportunity to read and sign the interview record (or any written statement taken down by a police officer).

11.12 Any refusal by a person to sign an interview record when asked to do so in accordance with the provisions of the code must itself be recorded.

11.13 A written record shall also be made of any comments made by a suspected person, including unsolicited comments, which are outside the context of an interview but which might be relevant to the offence. Any such record must be timed and signed by the maker. Where practicable the person shall be given the opportunity to read that record and to sign it as correct or to indicate the respects in which be considers it inaccurate. Any refusal to sign shall be recorded.

(c) Juveniles. mentally disordered people and mentally handicapped people

11.14 A juvenile or a person who is mentally disordered or mentally handicapped, whether suspected or not, must not be interviewed or asked to provide or sign a written statement in the absence of the appropriate adult unless paragraph 11.1 of Annex C applies.

11.15 Juveniles may only be interviewed at their places of education in exceptional circumstances and then only where the principal or his nominee agrees. Every effort should be made to notify both the parent(s) or other person responsible for the juvenile's welfare and the appropriate adult (if this is a different person) that the police want to interview the juvenile and reasonable time should be allowed to enable the appropriate adult to be present at the interview. Where awaiting the appropriate adult would cause unreasonable delay and unless the interviewee is suspected of an offence against the educational establishment, the principal or his nominee can act as the appropriate adult for the purposes of the interview.

11.16 Where the appropriate adult is present at an interview, he shall be informed that he is not expected to act simply as an observer, and also that the purposes of his presence are, first, to advise the person being questioned and to observe whether or not the interview is being conducted properly and fairly, and secondly, to facilitate communication with the person being interviewed.

Notes for Guidance

11D When a suspect agrees to read records of interviews and other comments and to sign them as correct, he should be asked to endorse the record with words such as "I agree that this is a correct record of What was said" and add his signature. Where the suspect does not agree with the record, the officer should record the details of any disagreement and then ask the suspect to read these details and then sign them to the effect that they accurately reflect his disagreement. Any refusal to sign when asked to do so shall be recorded.

Clean Air Act 1993

1. Dark Smoke—Prohibition of dark smoke from chimneys

(1) Dark smoke shall not be emitted from a chimney of any building, and if, on any day, dark smoke is so emitted, the occupier of the building shall be guilty of an offence.

(2) Dark smoke shall not be emitted from a chimney (not being a chimney of a building) which serves the furnace of any fixed boiler or industrial plant, and if, on any day, dark smoke is so emitted, the person having possession of the boiler or plant shall be guilty of an offence.

(3) This section does not apply to emissions of smoke from any chimney, in such classes of case and subject to such limitations as may be prescribed in regulations made by the Secretary of State, lasting for not longer than such periods as may be so prescribed.

(4) In any proceedings for an offence under this section, it shall be a defence to prove—
- (a) that the alleged emission was solely due to the lighting up of a furnace which was cold and that all practicable steps had been taken to prevent or minimise the emission of dark smoke;
- (b) that the alleged emission was solely due to some failure of a furnace, or of apparatus used in connection with a furnace, and that—
    - (i) the failure could not reasonably have been foreseen, or, if foreseen, could not reasonably have been provided against; and
    - (ii) the alleged emission could not reasonably have been prevented by action taken after the failure occurred; or
- (c) that the alleged emission was solely due to the use of unsuitable fuel and that—
    - (i) suitable fuel was unobtainable and the least unsuitable fuel which was available was used; and
    - (ii) all practicable steps had been taken to prevent or minimise the emission of dark smoke as the result of the use of that fuel;

or that the alleged emission was due to the combination of two or more of the causes specified in paragraphs (a) to (c) and that the other conditions specified in those paragraphs are satisfied in relation to those causes respectively.

(5) A person guilty of an offence under this section shall be liable on summary conviction—

   (a) in the case of a contravention of subsection (1) as respects a chimney of a private dwelling, to a fine not exceeding level 3 on the standard scale; and
   (b) in any other case, to a fine not exceeding level 5 on the standard scale.

(6) This section has effect subject to section 51 (duty to notify offences to occupier or other person liable).

2. Prohibition of dark smoke from industrial or trade premises

(1) Dark smoke shall not be emitted from any industrial or trade premises and if, on any day, dark smoke is so emitted the occupier of the premises and any person who causes or permits the emission shall be guilty of an offence.

(2) This section does not apply—

   (a) to the emission of dark smoke from any chimney to which section 1 above applies; or
   (b) to the emission of dark smoke caused by the burning of any matter prescribed in regulations made by the Secretary of State, subject to compliance with such conditions (if any) as may be so prescribed.

(3) In proceedings for an offence under this section, there shall be taken to have been an emission of dark smoke from industrial or trade premises in any case where—

   (a) material is burned on those premises; and
   (b) the circumstances are such that the burning would be likely to give rise to the emission of dark smoke,

unless the occupier or any person who caused or permitted the burning shows that no dark smoke was emitted.

(4) In proceedings for an offence under this section, it shall be a defence to prove—

   (a) that the alleged emission was inadvertent; and
   (b) that all practicable steps had been taken to prevent or minimise the emission of dark smoke.

(5) A person guilty of an offence under this section shall be liable on summary conviction to a fine not exceeding level 5 on the standard scale.

(6) In this section "industrial or trade premises" means—

   (a) premises used for any industrial or trade purposes; or
   (b) premises not so used on which matter is burnt in connection with any industrial or trade process.

(7) This section has effect subject to section 51 (duty to notify offences to occupier or other person liable).

3. Meaning of "dark smoke"

(1) In this Act "dark smoke" means smoke which, if compared in the appropriate manner with a chart of the [1956 c. 52.] type known on 5th July 1956 (the date of the passing of the Clean Air Act 1956) as the Ringelmann Chart, would appear to be as dark as or darker than shade 2 on the chart.

(2) For the avoidance of doubt it is hereby declared that in proceedings—

    (a) for an offence under section 1 or 2 (prohibition of emissions of dark smoke); or

    (b) brought by virtue of section 17 (smoke nuisances in Scotland),

the court may be satisfied that smoke is or is not dark smoke as defined in subsection (1) notwithstanding that there has been no actual comparison of the smoke with a chart of the type mentioned in that subsection.

(3) Without prejudice to the generality of subsections (1) and (2), if the Secretary of State by regulations prescribes any method of ascertaining whether smoke is dark smoke as defined in subsection (1), proof in any such proceedings as are mentioned in subsection (2)—

    (a) that that method was properly applied, and

    (b) that the smoke was thereby ascertained to be or not to be dark smoke as so defined,

shall be accepted as sufficient.

Criminal Justice and Public Order Act 1994

Section 34—Effect of accused's failure to mention facts when questioned or charged

(1) Where, in any proceedings against a person for an offence, evidence is given that the accused—

    (a) at any time before he was charged with the offence, on being questioned under caution by a constable trying to discover whether or by whom the offence had been committed, failed to mention any fact relied on in his defence in those proceedings; or

    (b) on being charged with the offence or officially informed that he might be prosecuted for it, failed to mention any such fact,

being a fact which in the circumstances existing at the time the accused could reasonably have been expected to mention when so questioned, charged or informed . . .

    (c) the court, in determining whether there is a case to answer; and

    (d) the court or jury, in determining whether the accused is guilty of the offence charged,

may draw such inferences from the failure as appear proper . . .

(4) This section applies in relation to questioning by persons (other than constables) charged with the duty of investigating offences or charging offenders . . .

Noise Act 1996

Summary procedure for dealing with noise at night

1. Adoption of these provisions by local authorities

(1) Sections 2 to 9 only apply to the area of a local authority if the authority have so resolved or an order made by the Secretary of State so provides . . .

2. Investigation of complaints of noise from a dwelling at night

(1) A local authority must, if they receive a complaint of the kind mentioned in subsection (2), secure that an officer of the authority takes reasonable steps to investigate the complaint.

(2) The kind of complaint referred to is one made by any individual present in a dwelling during night hours (referred to in this Act as "the complainant's dwelling") that excessive noise is being emitted from another dwelling (referred to in this group of sections as "the offending dwelling").

(3) A complaint under subsection (2) may be made by any means.

(4) If an officer of the authority is satisfied, in consequence of an investigation under subsection (1), that—

    (a) noise is being emitted from the offending dwelling during night hours, and
    (b) the noise, if it were measured from within the complainant's dwelling, would or might exceed the permitted level, he may serve a notice about the noise under section 3.

(5) For the purposes of subsection (4), it is for the officer of the authority dealing with the particular case—

    (a) to decide whether any noise, if it were measured from within the complainant's dwelling, would or might exceed the permitted level, and
    (b) for the purposes of that decision, to decide whether to assess the noise from within or outside the complainant's dwelling and whether or not to use any device for measuring the noise.

(6) In this group of sections, "night hours" means the period beginning with 11 p.m. and ending with the following 7 a.m.

(7) Where a local authority receive a complaint under subsection (2) and the offending dwelling is within the area of another local authority, the first local authority may act under this group of sections as if the offending dwelling were within their area, and accordingly may so act whether or not this group of sections applies to the area of the other local authority.

(8) In this section and sections 3 to 9, "this group of sections" means this and those sections.

3. Warning notices

(1) A notice under this section (referred to in this Act as "a warning notice") must-
   (a) state that an officer of the authority considers—
      (i) that noise is being emitted from the offending dwelling during night hours, and
      (ii) that the noise exceeds, or may exceed, the permitted level, as measured from within the complainant's dwelling, and
   (b) give warning that any person who is responsible for noise which is emitted from the dwelling, in the period specified in the notice, and exceeds the permitted level, as measured from within the complainant's dwelling, may be guilty of an offence.

(2) The period specified in a warning notice must be a period—
   (a) beginning not earlier than ten minutes after the time when the notice is served, and
   (b) ending with the following 7 a.m.

(3) A warning notice must be served—
   (a) by delivering it to any person present at or near the offending dwelling and appearing to the officer of the authority to be responsible for the noise, or
   (b) if it is not reasonably practicable to identify any person present at or near the dwelling as being a person responsible for the noise on whom the notice may reasonably be served, by leaving it at the offending dwelling.

(4) A warning notice must state the time at which it is served.

(5) For the purposes of this group of sections, a person is responsible for noise emitted from a dwelling if he is a person to whose act, default or sufferance the emission of the noise is wholly or partly attributable.

4. Offence where noise exceeds permitted level after service of notice

(1) If a warning notice has been served in respect of noise emitted from a dwelling, any person who is responsible for noise which—
   (a) is emitted from the dwelling in the period specified in the notice, and
   (b) exceeds the permitted level, as measured from within the complainant's dwelling,
   is guilty of an offence.

(2) It is a defence for a person charged with an offence under this section to show that there was a reasonable excuse for the act, default or sufferance in question.

(3) A person guilty of an offence under this section is liable on summary conviction to a fine not exceeding level 3 on the standard scale.

5. Permitted level of noise

(1) For the purposes of this group of sections, the Secretary of State may by directions in writing determine the maximum level of noise (referred to in this group of sections as "the permitted level") which may be emitted during night hours from any dwelling.

(2) The permitted level is to be a level applicable to noise as measured from within any other dwelling in the vicinity by an approved device used in accordance with any conditions subject to which the approval was given.

(3) Different permitted levels may be determined for different circumstances, and the permitted level may be determined partly by reference to other levels of noise.

(4) The Secretary of State may from time to time vary his directions under this section by further directions in writing . . .

8. Fixed penalty notices

(1) Where an officer of a local authority who is authorised for the purposes of this section has reason to believe that a person is committing or has just committed an offence under section 4, he may give that person a notice (referred to in this Act as a "fixed penalty notice") offering him the opportunity of discharging any liability to conviction for that offence by payment of a fixed penalty.

(2) A fixed penalty notice may be given to a person—
   (a) by delivering the notice to him, or
   (b) if it is not reasonably practicable to deliver it to him, by leaving the notice, addressed to him, at the offending dwelling

(3) Where a person is given a fixed penalty notice in respect of such an offence—
   (a) proceedings for that offence must not be instituted before the end of the period of fourteen days following the date of the notice, and
   (b) he cannot be convicted of that offence if he pays the fixed penalty before the end of that period.

(4) A fixed penalty notice must give such particulars of the circumstances alleged to constitute the offence as are necessary for giving reasonable information of the offence.

(5) A fixed penalty notice must state—
   (a) the period during which, because of subsection (3)(a), proceedings will not be taken for the offence,
   (b) the amount of the fixed penalty, and
   (c) the person to whom and the address at which the fixed penalty may be paid.

(6) Payment of the fixed penalty may (among other methods) be made by pre-paying and posting to that person at that address a letter containing the amount of the penalty (in cash or otherwise).

(7) Where a letter containing the amount of the penalty is sent in accordance with subsection (6), payment is to be regarded as having been made at the time at which that letter would be delivered in the ordinary course of post.

(8) The fixed penalty payable under this section is £100.

Seizure, etc. of equipment used to make noise unlawfully

10. Powers of entry and seizure etc.

(1) The power conferred by subsection (2) may be exercised where an officer of a local authority has reason to believe that—

(a) a warning notice has been served in respect of noise emitted from a dwelling, and
(b) at any time in the period specified in the notice, noise emitted from the dwelling has exceeded the permitted level, as measured from within the complainant's dwelling.

(2) An officer of the local authority, or a person authorised by the authority for the purpose, may enter the dwelling from which the noise in question is being or has been emitted and may seize and remove any equipment which it appears to him is being or has been used in the emission of the noise.

(3) A person exercising the power conferred by subsection (2) must produce his authority, if he is required to do so.

(4) If it is shown to a justice of the peace on sworn information in writing that—
(a) a warning notice has been served in respect of noise emitted from a dwelling,
(b) at any time in the period specified in the notice, noise emitted from the dwelling has exceeded the permitted level, as measured from within the complainant's dwelling, and
(c) entry of an officer of the local authority, or of a person authorised by the authority for the purpose, to the dwelling has been refused, or such a refusal is apprehended, or a request by an officer of the authority, or of such a person, for admission would defeat the object of the entry,

the justice may by warrant under his hand authorise the local authority, by any of their officers or any person authorised by them for the purpose to enter the premises, if need be by force.

(5) A person who enters any premises under subsection (2), or by virtue of a warrant issued under subsection (4), may take with him such other persons and such equipment as may be necessary; and if, when he leaves, the premises are unoccupied, must leave them as effectively secured against trespassers as he found them.

(6) A warrant issued under subsection (4) continues in force until the purpose for which the entry is required has been satisfied.

(7) The power of a local authority under section 81(3) of the Environmental Protection Act 1990 to abate any matter, where that matter is a statutory nuisance by virtue of section 79(1)(g) of that Act (noise emitted from premises so as to be prejudicial to health or a nuisance), includes power to seize and remove any equipment which it appears to the authority is being or has been used in the emission of the noise in question.

(8) A person who wilfully obstructs any person exercising any powers conferred under subsection (2) or by virtue of subsection (7) is liable, on summary conviction, to a fine not exceeding level 3 on the standard scale.

(9) The Schedule to this Act (which makes further provision in relation to anything seized and removed by virtue of this section) has effect.

SCHEDULE

Section 10

Powers In Relation To Seized Equipment

Introductory

1.—In this Schedule—
  (a) a "noise offence" means—
    (i) in relation to equipment seized under section 10(2) of this Act, an offence under section 4 of this Act, and
    (ii) in relation to equipment seized under section 81(3) of the Environmental Protection Act 1990 (as extended by section 10(7) of this Act), an offence under section 80(4) of that Act in respect of a statutory nuisance falling within section 79(1)(g) of that Act,
  (b) "seized equipment" means equipment seized in the exercise of the power of seizure and removal conferred by section 10(2) of this Act or section 81(3) of the Environmental Protection Act 1990 (as so extended),
  (c) "related equipment", in relation to any conviction of or proceedings for a noise offence, means seized equipment used or alleged to have been used in the commission of the offence,
  (d) "responsible local authority", in relation to seized equipment, means the local authority by or on whose behalf the equipment was seized.

Retention

2.—(1) Any seized equipment may be retained—
  (a) during the period of twenty-eight days beginning with the seizure, or
  (b) if it is related equipment in proceedings for a noise offence instituted within that period against any person, until—
    (i) he is sentenced or otherwise dealt with for the offence or acquitted of the offence, or
    (ii) the proceedings are discontinued.

(2) Sub-paragraph (1) does not authorise the retention of seized equipment if—
  (a) a person has been given a fixed penalty notice under section 8 of this Act in respect of any noise,
  (b) the equipment was seized because of its use in the emission of the noise in respect of which the fixed penalty notice was given, and
  (c) that person has paid the fixed penalty before the end of the period allowed for its payment.

Forfeiture

3.—(1) Where a person is convicted of a noise offence the court may make an order ("a forfeiture order") for forfeiture of any related equipment.

(2) The court may make a forfeiture order whether or not it also deals with the offender in respect of the offence in any other way and without regard to any restrictions on forfeiture in any enactment.

(3) In considering whether to make a forfeiture order in respect of any equipment a court must have regard—
- (a) to the value of the equipment, and
- (b) to the likely financial and other effects on the offender of the making of the order (taken together with any other order that the court contemplates making).

(4) A forfeiture order operates to deprive the offender of any rights in the equipment to which it relates.

Consequences of forfeiture

4.—(1) Where any equipment has been forfeited under paragraph 3, a magistrates' court may, on application by a claimant of the equipment (other than the person in whose case the forfeiture order was made) make an order for delivery of the equipment to the applicant if it appears to the court that he is the owner of the equipment.

(2) No application may be made under sub-paragraph (1) by any claimant of the equipment after the expiry of the period of six months beginning with the date on which a forfeiture order was made in respect of the equipment.

(3) Such an application cannot succeed unless the claimant satisfies the court—
- (a) that he had not consented to the offender having possession of the equipment, or
- (b) that he did not know, and had no reason to suspect, that the equipment was likely to be used in the commission of a noise offence.

(4) Where the responsible local authority is of the opinion that the person in whose case the forfeiture order was made is not the owner of the equipment, it must take reasonable steps to bring to the attention of persons who may be entitled to do so their right to make an application under sub-paragraph (1).

(5) An order under sub-paragraph (1) does not affect the right of any person to take, within the period of six months beginning with the date of the order, proceedings for the recovery of the equipment from the person in possession of it in pursuance of the order, but the right ceases on the expiry of that period.

(6) If on the expiry of the period of six months beginning with the date on which a forfeiture order was made in respect of the equipment no order has been made under sub-paragraph (1), the responsible local authority may dispose of the equipment.

Return etc. of seized equipment

5. If in proceedings for a noise offence no order for forfeiture of related equipment is made, the court (whether or not a person is convicted of the offence) may give such directions as to the return, retention or disposal of the equipment by the responsible local authority as it thinks fit.

6.—(1) Where in the case of any seized equipment no proceedings in which it is related equipment are begun within the period mentioned in paragraph 2(1)(a)—

(a) the responsible local authority must return the equipment to any person who—
   (i) appears to them to be the owner of the equipment, and
   (ii) makes a claim for the return of the equipment within the period mentioned in sub-paragraph (2), and
(b) if no such person makes such a claim within that period, the responsible local authority may dispose of the equipment.

(2) The period referred to in sub-paragraph (1)(a)(ii) is the period of six months beginning with the expiry of the period mentioned in paragraph 2(1)(a).

(3) The responsible local authority must take reasonable steps to bring to the attention of persons who may be entitled to do so their right to make such a claim.

(4) Subject to sub-paragraph (6), the responsible local authority is not required to return any seized equipment under sub-paragraph (1)(a) until the person making the claim has paid any such reasonable charges for the seizure, removal and retention of the equipment as the authority may demand.

(5) If—
   (a) equipment is sold in pursuance of—
      (i) paragraph 4(6),
      (ii) directions under paragraph 5, or
      (iii) this paragraph, and
   (b) before the expiration of the period of one year beginning with the date on which the equipment is sold any person satisfies the responsible local authority that at the time of its sale he was the owner of the equipment,

the authority is to pay him any sum by which any proceeds of sale exceed any such reasonable charges for the seizure, removal or retention of the equipment as the authority may demand.

(6) The responsible local authority cannot demand charges from any person under sub-paragraph (4) or (5) who they are satisfied did not know, and had no reason to suspect, that the equipment was likely to be used in the emission of noise exceeding the level determined under section 5.

Magistrates' Courts (Advance Notice of Expert Evidence) Rules 1997, SI 1997/705

3.—(1) Where a magistrates' court proceeds to summary trial in respect of an alleged offence and the person charged with that offence pleads not guilty in respect of it, if any party to the proceedings proposes to adduce expert evidence (whether of fact or opinion) in the proceedings (otherwise than in relation to sentence) he shall as soon as practicable after the person charged has so pleaded, unless in relation to the evidence in question he has already done so—
   (a) furnish the other party or parties with a statement in writing of any finding or opinion which he proposes to adduce by way of evidence; and
   (b) where a request in writing is made to him in that behalf by any other party, provide that party also with a copy of (or of it appears to the party proposing to adduce the

evidence to be more practicable, a reasonable opportunity to examine) the record of any observation, test, calculation or other procedure on which such finding or opinion is based and any document or other thing or substance in respect of which any such procedure has been carried out.

. . .

5. A party who seeks to adduce expert evidence in any proceedings and who fails to comply with rule 3 above shall not adduce that evidence in those proceedings without the leave of the court.

Magistrates' Courts (Hearsay Evidence in Civil Proceedings) Rules 1999, SI 1999/681

2. Application and interpretation

(1) In these Rules, the "1995 Act" means the Civil Evidence Act 1995.

(2) In these Rules—

"hearsay evidence" means evidence consisting of hearsay within the meaning of section 1(2) of the 1995 Act;
"hearsay notice" means a notice under section 2 of the 1995 Act.

(3) These Rules shall apply to hearsay evidence in civil proceedings in magistrates' courts.

3. Hearsay notices

(1) Subject to paragraphs (2) and (3), a party who desires to give hearsay evidence at the hearing must, not less than 21 days before the date fixed for the hearing, serve a hearsay notice on every other party and file a copy in the court by serving it on the justices' clerk.

(2) Subject to paragraph (3), the court or the justices' clerk may make a direction substituting a different period of time for the service of the hearsay notice under paragraph (1) on the application of a party to the proceedings.

(3) The court may make a direction under paragraph (2) of its own motion.

(4) A hearsay notice must—
   (a) state that it is a hearsay notice;
   (b) identify the proceedings in which the hearsay evidence is to be given;
   (c) state that the party proposes to adduce hearsay evidence;
   (d) identify the hearsay evidence;
   (e) identify the person who made the statement which is to be given in evidence; and
   (f) state why that person will not be called to give oral evidence.

(5) A single hearsay notice may deal with the hearsay evidence of more than one witness.

4. Power to call witness for cross-examination on hearsay evidence

(1) Where a party tenders as hearsay evidence a statement made by a person but does not propose to call the person who made the statement to give evidence, the court may, on application, allow another party to call and cross-examine the person who made the statement on its contents.

(2) An application under paragraph (1) must—
- (a) be served on the justices' clerk with sufficient copies for all other parties;
- (b) unless the court otherwise directs, be made not later than 7 days after service of the hearsay notice; and
- (c) give reasons why the person who made the statement should be cross-examined on its contents.

(3) On receipt of an application under paragraph (1), the justices' clerk must—
- (a) unless the court otherwise directs, allow sufficient time for the applicant to comply with paragraph (4);
- (b) fix the date, time and place and endorse them on the copies of the application filed by the applicant; and
- (c) return the copies to the applicant forthwith.

(4) Subject to paragraphs (5) and (6), on receipt of the copies from the justices' clerk under paragraph (3)(c), the applicant must serve a copy on every other party giving not less than 3 days' notice of the hearing of the application.

(5) The court or the justices' clerk may give directions as to the manner in which service under paragraph (4) is to be effected and may, subject to giving notice to the applicant, alter or dispense with the notice requirement under paragraph (4) if the court or the justices' clerk, as the case may be, considers it is in the interests of justice to do so.

(6) The court may hear an application under paragraph (1) ex parte if it considers it is in the interests of justice to do so.

(7) Subject to paragraphs (5) and (6), where an application under paragraph (1) is made, the applicant must file with the court a statement at or before the hearing of the application that service of a copy of the application has been effected on all other parties and the statement must indicate the manner, date, time and address at which the document was served.

(8) The court must notify all parties of its decision on an application under paragraph (1).

5. Credibility and previous inconsistent statements

(1) If—
- (a) a party tenders as hearsay evidence a statement made by a person but does not call the person who made the statement to give oral evidence, and
- (b) another party wishes to attack the credibility of the person who made the statement or allege that the person who made the statement made any other statement inconsistent with it,

that other party must notify the party tendering the hearsay evidence of his intention.

(2) Unless the court or the justices' clerk otherwise directs, a notice under paragraph (1) must be given not later than 7 days after service of the hearsay notice and, in addition to the requirements in paragraph (1), must be served on every other party and a copy filed in the court.

(3) If, on receipt of a notice under paragraph (1), the party referred to in paragraph (1)(a) calls the person who made the statement to be tendered as hearsay evidence to give oral evidence, he must, unless the court otherwise directs, notify the court and all other parties of his intention.

(4) Unless the court or the justices' clerk otherwise directs, a notice under paragraph (3) must be given not later than 7 days after the service of the notice under paragraph (1).

. . .

Regulation of Investigatory Powers Act 2000

Part II
Surveillance And Covert Human Intelligence Sources

Introductory

Section 26—Conduct to which Part II applies

(1) This Part applies to the following conduct—
   (a) directed surveillance;
   (b) intrusive surveillance; and
   (c) the conduct and use of covert human intelligence sources.

(2) Subject to subsection (6), surveillance is directed for the purposes of this Part if it is covert but not intrusive and is undertaken—
   (a) for the purposes of a specific investigation or a specific operation;
   (b) in such a manner as is likely to result in the obtaining of private information about a person (whether or not one specifically identified for the purposes of the investigation or operation); and
   (c) otherwise than by way of an immediate response to events or circumstances the nature of which is such that it would not be reasonably practicable for an authorisation under this Part to be sought for the carrying out of the surveillance.

(3) Subject to subsections (4) to (6), surveillance is intrusive for the purposes of this Part if, and only if, it is covert surveillance that—
   (a) is carried out in relation to anything taking place on any residential premises or in any private vehicle; and
   (b) involves the presence of an individual on the premises or in the vehicle or is carried out by means of a surveillance device.

(4) For the purposes of this Part surveillance is not intrusive to the extent that—
   (a) it is carried out by means only of a surveillance device designed or adapted principally for the purpose of providing information about the location of a vehicle; or

(b) it is surveillance consisting in any such interception of a communication as falls within section 48(4).

(5) For the purposes of this Part surveillance which—

(a) is carried out by means of a surveillance device in relation to anything taking place on any residential premises or in any private vehicle, but

(b) is carried out without that device being present on the premises or in the vehicle,

is not intrusive unless the device is such that it consistently provides information of the same quality and detail as might be expected to be obtained from a device actually present on the premises or in the vehicle.

(6) For the purposes of this Part surveillance which—

(a) is carried out by means of apparatus designed or adapted for the purpose of detecting the installation or use in any residential or other premises of a television receiver (within the meaning of section 1 of the Wireless Telegraphy Act 1949), and

(b) is carried out from outside those premises exclusively for that purpose,

is neither directed nor intrusive.

(7) In this Part—

(a) references to the conduct of a covert human intelligence source are references to any conduct of such a source which falls within any of paragraphs (a) to (c) of subsection (8), or is incidental to anything falling within any of those paragraphs; and

(b) references to the use of a covert human intelligence source are references to inducing, asking or assisting a person to engage in the conduct of such a source, or to obtain information by means of the conduct of such a source.

(8) For the purposes of this Part a person is a covert human intelligence source if—

(a) he establishes or maintains a personal or other relationship with a person for the covert purpose of facilitating the doing of anything falling within paragraph (b) or (c);

(b) he covertly uses such a relationship to obtain information or to provide access to any information to another person; or

(c) he covertly discloses information obtained by the use of such a relationship, or as a consequence of the existence of such a relationship.

(9) For the purposes of this section—

(a) surveillance is covert if, and only if, it is carried out in a manner that is calculated to ensure that persons who are subject to the surveillance are unaware that it is or may be taking place;

(b) a purpose is covert, in relation to the establishment or maintenance of a personal or other relationship, if and only if the relationship is conducted in a manner that is calculated to ensure that one of the parties to the relationship is unaware of the purpose; and

(c) a relationship is used covertly, and information obtained as mentioned in subsection (8)(c) is disclosed covertly, if and only if it is used or, as the case may be, disclosed in a manner that is calculated to ensure that one of the parties to the relationship is unaware of the use or disclosure in question.

(10) In this section "private information", in relation to a person, includes any information relating to his private or family life.

(11) References in this section, in relation to a vehicle, to the presence of a surveillance device in the vehicle include references to its being located on or under the vehicle and also include references to its being attached to it.

Authorisation of surveillance and human intelligence sources

Section 27—Lawful surveillance etc.

(1) Conduct to which this Part applies shall be lawful for all purposes if—
   (a) an authorisation under this Part confers an entitlement to engage in that conduct on the person whose conduct it is; and
   (b) his conduct is in accordance with the authorisation.

(2) A person shall not be subject to any civil liability in respect of any conduct of his which—
   (a) is incidental to any conduct that is lawful by virtue of subsection (1); and
   (b) is not itself conduct an authorisation or warrant for which is capable of being granted under a relevant enactment and might reasonably have been expected to have been sought in the case in question.

(3) The conduct that may be authorised under this Part includes conduct outside the United Kingdom.

(4) In this section "relevant enactment" means—
   (a) an enactment contained in this Act;
   . . .

Section 28—Authorisation of directed surveillance

(1) Subject to the following provisions of this Part, the persons designated for the purposes of this section shall each have power to grant authorisations for the carrying out of directed surveillance.

(2) A person shall not grant an authorisation for the carrying out of directed surveillance unless he believes—
   (a) that the authorisation is necessary on grounds falling within subsection (3); and
   (b) that the authorised surveillance is proportionate to what is sought to be achieved by carrying it out.

(3) An authorisation is necessary on grounds falling within this subsection if it is necessary—
   (a) in the interests of national security;
   (b) for the purpose of preventing or detecting crime or of preventing disorder;
   (c) in the interests of the economic well-being of the United Kingdom;
   (d) in the interests of public safety;
   (e) for the purpose of protecting public health;

(f) for the purpose of assessing or collecting any tax, duty, levy or other imposition, contribution or charge payable to a government department; or

(g) for any purpose (not falling within paragraphs (a) to (f)) which is specified for the purposes of this subsection by an order made by the Secretary of State.

(4) The conduct that is authorised by an authorisation for the carrying out of directed surveillance is any conduct that—

(a) consists in the carrying out of directed surveillance of any such description as is specified in the authorisation; and

(b) is carried out in the circumstances described in the authorisation and for the purposes of the investigation or operation specified or described in the authorisation.

(5) The Secretary of State shall not make an order under subsection (3)(g) unless a draft of the order has been laid before Parliament and approved by a resolution of each House.

Section 29—Authorisation of covert human intelligence sources

(1) Subject to the following provisions of this Part, the persons designated for the purposes of this section shall each have power to grant authorisations for the conduct or the use of a covert human intelligence source.

(2) A person shall not grant an authorisation for the conduct or the use of a covert human intelligence source unless he believes—

(a) that the authorisation is necessary on grounds falling within subsection (3);

(b) that the authorised conduct or use is proportionate to what is sought to be achieved by that conduct or use; and

(c) that arrangements exist for the source's case that satisfy the requirements of subsection (5) and such other requirements as may be imposed by order made by the Secretary of State.

(3) An authorisation is necessary on grounds falling within this subsection if it is necessary—

(a) in the interests of national security;

(b) for the purpose of preventing or detecting crime or of preventing disorder;

(c) in the interests of the economic well-being of the United Kingdom;

(d) in the interests of public safety;

(e) for the purpose of protecting public health;

(f) for the purpose of assessing or collecting any tax, duty, levy or other imposition, contribution or charge payable to a government department; or

(g) for any purpose (not falling within paragraphs (a) to (f)) which is specified for the purposes of this subsection by an order made by the Secretary of State.

(4) The conduct that is authorised by an authorisation for the conduct or the use of a covert human intelligence source is any conduct that—

(a) is comprised in any such activities involving conduct of a covert human intelligence source, or the use of a covert human intelligence source, as are specified or described in the authorisation;

(b) consists in conduct by or in relation to the person who is so specified or described as the person to whose actions as a covert human intelligence source the authorisation relates; and

(c) is carried out for the purposes of, or in connection with, the investigation or operation so specified or described.

(5) For the purposes of this Part there are arrangements for the source's case that satisfy the requirements of this subsection if such arrangements are in force as are necessary for ensuring—

- (a) that there will at all times be a person holding an office, rank or position with the relevant investigating authority who will have day-to-day responsibility for dealing with the source on behalf of that authority, and for the source's security and welfare;
- (b) that there will at all times be another person holding an office, rank or position with the relevant investigating authority who will have general oversight of the use made of the source;
- (c) that there will at all times be a person holding an office, rank or position with the relevant investigating authority who will have responsibility for maintaining a record of the use made of the source;
- (d) that the records relating to the source that are maintained by the relevant investigating authority will always contain particulars of all such matters (if any) as may be specified for the purposes of this paragraph in regulations made by the Secretary of State; and
- (e) that records maintained by the relevant investigating authority that disclose the identity of the source will not be available to persons except to the extent that there is a need for access to them to be made available to those persons.

...

(7) The Secretary of State may by order—

- (a) prohibit the authorisation under this section of any such conduct or uses of covert human intelligence sources as may be described in the order; and
- (b) impose requirements, in addition to those provided for by subsection (2), that must be satisfied before an authorisation is granted under this section for any such conduct or uses of covert human intelligence sources as may be so described.

(8) In this section "relevant investigating authority", in relation to an authorisation for the conduct or the use of an individual as a covert human intelligence source, means (subject to subsection (9)) the public authority for whose benefit the activities of that individual as such a source are to take place.

(9) In the case of any authorisation for the conduct or the use of a covert human intelligence source whose activities are to be for the benefit of more than one public authority, the references in subsection (5) to the relevant investigating authority are references to one of them (whether or not the same one in the case of each reference).

INDEX

abandoned premises 5.50–5.53
abatement notices *see also* **abatement orders, appeals against abatement notices, services of notices**
abatement *versus* specifying works 12.50–12.56, 13.17
amendment of 12.33, 12.42 (fn 72), 12.81, 13.76–13.77
animals 8.09–8.10, 8.12
breach of 14.04–14.12
consultations prior to serving 6.78, 6.113, 12.12–12.16
defects in 13.17–13.26
drafting of 4.37 (fn 58), 6.75–6.78, 12.17–12.57
duty to serve 12.16, 17.07
European Convention on Human Rights 11.03–11.04, 11.26–11.29, 11.52
failure to comply with 14.04–14.12
form 12.21
generally 12.01–12.81
issued under previous legislation 12.80
multiple notices 12.36
noise 6.32–6.35, 6.75–6.78, 12.40–12.43
reasonable excuse for failing to comply 4.57, 15.29–15.43, 18.02
reasonableness of steps to be taken 4.60–4.63
schedules to 12.49
second or subsequent notices 12.54
separate letters (etc) together with 12.49
separate notices for separate nuisances 12.36
specifying alternative works 12.44–12.45
specifying ineffective steps 12.54
specifying nuisance 12.35–12.38
specifying obligation to use a consultant 12.48, 12.52
specifying officer's satisfaction 12.46
specifying unreasonable requirements 13.32–13.36
specifying works 12.39–12.59
survives abatement of nuisance 12.79
suspension of 12.75–12.77, 13.06–13.11
technical requirements 12.17–12.57
time-limit for compliance 12.58–12.59, 13.37–13.40
vehicles 12.28
void and invalid notices 13.19–13.26
whether can be served on housing authority 5.46

withdrawal of 12.78–12.81, 17.31–17.32
abatement orders 16.10, 16.35–16.40
abattoirs *see* **slaughterhouses**
abuse of process 14.26
access *see* **local authorities**: powers of entry; **occupiers**: failure to allow access; **tenants**: failure to allow access
accidents *see* **'injurious to health'**
accommodation *see* **housing, inhabited structures, vans, etc**
accumulations and deposits
generally 4.04, 4.33. 4.35. 4.43 (fn 68), 4.91–4.93, 4.96, 9.01–9.15
pigeon-droppings 8.07, 17.23
public nuisance 17.23
'acid-house' parties *see* **parties (noisy)**
acoustic experts *see* **expert witnesses, consultants**
'act, default, or sufferance'
'act or default' 10.19–10.21
'act, default, or sufferance' 5.15–5.16, 10.25, 12.22, 16.11
'default or sufferance' 14.57–14.60
actual knowledge *see* **knowledge**
'additional owner' (mines, quarries, etc.) 10.35
administrators 12.72
adopting or continuing a nuisance *see also* **'person responsible', trespassers**
liability for 5.61, 5.71, 12.29
Agricultural Land Tribunal 10.24
air pollution
air quality 2.35
history 3.07–3.08, 7.02–7.04
in streets 4.04
statutory nuisance 4.34
aircraft noise *see also* **noise**
European Convention on Human Rights 11.38
generally 6.120–6.123
alarms *see also* **noise**: from premises; **noise**: from vehicles
4.54, 6.63
alternative dispute resolution 17.02–17.10
'always speaking' principle *see* **statutory interpretation**
amendments
to abatement notices 12.33, 12.42 (fn 72), 12.81
to grounds of appeal (against abatement notices) 13.63–13.64

INDEX

amenity nuisances 4.31–4.33, 9.12–9.13
amplified music *see* **noise**: music, entertainment noise
animals 4.04, 6.132, 8.01–8.20
annoyance *see* discomfort
appeals against abatement notices
   amending grounds of appeal 13.63–13.64
   appeals by one recipient (if one or more served) 12.30
   best practicable means 1.36, 13.41–13.46, 15.07–15.09, 15.15
   costs 13.40 (fn 45), 13.71–13.94
   failing to accept alternative solutions 13.27–13.36
   generally 13.01–13.93
   grounds of appeal 13.12–13.56
   officers' authority to respond to 2.17
   onerous requirements 13.47–13.48
   procedures 13.65–13.70
   service on wrong person 13.49–13.56
   suspension of notice 12.75–12.77, 13.06–13.11
   time for considering 'prejudice to health' 5.50, 13.04, 13.43
   where more than one nuisance specified 12.36
   who may appeal 13.03
appeals from magistrates *see* **Crown Court, Divisional Court; application for judicial review**
architects 5.104, 6.105
armed forces 6.93, 7.11
arrangements of rooms *see* **layout**
asbestos 5.28
ash 9.06
asses 8.03
asthma 4.67
atmospheric emissions *see* **air pollution**
Attorney-General 2.10 (fn 18), 4.22, 6.14, 11.58 (fn 58), 11.61, 11.67 (fn 68), 14.30–14.33
audio-tapes *see* **tape recorders**

bad faith 13.26
beaches *see also* **estuaries and tidal waters**
   pollution of 4.98, 9.06
'Belgravia versus Bermondsey' test 4.79
'best practicable means' (trade, business, and industrial premises)
   accumulations and deposits 9.14
   and appeals against abatement notices 13.36, 13.41–13.46
   animals 8.09
   availability as a defence 15.09 (and Table 15.1)
   burden and standard of proof 11.47, 15.06–15.07, 15.20, 15.34

dogs 15.27
   evidence 15.06–15.07, 15.18–15.20, 15.34
   generally 4.56, 5.80, 6.38–6.39, 12.16, 12.20, 14.03, 14.10, 14.32, 15.01–15.28, 18.02, 18.81
   noise 6.34, 6.38–6.39, 6.82–6.90, 15.27
   planning permission 15.25–15.26
   question of fact 15.17
   smoke 7.13, 7.28, 10.01
   trade practices 15.23
bias 14.90, 17.47–17.48
birds *see also* **accumulations and deposits, pigeons**
   8.03, 8.07 (fn 10), 9.03 (fn 1)
blasting *see also* **quarries and excavations**
   4.35, 17.23
blocks of flats *see* **flats**
boats *see* **vessels**
bones and bone crushing 4.43, 7.25
bonfires 7.08
branches *see* **trees**
breach of abatement notice *see* **abatement notices: breach of**
bridges *see also* **pigeons**
   4.41 (fn 63), 9.09
British Standards Institution (noise measurements) 6.07
brothels 4.32 (fn 44)
builders' rubble *see also* **accumulations and deposits**
   9.12
Building Act notices 5.84–5.97
Building Research Establishment (Medical Advice Panel) 4.104
building sites *see* **construction sites, demolition sites**
burden and standard of proof
   appeals against abatement notices 13.45, 13.71–13.84
   best practicable means defence 15.06–15.07, 15.20, 15.34
   reasonable excuse for failing to comply with abatement notice 15.30–15.34
   reversal of burden of proof and European Convention on Human Rights 11.47
burglar alarms *see* **alarms**
business documents *see also* **hearsay evidence**
   18.31–18.34
business premises *see also* **'best practicable means'**
   dust (etc) 7.17–7.27
   generally 4.04, 12.68
   noise 6.79–6.81
bye-laws
   animals 8.13, 8.18–8.20

INDEX

bye-laws (*cont*):
   generally   4.50, 6.130–6.132
   inhabited structures   10.28

cameras   18.06–18.08
canals   *see also* **watercourses**
   10.20
caravan dwellers   11.37
carbon monoxide   5.28
cars   *see* **alarms**; **noise**: from street, from vehicles
'case stated'   *see* **Divisional Court**
cats   8.03, 8.15
cattle   8.03
cautions (formal)   14.40–14.50
cautions (in interviews)   18.47–18.50, 18.79
caves   5.75
certainty in the criminal law   *see* **no punishment without law, right to**
Chadwick, Sir Edwin (1801–1890)   3.13
charity shops   15.12
Chartered Institute of Environmental Health
   2.29–2.30
chickens (poultry)   8.03
   chicken processing   4.35, 17.23
children
   as perpetrators   12.70, 14.60
   as victims   4.67, 4.93
   European Convention on Human Rights
     11.37
   parents of   14.60
chimneys and chimney smoke   *see also* **smoke**
   7.06, 7.13–7.14, 7.19
cholera   *see* **history of environmental health legislation**
cinders   9.06
cisterns   4.06, 10.30–10.32
City of London Corporation   2.10 (fn 3)
civil proceedings
   against landlords   5.106–5.108
   by or against local authorities   2.09–2.10, 2.15–2.17, 6.14, 8.07
   distinguished from criminal proceedings
     11.51–11.52
'class' of the public at large   6.29
cliff falls   *see* **landslips**
closing orders   5.100
coastal erosion   *see* **landslips**
codes of practice   6.133, 11.66, 18.79
collapse of land   *see* **dangerous structures, landslips**
comfort   *see* **discomfort**
commercial premises   *see also* **'best practicable means'**
   fumes   7.15–7.20
   generally   4.04

   noise   6.79–6.81
Commission for Local Administration
   2.20–2.26, 6.35, 12.08
Common Council (City of London)   2.01
   (fn 3)
common law   *see* **history of environmental health legislation; negligence; private nuisance; public nuisance**
companies
   and European Convention on Human Rights
     11.16, 11.30, 11.37, 11.41
   prosecution of   14.63–14.65
   service on   12.62, 12.72–73, 16.22
compensation orders   14.91–14.93, 16.15, 16.41–16.50
complaints to local authorities   12.02, 12.04, 12.06–12.11
complaints to magistrates   5.46, 12.06, 12.09, 16.01–16.63
computers   18.08, 18.24
concordat (enforcement)   14.37–14.39, 17.06
condensation   4.33, 4.49, 4.99, 5.27, 5.39–5.49, 5.104, 16.13
construction sites   6.102–6.118, 17.15
constructive knowledge   5.69
consultants (obligation to engage)   12.48, 12.52
consultations   *see* **abatement notices: consultations prior to serving**
contaminated land   17.58–17.60
contaminated water   *see* **water pollution**
continuing or adopting a nuisance   *see also* **'person responsible . . .'; trespassers**
   5.61, 5.71, 12.29
contractors (mining)   10.35
contracts with local authorities   2.08
coprolites   7.25 (fn 36)
corporations   *see also* **companies**
   local authorities as corporations   2.07–2.08
   prosecution of   14.63–14.65
cost of abating nuisance   *see* **financial implications**
costs (legal)   12.52 (fn 92), 14.68–14.90, 14.101, 16.52–16.56
   in appeals against abatement notices   13.40 (fn 45), 13.71–13.84, 13.90–13.92
councillors   *see* **local authorities**: members
councils   *see* **local authorities**
County Courts   14.92, 17.24
covenants   *see* **leases**
'covert human intelligence sources'
   11.85–11.86, 11.89
'covert surveillance'   11.74, 11.80–11.81
criminal proceedings   *see also* **abatement notices**: breach of; **evidence; prosecutions**

criminal proceedings (*cont*):
  complaints to magistrates 16.15,
    16.31–16.33
  costs 14.68–14.90, 14.101
  distinguished from civil proceedings
    11.51–11.52
  'equality of arms' 11.58
crocodiles 8.03
Crown Court
  appeals to 13.85–13.92, 14.91,
    14.94–14.101, 16.59–16.60
  European Convention on Human Rights
    11.10–11.12
cross-examination 11.63
**Crossman, Richard Howard Stafford
  (1907–1974)** 2.21 (fn 33)
Crown immunity and Crown property
  6.106, 7.11. 12.31, 14.66–14.77
culverts *see also* **land drainage;
  watercourses**
  10.21–10.22, 10.24

d.a.t. recorders (digital audio tape recorders)
  18.16
dampness *see* **condensation, water
  penetration**
dams *see also* **watercourses**
  10.22
dangerous structures *see also* **housing;
  landslips**
  5.57, 5.84–5.97
dark smoke 7.05–7.08
date *see* **time**
death of a witness 18.22
decibel readings *see* **noise**; **abatement
  notices**: **noise**; **noise**: monitoring or
  measuring
decisions to prosecute *see also* **cautions
  (formal)**
  by local authorities 2.10, 2.14,
    14.26–14.39
  European Convention on Human Rights
    11.03, 11.18–11.19
declarations of incompatibility 11.10–11.13
declaratory judgements (High Court) 12.31,
  17.54
deer 8.03
'default' *see* **'act, default, or sufferance'**
**'default proceedings' against local authorities
  16.61–16.62**
defects *see* **housing; internal nuisances;
  latent defects; layout; 'premises';
  sanitation; staircases**
defences *see also* **'best practicable means';
  'reasonable excuse'; statutory
  authority**
  15.01–15.43, 16.57–16.58

delay
  by prosecutors 11.55
delegation of local authority powers
  2.11–2.14
demolition orders 5.100
demolition sites 9.12–9.13
demolition works 4.69, 5.53
demonstrations (political) 6.93–6.95
Department of the Environment 2.32
deposits *see* **accumulations and deposits;
  waste**
derogation from grant 5.106
devolution 2.04–2.06
digital audio tape recorders 18.16
digital cameras 18.07–18.08
'directed surveillance' 11.74–11.75,
  11.80–11.81, 11.87
disclosure of evidence *see* **evidence**: advance
  disclosure
discomfort
  and statutory nuisance 4.38, 4.43–4.51,
    4.105, 5.72
  European Convention on Human Rights
    11.41
discretion (fettering of) 17.43–17.46
disease *see* **'health' limb**
disproportionality *see* **proportionality**
disrepair *see* **dangerous structures; housing;
  internal nuisances; 'premises'**
district councils 2.01
ditches *see also* **watercourses**
  4.06, 10.02, 10.24
Divisional Court 14.102–14.110, 16.59–16.60
  appeals to 13.93
documentary evidence *see also* **evidence;
  witness statements**
  18.22–18.34
dogs 4.61, 6.86, 8.03, 8.09, 8.13–8.15, 8.17,
  15.27
domestic fires and grates 7.09, 7.17
domestic waste 9.03, 9.06, 9.12–9.13, 12.45
domestic water supply 10.30–10.32
doves 8.07 (fn 10)
drains and drainage *see* **land drainage;
  sanitation**
dry rot *see* **fungi**
dung 9.06, 9.08
duration of nuisance *see also* **noise**:
  duration
  4.72–4.76
dust 7.14, 7.17–7.20, 18.21
'dwelling' *see also* **housing; layout;
  'premises in such a state . . .; unfitness
  for human habitation**
  and business use 15.13
  and residential use 5.32 (fn 27), 5.54, 6.56,
    6.61, 7.15

economic considerations *see* **financial implications; social utility of land use**
effluvia 4.04, 4.43, 5.29, 7.17, 7.25–7.27
electrical wiring and electricity supply 4.105, 5.41 (fn 42), 5.108
emanations from land *see* **effluvia; transmission of nuisances**
emergencies *see also* **injunctions**
  warrant for entry onto land 14.16
emissions *see* **air pollution; effluvia**
empty premises 5.50–5.53
encroachments onto land *see* **land affected by nuisance; landslips; trees**
enforcement action *see* **abatement notices**
Enforcement Concordat 14.37–14.39, 17.06
enforcement authorities *see* **Environment Agency; local authorities; ports and harbours**
engineering sites *see* **construction sites**
entry, powers of *see* **local authorities**: powers of entry
Environment Agency 2.31–2.33, 7.12, 9.04, 10.17, 10.22 (fn 25), 11.05
Environment, Department of 2.32
environmental health officers *see also* **expert witnesses**: environmental health officers, **local authorities**: powers of entry
  abatement notices referring to 12.46
  evidence and opinions of 5.42, 6.33, 12.17–12.21
  negligence by 12.19
  notebooks 18.43–18.45
  obstruction of 6.62
  odour nuisance 18.18
  organisational structure within local authorities 2.27–2.28
  qualifications 2.29–2.30
environmental health technicians 2.29–2.30
'equality of arms' 11.58
equipment
  seizure of noise equipment 6.53–6.62
  street noise 4.04
  street smoke, fumes, or gases (London) 7.29
erosion *see* **landslips**
escapes 4.76, 5.02, 5.56–5.72
established uses ('prior appropriation') 3.09–3.10
estuaries and tidal waters *see also* **ports and harbours; territorial sea; watercourses** 10.11–10.18
European Convention on Human Rights
  and local authorities 2.10, 11.03, 11.17–11.29
  and Noise Act 1996 6.57
  and rules of evidence 18.26
  generally 11.01–11.89
European Court of Human Rights 11.01, 11.14, 11.28, 11.38, 17.39
European Union *see* **Treaty of European Union**
evidence *see also* **computers; expert witnesses; photographs; tape recorders**
  advance disclosure 11.58–11.61, 18.55–18.77
  'best practicable means' defence 15.06–15.07, 15.18–15.20, 15.34
  burden and standard of proof 15.06–15.07, 15.20, 15.30–15.34
  business documents 18.31–18.34
  competence of officers to give evidence on behalf of local authority 2.16–2.30
  complaints to magistrates 16.15
  contemporaneous notes 6.43
  defendant's bad character 18.82
  discretion of court to exclude prosecution evidence 18.25, 18.78–18.79
  generally 18.01–18.83
  hearsay 11.62–11.64, 14.01, 18.22–18.34
  notebooks 18.43–18.45
  rebuttal evidence 18.80–18.82
  'sensitive material' 18.72
  unlawfully obtained evidence 11.65–11.66
excavations *see* **quarries and excavations**
excreta of cats or dogs 8.15
exotic animals 8.03, 8.16
expert witnesses
  best practicable means 13.44
  disclosure of evidence 18.73–18.77
  duties of 18.38
  environmental health technicians 2.30
  environmental health officers 4.103, 5.42–5.43, 18.37–18.39
  no need to be medically qualified 4.102–4.103, 5.42
  noise 18.14
  opinion evidence 18.35–18.42
  'prejudicial to health' evidence 4.101, 5.42
external factors *see also* **traffic noise** 5.14–5.23
eyesores *see* **amenity nuisances**

factories *see* **industrial premises**
failure to comply with abatement notice 14.04–14.12
fair trial, right to 11.46–11.68, 13.24
false statements 14.02
family life, right to *see* **private and family life, right to**
fat smelting 4.55 (fn 80)

fear *see* witnesses in fear
fencing (lack of) *see also* trespass to land:
   by animals
   10.01, 10.33–10.35
feral animals and birds 8.03
fettering discretion 17.43–17.46
filthy premises *see also* accumulations and
   deposits; housing; waste
   5.89–5.99
financial implications 15.21–15.22
fines *see also* sentencing
   15.21 (fn 29), 16.51
fire brigades 4.04, 7.29
fires and grates (domestic) 7.09, 7.17
fireworks 4.69 (fn 97), 4.74
fitness for human habitations *see* unfitness
   for human habitation
flats *see also* sound insulation
   5.54–5.55, 5.103, 10.31–10.32, 12.23
flies 8.09, 9.06
flooding *see* land drainage; water
   penetration
flushing (defective) *see* sanitation
fly-tipping *see also* accumulations and
   deposits
   4.93, 9.12
food preparation *see also* kitchens; layout
   (of premises)
forcible entry 14.16
forklift trucks 15.15
fouling of land by cats or dogs 8.15
fumes 4.04, 5.29, 7.14–7.16
fungi *see also* condensation, internal
   nuisances
   4.96, 5.39

gallops 5.76
game birds 8.03
gardens 5.32 (fn 27), 5.79, 6.61, 9.03 (fn 3)
gas installations 4.105, 5.41 (fn 42), 5.108
gases 4.04, 4.09, 5.29, 7.14
'give and take' principle 4.34, 4.55, 4.79, 6.45
glare (of light) 4.32 (fn 44)
glass (broken) 9.12–9.13, 12.29 (fn 49)
goats 8.03
Grant Report 6.06 (fn 4)
Greater London 2.01, 6.136
grit *see* smoke
groups of individuals 11.16
grouse 8.03
gutters 4.06, 4.97, 10.02

harassment
   of neighbours and others 6.50,
   17.68–17.72
   of tenants 4.47 (fn 73), 17.73–17.74
harbours *see* ports and harbours

'health' 4.38, 4.43, 6.30
'health' limb (of statutory nuisance) 4.03,
   4.08–4.15, 4.33, 4.37–4.40, 4.48–4.54,
   4.82–4.105, 5.01, 5.27, 5.42–5.45,
   5.50–5.53, 5.72, 5.98–5.99, 6.25–6.26,
   6.30–6.31, 6.42, 8.05–8.06, 9.12–9.13
hearsay evidence *see* evidence: hearsay
heaters (domestic) *see* carbon monoxide;
   landlords: repairing obligations
heating (lack of) 4.33, 4.96, 5.12, 5.39, 5.47,
   16.13
hedges 4.02 (fn 2), 17.10
Her Majesty's Inspectorate of Pollution
   2.32
High Court *see* Divisional Court;
   injunctions; judicial review; public
   nuisance
highway authority 10.21 (fn 24)
highways *see also* bridges; pigeons; street
   noise; street smoke, fumes, or gases
   (London)
   as a 'public place' 6.95
   obstruction of 4.41 (fn 63), 4.55 (fn 80),
   8.08
   sheep droppings on 9.06
   trees 5.59
hinnies 8.03
history of environmental health legislation
   see also statutory interpretation
   accumulations and deposits 9.02–9.03
   animals 8.02
   effluvia 7.24–7.25 (fn 38)
   generally 2.27, 3.01–3.25, 4.02,
   4.04–4.06, 4.11–4.16, 4.41, 4.43–4.45,
   4.50–4.54, 4.88–4.89, 4.91
   noise 6.18–6.21
   premises 5.09–5.10
   watercourses 10.12–10.18
holiday camps 5.78
'home' 11.37, 11.40
horses 5.76, 8.03
hospitals
   service of notices on 12.74
   whether 'business premises' 15.14
houseboats *see* vessels
household waste *see* domestic waste
houses in multiple occupation 5.102–5.103
housing *see also* internal nuisances; layout;
   'premises in such a state . . .';
   sanitation; staircases (dangerous);
   unfitness for human habitation
   housing defects (alternative procedures)
   5.83–5.105
   inhabited structures, vans, etc 4.06, 10.01,
   10.26–10.29, 16.10
   magistrate's order prohibiting human
   habitation 16.02, 16.05

INDEX

housing department
whether abatement notice can be served on 5.46
housing executive (Northern Ireland) 2.02
housing officers (evidence of) 5.42
human habitation *see* **housing; unfitness for human habitation**
Human Rights Act 1998 *see* **European Convention on Human Rights**
hygiene *see* **food preparation; layout; sanitation**
hypersensitivity 4.64–4.67, 5.45, 6.10

ice-cream vans (chimes) 6.133
imputed knowledge 5.69
incompatibility *see* **declarations of incompatibility**
industrial revolution 3.07–3.10
'industrial, trade, and business premises'
see also **'best practicable means'**
business 15.13
dust (etc) 7.17–7.27
industry 4.04, 4.55
noise 6.79–6.90
trade 15.12
inert and inorganic waste 9.12–9.13
inflammable material (storage of) 17.23
information *see* **laying an information**
inhabited structures, vans, etc 4.06, 10.26–10.29
injunctions 2.10, 3.06, 4.22, 6.14 (fn 11), 6.72, 6.102, 6.109, 17.08, 17.11–17.21, 17.54, 17.73–17.74
'injurious to health' *see also* **'health' limb**
4.85–4.89, 4.104, 5.27, 5.42–5.45, 5.105, 8.05–8.06, 16.06
Inner Temple 2.01 (fn 3)
inorganic waste *see* **inert and inorganic waste**
insolvent companies 12.72
inspection of land *see* **local authorities**: duty to inspect
insulation (sound) 5.14–5.23
insulation (thermal) 5.12
integrated pollution prevention and control
6.20 (fn 22), 7.12, 7.25 (fn 33), 9.04 (fn 6)
intensification of activities 15.24
intensity of nuisance *see also* **noise**: intensity
4.72–4.76
interests in land (requisitions as to) 5.41 (fn 43), 12.68
'internal nuisances' *see also* **condensation; water penetration**
4.33, 4.49, 4.82, 4.87–4.92, 4.96–4.97, 4.104–4.105, 5.01, 5.39–5.49, 7.18 (fn 24)

interpretation of statutes *see* **statutory interpretation**
interviews with witnesses and suspects
11.67–11.68, 18.47–18.54
'intimation notices' 12.13
intimidation *see* **harassment; witnesses in fear**
intruder alarms *see* **alarms**
'intrusive surveillance' 11.78–11.81
invertebrates 8.03
investigatory powers (regulation of)
11.69–11.89
irrationality 17.36–17.38
irrelevance 17.33–17.35
Isles of Scilly 2.01 (fn 3)

judicial review
and European Convention on Human Rights 11.14–11.16, 17.39–17.51
generally 2.19, 12.08, 14.107, 17.26–17.56
grounds for seeking 17.30–17.38
procedure for applying 17.52–17.56
justices of the peace *see* **magistrates**

kitchens 4.105, 5.06
knowledge of nuisance 5.58–5.72, 9.09, 10.21, 12.29

lakes (artificial) 10.10
lakes (natural) 10.18
land *see also* **contaminated land; 'premises'**
local authority land 2.08
land affected by nuisance
encroachment on 4.31–4.33, 4.43, 5.56–5.72
injury to 4.31
interference with enjoyment of 4.31
interest in that land (whether necessary) 4.22, 4.28–4.30
'making sick people worse' 4.43 (fn 66), 7.25
land causing nuisance *see* **escapes; land drainage; landslips; trees**
land drainage 9.07, 10.21, 10.22–10.25
landlords
domestic water supply 10.32
offering suitable alternative accommodation to tenant 5.49
repairing obligations 5.41, 5.106–5.108, 12.23, 16.07
landslips 5.02, 5.56–5.57, 5.63, 5.65
latent defects 5.58–5.59
laundry (as a cause of condensation) 5.48
lavatories *see* **sanitation**
lawyer (right of access to) 11.53–11.54, 11.68

INDEX

'laying an information' 16.32–16.34
layout (of premises) 4.92, 4.105, 5.06–5.08, 5.11–5.12, 5.22
leaseholders *see* **tenants**
leases *see also* **landlords; tenants** 5.106–5.108, 12.23–12.24
legionnaires' disease 17.57 (fn 82)
legitimate expectations 12.14–12.15, 17.49–17.51
lessees *see* **tenants**
letter of intention to complain to magistrate 16.18–16.30
leylandii *see* **hedges**
licensing (and noise) 6.66–6.69, 6.134–6.137
light pollution 4.32 (fn 44), 17.10
liquidators (of mining companies) 10.35
'livestock' 8.03
local authorities *see also* **bye-laws**
   and European Convention on Human Rights 2.10, 11.03, 11.17–11.29
   and territorial sea 5.38
   appearance in legal proceedings 2.15–2.17
   authority to represent in criminal proceedings 2.15–2.17
   civil proceedings, by or against 2.09–2.11, 2.15–2.17, 6.14, 8.07
   committees and sub-committees 2.11
   contracts 2.08
   consent required of Secretary of State to bring proceedings 6.20, 7.12, 9.04
   default powers of the Secretary of State 12.05
   default proceedings against 16.61–16.62
   delegation of powers and decisions 2.11–2.14, 17.16
   discharge of functions by another local authority 2.11
   duty to inspect 12.02–12.11
   enforcement of statutory nuisance legislation 2.01, 10.01–10.35
   implied powers 2.18
   members 2.14–2.17
   minutes 2.15
   negligence by 12.19
   notices served without authority 2.15 (fn 26)
   officers 2.11–2.17
   organisational structure (environmental health) 2.27–2.28
   powers 2.18–2.19
   powers of entry 5.97, 5.99, 6.53–6.55, 6.62, 6.64, 10.02, 12.47, 14.14–14.16, 14.67
   prosecutions 2.09–2.11, 2.14–2.18
   requisitions as to interests in land 5.41 (fn 43), 12.68
   residents 12.10–12.11
   resolutions 2.15

   service of abatement notice on 5.46, 16.04
   standing orders 2.12, 2.14
   status 2.07–2.08
   surveillance by 11.72–11.89
   'ultra vires' rule 2.08, 2.18–2.19, 8.18
   undertaking works under Building Act 1984 5.85–5.97
   undertaking works under Public Health Act 1936 5.99, 10.02
local drainage boards 10.22–10.24
local government ombudsman *see* **Commission for Local Administration**
locality 4.58, 4.78–4.81, 6.34, 6.42 (fn 42), 15.24 (fn 32)
locomotives *see* **railways**
'locus standi' *see* **standing to seek judicial review**
lodgers 5.104
London 2.01, 4.04, 7.28
loudspeakers 6.100–6.101

machinery (street noise) 4.04, 4.54, 6.24
magistrates *see also* **complaints to magistrates; 'person aggrieved'**
   abatement orders 16.35
   appeals against abatement notices 13.05, 13.21, 13.35, 13.57–13.64
   bias 14.90
   Building Act 1984 5.95
   closing off domestic water supply 10.31–10.32
   compensation orders 14.91–14.93
   construction works 6.111–6.112
   declarations of incompatibility (no power to make) 11.10, 11.12
   default proceedings against local authorities 16.61–16.62
   prohibiting human habitation of premises 16.02–16.36
   varying abatement notice 13.76–13.77
   warrant of forcible entry 14.16
'maladministration' 2.21, 2.23–2.24
malice *see also* **noise**: motive for causing 4.70–4.71
managers (mining) 10.35
managing agents 10.32, 12.27
mandatory orders 17.54
manure 4.43, 7.22, 7.25, 9.06, 9.08
mediation 17.02–17.10
medical officers of health 2.27
mental health *see also* **'health'** 5.105, 12.69
metropolitan district councils 2.01 (fn 1)
Middle Temple 2.01 (fn 3)
military and naval forces *see* **armed forces**
milk processing 7.25 (fn 34)
mills (water mills) 10.22

INDEX

mines *see* **caves; quarries and excavations**
mitigation of sentences 18.85–18.86
model aircraft 6.121, 6.133
motive (of defendant) *see also* **noise**: motive for causing
 4.70–4.71
motor vehicles *see* **traffic noise; vehicles**
mould *see* **condensation; fungi**
mules 8.03
musical instruments *see also* **noise**: music, entertainment noise
 6.130, 6.134–6.137

National Health Service 12.74
National Rivers Authority 2.32
national security 14.67
naturally occurring nuisances *see also* **landslips; trees**
 5.58, 5.62, 5.71, 9.09–9.10, 10.20
nausea (nuisance causing) 4.43 (fn 66), 7.25
naval and military forces *see* **armed forces**
negligence (by environmental health officer)
 12.19
neighbourhood *see* **locality**
'Nelsonian blindness' *see* **knowledge of nuisance**
'Newton hearings' 18.86
night-time working *see* **noise**: time of day
no punishment without law, right to
 11.42–11.45, 12.56, 13.24
noise *see also* **abatement notices**: noise
 animals 6.40, 8.08–8.09, 8.11–8.14, 8.19–8.20
 bye-laws 4.50, 6.14, 6.130–6.132
 construction sites 6.102–6.118
 duration 4.55, 4.58, 6.34, 6.49, 6.65
 entertainment noise 6.37, 6.65–6.74, 6.134–6.137
 from premises 4.32, 4.34, 4.50, 4.55, 6.22–6.23
 from street 4.04, 4.34, 4.50 (fn 77), 4.54, 6.24, 6.91–6.95, 6.124, 14.55
 from vehicles 4.04, 4.54, 6.93, 6.124, 12.28
 generally 6.01–6.140
 in ports 2.03
 industrial noise 3.08
 licenses and permissions 6.66–6.69
 low frequency 6.80
 monitoring or measuring 4.66, 6.05, 6.07, 6.43, 6.62, 11.08, 11.31–11.41, 11.69–11.89, 12.42 (fn 71), 18.09
 motive for causing 4.58, 4.70–4.71
 music 6.02, 6.40, 6.53–6.62, 6.132, 15.41
 neighbourhood, or domestic noise
 6.40–6.49, 6.51

 Noise Abatement Act 1960 3.18, 4.50, 6.13, 6.18, 8.14
 occupational noise 6.81, 6.128–6.129
 'one-off events' 4.55, 4.58, 6.34, 6.49, 6.65
 opinion of environmental health officer
 12.17–12.21
 seizure of equipment 6.53–6.62, 6.71
 sound insulation 5.14–5.23, 6.41, 6.46
 statutory authority 6.125–6.127
 time of day 4.58, 4.77
 traffic-related noise 2.35
 weather conditions 18.14
 workplace noise 6.81, 6.128–6.129
noise abatement zones 6.21
Noise Advisory Council 6.37
noise diaries *see* **noise**: monitoring or measuring
non-governmental organisations 11.16
'normal user' *see* **reasonableness of activities**
Northern Ireland 2.02, 2.04, 3.04, 11.01
notebooks 18.43–18.45
notices *see* **abatement notices; Building Act notices; bye-laws; construction sites; 'intimation notices'; letter of intention . . .; Public Health Act notices; repairs notices; service of notices**
nuisance *see* **'nuisance' limb; private nuisance; public nuisance; statutory nuisance; warning notices**
'nuisance limb' of statutory nuisance 4.03, 4.08–4.11, 4.16–4.33, 4.37–4.81, 6.25–6.26, 7.18 (fn 24)

obstruction (of environmental health officer)
 6.62, 14.02, 14.13–14.22, 14.25
obstructions (to highway) 4.41 (fn 63), 4.55 (fn 80), 8.08
obstructions (to watercourses) 10.03–10.04, 10.22–10.25
occupational noise *see* **noise**: occupational noise
'occupier' *see also* **'person responsible . . .'**
 failing to allow access 12.16
 habitations 10.27, 12.24–12.25
 vessels 5.38
odometers 18.17
odours *see* **smells**
offences *see* **abatement notices**: breach of; **false statements; obstruction (of environmental health officer); prosecutions**
officers of local authority *see also* **environmental health officers**
 authority to prosecute (etc) 2.15–2.17

officers of local authority (*cont*):
  delegation to 2.11–2.14
  expert witnesses (whether entitled to be) 5.42–5.43
  warrant card 2.15
off-road activities (vehicle noise) 6.124
oil 4.32
olfactory tests 18.18
ombudsman (local government) *see* Commission for Local Administration
'original intent' doctrine *see* history of environmental health legislation; statutory nuisance
overcrowding *see also* housing
  10.26
over-sensitivity 4.64–4.67, 5.45, 6.10
'owner' 10.35, 12.23, 12.25–12.26

parties (noisy) 4.35, 4.69 (fn 97), 4.74, 6.49, 6.96, 6.137, 11.77, 15.36–15.37, 17.13
partnerships (service on) 12.62–12.63, 16.22
partridges 8.03
'pay parties' *see* parties (noisy)
penalties *see* sentencing
'person aggrieved' *see also* complaints to magistrates
  2.01 (fn 2), 5.44, 5.46, 5.55, 11.04, 14.91, 15.28, 16.08–16.10
'person living within area' 12.10–12.11
'person responsible' for statutory nuisance
  see also prosecutions: who to prosecute
  generally 5.41, 5.47–5.49, 12.22–12.31, 14.56–14.62, 16.11–16.14
  knowledge of nuisance 5.58–5.72, 9.09
  trespassers 5.61–5.62
  vehicles, machinery, or equipment 12.28
  watercourses 10.19–10.21, 10.23
personal comfort *see* discomfort
pests *see* vermin and other pests
petrol tankers (vehicles) 5.77
pets *see* animals; cats; dogs; exotic animals
pheasants 8.03
photocopies (as evidence) 18.06
photographs (as evidence) 18.03–18.08
physical injuries *see* 'health'; 'health limb'; 'injurious to health'
pigeons 4.43 (fn 68), 5.71 (fn 86), 8.03, 8.07, 9.03, 9.09, 17.23
pigs 7.22 (fn 28), 8.03, 8.18, 17.65–17.66, 18.18, 18.20
pipes (hot) 4.105
planning permission
  and 'best practicable means' defence 15.25–15.26
  and noise 6.66–6.69, 15.25–15.26
  relevance of 4.80–4.81, 17.61–17.67

policy considerations *see* fettering discretion
political demonstrations 6.93–6.95
'polluter pays' principle 2.35
pollution *see* air pollution; water pollution
ponds and pools 4.06, 10.02
ports and harbours 2.03, 9.06, 9.10, 10.07
poultry 8.03
'precautionary principle' 2.35
'prejudicial to health' *see* 'health' limb
'premises' *see also* 'industrial, trade, and business purposes'; local authorities: powers of entry
  and animals 8.05–8.06
  bridges 4.41 (fn 63), 9.09
  empty 5.50–5.53
  identification of 5.54–5.55, 12.34
  meaning of 5.03, 5.30–5.79, 5.106–5.108
'premises in such a state . . .' *see also* accumulations and deposits; animals; condensation; water penetration
  4.04, 4.45–4.47, 4.82, 4.96, 5.01–5.108
'preventive principle' 2.35
'prior appropriation' 3.09–3.10
privacy *see* private and family life, right to
private bodies and European Convention on Human Rights 11.07–11.08, 11.23
private and family life, right to 11.08, 11.16 (fn 26), 11.33–11.41, 11.71–11.89
private nuisance 3.06, 4.11–4.24, 4.28–4.36, 5.40, 5.57–5.60, 6.27–6.28
privatised utilities and European Convention on Human Rights 11.06
privies *see* sanitation
prohibiting order 17.54
property, right to 11.30–11.32
proportionality 11.25, 17.40–17.42
prosecutions *see also* 'best practicable means'; decisions to prosecute
  by local authorities 2.08–2.10, 2.15–2.18, 14.01–14.110
  consent required of Secretary of State 6.20, 7.12, 9.04
  private prosecutions 2.01 (fn 2)
  who to prosecute 14.51–14.65
prostitutes 4.32 (fn 44)
'proximity principle' 2.35
'public authorities' 11.02, 11.04
Public Health Act notices 5.98–5.99
public nuisance
  and statutory nuisance 4.16, 4.22, 4.24–4.27, 4.34–4.36, 5.40
  animals 8.08
  noise 6.15–6.18, 6.29, 6.99
  private proceedings for 17.22 (fn 27)
  proceedings brought by local authorities 2.10, 6.14, 17.22–17.24
  prosecutions for 3.06, 4.36 (fn 56)

INDEX

public order 6.95–6.99
'public place' 6.95
punishment without law *see* **no punishment without law, right to**
'purposive approach' *see* **statutory interpretation**

quarries and excavations 4.35, 5.73, 10.01, 10.33–10.35, 17.23
quashing order 17.54
quiet enjoyment (covenant for) 5.106
  rivers 10.04

racehorses 5.76
radioactive substances 10.27, 10.32
Railtrack 11.06 (fn 9)
railways *see also* **bridges**
  5.15, 6.120, 6.126–6.127, 7.06, 7.20, 9.06
rats *see* **vermin and other pests**
'raves' *see* **parties (noisy)**
'reasonable excuse' (for failing to comply with abatement notice)
  4.57, 15.29–15.43, 18.02
reasonableness of activities *see also* **noise: motive for causing; social utility of land use**
  4.34, 4.55, 4.70–4.71, 4.94–4.95, 6.45–6.48
reasonableness of precautions see also **'best practicable means'; financial implications**
  4.55–4.56
reasons, right to 11.46–11.57
receivers (mines) 10.35 *see also* **insolvent companies**
recordings (of noise) *see* **noise: monitoring or measuring**
refuse *see* **accumulations and deposits; domestic waste**
regulatory bodies and European Convention on Human Rights 11.05
relator actions 2.10 (fn 18), 4.22
repairs notices 5.94, 5.100
representative bodies and European Convention on Human Rights 11.16
requisitions as to interests in land 5.41 (fn 43), 12.68
residential premises *see* **housing**
'residents' of local authority area 12.10–12.11
responsibility for statutory nuisance *see* **'person responsible…'**
Ringelmann chart 7.05
riparian owners 10.19–10.20, 10.23
rivers (obstruction of) *see also* **watercourses**
  10.03–10.04, 10.20–10.25
road traffic *see* **traffic noise vehicles**
road works 6.103

roads *see* **highways; street noise; street smoke, fumes, or gases (London); traffic noise**
rockfalls *see also* **landslips**
  5.02
roots *see* **trees**
rubbish *see* **accumulations and deposits; household waste; waste and waste sites**
rubble *see* **accumulations and deposits; amenity nuisances; inert and inorganic waste**
Rylands v Fletcher liability 5.70

sanitation (and sanitary fittings) 4.96, 4.104–4.105, 5.06–5.23, 5.27, 5.41 (fn 42), 5.108, 10.27
'sanitary inspectors' 2.27
sanitary legislation (19th century) 3.11–3.16, 3.19–3.20, 3.22–3.23
schools 15.14
Scilly, Isles of 2.01 (fn 3)
Scotland 2.02, 2.05, 6.51, 11.01, 11.05
Scottish Environmental Protection Agency 2.31, 2.33, 9.04
sea *see* **landslips; territorial sea**
searches of premises 18.79
seaweed 5.71 (fn 86), 9.06–9.10
'section 82 proceedings' *see* **complaints to magistrates**
security of premises (inadequate) 4.104
seizure of equipment (noise nuisance) 6.53–6.62, 14.23–14.25
'sensitive material' (evidence) 18.72
sensitive trades and sensitive occupiers of land 4.64–4.67
sentencing
  appeals against sentence 14.99–14.100
  breach of injunction 17.21
  environmental health offences 14.11–14.12, 15.21 (fn 29), 18.83–18.86
service of notices
  by leaving at proper address 12.61
  by post 12.60
  generally 12.60–12.74, 16.19–16.24
  not authorized by local authority 2.15 (fn 26)
  on alternative address 12.64, 16.23
  on companies 12.62, 12.72–12.73
  on hospitals 12.74
  on housing authority 5.46, 16.04
  on mentally sick persons 12.69
  on partnerships 12.62–12.63
  on persons who cannot read English 12.71
  on wrong person 13.49–13.56
  vehicles, machinery, or equipment 12.28
  where landowner or occupier cannot be identified 12.67

INDEX

sewage
  on beaches and in estuaries 4.98, 9.06, 10.11–10.18
  sewage tanks and works 5.73, 7.22 (fn 30)
sewers 5.36, 5.73
sheds (inhabited) 4.06, 10.01, 10.26–10.29
sheep 8.03, 9.06
ships *see* **vessels**
shops 15.12
silence, right of 11.67–11.68, 18.49–18.51
silt *see also* **obstructions (to watercourses)** 10.03
skirting-boards 4.97
slaughterhouses (history) 3.09
sleep (loss of)
  from noise 4.74, 6.12, 6.31
  from smells 18.18
slums *see* **housing; 'premises in such a state...'; unfitness for human habitation**
smells 4.04, 4.32, 4.34–4.35, 4.96, 7.16, 7.22–7.25, 9.10, 18.17
smoke 4.04, 7.01–7.02, 7.05–7.13, 7.23, 18.21
smoke control areas 7.06
snakes 8.03, 8.06
social utility of land use 4.68–4.69, 7.22 (fn 30)
soot *see* **smoke**
sound insulation 5.15–5.23, 6.41, 6.46
soya meal dust 7.20
sparrows 8.07 (fn 10)
special damage 4.22
specific performance 5.108
squatters 5.53, 11.37, 12.11
staircases (dangerous) 4.87–4.89, 4.105, 5.24–5.29, 12.17 (fn 27)
standard of proof *see* **burden and standard of proof**
standing to seek judicial review 17.55–17.56
starlings 8.07 (fn 10)
'state' of the premises 5.05–5.29
statements of witnesses *see* **witness statements**
statutory authority (to commit nuisance) 6.125–6.127, 17.61–17.67
statutory interpretation *see also* **history of environmental health legislation** 4.11–4.15, 4.41 (fn 63), 5.08–5.13, 5.28, 5.34, 10.16
statutory nuisances *see also* **abatement notices; complaints to magistrates; history of environmental health legislation; planning permission**
  and trespass to land 4.31 (fn 42)
  defences to 5.80–5.82, 6.125–6.127
  definition (finite list) 4.04–4.06
  enforcement authorities 2.01–2.02
  generally 4.01–4.105
  inspections 12.02–12.05
  knowledge of 5.68–5.72
  likelihood of occurrence or recurrence 12.32–12.33
  miscellaneous legislation 10.01–10.35
  Northern Ireland 2.02
  not yet occurring 16.02
  overlap with private and public nuisance 4.34
  persons responsible for 5.41, 5.47–5.49
steam 4.04, 7.21
steam railways 7.06–7.07
steamships 5.37 (fn 33)
'steps' to be taken 4.60–4.63, 15.28
streams *see* **watercourses**
street noise 2.35, 4.04, 6.24, 6.91–6.101, 6.132
street smoke, fumes, or gases (London) 4.04, 7.29
'strict liability offences' 14.02–14.03
structural defects *see* **dangerous structures; housing; internal nuisances; layout of premises; sanitation; staircases (dangerous)**
subsidence *see* **landslips**
'sufferance' *see* **'act, default, or sufferance'**
summary proceedings *see* **complaints to magistrates**
summons, issuing of 16.32–16.34
support (loss of) *see* **landslips**
surveillance (regulation of) 11.69–11.89
surveyors 4.102, 5.42, 6.105, 16.06
suspects *see* **interviews with witnesses and suspects**
'sustainable development' 2.35

tanks (water storage) 4.06, 10.30–10.32
tape recorders 11.84, 11.87, 18.16, 18.45
Temple (Inner and Middle) 2.01 (fn 3)
temporary nuisances *see also* **duration of nuisance; noise: duration** 4.69 (fn 97)
tenancies *see* **leases**
tenants
  failure to allow access 5.47, 12.26
  failure to use heating 4.99, 5.47–5.48, 16.13
  harassment of 4.47 (fn 73), 17.73–17.74
  offer of suitable alternative accommodation to 5.49
  'person aggrieved' 5.44, 5.46, 14.91, 16.04, 16.09
  'person responsible' for statutory nuisance 5.47–5.48, 12.24
  rights under Defective Premises Act 1972 5.104

INDEX

tents 4.06, 10.01, 10.26–10.29
territorial sea 5.38
tidal waters *see* **estuaries and tidal waters; ports and harbours**
time
  for appealing against abatement notice 13.02
  for compliance with abatement notice 13.37–13.40
  for considering 'prejudice to health' 5.50–5.53, 13.04
  for considering whether abatement notice is justified 13.04, 13.43
  for establishing 'best practicable means' 13.43, 15.15–15.16, 15.38–15.40
  for laying an information before a magistrate 16.34
  for undertaking work specified in abatement notice 12.58–12.59
time of day (and noise nuisance) 6.34, 6.49, 6.65
trade practices (and 'best practicable means') 15.23
trade premises *see also* **'best practicable means'** 4.04, 6.79–6.81, 7.17–7.27
traffic noise 2.35, 4.04, 5.14–5.23, 6.93, 6.120
transmission of nuisances 4.32–4.33, 4.48–4.49, 5.26 (fn 23), 5.40, 9.12–9.13
Treaty of European Union 1997 2.34–2.35
trees 5.59, 5.64, 5.71 (fn 86)
trespass to land
  and statutory nuisance 4.31 (fn 42)
  by animals 8.05–8.06
trespassers 4.93, 5.60–5.61
trunk roads *see* **road works**
tunnels *see* **caves**

'ultra vires' rule
  bye-laws 8.18
  local authorities 2.08, 2.18–2.19, 17.31–17.32
undertakings in damages 17.20
unfitness for human habitation 4.45 (fn 71), 5.50, 5.53, 5.81, 5.98–5.99, 5.100–5.102, 5.106, 16.05–16.06, 16.36
unincorporated associations and European Convention on Human Rights 11.16
unitary authorities 2.01–2.02
unlawfully obtained evidence *see* **evidence**: unlawfully obtained evidence
unoccupied premises 5.50–5.53
'unreasonableness' *see* **irrationality; 'Wednesbury unreasonableness'**
unused material, disclosure of *see* **evidence**: advance disclosure

vans (inhabited) 4.06, 10.01, 10.26–10.29
vapours *see* **gases**
vehicles
  alarms 4.54
  definition 7.29 (fn 41)
  exhausts 4.04 (fn 4), 7.29
  inhabited vans 4.06
  street noise 4.04, 4.54, 6.91–6.95, 12.28
  street smoke, fumes, or gases (London) 4.04, 7.29
  whether or not 'premises' 5.77
ventilation (lack of) 4.33, 4.96, 4.104, 5.12, 5.39, 5.47
vermin and other pests *see also* **pigeons** 4.93, 5.27, 5.98–5.99, 8.05, 9.03. 9.08
vessels
  and dust 7.20
  and smoke 7.10
  and noise 6.23
  generally 5.37–5.38
vibrations 5.15, 6.10, 6.22
videos *see also* **photographs** 18.03
visitors 7.18
visual impact *see* **amenity nuisances; light pollution**

Wales 2.02, 2.06, 11.01, 11.05
'warehouse parties' *see* **parties (noisy)**
warning notices (Noise Act 1996) 6.55
warrant card 2.15
warrant of forcible entry 14.16
washing facilities (lack of) 4.13
waste and waste sites *see also* **accumulations and deposits**
  as industrial, trade, or business premises 15.11
  household waste 9.03, 9.06, 9.12–9.13, 12.45
  inert and inorganic waste 9.12
  regulation of 2.32, 2.36, 9.04, 11.23
water-butts and water tanks 4.06, 10.30–10.32
water closets *see* **sanitation**
water-heaters (defective) 4.96, 5.41 (fn 42), 5.108
water penetration 4.41 (fn 63), 4.49, 4.96, 4.104, 5.27, 5.39–5.49, 5.104, 16.10
water pollution 3.08, 5.27, 10.30–10.32
water supply (domestic) 10.30–10.32
watercourses 4.06, 10.01–10.25
'Wednesbury unreasonableness' 17.36–17.42
weirs *see also* **watercourses** 10.22
wells 4.06, 10.30–10.32
wild animals 8.03–8.04, 8.17

wilful obstruction *see* **obstruction of environmental health officer**
'without reasonable excuse' *see* **'reasonable excuse'**
witness statements 18.22–18.23, 18.46–18.54
witnesses
   absent from trial 18.22–18.34
   and European Convention on Human Rights 11.63
   in fear 18.27–18.30
   interviews with 11.67–11.68, 18.47–18.54
   paid witnesses (private investigators, etc) 11.85, 11.89
'works' 12.39–12.59
World Health Organisation 6.30, 18.11

yachts *see* **vessels**